Contents

Foreword

Almost 40 years ago, a small group of companies in the UK decided to do something different. It was time, they believed, to look beyond their own bottom line and to start thinking about what part they could play in making the world a better place. Business in the Community (BITC) was born.

Since then, the UK has changed a lot. From the devastating effects of the global financial crisis to the radical changes which the internet and technology have brought about, BITC has watched our country redefine itself time and again. But over the years, one trend has emerged strongly; people have begun increasingly to look to the private sector for help in tackling the world's hardest problems. After all, companies have the resources, the reach and the reason to do so.

The twelfth edition of *The UK Guide to Company Giving* lays bare the scale of that expectation for responsible business in 2019. 400 companies contributing around £400 million in cash and in-kind support is a staggering level of community support. It is something that as a nation we should be immensely proud of.

When BITC was founded in the 1980s, cash-giving was the watchword. Today, we still see enormous value in the ability of companies to financially support charities or causes which their employees care about and I am pleased to read in this year's guide that that tradition is alive and well. But I was also happy to see that the entries in the guide highlight the fact that giving is about far more than money.

Donating money is a good start, but it is when we begin to really consider what is within our power to give away that things get interesting. As well as being able to offer financial support, companies have the resource, talent, skills and – most important of all – the perspective to give charities and communities the best chance of succeeding. Thoughtful giving is a powerful act.

I am particularly happy to see that the guide has emphasized the importance of partnerships which bring this type of giving to life. Understanding the give and take of long-term relationships with community groups or the third sector is something which marks out a business as being not only responsible but really remarkable.

The beauty of responsible business is that it really does work for everyone. By giving more, each company on this list is helping communities, taking care of its employees and securing all of our futures. This guide is a brilliant and invaluable resource for charities and companies alike. Looking at it, I feel more confident than ever that the chorus of responsible businesses is on the brink of becoming a roar. I hope that – like me – you can't wait to hear it.

Amanda Mackenzie OBE
Chief Executive, Business in the Community

About the Directory of Social Change

The Directory of Social Change (DSC) has a vision of an independent voluntary sector at the heart of social change. We believe that the activities of independent charities, voluntary organisations and community groups are fundamental to achieve social change. We exist to help these organisations in achieving their goals.

We do this by:

- Providing practical tools that organisations and activists need, including online and printed publications, training courses, and conferences on a huge range of topics
- Acting as a 'concerned citizen' in public policy debates, often on behalf of smaller charities, voluntary organisations and community groups
- Leading campaigns and stimulating debate on key policy issues that affect those groups
- Carrying out research and providing information to influence policymakers

DSC is the leading provider of information and training for the voluntary sector and publishes an extensive range of guides and handbooks covering subjects such as fundraising, management, communication, finance and law. Our subscription website, Funds Online, contains a wealth of information on funding from grant-making charities, companies and government sources. We run more than 300 training courses each year, including bespoke in-house training provided at the client's location. DSC conferences and fairs, which take place throughout the year, also provide training on a wide range of topics and offer a welcome opportunity for networking.

For details of all our activities, and to order publications and book courses, go to www.dsc.org.uk, call 020 7697 4200 or email cs@dsc.org.uk.

Introduction

Welcome to the twelfth edition of *The Guide to UK Company Giving* which continues to provide relevant, updated commentary on the current state of corporate community involvement in the UK.

This edition features 400 companies, which collectively gave around £400 million in community support, mostly in the financial years 2016/17, 2017 or 2017/18. The edition also includes full details of 128 associated corporate charities which together gave over £200 million. This figure was derived from the combined grant totals of each of the corporate charities listed and does not represent what was given by the companies themselves.

Since reforms were made to the Companies Act 2006 companies no longer have a legal obligation to declare charitable donations. We have monitored how this transformed companies reporting on their community involvement since the changes took place in 2013. There has been a recognisable shift towards embedding corporate social responsibility (CSR) into company culture, by encouraging staff involvement, providing services pro bono, or by gifting products. We continue to see how this can have a positive effect on both those receiving the support and the givers themselves.

The corporate charities section on page 229 contains information on 128 corporate charities established by and closely associated with a company listed in the guide, often acting as a channel for its charitable giving. We hope that this will be of real use to our readers when looking for charitable funding given by companies.

Each of the 400 company records provide essential information for accessing funding and other resources. Throughout our research we look at thousands of pages of annual reports, accounts and CSR reports as well as the companies' own websites, with the aim of providing a comprehensive overview of the community-related activities by a particular business. The records focus on a company's contributions to its local community and/or society as a whole, which include both cash donations (where figures are available) and all forms of in-kind support from pro bono work to equipment. We also make a note of commercially led yet community-related initiatives, or other community-orientated contributions by the company.

Most of the guide consists of individual company records, but it also contains additional sections offering advice and information for fundraisers, voluntary organisations, community groups, companies and individuals.

Corporate social responsibility

Corporate social responsibility (CSR), also known as social or community investment, corporate citizenship or sustainable/responsible business, is a much-used term which covers a holistic attempt by businesses to act in an ethical manner, considering the effects they have on communities, people and the environment.

Initially self-regulated, there are now several legal requirements to report on various activities that fall under the CSR banner, including reporting on a company's gender pay gap, responding to the risk of modern day slavery in the supply chain, and ensuring that environmental damage is reduced or avoided. A CSR strategy should include the monitoring and review of a company's ethical policies and procedures, environmental policy, health and safety procedures, employees' welfare, and the effect the company's business has on its customers, suppliers, communities and stakeholders.

Many companies, depending on the nature of their business, quite naturally focus on the impact they have on the environment and what measures they are taking to try to redress the negative aspect of their activities. These programmes are often under the heading of sustainability as opposed to CSR.

For the benefit of our readers, we focus our research on companies' contributions to UK voluntary organisations. Where a company gives abroad and provides information, we include this information, however this guide has been written for the small and medium-sized charities working with beneficiaries in the UK and so we have tried to focus on the aspects of giving that will be of most use to them.

From our research we know that companies which establish partnerships or close relationships with the charities they support appreciate those organisations, their staff and the needs which they meet. This is probably more so for those that have a link to the nature of the company's business; for example, a sports clothing retailer has a very direct link with the beneficiaries of a voluntary group supporting young people. In this way, the beneficiaries of the voluntary organisation are often the company's customers or potential customers – 'a win–win situation' in the eyes of the company.

Companies are also realising that there are substantial benefits to be gained in supporting such voluntary groups. These benefits include:

- Getting good publicity and building brand awareness through association with an organisation or cause
- Gaining a deeper understanding of their own customer base
- Receiving the advantages of staff development opportunities where employees are involved in volunteering such as mentoring or pro bono work

Working in partnership can be of mutual benefit: companies bring their core business skills, including financial or logistical expertise, and access to supply chains and high-level contacts; charities can provide their own professional skills and a real knowledge of what is needed on the ground and what approaches will be most effective. We know that companies continue to set up corporate charities through which to channel their community/ charitable contributions as this is an efficient way to show their commitment to the voluntary sector.

The companies in this guide

In previous editions of this guide, cash donations have been the primary, albeit not the only, way in which DSC has measured companies' community involvement. While DSC maintains that it is good practice for companies to declare charitable donations, and applauds those companies that continue to do so, the shift in focus away from cash donations and towards corporate community contributions has presented us with the opportunity to draw attention to the other, sometimes very innovative, ways in which companies contribute to communities – the value of such contributions cannot always be properly translated into monetary terms.

Methodology

As it was no longer possible to use a threshold for financial contributions as we had done in previous years, we have opened up our basic criteria and have included companies whose CSR activities benefit communities in the UK directly. Generally, this would include any of the following: charitable contributions (either cash or gifts in kind such as equipment, employee volunteering, mentoring or secondment of staff); community partnerships; or activities of an affiliated grant-making corporate charity.

We started the research process by comparing a list of companies on the FTSE All-Share (taken on 10 August 2018) to the list of companies already on our database for which we hold historical information of charitable giving. An initial sift was then carried out of those FTSE All-Share companies not yet featured on our database to determine whether or not they fit within our criteria. Over many years of research we have noticed that the banking and finance sector and legal firms tend to have well-defined CSR programmes so we looked at other businesses in those areas to see if there were companies that had not been included in our research before.

From the companies that satisfied our basic criteria, more in-depth research was carried out to determine whether or not they should be included in the guide. The decision to include or exclude a company from the guide was rooted in its relevance and usefulness for fundraisers. Our guiding research question was – what is the company doing for charitable causes in the UK? We did not include companies whose CSR is geared mainly towards environmental sustainability or those companies whose community support is given on a long-term basis to one or a limited group of named charities, or those whose employees' fundraising or volunteering is the sole source of community contributions since the the recipients of funds such as these are nearly always predetermined.

Football clubs

This edition contains information about the community activities of 14 Premier League Football Clubs that met our criteria for inclusion. Football clubs were included for the first time in the previous edition of this guide and the decision to include them was based on a number of factors.

Firstly, many of the first football clubs had their origins as community organisations; they were Saturday social clubs for working class men, and were often managed by democratically elected local committees. Given DSC's extensive data on the charitable and community giving in other corporate sectors it seems appropriate that we should try to highlight the community involvement of an industry that has a natural and historic link to our local communities.

Furthermore, in 2015 it was announced that Sky and BT Sport agreed to pay a record sum of £5.14 billion for Premier League TV rights over three seasons beginning from 2016/17 (Premier League, 2015). This continued a general trend of increasingly lucrative TV deals since the Premier League's formation in 1992. As part of the deal, the Premier League agreed to use a proportion of the money in a socially responsible way. By setting out the community initiatives of Premier League football clubs, our intention was to monitor the impact that this influx of money has had on the clubs' community programmes during this period.

Since the publication of the previous guide, several clubs have been promoted to and relegated from the Premier League. Furthermore, since the last guide was written, the Premier League has successfully negotiated a new and even more lucrative TV deal with broadcasters (Premier League, 2018). At this stage, it remains too early to draw any definitive conclusions about the long-term impact of the revenue generated by the 2016/17 TV deal or the most recent deal. However, over the next few years we will continue to monitor any changes to the nature and scope of the community activities of Premier League clubs as further funds are made available.

Accreditation schemes and membership bodies

As in previous editions, during our research for this guide we recorded which companies are members of CSR membership bodies, specifically Business in the Community (BITC) and the London Benchmarking Group (LBG). We include this information to demonstrate that there are large organisations encouraging transparency and openness in order to assist voluntary sector and community organisations looking for corporate support.

Within the guide there were 62 companies signed up to the membership of LBG representing a 1.5% decrease since the last edition; however, we cannot say how many of these are truly compliant with the LBG reporting standard. For more information on LBG, see page 294.

Our research found that there are 120 (compared with 157 in the last edition) companies within our sample that hold the membership of BITC, with 12 (compared with 19 in the last edition) achieving the CommunityMark status. For more information, see page 294.

New to this edition is information on whether the company has been recognised by Stonewall or has been accredited by the Living Wage Foundation. We have also collected information on whether the company is a member of the Business Disability Forum.

We have also included information on the FTSE4Good index which is one of a range of ethical investment indices launched in 2001 by the FTSE Group. The indices are designed to measure the performance of companies demonstrating strong Environmental, Social and Governance (ESG) practices. We have included this as many charities are moving towards or already have ethical investment policies. However, some companies included may not meet the ethical standards or expectations of your own organisation and we would advise that you conduct your own research before relying on external benchmarking or accreditation bodies.

There are numerous accreditation schemes and membership bodies that companies can join and we hope to keep expanding our information so that in the future we can build a complete picture of a company's CSR strategy.

The corporate charities section

The corporate charities chapter focuses on grant-making charities associated with the companies in this guide. The 128 charities listed have an association, either historically or currently, with a company and each record includes full details of the charity, its purposes and contact details. Information is provided on how much the charities donate, to which organisations they give and the areas in which they focus their giving.

To be deemed a corporate charity in line with DSC's criteria and consequently to have a place in this guide, these charities should also receive all, or a substantial amount of their income from a connected company through an annual donation from the company's profits. We made our criteria more stringent for this edition as previously we included several charities that had received historic investments from a company or the founder of a company, but with which the company does not appear to have a current relationship. As the focus of the book is on current levels of company giving we chose to exclude them from our sample. Similarly as we look at how companies can support charities in the UK, we excluded corporate charities that mainly work overseas.

We have only included corporate charities that are linked to the companies in the main section of this guide; furthermore, we have focused solely on those that make grants to organisations. Some companies have corporate charities which do not make grants, instead delivering their own activities directly or offering support in other forms. Where applicable, these are detailed in the main section of the guide under the relevant company.

As well as the traditional method of receiving donations directly from the yearly profits of the company, corporate charities can also receive income from other sources, for example from staff/customer fundraising. All income streams contribute towards grant-making unless they have a predetermined restriction which prevents this. Many corporate charities also receive in-kind support from the company, such as staff time and expertise, and facilities and office space on the premises of the company.

Corporate charities can be an excellent vehicle for corporate giving. They:

- Provide a professional, structured and effective channel for charitable donations with trustees acting in the best interest of the charity (and not the company)
- Often employ skilled, motivated staff
- Apply the Charities SORP, which provides openness and transparency often lacking in companies' reporting
- Are often a way for companies to focus their charitable giving while demonstrating long-term support for their communities through the voluntary sector

Corporate organisations can contribute to the communities in which they operate through the charity's activities while also seeing an indirect benefit to their business. For example, a finance company might want to fund debt advice agencies and can do so through its corporate charity, provided this falls within the charity's objects.

Most corporate charities form part of a company's wider CSR programme and often focus on the same causes. Some are used as a vehicle to deliver other aspects of the company's CSR activities – for example, providing matched funding for employee-led fundraising initiatives or supporting a nominated Charity of the Year. In some cases there may be multiple corporate charities associated with one company, each delivering different aspects of the company's community involvement.

The ways in which corporate charities offer support may vary as much as their relationship with the company. In this edition there are corporate charities listed that give nationally and internationally as well as those that give only in the areas in which the company or their parent company has a local presence. Some charities focusing on local communities might also offer in-kind support, such as employee volunteering, to complement a financial grant. Application procedures can vary too; some may favour charities or causes with which employees of the company are already involved or may allow customers to nominate charities for support. Others may welcome applications from any charity working in a particular area or for any cause. As when applying to any grant-maker, we advise that you consider the eligibility criteria and exclusions of each funder carefully, and tailor your approach appropriately.

The corporate charities section of this guide is a valuable component of DSC's examination of UK companies' charitable giving. It is a traditional and straightforward way of giving but, nevertheless, an important and worthwhile avenue for charities to consider when searching for funding. These grant-makers have the advantage of being familiar to fundraisers who will understand their protocols and processes.

Conclusion

At this point in previous editions we would normally comment on whether the companies listed in this guide have given more or less than in our last edition, providing a narrative on any change in the companies' funding landscape. In light of decreasing transparency in company reporting we are no longer able to make a meaningful comparison of purely financial contributions by corporates. However, what we have seen during our research for this edition of the guide is how companies' charitable cash donations are only one part of the multi-faceted approach companies now take to their corporate social responsibilities. While declaring cash donations can provide a categorical and measurable way to evaluate companies' input, they are not necessarily the best way to measure impact.

Over the course of our research, we have seen the direct benefits of non-cash contributions, particularly of pro bono time and skills, gifts in kind, and unique and productive charity partnerships. In many ways, this sort of involvement demonstrates a commitment that a straightforward signing of a cheque does not. What is apparent is that many companies in this guide appear to be increasingly willing to facilitate and support their employees' community involvement – whether this is in the form of a volunteering policy, a payroll giving scheme, or by matching funds or time. Furthermore, it is particularly encouraging that there are a high number of companies willing to work in partnership with charities. The success of many of the charity partnerships we looked at in this guide is testament to the unique creativity and innovation that can be produced when two very different sectors come together to exchange their professional knowledge and values.

Good communication between charities and companies is mutually beneficial. It means that companies can find like-minded organisations to work with to fulfil their CSR objectives, and that charities can access valuable support. Some very simple information, published on a company's website, can make a big difference. Does the company make donations to charities or provide in-kind support? Who is the best person to contact about the company's community contributions? It is equally helpful if companies state clearly that they do not support unsolicited requests from charities – this prevents charities using valuable time and resources on an ineligible application and avoids the company having to field queries from ineligible applicants.

As always, however, there remains a long way to go for companies in terms of transparency in their CSR reporting and in publicising their social responsibility policies. DSC campaigns to achieve better funding relationships between charities and their funders. We want to develop good funding practice among those organisations which give to charities and other voluntary organisations. We use research to develop recommendations and practical tools for funders and fundraisers to positively change behaviour and practice. DSC calls on companies to give more, for more companies to give, and for more companies to be more transparent givers.

Some companies continue to use their marketing expertise to promulgate an image of their community involvement that is not a truthful depiction of what they actually do. Our research frequently flies in the face of the headline-grabbing spin that companies give billions of pounds to charities each year.

The aim of this guide is to provide the knowledge necessary to obtain corporate support through the provision of profile information on individual companies, identifying the kind of support available and how to access it effectively. We hope that this guide will continue to be an invaluable and comprehensive source of information for all of those with an interest in corporate giving in the UK.

References

Premier League (2015), 'League awards UK live broadcast rights for 2016/17 to 2018/19' [news release], available on www.premierleague.com/news/60495, dated 10 February 2015

Premier League (2018), 'Sales of UK and Ireland live TV rights decided' [news release], available on https://www.premierleague.com/news/708008, dated 7 June 2018

Acknowledgements

We would like to thank all the companies that have helped to compile this guide: both those which we have contacted directly and those which have made their annual reports and accounts and/or their websites informative and accessible.

How to use this guide

Types of company

A company may be: a public limited company (designated plc), normally a company with shares quoted on the stock exchange; a privately owned company; or a subsidiary company. If it is a subsidiary it may have retained its own identity for charitable donations and we would include a record in this guide. Other subsidiaries included are UK-based subsidiaries of an overseas-based company.

Where a company has been recently acquired it may not yet have decided whether it will continue to manage its own charitable donations budget.

Through acquisitions and mergers, companies may now be owned by a holding company, a conglomerate, or a transnational company. You may have to do your own research to link local companies and plants with the head office that may have ultimate control over their donations. The company's annual report, usually available free online or on request, lists subsidiary and associate (less than 50% owned) companies and reports on the activity of the company during the year.

Interpreting charitable giving information

Where information was available – either from an annual report and accounts, a CSR report or from a website – we have included a figure for total UK community contributions. This includes cash donations as well as the value of employee time and skills and gifts in kind, given in the UK. Where a separate figure for cash donations was available – albeit for the minority of companies in this guide – we have specified it.

A company's present level of donations does not necessarily indicate future commitments. Sending an appeal to comparatively less generous companies may actually persuade them to increase their donations. Certainly if they never receive appeals there will be no outside pressure on them to change their policy, although, in general, if a company is only giving a little your chances of success are reduced.

Normally, a co-ordinated corporate donor will budget a certain sum for its charitable contributions and stick to this amount. Some allocate their entire budget at an annual meeting; others spread contributions throughout the year. Some give to causes they wish to support until the budget is used up and then stop; others continue to give even after the budget is spent if an appeal takes their fancy. If companies reply to your appeal, many will write and say that their budget is fully committed.

The year end is important in that if you get your appeal in soon afterwards, the company may not have spent its charitable budget for the coming year. However, if a company allocates its budget evenly throughout the year and receives a flood of applications at the start of its new financial year, some, which would have been supported later in the year, now miss out. There is no fail-safe answer to this problem. Nevertheless, your chances of success are usually improved by sending the application earlier rather than later in the company's financial year.

Record layout

The layout used for the records in this guide is described in the breakdown of the fictional company record, Fictitious Productions plc, on page xii. We hope that this example will help users in accessing the information they require on the various types of support that each company offers.

Caution – please note

We are told that companies continue to receive many unsolicited or inappropriate appeals for support. While many bring this upon themselves due to a lack of clear guidelines for potential applicants, this should not be seen as an excuse to conduct blanket mailings. It is vitally important for success to do your research thoroughly and only apply to those companies which are likely to consider your application or request.

Before approaching any company in this guide, its record should be read carefully. As we have stated previously, unless there is some clear link with a company, or your project is clearly within its defined areas of support, you are unlikely to be successful.

We also recommend that you read the guidance on corporate fundraising provided by the Institute of Fundraising on its website. This gives a good overview of the issues involved in undertaking a relationship with a company and is available at: www.institute-of-fundraising.org.uk.

Fictional company record

Below is a typical company record, showing the format we have used to present the information obtained from each of the companies. Remember to always check the company's website for information before making an application. You should submit your request in writing, but may wish to ask for details of the grants procedure, check the contact for charitable donations or request a copy of the latest annual report. The latter, along with community support information, may also be obtained via the quoted website address.

This section provides a summary of the charitable causes that the company is likely to support.

Company registration numbers are taken from Companies House. In the case of a financial institution, such as a building society, FSA numbers are used.

Some companies in the guide have dedicated staff to deal with appeals (in these cases, where available, we have included direct contact details). However, in other companies appeals are dealt with by the company secretary, or public relations or marketing departments. The address refers to the most relevant address to send requests; whether this is the company's head office, the office where the CSR department is located, or the company's corporate charity.

The main area of the company's activity.

These figures give an indication of the scale of the company's giving relative to its size (figures in brackets denote a loss). Some figures have been converted into GBP.

This section provides information about the company's area of operation and the location of its offices.

This section highlights any relevant memberships or accreditations held by the company. Descriptions of these are provided on p. 294.

The 'community involvement' section provides an overview of the companies community strategy and activities.

Here we provide a summary of the types of in-kind support offered by the company. Examples of in-kind support might include the distribution of used stock, free access to company facilities or pro bono work.

Fictitious Productions plc

Social welfare, education, economic development

Company registration number: 111666

Correspondent: A. Grant, CSR Manager, 68 Nowhere Street, Anytown AN6 2LM (tel: 01510 000000; website: www.fictprod.co.uk)

Directors: Terence Story; Shelley Yarn; Luther Tale (female 33%; male 67%).

Nature of business: The company is involved in the production of fictitious information.

Year end	31/12/2017
Turnover	£837,300,000
Pre-tax profit	£292,000,000

Total employees: 7,689

Main locations: Bristol (head office), Grimsby, Liverpool, Perth.

Community involvement

Much of the companies charitable contributions are channelled through its corporate charity the Fictitious Productions Foundation, which provides cash donations to a wide range of local and national charities. The company also provides in-kind donations to charities local to its offices in Bristol, Grimsby, Liverpool and Perth. The company also allows its employees to undertake secondments to local economic development initiatives and social enterprises.

In-kind support

The company donates surplus or used furniture/equipment to local causes.

Employee-led support

A charity is selected each year to benefit from employee fundraising, with the company making a contribution by way of matched funding.

Payroll giving

A scheme is operated by the company.

The 'employee-led support' section provides details of any charitable activities undertaken by company employees. Such activities may include donations made through payroll giving schemes, fundraising or volunteering.

Commercially led support

Sponsorship

The arts: The typical sponsorship range is from £1,000 to £25,000. The company sponsors Southport Sinfonietta and supported music festivals in Grimsby and Perth.

Here we provide details of any of the company's charitable activities, which have a commercial focus. Such activities may include, sponsorship of local sports or cultural events, or the sale of 'charity products'.

Exclusions

No response is given to circular appeals. No grants are given for fundraising events, purely denominational religious appeals, local appeals not in areas of the company's presence, large national appeals, overseas projects, political activities or individuals. Non-commercial advertising is not supported. The company does not sponsor individuals or travel.

The 'exclusions' section lists any causes or types of grants that the company will not consider funding.

Applications

Apply in writing to the correspondent. Applications are considered by a donations committee which meets three times a year.

This section provides details of how and when to submit an application.

Corporate charity

Fictitious Productions Foundation (Charity Commission no. 123456) – see page 229.

Here we list the names and charity numbers of any of the companies associated corporate charities, details of which can be found in the corporate charities section of the book (pp. 229–291).

Community contributions

Cash donations UK	420,000
In-kind support UK	£155,000
Total contributions (cash and in kind)	£575,000

The company's community contributions totalled £575,000 in 2017. This included charitable donations totalling £420,000.

Here we provide a summary of the company's charitable contributions, including (where available) the value of their cash and in-kind donations in the UK and overseas.

And finally . . .

If you have any comments about the guide please get in touch with us at the Research Department, DSC, Suite 103, 1 Old Hall Street, Liverpool L3 9HG; email: research@dsc.org.uk.

Companies in alphabetical order

3i Group plc

Children and young people, education, older people, poverty and social exclusion

Company registration number: 1142830

Correspondent: Kathryn van der Kroft, Communications Director, 16 Palace Street, London SW1E 5JD (tel: 020 7975 3021; email: Kathryn.VanDerKroft@3i.com; website: www.3i.com)

Directors: Caroline Banszky; David Hutchison; Jonathan Asquith; Julia Wilson; Peter Grosch; Simon Borrows; Simon Thompson; Stephen Daintith (female 25%; male 75%).

Nature of business: 3i is an investment company with three complementary businesses, private equity, infrastructure and debt management, specialising in core investment markets in northern Europe and the USA.

Year end	31/03/2018
Turnover	£1,425,000,000
Pre-tax profit	£1,488,000,000

Total employees: 243

Main locations: The group's UK head office is based in London but it also has offices in Amsterdam, Frankfurt, Luxembourg, Madrid, Mumbai, New York, Paris and Singapore.

Community involvement

The group focuses its charitable activities on disadvantaged people, young people, older people and education. There is a preference for supporting both national charities and those local to the London office. It has a partnership with the following charities: Community Links, Contact the Elderly, Historic Royal Palaces, National Youth Orchestra, Snowdon Trust and The Passage. The group makes regular contributions to each charity, usually to support a particular activity or programme.

In-kind support

3i has a policy of matching the amount raised by UK staff through sponsorship by family and friends of their fundraising efforts for registered charities. 3i contributed £30,000 in matched donations in 2017/18.

Employee-led support

Staff contribute via the Give As You Earn scheme in the UK, administered by the Charities Aid Foundation. 3i matches employee donations through this scheme which totalled £50,000 in 2017/18.

3i's London-based employees have been contributing to the Community Links Christmas Toy Appeal for a number of years and donated in excess of 100 presents to the charity's 2017 appeal, which resulted in the collection of 18,000 presents in total for local children.

Applications

Contact the correspondent for further information.

Community contributions

Cash donations UK	£340,000

According to the 2017/18 CSR report, charitable donations totalled £340,000, which includes £30,000 from matched funding.

Abellio ScotRail Ltd

Arts and culture, community development, the environment, health

Company registration number: SC450732

Correspondent: ScotRail in the Community, 5th Floor, Culzean Building, 36 Renfield Street, Glasgow G2 1LU (tel: 0344 811 0141; website: www.scotrail.co.uk/about-scotrail/scotrail-community)

Directors: Alan Pilbeam; Alexander Hynes; Angus Thom; David Lister; Dominic Booth; James Downey; Julian Edwards (female 0%; male 100%).

Nature of business: Abellio ScotRail is a passenger railway service operator in Scotland.

Year end	31/12/2017
Turnover	£668,914,000
Pre-tax profit	(£17,907,000)

UK employees: 4,874

Main locations: The company operates rail services across Scotland.

Community involvement

ScotRail supports community groups and charities through a number of grant programmes focused on biodiversity, regeneration, arts and culture, health and literacy and numeracy. The company also offers groups and individuals the opportunity to utilise and develop station facilities for the benefit of their local communities through its 'Adopt-a-station' scheme.

Station Community Regeneration Fund

The Stations Community Regeneration Fund enables business and community groups to transform redundant station rooms into facilities to benefit local communities.

Any projects that will aid communities or rail passengers will be considered. Grants typically range between £5,000 and £75,000. Bids may also be made for larger sums, but these will be dependent on in-depth feasibility studies.

Grants can be used to contribute towards the costs of any structural repairs and to assist with the costs of fitting out station premises for their intended use. Applications will be assessed on whether they fit with the existing building, businesses and local area, how they meet a market or community demand, and the future benefits expected from the proposal.

The fund is jointly managed and administered by ScotRail and Transport Scotland.

ScotRail Foundation

The ScotRail Foundation aims to empower residents to make a positive difference in their local community by providing grants to community organisations. The foundation's grant programmes are administered by the Scotland Foundation. Recent examples of the foundation's grant programmes include The ScotRail Cultural and Arts Fund and the ScotRail Employee Charitable Giving Fund (see Employee-led section).

For information about the latest funding opportunities from the ScotRail Foundation, check the Scotland Foundation website at: www.foundationscotland.org.uk/programmes/scotrail.

'Adopt-a-station' scheme

The company's 'Adopt-a-station' scheme allows community groups and individuals to utilise and develop station facilities in order to transform the way that communities interact with their local station. According to the company's website, 'station adoption takes many forms including gardening and other tasks'. Charities and community groups are encouraged to participate in the scheme to help raise their profile or to 'showcase their services while promoting interaction with members of the travelling public'.

Participants in the scheme can claim back their expenses from the company and are rewarded with complimentary train tickets and passes. See the website for details.

Previously ScotRail offered participants the opportunity to apply for grants of between £100 and £5,000 to help deliver biodiversity projects. At the time of writing (November 2018), this fund was closed. See the website for updates.

Cycle Fund

Over a period of four years, £100,000 a year is being made available in order to help local councils and community organisations to deliver projects, which enhance cycling infrastructure and encourage as many people as possible to use bikes as an alternative form of everyday transport.

According to the website, the Cycle Fund will provide up to 50% of project costs, and can be used to support projects which:

- Improve directions and signs for cyclists to and from stations
- Upgrade connections between stations and other local services such as schools and town centres
- Improve marketing and promotion of cycling to stations including digital
- Introduce new facilities for customers accessing stations by bike

Employee-led support

The company matches employee fundraising up to £250 per application through its £10,000 Employee Charitable Giving Fund.

Applications

Station Community Regeneration Fund

Phase one application forms and guidance notes can be downloaded from the company's website at: www.scotrail.co.uk/about-scotrail/scotrail-community/stations-community-regeneration-fund For more information, email: SCRF@scotrail.co.uk.

Adopt-a-station scheme

Community groups interested in adopting a station can register their interest by emailing: adoptastation@scotrail.co.uk. Emails should include your name, contact details and the station you are interested in adopting.

Cycle Fund

For further information and to apply, contact cycling manager Kathryn Mackay at: cycle.fund@scotrail.co.uk.

Community contributions

Cash donations UK	£14,500

According to its 2017 annual report, the company made charitable donations of £14,500.

Accenture UK Ltd

Education (particularly financial education), enterprise and training, equal opportunities, projects outside the UK

Company registration number: 4757301

Correspondent: Corporate Citizenship Team, 30 Fenchurch Street, London EC3M 3BD (tel: 020 7844 4000; email: corporatecitizenship@accenture.com; website: www.accenture.com)

Directors: Daniel Burton; Emma McGuigan; Oliver Benzecry; Patrick Rowe; Simon Whitehouse; Zahra Bahrololoumi (female 33%; male 67%).

Nature of business: Accenture provides management consulting, technology and outsourcing services, with more than 305,000 employees; offices and operations in more than 200 cities in 56 countries. Accenture (UK) Ltd is a wholly owned subsidiary of the Accenture group and the main trading entity for Accenture in the United Kingdom.

Year end	31/08/2017
Turnover	£2,644,000,000
Pre-tax profit	£195,000,000

Total employees: 442,000

Main locations: Accenture has offices in Belfast, Edinburgh, Dublin, London, Manchester and Newcastle. The company has a global presence with offices in over 120 countries.

Community involvement

In the UK, the company's corporate citizenship programme, 'Skills to Succeed', focuses on environmental and social sustainability issues, with a particular emphasis on helping young people gain employability and entrepreneurial skills. The programme focuses on young people aged 18–24 who are not in education, employment or training and provides them with support to build skills and obtain work.

Partnerships

Accenture works with multiple partners to deliver the programme. Globally, Accenture want to reach three million people with the programme by 2020. The company has the following strategic partners:

- Bright Ideas Trust
- Business in the Community
- Cherie Blair Foundation for Women
- DePaul
- East London Business Alliance
- Fashion Retail Academy
- Global Action Plan
- OnSide
- The Prince's Trust
- Tomorrow's People

Accenture develops and sponsors programmes with its charity partners, as well as providing its own programme of apprenticeships. The company supports its corporate citizenship programme through cash donations and pro bono work. Employees are encouraged to fundraise and volunteer and in 2017 Accenture released a report – *A 2020 Vision for Employer-Supported Volunteering* – which demonstrated the positive impact that employee volunteering can have on both the business and the wider community.

In-kind support

Employees are given three days paid leave a year for volunteering. In 2016/17 employees contributed more than 726,000 hours to global Accenture-sponsored corporate citizenship activities during work hours, including pro bono consulting projects.

Employee-led support

Employees are encouraged to volunteer and fundraise for community organisations, charities and voluntary groups. In 2016/17 the company's employees contributed more than 185,000 hours of their own time through Accenture-facilitated volunteer events.

Applications

Contact the correspondent for further information.

Community contributions

Cash donations UK	£1,000,000

In 2016/17 Accenture (UK) Ltd made charitable donations totalling over £1 million.

Addleshaw Goddard LLP

Children and young people, community development, education, poverty and social exclusion

Company registration number: OC318149

Correspondent: Claire Cunningham, CSR Manger, Milton Gate, 60 Chiswell Street, London EC1Y 4AG (tel: 020 7606 8855; email: Claire.Cunningham@addleshawgoddard.com; website: www.addleshawgoddard.com)

Directors: Adrian Collins; Charles Penney; John Joyce; Justine Delroy; Malcolm McPherson; Michael Leftley; Michael Lowry; Paul Salsbury; William Wastie (female 11%; male 89%).

Nature of business: Addleshaw Goddard is an international business law firm.

Year end	30/04/2017
Turnover	£188,000,000
Pre-tax profit	£63,644,000

Main locations: In the UK the company has offices in Aberdeen, Edinburgh, Glasgow, London, Leeds and Manchester.

Community involvement

The company's CSR strategy is framed around its objective of 'Unlocking Young Potential'. Young people and communities are supported through the company's three CSR pillars:

- Access to education
- Access to the legal profession
- Access to work

As well as firm-wide programmes, there are local CSR leadership teams which oversee each office's efforts in the local community, such as pro bono work. Each office nominates and fundraises for its own Charity of the Year.

All of this is underpinned by a wider commitment and investment from the firm through the Addleshaw Goddard Charitable Trust (Charity Commission no. 286887), which was established in 2003 to support local charities and CSR-related projects.

Partnerships

The company has 18-month partnerships with charities that align with its objective of 'Unlocking Young Potential'. The four charities it will work with from July 2018 are Centrepoint – Soho, Changing Faces, NSPCC – Leeds and Street League. Employees choose which charities their local office will support and then campaign and fundraise for them.

In-kind support

Employees are able to undertake pro bono legal work.

Employee-led support

Employees have the opportunity to volunteer, campaign and fundraise for charities that meet the company's main CSR objective. The company matches employee's fundraising efforts; in 2016/17 matched funding totalled £29,500.

Applications

Contact the correspondent for further information.

Corporate charity

The Addleshaw Goddard Charitable Trust (Charity Commission no. 286887) – see page 230.

Community contributions

Cash donations UK	£31,000

In 2016/17 the company donated £31,000 to its corporate trust. The trust awarded grants of £45,500 to charities and contributed £29,500 in matched funding.

Admiral Group plc

Children and young people, general charitable purposes, health and medical research, housing and homelessness, older people

Company registration number: 3849958

Correspondent: CSR Team, Ty Admiral, David Street, Cardiff CF10 2EH (tel: 0871 882 8282; website: www.admiralgroup.co.uk)

Directors: Andy Crossley; Annette Court; Colin Holmes; David Stevens; Geraint Jones; Jean Park; Justine Roberts; Manning Rountree; Owen Clarke (female 33%; male 67%).

Nature of business: The group sells and underwrites private car insurance in the UK.

Year end	31/12/2017
Turnover	£1,128,900,000
Pre-tax profit	£403,500,000

Main locations: In the UK the group's principal offices are located in Cardiff, Newport and Swansea. It also has offices in Europe, Canada and Asia.

Community involvement

The group supports communities where it has a presence through charitable donations, matched funding and sponsorship. Most of its CSR is directed through the Admiral Community Chest and the Ministry of Giving. The following information was taken from the group's 2017 CSR report.

Admiral Community Chest

Admiral Community Chest is a fund set up for charities and local organisations which employees and their families are involved with. Employees' fundraising endeavours are matched by the group from this community fund. During 2017, there were 280 successful applications for funding. This included 141 football and rugby teams, 22 schools and nurseries and a variety of other clubs, societies and charities. Examples of donations were given in the CSR report and included:

- Buying a generator for Labradors in Need to use at future fundraising events
- A £600 donation to Growing Space, a charity based in Tredegar park and gardens in Newport to build a compost bin
- A £950 [donation] to help fund ballet classes run by Flamingo Chicks at Ty Gwyn School in Ely for children with disabilities or additional needs
- Buddy benches for a local school. (Buddy benches are put in the playground and children sit on these if they are feeling lonely, and as a result other pupils will see this and offer to play with them)
- A set of underwater speakers for a synchronised swimming club

Ministry of Giving

In 2017 the group started a new initiative: the Ministry of Giving. Through the Ministry of Giving the group will be giving sizeable donations to a small number of charities in South Wales over two years, totalling £400,000. Funding will benefit the areas where the group is based (Cardiff, Swansea or Newport). Employees throughout the UK voted for the following to be supported during 2018:

- Brightening the lives of children with life-limiting illnesses
- Supporting cancer care facilities and charities

- Improving the lives of vulnerable elderly people
- Helping local homeless people

Employee-led support

The group encourages payroll giving and volunteering.

Commercially led support

Sponsorship

The group works with Cardiff Council to provide uniforms for school crossing officers and to raise awareness of road safety in Cardiff. It also sponsors the following:

- Welsh Rugby Union
- Chapter Arts Centre
- NoFit State Circus
- Swansea Waterfront Winterland Open Air Ice Rink
- Techniquest After Hours
- Pride Cymru
- Jermin Productions Theatre Company
- Admiral Ice Rink – Cardiff Winter Wonderland

The group sponsors several races and marathons in Newport, Swansea and Cardiff.

Applications

Apply in writing to the correspondent making reference to either the Ministry of Giving or the Admiral Community Chest. Note: the group prefers to support organisations with which Admiral employees or their immediate family are involved.

Community contributions

Cash donations UK	£140,000

In 2017 Admiral Group donated £140,000 to local and national charities.

Adnams plc

Arts and culture, education, the environment, health, sports and recreation,

Company registration number: 31114

Correspondent: Rebecca Abrahall, Charity Administrator, Sole Bay Brewery, Southwold, Suffolk IP18 6JW (tel: 01502 727200; email: charity@adnams.co.uk; website: www.adnams.co.uk)

Directors: Bridget McIntyre; Dr Andy Wood; Dr Karen Hester; Guy Heald; Jonathan Adnams; Nicky Dulieu; Stephen Pugh; Steven Sharp (female 38%; male 63%).

Nature of business: The principal activities of the company are brewing and distilling; retailing and wholesaling beer, wines, spirits and minerals; pub and hotel ownership and management.

Year end	31/12/2017
Turnover	£74,765,000
Pre-tax profit	£2,109,000

Main locations: The main office and brewery is located in Southwold, Suffolk.

Community involvement

The company's charitable giving is channelled through its corporate charity The Adnams Community Trust (Charity Commission no. 1000203). The company also donates its carrier bag charge to the Suffolk Wildlife Trust.

Commercially led support

The company supports cultural events, such as the Norfolk and Norwich Festival and the Soho Theatre, and sporting events such as the Oxford and Cambridge Boat Race or the Tour of Britain. It is also prepared to sponsor local events and sports teams within a 25-mile radius of Southwold.

Applications

Contact the correspondent for further information.

Corporate charity

The Adnams Community Trust (Charity Commission no. 1000203) – see page 230.

Community contributions

Cash donations UK	£22,000

Adnams gives 1% of its annual profits to charitable causes through The Adnams Community Trust. Donations to the trust during the year amounted to £22,000.

Aggregate Industries Ltd

Community development, education, the environment

Company registration number: 5655952

Correspondent: Local Community Liaison Group, Bardon Hall, Copt Oak Road, Markfield, Leicestershire, United Kingdom LE67 9PJ (tel: 01530 816600; website: www.aggregate.com)

Directors: Francois Petry; John Bowater; Roland Köhler (female 0%; male 100%).

Nature of business: Aggregate Industries and its subsidiaries are engaged in the exploitation of land and mineral reserves principally for the supply of heavy building materials for construction activities. Operating at locations across the UK, Channel Islands, Norway and Northern Europe it employs over 3,500 people.

Aggregate Industries Ltd itself is a holding company with no employees. In 2005 it became part of the Holcim Group which is incorporated in Switzerland.

Year end	31/12/2017
Pre-tax profit	£41,000,000

Total employees: 4,008

Main locations: The company has sites throughout the UK. Community giving appears to be focused around the group headquarters in Leicestershire.

Community involvement

The company carries out a number of community engagement initiatives at their quarries, including working with local schools to provide visits to sites so children can learn more about the industry.

Bardon Hill Community Fund

This will provide £400,000, released in £40,000 tranches over ten years, to support local community initiatives around Bardon Hill Quarry. Eligible organisations include voluntary and community groups. The following is taken from the guidance document:

> The type of project that is likely to be supported is one that includes some or all of the following aspects:
>
> - Shows a direct and reasonable relationship with Bardon Hill Quarry
> - Provides a clear and sustainable benefit to the people of the area
> - Encourages involvement for a wide range of age groups
> - Supports a generally unsupported cause
> - Provides the seed capital to a much larger project
> - Includes match funding from other funding source(s)
>
> There is no minimum application level, but careful consideration should be given to applications of less than £500. It is likely that those applications which cover the following or similar, would not be supported:
>
> - Ongoing contributions for revenue costs such as rent, staff, vehicle running costs etc.
> - Party political motivated projects
> - Projects that implicitly or explicitly discriminate against any group or individual within the community
> - Projects that have a negative or divisive impact in the area

Previous beneficiaries have included: Markfield Parish Council (£30,000); Bardon Sports Club (£13,800); North West Leicestershire District Council (£9,800); Rutland Wildlife Trust (£4,100); Copt Oak Church (£2,000).

Partnerships

The company partnered with Leicester Tigers in 2017 to deliver Concrete Rugby, a free programme for school pupils in years 7, 8 and 9 to be coached by professional Tigers coaches and learn more about living a safe and healthy lifestyle. The 2017 Sustainability Report states that almost 2,000 schoolchildren were reached through the programme during the year.

In-kind support

Goods and materials donated during the year totalled £12,300. The company has an agreement with all UK employees that every year they can spend a day volunteering in company time. The 2017 sustainability report notes that during the year 2,747 hours of labour were volunteered to support community projects.

Employee-led support

Employees are encouraged to fundraise and volunteer for community projects and local charities.

Applications

Apply in writing to your local site addressed 'Community Liaison Group' and referenced 'Community Giving'.

Dates for future meetings of the Bardon Hill Community Fund committee can be found on the guidance documents on the company's website. Application forms can be downloaded from the website and should be returned to: Bardon Hill Quarry Community Fund, c/o Aggregate Industries, Bardon Hill Quarry, Coalville, Leicestershire LE67 1TL.

For more information on the Concrete Rugby Programme, or to find out how your school can take part, email Joe Reynolds, Leicester Tigers Rugby Development Officer, at: joe.reynolds@tigers.co.uk or telephone on 0771 585 6901.

Community contributions

Cash donations UK	£37,500
In-kind support UK	£12,300
Total contributions (cash and in kind)	£50,000

In 2017 cash donations totalled £37,500 and in-kind donations totalled £12,300.

Allen & Overy LLP

Children and young people, community development, disaster relief, education, enterprise and training, equal opportunities, human rights, older people, poverty and social exclusion

Company registration number: OC306763

Correspondent: See 'applications', Bishops Square, One Bishops Square, London E1 6AD (website: www.allenovery.com)

Directors: Andrew Ballheimer; Daniel Shurman; David Lee; Denise Gibson; Jason Haines; Wim Dejonghe (female 17%; male 83%).

Nature of business: Allen & Overy is an international law firm.

Year end	30/04/2017
Turnover	£1,519,000,000
Pre-tax profit	£716,000,000

UK employees: 2,400

Total employees: 5,500

Main locations: The company has 44 offices in 31 countries. In the UK it has offices in London and Belfast.

Community involvement

The company CSR strategy is focused on two major themes: access to justice and access to education and employment. The company's corporate charity, The Allen & Overy Foundation (Charity Commission no. 1153738), is funded by contributions from all Allen & Overy partners around the world. Around 75% of funds are allocated to support local projects with the remaining 25% being donated to international causes.

Access to justice

The company's programmes vary from community to community to reflect local cultures and priorities. It also advises charities and community groups on legal, strategic and business issues. The company undertakes pro bono work in the following areas:

- **Rule of Law** – Allen & Overy work with emerging economies to develop legal and justice systems
- **Free Legal Advice** – free legal advice is provided to vulnerable people in a number of countries, either by providing in-person advice, end-to-end casework or organisational development assistance. In 2015 Allen & Overy, DLA Piper and Coram Children's Legal Centre launched the first Children's Pro Bono Legal Service in the UK to help children gain British Citizenship
- **Human Rights Working Group** – pro bono support is provided to human rights charities and non-governmental organisations, such as Liberty, Amicus, INTERIGHTS and Fair Trials International. This ranges from representing marginalised communities in court and submitting interventions and amicus curiae briefs, to undertaking international comparative research projects to inform policy work
- **Microfinance and Social Investment Group** – advice is provided to microfinance institutions and social enterprises in developing economies around the world

Access to education and employment

The company forms long-term partnerships with schools local to its offices to advise them on issues around governance and financial sustainability, as well as supporting pupils' academic achievement. In London, the local office's current partner is Raine's Foundation School, following a successful ten-year partnership with Bethnal Green Academy. In addition the company runs the following programmes:

- **Artbeat** – students in London and New York are given the opportunity to work with professional artists to create a range of art to be displayed at Allen & Overy's offices and their schools
- **ReStart** – a skills development and mentoring programme for over-50s living in London who have been unemployed between six months and a year. The programme supports people from any background or profession
- **Smart Start** – a work experience scheme that gives year 12 students from non-privileged backgrounds the opportunity to work at Allen & Overy's offices for a week. In 2016 the scheme launched in Hong Kong, India and South Africa

Charity partnerships

In October 2016 the company's two year partnership with Amref Health Africa ended. The 2016/17 accounts note that the company raised £930,000 for the charity through fundraising and donations and contributed £786,000 of pro bono and in-kind support. Through its pro bono work, Allen & Overy helped build Amref's legal advocacy skills to help it campaign more effectively for changes to sexual and reproductive health at community and government level.

Following the success of the partnership with Amref, the company began a new two year partnership with War Child, to support its 'Rescue Childhood' programme. Through a global fundraising campaign, £500,000 was raised in the first six months of partnership. The aim is to raise enough money to fully fund a child-friendly space in one of Jordan's largest refugee camps.

In-kind support

The company's website states that Allen & Overy have provided £16.4 million in pro bono legal support. It also notes that 36,649 hours were spent on pro bono and community investment work by its lawyers globally. Grant recipients of The Allen & Overy Foundation are also offered pro bono support, which in 2016/17 totalled £500,000.

Applications

For more information about pro bono work, or the Artbeat and Start Smart programmes, contact the relevant correspondent.

Corporate charity

The Allen & Overy Foundation (Charity Commission no. 1153738) – see page 231.

Community contributions

Cash donations worldwide	£1,500,000
In-kind support worldwide	£16,400,000
Total contributions (cash and in kind)	£17,900,000

In 2016/17 pro bono support equivalent to £16.4 million was given by the company. The company donated £1.5 million to its corporate charity.

Allianz Insurance plc

General charitable purposes, animal welfare, projects outside the UK

Company registration number: 84638

Correspondent: CSR Team, 57 Ladymead, Guildford, Surrey GU1 1DB (website: www.allianz.co.uk/about-allianz-insurance/social-responsibility.html)

Directors: Christian Dinesen; David Torrance; Jonathan Dye; Mark Churchlow; Richard Hudson; Rosanne Murison (female 17%; male 83%).

Nature of business: Allianz is a financial services company. Its core businesses are insurance and asset management.

Year end	31/12/2017
Turnover	£1,582,400,000
Pre-tax profit	£150,400,000

UK employees: 4,500

Main locations: Allianz has 26 offices throughout the UK.

Community involvement

Allianz provides financial and in-kind support to local and national charities. The company aims to:

- Support charities and voluntary initiatives in the community that are relevant to its business objectives and brand values
- Increase financial contributions through company donations, employee fundraising and payroll giving
- Maximise contributions delivered through non-financial means, such as employee volunteering
- Create lasting value for community partners and employees through training and skills development

Partnerships

Allianz works with a number of charities in the UK aligned to its business. Partner charities receive donations from the company and matches employees' fundraising efforts. Examples of current partnerships include:

- **The Prince's Trust** – The company has supported The Prince's Trust since 2005. Employees volunteer to deliver workshops on work placements and CV and interview skills
- **Association of Air Ambulances Charity (AAAC)** – The AAAC works with all 20 regional air ambulance charities in the UK. The company aims to raise £1 million to support air ambulance services across the country. In 2017 employee fundraising and company contributions raised a total of £358,000
- **Disasters Emergency Committee (DEC)** – In the event of a natural disaster that prompts an appeal by DEC, Allianz will respond by offering an immediate one-off payroll giving facility through which employees can make a tax-efficient donation to the disaster appeal. This donation will be channelled through Care International, the company's chosen international emergency partner for employee donations in the UK

Allianz foundations

There is an international network of 14 Allianz affiliated corporate foundations. In the UK, the corporate foundation is related to Petplan, a subsidiary of Allianz Insurance, which raises funds by requesting a donation with the premiums paid by policyholders. The Petplan Charitable Trust (Charity Commission no. 1032907) received £50,000 from the company in 2017.

In-kind support

Each employee is able to take ten hours of paid time annually to support a local charity or organisation. In 2017, 658 employees gave 5,387 hours of their time to their local communities. This equates to 15% of employees using their volunteering time.

Employee-led support

Employees are encouraged to fundraise and volunteer for the company's charity partners as well as local organisations. Allianz offices are paired with their nearest air ambulance and employees fundraise to support life-saving services in their local area. The company also operates a payroll giving scheme.

Applications

For further details contact the correspondent.

Corporate charity

Petplan Charitable Trust (Charity Commission no. 1032907) – see page 273.

Community contributions

Cash donations UK	£419,000

In 2017 cash donations totalled £419,000. A list of beneficiaries was not available.

Alun Griffiths (Contractors) Ltd

Education, general charitable purposes

Company registration number: 1493003

Correspondent: CSR Team, Waterways House, Merthyr Road, Llanfoist, Abergavenny NP7 9PE (tel: 01873 857211; website: www.alungriffiths.co.uk)

Directors: Anthony Morgan; Huw Llywelyn; Martyn Evans; Nick Mason; Paul Fleetham; Shaun Thompson (female 0%; male 100%).

Nature of business: Alun Griffiths is a civil engineering and construction company.

Year end	31/12/2017
Turnover	£182,400,000
Pre-tax profit	£966,000

Main locations: The company's headquarters are in Abergavenny. There are also offices in Gwynedd, Carmarthenshire, Swansea and Bristol.

Community involvement

The company makes donations to local charities and runs health and safety and careers programmes in local primary schools.

Applications

Contact the correspondent for further information.

Community contributions

Cash donations UK	£202,000

According to the company's website, it donated £202,000 to local charities, clubs and organisations in 2016/17.

Amey UK plc

Children and young people, community development, economic generation, education, enterprise and training, the environment, projects outside the UK

Company registration number: 4736639

Correspondent: Social Responsibility Department, Sherard Building, Edmund Halley Road, Oxford OX4 4DQ (tel: 0800 521660; website: www.amey.co.uk)

Directors: Alfredo García; Andres Camacho; Andrew Milner; Andrew Nelson; Carol Hui; Fernando Gonzalez De Canales Moyano; Fidel Lopez Soria; Ian Tyler (female 13%; male 88%).

Nature of business: Amey provides support services in the UK, ranging from transportation and education, to defence and health.

Year end	31/12/2017
Turnover	£2,200,000,000
Pre-tax profit	£188,900,000

UK employees: 16,966

Main locations: The company has sites across the UK as well as Australia and Qatar.

Community involvement

The company's community involvement centres around employment, skills and training programmes aimed at disadvantaged people. Through local community partnerships, Amey works with over 300 ex-offenders, homeless and disadvantaged young people to provide them with skills and support to find employment.

The company supports STEMNET, an ambassador programme to inspire young people into science, technology, engineering and mathematics (STEM).

Partnerships

Amey has supported a youth charity, The Duke of Edinburgh's Award, for almost 15 years to improve the life chances and employability of young people.

The company is also partnered with the Buy Social Corporate Challenge to promote and support social enterprises in its supply chain. This is complemented by its Gold Partnership with Enactus UK, an international charity that encourages teams of students to create new social enterprises that tackle the UN Sustainable Development Goals. Employees provide mentoring, coaching and advice for Enactus students.

The company has an ongoing partnership with SSAFA and has signed the Armed Forces Covenant to provide employment opportunities to ex-veterans.

In 2017 Amey partnered with Scope to help incorporate better working practices for its employees with disabilities.

In-kind support

The company provides one paid day a year for employees to participate in charities and community projects of their choice. In 2017 around 1,700 employees – about 15% of the workforce – took volunteering leave.

Employee-led support

Employees are encouraged to fundraise and volunteer for charities. In 2017 employees volunteered for a range of organisations including the YHA (Youth Hostel Association), the Trussell Trust, the Wildlife Trusts and the Poppy Factory.

The Amey Foundation (not a registered charity) is a fund held by the company to support employee fundraising activities in their local communities. Any employee taking part in an event to raise money for charity can apply for additional fundraising from the foundation which will match their efforts up to a total of £500.

Applications

Contact the correspondent for further information.

Community contributions

Total contributions (cash and in kind)	£3,800,000

In Amey's parent company's (Ferrovial) 2017 Integrated Annual Report it states that worldwide community investment totalled €4.3 million (≈ £3.8 million as at November 2018). Most of Ferrovial's contributions are in cash (76% in 2017). As 21% of its community investment is in the UK, we have estimated that around €903,000 (≈ £797,000 as at November 2018) was spent on community investment in the UK.

MS Amlin plc

Community development, general charitable purposes

Company registration number: 2854310

Correspondent: Community & Charities Panel, 122 Leadenhall St, London EC3V 4AG (tel: 020 7746 1000; website: www.amlin.com/about-amlin/responsibility.aspx)

Directors: Hironori Morimoto; James Illingworth; Kenichi Fukuhara; Kiyotaka Shuto; Martin Albers; Oliver Peterken; Philip Calnan; Robin Adam; Shinichi Imayoshi; Shonaid Jemmett-Page; Simon Beale (female 9%; male 91%).

Nature of business: Amlin is an independent insurer specialising in providing insurance cover to commercial enterprises and reinsurance protection to other insurance companies around the world.

In late 2015 it was announced that Amlin plc had been acquired by the Mitsui Sumitomo Insurance Company Ltd, which is a wholly owned subsidiary of MS and AD Insurance Group Holdings Inc. The group's name was then changed from Amlin plc to MS Amlin plc.

Year end	31/12/2016
Turnover	£2,627,500,000
Pre-tax profit	£16,100,000

Main locations: The group's UK offices are located in London, Chelmsford and West Malling. The group also has a presence in Europe, the Middle East, Asia and the USA.

Community involvement

Support is given in the communities in which MS Amlin operates, for the education and development of young people, as well as charities that have a connection with employees. In the UK, charitable giving is co-ordinated through a community and charities panel, which is chaired by a senior underwriter. Outside the UK, community and charity budgets are managed by local boards.

During 2016, the group partnered with Macmillan Cancer Support and The Outward Bound Trust.

Employee-led support

Under its CSR policy MS Amlin also encourages individual employees to fundraise on behalf of charities and matches donations.

Commercially led support

Amlin has a dedicated website, Amlin World (www.amlinworld.com) which shares 'in-depth stories' about the activities sponsored and supported by the group and 'showcases everything from sport and the arts, to research and philanthropy'. MS Amlin is also a supporter of the National Open Art Competition.

Applications

Contact the correspondent for further information.

Community contributions

Cash donations UK	£150,000

The 'Community' section of the annual report states: 'In 2016, MS Amlin supported more than 40 UK charities with a total budget of £150,000.' We have taken this figure as the group's cash donations for the year.

We were not able to determine a value for in-kind support provided by the group.

Anglian Water Services Ltd

Community development, education, the environment

Company registration number: 2366656

Correspondent: Community Ambassador, Lancaster House, Lancaster Way, Ermine Business Park, Huntingdon, Cambridgeshire PE29 6XU (tel: 0345 714 5145; website: www.anglianwater.co.uk)

Directors: Dr Stephen Billingham; Duncan Symonds; John Hirst; Natalie Ceeney; Niall Mills; Paul Good; Paul Whittaker; Peter Simpson; Scott Longhurst; Veronica Courtice (female 17%; male 83%).

Nature of business: Anglian Water supply and distribute water, collect and treat waste water, and provide social housing repairs and property development.

Year end	31/03/2018
Turnover	£1,248,900,000
Pre-tax profit	£320,000,000

UK employees: 4,692

Main locations: The company is based in Cambridgeshire; however, there are a number of locations worldwide.

Community involvement

The company is mainly engaged in environmental work around the sites from which it operates. It supports its communities in various ways including:

- Providing a stimulating and hands-on experience of the industry, linked to the National Curriculum, through its education programme delivered at dedicated centres or through school visits
- Raising community awareness of the value of water and encouraging everyone to do their bit
- Promoting Drop 20 and Keep it Clear campaigns through open days at its local sites and community presentations
- Supporting local communities through the employee volunteering scheme – Love to Help
- Involvement in charitable giving through the company's Give As You Earn scheme
- Working in partnership with regional and national bodies to add to the sustainability of the local environment

The company has established the Anglian Water Assistance Fund to support customers in financial hardship. The fund is administered by Charis Grants Ltd on behalf of Anglian Water and the aims are:

- To administer a grants programme aimed at reducing water and sewerage debt for customers experiencing poverty and hardship throughout the region
- To make awards that will help people recover from the burden of debt and become financially more stable
- To make a positive long-term difference to an applicant's financial situation

Further information can be found on Anglian Water's website.

Partnerships

Anglian Water formally recognises WaterAid as its nominated charity and as such it does not offer charitable donations or sponsorship to other charities and bodies.

The company also funds the RiverCare and BeachCare programme that is delivered in partnership with Keep Britain Tidy and local Wildlife Trusts. Voluntary groups establish ownership of a stretch of their local watercourse and undertake a suite of activities including litter picking, removal of non-native species, survey and monitoring flora and fauna and carrying out habitat management and restoration.

Education centres

These purpose-built centres at water recycling sites offer tours at no charge to schools/organisations and offer talks on water, the environment and biodiversity. The education centres can be found at Chelmsford in Essex and Leighton Linslade in Bedfordshire. The website also provides free resources and games for schools to use when teaching about water and the environment.

In-kind support

Love to Help is the company's employee volunteering scheme. Employees can choose one of three ways to volunteer through the programme and the company pledges to match up to thirty hours per year of work time to help staff do more volunteering.

Employee-led support

Employees are able to donate to their chosen charity through a Give As You Earn scheme administered through the Charities Aid Foundation. Employees also fundraise for the company's charity partner – WaterAid. In 2017/18 they raised £902,000.

Applications

Anglian Water only supports WaterAid and does not offer charitable donations or sponsorships to other charities.

Community contributions

Cash donations UK	£40,000

In 2017/18 the company donated £40,000 to WaterAid.

Anglo American plc

Community development, education and training, the environment, health (particularly HIV/AIDS), projects outside the UK

Company registration number: 3564138

Correspondent: Hermien Botes, Head of Sustainability Engagement, 20 Carlton House Terrace, London SW1Y 5AN (tel: 020 7968 8888; email: Hermien.botes@angloamerican.com; website: www.angloamerican.co.uk)

Directors: Anne Stevens; Byron Grote; Ian Ashby; Jack Thompson; Jim Rutherford; Mark Cutifani; Mphu Ramatlapeng; Nolita Fakude; Sir Philip Hampton; Stephen Pearce; Stuart Chambers; Tony O'Neill (female 25%; male 75%).

Nature of business: Anglo American is a global mining business.

Year end	31/12/2017
Turnover	£22,300,000,000
Pre-tax profit	£4,290,000,000

UK employees: 2,000

Total employees: 67,095

Main locations: Anglo American's only UK office is in London. It also has offices and operations in Canada; Europe; South America; South Africa; East Asia; and Australia.

Community involvement

The group focuses mainly on supporting community development, education and health, through its corporate charity, the Anglo American Group Foundation (Charity Commission no. 1111719). Globally, much of the group's community investment is focused on supporting community and health programmes in the areas where it operates, particularly in South Africa and South America.

Partnerships

The group works with a number of organisations to deliver its sustainability goals to support community development activities and to manage biodiversity in its operations. It has partnerships with Business Action for Africa, Danish Institute for Business and Human Rights, Fauna and Flora International, International Alert, TechnoServe, Shift, UNAIDS, and Women in Mining.

Employee-led support

Employee volunteering is organised by each individual business within the group, with a particular focus on: education, skills and youth development; the environment; sustainable community development.

The group is using its 'Ambassadors' volunteering programme in Chile as a model for a group-wide approach. The scheme involves employee teams partnering with local community groups to run projects which can receive up to $5,000 in funding, as well as capacity-building training for community development.

The Anglo American Group Foundation also provides matched funding for funds raised by employees in London and Luxembourg.

Applications

Contact the correspondent for further information.

Corporate charity

Anglo American Group Foundation (Charity Commission no. 1111719) – see page 232.

Community contributions

Total contributions (cash and in kind)	£68,500,000

The 2017 Sustainability Report states that during the year the group's total Corporate Social Investment, including cash and in-kind contributions from the Anglo American Chair's Fund, the Anglo American Group Foundation, and the group's enterprise development programmes, amounted to $88 million (≈ £68.5 million as at November 2018). Corporate Social Investment in the UK totalled $444,000 (≈ £346,000 as at November 2018); however, there was no breakdown of charitable giving available. We have taken this figure as the company's total charitable contributions.

A further $260,000 (≈ £202,500 as at November 2018) was given globally to employee-matched giving and fundraising.

Apax Partners LLP

Education, enterprise and training, projects outside the UK, poverty and social exclusion

Company registration number: OC303117

Correspondent: Ellen de Kreij, Head of London Sustainability Programme, 33 Jermyn Street, London SW1Y 6DN (tel: 020 7872 6300; website: www.apax.com)

Directors: Andrew Sillitoe; Mitch Truwit (female 0%; male 100%).

Nature of business: Apax is an independent global private equity advisory firm.

Year end	31/03/2017
Turnover	£184,245,000
Pre-tax profit	£112,151,000

Total employees: 150,000

Main locations: The firm's UK office is located in London. There are also seven offices worldwide: Hong Kong; Mumbai; Munich; New York; Shanghai; Tel Aviv.

Community involvement

The firm channels its community involvement through its corporate charity, the Apax Foundation (Charity Commission no. 1112845), which supports social entrepreneurship and social mobility. The foundation also has a proportion of its assets in social investment. These include East London Bond and Finance in Motion.

Employee-led support

In 2016/17 the Apax Foundation extended the staff matched funding scheme to match donations made by members of the Apax team 1:1 up to $50,000, as well as continuing to support the efforts of members of the Apex team who give significant time to charitable commitments. The foundation provided £493,500 in matched funding in 2016/17.

Applications

Contact the correspondent for further information on the firm's sustainability programme.

Corporate charity

The Apax Foundation (Charity Commission no. 1112845) – see page 232.

Community contributions

Cash donations UK	£793,500

No figure was given for the firm's charitable contributions. The foundation receives a percentage of the firm's profits which in 2016/17 totalled £793,500. We have taken this figure as the firm's cash donation.

Arla Foods Ltd

Community development, health, general charitable purposes

Company registration number: 2143253

Correspondent: Community Involvement Team, Arla House, 4 Savannah Way, Leeds Valley Park, Leeds LS10 1AB (tel: 0113 382 7000; website: www.arlafoods.co.uk/overview/arla-in-the-uk/community-involvement)

Directors: Afshin Amirahmadi; Ivar Vatne; Kent Skovsager; Kingsley Ajerio; Lucy Williams; Pauline Hogg; Peter Gioertz-Carlsen; Tomas Pietrangeli (female 25%; male 75%).

Nature of business: This company is a subsidiary of Arla Foods UK plc, which is a leading supplier of milk and dairy products in the UK market. The group supplies liquid milk, cream, butter, spreads, cheeses, fresh dairy products, yoghurts and desserts to the major supermarkets.

Year end	31/12/2017
Turnover	£2,536,173,000
Pre-tax profit	£15,483,000

Main locations: The company's head office is in Leeds. It also has sites in Aylesbury, Cheshire, Cornwall, Devon, Hatfield, Leeds, Leicester, Llandyrnog, Lockerbie, London, Oswestry, Settle and Wiltshire.

Community involvement

In the UK, Arla is a corporate partner to Marie Curie Cancer Care and each site supports its local branch of the charity. There is also a Community Challenge initiative which allows employees to have an input into how the company's community involvement budget is used. Community Challenge supports employees' communities in two ways: firstly, funds raised by Arla employees for causes important to them are matched; secondly, funding is given to causes with which employees volunteer.

Applications

Contact the correspondent for further information.

Community contributions

Cash donations UK	£58,000

In 2017 the company declared donations of £58,000 to UK charities.

Arsenal Holdings plc

Children and young people, education, enterprise and training, disability and health, projects outside the UK, poverty and social exclusions, sports and recreation

Company registration number: 4250459

Correspondent: Arsenal in the Community, Highbury House, 75 Drayton Park, London N5 1BU (tel: 020 7619 5003; website: www.arsenal.com/community)

Directors: Chips Keswick; Ivan Gazidis; Josh Kroenke; Kenneth Friar; Lord Harris of Peckham; Stan Kroenke (female 0%; male 100%).

Nature of business: Arsenal FC is a professional football club competing in the Premier League.

Year end	31/05/2017
Turnover	£424,000,000
Pre-tax profit	£44,600,000

Total employees: 695

Main locations: The football club is based in North London.

Community involvement

Arsenal Holdings supports charities and community groups in North London and overseas through partnerships and the delivery of sport and education programmes. Support is also provided through the club's grant-making charity, the Arsenal Foundation.

Arsenal in the Community

Arsenal in the Community was set-up in 1985 and today delivers sport, social and educational programmes to over 5,000 individuals each week. Details of all of the club's current programmes are available on its website.

Sport

Arsenal in the Community runs football programmes for women's football, people with disabilities, young people and walking football. There are also programmes for other sports including hockey and bowls.

Education and training

Arsenal in the Community runs a broad range of education and training programmes from numeracy and literacy classes to further education and employability training. Recent examples of the club's education programmes include:

- **Arsenal Double Club:** A scheme aimed at 'reluctant' learners that combines classroom based teaching with football coaching sessions
- **Enterprise Programme:** A scheme that provides careers advice to students in North London secondary schools about the different jobs that exist at the football club
- **The Arsenal Football and Community Sports Coaching Foundation Degree:** A two-year course, which prepares students for careers in community football coaching and PE teaching

Social inclusion

Arsenal in the Community's social inclusion programmes seek to engage with and support young people who find themselves drawn into the criminal justice system or exposed to substance abuse. Recent examples of the club's social inclusion programmes include:

- **Positive Futures:** This programme runs on ten estates in Islington. It includes youth engagement football sessions that offer additional activities such as trips, workshops, homework clubs and volunteer placements
- **Freedom from Torture:** A joint project between Arsenal in the Community and Freedom from Torture, a medical foundation that helps rehabilitate survivors of torture. The programme is made up of football and classroom sessions, designed to help participants develop confidence as well as language and social skills

Healthy living

Arsenal in the Community works in partnership with Jamie Oliver's Ministry of Food campaign to provide cooking classes to communities in North London.

The Arsenal Foundation (Charity Commission no. 1145668)

The Arsenal Foundation is the club's grant-making charity. In 2016/17 the foundation made grants of £1.2 million to international charity partners such as Save the Children as well as smaller local charities and community groups working in North London.

Applications

Contact the correspondent for more information.

Corporate charity

The Arsenal Foundation (Charity Commission no. 1145668) – see page 233.

Community contributions

Cash donations UK	£54,000

According to the Arsenal Foundation's 2016/17 accounts, during the year Arsenal Holdings donated £54,000 to the charity. The foundation's accounts also state that a further £1.05 million was raised and donated by Arsenal FC; however, this figure is believed to include funds donated by fans, staff members and players as well as money raised through various fundraising events. The club's accounts do not quantify the value of its community programmes or provide any figure for the club's total community contributions. As such, the figure of £54,000 has been taken as the club's total community contribution for 2016/17.

Artemis Investment Management LLP

Education, the environment, health, poverty and social exclusion

Company registration number: OC354068

Correspondent: CSR Team, Cassini House, 57 St James's Street, London SW1A 1LD (tel: 020 7399 6000; website: www.artemisfunds.com/en/about-artemis/artemis-charitable-foundation)

Directors: Alexandra McAndie; Andrew Gray; Antony Page; Cormac Weldon; Derek Stuart; Edward Legget; Elaine Vincent; Graeme Mitchell; Harry Paterson; Jacob De Tusch-Lec; Jane Foster; John Dodd; Johnathan Rigler; Jonathan Loukes; Lesley Cairney; Lindsay Whitelaw; Mark Murray; Mark Niznik; Mark Tyndall; Peter Leckie; Peter Saacke; Philip Wolstencroft; Richard Turpin; Simon Edelsten; Stephen Moore; Stewart Brown; William Littlewood; William Warren; Adrian Frost (female 17%; male 83%).

Nature of business: Artemis is a fund management company.

Year end	31/12/2017
Turnover	£184,902,000

UK employees: 138

Main locations: The company's UK headquarters are in London.

Community involvement

The company's corporate charity, The Artemis Charitable Foundation (OSCR no. SC037857) manages its charitable activities which include grant-making, Charity of the Year schemes and event sponsorship. Grants are made for health, poverty, education and environment in the UK and internationally.

Charity of the Year

The company supports a staff-nominated charity and cancer Charity of the Year. In 2017 the foundation awarded £40,000 to The Rock Trust and £10,000 awards each to the Beatson Cancer Charity, Brain Tumour Research, Cancer Support Scotland, Farleigh Hospice, Royal Marsden Cancer Charity and Teens Unite Facing Cancer.

Employee-led support

Staff volunteer with partner charities and company-sponsored events. The company also encourages staff to participate in charitable events by covering their registration fees and other related costs while encouraging personal fundraising for the event. The company's Give As You Earn scheme is match funded (up to an annual limit) by partners of the company.

Commercially led support

Artemis sponsor several charity-related events each year such as The Artemis Great Kindrochit Quadrathlon and The Balmoral Challenge.

Applications

Contact the correspondent for further information.

Corporate charity

The Artemis Charitable Foundation (OSCR no. SC037857) – see page 233.

Community contributions

According to the Artemis Charitable Foundation's 2017 accounts, it received £1.04 million from Artemis Investment Management LLP. This figure included Gift Aid and corporate sponsorship.

Arup Group Ltd

Children and young people, community development, disaster relief, education (particularly STEM subjects and the built environment), health, poverty and social exclusion

Company registration number: 1312454

Correspondent: Alison Ball, Associate Director, Sustainability, 13 Fitzroy Street, London W1T 4BQ (tel: 0151 227 9397; email: alison.ball@arup.com; website: www.arup.com)

Directors: Alan Belfield; Dervilla Mitchell; Fiona Cousins; Genevieve Shore; Gregory Hodkinson; Jerome Frost; Matthew Tweedie; Michael Kwok; Peter Bailey; Peter Chamley; Thomas Whyte; Timothy Stone; Tristam Carfrae (female 23%; male 77%).

Nature of business: Arup is an independent firm of planners, designers, engineers and consultants working across the built environment. It is a wholly independent organisation, which is owned in trust for the benefit of its employees and their dependants and has no shareholders or external investors. Each of Arup's employees receives a share of the firm's operating profit each year.

Year end	31/03/2017
Turnover	£1,509,500,000
Pre-tax profit	£66,500,000

Total employees: 13,346

Main locations: The group's head office is in London and it has various offices around the UK in Belfast, Bristol, Cardiff, Edinburgh, Glasgow, Leeds, Liverpool, Manchester, Newcastle, Nottingham, Sheffield, Solihull, Winchester and York. The group also operates in a further 35 countries around the world.

Community involvement

The annual report for 2016/17 notes that one of Arup's core values is social usefulness, which the group expresses in its commitment to various charitable causes. Donations are made by the group and also through its various corporate charities. Employees around the world also volunteer their time, undertake pro bono work and fundraise for various causes that share the same values as the group.

UK corporate charities

Arup has two corporate charities which receive income from the group. The Ove Arup Partnership Charitable Trust (Charity Commission no. 1038737) makes grants for general charitable purposes and The Ove Arup Foundation (Charity Commission no. 328138) supports academic research into the built environment.

Arup Education Trust, South Africa

The Arup Education Trust (AET) provides financial assistance to eligible beneficiaries in tertiary and secondary education. AET places qualified students into the corporate environment, eliminating the gap between study and employment.

Charity partners

The company's founder, Ove Arup, was also a founder member of RedR, a UK-based international charity that deploys skilled professionals in emergency situations around the world. The company has a long-standing partnership with this charity, with its own engineers providing support during disasters such as earthquakes and hurricanes. Employees also regularly fundraise for the charity.

In the UK, the company's current partners include: Arup Educational Trust, Bridges to Prosperity, Engineering Development Trust, Engineers Without Borders UK, FRANK Water and The Prince's Trust.

In-kind support

Employees can undertake pro bono work which is sponsored by Arup. Arup then make contributions towards the costs of approved projects. In 2016/17 employees volunteered 9,300 hours of company time to this programme.

Employee-led support

Employees are encouraged to participate across a broad range of activities in the local communities where the company operates by donating their skills and expertise. The employee engagement programme is made up of three strands:

- **Local Engagement:** providing support to organisations and communities that are local to Arup offices and for whom its skills are particularly relevant
- **Development:** providing technical assistance to community-based and international organisations; delivering projects that improve people's lives in developing and newly industrialised countries
- **Disaster Response and Recovery:** enabling employees to respond to humanitarian needs by supporting fundraising initiatives and responding to requests for technical support

For further information visit: www.arupcommunity.org

Applications

For further information contact the correspondent or your local Community Engagement team.

Corporate charity

Ove Arup Partnership Charitable Trust (Charity Commission no. 1038737) – see page 234. The Ove Arup Foundation (Charity Commission no. 328138) – see page 234.

Community contributions

The group's website notes the following:

> Arup's Community Engagement programme invests about 3% of our profits on community engagement work each year, in five fields of activity. We support local community engagement work, a development fund, disaster relief and recovery work, our Global Challenge, education work, and carbon reduction initiatives.

In 2016/17, £5 million was invested in the Global Challenge Fund and an additional £438,000 was donated to The Ove Arup Partnership Charitable Trust. We were unable to determine a figure for charitable donations in the UK during the year.

Asda Stores Ltd

Children and young people, community development, education, health, sports and recreation, women

Company registration number: 464777

Correspondent: Local Community Champion, Asda House, Southbank, Great Wilson Street, Leeds LS11 5AD (tel: 0113 243 5435; website: www.asda.com)

Directors: Alexander Simpson; Roger Burnley (female 0%; male 100%).

Nature of business: Asda is a food, clothing and general merchandise retailer with stores and services throughout the

UK and online. In 1999 Asda became part of Wal-Mart Stores Inc.

Year end	31/12/2017
Turnover	£21,951,800,000
Pre-tax profit	£379,000,000

UK employees: 145,000

Main locations: Asda has locations throughout the UK.

Community involvement

The majority of Asda's charitable giving is made through its charity, The Asda Foundation (Charity Commission no. 1124268), which makes grants to charities nominated by store employees. The foundation supplements the good causes that employees support locally, as well as a number of bigger ad hoc projects. The general public can nominate local voluntary and not-for-profit schools to receive a donation of £200 or £500 through the Green Token scheme in stores.

You can find information for your local area, including community initiatives, your local community champion and details on how to nominate an organisation for support, by visiting the 'Find your nearest Asda' facility on the community webpage.

In-kind support

Asda stores are FareShare partners and from 2013 to 2016, Asda provided FareShare with 2,195 tonnes of surplus food to redistribute to UK charities and community groups across the country, enough to make over 5.2 million meals for people in need. In-kind support is also given to the Salvation Army Trading Company. Asda has other partnerships with In Kind Direct and the Company Shop to pass on surplus stock. Asda also provides space in its stores for charities and community groups to use free of charge.

Employee-led support

Asda employees support their local communities in the following ways:

- **In-store fundraising** – community groups can raise funds through activities such as bag packing
- **Employee fundraising** – employees organise fundraising events and can also apply for additional funding from the Asda Foundation
- **Healthy eating sessions in schools** – Asda Community Champions deliver talks and workshops on what makes a healthy, balanced diet and how to cook healthy snacks in schools
- **Volunteering** – Asda employees spent 150,517 hours volunteering for local organisations in 2017

Commercially led support

Asda donates some of the proceeds from the carrier bag charge to social investment initiatives in Scotland and Wales as well as to its partner charities in England.

Applications

Applicants should approach the Community Champion at their local store to see if they are eligible for support.

Corporate charity

The Asda Foundation (Charity Commission no. 1124268) – see page 234.

Community contributions

In 2017 the company's total cash donation, including monies raised through store collections and product sales, totalled £6.2 million. This includes donations to the Asda Foundation of £4 million. Unfortunately, there is no breakdown between cash raised by customers and staff and cash donated by the company.

Ashmore Group plc

Children and young people, disaster relief, economic generation, education, enterprise and training, general charitable purposes, projects outside the UK

Company registration number: 3675683

Correspondent: CSR Team, 61 Aldwych, London WC2B 4AE (tel: 020 3077 6000; email: ashmail@ashmoregroup.com; website: www.ashmoregroup.com)

Directors: Clive Adamson; Dame Anne Pringle; David Bennett; Jennifer Bingham; Mark Coombs; Peter Gibbs; Tom Shippey (female 29%; male 71%).

Nature of business: Ashmore Group is a specialist emerging markets fund manager across six core investment themes: external debt, local currency, special situations, equity, corporate high yield and multi-strategy.

Year end	30/06/2017
Turnover	£257,200,000
Pre-tax profit	£206,200,000

Total employees: 270

Main locations: The group's head office in the UK is in London. It also has a number of worldwide locations.

Community involvement

The majority of the group's CSR is channelled through the work of its corporate charity, The Ashmore Foundation (Charity Commission no. 1122351). Local charities benefit from employee fundraising and volunteering, which the group supports through matched donations. According to its 2016/17 annual report, the group continues to make 'an annual donation of foreign coins and banknotes' to the Alzheimer's Society, and to support local charities with gifts in kind. The group also responds to emergency appeals from the Red Cross if there is a link to a country where it has a presence.

The Ashmore Foundation (Charity Commission no. 1122351)

The Ashmore Foundation currently has seven priority countries (Brazil, Colombia, India, Indonesia, Mexico, Philippines and Turkey) based on the location of Ashmore offices and the existence of a strong civil sector and clear social needs on which the foundation can focus. Grants are available for NGOs staffed by local people that are working in the following areas:

- **Education** – specifically, local organisations bringing children and young people who are marginalised from mainstream education into regular education, improving their educational attainment and job prospects
- **Livelihoods** – specifically, local organisations providing vocational training for disadvantaged young people, building local capacity for sustainable enterprises and supporting social enterprises benefitting disadvantaged groups

Grants are usually multi-year and range in size depending on the scale and nature of the programme and the organisation's capacity, but a typical partnership grant is between £20,000 and £50,000 per year over three years. In 2017 the foundation awarded grants of $905,000 (≈ £709,000 as at November 2018).

In-kind support

Ashmore also supports the foundation's charitable activities through the provision of pro bono office space, administrative support and a matched funding commitment for employee donations to the Ashmore Foundation. The group allows employees to take one day annually to support charitable projects.

Employee-led support

The Ashmore Foundation is supported solely by Ashmore and its employees globally. Income to the foundation is supported by a matched giving scheme, whereby Ashmore will match individual donations to the foundation of up to £2,000 per Ashmore employee per year and match employee group fundraising donations (for example through Ashmore Challenge events) of up to £50,000 per year. The foundation matches donations made directly to foundation grantees of up to £500 per

Ashmore employee per year. Voluntary donation income for 2017 was $145,000 (≈ £113,500 as at November 2018) from Ashmore employee bonus waivers, direct donations to the foundation via the payroll giving scheme and fundraising activities.

Support from employees extends beyond financial aid through to active engagement in fundraising and a network of support which includes volunteering, mentoring and helping NGOs expand their network of contacts. The group also matches employees' fundraising efforts. Charities that have been supported recently include the Alzheimer's Society and Resurgo, a London-based charity that supports young people.

Applications

For further information on how your charity can work with the group, contact your local office's CSR team.

Community contributions

Cash donations UK	£100,000

The 2016/17 annual report notes that the group made charitable donations of £100,000 to its corporate charity.

Ashtead Group plc

Education, enterprise and training, disaster relief, general charitable purposes, housing and homelessness, projects outside the UK

Company registration number: 1807982

Correspondent: Local Service Centre CSR Team, 100 Cheapside, London EC2V 6DT (tel: 020 7726 9700; website: www.ashtead-group.com)

Directors: Brendan Horgan; Chris Cole; Geoff Drabble; Ian Sutcliffe; Lucinda Riches; Michael Pratt; Paul Walker; Tanya Fratto; Wayne Edmunds (female 22%; male 78%).

Nature of business: Ashtead is an international equipment rental company with national networks in the USA and the UK and a small presence in Canada. The group rents a full range of construction and industrial equipment across a wide variety of applications to a diverse customer base.

Year end	30/04/2018
Turnover	£3,706,000,000
Pre-tax profit	£862,100,000

UK employees: 3,571

Total employees: 15,981

Main locations: The group's head office is in London but it has 187 locations nationwide. It also operates in Canada and the USA.

FTSE4Good

Community involvement

The group comprises of three brands: Sunbelt Rentals US, Sunbelt Rentals Canada and A-Plant in the UK. We have focused on the charitable activities of the UK brand A-Plant, although the group's CSR strategy is equally as involved overseas. In the USA and Canada it supports ex-veterans through The Gary Sinise Foundation and has a partnership with the American Red Cross and Second Harvest Food Bank. The group provides in-kind support to communities affected by natural disasters in the USA.

In the UK, A-Plant is a patron of, and provides support for, CRASH, the construction and property industry's charity for homeless people. A-Plant delivers improved accommodation to homeless people through professional expertise, building materials and financial donations.

It is also a partner of The Prince's Trust, helping young people gain access to jobs in construction, civil engineering and other sectors associated with the built environment. The Ashtead Group forms part of The Prince's Trust Built Environment Leadership Group and donations from this group helped 800 young people move into the sector in 2017.

In-kind support

A-Plant supplies equipment free of charge for projects at nature reserves, community centres, schools and gardens. It also works with BBC's DIY SOS for a variety of refurbishment projects including a support centre to help veterans find homes and new careers.

Employee-led support

The group's employees are encouraged to volunteer and fundraise for their chosen charities, as well as contribute to group-wide initiatives.

Applications

Contact the correspondent for further information. You can find your local centre on A-Plant's website: www.aplant.com/service-centres.

Community contributions

Cash donations worldwide	£1,800,000

The 2017/18 accounts state that charitable donations in the year totalled £1.8 million and we have taken this as the overall figure for the total worldwide cash donation. A-Plant makes an annual donation to The Prince's Trust of £15,000.

Associated British Ports

Arts and culture, children and young people, community development, disability, education, enterprise and training, the environment, health, sports and recreation

Company registration number: ZC000195

Correspondent: Corporate Communications Manager, 25 Bedford Street, London WC2E 9ES (email: csr@abports.co.uk; website: www.abports.co.uk)

Directors: James Bryce; Sebastian Bull; Philippe Busslinger; Philip Butcher; John Coghlan; Hakim Drissi; Stewart Hicks; Peter Hofbauer; George Kay; Eric Machiels; John Morea; Philip Nolan; Henrik Pedersen; Gregory Pestrak; John Rishton; Dmitry Yashnikov (female 0%; male 100%).

Nature of business: The principal activities of the company comprise the ownership, operation and development of port facilities and the provision of related services in the UK where it owns 21 general cargo ports. The group also provides other transport facilities and related services including the Hams Hall rail freight terminal in the Midlands.

Year end	31/12/2017
Turnover	£540,100,000
Pre-tax profit	£247,500,000

UK employees: 2,076

Main locations: The Associated British Ports (ABP) group has sites across the UK. For more information see: www.abports.co.uk/our_locations.

Community involvement

The ABP group assists the causes that their employees support on a local, regional and national level.

ABP Southampton Sailing Academy

In 2014 the company launched the ABP Southampton Sailing Academy. The Sailing Academy gives local youngsters the opportunity to take to the water and learn new skills such as teamwork, communication and self-reliance.

Charities of the year

In 2017, two local hospices located on the north and south bank of the Humber that offer support and respite for people with life limiting illnesses were announced as the charities of the year for ABP Humber.

St Andrew's Hospice cares for both adults and children with life-limiting illnesses under one roof in Grimsby. Adult patients are aged 18 and over, and come mainly from North East

Lincolnshire for overnight stays or respite. There is also a comprehensive well-being programme for people to participate in, such as creative writing, cooking and gardening.

Andy's at St Andrew's Hospice is the only children's hospice in Lincolnshire and East Yorkshire, so many families travel to use its services.

Dove House Hospice is maintained by funds raised in the local community and as such, there are no charges for any services offered.

The ABP Social Team will be liaising with both charities to arrange and facilitate fundraising events as well as supporting existing events which will be directly led by each charity.

In-kind support

In-kind support includes staff volunteering and the provision of free access to some of the group's facilities.

Employee-led support

Employees are very involved in fundraising within their local communities.

A team drawn from across ABP's 21 ports entered the 30th annual Macmillan Cancer Support House of Lords vs House of Commons Tug of War fundraising event at Westminster in June.

Also in this year a group of employees from Humber has given up a few hours each week to help children in Humber improve their reading skills. Each of the volunteers has been trained by Beanstalk (a charity that trains people to help with reading in primary schools) and provided with appropriate books and literacy materials. Normally schools are asked for a donation, but ABP has covered these costs meaning the programme is free to the schools that use ABP employees.

Give As You Earn: Through the scheme ABP continues to match employee donations and meet the administration costs.

Commercially led support

Sponsorships

The group has sponsored the Welsh National Opera (WNO) continuously for 30 years.

Following on from the inaugural ABP Southampton Half Marathon and 10K in 2015, ABP Southampton has announced that it will return as headline sponsor for the second-year running.

ABP and the organisers are 'building up an army of ABP Milemakers to line the route and cheer on the runners'. In addition, ABP is donating £200 to every charity or community group that acts as an ABP Milemaker.

Associated British Ports (ABP) will once again sponsor Immingham's East Midlands in Bloom campaign.

Applications

Apply in writing to the correspondent. There is a contact list for all of the company's ports at: www.abports.co.uk/Contact_Us/Contact_Ports_Direct.

Community contributions

Cash donations UK	£112,500

In 2017 cash donations as declared in the report and accounts were £112,500. We were unable to determine the total value of cash donations and in-kind contributions.

AstraZeneca plc

Education (particularly STEM subjects), disaster relief, health and medical research, projects outside the UK

Company registration number: 2723534

Correspondent: Corporate Responsibility Team, 1 Francis Crick Avenue, Cambridge Biomedical Campus, Cambridge CB2 0AA (tel: 0800 783 0033; website: www.astrazeneca.com)

Directors: Deborah Eldracher; Genevieve Berger; Graham Chipchase; John Broadley; Leif Johansson; Marc Dunoyer; Marcus Wallenberg; Pascal Soriot; Rudolph Markham; Sabera Rahman; Sherilyn McCoy; The Rt Hon Baroness Shriti Vadera (female 42%; male 58%).

Nature of business: The group's principal activities are the research, development and marketing of medicines for serious health conditions.

Year end	31/12/2017
Turnover	£17,300,000,000
Pre-tax profit	£1,714,000,000

UK employees: 6,600

Total employees: 61,100

Main locations: AstraZeneca has various locations throughout the UK and overseas.

Community involvement

The group's community investment strategy focuses on community healthcare and STEM education. It also supports disaster relief.

Partnerships

The British Red Cross continues to be the group's global disaster relief partner, with the majority of disaster relief donations channelled through it. In 2017 the group funded a deployment of a mass sanitation unit to Northern Uganda where it provided more than 13,000 refugees with access to a safe latrine and reached more than 19,000 refugees with hygiene promotion activities.

The group is also partnered with the UK educational charity Career Ready to support increased participation by 16- to 19-year-olds in STEM subjects.

Patient organisations

The group works with patient groups and health charities to share knowledge and information. It provides charitable donations and sponsorship to organisations benefitting healthcare, health promotion and the NHS.

In-kind support

The group provides in-kind support of product donations to charitable organisations and has a global volunteering allowance of one day for all employees. In 2017 employees volunteered more than 29,000 hours on community projects around the world.

Employee-led support

In the UK, the group offers a Give As You Earn programme that allows local employees to manage their own charitable giving fund. In 2017 more than 550 employees made almost 6,000 donations to UK charities for a total of more than £390,000 in charitable funding. Employees also act as STEM mentors and, at the Cambridge site in the UK, staff joined the BioVenture weekend to support young entrepreneurs and help them take their innovative ideas from academia into commercial research.

Applications

Contact the correspondent for further information.

Community contributions

Total contributions (cash and in kind)	£331,000,000

According to AstraZeneca's annual report, in 2017 the group spent over \$426 million (≈ £331 million as at September 2018) worldwide in community investment sponsorships, partnerships and charitable donations worldwide, including product donation and patient assistance programmes that make its medicines available free of charge or at reduced prices. Of this, \$25 million (≈ £19 million as at September 2018) in 'community investment contributions' were made to more than 900 non-profit organisations in 61 countries around the world. The remaining \$401 million (≈ £308.5 million as at September 2018) comprises medicines donated in connection with patient assistance programmes around the world. We were unable to determine a figure for cash donations.

Autonomous Research LLP

Arts and culture, community development, disability, education (particularly financial education), health, projects outside the UK, poverty and social exclusion

Company registration number: OC343985

Correspondent: c/o Moore Stephens, 150 Aldersgate Street, London EC1A 4AB (tel: 020 7334 9191; email: info@autonomous-research.com; website: www.autonomous-research.com)

Directors: Erickson Davies; Lord Myners.

Nature of business: Autonomous Research is one of the leading independent stock analysis firms in the City of London.

Year end	31/03/2018
Turnover	£30,000,000
Pre-tax profit	£15,400,000

Main locations: The company's UK office is in London. There are also offices in Hong Kong and New York.

Community involvement

The company's website states that it partners with a small number of charities, and also allocates a share of its profits to charitable causes through its corporate charities: the Autonomous Research Charitable Trust in the UK and the Autonomous Research Foundation in the USA.

Partner charities

The company's website states that its current core charities are: Auditory Verbal, a UK-registered charity which provides services and advice to families with deaf babies and children; WellFound, a UK-registered charity which delivers clean water projects in remote parts of Africa; and W!SE (Working In Support of Education), a US-based charity which provides financial education. Previous partner charities have included: Food Cycle; Find Your Feet; Five Talents; One Degree; Plan International; Smart Works.

Corporate charity

Autonomous Research Charitable Trust (Charity Commission no. 1137503) – see page 235.

Community contributions

Cash donations UK	£301,500

In 2017/18 the company made charitable donations totalling £301,500 to UK-registered charities.

Autotrader Group plc

Community development and general charitable purposes

Company registration number: 9439967

Correspondent: Christos Tsaprounis, Head of People and Culture, 1 Tony Wilson Place, Manchester M15 4FN (tel: 0161 669 9888; website: plc.autotrader.co.uk/responsibility)

Directors: Claire Baty; David Keens; Ed Williams; Jeni Mundy; Jill Easterbrook; Nathan Coe; Trevor Mather (female 43%; male 57%).

Nature of business: Auto Trader is an automotive classified advertising business.

Year end	31/03/2018
Turnover	£330,100,000
Pre-tax profit	£210,800,000

Main locations: The company has offices in Manchester and London.

Community involvement

The company provides support through its community fund and matched funding initiatives.

The Auto Trader Community Fund

The fund makes grants of up to £1,000 for grassroots community activity in any of the ten boroughs of Manchester. Organisations applying to the fund should have an annual income of less than £60,000.

Partnerships

The company has a partnership with HOME arts centre in Manchester. The company supports various initiatives including arts festivals and the Bring the Family film programme.

In-kind support

Staff receive two volunteering days per year.

Employee-led support

Around 11% of staff are enrolled on the company's Give As You Earn scheme.

Matched funding

Direct donations to charities through the Auto Trader Sponsorships initiative totalled £60,000. The initiative provides matched funding to employees, customers and partners fundraising for charities.

Applications

The Auto Trader Community Fund

The fund is administered by Forever Manchester. Visit the website for further information: www.forevermanchester.com/auto-trader-community-fund

For all other enquiries, contact the correspondent.

Community contributions

Cash donations UK	£120,000

In 2017/18 the company donated £60,000 through its community fund and a further £60,000 through matched funding.

Aveva Group plc

Children and young people, education (particularly STEM subjects), general charitable purposes, projects outside the UK

Company registration number: 2937296

Correspondent: Corporate Responsibility Team, High Cross, Madingley Road, Cambridge CB3 0HB (tel: 01223 556655; website: www.aveva.com)

Directors: Christopher Humphrey; Craig Hayman; Emmanuel Babeau; James Kidd; Jennifer Allerton; Peter Herweck; Philip Aiken; Ron Mobed (female 13%; male 88%).

Nature of business: The principal activities of the group are the marketing and development of computer software and services for engineering and related solutions.

Year end	31/03/2018
Turnover	£704,633,000
Pre-tax profit	£64,643,000

Total employees: 4,400

Main locations: Aveva has offices in more than 40 countries. The group's UK offices are in Cambridge.

Community involvement

The group's charitable giving centres around promoting STEM subjects and supporting employees' charitable activities.

Employee-led support

The group supports employees' fundraising efforts for charities of their choice by matching the funding raised. Charities that benefitted during the year included Sarcoma UK, Macmillan Cancer Support and East Anglia Children's Hospice.

Employees volunteer as STEM ambassadors to deliver talks in schools and university and mentor students. In the UK, the company has worked with the Engineering Development Trust to help deliver different initiatives aimed at encouraging students to take more STEM subjects.

Applications

Contact the correspondent for further information.

Community contributions

Cash donations UK	£50,000

In 2017/18 the group donated nearly £50,000 to charities and good causes.

Beneficiaries included: the British Red Cross, Arthur Rankin Hospice, Guide Dogs for the Blind, and the Alzheimer's Society.

Aviva plc

Children and young people, community development, disability, disaster relief, the environment, health, older people, poverty and social exclusion, safety and crime prevention, sports and recreation

Company registration number: 2468686

Correspondent: Corporate Responsibility Team, Aviva, Wellington Row, York YO90 1WR (tel: 020 7283 2000; email: cccc@aviva.com or cr.team@aviva.com; website: community-fund.aviva.co.uk)

Directors: Andy Briggs; Belén García; Claudia Arney; Glyn Barker; Keith Williams; Maurice Tulloch; Michael Hawker; Michael Mire; Patricia Cross; Sir Adrian Montague; Thomas Stoddard (female 27%; male 73%).

Nature of business: The company transacts life assurance and long-term savings business, fund management, and all classes of general insurance through its subsidiaries, associates and branches in the UK, Europe, Asia and Canada.

Year end	31/12/2017
Turnover	£49,653,000,000
Pre-tax profit	£2,374,000,000

UK employees: 15,000

Total employees: 30,000

Main locations: The group has offices across the UK, as well as in a number of countries worldwide.

Community involvement

The majority of support is given through the Aviva Community Fund (not a registered charity), which provides grants for organisations to run community projects, focusing on: health; disability; children and young people; older people; sport; environment; community.

Aviva Community Fund UK

Community projects can be submitted online by, or on behalf of, a community organisation or charity in the UK. Projects can then be voted for online and the final winners are picked by a judging panel and awarded funding.

There are four categories of grants that can be awarded: up to £1,000; up to £5,000; up to £10,000; and up to £25,000. The categories change each year. In 2018 the categories were:

- **Environment** – funding for community projects trying to improve their natural surroundings, increase sustainability or regenerate community areas to create habitats for wildlife
- **Health and well-being** – funding for projects aiming to help people take control of their physical and mental health, regardless of age or situation
- **Skills for life** – funding for communities and individuals to help improve their lives by learning new skills, particularly financial literacy and digital skills

In 2017 2,400 projects were supported across the UK.

There is a separate set of awards for projects submitted and supported by an insurance broker. The broker awards are open to any UK-based insurance broker. You do not need to have an existing account or relationship with Aviva to enter into the broker awards.

The first 1,000 customer entries and the first 1,000 employee entries also receive £200 if they do not win any of the funding awards. Aviva have partnered with Crowdfunder to increase the amount of money received even if you do not get through to the judging round.

Partnerships

In early 2016, the group began a three year partnership with the British Red Cross (BRC), working to support community resilience to disasters in the UK and globally. The group is a member of the Disaster Relief Alliance, investing in BRC's work in preparedness, response, recovery and innovation, and has sponsored the BRC Community Reserve Volunteer project which aims to create a network of 10,000 people to help when disaster strikes their local community. Aviva also repeated its Aviva Global Mapathon which creates digital up-to-date maps, helping aid organisations reach families who live in remote areas of countries like Nepal and Bangladesh. The group will also offer its expertise in risk management, employee volunteering and matched funding for employee fundraising.

In-kind support

The group offers paid volunteering leave to employees, and also provides matched funding for employee fundraising. In 2017 employees volunteered for a total of almost 48,500 hours and raised over £1.2 million. The group has set an aim of reaching 200,000 hours of volunteering by 2020.

Employee-led support

Employees are encouraged to fundraise and volunteer for charitable organisations.

Exclusions

A full list of exclusions from the Aviva Community Fund is provided on the fund's website.

Applications

Apply in writing via post or email to the Corporate Responsibility Team.

Community contributions

Total contributions (cash and in kind)	£11,900,000

In 2017 the group contributed a total of £11.9 million worldwide mainly through its community funds. The annual report notes that 2,400 projects were supported during the year.

Avon Cosmetics Ltd

Breast cancer, domestic violence, women

Company registration number: 592235

Correspondent: UK Causes Team, Avon Products Inc., Global Headquarters, Building 6, Chiswick Park, London W4 5HR (email: avoncr@avon.com or uk.contact@avon.com; website: www.avon.uk.com/Causes)

Directors: James Wilson; Jonathan Myers; Susan Ormiston (female 33%; male 67%).

Nature of business: Avon distributes and sells beauty, gift and decorative products. Core trading continues to be the marketing of products through an established network of active sales representatives. Avon products are sold and distributed in approximately 70 countries worldwide.

Year end	31/12/2017
Turnover	£210,000,000
Pre-tax profit	£909,600,000

Total employees: 6,000,000+

Main locations: The company operates in approximately 70 countries worldwide. In the UK, Avon's head office is in Northampton and the global head office is in London.

Community involvement

Avon markets itself as the company for women and is therefore committed to supporting causes that are more likely to affect women, such as breast cancer and domestic violence. The company's website notes that globally, Avon has donated 'more than $957 million to date as one of the world's largest supporter of women's causes'.

The Avon Foundation (USA)

In 1955 the company formalised its philanthropic efforts with the creation of the Avon Foundation, which aims to improve the lives of women and their families, with particular focus on breast cancer and domestic violence. The foundation has funded the Justice Institute on Gender-Based Violence, an innovative and interactive training programme that provides participants with the tools needed to better identify, investigate and prosecute gender-based violent crimes. The latest annual report for the foundation, and details on programmes, grants and educational materials, can be found on the Avon Foundation website: www.avonfoundation.org.

In-kind support

Avon provide hampers to anyone fundraising for one of their partner charities.

Commercially led support

Representatives around the world sell specially designed 'pink ribbon' products which Avon and the Avon Foundation award a portion of the proceeds of to organisations and institutions working to eradicate breast cancer. Grants are made within the country in which the funds are raised. The company also sells products that raise money for domestic violence charities.

Applications

Apply in writing to the correspondent or contact your nearest Avon representative.

Community contributions

Cash donations UK	£402,000

In 2017 the company made charitable donations amounting to £385,000 to breast cancer charities and organisations working with survivors of domestic violence. The company spent an additional £17,200 on campaigns and other charitable activities.

Beneficiaries included: Breakthrough; Children are Butterflies; Crazy Hats; Coppafeel; Kettering General Hospital; Northamptonshire Community Foundation; Refuge; Women's Aid.

Axis Europe plc

Poverty and social exclusion

Company registration number: 1991637

Correspondent: 145–149 Vauxhall Street, London SE11 5RH (website: www.axiseurope.com)

Directors: John Hayes; Sally Hayes; Stephen Lang; Stephen Lang; Timothy Hayes; Yusuf Ibrahim (female 17%; male 83%).

Nature of business: Axis Europe is a property improvement and maintenance contractor.

Year end	31/03/2017
Turnover	£137,700,000
Pre-tax profit	£7,437,000

UK employees: 860

Main locations: The company has ten offices throughout London, the West Midlands and the South East.

Community involvement

The company provides support to welfare projects in London, the South East and West Midlands through its corporate foundation, Axis Foundation (Charity Commission no. 1126117).

In-kind support

Employees are given paid leave to volunteer for local charities.

Corporate charity

Axis Foundation (Charity Commission no. 1126117) – see page 235.

Community contributions

Cash donations UK	£106,000
In-kind support UK	£76,500
Total contributions (cash and in kind)	£182,500

In 2016/17 the company declared cash donations of £106,000 which was given to Axis Foundation, the company's corporate charity. Employee time was valued at £76,500.

BAE Systems plc

The armed forces and military heritage, community development, STEM subjects, projects outside the UK

Company registration number: 1470151

Correspondent: Corporate Responsibility Team, Corporate Responsibility Head Office, 6 Carlton Gardens, London SW1Y 5AD (email: corporate.responsibility@baesystems.com; website: www.baesystems.com)

Directors: Charles Woodburn; Chris Grigg; Elizabeth Corley; Harriet Green; Ian Tyler; Jerry DeMuro; Nick Rose; Paula Rosput Reynolds; Peter Lynas; Revathi Advaithi; Sir Roger Carr (female 36%; male 64%).

Nature of business: The main activity of the group is defence, comprising the design and manufacture of civil and military aircraft, surface ships, submarines, space systems, radar, communications, electronics and guided weapon systems.

Year end	31/12/2017
Turnover	£18,322,000,000
Pre-tax profit	£1,480,000,000

UK employees: 34,300

Total employees: 83,200

Main locations: BAE Systems has offices throughout the United Kingdom, Australia, India, Saudi Arabia and the USA.

Community involvement

Support is mainly focused on communities where the company operates and issues connected to the group's business such as the armed forces and STEM education. The group provides one-off support as well as undertaking longer projects that help charities plan work in advance.

Armed forces

In the UK the group supports five leading armed forces charities – ABF The Soldiers' Charity, Combat Stress, the RAF Benevolent Fund, the Royal Navy and Royal Marines Charity, and SSAFA.

The group has also made a donation of £5 million over five years to the new Defence and National Rehabilitation Centre (DNRC) which will replace the UK's current facility at Headley Court.

Education

The group's UK businesses are involved in programmes that encourage young people to follow careers in engineering. It also partners with The Prince's Trust to help deliver the Movement to Work scheme which provides work experience for young people.

Communities

The Big Build scheme is run by BAE's land UK business. Its aim is to build STEM into projects, helping local communities while encouraging apprentices and graduates to follow engineering and technical careers. For example, in 2017 employees built a playground suitable for children with disabilities at the Grace House respite charity in Sunderland.

In-kind support

Where possible, volunteering is integrated into formal career development programmes. During 2017, employees volunteered 15,000 hours in work time, contributing to various company-endorsed projects and activities. The 2017 annual report notes that global in-kind contributions totalled £600,000.

Employee-led support

Employees contribute their time, knowledge and skills to fundraise and volunteer for local schools and charities. In the UK, BAE has a matched funding programme which matches employee contributions within specific capped levels via payroll giving.

Exclusions

Funding and support is not provided to individuals or non-charitable organisations involved in fundraising activities.

Applications

Apply in writing to the correspondent. Requests for funding or support should fall within one of the four following areas:

- The armed forces and their families
- Science, technology, engineering and maths education
- Local communities
- Employee fundraising and volunteering

Community contributions

Total contributions (cash and in kind)	£11,300,000

In 2017 the group and its employees contributed £11.3 million globally through its community investment programme. Over £4.3 million was donated in support of the armed forces, £3.5 million was donated to support education initiatives in STEM subjects, £3.2 million was donated to community projects and £300,000 was awarded to heritage projects. We were unable to determine a figure for cash donations, or specific contributions in the UK. Global in-kind contributions totalled £600,000.

Baillie Gifford and Co. Ltd

Arts and culture, community development, sports and recreation, projects outside the UK

Company registration number: SC069524

Correspondent: Sponsorship Committee, Calton Square, 1 Greenside Row, Edinburgh EH1 3AN (tel: 0131 275 2000; website: www.bailliegifford.com/en/uk/about-us/corporate-citizenship)

Directors: Alan Paterson; Andrew Telfer; Colin Fraser; Derek McGowan; Evan Delaney; Michael Wiley; Patrick Edwardson; Richard Letham; Susan Swindells (female 11%; male 89%).

Nature of business: Baillie Gifford is an investment management company.

Year end	31/03/2018
Turnover	£137,435,000
Pre-tax profit	£10,074,000

Main locations: The company is based in Edinburgh.

Community involvement

The company supports organisations through its sponsorship programme.

Sponsorship

The company currently sponsors around 50 organisations throughout the UK and internationally. In the UK support is provided for: communities and citizenship, arts and culture and grassroots sports. There is a focus on Scottish organisations. International support includes education initiatives and help for refugees. In 2017/18 the sponsorship budget was spent as follows:

Communities and citizenship	45%
Arts and culture	45%
International	5%
Grassroots sports	5%

Beneficiaries included: Lothian Derby Dolls; ProjectScotland; Scottish Ballet; United World Schools; V&A Dundee.

Applications

The company's website states:

> Before submitting your proposal, we recommend you read our Focus on Sponsorship brochure, which features case studies from a number of our sponsorship partners. It's worth bearing in mind that we steer away from sponsoring elite sports or capital projects.
>
> If you have an initiative you would like us to consider, please get in touch with the relevant team:
>
> **The Arts –** SponsorshipArtsGroup@BaillieGifford.com
>
> **Grassroots sport –** SponsorshipSportsGroup@BaillieGifford.com
>
> **International sponsorship –** SponsorshipInternationalGroup@BaillieGifford.com
>
> For all proposals relating to communities and citizenship, or general sponsorship enquiries, get in touch with Sponsorship Manager, Samantha Pattman, at Samantha.Pattman@bailliegifford.com.

Community contributions

We were unable to determine the company's charitable contributions for 2017/18.

Balfour Beatty plc

Children and young people, education, enterprise and training, general charitable purposes

Company registration number: 395826

Correspondent: Balfour Beatty Community Engagement Working Group, 5 Churchill Place, Canary Wharf, London E14 5HU (tel: 020 7216 6800; email: sustainability@balfourbeatty.com; website: www.balfourbeatty.com)

Directors: Barbara Moorhouse; Iain Ferguson; Leo Quinn; Michael Lucki; Philip Aiken; Philip Harrison; Stephen Billingham; Stuart Doughty (female 13%; male 88%).

Nature of business: Balfour Beatty is an international infrastructure group that delivers services essential to the development, creation and care of infrastructure assets; from finance and development, through design and project management to construction and maintenance; either alone or in partnership and by integrating local supply chains.

Year end	31/12/2017
Turnover	£6,916,000,000
Pre-tax profit	£117,000,000

Total employees: 28,000

Main locations: The group operates across the UK. Its head office is in London.

Community involvement

Balfour Beatty aims to improve social cohesion and inclusion in local communities through cash donations, in-kind support and employee-led initiatives. Much of its charitable giving is through The Balfour Beatty Charitable Trust (Charity Commission no. 1127453) which is funded through a combination of employee fundraising and financial support from the group.

The group was a founding member of the Health in Construction Leadership Group and supports the Mates in Mind charity, which aims to improve and raise awareness of mental health in the construction industry. The group also provides work placements and mentors for people nominated by charities, such as Leonard Cheshire Disability and The Amos Bursary.

In-kind support

The company has provided in-kind support to several projects during the year, totalling £95,000.

Employee-led support

Employees volunteer for local organisations to help deliver construction projects. Across the company's operations, employees volunteered 12,400 hours for charitable causes in 2017. Employees raised £157,500 during the year.

Applications

Contact the correspondent for further information.

Corporate charity

The Balfour Beatty Charitable Trust (Charity Commission no. 1127453) – see page 235.

Community contributions

Cash donations UK	£102,000
Cash donations overseas	£577,000
In-kind support UK	£95,000
Total contributions (cash and in kind)	£774,000

In 2017 the UK business made direct cash donations of £102,000. The 2017 accounts note that the USA branch contributed $430,000 (≈ £337,000 as at November 2018) to charitable causes and the Hong Kong, mainland China and Singapore branches provided over HK$2.4 million (≈ £240,000 as at November 2018) in sponsorships, scholarships and charitable donations. We have taken the overseas figures, as well as the cash and in-kind donations in the UK as the group's total charitable contribution (£774,000).

Bank of Ireland (UK) plc

Arts and culture, children and young people, education, poverty and social exclusion, projects outside the UK

Company registration number: 7022885

Correspondent: Corporate Responsibility Officer, Head Office GB, Bow Bells House, 1 Bread Street, London EC4M 9BE (email: responsiblebusiness@boi.com; website: www.bank-of-ireland.co.uk)

Directors: Desmond Crowley; Donal Collins; John Baines; John Maltby; Mimi Kung; Neil Fuller; Philip Moore; Robert Sharpe; Susan Harris; Thomas McAreavey (female 20%; male 80%).

Nature of business: Bank of Ireland provides an extensive range of banking and other financial services in Great Britain and Northern Ireland.

Year end	31/12/2017
Turnover	£471,000,000
Pre-tax profit	£151,000,000

UK employees: 177

Main locations: The company has offices throughout the UK.

Community involvement

Much of the bank's charitable work is employee-led, although it also contributes a lot of in-kind support and gives charities opportunities to feature their branding on its sponsorship of sports teams.

Give Together

The company's main approach has been to channel community investment through an initiative called Give Together. Employees are allowed to take one day's paid volunteering leave a year, and the company matches the funds they raise for charities, as well as facilitating payroll giving. Since its launch in 2007, Give Together has raised €33.6 million (≈ £30.2 million as at September 2018) and resulted in 8,700 volunteer days of support for charitable organisations.

The bank has four partner charities: Age Action, The Alzheimer's Society, The Jack and Jill Foundation and The Irish Heart Foundation. Examples of how the company and its employees worked with these charities can be found in the 2017 Responsibility Report.

In-kind support

The bank offers in-kind support to its partnership charities as well as charities local to its branches. It offers one-day training courses to community groups and charities in partnership with Business in the Community Ireland. In 2017 it welcomed 160 charity employees to its learning centre in Dublin for facilitator-led training in a number of different areas, including negotiation, leadership development, people management and PC skills.

As well as supporting charities through volunteering and fundraising, the bank halves its current account fees and charges for charities and not-for-profit organisations in Ireland and Northern Ireland. In 2017 this saved organisations approximately €2.9 million (≈ £2.6 million as at September 2018).

Employees are given one day's paid volunteering leave per year. In 2017 employees volunteered a total of over 1,300 days.

Employee-led support

Employees participate in payroll giving schemes and fundraising events which provide funding for the bank's Florin Fund and its Third World Fund which supports projects in developing countries. During the year €846,000 (≈ £753,500 as at September 2018) was given by the fund in support of 44 overseas projects.

Commercially led support

Sponsorship

The bank has community sponsorships in rugby, soccer, the Gaelic Athletics Association (GAA), golf and other areas and supports more than 5,200 sports clubs. As well as sponsoring larger clubs like Leinster, Munster and Ulster rugby, the bank invests in smaller, amateur clubs and primary and secondary school communities.

The bank also supports arts and culture through its Cultural and Heritage Centre in College Green and sponsors the Bank of Ireland Junk Kouture initiative.

Applications

Contact the correspondent for further information.

Community contributions

In 2017 charitable giving totalled €2.8 million (≈ £2.5 million as at September 2018) but we were unable to determine how much of this was directly from the company or raised by employees and customers.

The Banks Group Ltd

Community development, the environment, general charitable purposes

Company registration number: 2267400

Correspondent: James Eaglesham, Fund Manager, Inkerman House, St John's Road, Meadowfield, Durham DH7 8XL (tel: 0191 378 6100; email: enquiries@banksgroup.co.uk; website: www.banksgroup.co.uk)

Directors: Andrew Cunningham; Andrew Fisher; Christopher Gill; David Martin; Gavin Styles; Harry Banks; Richard Dunkley (female 0%; male 100%).

Nature of business: The Banks Group is a family-owned energy and property development business. The group's activities are undertaken under three operational divisions: Banks Mining, Banks Renewables, and Banks Property.

Year end	01/10/2017
Turnover	£94,749,000
Pre-tax profit	(£3,025,000)

Total employees: 334

Main locations: The group's main office locations are in Durham and Lanarkshire. The group also operates in various locations in the Midlands; North East England; North West England; Scotland; and Yorkshire.

Community involvement

The Banks Group channels its charitable giving through the Banks Community Fund, which awards grants to voluntary organisations in the communities in which it operates. Preference is given to community projects that provide physical benefits (including improvements to community buildings, community renewable energy projects, biodiversity projects, club or sporting facilities) or social benefits (such as increasing employment opportunities, skills and training).

The Banks Community Fund

The Banks Community Fund was established in 1997 and provides support to community groups, voluntary organisations and environmental projects located near to current or proposed Banks Group developments. It is administered by the County Durham Community Foundation.

The fund gains its income from a variety of sources from within the Banks Group. A funding panel, which includes representatives from local communities, oversees the fund. Grants are normally of up to £5,000 but in exceptional circumstances can be more. To be eligible projects must aim to:

- Bring land back into use
- Reduce or prevent pollution
- Provide information on sustainable waste management
- Build, improve or maintain public parks or amenities
- Build, improve or maintain community buildings or amenities
- Improve quality of life in a local environment
- Promote or conserve biological diversity through the provision, conservation, restoration or enhancement of a natural habitat or the maintenance or recovery of a species in its natural habitat

To receive funding, applicant organisations must be open to the public for a minimum of four evenings per week, two days per week or 104 days per year and be located within an area where the Banks Group is currently operating. To check if your organisation or project is located within an area of benefit visit: www.banksgroup.co.uk/projects/all.

Examples of previously funded projects are available on the group's website.

Connect2Renewables

Connect2Renewables is an initiative between the local communities, Banks and South Lanarkshire Council which seeks to maximise the social and economic benefit of developments to the local area. The scheme focuses on supporting local people to gain apprenticeships and workplace learning placements. The scheme is administered by South Lanarkshire Council.

Employee-led support

According to the news section of the company's website, employees regularly hold fundraising events to support local community groups and charities.

Applications

To apply to any of the community funds, first contact the group's Fund Manager by phone or email. Applicants may then be able to make a full application via the County Durham Community Foundation's website, where application guidelines and deadline dates are available: www.cdcf.org.uk/apply-for-a-grant/grants-for-groups/banks-community-fund.

Community contributions

The group did not declare its charitable or community contributions in its latest accounts for 2016/17.

Previous beneficiaries of the Banks Community Fund have included: Hazelrigg Victory Football Club (£8,000); Hawick and Wilton Cricket Club (£6,000); Cramlington Town Council, Dinnington Village Social Club, The Bill McLaren Foundation and The Briardale Community Centre (£5,000 each); Ashington Amateur Boxing Club (£3,900); Hickleton Village Hall (£3,000); Groundwork Cresswell, Ashfield and Mansfield (£2,000); Avondale Community Beekeepers (£1,400); Barnburgh Church (£975); Rotherham Brownie Pack (£250).

J. Barbour and Sons Ltd

Animal welfare, the armed forces, arts and culture, community development, disability, education, the environment and rural heritage, housing and homelessness, medical research, older people

Company registration number: 124201

Correspondent: Audrey Harvey, Barbour Foundation Grants Administrator, PO Box 21, Guisborough, Cleveland TS14 8YH (tel: 0191 427 4221; email: barbour.foundation@barbour.com; website: www.barbour.com/uk/corporate-social-responsibility/charities)

Directors: Dame Margaret Barbour; Helen Humphrey; Ian Beattie; Ian Sime; Stephen Buck (female 40%; male 60%).

Nature of business: J. Barbour and Sons (Barbour) is a British luxury and lifestyle brand that designs, manufactures and markets clothing, footwear and accessories.

Year end	30/04/2017
Turnover	£184,300,000
Pre-tax profit	£29,300,000

Main locations: The head office and main production site is in South Shields.

Community involvement

Barbour's CSR is focused on supporting causes in the North East, where its head office and factory is located and where the company has historic roots. The Barbour Foundation (Charity Commission no. 328081) was formed in 1988 by Dame Margaret Barbour. Barbour also donates clothing and jackets in kind to support agricultural and rural workers and craftspeople, as well as to young homeless people through Centrepoint.

The Barbour Foundation

The foundation supports charitable causes, cultural and community projects and women's groups primarily in the North East. In 2016/17 the foundation awarded 552 grants totalling £845,500. The accounts provided the following breakdown:

Medical	£226,500
Community welfare	£140,500
Children and young people	£124,000
Housing/homeless	£86,500
The arts	£73,500
Disability	£55,000
Education	£55,000
Service charities	£25,000
Conservation/horticultural	£21,000
Older people	£14,500
Animal welfare	£13,000
Maritime	£5,700
Special appeals	£3,500
Heritage/museums	£1,000

Beneficiaries included: West End School (£62,500); Hospitality and Hope South Tyneside and North Music Trust (£50,000 each); Elton John Aids Foundation (£20,000); The Royal British Legion (£10,000); North of England Refugee Service and Young Asian Voices (£5,000 each); Fire Fighters Charity, Jesmond Library and Middleton in Teesdale Methodist Church (£2,000 each); Byker Community Association, Evenwood Family Support Project, Northern Children's Book Festival and South Tyneside Women's Aid (£1,000 each).

In-kind support

At the time of writing (November 2018), Barbour donate clothing and jackets to the following charities: Broads Reed and Sedge Cutters Association; Centrepoint; Dry Stone Walling Association; Freshwater Habitats Trust; Groundwork South Tyneside and Newcastle; Upper Teesdale Agricultural Support Services. It also donates clothing and jackets to two Princes Countryside Fund apprentices each season. In 2016/17 in-kind donations worth £5,500 were made through the Barbour Foundation.

Exclusions

The foundation does not support the following:

- Requests from outside the geographical area
- Individual applications, unless backed by a particular charitable organisation
- Capital grants for building projects

Applications

Grant applications should be made in writing and sent to the correspondent. The application should include detailed information of what the grant will be used for, a statement of accounts and the official charity number of the applicant. A main grants meeting is held every three to four months to consider applications for grants of more than £500; smaller grants are considered on a monthly basis.

For further information on corporate partnerships or sponsorship, contact Barbour's CSR Team.

Community contributions

We were unable to determine a figure for the company's community contributions.

Barclays plc

The armed forces, arts and culture, children and young people, disability, education (particularly financial education), sports and recreation

Company registration number: 48839

Correspondent: Barclays Community Affairs, 1 Churchill Place, Canary Wharf, London E14 5HP (tel: 020 7116 4451; email: ukcommunity@barclays.com; website: www.barclays.com)

Directors: Crawford Gillies; Diane Schueneman; Dr Dambisa Moyo; James Staley; John McFarlane; Mary Citrino; Mary Francis; Matthew Lester; Michael Turner; Mike Ashley; Reuben Jeffery III; Sir Gerald Grimstone; Sir Ian Cheshire; Tim Breedon; Tushar Morzaria (female 27%; male 73%).

Nature of business: Barclays is a British multinational investment bank and financial services company. Apart from investment banking, Barclays is organised into four core businesses: personal banking, corporate banking, wealth management, and investment management.

Year end	31/12/2017
Turnover	£21,076,000,000
Pre-tax profit	£3,541,000,000

UK employees: 47,000

Total employees: 97,418

Main locations: Barclays has two offices in London and branches across the UK. The company has a presence in over 50 countries across the world.

Community involvement

Barclays is committed to playing a broader role in the communities where the group has a presence. This is undertaken through its community investment programmes and the direct efforts of its employees. The Shared Growth Ambition is the group's strategy on citizenship and sustainability. It is focused on three areas: access to employment; access to financial and digital empowerment; and access to financing. Barclays runs a number of community investment programmes globally and in the UK. The website provides examples of Barclays' latest projects.

The Armed Forces Transition Employment and Resettlement (AFTER) programme

AFTER was launched in partnership with the Ministry of Defence and a number of service charities to support the transition of armed forces personnel in their transition to civilian employment. Barclays Military Services Network run two or three Military Talent Days each year outlining opportunities within their organisation for veterans. It also runs CV and interview workshops and there is a Military Internship Programme.

Charity partners also run education and vocational courses funded by Barclays. Partners have included ABF The Soldiers' Charity, The Royal Air Force Benevolent Fund, RFEA, The Royal Navy Benevolent Trust, Stoll and Support Our Paras.

Partnerships

In September 2016, Barclays, in partnership with Shelter, set up a pilot programme called Sustainable Home Ownership and Resettlement (SHOR) to provide customers at risk of losing their home with full debt advice. In situations when financial solutions such as interest rate reductions or mortgage term extensions are no longer suitable, the customer is referred to Shelter to help them get more income via benefits they do not realise they are eligible for, allowing the customer to keep their home. Where homeownership is not sustainable, customers receive a housing advice and support service that seeks to achieve a 'soft landing' out of homeownership, including sourcing alternative accommodation.

Employee-led support

Employees engage in fundraising and volunteering activities. In 2017 over 50% of employees participated in volunteering, fundraising or regular giving activities, with 43,700 unique participants.

Commercially led support

Barclays looks for sponsorship opportunities which help form positive associations with its brand. It is the principal sponsor of the Donmar Warehouse and the annual Barclaycard presents the British Summer Time Hyde Park. Barclays has sponsored the Premier League since 2001 when it first sponsored the league under the Barclaycard brand. Barclays was sponsor of the league until the end of the 2015–16 season when it agreed a new sponsorship until the end of the 2018–19 season.

Exclusions

According to its website, Barclays does not sponsor the following:

- Political or religious associations
- Sponsorship properties which have already given significant exposure for our competitors in banking
- Sponsorship properties which are perceived to have or encompass a dangerous or violent nature (e.g. boxing)
- Sponsorships where Barclays or its employees have or are perceived to have a conflict of interest
- Sponsorships of teams (by exception only)
- Sponsorship of individuals (by exception only)
- An event which is due to commence in the next two months

Applications

Barclays Community Affairs

Enquiries for charitable or community sponsorship should be made by email to ukcommunity@barclays.co.uk or by phone to 020 7116 4451.

Event Sponsorship

Enquiries for event sponsorship should be made by email to sponsorshipenquiries@barclays.co.uk. Consult the 'Applying for sponsorship' section on the website (www.home.barclays/about-barclays/sponsorship.html) for application details.

Community contributions

Cash donations worldwide	£30,300,000
In-kind support worldwide	£9,200,000
Total contributions (cash and in kind)	£39,500,000

The group uses the London Benchmarking Group framework and reports that globally Barclays spent £42.1 million in community investment, of which cash donations totalled £30.3 million (72%) and staff volunteering amounted to £9.2 million (22%). A further £2.5 million was spent on management costs (6%) but for the purposes of this book we do not include this figure. In the 2017 annual report the group states that over £4.25 million was awarded to military charities to assist wounded and injured service personnel in employment transition. A further breakdown of giving was not included.

A. G. Barr plc

Community development, the environment, health, poverty and social exclusion, sports and recreation

Company registration number: SC005653

Correspondent: CSR Committee, Westfield House, 4 Mollins Road, Cumbernauld G68 9HD (tel: 01236 852400; website: www.agbarr.co.uk)

Directors: Andrew Memmott; David Ritchie; John Nicolson; Jonathan Kemp; Julie Barr; Martin Griffiths; Pamela Powell; Robin Barr; Roger White; Stuart Lorimer; Susan Barratt (female 27%; male 73%).

Nature of business: The group trades principally as a manufacturer, distributor and seller of soft drinks.

Year end	27/01/2018
Turnover	£277,700,000
Pre-tax profit	£44,900,000

UK employees: 900+

Main locations: The company has offices and distribution centres across the UK in Bolton, Cumbernauld, Dagenham, Forfar, London, Manchester, Milton Keynes, Newcastle, Sheffield and Wednesbury.

Community involvement

Local and national charities are supported through financial support, in-kind support and long-term partnerships. According to the company website, support is focused in three main areas:

- Encouraging health, well-being and physical activity
- Protecting the environment and championing sustainability
- Tackling social inequality

Partnerships

The company works in partnership with local schools, taking part in a variety of events to help pupils develop their business awareness as well as supporting them to develop some of the softer skills required in the workplace.

In 2016 Macmillan Cancer Support became the company's charity partner following a company-wide vote. The partnership will continue for three years. Every employee sets out to raise £27 each during each year of the partnership which will fund one hour of cancer care.

The company has a long-term partnership with Keep Scotland Beautiful and is one of the founding funders of its Roadside Litter Campaign.

Cumbernauld Community Fund

Following the installation of a wind turbine at the Cumbernauld site, a community benefit fund of around £120,000 is available to local charities and groups. Employees can nominate local charities to receive a share of around £6,000 per year. Organisations that have received grants from the fund include the Craighalbert Centre in Cumbernauld, Condorrat City Youth Football Team, High Barrwood Respite in Kilsyth and the Friends of Merkland School in Kirkintilloch. Previous research has suggested that similar funds may be available to communities local to the company's sites.

In-kind support

In-kind support is normally provided through donations of products. In 2017/18 over 500,000 bottles of Strathmore water were provided to community and charity road races. The company developed a new employee volunteering policy in 2017/18 which allows employees paid time off to take part in activities which support Macmillan.

Employee-led support

Employees are encouraged to fundraise and volunteer for the company's partner charities.

Applications

Requests for support can be made through the Community and Charity Enquires section of the company's website: www.agbarr.co.uk/contact-us/community-charity-enquiries.

Community contributions

The company does not declare its cash donations and we were unable to determine how much was given in the year. It has previously stated in past annual reports that it gives 1% of profits after tax to charitable causes.

Bayer plc

Arts and culture, children and young people, community development, education, enterprise and training, the environment, health and medical research, projects outside the UK

Company registration number: 935048

Correspondent: Corporate Grants Committee, 400 South Oak Way, Green Park, Reading, Berkshire RG2 6AD (email: communications.ukireland@bayer.com; website: www.bayer.co.uk)

Directors: Arun Kurdikar; Lars Bruening; Vera Hahn (female 67%; male 33%).

Nature of business: Bayer in the UK and Ireland is part of the global company Bayer AG, based in Leverkusen, Germany. In the UK and Ireland, the business includes: pharmaceuticals; consumer health; crop science; animal health; and material sciences.

Year end	31/12/2017
Turnover	£720,400,000
Pre-tax profit	£86,700,000

UK employees: 739

Main locations: The group's locations in the UK and Ireland are: Cambridge; Dublin; Newbury (headquarters). Internationally, the group is based in Germany and has operations across the world.

Community involvement

Bayer has been involved in social, community and environmental programmes across the UK and Ireland for a number of years. It supports numerous social responsibility programs, often in partnership with other organisations. The company supports activities that are local to its operations, and are also linked to employees' community activities or connected to the company's products or services.

Charitable giving

The website provides detailed information on eligibility criteria. Support is given for activities which enhance local quality of life through:

- The environment
- Community care
- Culture and the arts
- Education
- Projects in line with [Bayer's] purpose
- Projects benefiting groups and not individuals

While activities meeting the above criteria will be considered, other factors (such as budget already committed) will also be taken into account.

Grants to patient groups and healthcare organisations

Bayer also makes grants to patient advocacy and other voluntary health groups to raise awareness of diseases and develop interventions for at-risk populations.

The group also provides funding and in-kind support for organisations involved with health professionals or research for the purposes of improving patient care.

Beneficiaries included: RNIB (£50,000 in four grants); Endometriosis UK (£15,000); Heart Failure Alliance (£6,600); Atrial Fibrillation Association (£1,700); Men's Health Forum (£500).

Education

Bayer has opened a free laboratory (Baylab) for schools in the UK. Based in Green Park, Reading, it offers pupils in key stage 1–5 the opportunity to use equipment, conduct experiments, solve tasks and develop solutions.

Since 2001, Bayer's Crop Science business in the UK has been collaborating with long-term partners who are committed to the future of farming and has set up educational events and award schemes to support these partnerships.

International Bayer Foundations

The group has two corporate foundations, based in Leverkusen, Germany. The Bayer Science and Education Foundation supports science fellowships, science programmes in schools and other science awards. The Bayer Cares Foundation supports volunteering programmes, disaster relief and social innovation in health.

In-kind support

In the past the company has provided in-kind support to charities by donating healthcare products to humanitarian charities.

Employee-led support

Fundraising and volunteering

The group encourages employee volunteering and works with Volunteer Centre West Berkshire to develop volunteering opportunities. These have included team challenges at local charities Growing2Gether, Headley, and the Five a Day market garden at Englefield. Employees also planted indigenous trees and shrubs at Goldwell Park, Newbury.

Bayer employees have ongoing annual challenges to raise funds for local charities and previous events include several London to Paris cycles. During the year, employees raised almost £26,000 for Together for Short Lives, a UK charity which supports seriously ill children and their families.

Commercially led support

Sponsorship

The group sponsors the Cultivate Programme for young people in the Thames Valley to develop their business ideas, with prizes worth £1,000. The programme is run by the Education Business Partnership, West Berkshire, and involves young people working with assigned mentors over a period of four months. Around ten shortlisted candidates and groups from local schools then present their ideas and business plans to a judging panel at a grand awards ceremony.

Exclusions

According to the website, Bayer is unable to support:

- Individuals
- Religious, political or racially aligned movements
- Projects or activities bridging a gap in government or local authority funding
- Sporting or recreational activities unless closely associated to Bayer
- Entries in log books, year books or support advertising
- Projects of a local nature which are outside key locations of Berkshire, Cambridge and Dublin
- Conferences, lectures, trips, respite breaks or holidays

Applications

Applications for support can be made using a form available to download from the website, along with eligibility criteria. Forms should be submitted by post or by email. The company asks that applicants do not telephone to discuss applications. The Corporate Grants Committee reviews applications on a monthly basis. The committee will contact applicants by email or letter to inform them of its decision.

Community contributions

Total contributions (cash and in kind)	£187,000

The 2017 annual report states that the company spent £187,000 on its corporate social responsibility programmes during the year.

BBA Aviation plc

Children and young people, community development, disaster relief, education (particularly STEM subjects), projects outside the UK

Company registration number: 53688

Correspondent: Charitable Giving Committee, 105 Wigmore Street, London W1U 1QY (tel: 020 7514 3999; email: info@bbaaviation.com; website: www.bbaaviation.com)

Directors: Amee Chande; David Crook; Emma Gilthorpe; Mark Johnstone; Nigel Rudd; Peter Edwards; Peter Ventress; Susan Kilsby; Wayne Edmunds (female 33%; male 67%).

Nature of business: BBA is an international group of aviation services and materials technology businesses.

Year end	31/12/2017
Turnover	£1,800,000,000
Pre-tax profit	£128,000,000

Total employees: 6,700

Main locations: The group operates in more than 220 locations across five continents.

Community involvement

BBA's Community Involvement and Charitable Giving Framework sets out the approach it takes in choosing partnerships with organisations that benefit the communities in which it operates and in the following key areas:

- Aviation-related activities
- Education programmes
- Engineering activities

The group also supports disaster relief.

In-kind support

Employees are permitted to volunteer during company time.

Employee-led support

Employees are encouraged to fundraise and volunteer for local community and charitable groups. The Charitable Giving Programme states the following:

> Where 10% or more of the employees in a facility are participating in a fundraising event in their own time, the company may make a donation up to matching the funds the employees have raised from other sources, subject to locally set limits. The company may support a group of employees participating in an event fundraising for any registered charity, not necessarily one that is local to the facility.

Exclusions

Donations are not made to individuals, unregistered organisations or associations, or to political or religious organisations.

Applications

Under the Charitable Giving Programme employees or sites can, on behalf of a charity or not-for-profit organisation, apply to the BBA Aviation Charitable Giving Committee for a donation. Priority is given to organisations with a strong local connection to sites and/or those connected with aviation, engineering or education. Applications are invited every six months.

Community contributions

Cash donations worldwide	£699,500

In 2017 the group's charitable donations totalled \$877,000 (≈ £699,500 as at September 2018). We were unable to determine a figure for UK contributions.

Previous beneficiaries have included: National Star College – Cheltenham (£6,600); Age Concern – Luton (£6,500); Aberdeen Stillbirth and Neonatal Death Society (£2,000 each).

BC Partners LLP

Arts and culture, community development, education, the environment, general charitable purposes, projects outside the UK

Company registration number: OC404426

Correspondent: 40 Portman Square, London W1H 6DA (tel: 020 7009 4800; email: bcpfoundation@bcpartners.com; website: www.bcpartners.com)

Nature of business: BC Partners is an international investment firm.

Year end	31/12/2017
Turnover	£108,300,000
Pre-tax profit	£41,000,000

Main locations: BC Partners has offices in London, Hamburg, New York and Paris.

Community involvement

The firm's charitable giving is channelled through its corporate charity, the BC Partners Foundation (Charity Commission no. 1136956). The foundation supports charities nominated by employees and provides matched funding for their own initiatives. There is a focus on the following areas:

- Community development, including infrastructure, overseas aid and healthcare
- Environmental conservation
- Arts and education

The firm also has a sister charity in the USA, the BC Partners Foundation (US) Inc.

Employee-led support

The BC Partners Foundation provides matched funding for employee fundraising initiatives and supports charities proposed by the employees of BC Partners or trustees of the BC Partners Foundation. The foundation's 2017 annual report states that each office nominates two charities per year to support through donations and, where possible, volunteering.

Corporate charity

BC Partners Foundation (Charity Commission no. 1136956) – see page 236.

Community contributions

Cash donations UK	£409,000

In 2017 the firm donated £409,000 to its corporate charity.

Beazley plc

Children and young people, community development, education (particularly STEM subjects), general charitable purposes, health, housing and homelessness, medical research, older people

Company registration number: 102680

Correspondent: UK Charity Committee, Plantation Place South, 60 Great Tower Street, London EC3R 5AD (tel: 020 7667 0623; email: info@beazley.com; website: www.beazley.com)

Directors: Adrian Cox; Andrew Horton; Angela Crawford-Ingle; Catherine Woods; Christine LaSala; David Roberts; George Blunden; John Sauerland; Martin Bride; Neil Maidment; Robert Stuchbery; Sir Andrew Likierman (female 25%; male 75%).

Nature of business: Beazley is the parent company of specialist insurance businesses with operations in Europe, the USA, Asia, Middle East and Australia. Beazley manages six Lloyd's syndicates.

Year end	31/12/2017
Turnover	£1,572,000,000
Pre-tax profit	£129,000,000

Total employees: 1,200

Main locations: The group operates in Europe, the USA, Asia, Latin America and Australia. In the UK its offices are located in Birmingham, Ipswich, Leeds, London and Manchester.

Community involvement

The group's charitable work is focused on improving the skills of young people (six years old to graduate level) from disadvantaged backgrounds to help them enter the workforce. The group also supports disaster relief appeals and encourages employees to support local charities through fundraising and volunteering. The group has a global charity partnership with All Hands and Hearts, which support the needs of communities impacted by natural disasters by restoring and rebuilding homes, schools and so on.

The group takes on interns through its partnership with the charity, The Brokerage CityLink. Internships are also available in the London, New York and San Francisco offices. In 2017 employees mentored Year 10 students in East London, and volunteered to help improve the reading and numerical skills of children in Tower Hamlets.

In-kind support

The group allows employees to take leave to volunteer for charities or to undertake mentoring positions within charities.

Employee-led support

Employees volunteer for local charities and for the group's charity partner as well as taking part in fundraising events. The company matches employees' fundraising efforts up to $750 (or local currency equivalent).

Applications

Contact the correspondent for further information.

Community contributions

Cash donations worldwide	£319,500

In 2017 the group made charitable donations in the UK and the USA of around $417,000 (≈ £319,500 as at September 2018). We were unable to determine how much of this was donated in the UK or how much came from the company.

Bellway plc

Health, young people, older people, housing and homelessness, the environment, community development

Company registration number: 1372603

Correspondent: Charity Committee, Bellway Head Office, Seaton Burn House, Dudley Lane, Seaton Burn, Newcastle upon Tyne NE13 6BE (tel: 0191 217 0717; email: charities@bellway.co.uk; website: www.bellway.co.uk)

Directors: Denise Jagger; Jason Honeyman; Jill Caseberry; John Cuthbert; John Watson; Keith Adey; Mike Toms; Paul Hampden Smith; Simon Scougall; Ted Ayres (female 20%; male 80%).

Nature of business: The company provides housebuilding and related services.

Year end	31/07/2017
Turnover	£2,558,561,000
Pre-tax profit	£560,723,000

Main locations: Bellway has a number of locations throughout the United Kingdom. The company's head office is in Newcastle upon Tyne.

Community involvement

Bellway supports the communities in which it operates by making financial donations to registered local and national charities. The main charitable budget is allocated at Head Office under the direction of Bellway's Charity Committee. The budget comprises both small donations to local charities across the group's areas of operation, as well as any larger donations to the national Charity of the Year partner. The group is keen to support charities which are connected to the construction industry as well as those with the following purposes:

- Health
- Young people
- Older people
- Housing and homelessness
- Environment
- Community welfare

In Newcastle the group makes small donations through the Community Foundation of Tyne and Wear and Northumberland. It also financially supports the running of a breakfast club in a local primary school as part of the Greggs Foundation Breakfast Club programme.

Charity of the Year

Bellway's Charity of the Year for 2017 and 2018 was Cancer Research UK and it has committed to double every pound raised by employees in addition to donating £10 for every completed customer survey.

Employee-led support

Bellway supports employees fundraising efforts and each division has its own budget for donations to local charities and community groups. In 2017 employees raised a total of £44,500 for various charities and causes of their choice. The group intended to roll out a payroll giving scheme in 2018 to help facilitate employee giving.

Bellway also supports its employees' fundraising efforts and gives £2 for every £1 raised by an employee, a supplier, or subcontractor.

Exclusions

Note that Bellway does not provide support for religious organisations (unless they can demonstrate that services are provided to the wider community), organisations that operate discriminatory practices (with respect to employment or the provision of services), or political organisations.

Applications

Requests from registered charities seeking small donations (of around £500) should be sent by email to charities@bellway.co.uk. These will be considered on a quarterly basis, and only those charities selected will be contacted.

For other enquiries, the address and contact details of each division can be found on the group's website.

Community contributions

Cash donations UK	£293,000

In 2016/17 Bellway's total donations, comprised of employee fundraising, matched funding and direct donations, amounted to £522,000, of which £229,000 was raised by its employees and colleagues in its supply chain. This figure includes donations to its national charity partner which totalled £386,000 during the year, of which employees, sub-contractors and suppliers raised £185,000.

Berkeley Group plc

Children and young people, community development, disability, health, the environment and heritage, housing and homelessness

Company registration number: 1454064

Correspondent: Berkeley House, 19 Portsmouth Road, Cobham, Surrey KT11 1JG (tel: 020 7720 2600; email: info@berkeleyfoundation.org.uk; website: www.berkeleygroup.com)

Directors: Adrian Li; Alison Nimmo; Andy Myers; Diana Brightmore-Armour; Glyn Barker; Justin Tibaldi; Karl Whiteman; Paul Vallone; Peter Vernon; Rachel Downey; Richard Stearn; Rob Perrins; Sean Ellis; Sir John Armitt; Tony Pidgley; Veronica Wadley (female 25%; male 75%).

Nature of business: Berkeley is a developer of residential-led, mixed-use schemes building homes and neighbourhoods in its core markets of London and the south of England.

Year end	30/04/2017
Turnover	£2,723,500,000
Pre-tax profit	£812,400,000

Main locations: Berkeley mainly operates around London and the South East England, particularly Berkshire, Buckinghamshire, Kent and Surrey.

Community involvement

The group channels all of its charitable and community giving through its corporate charity, The Berkeley Charitable Foundation (Charity Commission no. 1152596) which supports the following: children and young people; the environment and heritage; health, particularly mental health; homelessness; people with disabilities.

Employee-led support

Employees raised £876,000 through the Give As You Earn scheme in 2016/17. Staff also engage in fundraising activities and volunteer their time and skills to support local and national charities.

Corporate charity

The Berkeley Charitable Foundation (Charity Commission no. 1152596) – see page 237.

Community contributions

Cash donations UK	£1,800,000

In 2016/17 the group donated £1.8 million to its corporate charity.

Bestway (Holdings) Ltd

Arts and culture, community development, disability, disaster relief, education, health, older people, projects outside the UK, poverty and social exclusion, sports and recreation

Company registration number: 1392861

Correspondent: CSR Team, Bestway Foundation, 2 Abbey Road, Park Royal, London NW10 7BW (tel: 020 8453 1234; website: www.bestway.co.uk)

Directors: Dawood Pervez; Haider Choudrey; Rizwan Pervez; Sir Anwar Pervez; Younus Sheikh; Zameer Choudrey (female 0%; male 100%).

Nature of business: Bestway is a family-owned business with operations in the wholesale, cement, banking, real estate and pharmacy sectors.

Year end	30/06/2017
Turnover	£2,900,000,000
Pre-tax profit	£440,800,000

Main locations: The company has locations throughout the UK and South Asia (particularly Pakistan).

Community involvement

Bestway donates 2.5% of its yearly profits to charitable causes, almost all of which is channelled through the group's charities, The Bestway Foundation (Charity Commission no. 297178) and the Bestway Foundation Pakistan. Bestway's website states that the group's CSR programme is focused on education, health, humanitarian aid for victims of natural disasters, and poverty relief in Pakistan.

The group supports several charities on a long-term basis and some of its subsidiaries elect to support charities for a year. In 2017 Well Pharmacy nominated the Stroke Association as its charity partner for the year. The group's depots around the UK work closely with local charities and places of worship to provide support through sponsorship, in-kind and cash donations.

Royal Ascot Charity Race Day

Bestway has staged this annual event for several years and selects a charity each year to receive the proceeds. The following have been previous beneficiaries of the event: Barnardo's, Crimestoppers, Great Ormond Street Hospital Charity, GroceryAid, Imran Khan Cancer Appeal, National Hospital Development Fund, President of Pakistan Earthquake Relief Fund, Save the Children and Sports Aid. In 2017 the event raised £100,000 for the NSPCC.

In-kind support

The group encourages individual depots to donate goods to local charitable organisations.

Applications

Applications should be made in writing to the foundation and should enclose an sae. The foundation has previously noted that telephone calls are not invited.

Corporate charity

The Bestway Foundation (Charity Commission no. 297178) – see page 237.

Community contributions

Cash donations UK	£176,000
Cash donations overseas	£224,000
Total contributions (cash and in kind)	£400,000

The 2016/17 accounts state that the United Bank Ltd, a subsidiary of Bestway, donated £224,000 to the education and healthcare causes in Pakistan. In the UK, The Bestway Foundation received £176,000 from the company. A figure for in-kind donations was not available.

Bettys and Taylors of Harrogate Ltd

 General charitable purposes, the environment

Company registration number: 543821

Correspondent: CSR Team, 1 Parliament Street, Harrogate, North Yorkshire HG1 2QU (tel: 01423 814000; website: www.bettysandtaylors.co.uk)

Directors: Andrew Wildsmith; Berenice Smith; Clare Morrow; Lesley Wild; Paul Cogan; Philip Hanson; Rachel Fellows (female 57%; male 43%).

Nature of business: The company owns the Yorkshire Tea and Taylors of Harrogate brands and runs a small chain of tea rooms in Yorkshire.

Year end	31/10/2017
Turnover	£189,653,000
Pre-tax profit	£17,663,000

UK employees: 1,373

Main locations: The company's headquarters are in Harrogate. Support is provided to charities in Yorkshire.

Community involvement

Support is provided to charities in Yorkshire through the Good Cause Awards. The company also runs tree planting and environmental education schemes for schoolchildren.

Trees for Life

The Trees for Life programme supports tree planting activities in the Yorkshire Dales and school environmental projects.

Charity partnerships

The company has a partnership with cricket charity Chance to Shine.

Cone Exchange

The company's website states:

> The Cone Exchange encourages school children to recycle in exchange for Cone Exchange rewards; supports social enterprises by providing waste from our own and other businesses to use for crafts; provides meaningful work experience and placements for young people with additional learning needs; and raises funds through sales of waste for local good causes.

Employee-led support

Staff raise money for charities in Yorkshire which is matched through the Good Cause Awards. In total staff raised £97,000 in 2016/17.

Applications

Contact the correspondent for further information.

Community contributions

Cash donations UK	£56,500
Total contributions (cash and in kind)	£307,500

In 2016/17 the company's UK charitable contributions totalled £307,500. This was measured in accordance with the London Benchmarking Framework and excluded management costs. Cash donations through the Good Cause Award scheme totalled £56,500.

BGL Group Ltd

 General charitable purposes

Company registration number: 2593690

Correspondent: CSR Team, Pegasus House, Bakewell Road Orton Southgate, Peterborough, Cambridgeshire PE2 6YS (tel: 01733 374444; email: csr@bglgroup.co.uk; website: www.bglgroup.co.uk/csr/community)

Directors: Debbie Hewitt; Dominic Platt; Inaki Echave; Katherine Chung; Lord Gadhia; Matthew Donaldson; Patricia Jackson; Seamus Keating; Stephen Klinkert; Stephen Van Rooyen (female 30%; male 70%).

Nature of business: BGL Group is a financial services company specialising in vehicle and home insurance.

Year end	30/06/2018
Turnover	£162,600,000
Pre-tax profit	(£17,400,000)

Total employees: 2,608

Main locations: In the UK the group has offices in London, Peterborough, Sunderland and Wakefield.

Community involvement

According to its website, the group has a community programme that operates through the three main areas of 'Partnerships, Community and Personal'. The group offers financial and in-kind support to charities operating in the areas the group have an office.

Partnerships

The group's partnerships are set up to encourage education, entrepreneurship and empowerment. The group works with four charities in the UK, local to its offices in Peterborough, Sunderland, Wakefield and London.

Community Teams

The group has dedicated Community Teams at its offices in Peterborough, Sunderland, Wakefield, London and Paris. Meeting monthly, the Community Teams encourage, support and review applications for funding and volunteering, allocating BGL resources to worthy causes and establishing relationships with local charities.

BGL Make a Difference Fund

As part of the group's community programme it has launched the BGL Make a Difference Fund, an additional £160,000 funding pot distributed between its five key sites in Sunderland, Wakefield, Peterborough, London and Paris. All five sites select a partner charity to support with Make a Difference funding and volunteering for a key project or initiative to be delivered over the next two years.

In-kind support

The group offers employees a 'paid day out' to volunteer for a charity of their choice.

Employee-led support

The group has an employee volunteering programme through which employees volunteer during the year for worthy causes. BGL Group also matches any funds raised by employees up to £1,000. People fundraising as part of a group can each claim up to £1,000 matched funding. The website states: 'So far we've matched fundraising by our colleagues of £220,000 over the last couple of years.'

The group's website also notes that it has a payroll giving scheme.

Commercially led support

The group has a sponsorship programme that has evolved to support a range of sports teams, clubs and events in its communities.

Applications

Contact the correspondent for further information.

To discuss how BGL might be able to support your organisation through sponsorship, email: sponsorship@bglgroup.co.uk.

Community contributions

The group's annual report and accounts for 2017/18 provided no information on how much it gave in donations.

Bibby Line Group Ltd

General charitable purposes

Company registration number: 34121

Correspondent: Corporate Social Responsibility Department, 105 Duke Street, Liverpool L1 5JQ (tel: 0151 708 8000; website: bibbylinegroup.co.uk)

Directors: Caroline Hoare; David Anderson; Geoffrey Bibby; John Cresswell; Mark Lyons; Paul Drechsler; Sir Michael Bibby; Timothy Lebus (female 13%; male 88%).

Nature of business: Bibby Line Group Ltd is the parent company of a group of trading businesses. The group is 90%

owned by the Bibby family. Bibby Financial Services, Bibby Distribution, Bibby Marine, Costcutter and Garic are its constituents.

Year end	31/12/2017
Turnover	£1,004,216,000
Pre-tax profit	(£19,992,000)

Total employees: 4,656

Main locations: The group's head office is in Liverpool and its areas of operation span the UK and overseas.

Community involvement

The group operates a 'Give Something Back' initiative which supports employees in their fundraising and volunteering activities.

In-kind support

Bibby Line Group provides matched-funding for employees' fundraising activities. The annual report for 2017 states:

> Through match funding, payroll giving and Group challenges, we supported colleagues to raise just under a quarter of a million pounds for charity, and volunteer hundreds of hours for good causes.
>
> In 2017, Bibby Line Group and Bibby Financial Services also provided support and expertise through skill sharing including employees helping young people to learn both finance and CV skills. This support follows a longstanding commitment by the Bibby family to young people in Wirral.

Employee-led support

In 2017 employees' efforts resulted in £310,000 donated to 150 charities. The group's annual report states that:

> Employees trekked, cycled, baked, and danced for their chosen charities, as well as helping many beneficial yet difficult to reach causes such as local hospices, school and sports groups. Employees continued to regularly support their favourite charities through the Group's Payroll Giving scheme, and in 2017, with the support of Bibby Line Group, our employees donated over £40,000 to their chosen charities through the scheme.

Commercially led support

The Local Pride initiative, operated by Costcutter, one of Bibby Group's subsidiaries, enables Costcutter retailers to nominate a charity and raise funds through pence per pack donations, carrier bag sales and local fundraising. Costcutter's website states that: 'During the short time Local Pride has been live we have raised a staggering £250,000 for local charities up and down the country; from children's football teams to local hospices we've helped 100s of charities'.

Applications

Apply in writing to the correspondent. For Costcutter stores, apply locally to the Manager.

Community contributions

Cash donations UK	£216,000

In 2017 the group declared charitable donations of £216,000.

Big Yellow Group plc

Community development, health

Company registration number: 3625199

Correspondent: Paul Donnelly, Corporate Social Responsibility Manager, 1 The Deans, Bridge Road, Bagshot, Surrey GU19 5AT (tel: 01276 470190; email: csr@bigyellow.co.uk; website: corporate.bigyellow.co.uk/csr.aspx)

Directors: Adrian Lee; Dr Anna Keay; Georgina Harvey; James Gibson; John Trotman; Nicholas Vetch; Richard Cotton; Steve Johnson; Vince Niblett (female 22%; male 78%).

Nature of business: Big Yellow provides self-storage facilities across the UK.

Year end	31/03/2018
Turnover	£116,660,000
Pre-tax profit	£134,139,000

UK employees: 335

Main locations: The company's head office is located in Surrey but it has 45 stores in London and over 60 locations across the UK.

Community involvement

After a trial period in 2017, the company launched The Big Yellow Foundation (Charity Commission no. 1171232) in February 2018. The foundation works with six charity partners to support vulnerable people, such as ex-offenders, refugees, ex-service personnel and people with disabilities to find employment. The company matches every £1 donated by customers up to £1,000. The six partner charities are: the Back-Up Trust, Breaking Barriers, Bounce Back, Down's Syndrome Association, Hire a Hero and the St Giles Trust.

In-kind support

The company allows charities to use its storage facilities. In 2017/18 the value of free space donated for community or charity use totalled £684,000.

Employee-led support

Employees fundraise for The Big Yellow Foundation.

Applications

Contact the correspondent for more information about using the company's storage facilities. For further information about the foundation, contact Nicky Martin, either by telephone: 01276 477136 or email: foundation@bigyellow.co.uk.

Community contributions

Cash donations UK	£11,000
In-kind support UK	£684,000
Total contributions (cash and in kind)	£695,000

In 2017/18 the company matched funds of £11,000 raised by employees and customers. It made payments of £5,000 to social enterprise organisations, but a list of beneficiaries was not available. In-kind support totalled £684,000.

Birketts LLP

Community development, general charitable purposes

Company registration number: OC317545

Correspondent: CSR Team, Providence House, 141–145 Princes Street, Ipswich, Suffolk, United Kingdom IP1 1QJ (tel: 01473 232300; website: www.birketts.co.uk/about-us/corporate-social-responsibility)

Nature of business: Birketts is a law firm based in the East of England.

Year end	31/05/2018
Turnover	£49,063,809
Pre-tax profit	£16,382,829

UK employees: 542

Main locations: Birketts is based in the East of England, with offices in Cambridge, Chelmsford, Ipswich and Norwich.

Community involvement

The group offers financial and in-kind support to charities operating in Suffolk, Norfolk, Cambridgeshire and Essex whose primary aim is to 'improve the quality of people's lives'. The group has a community fund in its operating areas administered by the Suffolk Community Foundation, the Norfolk Community Foundation, the Cambridge Community Foundation and the Essex Community Foundation. According to its website, grants are awarded twice a year by a committee comprising a cross-section of staff and partners of the firm.

In-kind support

The group is a member of the Suffolk, Norfolk and Cambridgeshire branches of the Pro-Help Group, a scheme created by the Business in the Community organisation. The aim is to provide a broad range of professional services to locally based charities and the voluntary sector free of charge and the group's members include local firms of solicitors, accountants, surveyors and a host of other professionals.

The group also participates in a local pro bono initiative with the object of providing legal assistance and support to small local groups principally concerned with the interests of 'ethnic minorities and the disadvantaged'.

Employee-led support

Employees take part in various pro bono and fundraising initiatives.

Commercially led support

The group sponsors the annual 'Race4Business', where different businesses race on behalf of charity. In 2018 nearly 1,000 runners took part in support of local charity Farleigh Hospital.

Applications

Suffolk Community Foundation

Full guidelines on how to apply are available at: www.suffolkcf.org.uk/apply-for-a-grant-introduction/apply-for-a-grant

Norfolk Community Foundation

For more information on how to apply, contact the Grants Team on:

Email: grants@norfolkfoundation.com

Telephone: 01603 623958

Cambridge Community Foundation

For more information on how to apply, contact the Grants Team on:

Telephone: 01223 410535

Email: info@cambscf.org.uk

Essex Community Foundation

Full guidelines on how to apply are available at: www.essexcommunityfoundation.org.uk/grants/our-grant-making/apply.

Community contributions

Cash donations UK	£83,000

In its annual report he group declared cash donations for charitable causes totalling £83,000 during 2017/18. We believe this amount was donated to the group's community funds.

Birmingham Airport Ltd

Children and young people, community development, education, enterprise and training, the environment, health, older people, poverty and social exclusion, sports and recreation

Company registration number: 2078273

Correspondent: Abigail Redmond, Sustainability Assistant, Diamond House, Birmingham Airport, Birmingham B26 3QJ (tel: 0871 222 0072; email: community@birminghamairport.co.uk; website: www.bhx.co.uk)

Directors: Cllr David Welsh; Cllr George Richards; Cllr Gurmukh Singh; Cllr Paul Tilsley; Cllr Steven Clark; Cllr Waseem Zaffar; David Stanton; Michael Bird; Michael Toms; Robert Piper; Rosemarie McClean; Timothy Clarke; Tristan Chatfield; Waheed Nazir (female 7%; male 93%).

Nature of business: The principal activity of the company is the operation and management of Birmingham International Airport and the provision of associated facilities and services.

Year end	31/03/2018
Turnover	£155,500,000
Pre-tax profit	£42,100,000

UK employees: 850

Main locations: The company's head office is in Birmingham.

Community involvement

The airport's charitable involvement is focused on disadvantaged communities in the area where it operates. Support is given for education, community welfare and cohesion, and children and young people. In 2015/16 the company reviewed its CSR strategy and decided that 30% of the company's community investment would be targeted at disadvantaged communities in East Birmingham, while another 30% would be focused on disadvantaged communities in North Solihull. The remaining 40% would be shared among other communities that are impacted by the airport's activities. This support is distributed through the airport's corporate charity, The Birmingham Airport Community Trust Fund (Charity Commission no. 1071176), which receives around £75,000 investment from the company every year, in addition to any fees charged to airlines breaching noise regulations.

Partnerships

The company have an established charity partner, Acorns Children's Hospice Trust, which employees fundraise for. The company's website notes that it has 'no immediate plans to change this relationship'.

The company also provides support for projects which do not meet the criteria of its corporate charity. For example, in 2017, the airport supported 'The Big Sleuth', an arts project raising money for Birmingham Children's Hospital Charity. Support was also given to The Holiday Kitchen scheme which provides a structured summer programme providing food and activities for schoolchildren and families on low incomes. To help make the airport more accessible the company partnered with Autism West Midlands and The Alzheimer's Society to ensure that customers with hidden disabilities get the help they need.

Education and training

The company has a dedicated education facility, The Learning Hub, for activities such as workshops with partner schools, school holiday projects and CPD sessions for teachers. The airport also worked with Enabling Enterprise, The Wonder Why Society and UpRising to deliver free programmes for children and young people, to help them develop vocational skills and experience. The company has a long-term partnership with The Prince's Trust through the 'Get into Airports' programme which provides vocational experiences for young people aged 16 to 25.

Employee-led support

Employees fundraise for the company's nominated charity partner and give talks and presentations to community groups.

Commercially led support

The company sponsors sporting events taking place in Birmingham.

Applications

There is a form on the website for charities to request support: birminghamairport.custhelp.com/app/applications/charities/p/51.

There is also a form on the website for arranging educational visits.

Corporate charity

The Birmingham International Airport Community Trust (Charity Commission no. 1071176) – see page 238.

Community contributions

No overall figure was given for the company's total charitable contributions. The company gives at least £75,000 each year to its corporate charity.

A. F. Blakemore and Son Ltd

General charitable purposes, education, enterprise and training

Company registration number: 391135

Correspondent: Liz Blakemore, Community Affairs Officer, Long Acres Industrial Estate, Rosehill, Willenhall, West Midlands WV13 2JP (tel: 0121 568 2910; email: lblakemore@afblakemore.co.uk; website: www.afblakemore.com/our-community)

Directors: Caoire Blakemore; Geoff Hallam; Ian Diment; Jerry Marwood; Peter Blakemore; Scott Munro-Morris; Tomas Blakemore (female 14%; male 86%).

Nature of business: The principal activity of the group is the wholesale and retail distribution of grocery products and the operation of grocery convenience stores, such as SPAR.

Year end	30/04/2017
Turnover	£1,300,000,000
Pre-tax profit	£7,354,000

Main locations: The company's head office is in Willenhall. A map of the area the foundation supports can be found on the foundation's website.

Community involvement

All of the company's community giving is supported by its charitable trust, the Blakemore Foundation (Charity Commission no. 1015938). The foundation supports general charitable purposes in the area the company has a presence. SPAR retailers can also apply for grants to support charities local to their store.

During the year, Blakemore Retail's Charity of the Year was NSPCC ChildLine and employees raised over £301,500 through various fundraising initiatives.

Branching Out

In 2016/17, the group launched a new community programme 'Branching Out', with the aim to engage and motivate young people into the world of work. It is made up of five key themes:

- Reading partnerships
- Workplace insights
- Employability workshops
- Career support
- Work experience

The programme is led by employees, who volunteer their time to help deliver the programme to local young people.

In-kind support

In-kind donations are given in the form of food, drink or supplies from Blakemore Retail SPAR stores.

Employee-led support

Employees fundraise for their chosen charities and in 2017/18 raised £656,000. The company matches funds up to £200. Employees also volunteer for community organisations and in 2016/17 a total of 1,237 employees volunteered 11,981 hours.

Applications

There are different application forms and processes depending on the type of support requested but all information, including upcoming deadlines, can be found on the company's helpful website.

Corporate charity

Blakemore Foundation (Charity Commission no. 1015938) – see page 238.

Community contributions

Cash donations UK	£356,500

In 2016/17 the company donated £356,500 to its corporate charity. We have taken this figure as the total cash contribution from the company.

Bloomsbury Publishing plc

Arts and culture, children and young people, community development, education, housing and homelessness, general charitable purposes

Company registration number: 1984336

Correspondent: CSR Team, 31 Bedford Avenue, London WC1B 3AT (tel: 020 7631 5600; email: contact@bloomsbury.com; website: www.bloomsbury.com)

Directors: Jill Jones; John Warren; Jonathan Glasspool; Nigel Newton; Penny Scott-Bayfield; Sir Richard Lambert; Steven Hall (female 29%; male 71%).

Nature of business: Bloomsbury Publishing is an independent worldwide publisher with offices in London, New York and Sydney.

Year end	28/02/2018
Turnover	£161,510,000
Pre-tax profit	£11,644,000

Total employees: 627

Main locations: In the UK the group has offices in London and Oxford. There are also offices in New Delhi, New York, and Sydney.

Community involvement

The group has a focus on supporting causes relating to literacy, literature and education. The annual report states that it makes a small number of cash donations to charitable organisations supporting these purposes and also works with schools, universities, libraries and charities worldwide. The group sometimes works in partnerships with charities. Previously the group's Methuen Drama publisher worked in partnership with Prison Reading Groups to support the reading of plays in prisons, as well as providing books and arranging drama workshops. In 2017/18 the group responded to requests from prisoners to help stock their prison library.

In-kind support

In the UK, the USA and Australia the group donates, or provides at a reduced cost, a substantial quantity of books and games each year, which includes donations of mainstream titles to schools, libraries and organisations supporting education. Charities such as Book Trust, Barnardo's, Oxfam and Red Cross, and smaller organisations local to its offices also receive in-kind support and discounted books. For example, the group's London office donates books to disadvantaged children in London and the group's nautical publisher, Adlard Coles Nautical, donates relevant books to RNLI for fundraising purposes.

The Bloomsbury Institute, which organises events in the group, has run fundraising events for charitable causes such as Book Aid and International Women's Day.

Employee-led support

Employees volunteer in their own time for good causes sometimes either directly or indirectly assisted by the business. Employees also volunteer to visit schools and colleges to deliver talks on careers and reading skills in the workplace, and to assist with practice interviews and producing school magazines.

Commercially led support

The group is both a sponsor and partner of World Book Day. It also sponsors achievement prizes in UK and US universities.

Applications

Contact your local office for further information.

Community contributions

Cash donations worldwide	£24,500

In 2017/18 the group's cash donations to charities totalled £24,500. The beneficiaries were chosen by employees through separate online polls in the UK, the USA and India.

BMW UK Ltd

Children and young people, community development, education, health

Company registration number: 1378137

Correspondent: Corporate Responsibility Team, Summit One, Summit Avenue, Farnborough, Hampshire GU14 0FB (email: sustainability@bmwgroup.com; website: www.bmw.co.uk)

Directors: Graeme Grieve; Jean-Phillipe Parain; Michael Kreeft (female 0%; male 100%).

Nature of business: The principal activity of the company is the importation, storage and distribution of BMW products in the UK.

Year end	31/12/2017
Turnover	£5,659,000,000
Pre-tax profit	£76,300,000

UK employees: 8,000+

Main locations: As a global company, the BMW Group operates 30 production and assembly facilities in 14 countries and has a global sales network in more than 140 countries. A list of locations can be found on its website.

Community involvement

The company's CSR focuses mainly on environmental issues although there is some support for charities. Support is currently given to BEN – Motor and Allied Trades Benevolent Fund, Community Matters Partnership Project and Macmillan. In recent years the company has supported Whizz-Kidz, raising over £315,000 for the charity.

Applications

Contact your local dealership for information.

Community contributions

Cash donations UK	£215,000

During the year the company made charitable donations of £215,000 of which BEN – Motor and Allied Trades Benevolent Fund received £207,000.

Boodle & Dunthorne Ltd

Children and young people, projects outside the UK

Company registration number: 472968

Correspondent: Boodles House, 35 Lord Street, Liverpool L2 9SQ (tel: 0151 224 0580; website: www.boodles.co.uk)

Directors: Elizabeth Wainwright; Frances Wainwright; James Amos; Jonathan Wainwright; Michael Wainwright; Nicholas Wainwright (female 33%; male 67%).

Nature of business: Boodles is a family-owned luxury jewellers with stores in London, Liverpool, Manchester, Chester and Dublin.

Year end	28/02/2018
Turnover	£70,800,000
Pre-tax profit	£7,300,000

Main locations: There are stores in Chester, Liverpool, London, Manchester, and the head office is in London.

Community involvement

The majority of the company's charitable giving is channelled through its corporate charity, The Boodle & Dunthorne Charitable Trust (Charity Commission no. 1077748). Boodles has a partnership with Street Child to provide funds for projects in the rural east of Sierra Leone that have been affected over the years by irresponsible diamond-mining practices.

Employee-led support

Employees fundraise for the company's partner charity and corporate charity.

Corporate charity

The Boodle & Dunthorne Charitable Trust (Charity Commission no. 1077748) – see page 239.

Community contributions

Cash donations UK	£387,500

In 2017/18 the company declared charitable donations totalling £387,500, of which £182,000 was given to The Boodle & Dunthorne Charitable Trust. A list of beneficiaries for the remaining £205,500 was not provided.

Boots UK Ltd

Community development, education, health, women

Company registration number: 928555

Correspondent: Essi Linderborg-Gooding, CSR Manager, 1 Thane Road West, Nottingham NG2 3AA (tel: 0345 070 8090; website: www.boots-uk.com/csr)

Directors: Elizabeth Fagan; George Clements; Paul Dunne; Richard Bradley (female 25%; male 75%).

Nature of business: The company's principal activity is pharmacy-led health and beauty retailing. Boots UK is part of the Retail Pharmacy International Division of Walgreens Boots Alliance, Inc. (NASDAQ: WBA), the first global pharmacy-led, health and well-being enterprise.

Year end	31/08/2017
Turnover	£6,837,000,000
Pre-tax profit	£498,000

UK employees: 57,000

Main locations: The group has offices across the UK. Its head office is in Nottingham.

Community involvement

Much of the company's CSR strategy focuses on the local area around the offices in Nottingham. It awards grants through its corporate charity, The Boots Charitable Trust (Charity Commission no. 1045927), which is wholly funded by the company.

Charity partners

In the UK Boots is working with two key charity partners – Macmillan Cancer Support and BBC Children in Need (which it has supported for a number of years).

Employability

Boots runs several employability schemes to support people into work. These include work experience, apprentice and graduate schemes and an ex-military work placement scheme. Recently the company has also started to employ more people who have experienced the criminal justice system.

Boots Benevolent Fund (Charity Commission no. 1046559)

The Boots Benevolent Fund is a registered charity which provides financial help and support to serving and retired employees who are unexpectedly experiencing financial hardship. The fund is open to all current and former employees of the company in the UK and is funded through staff's payroll giving. It aims to help when unexpected events happen and staff are faced with homelessness, debts involving bailiffs, large utility bill arrears or essential living requirements where they are facing financial hardship.

In-kind support

In 2017 Boots donated 12,000 wash bags to forty-seven UK Sexual Assault Referral Centres (UK SARCs) across the country as part of the three-year Wash Bags Initiative between Boots and UK SARCs. Every survivor of rape and sexual abuse who receives support at a UK SARC will receive a wash bag, following the forensic examination.

Employee-led support

Supporting charity partners

Employees, customers and suppliers fundraise and campaign for the two core charities, Children in Need and Macmillan Cancer Support. Since support for these partners began, over £12 million has been raised. Employees also volunteer to support different Macmillan initiatives:

- **Macmillan in Every Community** – A volunteer-led scheme that offers practical support to people affected by cancer. The scheme helps those affected by cancer get access to the services they need and to maintain independence and control over their lives
- **Look Good Feel Better** – Many of the company's No7 beauty advisors give their time and expertise to support beauty workshops for women affected by cancer. This is an initiative sponsored by the cosmetics industry. Advisors receive training on how to give advice to people experiencing the visual side effects of cancer treatment as well as giving advice on skin changes
- **Event support** – Boots UK volunteers marshal and support fundraising marathons and events for Macmillan

Matched funding

Employees fundraising efforts are matched up to £500 through the Boots UK 'Make the Difference Fund'. Typically, around 500 awards are granted each year providing additional funding to benefit the charities supported by staff.

Applications

Contact the correspondent for more information.

Corporate charity

Boots Charitable Trust (Charity Commission no. 1045927) – see page 239.

Community contributions

Cash donations UK	£250,000

We were unable to find details of the company's charitable giving for 2016/17. However, The Boots Charitable Trust's accounts state that it received £250,000 from the company during this period.

AFC Bournemouth Ltd

Sports and recreation, disability and health, education

Company registration number: 6632170

Correspondent: Andrew Battison, Community Operations Co-ordinator, Vitality Stadium, Dean Court, Bournemouth BH7 7AF (tel: 0344 576 1910; email: community@afcb.co.uk; website: www.afcb.co.uk/community-sports-trust)

Directors: Jay Coppoletta; Jeffrey Mostyn; Matt Hulsizer; Neill Blake; Nicholas Rothwell; Rico Seitz (female 0%; male 100%).

Nature of business: AFC Bournemouth is a professional football club competing in the English Premier League.

Year end	30/06/2017
Turnover	£136,450,000
Pre-tax profit	£14,650,000

Total employees: 575

Main locations: The football club is based in Bournemouth.

Community involvement

AFC Bournemouth Ltd supports sport, education and community projects in Bournemouth, Poole and Dorset. Many of the club's community activities are delivered through its charity, the AFC Bournemouth Community Sports Trust (Charity Commission no. 1122693). Support is provided through, sports and educational programmes, charity partnerships and in-kind and cash donations.

AFC Bournemouth Community Sports Trust

The Community Sports Trust is the charitable arm of AFC Bournemouth. The trust works with people of all ages to help them achieve their goals through the delivery of sports sessions and educational programmes across Bournemouth Poole and Dorset. The trust has four main themes: sports participation, education, disability and health.

Sports participation

The trust offers weekly coaching sessions for a range of age groups and abilities. Full details can be found on the club's website.

Education

The trust works with local schools to deliver a variety of educational programmes for young people. Recently these have included:

- **Premier League Primary Stars:** A Premier League-led programme, which uses the power of football to inspire children to learn, be active and develop important life skills. The club's own Premier League Primary Stars project consists of a ten-week PE programme, which is free to Year 5 and 6 children in Bournemouth Schools
- **Connect with Care:** A programme offering one-hour Internet safety lessons, which educate young people about how to remain safe while using the internet
- **Healthy Lifestyle:** A series of workshops intended to educate young people about the importance of a healthy diet and lifestyle

Details of all other education programmes are available on the club's website.

Disability

The club currently runs a number of training sessions and weekly activity programmes designed to enable individuals with any form of physical or learning disability to stay active and have fun in an environment suited to their needs. For more details, see the club's website.

Health

The club is currently involved in a number of initiatives to promote health and well-being within its local communities. Recently these have included fitness schemes for men and women, and activity programmes for the residents of local care homes. See the club's website for full details.

Charity partners

Each year, the club partners with local registered charities whose work benefits people living in the Dorset and Hampshire area and who support AFC Bournemouth's positive stance on equality. According to its website, AFC Bournemouth's chosen charities benefit from:

- Increased awareness
- Fundraising through selected club events
- Signed football club merchandise
- Engagement with AFC Bournemouth corporate partners and AFC Business members
- Match tickets
- Player appearances

The club's chosen charities for 2017/18 season were: Dorset Children's Foundation; Cherry Tree Nursery; The Fortune Riding Centre; The Dorset Cancer Care Foundation.

Player Appearances

Members of AFC Bournemouth's first team regularly make appearances at local schools and events.

Cherries Community Fund

The Cherries Community Fund was set up by the club in 2016 and provides grants of up to £1,000 to community groups and charities supporting young and vulnerable people, sport and healthy living in Dorset. The fund is financed from the proceeds of the Cherries Community Draw and other donations received by the club.

Applications

Charity partners

Each season charities can nominate themselves to be one of AFC Bournemouth's chosen charities. Application and selection processes are announced on the club's website in spring.

Player appearances

Groups can request an appearance by a player using an online form on the club's website: www.afcb.co.uk/community-sports-trust/player-appearance-requests.

Cherries Community Fund

Applications to the Cherries Community Fund should be submitted via email to cherriescommunityfund@afcb.co.uk. Applications are judged by a three-person panel, comprised of AFC Bournemouth chair Jeff Mostyn, head of AFC Bournemouth's Community Sports Trust Steve Cuss and first team player Marc Pugh. Funding is allocated in March, June, September and December of each year with the application deadline set at the end of the month prior to the next panel meeting.

Community contributions

The club's total charitable contributions were not declared in its 2016/17 accounts.

BPI (British Recorded Music Industry)

Music

Company registration number: 1132389

Correspondent: Riverside Building, County Hall, Westminster Bridge Road, London SE1 7JA (tel: 020 7803 1300; email: general@bpi.co.uk; website: www.bpi.co.uk/about-bpi)

Directors: Adam Barker; Alice Dyson-Jones; David Joseph; Geoffrey Taylor; Gerald Doherty; Henry Semmence; Iain McNay; James Radice; Jason Iley; Kiaron Whitehead; Max Lousada; Nicholas Hartley; Nicola Tuer; Vanessa Higgins (female 21%; male 79%).

Nature of business: BPI acts as a trade association, representing the producers and sellers of recorded music, including devising and implementing strategies to protect digital and physical music content.

Year end	31/12/2017
Turnover	£15,700,000
Pre-tax profit	£413,300,000

Main locations: The group's head office is in London.

Community involvement

Through the staging of the annual BRIT Awards and Classical BRIT Awards shows, the BPI contributes substantially to its corporate charity the BRIT Trust (Charity Commission no. 1000413). The trust supports young people through music and education and also supports Nordoff Robbins and the BRIT School. BPI works with the charity Julie's Bicycle to reduce CD packaging emissions among other sustainable initiatives.

Corporate charity

BRIT Trust (Charity Commission no. 1000413) – see page 240.

Community contributions

Cash donations UK	£1,600,000

In 2017 the group donated £1.6 million to its corporate charity, the BRIT Trust.

Brewin Dolphin Holdings plc

General charitable purposes, education, enterprise and training

Company registration number: 2135876

Correspondent: Corporate Responsibility Ambassadors, 12 Smithfield Street, London EC1A 9BD (website: www.brewin.co.uk/corporate-responsibility)

Directors: Caroline Taylor; David Nicol; Ian Dewar; Kathleen Shailer; Michael Kellard; Paul Wilson; Simon Miller; Simonetta Rigo (female 38%; male 63%).

Nature of business: Brewin Dolphin is a British investment management and financial planning firm.

Year end	30/09/2017
Turnover	£303,896,000
Pre-tax profit	£57,643,000

UK employees: 1,614

Main locations: The company has offices across the UK.

Community involvement

Each office has a nominated corporate responsibility ambassador who helps to organise a calendar of activities throughout the year and encourages staff to get involved in a variety of ways including fundraising, sponsorships and volunteering.

Partnerships

The company has charitable partnerships with three organisations working to improve young people's educational attainment and employability. The company has partnered with Enabling Enterprise in England, the Winning Scotland Foundation in Scotland, and AnCosán in Ireland. The company has also partnered with Dress for Success Ireland which promotes economic independence for women.

Small grants programme

Employees are invited to nominate local charities that they are personally involved with for a small grant of up to £1,000. In the year 2016/17 over £20,000 was donated to 25 charities.

In-kind support

Every employee is offered one paid day off per year to volunteer for the charity or organisation of their choice. In 2016/17 employees volunteered for more than 3,000 hours.

Employee-led support

Every employee can claim a £100 donation from Brewin Dolphin for their chosen cause if they raise over £100, or £200 if they raise more than £1,000. According to the 2016/17 annual report, 170 employees collectively raised £136,000. Employees can donate to charities from their pre-tax salary. Brewin Dolphin matches payroll donations by up to £20 every month.

Applications

Contact your local Corporate Responsibility Ambassador for more information.

Community contributions

Cash donations UK	£39,500

In 2016/17, £20,000 was awarded through the small grants programme and the company gave £19,500 in matched funding.

Bristol Airport Ltd

Community development, the environment, health, general charitable purposes

Company registration number: 2078692

Correspondent: See 'Applications', Bristol Airport, Bristol BS48 3DY (tel: 01275 473615; email: communityfund@bristolairport.com; website: www.bristolairport.co.uk/about-us/community)

Directors: Andrew Goodenough; Dave Lees; Debbie Hartshorn; Jason Clark; Nigel Scott; Paul Davies; Simon Earles; Simon Preece (female 13%; male 88%).

Nature of business: Bristol Airport, located at Lulsgate Bottom in North Somerset, is the commercial airport serving the city of Bristol, England, and the surrounding area.

Year end	31/12/2017
Turnover	£100,073,000
Pre-tax profit	£36,011,000

UK employees: 283

Main locations: The airport is in Bristol and supports surrounding areas affected by the airport's operations.

Community involvement

Bristol Airport makes grants to community groups in the local area most affected by the airport's operations. Two schemes are available: the Bristol Airport Environmental Improvement Fund; and for 2018 a newly created Diamond Fund.

Bristol Airport Environmental Improvement Fund

This fund focuses on a number of core local parishes including the villages of Winford, Wrington, Backwell, Brockley, Cleeve and Barrow Gurney. Its main purpose is to mitigate the environmental and social impacts of the Airport's operations. The following criteria is taken from the company's website:

> The Fund will support projects in the following areas:
>
> - Initiatives to mitigate the impact of aircraft and ground noise on the local community which may include but not be limited to noise insulation for schools and homes in affected areas, the construction of additional noise insulation barriers and the funding of school trips
> - The on-going improvement of transport infrastructure and services to and from Bristol Airport with an emphasis on reducing the impact of airport traffic in the community and villages surrounding the Airport which may include but not be limited to road

improvements, public transport initiatives and measures to reduce community severance; and
- Nature conservation, educational projects and sustainability initiatives in the locality of the Airport

Over £100,000 is contributed to the fund each year.

Diamond Fund

The Diamond Fund was **only available in 2018**, to celebrate Bristol Airport's 60th anniversary on the current site. The fund supported smaller-sized projects in the core area which did not meet the criteria for the Bristol Airport Environmental Improvement Fund, or which were situated outside the core area.

Charity of the Year

Each year the Bristol Airport team vote and select one charity to support. This year, the airport's nominated local charity is Children's Hospice South West (Charlton Farm).

Employee-led support

Employees take part in various fundraising activities on behalf of the airport's Charity of the Year.

Applications

Bristol Airport Environmental Improvement Fund

Applicants can apply using the online application form available at: forms1.thrive-csr.com/bristol_airport/apply_for_community_fund.html.

Contact the Local Community Fund Administrator for further information.

Diamond Fund

Applicants can apply using the online application form available at: forms1.thrive-csr.com/bristol_airport/apply_for_diamond_fund.html.

Contact the Diamond Fund Administrator for further information.

Community contributions

Cash donations UK	£145,000

According to the 2017 Annual Report, the airport donated £145,000 to local community groups during the year.

Beneficiaries included: Backwell Parish Council; Cleeve Parish Council; Wrington Scout Hall; Community of Purpose; Winford Toddler Group; Yatton Rugby Club.

Brit Ltd

General charitable purposes, health, projects outside the UK

Company registration number: 8821629

Correspondent: Social Committee, The Leadenhall Building, 122 Leadenhall Street, London EC3V 4AB (tel: 020 3857 0000; website: www.britinsurance.com)

Directors: Andrea Welsch; Andrew Barnard; Gordon Campbell; Jeremy Ehrlich; Mark Allan; Mark Cloutier; Matthew Wilson (female 14%; male 86%).

Nature of business: Brit provides global specialty insurance and reinsurance.

Year end	31/12/2017
Turnover	£1,549,000,000
Pre-tax profit	£4,200,000

Total employees: 562

Main locations: Brit's head office is in the City of London, as well as offices in various locations overseas.

Community involvement

Brit supports the communities in which it operates and charities chosen by its employees. According to the 'Social and community' section within the annual report for 2017, the group supports causes based on the following three criteria:

- Projects should be for a good cause and operate in an area relevant to us
- Financial involvement should be for the benefit of the good cause
- Projects should offer alignment with our strategic priorities

Brit employees select the charities that receive support. The charities benefit from an initial one-off donation and support continues throughout the year in the form of fundraising activities and events.

Employees are also supported in their charitable involvement in their local areas and there is a 'cross-functional' Social Committee which organises, among other things, community and charitable events.

In-kind support

Employees are given two additional days of paid leave for volunteering activities with registered charities in their local areas. During 2017, 67 employee volunteering days were taken.

Employee-led support

The company's Social Committee organises a range of community and charitable events for employees, including volunteering days. Employees can support good causes through a payroll giving scheme. Money raised by employees through charitable activities is matched by Brit.

Applications

Support is given to charities chosen by the employees.

Community contributions

Cash donations worldwide	£527,500

The 2017 annual report states: 'During 2017, Brit donated US$0.7 million under its charitable initiatives.' We have taken the figure declared (≈ £527,500 as at September 2018) as our figure for the group's worldwide cash donations. We believe the majority of this to have been given in the UK (seven of the ten charities supported were based in the UK); however, we could not determine the exact amount.

The ten charities chosen by employees for 2017 were: Action Duchenne (UK), Autistica (UK), Blossom Trust (India), Bountiful Blessings (US), The Disability Foundation (UK), Horatio's Garden (UK), Motor Neurone Disease Association (UK), Ordinary 2 Extraordinary (UK), Philabundance (US), and the Rockinghorse (UK).

British American Tobacco plc

Education, the environment, general charitable purposes, projects outside the UK

Company registration number: 3407696

Correspondent: Corporate Social Investment Committee, Globe House, 4 Temple Place, London WC2R 2PG (tel: 020 7845 1000; website: www.bat.com)

Directors: Ben Stevens; Dimitri Panayotopoulos; Dr Marion Helmes; Holly Koeppel; John Stevens; Kieran Poynter; Lionel Nowell; Luc Jobin; Nicandro Durante; Richard Burrows; Savio Kwan; Sue Farr (female 27%; male 73%).

Nature of business: The company's principal activities are the manufacture, market and sale of cigarettes and other tobacco products.

Year end	31/12/2017
Turnover	£20,292,000,000
Pre-tax profit	£29,591,000,000

Total employees: 55,000

Main locations: The company headquarters are in London and it has various locations worldwide.

Community involvement

The company's approach toward corporate social investment (CSI) is focused around three key themes:

- Sustainable agriculture and environment
- Empowerment
- Civic life

At group level, the major activities supported by the company are the British American Tobacco Biodiversity Partnership and the Eliminating Child Labour in Tobacco Growing Foundation. Much of the company's community involvement is in the countries where it has a presence.

Applications

Contact the correspondent for further information.

Community contributions

Cash donations worldwide	£18,700,000
In-kind support worldwide	£14,300,000
Total contributions (cash and in kind)	£33,000,000

The 2017 annual report notes that the company:

> Invested a total of £18.7 million in cash, and a further £14.3 million in-kind charitable contributions and CSI projects, including £1.09 million given for charitable purposes in the UK. Much of this investment is delivered through partnerships with external stakeholders including communities, NGOs, governments, development agencies, academic institutions, industry associations and peer companies.

No further breakdown was given and a list of beneficiaries was not available.

British Land Company plc

Arts and culture, children and young people, community development, education, enterprise and training

Company registration number: 621920

Correspondent: Joanne Hammond, Community Investment Executive, York House, 45 Seymour Street, London W1H 7LX (tel: 020 7467 3452; email: jo.hammond@britishland.com; website: www.britishland.com/sustainability)

Directors: Alastair Hughes; Charles Maudsley; Christopher Grigg; John Gildersleeve; Laura Wade-Gery; Nicholas Macpherson; Preben Prebensen; Prof. Lynn Gladden; Rebecca Worthington; Simon Carter; Timothy Roberts; Timothy Score; William Jackson (female 23%; male 77%).

Nature of business: British Land is a real estate investment trust with a portfolio of office and residential properties in London and retail and leisure properties across the UK.

Year end	31/03/2018
Turnover	£639,000,000
Pre-tax profit	£501,000,000

Main locations: The company's head office is in London. Local team's contact details can be found at: www.britishland.com/our-places.

Community involvement

British Land supports national, regional and local initiatives in the areas around its properties and developments, with a particular focus on those that benefit:

- Local communities
- Education and training
- Well-being and community infrastructure

Grants programme

The company takes a structured and transparent approach to community contributions and its policy and processes are outlined in a document available to download from the website. Titled 'Community Funding Guidelines', the document explains that the company funds projects that:

> - Make positive contributions locally around our places.
> - Support at least one of our Local Charter commitments to:
>   - Connect with communities so we understand local needs.
>   - Help local people progress by supporting local jobs and training.
>   - Support educational initiatives for local people.
>   - Promote wellbeing and enjoyment at our places.
>   - Offer the local community opportunities at our places.
> - Are backed by our local teams.

It goes on to state that it particularly welcomes:

> - Opportunities for local teams to get actively involved, e.g. through volunteering.
> - Lasting partnerships, as these can bring the greatest benefits for our communities and places

Grants can be made from £500 upwards and local teams are available to work with community partners on funding applications.

In addition to funding projects within these guidelines, British Land also supports its employees' charitable involvement by providing matched funding for their payroll giving and fundraising efforts.

Community Day

The company runs an annual 'Community Day' where employees from the company's head office and other London sites take part in the event. Activities include: providing charity partners with mentoring support, running mock interviews and providing support for job seekers, creating outdoor learning spaces for schoolchildren, and organising social events for older people living in local care homes.

In-kind support

In 2017/18 the value of employee time contributed by the company through volunteering amounted to £203,500 and other in-kind contributions amounted to £204,000.

Employee-led support

Matched funding

The company supports employee charitable involvement with matched funding in three ways:

- 50% matched funding is given for all employee payroll giving donations, up to a maximum of £5,000 per employee per year
- Up to £750 per person per year is given in matched funding for money raised by staff
- Each year, the company matches fundraising initiatives at each of the company's retail properties, up to a value of £1,000 per initiative per year

This matched funding scheme is also available to on-site employees of Broadgreen Estates Ltd, a subsidiary of the company.

Employee volunteering

In 2017/18 employees spent 2,422 hours volunteering for charity and community causes, an average of 9.7 hours per employee. During the year, 79% of British Land employees volunteered. Of the volunteering work carried out by employees, 16% was skills based, e.g. mentoring students.

Exclusions

The funding guidelines state that British Land does not make donations to political organisations or religious, nor will it support:

- Programmes outside the communities local to its offices
- Initiatives that do not support one or more Local Charter commitments
- Projects that are not backed by local teams
- Applications for commercial sponsorship

Applications

In the first instance, read the helpful 'Community Funding Guidelines' which are available to download from the website. The document can be found in the 'Governance and policies' area of the website under the heading 'Community'.

All applications must be made through the local teams, there is no open grant application process. If your proposal falls into the funding criteria, you should locate your local team (contact details: www.britishland.com/our-places). Funding application forms will be provided and the Community Investment Committee approves grants on a quarterly basis.

Community contributions

Cash donations UK	£1,690,000
In-kind support UK	£407,500
Total contributions (cash and in kind)	£2,098,000

The company publishes a detailed breakdown of its community

contributions in the form of sustainability accounts, which can be downloaded from the website.

The sustainability accounts show that, in 2017/18 the company made total community contributions of £2.09 million. As is our usual practice, we have not included the figure for management costs in our total for the company's community contributions.

The company uses the London Benchmarking Group's framework:

Direct community investment	Amount
Cash	£1.69 million
British land employee time	£203,500
In-kind contributions	£204,000
Management costs	£582,000
Total	**£2.68 million***

*This contribution equates to 0.53% of pre-tax profits.

In addition, the accounts also provide a breakdown of 'leveraged' community investment. We have taken this to represent contributions from employees and suppliers. As is our usual practice, we have not counted it in the company's total contributions made during the year. This amounted to £1.07 million (£720,500 in cash and £127,000 in 'key supplier workforce time').

In total 39,798 beneficiaries – including apprentices, jobseekers, and schoolchildren – were reached through the company's community programmes: 19,684 in the well-being, culture and leisure category; 19,602 in the education category; and 512 in the employment and training category.

British Sugar plc

Education, enterprise and training, the environment, health

Company registration number: 315158

Correspondent: One Team One Community, Sugar Way, Peterborough PE2 9AY (tel: 01733 563171; email: communications@britishsugar.com; website: www.britishsugar.co.uk)

Directors: Colm McKay; Mark Carr; Paul Kenward; Robert Conn (female 0%; male 100%).

Nature of business: British Sugar's principal activities are the processing of sugar beet and the manufacture and sale of sugar, animal feeds, bio-ethanol and other co-products of the sugar manufacturing process. It is a wholly owned subsidiary of international food, ingredients and retail group, Associated British Foods plc (ABF).

Year end	16/09/2017
Turnover	£729,900,000
Pre-tax profit	£73,500,000

Total employees: 1,717

Main locations: The company's head office is in Peterborough. It has sites in Bury St Edmunds, Cantley, Newark and Wissington.

Community involvement

Each company site is allocated an amount for charitable spending; however, we have been unable to determine the figure. There is also a Charity of the Year programme at the Peterborough site. At the time of writing (October 2018), Magpas Air Ambulance is the current charity supported. British Sugar encourages employees at its sites to play an active role in local communities through media visits, schools activities, agricultural and environmental events.

One Team One Community

Through this scheme funds are allocated to factories in Bury St Edmunds, Cantley, Newark and Wissington and the head office in Peterborough.

Individuals apply for funding for causes that they're either directly involved in, or indirectly through family and friends. This funding is then either approved or declined by a committee made up of peers from across the five sites of the company's operations. The company's website notes: 'The flexibility of the scheme means that while the full funding requested may not be allocated, in most cases a sum is granted meaning that more people can make use of the scheme.'

Employee-led support

Employees are encouraged to donate their time and examples include converting an abandoned piece of land into a kitchen garden, re-designing a day care centre and improving the efficiency of local food banks. The company matches employees' fundraising efforts up to £500 per person.

Applications

For information about the Charity of the Year scheme, contact the company's head office in Peterborough.

For information regarding the company's One Team One Community initiative, contact your nearest area of operation in Cantley, Newark, Wissington or Bury St Edmunds.

Community contributions

We could find no figure for the company's cash donations nor costings for its charitable or community giving during 2016/17. The company's website states: 'Over the past five years we've given £150,000 to local community groups and projects, charities, schools, sporting teams and other great causes across East Anglia and the East Midlands'. It also states that it has, over the last five years (ending 2017), supported over 193 individuals or team events through matched funding, donating a further £50,000.

We have therefore put its cash donation at £40,000.

Britvic Soft Drinks plc

Community development, education, the environment, health

Company registration number: 5604923

Correspondent: Sustainable Business Committee, Britvic Head Office, Breakspear Park, Breakspear Way, Hemel Hempstead HP2 4TZ (tel: 0121 711 1102; email: SustainableBusiness@britvic.com; website: www.britvic.co.uk)

Directors: Christopher Eccleshare; Euan Sutherland; Ian McHoul; John Daly; Mathew Dunn; Peter Litherland; Suniti Chauhan; Susan Clark (female 25%; male 75%).

Nature of business: Britvic supplies branded still soft drinks and branded carbonated soft drinks in Great Britain, Ireland and Europe. Through franchising, export and licensing, Britvic has also been growing its reach into other territories, particularly the USA.

Year end	01/10/2017
Turnover	£1,540,800,000
Pre-tax profit	£138,800,000

Main locations: Britvic has various locations throughout the UK and worldwide.

Community involvement

As part of its overall policy on corporate responsibility and long-term corporate vision of supporting local communities, Britvic established the Britvic Community Fund administered by the Essex Community Foundation (ECF). The fund focuses on supporting charities and voluntary groups in Essex, with a particular focus on those working with families in the Chelmsford area. Grassroots projects, such as local breakfast clubs and local charities receive funding. The 2016/17 accounts for the ECF note that grants from the fund totalled £6,700 during the year.

Partnerships

In Great Britain, the company has a long-term partnership with The Wildlife Trust and Sported which employees support through volunteering and fundraising.

In-kind support

The company encourages employees' volunteering efforts to support local communities by offering three paid days a year. Surplus stock is donated to charities and community organisations.

Employee-led support

Employees fundraise and volunteer for the company's charity partners and other causes local to the areas where the company operates. The company operates a Give As You Earn scheme.

Commercially led support

The company's brands support charities through special charity products, such as Ballygowan's gold label bottles which raised €144,000 (≈ £128,500 as at September 2018) for the Irish Cancer Society in the Republic of Ireland and Marie Curie Cancer Care in Northern Ireland.

In 2016 the company set up a new charity initiative, the Britvic Lifting Spirits Foundation, to celebrate the new branding for its mixers and juices range. The 2016/17 annual report notes that:

> This foundation has been specifically designed to further Britvic's heritage in supporting local communities and social projects. For every bottle of new look mixers & juices sold by participating customers, Britvic has committed to give back to local initiatives and projects, chosen by publicans and bar owners.

No further information on how this might have been distributed was given.

Applications

Contact the correspondent for more information. The company states it is only able to respond to emails that are relevant to its Sustainable Business programme.

For more information on the Britvic Community Fund, contact the ECF's Grants Team via email: grants@essexcf.org.uk or phone: 01245 356018.

Community contributions

Community support activity undertaken by employees in Great Britain was valued at £67,000 in 2017. This figure was derived from a combination of volunteering time, matched funding, payroll giving, in-kind donations and money raised through the monthly employee lottery. We were unable to find a further breakdown of support given.

Brother UK Ltd

Arts and culture, education, enterprise and training

Company registration number: 29301

Correspondent: CSR Team, Shepley St, Audenshaw, Manchester M34 5JD (tel: 0333 777 4444; website: www.brother.co.uk/about-brother/corporate-social-responsibility-hub/community)

Directors: Ian Metcalfe; Isao Noji; Phillip Jones (female 0%; male 100%).

Nature of business: Brother UK are suppliers of home and office printers, business solutions, office supplies and accessories.

Year end	31/03/2018
Turnover	£98,843,000
Pre-tax profit	£3,466,000

Main locations: The company is based in Tameside, Greater Manchester.

Community involvement

Brother UK Ltd supports charities and community groups in and around Tameside, Greater Manchester. Support is provided through a community fund (administered by Forever Manchester) and employee volunteering. According to its website, the company's community engagement is centred around the following four key areas:

- **Enterprise:** Community and voluntary organisations developing projects that encourage income generation, which will be re-invested in the community to support social impact. E.g. start-up business and young entrepreneurs
- **Employability:** To support young people up to the age of 25 with personal development, bridge the aspirations attainment gap, boost their confidence and enable them to gain practical and life skills, to support long-term employability
- **Elderly:** To support community activities, giving a pathway for the over 50's to socialise and play a positive role in their community, not become isolated and have the support needed to maintain an independent lifestyle
- **The Arts:** To support local community groups looking to expand knowledge and life skills

Brother UK Fund

The Brother UK Fund is administered by Forever Manchester and its current priority is to encourage and support grassroots community activity. Applications are accepted for all types of projects from 'grassroots community groups' based in Tameside. The annual income of groups applying to the Fund should be less than £150,000 and the maximum award request that will be considered is £2,000. For more information see the Forever Manchester website: forevermanchester.com/brother-uk-fund.

Education and Employability

The company delivers a wide range of activities focused on developing the employability of people up to the age of 25, including: mentoring, mock interviews and workshops.

Exclusions

At this time the Brother UK Fund doesn't support applications from sports groups and clubs. The fund cannot support activities that have already taken place or been paid for, contributions to major appeals, activities promoting political or religious beliefs and activities which should be provided by statutory services.

Applications

Enquiries about Brother's community engagement projects can be submitted using an online form on the company's website: www.brother.co.uk/about-brother/corporate-social-responsibility-hub/contact-us.

Community contributions

Cash donations UK	£38,000

According to its 2017/18 annual report during the year Brother UK Ltd made charitable donations amounting to £38,000.

Bruntwood Group Ltd

General charitable purposes

Company registration number: 2825044

Correspondent: Kathryn Graham, Administrator for the Bruntwood Charity, Union, Albert Square, Manchester M2 6LW (tel: 0333 323 2240; email: info@bruntwood.co.uk; website: www.bruntwood.co.uk)

Directors: Christopher Oglesby; Katharine Vokes; Michael Oglesby (female 33%; male 67%).

Nature of business: Bruntwood is a family-owned and family-run property investment, development and management group with over 110 properties in four UK cities. It provides office space, serviced and virtual offices and meeting rooms and retail premises to companies across a range of different business sectors.

Year end	30/09/2017
Turnover	£131,500,000
Pre-tax profit	£71,600,000

UK employees: 642

Main locations: The group operates in the following areas: Birmingham; Cheshire; Greater Manchester; Leeds; and Liverpool.

Community involvement

The group focuses its community contributions primarily in the communities in which its business operates, particularly Greater Manchester. It donates over 10% of annual profits after tax to environmental, arts, medical and charity organisations in the cities in which it operates. The Oglesby Charitable Trust (Charity Commission no.1026669) is Bruntwood's corporate charity and supports registered charities in the North West.

Bruntwood has long-term partnerships with a wide range of 'innovative and ambitious' arts organisations, including the Manchester International Festival which it has supported since 2005. In 2016 the group became the headline sponsor of the Royal Horticultural Flower Show in Tatton Park, Cheshire East.

In-kind support

The group has a scheme called Bruntwood Cares where employees are entitled to two days per year to volunteer for community projects. In 2016/17 employees devoted over 2,000 hours to volunteering for local charitable causes.

Employee-led support

The Bruntwood Charity (Charity Commission no. 1135777)

Through The Bruntwood Charity, employee-nominated charities are supported across the regions the group operates in. Charities are selected on the basis of the real difference they can make to the lives of people in these communities. Bruntwood employees devise their own ways of raising money to reach fundraising targets and the company itself also makes donations. The charity does not accept any unsolicited requests for funding.

Previous beneficiaries have included: Candlelighters – Leeds; Children's Liver Disease Foundation; Claire House – Liverpool; Factory Youth Zone – Manchester; Whizz-Kidz – Birmingham.

Commercially led support

For the past decade the group has provided a platform to showcase creative talent by encouraging writers, through The Bruntwood Prize for Playwriting. The prize came about through a long-standing partnership between the group, the Oglesby Charitable Trust and the Royal Exchange Theatre. In 2016 the partners commissioned playwrights from seven different countries to write new plays on the subject of birth to promote discussions around global health inequalities.

Sponsorship

According to its website, Bruntwood sponsors a variety of organisations and cultural events 'that adds to the vibrancy of the cities' in which it operates. A list of organisations that it sponsors, or has sponsored, can be found on the group's website.

Applications

According to the Charity Commission record, **The Bruntwood Charity's** funds are fully committed and they do not seek unsolicited requests for funding. Enquiries can be addressed to Kathryn Graham, the Charity Administrator.

The Oglesby Charitable Trust has an application form on its website; however, the site currently notes that 'this form should only be used when requested by Trustees and any unsolicited requests will not be acknowledged and are unlikely to be read'. Enquiries can be addressed to the trustees. Visit: www.oglesbycharitabletrust.co.uk for further information.

Individuals can apply to **The Bruntwood Prize for Playwriting** via the website: www.writeaplay.co.uk. The prize is a biennial event, check the website for the latest deadline dates.

Any other enquiries regarding community involvement and contributions can be emailed to info@bruntwood.co.uk for the attention of the directors.

Corporate charity

Oglesby Charitable Trust (Charity Commission no. 1026669) – see page 269.

Community contributions

Total contributions (cash and in kind)	£4,789,000

The group donates over 10% of its annual profits each year to charitable causes. The 2016/17 annual report has a section on the group's corporate responsibility programme and notes that: 'Each year Bruntwood and the family shareholders donate a figure of over 25% of annual distributable profits to meet these aims (assessed by the directors to be profit after tax, less revaluation gain). This year that figure is £4,789,000.'

BT Group plc

Children and young people, community development, education, enterprise and training, projects outside the UK, poverty and social exclusion, sports and social exlusion

Company registration number: 4190816

Correspondent: CSR Team, 81 Newgate Street, London EC1A 7AJ (email: yourviews@bt.com; website: www.btplc.com/Purposefulbusiness)

Directors: Gavin Patterson; Iain Conn; Isabel Hudson; Jan Du Plessis; Jasmine Whitbread; Mike Inglis; Nick Rose; Simon Lowth; Tim Höttges (female 22%; male 78%).

Nature of business: BT provides fixed lines, broadband, mobile and TV products and services and networked IT services.

Year end	31/03/2018
Turnover	£23,723,000,000
Pre-tax profit	£2,616,000,000

UK employees: 82,200

Total employees: 105,800

Main locations: The group has offices throughout the UK and across the world.

Community involvement

BT looks to support communities in the UK and overseas by sharing skills, supporting fundraising and providing technology. It works with a variety of charities, schools and not-for-profit organisations through its Connecting Society strategy. Examples include:

- Through the **Building Infrastructure** programme, residents, businesses, charities and schools can club together and apply for funding to support the cost of building better broadband infrastructure in their community. Grants of up to £30,000 are available, to cover up to a maximum of three-quarters of the cost of installing fibre. This is delivered in partnership with Openreach
- The **Digital Inclusion For All** programme aims to reach digitally excluded communities. Examples of current initiatives include providing low-cost internet for social housing providers and working with SOS Children's Villages to connect villages in Africa via satellite technology
- The **Improving Accessibility** programme builds on BT's commitment to making its products and services accessible for all. In 2017/18 BT worked with Action on Hearing Loss to develop a range of mobile phones and tariffs aimed at Action on Hearing Loss beneficiaries
- The **Building Tech Literacy** programme aims to help children and adults receive better teaching in computing and tech skills. BT is a primary sponsor of the Barefoot programme (www.barefootcas.org.uk) which provides free resources for teachers. It also partnered with the charity 5Rights to run an event to help young people navigate the internet

In 2017/18 BT partnered with Unseen to run a 24/7 helpline for victims of modern day slavery.

BT also use new technology to help develop new means of fundraising for charities. In recent years this has included the MyDonate, a commission-free online fundraising and donation platform with no set-up fees, which BT intend to close by June 2019. In 2017 it trialled a new contactless fundraising technology, Digital Tin, in place of traditional cash collection tins. This raised an average of £276 a day for several charities including Unicef UK,

Comic Relief and Cancer Research UK. According to BT's 'Delivering Our Purpose' report, people used their cards to donate an average of £4.57 each – over 50% higher than the closest alternative. BT aim to launch the device for use by more charities in 2018.

In-kind support

BT contributes in-kind support to charities through technology and fundraising assistance, including:

- BT MyDonate – a free platform for online fundraising
- Support to telethons and large-scale fundraising appeals
- BT Community Web Kit – a free service for charities to host and manage their own website

It also provides phone lines, staff and technical support for charities to run telethons and online fundraising campaigns. In 2017/18 it supported BBC Children in Need, Sport Relief, Stand Up To Cancer and campaigns run by the Disasters Emergency Committee to help people in East Africa, Myanmar and Yemen. It also provided text donation services to charities raising funds for victims of the Grenfell Tower disaster in London and the Manchester Arena terrorist attack.

BT offers up to three days a year for staff to participate in volunteering activities. In 2017/18, 40,175 (39%) of employees spent 37,348 days volunteering to support charities and community groups around the world.

Employee-led support

Employees are able to donate to charities through payroll giving and in 2017/18 more than 10,000 staff gave £2.7 million. BT is a founding partner of the Geared for Giving campaign, calling on every UK employer with more than 250 staff to offer payroll giving by 2021.

BT encourages employees to get involved in local communities, and provides a wide range of volunteering opportunities.

Commercially led support

BT sponsor the Tech4Good Awards to support new ideas and technology that improve lives.

The Supporters Club

BT Sport raises money through donations from customer and the funds raised are used to make grants to projects for young people in the UK and abroad, with a particular focus on sport. In 2017/18 £1.8 million was raised. More information on the scheme can be found at: www.thesupportersclub.org.

Applications

BT Group

Apply in writing to the correspondent.

BT Supporters Club

Grants from the Supporters Club are administrated by Comic Relief; for further information, visit the website: www.thesupportersclub.org.

Community contributions

According to the 2017/18 annual report, the group's community investments totalled £35.9 million during the year, including: environmental work, cash donations, volunteering time and in-kind support. During the year, £109 million was raised for good causes, including: funds raised through MyDonate by fundraising, telethons and appeals; employee fundraising and volunteering in working hours; sponsorships; in-kind and pro bono support; matched funding; donations; partnerships; fundraising activities run by the company; investment in infrastructure such as MyDonate. The MyDonate platform accounts for nearly £63 million of this. We were unable to determine a figure for in-kind support or cash donations from the company.

Bunzl plc

Disability and health, education, the environment, poverty and social exclusion

Company registration number: 358948

Correspondent: Julia Battyll, Bunzl Communities Co-ordinator, York House, 45 Seymour Street, London W1H 7JT (email: responsibility@bunzl.com; website: www.bunzl.com/responsibility)

Directors: Brian May; Eugenia Ulasewicz; Frank Van Zanten; Jean-Charles Pauze; Lloyd Pitchford; Patrick Larmon; Philip Rogerson; Stephen Nanninga; Vanda Murray (female 22%; male 78%).

Nature of business: Bunzl provides outsourcing solutions and customer service orientated distribution and light manufacture, primarily of plastic and paper-based products.

Year end	31/12/2017
Turnover	£8,580,900,000
Pre-tax profit	£409,300,000

Main locations: Bunzl's global headquarters are based in London and the group has operations in 30 countries.

FTSE4Good

Community involvement

Bunzl supports charitable projects in the local communities where its businesses are based through monetary and in-kind product donations and sponsorship for fundraising activities carried out by employees. The company prefers to support charities working in healthcare and the environment. Some support is also given to benevolent societies, educational organisations and disability charities.

Bunzl has a long-term partnership with St John Ambulance (SJA). Since 2015 the group has funded two purpose-built mobile first aid vehicles that can be used by volunteer first aiders at major public and sporting events, as a night service in city centres, and to provide emergency support for disaster situations. Bunzl are also funding 100 first aid classes provided by SJA in primary and secondary schools, aiming to create a new generation of first aiders.

In-kind support

Bunzl donates stock free of charge to local community organisations and charities.

Employee-led support

Bunzl supports its employees in their volunteering and fundraising efforts and can provide matched funding.

Exclusions

It is Bunzl's policy not to donate to sectarian or political projects and parties.

Applications

Each business is encouraged to support its local community and it is company policy to continue to support appropriate local community activities. Write to your local Bunzl company with information about your project or alternatively use the details found in the 'Contact Us' section on the website. Further information can also be found in the CR FAQ's, also available online.

Community contributions

Cash donations worldwide	£742,000

The group donated a total of £742,000 to charitable causes during 2017. This does not include in-kind donations or employee fundraising.

Bupa Ltd

Children and young people, health, medical research, older people

Company registration number: 3956433

Correspondent: Anna Russell, Corporate Responsibility Director Bupa UK, 1 Angel Court, London EC2R 7HJ (website: www.bupa.co.uk)

Directors: Caroline Silver; Clare Thompson; Evelyn Bourke; Janet Voûte; John Tooke; Joy Linton; Julian Sanders; Lord Leitch; Martin Houston; Roger Davis; Simon Blair (female 45%; male 55%).

Nature of business: Bupa is an international healthcare group offering health insurance and medical subscription products. It runs care homes, retirement villages, hospitals, primary care and diagnostic centres and dental clinics. Bupa also provides workplace health services, home healthcare, health assessments and long-term condition management services.

Year end	31/12/2017
Turnover	£12,248,800,000
Pre-tax profit	£620,300,000

UK employees: 22,000

Main locations: Bupa has locations throughout the UK, details can be found on their website.

Community involvement

Much of the company's charitable giving is directed through its foundations in Australia, the UK and Spain. The Bupa UK Foundation (Charity Commission no. 1162759) has three priority funding areas: mental health, carers and young adults who live with health challenges.

Bupa Global Community Grants

The scheme is funded by Bupa Global and made donations to 13 separate projects in 2017 through its Community Grants scheme, including funding shelters for young homeless people in the UK, and repairing flood damaged housing in Sri Lanka.

Bupa Cares Community Fund

In August 2018 the company launched the scheme which gives employees the chance to nominate local charitable projects for grants of up to £1,000. Grants can be given to a single project or split between up to three groups. Six projects have already been chosen: Moodswings and the MS Therapy Centre in Manchester; Friends of Gledhow Valley Woods and Preparation for Birth and Beyond in Leeds; the Children's Adventure Farm Trust in Cheshire; and the Bolton Lads and Girls Club.

Partnerships

The company has partnered with the East London Business Alliance (ELBA) to support East London communities. ELBA connects the skills and resources of Bupa employees with local charities and programmes that promote community regeneration and social mobility.

Employee-led support

In the UK Bupa matches up to £250 per employee, when they fundraise for health and/or adult social care charities. It also operates the Give As You Earn Scheme. In 2017 employees raised £15,000 for the Movember Foundation and a further £15,000 for the Make a Wish Foundation. Volunteers in Salford Quays and Staines took calls for Sport Relief, taking donations of almost £70,000 and raising money through a spin-a-thon and a 'Beat the Boss on the Bike' competition.

Applications

Contact the correspondent for further information.

Corporate charity

Bupa UK Foundation (Charity Commission no. 1162759) – see page 241.

Community contributions

Cash donations UK	£379,000
Total contributions (cash and in kind)	£779,000

The 2017 annual report for the Bupa Foundation states that during the year the charity received £379,000 from Bupa UK. The annual report for the company notes that Bupa UK 'invested a further £400,000 through match funding, fundraising, donations and partnerships'. We have taken the figure for total community contributions to be £779,000.

Burberry Group

Design and textiles education, children and young people, enterprise and training, disaster relief

Company registration number: 3458224

Correspondent: Catherine Sukmonowski, Horseferry House, Horseferry Road, London SW1P 2AW (tel: 020 7806 1328; email: corporate.responsibility@burberry.com; website: www.burberryplc.com/corporate_responsibility/our_communities)

Directors: Dame Carolyn McCall; Dr Gerry Murphy; Fabiola Arredondo; Ian Carter; Jeremy Darroch; Julie Brown; Marco Gobbetti; Matthew Key; Orna Nichionna; Ron Frasch; Stephanie George (female 45%; male 55%).

Nature of business: The company designs, develops, makes and sells products under the Burberry brand. Product design and development are centred in Burberry's London headquarters. Fabrics and other materials are bought from, and finished products manufactured at, company-owned facilities in the UK and through an external supplier network, predominantly located in Europe.

Year end	31/03/2018
Turnover	£2,733,000,000
Pre-tax profit	£413,000,000

Total employees: 10,000+

Main locations: The company has headquarters in London and various locations throughout the UK and worldwide.

Community involvement

Most of the company's corporate social responsibility is based around helping young people into employment. The Burberry Foundation (Charity Commission no. 1154468) is the company's corporate charity and is dedicated to helping tackle educational inequality and enhancing career advice for young people in the UK. In August 2017, the Burberry Foundation launched partnerships with three organisations, Teach First, the Careers and Enterprise Company and MyKindaFuture, to support young people in disadvantaged communities across Yorkshire and London. Support is also given to overseas projects.

In-kind support

Burberry's in-kind donations range from one-off gifts of non-trademark fabric and materials to assist young people enrolled in creative courses, to donations of smart business clothing to support vulnerable people enrolled in employability programmes and preparing for interviews. It also allows employees to volunteer during working hours.

Employee-led support

Employees worldwide are encouraged to take part in community projects. Volunteering activities include anything from career inspiration events and employability workshops to long-term mentoring programmes and community revitalisation projects.

Commercially led support

Burberry donates leather offcuts to Elvis and Kresse, a sustainable luxury accessories company, which then creates products to sell. Half the profits from this range will be donated to charitable organisations promoting renewable energy.

Applications

Contact the correspondent for further information.

Corporate charity

The Burberry Foundation (Charity Commission no. 1154468) – see page 241.

Community contributions

Total contributions (cash and in kind)	£4,130,000

Burberry continues to donate 1% of group adjusted profit before tax (£413 million in 2017/18) to charitable causes. We have therefore taken the figure of £4.13 million as the company's overall worldwide charitable contribution. Donations range from supporting disaster relief efforts (for example the London Grenfell fire, South Asia Floods, hurricanes Harvey and Irma, and the 2017 Mexico earthquake) to nurturing emerging talent through scholarships at the Royal College of Art. A significant proportion goes to The Burberry Foundation to support its community programmes.

Burnley FC Holdings Ltd

Sports and recreation, education, enterprise and training, health, poverty and social exclusion, projects outside the UK

Company registration number: 8335231

Correspondent: Neil Hart, Community CEO, Turf Moor, Burnley, Lancashire BB10 4BX (tel: 01282 704716; email: community@burnleyfc.com; website: www.burnleyfccommunity.org)

Directors: Barry Kilby; Brendan Flood; Brian Nelson; Clive Holt; David Baldwin; John Banaszkiewicz; Mike Garlick; Terence Crabb (female 0%; male 100%).

Nature of business: Burnley FC is a professional football club competing in the English Premier League.

Year end	30/06/2017
Turnover	£121,169,000
Pre-tax profit	(£5,100,000)

UK employees: 188

Main locations: The football club is based in East Lancashire.

Community involvement

Burnley FC Holdings Ltd provides a range of community activities and programmes across East Lancashire and overseas. These activities are mainly delivered by its charity, Burnley in the Community (Charity Commission no. 1155856) and focus on the areas of health, education, inclusion and sport.

Burnley in the Community

Burnley in the Community delivers a wide range of community activities and programmes with a focus on sport, education, health and inclusion. Full details about of the charity's current programmes is available on the club's website.

Sport

Burnley in the Community run several schemes to help schoolchildren, young people and people with disabilities become more involved with sport. Recent examples include:

- **Danny Ings Disability Sports Project:** A project run in partnership with BT and the Premier League, which aims to engage and empower members of the community through sport. The project includes the creation of Burnley Disability Football Club
- **Soccer Schools:** A programme of school holiday activities for young people aged between 5 and 12

Education

The charity currently offers a wide range of educational programmes for young people. Recent initiatives include:

- **UCFB Burnley:** A collaboration between Burnley in the Community and Nelson and Colne College. The partnership offers education opportunities to students including BTEC (Business and Technology Education Council) provision for work-related qualifications, apprenticeships, adult learning courses and employability workshops
- **Premier League Enterprise:** A project jointly funded by the Premier League and Sport Relief, which uses the backdrop of professional football clubs' business models to deliver enterprise education
- **Turf Works:** A Premier League-led employability programme, which uses the power of football to engage young people who are not involved in education, training or employment

Inclusion

The club runs The Duke of Edinburgh Award, The National Citizen Service and Premier League Kicks. All of these programmes help promote inclusion and help build skills for work and life.

Health

A part of its commitment to health and well-being, Burnley in the Community delivers a wide range of community schemes including healthy eating programmes, weight management and health checks and a veterans programme. Recent initiatives include:

- **Active Clarets:** A project, which aims to support the reduction of health inequalities in Burnley and the surrounding areas. Delivered in partnership with Lancashire Care NHS Foundation Trust, Lancashire County Council and the Premier League, the programme provides physical activity sessions and workshops to a wide range of beneficiaries, from primary school pupils to people over the age of 50
- **Extra Time:** A programme of activities to help tackle issues such as loneliness and social isolation, as well as helping to increase participation in physical activity among the senior community

Brierfield Mill

Burnley in the Community is currently involved in the renovation of a former textile mill. Once completed the mill will be a state-of-the-art community leisure facility, including sports facilities, education suites, dance studios and a soft play area.

Themed matchdays

Each season Burnley FC hold themed matchdays to raise awareness of a wide range of charitable causes. Themed matchdays in 2017 included, 'Mental Health Awareness', 'Celebrating Inclusion' and 'Equality and Diversity'.

Player appearances

Members of Burnley FC's first team regularly make appearances at local schools and events.

Applications

Contact the correspondent for more information.

Community contributions

Cash donations UK	£250,000

The club did not declare its total charitable contributions for the 2016/17. However, according to the accounts of Burnley in the Community, the club donated £250,000 to the Whitehough Outdoor Centre project, which we have taken as the club's cash donation. In 2016/17 Burnley in the Community had a charitable expenditure of approximately £1.33 million.

Business Design Centre Group Ltd

Community development, education, poverty and social exclusion

Company registration number: 532103

Correspondent: Leanne Pettyfer, HR Manager, Business Design Centre, 52 Upper Street, Islington Green, London N1 0QH (tel: 020 7288 6272; email: leannep@bdc.london; website: www.businessdesigncentre.co.uk)

Directors: Andrew Morris; Dominic Jones; Gerald Morris; Jack Morris; Joseph Mullee; Paul Morris; Philip Morris (female 0%; male 100%).

Nature of business: The Business Design Centre (BDC) is a conference and exhibition venue based in Islington.

Year end	31/03/2017
Turnover	£2,500,000
Pre-tax profit	£4,700,000

Main locations: The BDC is in Islington.

Community involvement

The company's community involvement is focused on improving the community around its offices in Islington. Financial support is available from its corporate charity, The Morris Charitable Trust (Charity Commission no. 802290). It also partners with local charitable organisations and schools, examples of which include:

- Running an annual show in conjunction with Age UK, Islington Giving and Anna Fiorentini's Theatre and Film School to deliver a variety performance for free for disadvantaged people in Islington. Food is provided by the company's service partners
- Offering one to one mentoring for sixth form students at a local college over the course of a year, helping them with employability and social skills
- Offering space in BDC to the London Village Network, a grassroots charity working to improve social equality and community cohesion

The company is a founding member of Islington Giving, an independent group of funders, businesses, residents and voluntary organisations working together to tackle poverty and inequality in the borough.

Employee-led support

Employees take part in a variety of fundraising and volunteering activities for local and national charities.

Applications

If you are a local educational organisation and would like more information on how BDC can provide mentoring and employability sessions for your students, contact Leanne Pettyfer, HR Manager.

Corporate charity

The Morris Charitable Trust (Charity Commission no. 802290) – see page 266.

Community contributions

Cash donations UK	£112,000

The 2016/17 accounts state that charitable cash donations totalled £112,000.

Cadbury

Education, enterprise and training, sport and health, the environment, general charitable purposes

Company registration number: 52457

Correspondent: Cadbury Ltd, PO Box 12, Bournville, Birmingham B30 2LU (website: www.cadbury.co.uk/cadbury-foundation)

Nature of business: Cadbury is one of the largest confectionery brands in the world. In 2010 it was acquired by US-based Kraft Foods Inc. which was later restructured into two companies: the 'spin-off' company became Kraft Foods Group Inc., specialising in grocery products, and the remaining company was renamed Mondelez International Inc., focusing on confectionery and snacks. Cadbury is now owned by Mondelez International.

Given Cadbury's historical and recognisable links to philanthropy, we have made the decision to name this record using the brand name 'Cadbury', rather than the name of the Mondelez holding company whose annual report and accounts declared charitable donations for 2017. See 'Community involvement' for more information.

Year end	31/12/2017

Main locations: Mondelez International has sites in Birmingham, Chirk (Wrexham), Crediton (Devon), Marlbrook (in Herefordshire), Reading, Sheffield, Uxbridge and the Republic of Ireland.

Community involvement

Philanthropy is intertwined with the Cadbury name. In 1893 the owners of the company began building at their own expense the Bourneville Model Village. Although the Cadbury brothers, Richard and George, died in 1899 and 1922 respectively, Cadbury's dedication to philanthropy continued, notably with the founding of its charitable trust in 1935. Now known as The Cadbury Foundation (Charity Commission no. 1050482), the foundation continues to receive support in the form of cash donations and services from Mondelez UK Holdings and Services Ltd (formerly named Cadbury Holdings Ltd) which is a subsidiary company of Cadbury Ltd.

Employee-led support

Employees can have their charitable fundraising efforts matched by The Cadbury Foundation. Employees can apply to the foundation for funding to support a chosen charity.

Corporate charity

The Cadbury Foundation (Charity Commission no. 1050482) – see page 242.

Community contributions

Cash donations UK	£600,000

The 2017 annual report and accounts of Mondelez UK Holdings and Services Ltd, a company whose immediate parent undertaking is Cadbury Ltd, states that: 'During the year, the company contributed £600,000 to the not-for-profit Cadbury Foundation, which gives grants to projects and partner organisations, mainly in the fields of education and employment.' We have taken this as Cadbury's cash donations for the year.

Cadogan Group Ltd

The armed forces, children and young people, health, housing and homelessness, religion, sports and recreation

Company registration number: 2997357

Correspondent: Paul Loutit, Company Secretary and Correspondent to the Trustees, 10 Duke of York Square, London SW3 4LY (tel: 020 7881 1032 or 020 7730 4567; email: info@cadogan.co.uk or paul.loutit@cadogan.co.uk; website: www.cadogan.co.uk)

Directors: Charles Ellingworth; Francis Salway; Hugh Seaborn; Jeremy Bentley; John Gordon; The Hon. James Bruce; Viscount Chelsea Edward Cadogan (female 0%; male 100%).

Nature of business: Cadogan Group Ltd is the holding company for the UK property investment business of the family of Earl Cadogan. The company is ultimately owned by a number of charitable and family trusts.

Year end	31/12/2017
Turnover	£160,896,000
Pre-tax profit	£171,975,000

Main locations: The group is responsible for the stewardship of the Royal Borough of Chelsea, and its charitable work is for the benefit of the area.

Community involvement

The group supports charity and community projects in the area in which it operates through making corporate donations and via The Cadogan Charity (Charity Commission no. 247773). It hosts an annual sleepover to raise funds for Glass Door, a local homeless charity and supports The Kensington and Chelsea Foundation (Charity Commission no. 1125940) to help local charities operating at grassroots level.

In-kind support

The group's land and buildings around Chelsea are available for charitable and community purposes. This has included: churches; schools; and social housing. It also donates surplus furniture, bedding and crockery from its hotels to charitable causes.

Employee-led support

Cadogan's employees volunteer and fundraise for local charities, which is then 100% matched by the company.

Commercially led support

Cadogan has sponsored the following:

- Team GB at the 2012 Olympics
- The Thames Diamond Jubilee Foundation
- The Royal Philharmonic Orchestra, based at Cadogan Hall

- The Princes Foundation for Children and the Arts Carol Concert
- The Chelsea Gardens Exhibition by the Chelsea Society
- Chelsea in Bloom
- Chelsea Festival of Music
- The National Army Museum
- The Royal Court Theatre on Sloane Square

It has also supported several local churches and each year funds the Christmas lights in and around the Estate.

Applications

Applications can be made in writing to the correspondent, who represents both the group and its charity.

Corporate charity

The Cadogan Charity (Charity Commission no. 247773) – see page 242.

Community contributions

Cash donations UK	£259,000

In 2017 the group declared £259,000 in charitable donations. During the year, it donated £200,000 via 'The Big Give' to the Grenfell Tower Appeal fund.

Cairn Energy plc

Arts and culture, children and young people, community development, education, enterprise and training, the environment, health and projects outside the UK

Company registration number: SC226712

Correspondent: Paula Pratt, Charities Committee, 50 Lothian Road, Edinburgh EH3 9BY (tel: 0131 475 3000; email: paula.pratt@cairnenergy.com; website: www.cairnenergy.com/working-responsibly/charitable-giving)

Directors: Alexander Berger; Ian Tyler; James Smith; Keith Lough; Mary Sheppard; Nicoletta Giadrossi; Peter Kallos; Simon Thomson; Todd Hunt (female 22%; male 78%).

Nature of business: Cairn is an independent oil and gas exploration and development company.

Year end	31/12/2017
Turnover	£25,600,000
Pre-tax profit	£197,500,000

Main locations: Cairn has its headquarters in Edinburgh, Scotland, supported by operational offices in London, Norway, Senegal and Mexico.

Community involvement

Cairn support charities in the Lothian area, near to its headquarters in Edinburgh. Its website notes that Cairn 'looks to support charities that encourage the behaviours we value in our own organisation, such as teamwork, fostering individual potential and encouraging entrepreneurial spirit'. Although the company appears to support general charitable purposes, there is a preference for the following:

- Young people
- Communities
- Health
- Environment
- Arts and culture
- Education and learning

The company also has a partnership with The Hunger Project in Senegal which works with local women to improve access to clean water and sanitation, nutrition, maternal health and community health.

Exclusions

The application guidance on the website notes that the following are not funded:

- Charities with religious or political affiliations
- Political parties
- Places of worship
- Labour unions
- Organisations where there is a potential conflict of interest
- Organisations that discriminate
- Individual sponsorship

Applications

Application forms can be downloaded from the website and should be submitted via email to the correspondent. The application should be no longer than two sides; if it is longer, you will be asked to resubmit the application form as two sides. Application deadlines can be found online. Applications will be considered by the Charities Committee at its next meeting. All organisations that have applied for funding previously are welcome to do so again.

Community contributions

Cash donations UK	£285,000

According to Cairn's Corporate Responsibility Report 2017, the company gave £285,000 in the UK during the year. The following breakdown was provided:

Children	£104,000
Community development	£60,000
Health	£45,500
Other	£35,500
Culture	£20,000
Education	£10,000
Environment	£10,000

A list of beneficiaries was not included.

Social investment in Senegal and Mexico totalled £185,000 in 2017. Cairn defines social investment as 'pro-active contributions or actions taken by Cairn to help bring benefits to communities where we operate'. We have not included this figure in the total contributions for the company because it is not clear whether this relates to employee-led support or company giving.

Calor Gas Ltd

Rural communities, children and young people, the environment, education, health

Company registration number: 303703

Correspondent: Sustainability Team (Community), Athena House, Athena Drive, Tachbrook Park, Warwick CV34 6RL (email: sustainability@calor.co.uk; website: www.calor.co.uk/sustainability)

Directors: Adam Thompson; Geraldine Goddard; Jonathan Wood; Matthew Hicken; Paul Instrell (female 20%; male 80%).

Nature of business: The principal activity of the company is the processing, marketing and distribution of liquefied petroleum gas in the UK.

Year end	30/12/2017
Turnover	£422,600,000
Pre-tax profit	£53,900,000

Main locations: The company has various sites throughout the UK.

Community involvement

Calor's CSR strategy combines employee-led initiatives and corporate donations to support local communities and causes related to the business. In 2010 Calor started an energy advice initiative called FREE, aimed at tackling fuel poverty and promoting energy efficiency in off-gas rural communities across Britain. Advice and support is available for individuals, organisations working on behalf of individuals, and organisations aiming to improve their energy efficiency. For example, Energy Action Scotland (EAS) in partnership with Calor, developed a Strategic Affordable Warmth Fund aimed at helping rural housing associations map out their stock and draw up an affordable warmth strategy.

Calor Rural Community Fund

The company funds rural community projects that improve local life in rural areas, for example redecorating a community centre or village hall, funding new equipment for youth clubs, sports teams or uniformed groups. The projects and communities should be off the mains gas grid. There are 21 grants available each year and three levels of funding available: £5,000, £2,500 and £1,000. Funding applied for must equate to 50% or more of your total project cost. The following criteria is used to judge applications:

- How urgent is the need in the community?

- How many people will be impacted by this project?
- Is the idea appealing to a broad cross-section of the community?

Beneficiaries include: East Worlington School Garden – Devon, Ely Outdoor Sports Association – Cambridgeshire and Orkney Isles Music Instrument Bank (£5,000 each); Buckland Dinham Village Hall and Keen2Cook – Kent (£2,500 each); Hartington Rural Social Group, Hertfordshire and Essex Community Farm and Stockton Community Bus Shelters (£1,000 each).

Partnerships and Charity of the Year

The company states on its website that it has found it more valuable and effective to focus support on the work of one charity. A national charity is chosen by an all-staff voting process, typically for a three-year duration, for which the majority of corporate fundraising efforts are undertaken. Following a successful partnership with Make-A-Wish Foundation UK and the Alzheimer's Society, its new corporate charity for 2018 is Mind. The company has set a fundraising target of £100,000 through both corporate and individual employee-led initiatives.

The company also has a long-term partnership with the Woodland Trust. In 2011 local schoolchildren, Calor staff and their families planted 2,500 saplings on two hectares of unused scrubland at its Stoney Stanton site in support of the Woodland Trust's MOREwoods programme.

In-kind support

In-kind donations of liquid petroleum gas (LPG) appliances, such as BBQs or portable heaters may be offered as an alternative to cash donations. Calor gives employees one day's paid leave each year to do something which can make a difference to their community through the Start From The Heart programme.

Employee-led support

Employees fundraise and volunteer through the Start From The Heart programme. Employees can either choose to participate in an event coordinated by Calor or they are free to choose their own Start From The Heart activity, as long as they meet the criteria of education and sustainability. Team activities take place in June, July or August. Employees who undertake an individual activity for a registered charity will be offered a £50 donation from Calor.

Commercially led support

The company has a 'Gift of the Gas' scheme whereby it pledges to donate £5 (subject to terms and conditions) to its partner charity for every disused Calor cylinder returned to an approved Calor outlet.

Exclusions

Community grants are not available for projects or organisations that are political, discriminatory, or do not meet the 'off-grid' requirement. Individuals are not supported.

Applications

To apply for the Calor Rural Community Fund you must first register on the website: www.calor.co.uk/communityfund, where you can also find details about application deadlines and process, and see a full list of projects that previously received a grant. The fund has a comprehensive and helpful FAQ section which should be consulted before making an application. Applicants will be asked a series of eligibility questions before they complete an online application form.

For organisations local to a Calor site, the Site Manager responsible for the location can be contacted for further information on other CSR activities, or you can contact the Corporate Affairs Manager to discuss national or business-wide support.

Community contributions

Cash donations UK	£20,000

In 2017 the company did not declare its charitable donations in the annual report; however, the company's Sustainability Review notes that £20,000 was awarded to Rural Community Fund winners.

The Cambridge Building Society

General charitable purposes

Company registration number: 157223

Correspondent: The Marketing Team, PO Box 232, 51 Newmarket Road, Cambridge CB5 8FF (tel: 0345 601 3344; email: marketing@cambridgebs.co.uk; website: www.cambridgebs.co.uk)

Directors: Andrew Jones; Andrew Morley; Andy Lucas; Francis Burkitt; Jonathan Spence; Pauline Holroyd; Peter Burrows; Stephen Jack; Stephen Mitcham; Stuart Cruickshank; Victoria Stubbs (female 18%; male 82%).

Nature of business: The Cambridge Building Society is a UK mutual building society based in Cambridge.

Year end	31/12/2017
Turnover	£18,000,000
Pre-tax profit	£4,100,000

UK employees: 212

Main locations: The society has 13 branches across Cambridgeshire. Its headquarters are in Cambridge.

Community involvement

The society supports a wide range of charities and community groups working in the Cambridge area. Support is provided through cash donations, partnerships, sponsorship and employee volunteering and fundraising.

Community Partnership Programme

Through its Community Partnership Programme, the society works closely with four charities each year (each covering three months of the year). According to the society's website, participating charities each receive:

- Hands on help from the society's employees
- A cash donation
- Promotion via the society's social media channels
- Fundraising opportunities
- Access to the society's locations for promotional purposes

Applications are accepted from charities that operate within a 30-mile radius of Cambridge or national charities that can guarantee the funds will remain in the area.

In 2017 the society raised over £20,000 in total for four charities: East Anglian Air Ambulance, Eddie's (supporting people with learning disabilities), Alzheimer's Research UK and East Anglia's Children's Hospices.

According to the society's website, charities which aren't selected for partnership will be considered for other aspects of the community programme which include a donations initiative and an opportunity to be selected as the beneficiary voted for at the 2019 AGM where 25p is given for every member vote received.

Community donations scheme

The society makes monthly cash donations to charities voted for by its members in branches and online.

Employee-led support

The societies employees actively participate in fundraising and volunteering activities in support of charities participating in the Community Partnership Programme. During the year, employees volunteered for a total of 964 hours.

Commercially led support

The society regularly sponsors local community events.

Applications

Community Partnership Programme

Application forms can be downloaded from the website at: www.cambridgebs.co.uk/more/about-us/community-detail.

Completed applications forms should be returned by post, by email or at one of the society's local branches.

Sponsorship

Charities wishing to discuss sponsorship opportunity should contact the Marketing Team by email: marketing@cambridgebs.co.uk.

Community contributions

Cash donations UK	£36,500

According to its 2017 annual report, during the year the society provided charitable donations totalling £36,500.

Capgemini UK plc

General charitable purposes

Company registration number: 943935

Correspondent: Corporate Responsibility and Sustainability Team, Forge End, Woking, Surrey GU21 6DB (email: sustainability.reporting.uk@capgemini.com; website: www.capgemini.com/gb-en)

Directors: Aiman Ezzat; Christine Hogson; David Williams; Isabelle Roux-Chenu; James Gilshenan; Jean-Baptiste Massignon; Julie Mangan; Rosemary Stark (female 50%; male 50%).

Nature of business: Capgemini provides professional services and business consultation services.

Year end	31/12/2017
Turnover	£1,555,534,000
Pre-tax profit	£76,184,000

Main locations: The company's head office is in Woking. It also has offices in Birmingham, Bristol, Glasgow, Inverness, Telford, London, Liverpool, Manchester, Nairn, Rotherham, Treforest and Sheffield.

Community involvement

Support is provided through volunteering and the Community Spirit Awards which provide funding to projects supported by staff.

Community Spirit Awards

The awards provide grants of up to £2,500 for projects supported by staff members. Grants of up to £500 are also available for employees to help kick-start a fundraising or engagement activity. The awards support general charitable purposes. In 2017/18 donations to 42 projects through the award scheme totalled £36,500.

Employee-led support

There were 2,327 formal volunteering hours completed by staff in 2017/18.

In 2017/18 employee donations totalled £155,000 which includes payroll giving and donations made via company organised initiatives.

Applications

Contact the correspondent for further information.

Community contributions

Total contributions (cash and in kind)	£243,500

In 2017/18 corporate donations totalled £243,500. This includes contributions to charity partners, contributions through community award schemes and the cost of volunteering to the business.

Capita Group plc

Education, enterprise and training, health, general charitable purposes

Company registration number: 2081330

Correspondent: Corporate Responsibility Manager, 30 Berners Street, London W1T 3LR (email: corporate-responsibility@capita.co.uk; website: www.capita.co.uk)

Directors: Andrew Williams; Anthony Greatorex; Baroness Lucy Neville-Rolfe; Gillian Sheldon; John Cresswell; Jonathan Lewis; Matthew Lester; Sir Ian Powell (female 25%; male 75%).

Nature of business: The group provides a range of white-collar integrated professional support services to clients in local and central government, education, and the private sector. Services include: administrative services; consultancy; IT and software services; and human resource provision.

Year end	31/12/2017
Turnover	£4,234,600,000
Pre-tax profit	(£513,100,000)

Total employees: 70,000

Main locations: The group's head office is in London and it has various locations worldwide.

Community involvement

Capita's website states that: 'In each of the regions we operate, we look to understand the local socio-economic issues so that we can tailor our charitable and community activity to address these issues. These local initiatives are managed and delivered by the regional offices.' Much of the group's CSR strategy supports fundraising and pro bono work for the nominated charity partner. In 2017 the group began a partnership with the Alzheimer's Society. Through the partnership Capita aims to:

- Make 50% of UK employees Dementia Friends – a programme run by the Alzheimer's Society
- Become a dementia-friendly business
- Support research into dementia
- Raise £500,000 for the charity

According to the Corporate Responsibility Report 2017, 900 employees are Dementia Friends and over £100,000 was raised through fundraising events.

In-kind support

Capita allows employees one day off per year to volunteer or provide pro bono support to local charities. In 2017 employees volunteered 4,585 hours.

Employee-led support

Employees are encouraged to provide pro bono work and volunteer in their local communities. Many staff mentor at local colleges through Business in the Community's Business Class Programme, delivering workshops on interview skills, CV writing, time management and confidence. In addition to the work employees do with the Alzheimer's Society, the group supports employees' fundraising efforts for charities of their choice by offering a matched-funding programme and payroll giving scheme.

Applications

Contact the correspondent for further information.

Community contributions

Total contributions (cash and in kind)	£1,900,000

Capita's Corporate Responsibility Report 2017 notes that community investment totalled £1.9 million and supported around 150 charities, ranging from healthcare to improving education. A list of beneficiaries was not included.

Capital & Counties Properties plc (Capco)

The armed forces, children and young people, community development, education, enterprise and training, housing and homelessness

Company registration number: 7145051

Correspondent: CR Team, 15 Grosvenor Street, London W1K 4QZ (tel: 020 3214 9150; email: cr@capitalandcounties.com; website: www.capitalandcounties.com/responsibility/corporate-responsibility/charity)

Directors: Andrew Strang; Anthony Steains; Charlotte Boyle; Gary Yardley; Graeme Gordon; Henry Staunton; Ian Hawksworth; John Murphy; Ruth Pavey; Situl Jobanputra (female 20%; male 80%).

Nature of business: Capital and Counties (Capco), is a London-based property company with two key assets located at Earls Court and Covent Garden.

Year end	31/12/2017
Turnover	£87,700,000
Pre-tax profit	(£62,500,000)

UK employees: 119

Main locations: The group operates in London, primarily in the Covent Garden and Earls Court area.

Community involvement

According to its website, Capco works to develop long-standing relationships with selected charities in areas near to its assets at Earls Court and Covent Garden. Areas of special interest include young people, youth employment, homelessness and the armed forces. The group also works with schools in Earls Court and Covent Garden to deliver an educational programme for schoolchildren based around issues affecting their local areas.

Capco have a partnership with the London Community Foundation and donated £45,000 to provide grants to support community activity in the Earls Court area. The 2017 annual report notes that during the year the company 'supported a number of youth projects, computer coding classes, homework clubs, creative writing classes, boxing classes, nutrition and well-being projects and trips for older people'. During the year, Capco also partnered with BBC Children in Need for the official switch on of the 2017 Covent Garden Christmas lights.

Employee-led support

Capco employees are each given a corporate responsibility (CR) objective as part of their performance review. During 2017, Capco employees committed over 500 hours to CR-related activity. Employees also take part in a range of fundraising activities including sponsored bike rides and bake-offs. The website explains that funds raised by employees are often matched through the 'Capco staff recognition fund'.

Commercially led support

Capco sponsors local events such as the Covent Garden Community Association Christmas Carol concert held in St Paul's Church; the Poppy Day activities held on the Covent Garden Piazza; and the Chelsea Flower Show.

Applications

Contact the correspondent for further information.

Community contributions

Cash donations UK	£150,000

The 'Corporate Responsibility' section of the 2017 annual report states: 'This year we have developed close ties with selected charities which align with our overarching CR strategy and have donated over £150,000 to charitable causes.' As no breakdown was provided we have taken this as the overall figure for the group's charitable contributions.

Capital One (Europe) plc

Education (particularly financial education)

Company registration number: 3879023

Correspondent: UK Community Relations Team, Trent House, Station Street, Nottingham NG2 3HX (website: www.capitalone.co.uk)

Directors: Amy Lenander; Jeremy Penzer; Lucy Hagues; Michael Lynch; Neil Herbert; Richard Rolls; Robert Harding (female 29%; male 71%).

Nature of business: Capital One provides a range of financial services in the UK primarily comprising credit card lending.

Year end	31/12/2017
Turnover	£566,500,000
Pre-tax profit	£213,000,000

Main locations: Capital One has offices in London and Nottingham.

Community involvement

The majority of the company's CSR is dedicated to improving financial and digital literacy in the UK. Employees are encouraged to fundraise and volunteer for charities, as well as running school programmes such as 'Cheese Matters', a financial capability programme that follows the story of a young man who has got himself into debt, explores the consequences and then lets the students make decisions about what the outcome should be. It is run in partnership with two other businesses and Businesses in the Community to help bring secondary school pupils closer to the reality of financial management.

Capital One has had a partnership with YouthNet since 2012. The company has helped improve the work provided by the charity as well as helping with the development of online services.

In-kind support

Employees can take at least one day a year – or the equivalent in hours – to volunteer for charities and local schools.

Employee-led support

Employees are encouraged to volunteer their skills to benefit local charitable organisations for example by assisting with business plans, websites, databases, or by providing financial consultancy.

The company has several donation schemes for employees:

- A volunteer grant is available for employees who work on a regular basis for a local community group
- A 'Pennies From Heaven' scheme helps employees automatically donate the odd pence in their salaries to charity
- The Give As You Earn programme gives employees a tax efficient way of donating to their favourite charity straight from their salary

Previous research indicated that the company matches 100% of the money raised for charity.

Applications

Contact the correspondent for further information.

Community contributions

Cash donations UK	£500,000

The 2017 annual report notes that Capital One made 'charitable contributions of £0.5 million directly benefitting 3,190 individuals from 116 charitable organisations'.

Care UK Health and Social Care Holdings Ltd (Care UK)

Arts and culture, community development, health and medical research

Company registration number: 7158142

Correspondent: Foundation Administrator, Connaught House, 850 The Crescent, Colchester Business Park, Colchester, Essex CO4 9QB (tel: 01206 752552; email: well-beingfoundation@careuk.com; website: www.careukwell-beingfoundation.com)

Directors: Jonathan Hughes; Michael Parish; Philip Whitecross; Robert Moores (female 0%; male 100%).

Nature of business: Care UK provides health and social care services throughout the UK.

Year end	30/09/2017
Turnover	£655,800,000
Pre-tax profit	(£54,000,000)

Main locations: Care UK has offices in Colchester, London and Reading. It has 118 care homes and delivers services across the UK.

Community involvement

Care UK and its employees support good causes in the communities where they have a presence. It supports medical research and provides donations for charities working to improve well-being. In recent years charities providing art and music therapy have been supported including Creativity Works, Jessie's Fund, Nordoff Robins and Manchester Camerata.

Care UK Wellbeing Foundation

The company channels the majority of its charitable involvement through Care UK Wellbeing Foundation (not a registered charity) which works in partnerships with local grassroots charities and national charities working to promote health and well-being. In 2016 the foundation entered into a three-year partnership with the Rob George Foundation and will make annual donations to support its work. Local grassroots charities can apply for grants between £50 and £2,000.

The foundation also supports employees' fundraising efforts through its 'Working with the Community' matched funding scheme.

Recent beneficiaries listed on the foundation's website include: Activities, Respire, Rehabilitation Care Centres (ARRCC), Back on Track, Brogdale Collections, Carousel – Brighton, Fulham Good Neighbours and Global Arts Kingston (£2,000 each); Beau Halo Trust (£1,000).

Employee-led support

Care UK employees are actively involved with fundraising for charitable causes. The group matches donations up to £1,000 per employee. In 2017 employees helped raise £10,000 for the Care Workers Charity.

Applications

When a funding round is open, details are posted on the foundation's website. Local good causes can be nominated by non-employees using the online application form.

Employees can apply for matched funding at any time.

Community contributions

Cash donations UK	£42,000

In 2016/17 Care UK declared £42,000 in cash donations.

Cargill plc

Children and young people, education (particularly STEM subjects), the environment, health, poverty and social exclusion, projects outside the UK

Company registration number: 1387437

Correspondent: Cargill Cares, Velocity V1, Brooklands Drive, Weybridge, Surrey KT13 0SL (tel: 01932 861000; website: www.cargill.co.uk/en/sustainability)

Directors: Melanie Pollard; Michael Timewell; Paul Kingston; Peter de Braal; Richard Nield (female 20%; male 80%).

Nature of business: The company trades commodities and processes and distributes foodstuffs.

Year end	31/05/2017
Turnover	£1,000,000,000
Pre-tax profit	£47,000,000

UK employees: 1,200+

Total employees: 155,000

Main locations: The group has operations in Bathgate, Dalton, Farnborough, Hereford, Hull, Lichfield, Liverpool (five locations), London (two locations), Manchester, Weybridge, Witham St Hughs, Wolverhampton, Worcester, Worksop and York.

Community involvement

Cargill's community engagement programme supports local communities through economic development, partnerships and donations combined with the volunteer efforts of its employees. Support is given to select national and global non-profit and non-governmental organisations that serve communities in the areas the company operates. Cargill has three focus areas around food security, nutrition, and sustainability.

The following examples of projects supported in the UK are taken from the company's website:

- Cargill employees volunteer on an annual basis aboard the Irwell Pride litter boat, to help clean up the River Irwell in Manchester
- In the Lincolnshire area, the Cargill Global Food Challenge takes place every year in partnership with the Lincoln City FC Sport & Education Trust, to help children learn about nutrition, healthy eating and active lifestyles
- Cargill's Premix & Nutrition sites in the UK partner with the Country Trust's Children's Champion Scheme to help over 330 children from communities in need experience a farm day
- In the Liverpool area, Cargill has partnered with Ykids, a charity that helps improve opportunities for children, young people and families. Cargill's funding has helped support sports activities, kitchen gardens and meal provisions.
- Cargill employees in Weybridge have supported Painshill Park, in efforts to promote environmental awareness and understanding of local flora and fauna among school children

Cargill Cares Councils

Cargill businesses and facilities and their employees give through employee-led Cargill Cares Councils. The councils provide support for local charitable and civic organizations and programmes such as food relief agencies, schools and youth programmes, and local environmental projects. Cargill's five UK Cares Councils support initiatives and projects in the areas of health, education and environmental stewardship.

Partnerships

The group works with a range of different partners worldwide to deliver its corporate responsibility programmes.

In the UK Cargill has been working in partnership with the charity FareShare since 2009. The website states that the group has provided over £600,000 in funding to help establish regional centres in Merseyside and Greater Manchester.

Employee-led support

Employees volunteer with activities to support projects local to the area they work in.

Exclusions

The group will not support:

- Organisations without charitable status
- Capital campaigns/appeals
- Endowment campaigns
- Core costs
- Religious or political activities
- Sports events or athletic groups
- Medical research
- Individuals
- Advertising or media
- Fundraising events or sponsorship
- Travel

Applications

The following information was taken from the Cargill website: 'If your program or project is in a Cargill community contact the Cargill manager or Cargill Cares Council. They are typically responsible for reviewing local grant requests and making funding decisions.'

There is also an online form and guidelines for the group's global corporate giving, focusing on food security and nutrition; education; and environmental stewardship: www.cargill.com/corporate-responsibility/community-engagement/charitable-giving.

Community contributions

Cash donations UK	£145,000

The 2016/17 accounts state that charitable contributions during the year totalled £145,000.

CEMEX UK Operations Ltd

Community development, education, the environment

Company registration number: 658390

Correspondent: Harriet Aisthorpe, Community Fund Administrator, CEMEX House, Evreux Way, Rugby, Warwickshire CV21 2DT (tel: 07557 318038; email: harriettvictoria.aisthorpe@cemex.com; website: www.cemex.co.uk/cemexfoundation.aspx)

Directors: Christopher Leese; Larry Zea Betancourt; Laurence Dagley; Lex Russell; Michel Andre; Vishal Puri (female 0%; male 100%).

Nature of business: CEMEX is a global building materials company with a presence in more than 50 countries. CEMEX UK Operations Ltd is the principal CEMEX trading company in the UK.

Year end	31/12/2017
Turnover	£820,500,000
Pre-tax profit	£123,500,000

UK employees: 3,500

Total employees: 40,000

Main locations: CEMEX UK has sites throughout the UK. A searchable list can be found at: www.cemexcommunities.co.uk

Community involvement

The company channels its charitable contribution through the CEMEX UK Foundation (which is not a registered charity). It was created to provide a single point of focus for the company's charitable donations, community support and employee engagement activities. Both in-kind and financial support is available. The foundation will consider supporting small community and environmental projects within a three-mile radius of a CEMEX site. Projects that help educate children, students and stakeholders on CEMEX's business and the construction industry will also be considered.

The Rugby Group Benevolent Fund Ltd (Charity Commission no. 265669)

This fund was established in 1955 with the aim of supporting employees and former employees of Rugby Group Ltd, and their dependants. The Rugby Group is now a part of CEMEX UK, a global cement manufacturer, but the fund has kept its independence and is managed by a group of employees and former employees.

Partnerships

The company works with Groundwork UK to improve communities where the company operates. CEMEX UK has also had a partnership with the RSPB since 2009 which aims to create 1,000 hectares of priority habitat by 2020. Company staff also participate in wildlife initiatives and habitat maintenance schemes.

In-kind support

The foundation provides matched funding to employees that are raising money for charities and their communities up to a maximum of £200 per year.

Employee-led support

In the UK, employees from local CEMEX sites volunteer through the 'Lend-A-Hand' initiative to help carry out practical projects for local organisations, RSPB wildlife programmes and habitat maintenance schemes.

Applications

CEMEX UK Foundation

Application forms are available from the company's website.

Rugby Group Benevolent Fund (Charity Commission no. 265669)

Applications can be made through the fund's website: www.rugbygroupbenevolentfund.org.uk; or by contacting Ian Southcott, UK Community Affairs Manager at CEMEX House, Rugby.

Corporate charity

The Rugby Group Benevolent Fund Ltd (Charity Commission no. 265669) – see page 274.

Community contributions

Cash donations UK	£34,000

In 2017 CEMEX UK donated £34,000 to charitable organisations. The 2017 Sustainability Report notes that globally, CEMEX foundations have contributed over £5 million; however, a breakdown of support was not provided.

Center Parcs Ltd

Children and young people, health

Company registration number: 1908230

Correspondent: PR Team, One Edison Rise, New Ollerton, Newark, Nottinghamshire NG22 9DP (email: charity.requests@centerparcs.co.uk; website: www.centerparcs.co.uk)

Directors: Alan Park; Colin McKinlay; Colin Whaley; Kevin O'Donnell McCrain; Martin Dalby; Natalie Adomait; Paul Kent; Rajbinder Singh-Dehal; Zachary Vaughan (female 11%; male 89%).

Nature of business: Center Parcs is a network of holiday villages. In August 2015 it was purchased by Canadian asset management company Brookfield.

Year end	20/04/2017
Turnover	£440,300,000
Pre-tax profit	£75,700,000

UK employees: 7,500

Total employees: 8,200

Main locations: Center Parcs has villages in Bedfordshire, Cumbria, Nottinghamshire, Suffolk and Wiltshire in the UK and in Ballymahon in the Republic of Ireland. The company's head office is in Nottinghamshire.

Community involvement

Center Parcs' corporate responsibility programme focuses on supporting organisations that share its company ethos of bringing and keeping families together and supporting organisations local to the company's villages. Its Community Fund allows each of its villages and Head Office to sponsor local projects, whether delivered by employees or members of the community.

Occasionally the company pledges break donations to charities that support families in need. In 2018/19 the charities supported included the Ally Cadence Trust for Spinal Muscular Atrophy, Amy's Retreat, CLIC Sargent, Give Us Time, Josie's Dragonfly Trust, Lynsey Ivison Trust and Winston's Wish.

Partnerships

In June 2016, a new three-year partnership was formed with Together for Short Lives, a charity that raises money for childrens' hospices throughout the UK. Center Parcs matches donations made by guests and donates 25 breaks a year to the charity. As well as national support, each village fundraises for a local children's hospice, including Bluebell Wood Children's Hospice (Sherwood Forest village), East Anglia's Children's Hospice (Elveden Forest) and Jigsaw Children's Hospice (Whinfell Forest village).

In-kind support

In-kind support is given in the form of holiday breaks to disadvantaged families going through difficult times including those whose children are seriously ill. In 2016/17 the value of these breaks was more than £51,000.

Commercially led support

The company matches donations made by guests online and in the villages.

Exclusions

Center Parcs is unable to provide donations or prizes for raffles and auctions, or discounted breaks.

Applications

Requests for support can be made by contacting the PR team by emailing charity.request@centerparcs.co.uk including as much information as possible. Applicants will receive an automated response acknowledging the request. A response will be given within four weeks if the company can help. The company's website notes that it receives a huge volume of requests each week and is unable to support every application.

Community contributions

Cash donations UK	£15,500
In-kind support UK	£51,000
Total contributions (cash and in kind)	£66,500

Center Parcs did not provide any financial breakdown of support given in the accounts for 2016/17; however, the Annual Review 2017 notes that:

> During the year, Center Parcs donated nearly £15,500 to local community groups in and around our locations which makes a tangible difference to the lives of local people. Additionally, with the help of staff and guests and Center Parcs' matched contributions we have raised over £200,000 for our corporate charity partner, Together For Short Lives.

Central England Co-operative

Arts and culture, children and young people, community development, disability, education, the environment, health, older people, sports and recreation

Company registration number: IP10143R

Correspondent: Community Dividend Selection Committee, Central House, Hermes Road, Lichfield, Staffordshire WS13 6RH (website: www.centralengland.coop/community)

Directors: Dave Ellgood; Elaine Dean; Jane Avery; John Chillcott; Maria Lee; Marta Mayhew; Martyn McCarthy; Max Hunt; Paul Singh; Rachel Wilkinson; Richard Bickle; Sean Clothier; Sue Rushton; Tanya Noon (female 50%; male 50%).

Nature of business: Central England Co-operative's principal business activities are retail food stores (responsible for around 70% of total turnover), petrol filling stations, funeral services and property investment. The society also has trading interests in travel shops, coffin manufacture and optical services.

Central England Co-operative is independent from The Co-operative Group but is part of the wider co-operative movement. It trades across 16 counties from the Midlands to the East Coast.

Year end	27/01/2018
Turnover	£809,500,000
Pre-tax profit	£7,257,000

Main locations: The geographical area where support is given can be broken down into three regions: Western (West Midlands, Staffordshire, Warwickshire and Worcestershire); Central (Leicestershire, Derbyshire, Nottinghamshire, South Yorkshire and West Yorkshire); and Eastern (East and South Leicestershire, Lincolnshire, Northamptonshire, Cambridgeshire, Norfolk and Suffolk).

Community involvement

Central England Co-operative (the society) invests in communities where it has a trading presence, redistributing 1% of its trading profit each year. The society supports local charities and community causes through financial support, volunteering and partnerships.

Community Dividend Fund

Through the fund, Central England Co-operative makes charitable donations of between £100 and £5,000 to a wide range of local community groups in its trading area. The fund guarantees that at least 1% of the society's trading profit is reinvested in local communities in a bid to help projects to thrive across its trading area of 16 counties from the Midlands to the east coast. Grants are awarded every three months. Examples of projects recently supported are given on the website.

Charity partners

As well as making charitable donations to local community groups, the society also holds events to help raise money for its employee-nominated corporate charity partner. The society's current corporate charity is Dementia UK which it will continue to support in 2019. Employees, customers and members donated £280,000 to the charity in 2018, with an additional £500,000 raised through the 5p carrier bag levy. Previous charity partners have included Alzheimer's Research UK, Dementia Support South Lincolnshire, Louise Hamilton Centre and Newlife.

In-kind support

As part of the society's corporate responsibility strategy, it allows all employees to volunteer for up to three days each year.

Employee-led support

Employees nominate and fundraise for the society's corporate charity partners as well as volunteering for local organisations.

Exclusions

The website states that support cannot be given for:

- Vehicles
- Large scale projects
- Core costs
- Individuals

Applications

Applications for Community Dividend grants should preferably be made online where full information, including guidance and closing dates, can be found. Application forms can also be printed off from the website and submitted by post or handed in to your local Central England Co-operative store. Applicants who do not have access to a printer can obtain a Community Dividend application form by requesting one from an employee in store. Applications are considered every three months and applicants are normally informed of the decision 12–16 weeks after the closing date.

There are limited funds available and demand for awards is extremely high. The website states: 'Do not be too disappointed if your application is unsuccessful, but be assured that it will have received our full and proper consideration.'

Note that projects already in receipt of a Community Dividend Fund grant cannot submit a new application for two years.

Community contributions

Cash donations UK	£212,000

The 2017/18 annual report states that 120 community dividend grants were awarded to local organisations and totalled £212,000. The 2017/18 annual report states that investment in community and co-operative affairs totalled £1.22 million which included Community Dividend, Membership and Community funding, support for other co-operatives, grants, funds raised for charity and employee volunteering.

Recent beneficiaries detailed on the website include: Sunbeams (£2,500); Broxtoe Women's Project (£1,700); Rethink (£1,100); South Leicestershire Mobile Toy Library (£1,000).

Centrica plc

Community development, education, health, housing and homelessness, poverty and social exclusion

Company registration number: 3033654

Correspondent: Abi Robins, Director of Responsible Business, Millstream, Maidenhead Road, Windsor, Berkshire SL4 5GD (tel: 01753 494000; email: responsibility@centrica.com; website: www.centrica.com)

Directors: Carlos Pascual; Iain Conn; Jeff Bell; Joan Gillman; Margherita Della Valle; Mark Hanafin; Mark Hodges; Rick Haythornthwaite; Scott Wheway; Stephen Hester; Steve Pusey (female 18%; male 82%).

Nature of business: Centrica's principal activities are the provision of gas, electricity and energy related products and services in the UK, Ireland and the USA. The group also operates gas fields and power stations.

Year end	31/12/2017
Turnover	£28,023,000,000
Pre-tax profit	£142,000,000

UK employees: 32,592

Total employees: 33,000+

Main locations: Centrica operates in various locations through the UK and Ireland. It also operates worldwide.

Community involvement

Centrica invests in the local communities in which it operates through cash donations, in-kind support and employee volunteering. Centrica particularly focuses on the following areas:

- Climate change and the environment – particularly energy efficiency and investing in renewable power
- Fuel poverty and social inclusion – by working with public and voluntary sector partners to support Centrica's most vulnerable customers, particularly those affected by fuel poverty
- Education, skills and employability – by investing in education to promote learning about energy-related issues as well as supporting skills and training development
- Employee involvement – by encouraging charitable giving and volunteering

In the UK, the British Gas Energy Trust (Charity Commission no. 1106218) was established to award grants to organisations and individual British Gas customers.

Partnerships

Centrica has several flagship partnerships including:

- Shelter – Centrica works with Shelter to improve gas and electrical safety in the UK's private rented sector, alongside protection from retaliatory evictions
- The Alzheimer's Society – Since 2016, around 21,000 employees have become Dementia Friends
- Focus Ireland – Centrica donated €1.2 million (≈ £1 million as at October 2018) to prevent families in Ireland being affected by homelessness
- Children's Miracle Network Hospitals – In America, Centrica is supporting local hospitals through employee-led support

Employee-led support

Employees volunteer and fundraise for partner charities and local organisations. In 2017 employees volunteered a total of 57,340 hours and raised £700,000 across the group.

Applications

Contact the correspondent for further information. Note that the company has a preference for working in long-term partnerships with community organisations and charities that are closely aligned with its business principles.

Corporate charity

British Gas Energy Trust (Charity Commission no. 1106218) – see page 240.

Community contributions

Cash donations worldwide	£3,600,000

In 2017 Centrica's community contribution totalled £155.5 million of which £141.9 million was donated through mandatory contributions and £9.3 million was donated to support vulnerable customers. Centrica used the London Benchmarking Group framework to calculate that £700,000 was leveraged in employee fundraising. The remaining £3.6 million was donated to charitable organisations and we have taken this figure for the company's worldwide cash donation.

Channel 4 Television Corporation

Arts and culture, children and young people, disability, education, enterprise and training, equal opportunities

Correspondent: Corporate Responsibility Team, 124 Horseferry Road, London SW1P 2TX (website: www.channel4.com)

Directors: Alex Mahon; Althea Efunshile; Charles Gurassa; Christopher Holmes; Dan Brooke; Fru Hazlitt; Ian Katz; Jonathan Allen; Paul Geddes; Roly Keating; Simon Bax; Stewart Purvis; Tom Hooper; Uzma Hasan (female 29%; male 71%).

Nature of business: Channel 4 is a publicly-owned, commercially funded public service broadcaster. Channel 4 works across television, film and digital media to deliver its public service remit, as outlined in the 2003 Communications Act and the 2010 Digital Economy Act.

Year end	31/12/2017
Turnover	£960,000,000
Pre-tax profit	(£17,000,000)

Main locations: The group's head office is based in London.

Community involvement

The group has a focus on supporting education, training and equal opportunities in the creative, film, television and media industries. Support is provided through funding, partnerships and in-kind support. Employees are also encouraged to fundraise and volunteer for charitable causes.

Partnerships

The group works in partnership with a number of organisations to support training and skills in creative, film, television and media industries, including Creative Skillset and BRITDOC. The group also supports the RTS (Royal Television Society) Technology bursary scheme, which supports undergraduates from low-income backgrounds.

In-kind support

Channel 4 has worked in partnership with Disasters Emergency Committee for a number of decades, broadcasting international crisis appeals free of charge. The group has also offered the use of its premises and resources as in-kind support to charities.

Employee-led support

Channel 4 employees can make tax-free donations to charities through the group's Give As You Earn scheme. The group also supports staff teams to fundraise for charities by offering matched funding for team charitable fundraising efforts.

Applications

Contact the correspondent for further information.

Community contributions

No figure was given for the group's total charitable contributions.

Chelsea FC plc

Children and young people, disability, education, enterprise and training, poverty and social exclusion, sports and recreation, projects outside the UK

Company registration number: 2536231

Correspondent: Chelsea Foundation, Chelsea Football Club Training Facility, Stoke Road, Cobham KT11 3PT (tel: 01932 596193; email: enquiries@chelseafc.com; website: www.chelseafc.com/the-club/foundation.html)

Directors: Bruce Buck; Eugene Tenenbaum; Johnathan Laurence; Marina Granovskaia (female 25%; male 75%).

Nature of business: Chelsea FC is a professional football club competing in the English Premier League.

Year end	30/06/2017
Turnover	£361,308,000
Pre-tax profit	£15,646,000

Total employees: 812

Main locations: The football club is based in Central London. The Chelsea FC Foundation works across the UK with a preference for the south of England. The foundation also delivers projects in countries and cities across the world. A full list of locations can be found on the club's website at: www.chelseafc.com/en/foundation/where-we-work-map.

Community involvement

Chelsea supports a wide range of charitable causes including, social inclusion, education, sport, disability and equality and diversity. Support is provided through the club's charity, the Chelsea FC Foundation (Charity Commission no. 1129723).

The Chelsea Foundation

Formed in 2010, the Chelsea Foundation works on a broad range of initiatives focused on employment and education, social inclusion, crime reduction, and disability. The foundation also delivers a number of football development programmes in the UK and overseas and is involved in anti-discrimination projects aimed at improving equality and diversity in football. Full details of all of the foundation's current programmes are available on the club's website.

Social inclusion

The foundation delivers a number of programmes aimed at building stronger and safer communities. Recent examples of social inclusion programmes offered by the club include:

- **Chelsea Champions:** A Premier League-funded project that enables the foundation to place full-time staff within secondary schools in order to increase physical activity, support leadership qualities and improve emotional well-being and resilience of pupils through a number of universal, targeted and individual initiatives
- **Unlocking Potential:** An initiative designed to deter young people away from criminal behaviour and negative decision-making by taking them into Chelmsford prison to learn about prison life and the long-term consequences of committing crime and holding a criminal record

Education

The Chelsea FC Foundation education department works collaboratively with schools and businesses across Hammersmith and Fulham, Wandsworth, Westminster, Kensington and Chelsea and Brent to promote community cohesion, education, and lifelong learning. The club's education programmes focuses mainly on literacy, numeracy, employability, enterprise and technology.

Disability

The foundation's Disability Inclusion programme enables young people and adults with any disability to participate in regular, organised football matches and coaching sessions in a safe and enjoyable environment.

Chelsea Past Players Trust

The Chelsea Past Players Trust (Charity Commission no. 1120214) is a registered charity which provides funds to help support current or former members of Chelsea FC's playing, coaching, medical or scouting staff at first team, reserve team or youth academy level. In 2017 the charity received a £93,000 donation from the club and awarded funds for medical and general expenses worth a total of £113,500.

Building Bridges

According to its website, Building Bridges is Chelsea FC's campaign to 'promote equality, celebrate diversity and make everyone feel valued throughout the club, stadium and wider community'.

Partnerships

Since 2015, the club has worked in partnership with the international children's charity Plan International to help support the charity's Champions of Change programme in Columbia.

In-kind support

The club considers requests for signed merchandise from registered charities. However, the club states that due to high demand it is not possible to meet all requests.

Applications

General enquiries can be submitted in writing to the correspondent. Email addresses for local branches are available at: www.chelseafc.com/en/foundation/contact-us.

Charity requests

Applications for signed merchandise should be submitted by post or email. If applying via post it could take up to 28 days to receive a response. If applying via email the club will try to respond within five working days.

Community contributions

Cash donations worldwide	£93,000

The club's total charitable contributions are not detailed in its 2016/17 accounts. The 2016/17 accounts of the Chelsea Past Players Trust state that the club made a donation of £93,000. During the same period the club's foundation had charitable expenditure of approximately £6.34 million; however, it was not possible to determine what proportion of this figure was provided by the club itself.

Clifford Chance LLP

General charitable purposes

Company registration number: FCA LS 447778

Correspondent: The Clifford Chance Foundation, 10 Upper Bank Street, London E14 5JJ (tel: 020 7006 1000; website: www.cliffordchance.com/about_us/our-responsibilities/community-pro-bono/the-clifford-chance-foundation.html)

Nature of business: Clifford Chance LLP is a multinational law firm headquartered in London.

Year end	30/04/2017
Turnover	£1,540,000,000
Pre-tax profit	£532,000,000

Main locations: The firm has offices in London and Newcastle.

Community involvement

The firm channels its charitable giving through The Clifford Chance Foundation (not a registered charity). The firm offers pro bono support, community outreach and grant-making at a global and local level.

The Clifford Chance Foundation

The foundation provides funds at a global and local level to international and community charities covering long-term commitments and one-off payments. The firm provides its foundation with an annual budget of £1.2 million. Out of this budget, £700,000 supports the development of projects by its global pro bono and 'community outreach NGO clients', and funds disaster relief support for Save the Children and the group's Access to Justice Award. The remainder is distributed by each of its offices to local charitable projects.

Access to Justice Awards

The Clifford Chance Foundation donates money and time every year to a charitable organisation that promotes access to justice. The award is open to not-for-profit organisations that help individuals, groups or communities use the law to achieve significant social impact. Applicants should be involved in some way with the legal process to improve social justice in their communities. The winning organisation will receive a donation of £50,000 from the foundation and 500 hours of pro bono and volunteering work from lawyers and business services professionals across the firm.

In-kind support

The firm has a varied programme of community and pro bono activities, which focus on access to justice, access to education and access to finance.

Employee-led support

During 2016/17, the firm reported that each lawyer spent 19.48 hours providing pro bono and community support globally. In London, the firm participates in seven clinics each week, assisting local residents with issues such as Court of Appeal litigation, domestic violence, employment, welfare benefits, debt and housing. The firm also advise and represent the parents of children with autism, who are litigating in the Special Educational Needs Tribunal to secure better educational provision for their children.

Applications

The Clifford Chance Foundation

Applications to the Clifford Chance Foundation are welcome but must be championed by a member of the firm. All employees are able to download the application form from the firm's intranet site.

Access to Justice Awards

The winner of this award is selected by a judging panel comprising senior representatives from the firm's existing strategic pro bono partners, client base, and partners from Clifford Chance. More information is available at: www.cliffordchance.com/about_us/our-responsibilities/community-pro bono/access-to-justice-award-2018.html.

Community contributions

Cash donations worldwide	£50,000
Total contributions (cash and in kind)	£1,250,000

According to the firm's website, it awards £1.2 million every year to its foundation to further its charitable giving through financial and pro bono support. The firm also donates £50,000 every year through its Access to Justice Awards. We have taken £50,000 as the firm's total cash donations during the year, and £1.25 million as its total contribution.

Close Brothers Group plc

Arts and culture, community development, disaster relief, health and medical research

Company registration number: 520241

Correspondent: Rebekah Etherington, Group Head of Human Resources, 10 Crown Place, London EC2A 4FT (tel: 020 7655 3100; email: enquiries@closebrothers.com; website: www.closebrothers.com/charity)

Directors: Bridget Macaskill; Elizabeth Lee; Geoffrey Howe; Jonathan Howell; Margaret Jones; Michael Biggs; Oliver Corbett; Preben Prebensen (female 38%; male 63%).

Nature of business: Close Brothers is the parent company of a group of companies involved in merchant banking.

Year end	31/07/2018
Turnover	£486,100,000
Pre-tax profit	£271,200,000

Main locations: The group's main office locations are as follows: Doncaster; East Sussex; London; Manchester.

Community involvement

Close Brothers makes donations to a variety of charitable causes in the UK at a local level and to its staff-nominated charity partners. Cancer Research UK continues to be the group's health charity partner for the sixth year and the NSPCC was selected as the community charity partner. Funds raised from group-wide activities are split equally between the two charities. The group runs an annual charity week, consisting of a wide range of locally organised events for staff, which collectively raised over £126,000 during the 2018 event. A number of additional charities are also supported by its local businesses.

In-kind support

The group has launched a Trustee Leadership Programme to give their employees the skills to join a charity as a board member, with a particular focus on encouraging younger trustees. According to the 2017/18 annual report, 55 employees were appointed as trustees during the year.

Employee-led support

Employees are actively encouraged to participate in a range of events held during the company's designated charity week, and throughout the year, including sponsored fitness initiatives, dress down days, baking competitions and quizzes.

Employees are also encouraged to donate to charities of their own choice through the Workplace Giving scheme. Around 14% of employees across the group are signed up to the scheme and the group maintained its Payroll Giving Quality Mark Gold Award for the eighth consecutive year. The 2017/18 annual report notes that 199 different charities are now supported on an ongoing basis through the scheme.

The company's matched giving scheme matches 50% of funds raised or donates £8 per hour of voluntary time given by employees. It also matched funds raised by other local, organised fundraising activities, encouraging employees to work together to raise money for causes that are close to their hearts.

Commercially led support

Close Brothers are the exclusive sponsor of two Dogs for Good assistance puppies. The group's sponsorship will help support the puppies during their socialisation and training. This includes breeding and welfare costs, equipment and support to the volunteer socialisers. The puppies may go on to be autism assistance dogs, working with a child with autism and their family, or highly trained assistance dogs helping an adult or a child with disabilities.

Applications

Apply in writing to the correspondent. The CSR committee is chaired by the company's head of human resources and supported by employees across the group. There are also a number of local CSR committees which run initiatives to raise funds for charity.

Community contributions

Cash donations UK	£327,500

In 2017/18 the group's charitable cash donations in the UK were £327,500, raised through ongoing fundraising activities and matched funding.

CMC Markets plc

Children and young people, community development, education, enterprise and training, poverty and social exclusion

Company registration number: 5145017

Correspondent: CSR Committee, 133 Houndsditch, London EC3A 7BX (tel: 020 7170 8200; website: www.cmcmarkets.com/group)

Directors: David Fineberg; Grant Foley; James Richards; Malcolm McCaig; Manjit Wolstenholme; Peter Cruddas; Simon Waugh (female 14%; male 86%).

Nature of business: CMC Markets provides online financial trading.

Year end	31/03/2018
Turnover	£209,000,000
Pre-tax profit	£60,000,000

Main locations: The group's UK office is based in London, and there are also offices in Auckland; Beijing; Madrid; Milan; Oslo; Paris; Singapore; Stockholm; Sydney; Toronto.

Community involvement

The group supports employees fundraising efforts and activities and gives to The Peter Cruddas Foundation (Charity Commission no. 1117323). The foundation was established by Peter Cruddas, chief executive and founder of CMC Markets and he continues to make significant donations to it. The foundation makes grants in support of projects providing support for disadvantaged young people in England and Wales, particularly: support to get young people into education, training or employment; work experiences and skills projects for young people; and youth work in London. The foundation also provides mentoring support for charities.

Beneficiaries have included: Barnardo's; Duke of Edinburgh Trust; Great Ormond Street Children's Hospital Charitable Trust; Stroke Association; University College London Horizons Programme.

Employee-led support

The group provides matched funding for employee fundraising efforts.

Commercially led support

As part of its commitment to supporting local talent, the group and The Peter Cruddas Foundation sponsored Making The Leap for the second time to deliver its Social Mobility Careers Fair. A total of 15 employers attended and offered positions, while over 200 students attended on the day from across 24 London boroughs.

Applications

Contact the CSR Committee for further information on how the group can support you.

Application forms for The Peter Cruddas Foundation are available to download from the foundation's website (www.petercruddasfoundation.org.uk) along with guidance notes. Any queries before or during the submission of an application should be directed to Stephen Cox, the Foundation Administrator: s.cox@petercruddasfoundation.org.uk or 020 3003 8360.

Community contributions

Cash donations UK	£75,000

In 2017/18 the group donated £75,000 to The Peter Cruddas Foundation. No other information on community contributions was available.

Cobham plc

The armed forces, disability, health and medical research, disaster relief, education (particularly STEM subjects), projects outside the UK

Company registration number: 30470

Correspondent: Eleanor Smith, Vice President Corporate Responsibility and Sustainability, Brook Road, Wimborne, Dorset BH21 2BJ (tel: 01202 882020; email: crs@cobham.com; website: www.cobham.com)

Directors: Alison Wood; David Lockwood; David Mellors; John McAdam; Marion Blakey; Michael Wareing; Norton Schwartz; René Médori (female 25%; male 75%).

Nature of business: Cobham provides technologies and services to solve challenging problems across commercial, defence and security markets, such as: air-to-air refuelling; aviation services; audio, video and data communications, including satellite communications; defence electronics; life support; and mission equipment.

Year end	31/12/2017
Turnover	£2,052,000,000
Pre-tax profit	£66,900,000

Total employees: 11,000

Main locations: The group has a variety of business locations in the south of England, particularly London and the South East. Worldwide, it has business locations in: Australia; Denmark; Finland; France; Germany; Republic of South Africa; Sweden; and the USA. Contact information can be found on the group's website: www.cobham.com/the-group/locations.

Community involvement

Cobham states on its website that it invests in charitable causes that are relevant to its business and where the company can apply its skills and experience. Its focus is on supporting STEM education; ex-services personnel; causes in communities in which the company operates; and donating to disaster relief appeals.

In-kind support

The company has previously provided in-kind support for charities such as supplying computer monitors for schools in India and Zimbabwe and helping to equip Project Kaisei for the Pacific Ocean clean-up.

Employee-led support

Employees engage in fundraising activities on behalf of their chosen charities. The company operates a matched funding scheme to support employees' efforts.

Exclusions

No support is given for political appeals or for causes that are not relevant to the company's business.

Applications

Apply in writing to the correspondent. The central Corporate Responsibility and Sustainability team is overseen by a committee chaired by the CEO.

Community contributions

Cash donations worldwide	£275,500

In 2017 Cobham donated £275,500 to a range of causes including armed services, rescue and health-based charities, as well as to local community groups. No details were available regarding how much was donated in the UK.

Previous beneficiaries have included: Air League Trust; Combat Stress; Cancer Research UK; Help for Heroes; Make-A-Wish Foundation.

Compass Group plc

Education, enterprise and training, the environment, health

Company registration number: 4083914

Correspondent: Celine Ricord, Corporate Responsibility Manager, Compass House, Guildford Street, Chertsey, Surrey KT16 9BQ (tel: 01932 573000; email: global.HSE@compass-group.com; website: www.compass-group.com)

Directors: Anne-Francoise Nesmes; Carol Arrowsmith; Dominic Blakemore; Gary Green; Ireena Vittal; John Bason; John Bryant; Jonathan Thomson; Nelson Silva; Paul Walsh; Stefan Bomhard (female 27%; male 73%).

Nature of business: Compass provides contract food services to business and industrial organisations around the world. The company also provides support services such as cleaning, reception services and building maintenance.

Year end	30/09/2017
Turnover	£22,568,000,000
Pre-tax profit	£1,560,000,000

UK employees: 60,000

Total employees: 550,000

Main locations: The group has offices in Birmingham, Chertsey, London, Northampton and Uxbridge.

Community involvement

The group's corporate responsibility programme is primarily focused on improving the environment, education, health and well-being as well as engaging with local communities in the areas where the group has a presence. Employee fundraising and volunteering is supported by the group. The following is taken from the UK Corporate Responsibility Report 2017:

> In 2017, we revised our charity strategy to give more control to our different sectors. We set ourselves the target of donating £400,000 to charity every year and are pleased to have exceeded that in 2017 by raising almost £640,000. Each of our business sectors has chosen which charity it wishes to support and, typically, this is linked to our clients. For instance, our defence brand, ESS, raises money for the armed forces charity SSAFA, and Chartwells, which provides meals for young people, supports Young Minds, promoting strong mental health amongst young people. In addition to these individual relationships with charities, many of our sites also choose to support national campaigns.

In-kind support

In-kind donations of food totalling £106,000 was given to FareShare in 2017. According to the UK Corporate Responsibility Report 2017, this provided 32,000 meals for people in need.

Employee-led support

Employees use their skills to support community initiatives in areas where the company has a presence. Employees gave more than 1,700 hours volunteering for local and national charities in 2017. Compass supports a payroll giving scheme.

Commercially led support

Compass donates 5p form the sale of every EatFair product to raise money for growers and producers in the financially developing world. In May 2017, Compass introduced an expanded range of products and pledged to raise £50,000 to help improve gender equality in cocoa growing communities in Cote d'Ivore. The money will be given to Fairtrade Africa to help support the Women's Leadership School which empowers marginalised female farmers through a one-year course in business skills, economics and leadership.

Applications

Contact the correspondent for further information.

Community contributions

In-kind support UK	£106,000

In 2016/17 the group made worldwide charitable donations totalling £8.3 million; however, it is not clear how much of this was raised by employees or customers. In the UK, in-kind donations totalled £106,000 and Compass customers and employees raised a further £533,500 during the year.

Computacenter plc

General charitable purposes

Company registration number: 3110569

Correspondent: Charity Committee, Hatfield Avenue, Hatfield Business Park, Hatfield AL10 9TW (tel: 01707 631000; email: charity@computacenter.com; website: www.computacenter.com)

Directors: Dr Ros Rivaz; Francis Conophy; Gregory Lock; Michael Norris; Peter Ogden; Philip Hulme; Regine Stachelhaus; Ryan Peter; Timothy Powell (female 22%; male 78%).

Nature of business: Computacenter is an independent provider of IT infrastructure services in Europe offering services and solutions at every stage of infrastructure investment.

Year end	31/12/2017
Turnover	£3,800,000,000
Pre-tax profit	£111,700,000

Total employees: 14,652

Main locations: The company has a number of offices across England, plus an office in Cardiff and Edinburgh. Worldwide, the company operates in: Europe; Malaysia; Mexico; South Africa; and the USA.

Community involvement

In the UK, Computacenter's charity policy is to support three charities for a two-year period. At the end of that period, employees are asked to select alternatives from a shortlist that includes the current charity partners. The charities are approved by the charity committee and then receive considerable support from Computacenter during the period. Funds collected via fundraising activities within the programme are in most instances matched by Computacenter. The three charity partners for 2017, as nominated by the company's employees, were Alzheimer's Research UK, Mind and the Rainbow Trust.

The group also engages in charitable activities elsewhere in the world where its offices are based. In 2017 the group donated €50,000 (≈ £44,500 as at November 2018) to support refugee integration projects in Germany.

Education and employability

The company has a long-term partnership with the Hertfordshire Chamber of Commerce and a number of its UK employees have trained as ambassadors under its 'People Like Me' campaign. The ambassadors run activities in local schools to encourage girls to get into STEM subjects.

In 2017 the company partnered with the Muscle Help Foundation to support five young adults with muscular dystrophy through the Hertfordshire Chamber of Commerce's 'People Like Me' programme.

Employee-led support

Charitable activities and fundraising events are steered by the Charity Committee which comprises a cross section of employees. For example, in 2017 the HR Team in the UK opted to forgo the usual tradition of 'secret Santa' gifts, instead using the money that would have been spent on gifts for the team to donate toys to the Salvation Army to give to children in the UK. Employees also raise money each year for the company's chosen partners, which is usually matched by the company. The company also supports a Give As You Earn scheme.

Applications

Apply in writing to the company's Charity Committee. The committee is comprised of a cross section of employees throughout the company and any enquiries about the programme, fundraising activities or suggestions can be sent via email.

Community contributions

Cash donations overseas	£44,500

We were unable to determine a figure for cash contributions in the UK.

Construction Materials Online Ltd

Arts and culture, education, enterprise and training

Company registration number: 6755395

Correspondent: Community Fund Team, Burrington Business Park, Burrington Way, Plymouth, Devon PL5 3LX (tel: 01752 692769; email: enquiries@constructionmaterialsonline.co.uk; website: www.constructionmaterialsonline.co.uk)

Directors: Christopher Dorey; Andrew Dunkley; James Excell; Michael Fell; Adrian Saunders; Callum Tasker (female 0%; male 100%).

Nature of business: Construction Materials Online is an online supplier of construction materials in the UK.

Year end	31/12/2017
Turnover	£26,463,000
Pre-tax profit	£11,754,000

Total employees: 45

Main locations: The company is based in Plymouth, Devon.

Community involvement

The company supports charities and other community organisations through its Community Fund which provides discounted or free construction materials.

In-kind support

According to its website:

> The CMO Community Fund is a resource to which charities and other worthwhile organisations can apply in order to help source construction materials for their projects. Depending on the circumstances, applications can be made for a discounted order, or in some circumstances building materials may be donated free of charge.

Preference is shown for projects which do the following:

- Drive innovation and education
- Exemplify quality materials, design and workmanship
- Develop better communities

Prospective applicants are encouraged to visit the company's website to build a quote so that they can include their 'shopping list' as part of their application.

Applications

Applications to the Community Fund can be submitted using an online form on the company's website: www.constructionmaterialsonline.co.uk/cmo-community-fund.

Applications are considered on a monthly basis.

Community contributions

The company did not provide a figure for its total community contributions in its 2017 annual report.

Co-operative Group Ltd

Children and young people, community development, disaster relief, education, the environment

Company registration number: IP00525R

Correspondent: Local Community Fund Team, 1 Angel Square, Manchester M60 0AG (tel: 0800 023 4708; email: membershipcontactus@co-operative.coop; website: www.coop.co.uk/membership/local-causes)

Directors: Allan Leighton; Gareth Thomas; Hazel Blears; Ian Ellis; Lord Victor Adebowale; Margaret Casely-Hayford; Paul Chandler; Peter Plumb; Simon Burke; Sir Christopher Kelly; Steve Murrells; Stevie Spring (female 25%; male 75%).

Nature of business: The Co-operative Group is the UK's largest mutual business, owned not by private shareholders but by over six million consumers. The business areas of the group are: food retail and convenience store operation; financial and legal services; funeralcare; travel; property investment; electrical products; and banking.

Year end	31/12/2017
Turnover	£9,470,000,000
Pre-tax profit	£72,000,000

UK employees: 74,798

Main locations: The group has branches throughout the UK.

Community involvement

The Co-operative Group (Co-op) supports communities through partner charities which align with its subsidiaries businesses. For example, the Co-op Bank partners with Step Change and Citizens Advice Manchester to deliver debt advice. It has several products through which customers can donate to charities of their choice, partner charities or the Co-operative Community Investment Foundation. The group has partnered with the British Red Cross to tackle loneliness and isolation in communities across the UK.

In April 2017 the Co-op launched the Bright Future programme, which offers the opportunity of a paid work placement and a job in its food business to those who have been rescued from modern slavery. The programme was developed with City Hearts and is the first time a major UK business has offered work placements to survivors of modern slavery.

Co-operative Community Investment Foundation

The foundation (Charity Commission no. 1093028) is the Co-op's corporate charity and supports disadvantaged communities. In 2017 the foundation launched Belong, a new programme helping young people beat loneliness and created a £2 million #iwill fund to tackle loneliness through youth social action. The foundation aims to expand the Belong network through a second round of the #iwill fund as well as launch a new social investment and support programme for community-led enterprises.

In addition to its grant-making, the foundation also offers interest-free loans of up to £50,000 for ideas to improve community spaces. See the website for full details and information on how to apply.

In 2017 the foundation awarded 34 grants totalling £680,000 to 24 organisations.

Beneficiaries included: Youth Focus: North East (£70,000 in three grants); 42nd Street (£50,000); Royal Exchange Theatre (£35,000); Become Charity, Changing Our Lives and Whizz-Kidz (£20,000 each); Ovalhouse and Youth Action NI (£15,000 each); UK Youth (£5,000).

In-kind support

The group provides in-kind support by allowing employees to take volunteering leave.

Employee-led support

Employees take part in team challenges or volunteer on an individual basis with community organisations and charities. In 2017 employees volunteered 9,543 hours to their local communities. Examples included working with people who are unemployed for a long term, supporting children with their literacy and numeracy skills, and protecting the environment.

Commercially led support

The Co-op donates 3p from every litre of Co-op branded water it sells (previously, donations were only made for sales of Fairbourne Springs Water) to fund water projects in Africa. It is one of the UK founding members of the Global Investment Fund for Water, and will donate 1p per litre of branded water sold through its shops to fight water poverty across the developing world. In 2017 the Co-op donated £50,000 from sales of Co-op bottled water to help restore water and sanitation facilities for its banana supplier communities in the

Dominican Republic following Hurricanes Irma and Maria. A further £50,000 was donated to the Disasters Emergency Committee Rohingya appeal to support refugees fleeing conflict in Myanmar over the border into Bangladesh where water and sanitation provision is lacking.

Local Community Fund

Members of the Co-op support communities around its stores and funeral homes. The group gives 1% of what members spend on Co-op branded products in its stores, plus the proceeds of the 5p levy on single-use carrier bags, to local projects. Members can sign in to see and choose which projects to support.

Applications

Local Community Fund applications

New causes and organisations are chosen every 12 months. The application round opens in spring. To be accepted you must have a project in mind that will benefit your local community and your organisation must not be run for private profit. When the application round is open, further details are posted on the website.

Co-operative Community Investment Foundation applications

In the first instance, consult the foundation's website (www.coopfoundation.co.uk) where information on available funding, guidance and deadlines is posted. For further information email the Programmes and Partnerships Team at: foundation@coop.co.uk.

Community contributions

Cash donations UK	£14,500,000
Cash donations overseas	£2,070,000
In-kind support UK	£2,050,000
In-kind support overseas	£20,000
Total contributions (cash and in kind)	£18,640,000

The Co-op Way Report 2017 provides the following breakdown of community investment during the year using the London Benchmarking framework:

Type of community investment	Total
Cash	£14.5 million
Leverage	£10.6 million
Employee time	£2 million
Gifts in kind	£500,000

As is our usual practice, we have not included the amounts given in leverage in our figure for the group's community contributions. We have therefore calculated the total of the group's UK contributions to be £17 million. In addition to community investment in the UK, £2.1 million was given in support for communities overseas.

Costain Group plc

Children and young people, community development, education (particularly STEM subjects), the environment, health, older people

Company registration number: 1393773

Correspondent: Catherine Warbrick, Corporate Responsibility Director, Costain House, Vanwall Business Park, Maidenhead, Berkshire SL6 4UB (tel: 01628 842444; email: costainfoundation@costain.com; website: www.costain.com/our-culture)

Directors: Alison Wood; Andrew Wyllie; David McManus; Dr Paul Golby; Jacqueline De Rojas; Jane Lodge; Tony Bickerstaff (female 43%; male 57%).

Nature of business: Costain provides engineering and technology-led solutions operating in the rail, highway, power, oil and gas, water and nuclear sectors.

Year end	31/12/2017
Turnover	£1,684,000,000
Pre-tax profit	£38,900,000

Total employees: 4,008

Main locations: The group has offices in Aberdeen, Birmingham, London, Maidenhead and Manchester.

Community involvement

In 2017 Costain partnered with Cancer Research UK and supported the charity through cash donations and employee fundraising activities. Employees also act as STEM ambassadors, encouraging young people to choose a career in STEM.

The Costain Charitable Foundation (Charity Commission no. 1159056)

In 2015 Costain launched the '150 Challenge', a fundraising campaign with a target of £1 million, set to commemorate the group's 150th anniversary. The year-long challenge – in which employees, supporters and the company all took part – managed to raise more than £1.1 million. In 2018 the Costain Charitable Foundation was supporting the Samaritans.

The foundation only funds registered charities or activities with clearly defined charitable purposes. The foundation will support charities on an annual basis and the selection will be made by the board of trustees and employees. The selection criteria are aligned strategically to Costain's code of ethics and corporate governance.

At the time of writing (October 2018) it was not clear whether the foundation was still making grants or whether it was primarily supporting fundraising activities.

In-kind support

Every Costain employee is entitled to two days' annual volunteering leave. In 2017 a total of 30% of employees undertook a volunteering activity.

Employee-led support

Employees take part in volunteering and fundraising activities to support the company's charity partners. In 2017 over 2,500 hours of voluntary time was provided to community projects, ranging from creating community gardens to providing materials for the Bluebell heritage railway.

Commercially led support

Costain is a founding sponsor of the London Design and Technology UCT (University Technical College).

Applications

For information on how to apply to become a charity partner, in the first instance, see: www.costain.com/our-culture/the-costain-charitable-foundation.

Note that charity partners are selected according to criteria that are strategically aligned to Costain's code of ethics and corporate governance. The following guidance was obtained from the website:

> To be considered as one of the Foundation's sponsored charities the following requirements must be satisfied:
>
> - All recipients of the Foundation must be designated or registered as a charity or non-profit organisation; and are
>   - Not involved in the abuse of human rights
>   - Do not have employment policies or practices that discriminate on grounds of race, creed, sexual orientation, religion, gender, disability or age
>   - Do not discriminate unfairly in the allocation of their support according to race, creed, sexual orientation, religion, gender, disability or age
>   - Are not directly involved in gambling, recreational or illegal drugs, tobacco, armaments or alcohol (with the exception of those charities and organisations specifically dedicated to tackling addiction or drug abuse)
>   - Do not cause harm to animals for the purposes of either sport or entertainment
>   - Do not have, as their main purpose, the dissemination of political or religious information and do not otherwise use their charitable work to encourage support for political or religious causes
>   - Do not have activities which involve significant damage to the environment
>   - Fully disclose all relevant corporate and personal conflicts of interest

- The Costain Charitable Foundation's preference is to only support charities and other non-profit organisations that have long-term goals and objectives

Community contributions

Cash donations UK	£200,000

The 2017 annual report states that the company donated £200,000 to charities during the year. A list of beneficiaries was not provided.

Coutts & Co.

 Women and girls

Company registration number: 36695

Correspondent: Anna Hudson, Foundation Administrator, 440 Strand, London WC2R 0QS (tel: 020 7753 1000; email: coutts.foundation@coutts.com; website: www.coutts.com)

Directors: Francesca Barnes; Linda Urquhart; Lord Waldegrave of North Hill; Mark Lund; Mike Regan; Peter Flavel (female 33%; male 67%).

Nature of business: Coutts is a private bank specialising in supplying wealth management and banking services to high net worth individuals and their businesses. Coutts is a subsidiary of The Royal Bank of Scotland Group.

Year end	31/12/2017
Turnover	£560,000,000
Pre-tax profit	£165,000,000

Main locations: The bank's main location is London. There are offices across the UK in Birmingham, Bristol, Cambridge, Cardiff, Guildford, Hampshire, Leeds, Manchester, Newcastle upon Tyne, Norwich, Nottingham, Reading, Sheffield and Tunbridge Wells.

Community involvement

All of the Coutts's giving is directed through the Coutts Charitable Foundation (Charity Commission no. 1150784) which supports a small number of organisations that work to tackle the causes and consequences of poverty. At the time of writing (October 2018) the foundation was supporting organisations working with women and girls in the UK.

Employee-led support

Employees volunteer and organise fundraising activities to support charities and local community organisations. There is also a payroll giving scheme in place.

Commercially led support

Coutts sponsor exhibitions, festivals and events connected to the arts and design industries.

Applications

Sponsorship proposals can be submitted using the online form available at: www.coutts.com/sponsorship.

Corporate charity

Coutts Charitable Foundation (Charity Commission no. 1150784) – see page 244.

Community contributions

As the reporting period differs between the foundation and the company we were unable to determine the financial contributions for the 2017. The Coutts Foundation received £1 million from the company for the 2016/17 financial year.

Coventry Building Society

Children and young people, community development, education (particularly financial education), enterprise and training, general charitable purposes

Company registration number: FCA 150892

Correspondent: Christian Fleischmann, Foundation Correspondent, Economic House, PO Box 9, High Street, Coventry CV1 5QN (tel: 0845 766 5522; website: www.coventrybuildingsociety.co.uk)

Directors: Andy Deeks; Catherine Doran; Gary Hoffman; Iraj Amiri; Jo Kenrick; Mark Parsons; Martin Stewart; Michelle Faull; Peter Ayliffe; Peter Frost; Roger Burnell (female 20%; male 80%).

Nature of business: Coventry Building Society is the second largest building society in the UK.

Year end	31/12/2017
Turnover	£415,800,000
Pre-tax profit	£242,700,000

Main locations: The company is based in Coventry. There are branches across the West Midlands as well as in the East Midlands; Bath, Bristol and Somerset; Gloucestershire and Monmouthshire; Oxfordshire; Wiltshire; and Yorkshire.

Community involvement

Much of the society's CSR is centred on supporting organisations and causes local to Coventry Building Society's branches as well as supporting its charity partners. Branch and head office teams choose a local charity to work with and there are now over 75 partnerships in place. Its corporate charity, The Coventry Building Society Charitable Foundation (Charity Commission no. 1072244), is entirely funded by the society and makes donations to registered charities that are based or active within the region covered by Coventry Building Society's branch network.

Financial education and employability

The society offers support to schools, ranging from executives providing strategic advice as governors, to employees volunteering as Reading and Number Partners, or running budgeting lessons and mock interviews for sixth form colleges. The society also funds a Financial Inclusion Manager with Coventry Citizens Advice, who runs training sessions with branch staff to improve the support given to vulnerable members.

Partnerships

The society supports national charities and has partnered with The Royal British Legion for the past ten years. Since this partnership began in 2008, it has donated over £15 million, predominantly as a result of the society's portfolio of savings accounts. In addition, over 900 volunteering hours were provided by employees during the 2017 Poppy Appeal. Employees volunteer to operate the call centre for Children in Need each year, taking pledges for the charity.

In-kind support

The society supports employee's volunteering and fundraising efforts through paid volunteering time and matched funding. The 2017 annual report notes that employees volunteered over 7,500 hours.

Employee-led support

Over two-thirds of employees took part in the community programme through volunteering or fundraising during the year.

Commercially led support

The society opens 'Poppy Bonds' each year and pays 0.15% based on the total amount deposited as a donation to The Royal British Legion's Poppy Appeal. The total donated over the society's ten year relationship with the Legion is £15.4 million. Coventry Building Society was also a leading supporter of Coventry's bid to become the UK City of Culture in 2021.

Applications

Email community@thecoventry.co.uk for more information about how the society can work to benefit your school. Applications to the foundation must be sent through the appropriate community foundation, a list of which can be found on the society's website.

Corporate charity

Coventry Building Society Charitable Foundation (Charity Commission no. 1072244) – see page 244.

Community contributions

Cash donations UK	£1,600,000

In 2017 the society's charitable contributions totalled £1.6 million during the year. This included an amount of £1.5 million to The Royal British Legion's Poppy Appeal and £70,000 to its corporate charity, the Coventry Building Society Charitable Foundation. Unfortunately we have no definitive amount for the society's matched funding.

CPFC Ltd (Crystal Palace Football Club)

Children and young people, disability, education, enterprise and training, health, projects outside the UK, poverty and social exclusion, safety and crime prevention, sports and recreation

Company registration number: 7270793

Correspondent: Crystal Palace Foundation, Selhurst Park Stadium, Holmesdale Road, London, Greater London SE25 6PU (tel: 020 8768 6047; email: admin@palaceforlife.org; website: www.palaceforlife.org)

Directors: David Blitzer; Joshua Harris; Steve Parish (female 0%; male 100%).

Nature of business: Crystal Palace FC is a professional football club competing in the Premier League.

Year end	30/06/2017
Turnover	£142,735,000
Pre-tax profit	£11,876,000

UK employees: 196

Main locations: The club is based in South London, in particular the boroughs of Bromley, Croydon, Lambeth and Sutton.

Community involvement

The club's community activities are primarily channelled through its charity, Palace for Life Foundation (Charity Commission no. 1125878), which runs activities focusing on community development, social inclusion and crime prevention, disability, health and well-being, young people, and employability. It also offers in-kind support to charities through donations of signed memorabilia for fundraising purposes.

Palace for Life Foundation

According to its website, the foundation's work is focused around the following three priorities:

- Physical and mental health
- Early intervention for young people at risk
- Routes to employment

The foundation operates in South London and in particular in the boroughs of Bromley, Croydon, Lambeth and Sutton, with additional satellite sites outside London. It works with partners including local council, schools, voluntary sector and community organisations to deliver a wide range of programmes. Current example of the foundation's programmes include:

- **Community Inclusion:** This programme delivers sports sessions alongside pastoral support for young people in areas of deprivation
- **Route to Employment:** A series of programmes to help young people become ready for work
- **Active Adults:** A programme to inspire adults to lead healthier lifestyles in order to overcome problems of obesity and low self-esteem

Details of all of the foundation's current programmes can be found on its website.

In-kind support

The foundation can provide donations of merchandise for local registered charities or community groups that work within the boroughs of London in which the foundation works. It supports the following causes: young people; cultural relations; sporting activity or health; and education or literacy.

Applications

Applications for signed merchandise can be downloaded from the club's website at: www.cpfc.co.uk/club/faqs.

The website states that, although the club aims to help as many causes as possible, it is not able to grant every request due to the high volume it receives.

Community contributions

Cash donations UK	£63,000

In its 2016/17 accounts, no figure was given for the club's overall charitable contributions. However, in the 2016/17 accounts of the Palace for Life Foundation, it states that the club made a donation of £63,000. The foundation's accounts also reveal that it receives support from the club in the form of in-kind and administrative support, however the total value of this support was not quantified. In 2016/17 the foundation had a total charitable expenditure of £1.64 million.

Cranswick plc

General charitable purposes, community development

Company registration number: 1074383

Correspondent: CSR Team, 74 Helsinki Road, Sutton Fields Industrial Estate, Kingston Upon Hull HU7 0YW (tel: 01482 372000; email: info@cranswick.co.uk; website: cranswick.plc.uk)

Directors: Adam Couch; Jim Brisby; Kate Allum; Mark Bottomley; Mark Reckitt; Martin Davey; Pam Powell; Steven Esom; Tim Smith (female 22%; male 78%).

Nature of business: Cranswick is one of the largest food producers in Britain. The company has farms across Yorkshire and East Anglia.

Year end	31/03/2018
Turnover	£1,464,500,000
Pre-tax profit	£92,400,000

UK employees: 10,000+

Main locations: The company operates in various locations in the UK: Ballymena; Barnsley; Bury; Hull; Malton; Manchester; Milton Keynes; Norfolk; Preston; Sherburn; Suffolk; Watton.

Community involvement

The company engages in charitable activities predominantly in the UK but also elsewhere in the world. It does this through charitable donations, sponsorship and by encouraging employees to engage with their local communities through fundraising and volunteering. Cranswick supported a number of charities in 2017/18 including Bluebell Children's Hospice, the Yorkshire Air Ambulance, Macmillan Cancer Support and Life for a Kid. Both local and national charities are nominated by site employees through a local voting system. The company participates in the 'More Together' initiative, a charity project that encourages businesses based in East Yorkshire to fundraise for nominated charities.

In-kind support

Previous research has suggested that the company donates hampers and food parcels to charitable causes and local community events.

Employee-led support

Employees working at the company's various sites in the UK nominate local and national charities to support via a voting system and are encouraged to fundraise through sponsored events, competitions and cake sales. In 2017/18 employees raised over £13,000 for charities.

Commercially led support

Cranswick was a City Partner to Hull UK City of Culture 2017 and has sponsored the annual Freedom Festival in Hull for the past three years.

Applications

Contact the correspondent or your local Cranswick site for further information.

Community contributions

Cash donations UK	£80,000

At the time of writing (October 2018) the company's website noted that charitable donations made by the company at various UK sites totalled over £80,000. We have taken this to be the figure for UK cash contributions.

Credit Suisse AG

Arts and culture, community development, education (particularly financial education), enterprise and training, the environment, sports and recreation

Company registration number: FC007227

Correspondent: Corporate Citizenship Team, One Cabot Square, London EC14 4QJ (email: responsibility.corporate@credit-suisse.com; website: www.credit-suisse.com/uk/en)

Directors: Alexander Gut; Alexandre Zeller; Ana Pessoa; Andreas Gottschling; Andreas Koopmann; Iris Bohnet; Joaquin Ribeiro; John Tiner; Kai Nargolwala; Michael Klein; Seraina Macia; Severin Schwan; Urs Rohner (female 23%; male 77%).

Nature of business: Credit Suisse is a global financial services group based in Switzerland, with operations in 50 countries worldwide.

Year end	31/12/2017
Turnover	£20,900,000,000
Pre-tax profit	£1,793,000,000

Total employees: 46,840

Main locations: In the UK, Credit Suisse is based in London. The group operates in over 50 countries internationally.

Community involvement

The group has three areas of focus for its social commitments: education; microfinance; and employee engagement. The group has a global strategy for social commitments, which is implemented at a regional level depending on local needs, in co-operation with local partners. The group supports education at local and regional levels, as well as through its Global Education Initiative. Activities include a financial programme (in partnership with not-for-profit organisations), providing financial education and life skills support to girls in Brazil, China, India and Rwanda.

Credit Suisse Foundations

The group has a global Credit Suisse Foundation, which allocates funds to the group's Global Education Initiative and Financial Inclusion Initiative, and manages the Disaster Relief Fund. The Disaster Relief Fund provides short-term and long-term financial support to areas affect by disaster. The group is also a member of the Corporate Support Group for the International Committee of the Red Cross, offering financial contributions as well as support through expertise in areas like human resources or IT skills.

It also has a foundation for Europe, the Middle East and Africa. The Credit Suisse EMEA Foundation (Charity Commission no. 1122472) focuses on education, employability and aspirations among disadvantaged young people. Funding is given to organisations supporting these aims in the countries where Credit Suisse has offices. The foundation also supports the Charity of the Year scheme, and charities nominated by employees.

Youth unemployment

The group has a well-established programme to support young people who are unemployed, focusing on providing professional training through its Check Your Chance scheme.

In-kind support

The group's Global Citizens Programme, a leadership development scheme, allows employees to contribute their expertise pro bono to projects run by partner organisations, particularly in low- and middle-income countries.

All employees are entitled to four days paid volunteering leave each year to contribute to partner organisations' projects in the areas of health, education, social issues and environment. According to the 2017 corporate responsibility report, 18,410 employees volunteered during the year, dedicating more than 184,500 hours to volunteering.

Employee-led support

The group prefers to complement financial support that it provides to partner organisations with employee volunteering.

The group also has a global Board Training Programme which provides training for employees who are interested in becoming a trustee or board member of a charitable organisation.

Commercially led support

Sustainable or philanthropic products and services

The group offers services to charities and other not-for-profit organisations through 'strategic philanthropy' advice. This includes support with constructing a grant-making policy, help understanding charitable structures for individuals or families, and managing the operation of charitable foundations on behalf of clients. The group provides services for sustainable investment, impact investment and philanthropy.

Sponsorship

The group prefers to sponsor sports and arts events and organisations. Examples include the National Gallery in London, Sydney Symphony Orchestra and Roger Federer, tennis player.

Applications

Enquiries can be emailed to the Corporate Citizenship team at: responsibility.corporate@credit-suisse.com.

Corporate charity

Credit Suisse EMEA Foundation (Charity Commission no. 1122472) – see page 245.

Community contributions

Cash donations UK	£1,660,000

In 2017 the group gave £1.66 million to the Credit Suisse EMEA Foundation. It did not declare any other community contributions.

Cruden Holdings Ltd

Arts and culture, community development, education, the environment and conservation, health and medical research, housing and homelessness

Company registration number: SC339123

Correspondent: Michael Rowley, Secretary of the Cruden Foundation, Baberton House, Juniper Green, Edinburgh EH14 3HN (website: www.cruden-ltd.co.uk/group)

Directors: Alexander Hathorn; Graeme Bissett; Kevin Reid (female 0%; male 100%).

Nature of business: Cruden is one of Scotland's largest development and construction groups. The financial information and company details are for the holding company. For details of the other companies within the group consult Cruden's website.

Year end	31/03/2017
Turnover	£200,600,000
Pre-tax profit	£10,400,000

UK employees: 600+

Main locations: Cruden have offices in Edinburgh and Glasgow.

Community involvement

The majority of Cruden's giving is through the Cruden Foundation Ltd (OSCR no. SC004987) which is a shareholder of the group. The foundation makes grants to small and medium-sized Scottish charities to support community welfare, medical support and research, the arts, education and conservation. In 2016/17 grants totalled £326,000; of this amount, £103,000 was awarded to medical charities, £99,500 to social welfare charities, £92,000 to arts organisations, £17,500 to education charities and £14,500 to heritage and conservation projects.

Beneficiaries included: Edinburgh International Festival (£20,000); Marie Curie Cancer Care (£12,500); The Edinburgh Clothing Store (£10,000); The Cure Parkinson's Trust (£9,500); Scottish Ballet (£5,000); Habitat for Humanity GB (£3,500); St Columba's Hospice (£3,000); Bobath Scotland (£2,500).

In-kind support

The group offers pro bono support for projects that align with its business. In 2017 Cruden worked with Social Bite to develop the Social Bite Village using vacant land donated by the City of Edinburgh Council. The village provides a stable and supported communal way of living for 20 people at a time for around 12–18 months, acting as a stepping stone to permanent accommodation. Gill Henry from Cruden was appointed Project Director for the build and has co-ordinated and led the project from the outset, initially providing one day a week pro bono. The group allowed her to increase her commitment as the project developed.

Employee-led support

Employees fundraise and volunteer for local charities.

Applications

Applications can be made in writing to the correspondent and should be accompanied by most recent accounts.

Community contributions

We were unable to determine a figure for the group's charitable contributions.

Cumberland Building Society

General charitable purposes

Company registration number: 106074

Correspondent: Community Team, Cumberland House, Cooper Way, Carlisle CA3 0JF (tel: 01228 403141; email: communityfund@cumberland.co.uk; website: www.cumberland.co.uk)

Directors: Alex Windle; Des Moore; Gary Richardson; Jill Johnston; Paul Vines; Sam Lyon; Simon Whitwham; Susanne Parry; Will O'Carroll (female 22%; male 78%).

Nature of business: Cumberland Building Society is a building society based in Cumbria.

Year end	31/03/2018
Turnover	£44,895,000
Pre-tax profit	£21,405,000

UK employees: 322

Main locations: The society operates branches across Cumbria and the north of Lancashire. Its headquarters are in Carlisle.

Community involvement

The society provides support for a wide range of charitable initiatives in its area of operation. Support is provided through Community Fund grants and its corporate charity the Cumberland Building Society Charitable Foundation (Charity Commission no. 1072435).

Community Fund

Each year the society donates over £100,000 to local charities, neighbourhood groups, schools and voluntary organisations. The society supports a wide variety of causes, but has a particular preference for initiatives which relate to one or more of the following areas of focus:

- Health and well-being
- Vulnerability
- Financial education

According to the website, 'donations usually range from £25 to £1,500; however, funding of up to £10,000 can be awarded to specific educational projects or community events that involve a significant number of people'.

Previous beneficiaries have included: Eden Animal Rescue, Eden Valley Hospice, and CancerCare North Lancashire and South Cumbria.

Cumberland Building Society Charitable Foundation

The Cumberland Building Society Charitable Foundation was established by the society in 1998. Today the foundation awards grants of between £250 and £1,000 to support a wide range of charitable initiatives in the society's area of operation. The foundation is an independent organisation and is administered by Cumbria Community Foundation, but each year receives a substantial donation from the society.

Pledge for Votes

Each year the society makes a donation based on 50 pence for each vote recorded at its Annual General Meeting. In 2017, 21% of the eligible members voted, raising over £10,900 for Alzheimer's Society and Alzheimer Scotland.

Exclusions

According to its website, the society will not provide funding for any of the following:

- Organisations outside of our operating area
- Applications which have received a donation in the last six to twelve months
- Trips and holidays
- Events that have already occurred
- Sensitive, controversial or harmful requests, or those that could be a conflict of interest
- Political or pressure organisations
- Running costs including salaries and capital expenditure
- Individuals further education/tuition/course fees

Applications

Enquiries about the Community Fund can be submitted using an online form accessible via the society's website at: www.cumberland.co.uk/about/contact#community-funding.

Corporate charity

Cumberland Building Society Charitable Foundation (Charity Commission no. 1072435) – see page 245.

Community contributions

Cash donations UK	£101,500

According to the 2017/18 annual report, during the year, charitable donations of £101,500 were awarded. This figure included a £25,000 donation to the Cumberland Building Society Charitable Foundation.

P. Z. Cussons plc

Arts and culture, children and young people, community development, disability, education, health, projects outside the UK

Company registration number: 19457

Correspondent: Ngozi Edozien, Good4Business Committee, 3500 Aviator Way, Manchester Business Park, Manchester M22 5TG (tel: 0161 435 1000; email: pzccommunications@pzcussons.com; website: www.pzcussons.com/en_int/csr)

Directors: Alex Kanellis; Brandon Leigh; Caroline Silver; Dariusz Kucz; Helen Owers; Jez Maiden; John Nicolson;

Tamara Minick-Scokalo (female 38%; male 63%).

Nature of business: Principal activities of the group are the manufacture and distribution of soaps, toiletries, cleaning agents, pharmaceuticals, refrigerators and air conditioners.

Year end	31/05/2017
Turnover	£809,200,000
Pre-tax profit	£88,000,000

Total employees: 4,505

Main locations: In the UK the group has offices in Manchester, Salford and London. Internationally there are offices in Africa, Europe, Asia Pacific, the UAE and the USA.

Community involvement

As part of its 'Good4Business' strategy PZ Cussons supports local communities and charities in the places where it operates, with a particular focus on: children and families; education; well-being and hygiene; social welfare; people with disabilities; the arts and music. The group's website states: 'Our focus on Community & Charity is embedded into all our geographies and seeks to help and support the local communities which surround our factories and offices.'

Most support is given through The Zochonis Charitable Trust (Charity Commission no. 274769), a shareholding trust. Contributions are also made through staff time, fundraising and gifts in kind. In Manchester, where the global head office is based, the group supports the Seashell Trust (Charity Commission no. 1092655).

Charity partner

The group is in a long-term partnership with the Seashell Trust, a charity for children, young people and adults with disabilities. According to its website, employees have been involved with fundraising activities – such as sponsored runs, bike rides and cake bake sales to raise money for Seashell Trust's pupils who have severe learning and physical challenges. In addition to direct funding, the group has also been involved on a strategic level to help the charity to secure funding for their Transforming Lives Appeal which seeks to secure donations for 17 new children's homes and the £45 million needed for the new Royal School Manchester special school campus redevelopment.

PZ Cussons Nigerian Foundation

The foundation was established in 2007 and supports projects in Nigeria that improve education, health, water access and infrastructure. Support appears to be mainly in the form of in-kind donations (such as product packs) and employee volunteering and fundraising.

Employee-led support

The group embarked on a three-year association with Teach First in 2015/16 in which selected employees are being trained as coaches then paired with a teacher to mentor and support them during their two-year teacher training programme.

Commercially led support

This year the group's Carex brand again joined forces with United Purpose (formerly Universal Concern) to support Global Handwashing Day. This annual event, which was started by the United Nations eight years ago, touches over 200 million people and promotes a simple and life-saving message that handwashing with soap saves lives.

Applications

Contact the correspondent for further information.

Corporate charity

The Zochonis Charitable Trust (Charity Commission no. 274769) – see page 289.

Community contributions

Cash donations UK	£601,000

In 2017/18 the group declared cash donations of £601,000 to UK charities.

Beneficiaries included: Global Hand Washing Day; The Seashell Trust.

CYBG plc

Animal welfare, arts and culture, community development, education, the environment, health and medical research, poverty and social exclusion, sports and recreation

Company registration number: 9595911

Correspondent: Corporate Support Team, 20 Merrion Way, Leeds, West Yorkshire LS2 8NZ (website: www.cybg.com)

Directors: Adrian Grace; Amy Stirling; Clive Adamson; Darren Pope; David Bennett; David Duffy; Debbie Crosbie; Dr Teresa Robson-Capps; Fiona Macleod; Geeta Gopalan; Ian Smith; James Pettigrew; Paul Coby; Tim Wade (female 36%; male 64%).

Nature of business: CYBG is a banking group that owns Clydesdale Bank, established in Glasgow, and Yorkshire Bank, founded in Halifax, West Yorkshire. Both banks date back to the 19th century.

Year end	30/09/2017
Turnover	£1,036,000,000
Pre-tax profit	£268,000,000

UK employees: 6,040

Main locations: The group has offices in Glasgow, Leeds and London. Clydesdale Bank has branches across Scotland and Yorkshire Bank has branches has branches in the north of England and the Midlands.

Community involvement

The group awards grants to charities through its corporate charity, the Yorkshire and Clydesdale Bank Foundation (OSCR no. SC039747), which supports general charitable purposes. Employees donate to charities through payroll giving as well as fundraising for the group's partner charity. The group matches all employee donations. Employees volunteer days to contribute to associated projects, particularly in the area of education, and there are also grants available for charities that employees volunteer with in their spare time.

Charity partner

The group's charity partner since 2008 is Hospice UK. The group fundraises for both the national body and for local hospices. The group has raised over £5.8 million for the charity since its partnership began.

Education

The group's employees volunteer with local schools, delivering the Number Partners and Right to Read programmes run by Business in the Community. The group also works in partnership with Leeds City Council and Glasgow Life to deliver the Count Me In 123 and Count Me In Primary programmes, providing books and games for parents and teachers to help build numeracy skills.

In-kind support

Employees are entitled to two days' paid leave for volunteering on a bank-led volunteer activity. In 2016/17 employees volunteered a total of 7,000 hours.

Employee-led support

Payroll giving and matched funding

Around 20% of the group's employees support charities through the payroll giving scheme and the bank matches every donation. The group is part of the Geared for Giving campaign, which promotes payroll giving.

Volunteering

Employees are encouraged to volunteer for bank-organised activities. The group also has an Employee Volunteer Grant Programme, providing grants of up to £500 to charities. These are awarded quarterly to recognise employees volunteering in their own time. In 2016/17, 287 employee grants were awarded totalling over £141,000.

Fundraising

Employees organise fundraising initiatives for the group's partner charity, Hospice UK, which is matched by the group.

Commercially led support

Clydesdale Bank sponsors the Royal Zoological Society of Scotland's outreach programme, Wild about Scotland, with a bus that takes wildlife and environmental activities to schools across Scotland. The bank also sponsors and supports Scotland's Charity Air Ambulance.

Yorkshire Bank sponsors Cycle Yorkshire's bike libraries. The libraries allow people to donate unwanted bikes for reuse, providing a network of bikes that are free to hire.

Applications

Contact the correspondent for further information.

Corporate charity

Yorkshire and Clydesdale Bank Foundation (OSCR no. SC039747) – see page 288.

Community contributions

Cash donations UK	£710,000

No figure was given in the group's annual report and accounts for charitable contributions. According to the Yorkshire and Clydesdale Bank Foundation's 2016/17 annual report, the group donated £710,000 to the foundation during the year. We have taken this to be the figure for cash donations.

Daejan Holdings plc

Education, health and medical research, poverty and social exclusion

Company registration number: 305105

Correspondent: Mark Jenner, Company Secretary, Freshwater House, 158–162 Shaftesbury Avenue, London WC2H 8HR (tel: 020 7836 1555; email: mark.jenner@highdorn.co.uk; website: www.daejanholdings.com)

Directors: Alexander Freshwater; Benzion Freshwater; Chaim Freshwater; David Davis; Raphael Freshwater; Sander Srulowitz; Solomon Benaim; Solomon Freshwater (female 0%; male 100%).

Nature of business: Daejan Holdings is a property investment and trading company. The major part of the group's property portfolio comprises commercial, industrial and residential premises throughout the UK and in the USA.

Year end	31/03/2018
Turnover	£142,900,000
Pre-tax profit	£201,300,000

Main locations: The company's head office and location of the vast majority of its properties are based in London. The company also has properties across the UK, Wales and Scotland and in the USA.

Community involvement

The company makes cash donations, mainly to educational charities, in the areas in which the business operates.

Exclusions

Organisations dealing with professional fundraisers, large overhead expenses and expensive fundraising campaigns are avoided. Support is not given to the arts, enterprise or conservation.

Applications

Apply in writing to the correspondent. There is no donations or CSR committee.

Community contributions

Cash donations UK	£196,000

In 2017/18 the group made donations totalling £196,000 mainly to educational charities. The company also passed on dividend payments of £1 million from shares that were donated some years ago to charitable companies.

Daily Mail and General Trust plc

General charitable purposes, disaster relief, community development

Company registration number: 184594

Correspondent: CR Champions Network, Northcliffe House, 2 Derry Street, Kensington, London W8 5TT (tel: 020 7938 6000; email: enquiries@dmgt.com; website: www.dmgt.com/corporate-responsibility)

Directors: Andrew Lane; David Nelson; Dominique Trempont; François Morin; Heidi Roizen; J. P. Rangaswami; Kevin Beatty; Kevin Parry; Lady Keswick; Lord Rothermere; Paul Zwillenberg; Tim Collier (female 17%; male 83%).

Nature of business: Daily Mail and General Trust (DMGT) is a British media company, and the owner of The Daily Mail and several other titles.

Year end	30/09/2017
Turnover	£1,564,000,000
Pre-tax profit	£226,000,000

Main locations: DMGT's headquarters are based in London.

Community involvement

The group channels its charitable giving through its 'CR Champions' network which focuses on group-level partnerships, support for local community initiatives and disaster relief. The group provides financial donations, in-kind and employee-led support to the communities it serves.

CR Champions network

A network of employees representing each operating business meet by video call each quarter to discuss corporate responsibility at a grassroots level. The CR Champions share ideas and lessons learnt from CR initiatives they have carried out to encourage best practice. They promote group initiatives such as the Community Champions Awards and coordinate efforts for unexpected events and disasters in communities where the group's businesses operate.

Employee-led support

Community Champions Awards

The DMGT Community Champions Awards are designed to recognise the work employees carry out to support the communities they work and live within. The awards attracted over 100 nominations from across the group with winners for the 2017 awards selected by members of the DMGT CR Champions Network.

Volunteering and fundraising

The group has initiatives that allow employees to fundraise and volunteer their time to support local charities. Following the Grenfell Tower disaster, over 80 employees volunteered their time to help victims coordinated by DMGT's local charity partner the Kensington and Chelsea Foundation. In 2017 the group matched individual employee donations following Hurricane Harvey and the Grenfell Tower disaster.

Applications

Contact the correspondent for further information.

Community contributions

Cash donations worldwide	£817,000

The 2017 annual report states that the group gave £817,000 in charitable donations, additional to employee-led support. A list of beneficiaries was not available although £150,000 was donated to the Grenfell Tower Appeal.

Dairy Crest Group plc

Community development, education, enterprise and training, the environment, health, poverty and social exclusion, general charitable purposes

Company registration number: 3162897

Correspondent: Sue Farr, Chair of the Corporate Responsibility Committee, Claygate House, Littleworth Road, Esher, Surrey KT10 9PN (tel: 01372 472200; website: www.dairycrest.co.uk)

Directors: Adam Braithwaite; John Gibney; Mark Allen; Moni Mannings; Richard Macdonald; Stephen Alexander; Sue Farr; Tom Atherton (female 25%; male 75%).

Nature of business: Dairy Crest is a dairy company, processing and selling fresh milk and branded dairy products in the UK and Europe.

Year end	31/03/2018
Turnover	£456,800,000
Pre-tax profit	£179,200,000

Main locations: There are offices or operations in Esher, Surrey (head office); Cornwall; Frome; Kent; Kirkby; Newport; and Nuneaton.

Community involvement

Dairy Crest's CSR strategy focuses on supporting local charities and community groups in the areas where it has a presence. There is a preference for supporting health, education, youth engagement and employability skills, the environment and the countryside. Each Dairy Crest site is allocated an annual budget to support its local community.

Local Community Programmes

Local Community Programmes support local charitable causes that make a positive and direct contribution to the communities where Dairy Crest has a company presence. The programmes are run by local community committees made up of five or six employees from each place of work. Each committee has responsibility for their own budget and for the decisions they make. Each pot of money allocated to the local community committees reflects the size of the workforce, the socio-economic challenges of the area and the maturity of the programme.

Charity partners

Dairy Crest (together with other businesses and the Prince of Wales) contributed to setting up The Prince's Countryside Fund in 2010 to protect, improve and promote the British countryside and the businesses which work within it. The group has since maintained a long-term relationship with the charity, raising funds through brand partnerships, sponsored events and employee-led fundraising.

The group is also a long-term supporter of GroceryAid, a food industry charity that awards welfare assistance to people who are currently working or who have worked in the food industry.

The group has supported the charity Pub is the Hub since 2010. The charity encourages local authorities, local communities, licensees and pub owners to work together to support, retain and locate services within rural pubs. The group provides funding and assists pubs with setting up rural shops with the support of the local milkman.

The Prince's Rural Action Programme and The Dairy Initiative

The group supports the Prince's Rural Action Programme, which is run by Business in the Community. Its purpose is to engage businesses to make a positive difference to rural communities, through the way in which they do business, in order to sustain the rural economy, protect and enhance the environment and protect the nation's cultural heritage and landscape.

The Rural Action Award

The group sponsors the Dairy Crest Rural Action Award, run by Business in the Community. The award recognises companies that are helping to address issues faced by rural communities in order to maintain a vibrant, sustainable rural economy.

In-kind support

The group donates food products to assist charitable causes. For example, in 2017/18 the group donated over 1,150kg of Cathedral City cheese and 400kg of Country Life butter to the homeless charity Crisis at Christmas. Donations of cheese were also made to the Chelsea Pensioners to enjoy over the Christmas period. Employees can take one day paid volunteering leave each year and in 2017/18 employees completed around 80 volunteering days.

Employee-led support

Dairy Crest employees are encouraged to volunteer for local charities and community groups. The Local Community Programmes are owned and run by employees on a voluntary basis. The group also supports employees who wish to volunteer to deliver fresh food to vulnerable people in their local communities through Meals on Wheels.

Dairy Crest operates a staff lottery which is open to all employees. About £1,500 is donated to charitable causes each month through this scheme. In 2017/18 employees supported over 20 charitable causes through financial donations.

Beneficiaries included: Children with Cancer UK; NSPCC; The Cystic Fibrosis Trust.

Commercially led support

The group has brand partnerships with Davidstow cheddar and Country Life butter in order to raise £50,000 each year for The Prince's Countryside Fund.

Applications

Apply in writing to your local site, referenced, 'Local Community Committee'.

Community contributions

Cash donations UK	£290,000

In 2017/18 the annual report notes that the group donated £50,000 during the year to The Prince's Countryside Fund and a further £240,000 was spent supporting over 70 local causes. As no further information was available, we have taken £290,000 as the figure for the group's total charitable contributions. The annual report notes that beneficiaries included local schools, care homes, hospices, uniformed groups and health charities among others.

Darlington Building Society

General charitable purposes, medical research

Company registration number: 205895

Correspondent: CSR Team, Sentinel House, Morton Road, Darlington, County Durham DL1 4PT (tel: 01325 366366; website: www.darlington.co.uk)

Directors: Andrew Gosling; Chris Hunter; Christopher White; Ian Wilson; Jack Cullen; Jon Sawyer; Maxine Pott; Robert Cuffe (female 13%; male 88%).

Nature of business: Darlington Building Society is a UK building society.

Year end	31/12/2017
Turnover	£9,862,000
Pre-tax profit	£1,869,000

UK employees: 128

Main locations: The building society operates ten branches in locations across County Durham, North Yorkshire and Teesside.

Community involvement

The society supports a wide range of charitable causes in its area of operation with a particular preference for social welfare, older people, and medical research. Support is provided through cash donations, in-kind support, sponsorship and employee volunteering.

Sharing 5%

In 2017 the society pledged to support the communities local to its branches by donating 5% of its net profits after tax to charities and community organisations.

The society's members were invited to vote for the charitable causes that they would like to support. The three main areas of focus chosen by members in 2017 were as follows:

- People helping people
- Older people and loneliness
- Medical research

As a result of the pledge, in 2017 the society donated over £70,000 to 148 organisations.

The society works closely with the Durham Community Foundation to distribute the funds. For more information, see the community foundation's website: www.cdcf.org.uk.

In-kind support

The society allows local organisations to utilise available space within its branches to help them to promote themselves, meet new audiences or raise funds.

Employee-led support

All employees of the society are entitled to use two volunteering days to benefit their local communities.

Commercially led support

The society sponsors a range of sports and cultural events, including Bowes Museum exhibitions and the North Yorkshire and South Durham Cricket League. See the website for the latest information and opportunities.

Applications

Members can nominate causes they wish to support using on online form on the society's website: www.darlington.co.uk/community/nominate-a-worthy-cause.

Community contributions

Cash donations UK	£70,000

According to the 2017 annual report, during the year the society awarded over £70,000 in donations to 148 local charities and community organisations.

Deloitte LLP

Education (particularly STEM subjects), enterprise and training

Company registration number: OC303675

Correspondent: Responsible Business Team, 1 New Street Square, London EC4A 3HQ (tel: 020 7936 3000; website: www.deloitte.co.uk)

Directors: Andy Gwyther; David Sproul; Emma Codd; Kirsty Newman; Matt Ellis; Paul Robinson; Pauline Biddle; Richard Bell; Richard Houston; Stephen Griggs; Steve Ward; Vanessa Borchers (female 36%; male 64%).

Nature of business: Deloitte provides audit, tax, corporate finance and management consultancy services. In June 2017, Deloitte LLP combined with the Belgian, Danish, Dutch, Finnish, Icelandic, Norwegian and Swedish member firms to create Deloitte North West Europe. The information in this record refers to Deloitte's activities in the UK.

Year end	31/05/2017
Turnover	£3,503,000,000
Pre-tax profit	£416,000,000

Main locations: Deloitte has 30 offices based throughout the UK, the Channel Islands and the Isle of Man.

Community involvement

Deloitte's CSR framework focuses on employment, skills training and social mobility. It channels much of its work through the One Million Futures programme. There are three national charity partners, BeyondMe, Teach First and Volunteering Matters. Over 50 charitable organisations are supported through local offices across the UK, the Channel Islands and the Isle of Man.

A second programme, WorldClass, aims to empower 50 million people by 2030 through education, skills development and access to opportunity. The 2018 Impact Report notes that support has been given 'to social enterprises that help people with learning difficulties find employment, free English language classes for refugees, and schools workshops that encourage girls to consider careers in science, technology, engineering and maths'.

In-kind support

Deloitte undertakes pro bono research for charities as part of its One Million Futures programme. In 2016 the company formed a partnership with DePaul UK to help it expand its Nightstop service to new regions by providing a pro bono risk analysis heat-mapping initiative to identify areas most in need. The data Deloitte provided helped DePaul to secure government funding. Previous research suggests that the company also donates computers to charities.

Employee-led support

Employees provide pro bono services and volunteer for charities local to their office. For example, employees in Deloitte's Manchester office volunteered to help improve refugee women's English. The feedback was so positive that the office has partnered with Caritas International to continue the programme. According to the 2017 Impact Report, 3,449 employees volunteered during the year, giving a total of 31,258 hours of their time.

Staff also participate in fundraising activities, such as raffles, auctions, quiz nights, organised walks, runs and bike rides, as well as more challenging marathons and triathlons. The company also operates a Give As You Earn scheme.

Applications

Contact your local office for further information.

Community contributions

The 2018 Impact Report notes that the company's community contributions totalled £5.7 million in 2017/18; however, as this includes employee-led support and giving to social enterprises we were unable to determine the amount given to charities.

Dentons UK and Middle East LLP

General charitable purposes

Company registration number: OC322045

Correspondent: CSR Team, 1 Fleet Place, London EC4M 7WS (website: www.dentons.com/en/global-presence/united-kingdom/london)

Nature of business: Dentons UK and Middle East LLP (Dentons) is a global law firm with over 70 offices worldwide.

Year end	30/04/2017
Turnover	£170,312,000
Pre-tax profit	£48,306,000

Main locations: The firm's head office is in London and it has offices in Aberdeen, Edinburgh, Glasgow, Milton Keynes and Watford.

Community involvement

In the UK, Dentons channels its company giving through its corporate charity, the Dentons UKMEA LLP Charitable Trust (Charity Commission no. 1041204) which supports general charitable purposes in the areas where the company has a presence. Employees volunteer and fundraise for charities and local organisations as well as contribute to the company's global pro bono programme. In 2017 Dentons worked with over 170 organisations.

In-kind support

The company has a global pro bono initiative to support the work of charitable organisations and donated over 92,000 hours in 2017. Dentons has two pro bono legal clinics in London, one in Whitechapel which is open every Monday evening, and one in Poplar which is open every Tuesday evening.

In partnership with the National Centre for Domestic Violence, lawyers and trainee solicitors in several of the UK offices provide pro bono representation to individuals in abusive relationships who fear for their personal safety and/or the safety of their family. In 2017 it successfully obtained non-molestation orders in more than 24 cases.

Lawyers in the London office advised National Ugly Mugs (NUM) on a number of data protection and privacy issues associated with the development and use of an app that enables sex workers to alert each other to sexual predators in the area. Specific issues included the possible legal ramifications of posting the full name and other personal details of an alleged perpetrator on the app, including the risk of a defamation claim, and what should be included in the app's terms and conditions.

Overseas, Dentons has provided pro bono services on public international and local law that impacts refugees to the Norwegian Refugee Council and has interviewed refugees, translated documentation and prepared resettlement applications for the International Refugee Assistance Project.

Employee-led support

Employees engage in fundraising activities to support their chosen charities, as well as volunteering for local organisations and pro bono projects. For example, employees in the Milton Keynes office volunteer to read with children at a local primary school and staff in the firm's Scottish offices buy, cook, and serve food to the homeless through the Bethany Trust.

Applications

Contact the relevant legal team for further information about pro bono work.

Corporate charity

Dentons UKMEA LLP Charitable Trust (Charity Commission no. 1041204) – see page 246.

Community contributions

Cash donations UK	£103,000

The UK office donated £103,000 to its corporate charity. The 2016/17 annual report states that 'other offices have supported various other charities throughout the year', although no financial information was given.

Derwent London plc

Arts and culture, children and young people, disability, education, enterprise and training, the environment, equal opportunities, health, older people, sports and recreation

Company registration number: 1819699

Correspondent: Helen Joscelyne, Community Team, 25 Savile Row, London W1S 2ER (tel: 020 7659 3000; email: community@derwentlondon.com; website: www.derwentlondon.com)

Directors: Claudia Arney; Damian Wisniewski; David Silverman; Helen Gordon; Hon. Robert Rayne; John Burns; Nigel George; Paul Williams; Priscilla Snowball; Richard Dakin; Simon Fraser; Simon Silver; Stephen Young (female 23%; male 77%).

Nature of business: Derwent London is an office specialist property regenerator and investor. The group's investment portfolio comprises 6.2 million sq. ft., of which 98% is located in central London, specifically the West End and areas bordering the City of London.

Year end	31/12/2017
Turnover	£202,600,000
Pre-tax profit	£314,800,000

UK employees: 118

Main locations: There are offices in London and Glasgow.

Community involvement

Derwent London launched its Community Fund (not a registered charity) in 2013 which has two funding programmes, the Fitzrovia Community Fund and the Tech Belt Community Fund. The company defines the Tech Belt as the area extending from Kings Cross to Whitechapel, largely covering some EC1 and E1 postcodes. Local community groups, residents and local business owners are invited to apply for funding for their community projects, further details of which can be found in the community section of the company's website.

The projects must take place within the target areas, or sit just outside it, and fit within any of the following criteria:

- Local community events, supporting community programmes or activities
- Increasing employment opportunities/ apprenticeships for disadvantaged people in the area
- Well-being and health initiatives
- Small improvements to public space, street environment, community gardening, greening the streets
- Activities around arts and culture
- Educational and extra-curricular initiatives in schools

Since 2013, 56 projects have been supported and the fund has awarded over £450,000.

Beneficiaries of the Fitzrovia Community Fund include: All Souls Clubhouse; Fitzrovia Centre; Fitzrovia Chapel; Fitzrovia Neighbourhood Association; Fitzrovia Youth in Action; Upbeat Music and Mental Health.

Beneficiaries of the Tech Belt Community Fund include: Acting Freely; Islington Play; Ministry of Stories; The Spitz Charitable Trust.

In-kind support

Employees are entitled to one paid day per year to volunteer for a charity or community project.

Employee-led support

Many staff volunteer for projects already supported by the company, including beneficiaries of the Community Fund.

Exclusions

Applications to either the Tech Belt or Fitzrovia Community Fund must be from applicants based within the specified local areas in which the fund is allocated. Applicants based just outside the target area may be considered if their project benefits people living in the target area. See the 'Community involvement' section for more details.

The community funds will also not consider funding the following:

- Core costs
- Commercial costs
- Political activities and campaigns
- Religious activities
- Activities where people are excluded on the grounds of religious beliefs, ethnicity, sexual orientation or disability

Applications

Applications to the Tech Belt and Fitzrovia Community Funds can be made via an application form available to download from the company's website and should be addressed to the company's Community Team. In 2018 registered charities can apply for up to £5,000 and other organisations, businesses and individuals can apply for up to £2,000. Check the website for the latest application deadline dates.

Organisations that wish to enquire about the company's volunteering programme are advised to contact Susannah Woodgate by email: fitzrovia@ derwentlondon.com.

Community contributions

Cash donations UK	£108,000

In 2017, £108,000 was awarded to 19 organisations through the Community Fund. The 2017 annual report notes that the company also supported 'a wide range of charitable organisations through various sponsorships and donations, which during 2017 totalled £237,000'. As no further information was available, we have taken £237,000 to be a combination of commercially led, employee-led and in-kind support and have therefore not included it as a contribution from the company.

Deutsche Bank AG

Arts and culture, children and young people, education

Company registration number: FC007615

Correspondent: CSR Team, Winchester House, 1 Great Winchester Street, London EC2N 2DB (email: community.uk@db.com; website: www.db.com/unitedkingdom/responsibility.html)

Directors: Christian Sewing; Frank Strauss; Garth Ritchie; James Graf Von Moltke; Karl von Rohr; Nicolas Moreau; Stuart Lewis; Sylvie Matherat; Werner Steinmuller (female 11%; male 89%).

Nature of business: Deutsche Bank is the holding company of a group providing international merchant banking and investment management services.

Year end	31/12/2017
Turnover	£26,400,000,000

UK employees: 8,000+

Main locations: In the UK, the bank's head office is based in London. There are also offices in Birmingham and Bournemouth. The group's global headquarters are in Frankfurt, Germany and it operates in 70 countries worldwide.

Community involvement

The group supports charitable organisations and projects with a focus on education; social investment; and art and music. The current corporate citizenship programme, Born to Be, focuses on supporting young people to fulfil their potential.

Partnerships and programmes

The bank works in partnership with a number of organisations to deliver programmes supporting its Born to Be initiative, focusing on education, young people and youth unemployment.

Sporteducate

Working in partnership with the charity Sported, the bank has helped to develop an programme for disadvantaged young people which aims to provide education, employability skills and personal development through sport. The programme has been delivered by 33 sports clubs in London and employees also volunteer to support the programme.

Playing Shakespeare with Deutsche Bank

This programme offers educational workshops, tickets to performances and learning resources for school students in London and Birmingham to experience and engage with Shakespeare plays.

Design Ventura

Working in partnership with the Design Museum, Design Ventura gives school students the opportunity to learn about design and produce their own product in a competition, with the winning design going on sale for charity in the museum's shop.

Deutsche Bank Awards for Creative Design

The bank provides awards for students and recent graduates to pursue creative enterprise.

StreetSmart

The bank works in partnership with the StreetSmart and SleepSmart campaigns for homelessness charities, fundraising and covering administration costs for the campaign.

Charities of the Year

The group supports two charities each year, which are voted for by employees and support the Born to Be focus on young people. The group focuses on small charities and provides unrestricted funding, supported by employee fundraising. The group supports charities for a two year period and in 2018/19 it is supporting Cure Leukaemia and Rays of Sunshine Children's Charity.

Small grants fund

The bank provides small grants to local small charities and community groups in London and Birmingham whose work is related to the goals of the Born to Be initiative, supporting young people to fulfil their potential. Grants are distributed through the following partner organisations: the Community Foundation for Merseyside, Foundation Scotland and the London Community Foundation. Panels of Deutsche Bank employees decide which groups to support in their local areas.

Social enterprise and investment

The group's global enterprise programme, Made for Good, provides funding and expertise to help social entrepreneurs develop and grow their entrepreneurial ideas. The group also has an impact investment fund which invests in bodies providing funding for social enterprises.

In-kind support

In 2017 UK employees spent 2,179 hours volunteering for corporate programmes. Employees in the UK are entitled to up to two working days per year to volunteer.

Employee-led support

The bank runs an annual summer series of cycling events which employees can take part in to raise money for the Charities of the Year. The group also runs a 'Donate One Day' initiative in a number of countries including the UK, where employees are encouraged to donate a day's salary to charity. There is also a payroll giving scheme and matched funding available. In 2017, £2.4 million was raised for charities of the year.

Many employees volunteer with a number of the group's charitable projects under the Born to Be programme.

Applications

Charities of the Year

Charites need to be nominated by a Deutsch Bank employee. Details of how and when to apply can be found on the group's website.

Small grants fund

The website states that for information about the bank's small grants and whether they are currently available, you should contact The London Community Foundation: enquiries@londoncf.org.uk.

Contact the correspondent for all other enquiries.

Community contributions

The group's 2017 corporate responsibility report states that its global investments in corporate citizenship totalled €64.2 million (≈ £56.4 million as at October 2018). Of this, 8% was in the UK – around €5.14 million (≈ 4.5 million as at October 2018). It is unclear whether this includes employee fundraising.

DFS Furniture plc

General charitable purposes with a preference for children and young people

Company registration number: 7236769

Correspondent: CSR Team, 1 Rockingham Way, Redhouse Interchange, Adwick-le-Street, Doncaster DN6 7NA (website: www.dfscorporate.co.uk/responsibility/community)

Directors: Alison Hutchinson; Ian Durrant; Ian Filby; Julie Southern; Luke Mayhew; Nicola Bancroft (female 50%; male 50%).

Nature of business: DFS specialises in the retail of upholstered furniture with more than 100 stores across the UK and the Republic of Ireland. DFS also has a presence in mainland Europe.

Year end	29/07/2017
Turnover	£762,700,000
Pre-tax profit	£50,100,000

Main locations: There are stores across the UK. The head office is in Doncaster.

Community involvement

DFS works in partnership with three national charities and also supports local charities and initiatives in the communities where its stores are based. There is a particular emphasis on those that promote opportunities for young people.

The company also provides a matched funding plan for DFS employees raising money for their favourite charities.

Charity partners

During 2016/17, DFS continued its partnerships with:

- British Heart Foundation: DFS promotes the charity's furniture collection scheme to its customers. According to the website, more than £10 million has been raised by customers who have recycled their old sofas since 2012
- BBC Children in Need: Customers and staff helped to raise £750,000 through a wide range of activities. DFS runs monthly competitions for customers to have the chance of winning their order for free
- Duke of Edinburgh's Award: DFS is a Gold Partner of the Duke of Edinburgh's Award and its apprentices complete the award as part of their training. In the Republic of Ireland, DFS takes part in a similar scheme, Gaisce – The President's Award

Employee-led support

Employees raise money for DFS's partner charity BBC Children in Need through events and challenges.

Applications

We would suggest that requests are directed to your local DFS store.

Community contributions

Cash donations UK	£181,000

In 2016/17 DFS made charitable donations amounting to £181,000.

Dhamecha Holdings Ltd

Education, health, general charitable purposes

Company registration number: 6519903

Correspondent: Wembley Stadium Industrial Estate, First Way, Wembley HA9 0TU (tel: 020 8903 8181; email: info@dhamecha.com; website: www.dhamecha.com)

Directors: Jitendra Patel; Khodidas Dhamecha; Mukesh Vithlani; Shantilal Dhamecha (female 0%; male 100%).

Nature of business: Dhamecha is primarily a wholesale cash and carry business.

Year end	31/03/2017
Turnover	£702,891,000
Pre-tax profit	£12,620,000

UK employees: 574

Main locations: The head office is in Wembley, London. There are stores across Greater London and in Leicester.

Community involvement

The company makes its charitable contributions through The Laduma Dhamecha Charitable Trust (Charity Commission no. 328678).

Corporate charity

The Laduma Dhamecha Charitable Trust (Charity Commission no. 328678) – see page 246.

Community contributions

Cash donations UK	£503,000

In 2016/17 the company declared cash donations totalling £503,000 which were paid to The Laduma Dhamecha Charitable Trust.

Direct Line Insurance Group plc

The environment, safety and crime prevention

Company registration number: 2280426

Correspondent: Ashley Taylor, Sustainability Manager, Churchill Court, Westmoreland Road, Bromley, Kent BR1 1DP (tel: 01651 831653; email: ashley.taylor@directlinegroup.co.uk; website: www.directlinegroup.com)

Directors: Clare Thompson; Danuta Gray; Dr Richard Ward; Gregor Stewart; Jane Hanson; Mark Gregory; Mike Biggs; Mike Holliday-Williams; Paul Geddes; Penny James; Sebastian James (female 36%; male 64%).

Nature of business: The group provides a variety of insurance services such as motor, home, rescue and other personal lines and commercial insurance.

Year end	31/12/2017
Turnover	£3,489,000,000
Pre-tax profit	£539,000,000

UK employees: 10,808

Main locations: The head office is based in Bromley and there are offices across England and Scotland. See: www.directlinegroupcareers.com/About-Us/Our-Locations.

Community involvement

The group partners with road safety charities and makes small grants to UK charitable organisations with which its employees already have a connection.

Corporate social responsibility strategy

The group's current CSR strategy focuses on the following four areas:

- Helping to make society safe – this is focused on road safety initiatives, particularly those aimed at young drivers. The group develops partnerships with organisations to meet this strategic aim, see below for further details
- Proud to be here – to improve employee engagement such as the development of volunteer groups like the Community and Social Committees. See the 'Employee-led support' section for further details
- Being recognised as part of local communities – this includes group targets for volunteering, fundraising and matched payroll giving
- Reduce, reuse recycle – the group's environmental policy

Partnerships

In 2017 the group worked with various partners to highlight road safety issues. These included the Parliamentary Advisory Council for Transport Safety (PACTS), the Department for Transport and Brakes.

Grants

The group makes grants of £250 to organisations that its employees regularly volunteer or raise funds for in their own time.

In-kind support

Through the One Day Initiative, teams can spend a day engaging in a practical task for a charity or local community group. The annual report for 2017 notes that 34% of employees fundraised or volunteered for charitable organisations during company time.

Employee-led support

The group supports and funds a network of Community and Social Committees (CASCs) which its employees run on a voluntary basis. The CASCs create their own programme of events and activities at their local sites, including fundraising and building relationships with local charities and voluntary organisations. Examples of CASC support to charities in 2017 include: staffing the call centre to take pledges for Comic Relief and organising fundraising events such as quiz nights, cake sales and festivals. The group also encourages individual and team volunteering through the One Day Initiative.

Applications

Contact the local employee-run Community and Social Committees in the various sites in which the group's companies are based or the correspondent at head office for further information.

Community contributions

Cash donations UK	£170,000

In 2017 the group's employees donated £151,000 via payroll giving, which was matched with a further £104,000 by the group itself. The group also donated £66,000 in grants to organisations with which its employees already have a connection.

Dixons Carphone plc

Children and young people, projects outside the UK

Company registration number: 7105905

Correspondent: Corporate Responsibility Department, 1 Portal Way, London W3 6RS (tel: 0370 111 6565; email: CR@dixonscarphone.com; website: www.dixonscarphone.com)

Directors: Alex Baldock; Andrea Joosen; Fiona McBain; Gerry Murphy; Jock Lennox; Jonny Mason; Lord Livingston of Parkhead; Tony DeNunzio (female 23%; male 77%).

Nature of business: Dixons Carphone is an independent retailer of electrical and telecommunications devices and services.

Year end	30/04/2017
Turnover	£10,580,000,000
Pre-tax profit	£501,000,000

Total employees: 43,883

Main locations: The group's head office is based in London but the business operates in various locations across the UK and Ireland. Worldwide, the group has business locations in: Denmark; Finland; Greece; Norway; Spain; Sweden; and the USA.

Community involvement

The group, through its company Carphone Warehouse, has a long-term partnership with a The Mix with whom it directs its local and in-store charitable activities.

The Dixons Carphone Foundation

This fundraising account was established under the Charities Aid Foundation to enable the group to facilitate its employees' matched funding applications and one-off donations to emergencies and disaster funds.

The DSG International Foundation

This charity (Charity Commission no. 1053215) was established by the group in 1996 to distribute funds, primarily, to charitable organisations concerned with child welfare through Children in Need. No grants were made by the foundation in 2016/17.

Employee-led support

Employees take part in fundraising events in aid of the company's charity partner, The Mix, and the group's fundraising account, The Dixons Carphone Foundation. Employees also support a variety of charities and local causes through fundraising activities that are matched by the group. The group donates up to £100 or £300 for a team fundraising event.

Commercially led support

The group has sponsored Race to the Stones, a 100 km race along the ancient Ridgeway to Avebury Stone Circle.

Applications

Contact the correspondent for further information.

Community contributions

In 2016/17 the group donated £623,500 to its charity partner The Mix. This figure included gifts in kind and employee fundraising. A further £16,000 was given to the Dixons Carphone Foundation.

DLA Piper International LLP

Human rights, poverty and social exclusion, women and girls, medical research

Company registration number: OC305357

Correspondent: 160 Aldersgate Street, London EC1A 4HT (website: www.dlapiper.com/en/uk/aboutus)

Directors: Ana Garcia Fau; Bertold Bar-Bouyssiere; Claudine Vartian; Gerry Bean; Guillaume Penot; Janet Legrand; Jon Hayes; Jonathan Watkins; Joris Willems; Paul Edwards; Seán Mahon; Simon Levine (female 25%; male 75%).

Nature of business: DLA Piper is a global law firm with lawyers located in more than 40 countries throughout the Americas, Europe, the Middle East, Africa and Asia Pacific.

Year end	30/04/2017
Turnover	£876,800,000
Pre-tax profit	£307,400,000

Main locations: DLA Piper has offices in more than 40 countries throughout the Americas, Asia Pacific, Europe, Africa and the Middle East.

Community involvement

The majority of DLA Piper's community involvement in the UK is channelled through The DLA Piper Charitable Trust (Charity Commission no. 327280).

In-kind support

Employees are encouraged to take on pro bono work under DLA Piper's global initiative, New Perimeter. In 2017, 160 lawyers from 40 offices participated in 39 projects. At the time of writing (November 2018), the majority of projects took place in Africa, South East Asia and Central and South America. New Perimeter provides long-term legal assistance to support access to justice, social and economic development, and sound legal institutions. Its overarching goal is to support the advancement of women's rights. More information can be found at: www.newperimeter.com.

Corporate charity

The DLA Piper Charitable Trust (Charity Commission no. 327280) – see page 246.

Community contributions

We were unable to determine DLA Piper's charitable contributions for the year.

Drax Group plc

General charitable purposes, enterprise and training, STEM subjects

Company registration number: 5562053

Correspondent: Drax Power Ltd Charity Committee, Drax Power Station, Selby, North Yorkshire YO8 8PH (tel: 01757 618381; email: enquiries@drax.com; website: www.draxgroup.plc.uk)

Directors: Andy Koss; David Lindsell; David Nussbaum; Nicola Hodson; Philip Cox; Tim Cobbold; Tony Thorne; Vanessa Simms; Will Gardiner (female 22%; male 78%).

Nature of business: Drax Group has three principal activities: sourcing fuel (including sustainable biomass); electricity production; and electricity sales to the wholesale market and business customers.

Year end	31/12/2017
Turnover	£3,685,000,000
Pre-tax profit	(£183,200,000)

Total employees: 2,500

Main locations: The group has corporate offices in London and Yorkshire and operations in several locations around the world including Oxford, Northampton, Cardiff, Ipswich and Louisiana.

Community involvement

The group's businesses all support local projects through fundraising, partnerships and volunteering. Some businesses also run STEM initiatives in schools local to their operations.

Drax Inspire

The Drax Inspire programme focuses on STEM and digital outreach, innovating skills, transforming employability and creating a positive impact on the local community.

Applications

Applications to Drax Inspire can be made in writing to the correspondent or by using the enquiry form on the group's website. All requests are considered by the Drax Ltd Charity Committee. Funds can be allocated to charitable and non-charitable organisations based within a 30-mile radius of Drax Power Station in Selby.

Community contributions

Cash donations UK	£186,000

In 2017 the group donated £186,000 to charitable causes and £53,500 to non-charitable causes.

Dunelm Group plc

The armed forces, children and young people, health, projects outside the UK

Company registration number: 4708277

Correspondent: CSR Team, Watermead Business Park, Syston, Leicestershire LE7 1AD (tel: 0116 264 4400; email: enquiries@dunelm.com; website: www.dunelm-mill.com)

Directors: Andy Harrison; Bill Adderley; Dawn Durrant; Liz Doherty; Marion Sears; Nick Wilkinson; Peter Ruis; Will Adderley; William Reeve (female 33%; male 67%).

Nature of business: Dunelm is a specialist homewares retailer providing a range of products under the brand name Dunelm Mill.

Year end	30/06/2018
Turnover	£1,050,100,000
Pre-tax profit	£93,100,000

UK employees: 9,757

Main locations: There are stores across the UK. The head office is in Leicestershire.

Community involvement

In 2017/18 the group re-launched its charitable initiatives with a charity booklet containing details of activities which employees can participate in and fundraising ideas.

Charity of the Year

The group adopts a Charity of the Year biennially and facilitates collections in-store and specific fundraising events organised by its employees. The group also makes an annual cash donation to its Charity of the Year.

2017/18 is the second year of the group's partnership with Home-Start UK.

Regular donations

Regular local donations include supporting schools, communities and the town of Syston where the Dunelm Store Support Centre is based.

Sponsorship

The company is the main sponsor for the 7days 7irons challenge, supporting an individual to complete seven triathlons in seven days.

Employee-led support

Employees are involved in fundraising events and activities, the funds from which are often matched by the group. According to its website, the group aims to increase its matched funding in 2017/18. It also plans to establish payroll giving for its employees. Staff are given a paid day's leave to volunteer for local charities.

Exclusions

The company does not make any political donations.

Applications

Applications can be made by writing to the correspondent. For local fundraising and events enquiries, contact the charity committee at your local store.

Community contributions

Cash donations UK	£102,000

In 2017/18 the total value of charitable donations made by the group was £102,000. The total funds raised for charity by the group and its employees was £491,000. Of this, £456,000 was raised for Home-Start UK, the group's partner charity.

Dwr Cymru Welsh Water

Community development, the environment

Company registration number: 2366777

Correspondent: CSR Department, Pentwyn Road, Nelson, Treharris CF46 6LY (tel: 01443 452300; email: See 'Applications'; website: www.dwrcymru.com)

Directors: Alastair Lyons; Anna Walker; Chris Jones; Graham Edwards; Joanne Kenrick; John Warren; Menna Richards; Peter Bridgwater; Peter Perry; Prof. Tom Crick (female 30%; male 70%).

Nature of business: Dwr Cymru Welsh Water is a company which supplies drinking water and wastewater services to most of Wales and parts of western England.

Year end	31/03/2018
Turnover	£756,700,000
Pre-tax profit	(£14,800,000)

UK employees: 3,387

Main locations: The company's headquarters are based in Mid Glamorgan.

Community involvement

Dwr Cymru's Water Framework Directive provides financial contributions to not-for-profit organisations for projects that will deliver improvements to Welsh rivers, lakes and waterways. The aim is to create a more vibrant and healthy environment for people and wildlife.

The funding scheme aims to help implement the European Union's Water Framework Directive within Dwr Cymru's operational area. The directive aims to improve and ensure good quality of rivers, lakes, transitional waters, and coastal waters in all member states of the European Union.

Applications should:

- Describe how the proposal relates to Dwr Cymru operations or assets
- Be directly related to reducing the impacts/effects of the operation of assets or discharges or
- Involve 'upstream' or other work that could reduce the burden or risk of improvements being required at Dwr Cymru assets

The Independent Environmental Advisory Panel (IEAP) has been advising Dwr Cymru on the merits of projects submitted for funding.

Beneficiaries include: Loving our Lake working with Snowdonia-Active (aims to reduce phosphates in Llyn Padarn); The Monmouthshire Olway and Trothy project of the Wye and Usk Foundation (aims to reduce the adverse impact of agriculture in the catchments); Upper Tywi Catchment Restoration Project of the Carmarthenshire Rivers Trust (aims to reduce acidification); Alun and Chwiler Living Landscapes project of the North Wales Wildlife Trust (aims to increase the connectivity between habitats); River Schools educational programme by Groundwork North Wales (aims to raise awareness of the river environment); Clear Streams Swansea project (aims to reduce surface water entering the sewerage network and change attitudes and behaviours towards the water environment).

Biodiversity Fund

The company has launched a new Biodiversity Fund to give financial support to projects 'benefiting nature and enhancing biodiversity' at or near its sites. The fund is designed to help voluntary organisations develop and then implement ideas on how to help nature on those sites and also the wider community. The fund is open to any not-for-profit organisations in the areas Welsh Water serves in Wales, Herefordshire and Cheshire.

Welsh Water Community Fund

During 2017/18, the company launched the Welsh Water Community Fund to support those communities where its 'operational investment has caused disruption'. The Community Fund is a chance for communities to boost fundraising efforts for good causes in their area. In making awards from this fund, the Community Fund committee gives priority to areas where Welsh Water has been carrying out works that may have impacted the local community.

Recreational facilities

The company holds approximately 99,000 acres of land that is 'rich in scenery and biodiversity'. The land provides opportunities for public recreation, sporting and leisure facilities.

In-kind support

The company supports its staff in community schemes by providing their business/management expertise, mentoring or other skills. The company may offer assistance to communities in its area of operations that are experiencing flooding.

Employee-led support

Staff fundraise for a variety of charities including WaterAid.

Commercially led support

Education continues to be one of the main areas of community support. There is an ongoing outreach programme, combining both school visits and site visits to the company's education centres which demonstrate the importance of preserving water and protecting the environment. The available information, which is developed with educational experts, is linked to the national curriculum.

Applications

For information on the application process for the Welsh Water Community Fund visit: www.dwrcymru.com/en/Community-Fund.aspx or email: communityfund@dwrcymru.com.

For the Water Framework Directive, to discuss ideas for projects or to obtain an application form, visit: www.dwrcymru.com/en/Environment/Water-Framework-Directive-Projects.aspx.

Visit: www.welshwater.com/en/Environment/Biodiversity-Fund.aspx for further information on how to apply for funding from the Biodiversity Fund.

Community contributions

In 2017/18 the company did not declare its total charitable donations in its annual report and accounts. It did specifically declare, in the 2017/18 Annual Report, awards to two charities and stated that it disclosed those payments because it was required to by law, as both organisations campaigned for government policy change:

> During the year a payment of £33,750 was made to Citizens Advice, to fund a debt advisor providing advice to our customers in Rhondda Cynon Taff, and a payment of £18,000 was made to Step Change to support the work the charity does in providing debt advice to our customers.

Dyson Ltd

Education (particularly STEM subjects), medical research

Company registration number: 2627406

Correspondent: Tetbury Hill, Malmesbury, Wiltshire NS16 0RP (tel: 01666 827272; email: askdyson@dyson.co.uk; website: www.dyson.co.uk)

Directors: James Rowan; Jørn Jensen; Martin Bowen (female 0%; male 100%).

Nature of business: Dyson manufactures domestic appliances. The company began in 1978 when James Dyson invented the bagless vacuum. The group now operates in over 65 countries.

Year end	31/12/2017
Turnover	£374,000,000
Pre-tax profit	£177,000,000

Main locations: The UK head office is in Malmesbury, Wiltshire. It also operates internationally in over 65 countries.

Community involvement

All the company's community involvement is directed through The James Dyson Foundation (Charity Commission no. 1099709).

Corporate charity

The James Dyson Foundation (Charity Commission no. 1099709) – see page 247.

Community contributions

Cash donations UK	£1,500,000

According to its 2017 annual accounts, The James Dyson Foundation received £1.5 million from Dyson Ltd.

E.ON UK plc

Energy efficiency projects, fuel poverty, energy education and awareness

Company registration number: 2366970

Correspondent: Community Relations Team, Westwood Way, Westwood Business Park, Coventry CV4 8LG (tel: 024 7642 4000; email: EUKCommunityRelationsTeam@eon-uk.com; website: www.eon-uk.com)

Directors: Christian Barr; Christopher Norbury; Deborah Gandley; Michael Lewis; Sara Vaughan (female 40%; male 60%).

Nature of business: E.ON UK is an English energy company and a subsidiary of the German company E.ON.

Year end	31/12/2017
Turnover	£480,000,000
Pre-tax profit	£639,000,000

Total employees: 42,699

Main locations: The company's UK office is located in Coventry.

Community involvement

In the UK support is provided for energy efficiency projects, fuel poverty and energy education and awareness.

Energising Communities Fund

Funding is provided to all not-for-profit organisations in the UK for energy efficient projects and events. Grants range from £50 to £2,000 depending on the size and impact of the project. In 2017 the fund provided £74,000 in funding to 50 organisations.

STEM initiatives

The Energise Anything! programme provides free resources for schools to help inspire children in STEM.

Community relations

Working with partners such as charities, schools and councils, E.ON try and help people who need support with their energy usage. There are three issues that the company works on:

- Fuel poverty and how to reduce it
- Improving energy-awareness, education and skills for people of all ages
- Funding for local community energy projects

Charity partner

The company's two-year partnership with the Alzheimer's Society will involve a range of activities including fundraising and Dementia Friends sessions to help employees understand what it is like to live with dementia.

Employee-led support

Employees fundraise for the company's charity partner.

Applications

Energising Communities Fund

Further information including application deadlines can be found on the fund's webpage: www.eonenergy.com/About-eon/Community/energising-communities-fund.

Community relations

Contact the Community Relations Team for further information.

STEM

Resources can be found on the Energise Anything! section of the website: www.eonenergy.com/About-eon/Community/energise-anything.

Community contributions

Total contributions (cash and in kind)	£8,800,000

In 2017 E.ON made grants totalling £74,000 to UK organisations through its Energising Communities Fund. Worldwide, community investment totalled €10 million (≈ £8.8 million as at October 2018) and was broken down as follows:

Science and education	£2.53 million
Environment and sustainability	£2.04 million
Arts and culture	£1.54 million
Sports	£1.02 million
Other social projects	£890,500
Communities, customers and energy	£486,000
Healthcare	£388,500
Job creation projects	£168,000

East of England Co-operative Society Ltd

Community development, general charitable purposes

Company registration number: IP01099R

Correspondent: Community Engagement Team, Wherstead Park, The Street, Wherstead, Ipswich, Suffolk IP9 2BJ (tel: 01473 786000; email: enquiries@eastofengland.coop; website: www.eastofengland.coop/community)

Directors: Belinda Bulsing; Beverley Perkins; Chris Matthews; Chris Newbury; Claire Johnsen; Emma Howard; Fiona Powell; Frank Moxon; John Cook; John Hawkins; Judi Newman; Karla Powell; Nicola Fox; Richard Youngs; Sally Chicken; Steve Shaw (female 56%; male 44%).

Nature of business: The East of England Co-operative Society is the fourth largest consumer co-operative in the United Kingdom.

Year end	27/01/2018
Turnover	£353,622,000
Pre-tax profit	£3,247,000

UK employees: 4,305

Main locations: The society is headquartered in Ipswich and trading in the eastern counties of Essex, Suffolk and Norfolk.

Community involvement

The society supports local communities through a range of initiatives providing financial and in-kind support.

Community Token Support

The East of England Co-op supports its local communities by running a token scheme across its food stores giving local good causes a chance to collect a share of a £1,000 donation every three months. Each time a member shops with the society they are given a green token to place in the box of the cause they want to support. At the end of the three-month period the tally from each store across the cluster will be added together to show how the funding will be divided between the causes. The funding will be shared by the split of £500, £300 or £200. In 2017/18 over 384 charities and community groups received a donation through the scheme.

School Partnerships

The society works with a range of partners and stakeholders to support teachers, parents and students in the communities where it has a store. Teachers can download resources about the history of co-operatives or find local co-operative groups that can deliver learning sessions in schools.

In-kind support

Co-op Cuppa

This initiative gives local causes and communities throughout the east of England a free regular or one-off supply of Co-operative Fairtrade 99 Tea. In 2017/18 the society supported 1,199 community groups and good causes through this scheme.

Employee-led support

According to the website, employees carry out a variety of fundraising activities for good causes, including: marathons, sponsored fun runs, skydives and cycling challenges. During 2017, employees raised £4,800 for the Alzheimer's Society. The society contributes up to £50 per event when an employee is raising money for a charity or local community initiative through its pound-for-pound matched funding scheme.

Commercially led support

The society invites its customers and members to donate food through its stores. In 2017 over 23,000 items of food or essentials were donated to food banks across East Anglia.

Exclusions

Support is not available to the following:

- Individuals
- Political or lobbying organisations
- Religious groups
- Overseas organisations
- Statutory authorities and public bodies (unless co-ordinating a project on behalf of a charity)

In addition, the society is unable to support applications for core funding. Schools can only be supported for activities outside the scope of the general curriculum.

Applications

Community Token Scheme

Applicants need to demonstrate how their project will support at least three co-operative values and principles, details of which can be found online.

Applications can be made at any time but are assessed every three months. If you are not successful the first time your application will be held on file for the following three time periods and will be considered four times in total over a 12-month period; however, once this period is over you will be required to re-apply. The group asks applicants to be aware that it receives a large number of applications which means it may not be able to support all who apply.

You or your group must be an East of England Co-op member to apply. Applicants can join via the website.

Co-op Cuppa

Only members can apply for a free supply of tea. Applications can be for a one-off event or for ongoing support and there are separate application forms that can be downloaded from the society's website. Successful applicants are given a voucher for a nominated Co-op store where they can collect their tea.

Schools

For more information about how the society can support your school email: schools@eastofengland.coop.

Community contributions

Cash donations UK	£128,000

The annual report and accounts for 2017/18 state that £128,000 was awarded to over 384 charities during the year. A figure for in-kind donations was not provided.

Ecclesiastical Insurance Group plc

Heritage, religion

Company registration number: 1718196

Correspondent: Chris Pitt, Group CR Manager, Beaufort House, Brunswick Road, Gloucester GL1 1JZ (website: www.ecclesiastical.com)

Directors: Andrew McIntyre; Caroline Taylor; Chris Moulder; David Henderson; Denise Wilson; Ian Campbell; Jacinta White; John Hylands; Mark Hews; The Very Revd Christine Wilson; Tim Carroll (female 36%; male 64%).

Nature of business: Owned by a registered charity, Allchurches Trust (Charity Commission no. 263960), Ecclesiastical is a unique financial services organisation. With its main operations and headquarters in the UK, Ecclesiastical also operates in Australia, Canada and Ireland. Ecclesiastical is a specialist insurer of the faith, heritage, fine art, charities, education and private client sectors. Founded in 1887 to provide insurance for the Anglican Church, the company now offers a wide range of commercial insurances, as well as home insurance, selling through brokers and directly. The Ecclesiastical Group also includes broking and advisory businesses and an investment management business, EdenTree, which provides a range of ethically screened investment funds.

Year end	31/12/2017
Turnover	£207,200,000
Pre-tax profit	£82,200,000

Total employees: 1,415

Main locations: Ecclesiastical's head office is in Gloucester and it has offices in Birmingham, London, and Manchester. There are also offices in Ireland, Australian and Canada.

Community involvement

The Ecclesiastical Group is owned by Allchurches Trust and therefore gives a large proportion of its profits to the trust each year. The Ecclesiastical Group also supports charitable causes in its own right through charity partnerships, donations and employee-supported giving.

Charity partnerships

Ecclesiastical offices across the UK partner with local charities, as do its overseas businesses in Canada and Australia. Examples of charity partnerships include:

- The Landmark Trust – In 2016 Ecclesiastical established a partnership with the Landmark Trust to repair and restore a historic property on the at-risk register.
- Coram – Ecclesiastical continued its partnership with Coram to help develop its Life Education programme which promotes positive behaviour, mental and physical health, well-being, resilience and achievement in UK primary schools.

Employee-led support

Employee volunteering

In 2017 over 60% of Ecclesiastical's employees gave their practical and professional support through volunteering time.

Payroll giving

Ecclesiastical has a Gold standard Payroll Giving Quality Mark.

Matched funding

Ecclesiastical matches all money employees fundraise or donate through payroll giving.

'MyGiving'

Every employee is given a 'personal grant' of £125 which they can donate to a charity of their choice. Employees who volunteer with the same cause have their grant doubled.

Commercially led support

Through the Closer to You grants programme, insurance brokers on the Select Broker programme can apply for grants of up to £2,500 for their chosen charities.

Applications

Contact the correspondent for further information.

Corporate charity

Allchurches Trust Ltd (Charity Commission no. 263960) – see page 230.

Community contributions

Cash donations UK	£27,500,000

In 2017 the group's charitable giving totalled £27.5 million with £26 million given to its charitable owners Allchurches Trust and £1.5 million in direct charitable giving by the group. The group's direct charitable giving included £300,000 given towards heritage skills, £135,000 towards young people's mental health and £100,000 to 42 charities through its Closer to You grants programme.

The Economist Newspaper Ltd

Literacy and journalism, children and young people, education

Company registration number: 236383

Correspondent: CSR Team, 20 Cabot Square, London E14 4QW (tel: 020 7576 8000; website: www.economist.com)

Directors: Alex Karp; Brent Hoberman; Chris Stibbs; Eli Goldstein; John Elkann; Lady Heywood; Lord Deighton; Philip Malinckrodt; Rupert Pennant-Rea; Sir David Bell; Zanny Minton Beddoes (female 18%; male 82%).

Nature of business: The Economist Newspaper Ltd, trading as The Economist Group, is a British multinational media company specialising in international business and world affairs. It is best known as publisher of The Economist.

Year end	31/03/2017
Turnover	£366,603,000
Pre-tax profit	£40,231,000

Main locations: The group's UK offices are based in London. The group also has offices in a number of countries internationally.

Community involvement

The group's charitable contributions are channelled through its corporate charity, The Economist Charitable Trust, which supports a range of causes, as well as the group's matched funding and payroll giving scheme for employees. There is also a second charity, The Economist Educational Foundation, which works directly with young people to encourage them to engage with current affairs.

The Economist Charitable Trust (Charity Commission no. 293709)

The group channels its charitable activities through its corporate charity, The Economist Charitable Trust. The trust's 2016/17 accounts state the following:

> The principal activity of the Trust is the disbursement of monies received from The Economist Newspaper Ltd to various charities. 60–70% of the Trust's donations go to charities in the fields of communication, education, literacy and re-training for individuals and groups who are disadvantaged in some way. Approximately 30–40% of funds are used to match donations made by employees of The Economist Group. Remaining funds are utilised to make small donations to small and local charities.

The Economist Educational Foundation (Charity Commission no. 1147661)

The foundation works to give young people, particularly those who are disadvantaged, the opportunity to engage with current affairs and have their say on topical issues. The foundation's main programme the Burnet News Club is a network of school news clubs which helps develop young people's literacy and thinking skills through current affairs discussions.

Employee-led support

There is a payroll giving scheme and the group provides matched funding through The Economist Charitable Trust for employees' donations of both time and money donations to charities. Employees are also entitled to time out of work to take part in charitable and community activities.

Applications

Contact the foundation for further information at: foundationteam@economist.com.

Corporate charity

The Economist Charitable Trust (Charity Commission no. 293709) – see page 247.

Community contributions

Cash donations UK	£112,000

According to the 2016/17 accounts for The Economist Charitable Trust, The Economist donated £112,000 during the year.

EDF Energy plc

Education (particularly STEM subjects), the environment

Company registration number: 2366852

Correspondent: CSR Team, 40 Grosvenor Place, Victoria, London SW1X 7EN (tel: 020 7242 9050; website: www.edfenergy.com)

Directors: Colin Matthews; Henri Lafontaine; Jean-Bernard Levy; Pierre Todorov; Rob Guyler; Simone Rossi; Veronique Lacour; Xavier Girre (female 25%; male 75%).

Nature of business: EDF Energy (the group) is an integrated energy company with over 15,000 employees. It generates and supplies electricity and gas for the UK from a nuclear, coal, gas and renewable energy portfolio.

Year end	31/12/2017
Turnover	£5,393,300,000
Pre-tax profit	(£1,037,400,000)

Main locations: In the UK, the group has offices in London, Barnwood, Crawley, Exeter and Sunderland, as well as power stations around the UK (details can be found on the EDF website). EDF Energy is owned by the French state-owned EDF, with operations worldwide.

Community involvement

The group offers support through the EDF Energy Trust to individuals in need and through grants to organisations providing financial and debt advice and support. The group also supports a charity with a three year partnerships and has an extensive education programme, The Pod, which focuses on sustainability and STEM.

Charity partners

The group has established a three year partnership with Breast Cancer Now and hopes to raise around £450,000.

EDF Energy has also partnered up with the National Citizen Service – a youth empowerment programme available to 15- to 17-year-olds in England and Northern Ireland.

The Pod Programme for greener schools

The Pod is EDF's award-winning sustainable schools programme which has reached over 22,000 schools in the UK. Established in September 2008, the Pod aims to engage young people in energy, science and sustainability. It provides free curriculum-linked resources and runs campaigns to teach young people about these issues, empower them to act on their learning, and enable them to inspire others with their achievements.

The programme provides a wide range of resources for schools including lesson and assembly plans for different age groups, practical activity guides, films, games and resources linked to campaigns such as the Pods Waste Week and Switch Off Fortnight. Pod campaigns are designed to help get the whole school, parents and the local community engaged in living more sustainable lifestyles.

The Pod works with a number of partners to develop its resources including: Eco-Schools, the Met Office, Wastebuster and the British Trust for Ornithology.

Other STEM initiatives

Sites within the group also lead their own activities with local communities. For example, the group's Hinkley Point C site's Inspire Education programme focuses on encouraging local young people in Somerset to engage with STEM subjects.

The group has also launched a programme called Pretty Curious, which specifically aims to encourage girls to engage with STEM subjects and consider STEM careers.

In-kind support

Employees are entitled to two days of paid volunteering each year.

Employee-led support

Employees contribute to activities run by The Pod, the group's educational scheme, including STEM activities in schools and Helping Hands, which focuses on community action. Employees also fundraise to support the group's partner charity, which is voted on by employees.

Applications

Contact the correspondent for further information.

Corporate charity

EDF Energy Trust (Charity Commission no. 1099446) – see page 248.

Community contributions

Cash donations UK	£1,400,000

In 2016 the group donated £1.4 million to the EDF Energy Trust in relation to the Warm House Discounts scheme.

Edinburgh Airport Ltd

Education, the environment, health

Company registration number: SC096623

Correspondent: The Community Board, Edinburgh Airport, Edinburgh EH12 9DN (tel: 0844 448 8833; email: edicommunications@edinburghairport.com; website: www.edinburghairport.com/about-us/community-and-environment/community-board)

Directors: Adrian Witherow; Alastair Couper; David Feltham; David Gammie; Gilliam Pollock; Gordon Dewar; Gordon Robertson; John Watson; Stephen Swan (female 11%; male 89%).

Nature of business: Edinburgh Airport Ltd owns and runs Edinburgh Airport.

Year end	31/12/2017
Turnover	£184,877,000
Pre-tax profit	£86,435,000

Main locations: The airport is in Edinburgh.

Community involvement

Support is mainly provided through the company's Community Board grants programme. The company also provides matched funding and has an annual Charity of the Year.

The Edinburgh Airport Community Board

The board distributes £120,000 per year to projects in Edinburgh, Lothian and Fife that support local sport, health and well-being, environment and educational initiatives. Priority is given to applications benefitting those living within the communities closest to the airport or those most affected by aircraft noise.

Charity of the Year

In 2017 Children 1st received a donation of £65,000 made up from donations, foreign currency collections in the terminal and staff charity initiatives.

Employee-led support

Employees fundraise for the company's Charity of the Year. In 2017 the company made a donation of £13,200 to match the fundraising efforts of its staff.

Applications

The Edinburgh Airport Community Board

Applications can be made through the airport's website. Applications should be made two weeks before the board meeting date, information on which can also be found on the company website.

Charity of the Year

Details of how to apply for Charity of the Year can be found on the company website.

For all other enquires, contact the correspondent.

Community contributions

Cash donations UK	£146,000

In 2017 the company made charitable contributions of £146,000. The Community Board made grants totalling £120,000 to 62 charities. The company also made a donation of £13,200 to match fund the work of its employees, helping 50 charities and community groups. A further £6,500 was provided to charities at its annual Celebrating Success Awards Dinner.

The Entertainer (Amersham) Ltd

Children and young people, general charitable purposes

Company registration number: 2057757

Correspondent: CSR Team, Boughton Business Park, Bell Lane, Little Chalfont, Buckinghamshire HP6 6GL (email: Contact form on website; website: www.thetoyshop.com/charity)

Directors: Catherine Grant; Duncan Grant; Gary Grant; Mark Campbell; Stuart Grant (female 20%; male 80%).

Nature of business: The Entertainer is a toy retailer.

Year end	27/01/2018
Turnover	£163,855,000
Pre-tax profit	£11,914,000

Main locations: The company's headquarters are in Buckinghamshire. It has over 140 shops throughout the UK.

Community involvement

The company mainly provides charitable support through charitable donations.

Operation Christmas Child

The Entertainer is a drop-off location and partner for the Operation Christmas Child campaign

Charitable donations

The company's website states: 'Each year The Entertainer tithes 10% of its profits to supporting Children's charities.'

Employee-led support

The company's employees take part in events to raise money for children's charities and around 50% of employees give through payroll giving.

Applications

The company's website states: 'If you would like us to consider making a donation, please email us with details of your charity and event, including your charity number.'

Community contributions

Cash donations UK	£1,297,000

In 2017/18 the company's charitable donations totalled £1.3 million. The 2017/18 annual report states: 'It is the aim of the directors to donate 10% of each year's company trading profits to a range of charitable causes.'

Esh Group

Education (particularly STEM subjects), general charitable purposes

Company registration number: 3724890

Correspondent: Added Value Team, Esh House, Bowburn North Industrial Estate, Bowburn, Durham DH6 5PF (email: addedvalue@esh.uk.com; website: www.eshgroup.co.uk/added-value)

Directors: Andrew Radcliffe; Anna Urbanowicz; Chris Watson; Darren Warneford; Gareth Davies; Jack Lumsden; John Davies; Mark Sowerby; Meg Munn; Michael Hogan; Paul Watson; Phillip Coates; Simon Phillips; Tony Carroll Snr; William Stobbs (female 20%; male 80%).

Nature of business: The principal activities of the group are building, construction, civil engineering and property refurbishment.

Year end	31/12/2016
Turnover	£234,123,000
Pre-tax profit	£3,800,000

Total employees: 1,097

Main locations: The group operates in North East England, Yorkshire, North West England and Scotland. Its head office is in Durham, and there are also offices in Carlisle; Cramlington; Leeds; Livingston; and Newton Aycliffe.

Community involvement

The group provides support to charities in communities where it operates through its corporate charity, the Esh Foundation (Charity Commission no. 1112040). It also supports employability and STEM education initiatives.

Education and employability

Working in partnership with 83 schools and over 130 partner businesses, the group runs Building My Skills, a year-long programme which aims to equip students with employability skills and careers advice. The group also provides work experience opportunities.

The group has created Get into STEM kits in partnership with Northumbria University, providing resources for schools to encourage engagement with STEM subjects. The group also provides site visits and safety talks for schools.

Employee-led support

The group organises volunteering opportunities for its staff. In 2017 it launched a new system which promoted volunteering opportunities via the group's intranet.

Applications

Schools interested in Get into STEM or Building My Skills should contact their local added value co-ordinator. Contact details can be found on the Esh Group website: www.eshgroup.co.uk/added-value/community/building-my-skills.

Corporate charity

Esh Foundation (Charity Commission no. 1112040) – see page 248.

Community contributions

Cash donations UK	£130,000

No figure was given for the group's total charitable contributions in 2016. However, the Esh Foundation's accounts show it received £130,000 from the company during the year.

Everton Football Club Company Ltd

General charitable purposes, health, young people, employability and education, sports

Company registration number: 36624

Correspondent: Everton in the Community, Goodison Park, Goodison Road, Liverpool L4 4EL (tel: 0151 530 5253; email: community@evertonfc.com; website: www.evertonfc.com/community)

Directors: Alexander Ryazantsev; Bill Kenwright; Denise Barrett-Baxendale; Dr

Keith Harris; Jon Woods (female 20%; male 80%).

Nature of business: Everton FC is a professional football club competing in the Premier League.

Year end	31/05/2017
Turnover	£171,300,000
Pre-tax profit	£30,600,000

UK employees: 357

Main locations: Everton football club is based in Liverpool.

Community involvement

The club offers support through its charity, Everton in the Community (Charity Commission no. 1099366), which works with partners to deliver a wide range of projects in the local community, in the areas of health and well-being; young people; employability and education; and sports. The club also offers in-kind support to local charities including signed merchandise and memorabilia and visits from players.

Everton in the Community

The club's corporate charity, Everton in the Community, works in partnerships with organisations such as schools, charities and public services to delivers a wide range of community projects in the areas of health and well-being, young people, sports, employment and education.

Full details of all the charity's current programmes are available on the club's website.

Health and well-being

The charity works in partnership with a range of health organisations and partners to deliver projects aimed at improving the health and quality of life of some of the most hard-to-reach groups in the local community.

Young people

The charity runs youth engagement projects aimed at promoting community cohesion, positive life choices, and personal development. Projects are delivered in partnership with organisations such as The Prince's Trust and National Citizen Service, and are aimed at young people who are disadvantaged, including young people who look after children, have offended, or who are unemployed.

Sports

Everton in the Community runs a number of sports projects including: school programmes; development programmes for people with disabilities; activities with the local children's hospital; sports for young women with mental health problems; and football training for local people who have experienced homelessness.

Employment and education

The charity works in partnership with organisations such as government bodies, training and employment providers and the local NHS trust to provide educational programmes as well as employability training and support.

In-kind support

The club offers donations of merchandise and signed memorabilia to help charities raise funds. The club also organises visits by members of the first-team squad to help raise awareness of various good causes around the city. These activities are organised on behalf of the club by its charity, Everton in the Community.

Exclusions

Support can only be provided to charities within a 40-mile radius of Goodison Park. The club does not provide monetary support or sponsorship.

Applications

Applications for in-kind donations or player visits should be submitted using the club's online form for charity requests: www.evertonfc.com/community/fundraising/the-projects/everton-giving.

Community contributions

The club's 2016/17 accounts do not provide a figure for its overall community contribution.

Fenwick Ltd

General charitable purposes

Company registration number: 52411

Correspondent: CSR Team, Elswick Court, 39 Northumberland Street, Newcastle upon Tyne NE99 1AR (tel: 0191 232 5100; website: www.fenwick.co.uk)

Directors: Hugo Fenwick; Jill Anders; Mia Rose; Peter King; Richard Pennycook; Robert Feather; Stephen Barber (female 29%; male 71%).

Nature of business: Fenwick is a chain of department stores.

Year end	29/01/2017
Turnover	£426,366,000
Pre-tax profit	£30,413,500

Main locations: The group has stores located in Bond Street, Bracknell, Brent Cross, Canterbury, Colchester, Kingston, Newcastle, Tunbridge Wells and York.

Community involvement

The group makes donations in support of causes local to its stores.

Applications

Contact your local store for further information. Store contact details can be found on Fenwick's website.

Community contributions

Cash donations UK	£173,500

In 2016/17 the group made charitable donations of £173,500 to causes in the local areas of its stores. A list of beneficiaries was not provided.

FIL Holdings (UK) Ltd (Fidelity International)

Arts and culture, community development, education, the environment, health

Company registration number: 6737476

Correspondent: Corporate Citizenship Department, Oakhill House, 130 Tonbridge Road, Hildenborough, Tonbridge, Kent TN11 9DZ (email: corporate.citizenship@fil.com; website: www.fidelity.co.uk/investor/about/corporate-citizenship/default.page)

Directors: Anne Grim; Anthony Lanser; Bruce Weatherill; Cheryl Campbell; David Weymouth; Dominic Rossi; Dr Teresa Robson-Capps; Kristina Isherwood; Nicholas Birchall; Peter Horrell; Sally Nelson (female 45%; male 55%).

Nature of business: This is the holding company for a group of companies whose principal business is the management and distribution of collective investment funds, the management of defined benefit pension funds, and the management and administration of defined contribution pension funds.

Year end	30/06/2017
Turnover	£798,374,000
Pre-tax profit	£83,056,000

Main locations: The group's UK offices are in Hildenborough, Kent; Kingswood, Surrey; London; and Newport. There is also an office in Dublin.

Community involvement

Fidelity directs its community support through its two foundations and its Corporate Citizenship Programme. In the UK, financial support is given through The Fidelity UK Foundation (Charity Commission no. 327899) which makes grants to UK-registered charities for causes related to: arts and heritage; community; education; health; and environment.

Corporate Citizenship Programme

The programme supports local charities and employees in their efforts to contribute to their communities. Employees are encouraged to lend their support to good causes through volunteering, fundraising and payroll giving. The group sponsors charity fundraising events and has a small budget from which grants are made to support local charities that are working to benefit the communities in areas where the group has a presence.

The Fidelity International Foundation

Grants for projects outside the UK are made by the FIL International Foundation. The foundation is also funded by Fidelity International and has similar priorities to the UK foundation. Applications from established international charities serving beneficiaries in continental Europe, Australia, Bermuda, China, Hong Kong, India, Japan, Korea, Singapore and Taiwan are welcomed.

Employee-led support

Fidelity supports and encourages its employees to be active members of their communities. Through the employee grant-matching programme, funds raised for charitable organisations are matched by the company.

Commercially led support

Fidelity sponsors charity fundraising events in the areas local to its offices.

Exclusions

Corporate sponsorship

The company's website states that it does not support the following:

- Religious, political and animal-support charities (except environmental or conservation related animal causes)
- Individuals and individual schools
- Events for exclusive audiences such as black tie events
- High-risk activities, such as parachute jumps, motor racing and abseiling

Sports events, clubs and teams and advertisements in charity event programmes, diaries or directories are not usually supported.

Applications

Corporate sponsorship

The company's website states:

> We favour organisations that:
>
> - Support communities within 20km of any Fidelity office
> - Where we support national causes, we would expect the cause to have a local reach, where practicable
> - Have a good reputation in the local community
> - Provide the opportunity for the Fidelity International brand name to have a presence
> - Provide the opportunity for media activity
> - Are registered charities or not-for-profit organisations
> - Organise fundraising events that directly benefit their service users
> - Provide opportunities for employee involvement
> - Benefit the wider community rather than an exclusive audience
>
> Generally we like to be the sole sponsor of an event, and favour those that benefit the wider community rather than an exclusive audience.

Small grants for local charities

The company website states: 'We have a small dedicated budget to support local organisations who deliver services at a grass roots level. These funds must go to a project that directly benefits the local community.'

For more information on these programmes, contact Fidelity's Corporate Citizenship department.

FIL International Foundation

Information on the international foundation can found on the UK foundation's website.

For all other enquiries, contact the correspondent.

Corporate charity

The Fidelity UK Foundation (Charity Commission no. 327899) – see page 248.

Community contributions

Cash donations UK	£9,632,000

In 2016/17 FIL Holdings made donations of £9 million to The Fidelity UK Foundation. The group also made direct donations totalling £632,000 to a wide range of charities, including through the employee grant matching scheme. Individual donations were made to, for example, local children's charities, schools and hospitals.

We have taken our financial information from the annual report and accounts of FIL Holdings (UK Ltd) and have taken our CSR information from the website of FIL Ltd, which is the ultimate parent undertaking and controlling party FHL, registered in Bermuda.

FirstGroup plc

Education, the environment, general charitable purposes

Company registration number: SC157176

Correspondent: CSR Team, 395 King Street, Aberdeen AB24 5RP (email: communityfirst@firstgroup.com; website: www.firstgroupplc.com/responsibility.aspx)

Directors: David Robbie; Drummond Hall; Imelda Welsh; Jim Winestock; Jimmy Groombridge; Martha Poulter; Matthew Gregory; Warwick Brady; Wolfhart Hauser (female 11%; male 89%).

Nature of business: The company operates in the UK and the USA and provides passenger transport services primarily through bus and coach services and passenger railways.

Year end	31/03/2018
Turnover	£6,398,400,000
Pre-tax profit	£197,000,000

Total employees: 100,000

Main locations: The group serves areas across the UK. The headquarters are in Aberdeen.

Community involvement

The group supports local and national community and charitable organisations throughout the UK and the USA. Many sites where the group operates have developed community engagement plans and work in partnership with charitable organisations. According to the group's website, community investment is focused on the following:

- Developing long-term partnerships with charitable organisations most aligned with the business
- Mobilising employees to support these partnerships through charity committees and charity champion programmes and by encouraging personal commitments like fundraising and payroll giving

Partnerships

Action for Children is the group's charity partner until 2021 and has been chosen through an employee ballot. The 2017/18 annual report states that the group made a financial contribution of £1 million to its partner charity in 2018.

TransPennine express works with the Ahead Partnership to help young people across the Leeds City Region and the North East develop their employability skills.

Transform grants

The transform grants programme is run by TransPennine Express. Applicants can apply for grants of up to £5,000 for projects that projects that seek to tackle youth unemployment, promote social inclusion and improve the environment. Projects should be located within ten miles of any line of routes operated by TransPennine Express train services.

Employee-led support

Employees' fundraising efforts for charitable causes are also matched by the group. In 2017/18 almost £100,000 was donated to charity via payroll giving.

Be First Awards

The group holds an award evening called Be First Awards to celebrate the work of its employees. Winners of the award are given a donation made to a charity of their choice.

Applications

Transform Grants

Further information can be found on: www.tpexpress.co.uk/about-us/community/transform-grants.

Contact the correspondent for all other enquiries.

Community contributions

Cash donations worldwide	£1,400,000
In-kind support worldwide	£2,100,000
Total contributions (cash and in kind)	£3,500,000

In 2016/17 the group donated £4.1 million to charitable causes, measured by the London Benchmarking Group (LBG) model. These contributions were broken down in the 2016/17 Corporate Responsibility Data document, available from the group's website, as follows:

Community investment	Amount
In-kind	£1.8 million
Cash donations	£1.4 million
Leverage*	£586,000
Time	£302,500

*Leverage is defined as contributions from other sources such as employees, customers or suppliers.

No details were available regarding total community contributions made in the UK.

James Fisher and Sons plc

Arts and culture, children and young people, community development, education, health

Company registration number: 211475

Correspondent: Fisher House, PO Box 4, Michaelson Road, Barrow-in-Furness, Cumbria LA14 1HR (tel: 01229 615400; website: www.james-fisher.com)

Directors: Aedamar Comiskey; David Moorhouse; Fergus Graham; Justin Atkinson; Malcolm Paul; Michael Slater; Nick Henry; Stuart Kilpatrick (female 13%; male 88%).

Nature of business: The group provides marine-related engineering services and has four divisions: marine support; offshore oil; specialist technical; and tankships.

Year end	31/12/2017
Turnover	£505,400,000
Pre-tax profit	£50,300,000

UK employees: 2,645

Main locations: The group works across 19 countries, and has a number of offices and operations across the UK. Its headquarters are in Barrow-in-Furness.

Community involvement

As well as fundraising organised by employees or companies within the group, most of the group's charitable support is focused through its corporate charity, the Sir John Fisher Foundation.

Employee-led support

According to the 2017 annual report, examples of causes supported by employees or companies within the group in 2017 include: Scarborough Engineering Fair; Children's Cancer and Leukaemia Group; Cash for Kids; St Thomas Moore School for special needs; the University of Strathclyde.

Corporate charity

The Sir John Fisher Foundation (Charity Commission no. 277844) – see page 249.

Community contributions

Cash donations UK	£1,900,000

The company did not make any charitable contributions during the year. In 2016/17 the company's corporate charity, The John Fisher Foundation received £1.9 million in dividend income from its shareholding in James Fisher and Sons.

The Football Association Premier League Ltd

Armed forces, community development, disability, health, older people, projects outside the UK, sports and recreation

Company registration number: 2719699

Correspondent: Communities Team, 30 Gloucester Place, London W1U 8PL (tel: 020 7864 9000; website: www.premierleague.com/communities)

Directors: Claudia Arney; Kevin Beeston; Richard Scudamore (female 33%; male 67%).

Nature of business: The Football Association Premier League operates and promotes the Premier League – a professional football league.

Year end	31/07/2017
Turnover	£3,096,972,000
Pre-tax profit	£26,068,000

Total employees: 131

Main locations: The company delivers programmes worldwide.

Community involvement

The company channels the majority of its charitable support through its corporate charity the Premier League Charitable Fund, which delivers a wide range of education and sports programmes. The company also supports grassroots football through the Premier League and the FA Facilitates Fund and the Football Stadia Improvement Fund.

Community and School Programmes

Together with its charity the Premier League Charitable Fund (Charity Commission no. 1137208), the company delivers a wide range of sports and education programmes. Examples of the company's current programmes include:

- **Premier Skills** is a global coaching and referee development programme run by the Premier League and the British Council. To date, the programme has trained more than 20,000 coaches and referees in 29 countries
- **Premier League Primary Stars** is a programme designed to provide primary schools with support in improving the provision of physical education, sport and physical activities, both during curriculum and extra-curriculum time
- **Premier League Kicks** uses Premier League and Sport England funding to promote universal sports engagement in areas of disadvantage. Its primary focus is to encourage sports participation in deprived areas, targeting young people who traditionally do not participate in organised sporting activities
- **Premier League/BT Disability Fund** is a national programme that began at the start of the 2016/17 season. The programme is delivered by 25 clubs, which seek to create possibilities for people with disabilities to participate in sport
- **Premier League's Kit Scheme** provides kit and equipment for school teams, prioritising those in the most deprived areas or situations

For full details of all current programmes, see the website.

Premier League and the FA Facilities Fund

The company works with partners – the FA (Football Association), the Football Foundation and Sport England – to deliver new and renovated football facilities around the country including 3G Artificial Grass Pitches. Over the past 12 months, the fund has helped to support 300 facility projects.

Football Stadia Improvement Fund

The company is the sole funder of the Football Stadia Improvement Fund which provides grants to improve facilities for clubs in the Football League and further down the football pyramid. According to the website, grants can be used for 'the refurbishment and construction of new stands, provision for fans with disabilities, turnstiles, boundary fencing, perimeter barriers, dugouts, floodlights and changing rooms'. The fund is administered by the Football Foundation.

The Royal British Legion Shirt Auction

During Premier League matches played in the period leading up to Remembrance Sunday, players wear shirts embroidered with a poppy. The matchworn shirts are then signed and auctioned raising money for The Royal British Legion.

Applications

Football Stadia Improvement Fund

To apply to the Football Stadia Improvement Fund, visit the website: www.fsif.co.uk.

Premier League and the FA Facilities Fund

To apply to the Premier League and the FA Facilities Fund, visit the Football Foundation's website at: www.footballfoundation.org.uk/funding-schemes/premier-league-the-fa-facilities-fund.

Kit Scheme

Schools interested in applying for the Kit Scheme should register their interest at: plprimarystars.com.

Community contributions

Cash donations worldwide	£199,300,000

According to its 2016/17 annual report, during the year the company made charitable donations of around £199.3 million. This figure includes £74.1 million donated to football charities and £125.2 million contributed towards wider football support and other good causes. Donations of £24.3 million and £17.4 million were made to the Premier League Charitable Fund and the Football Foundation respectively.

Ford Motor Company Ltd

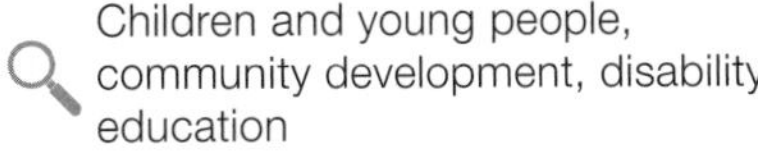

Children and young people, community development, disability, education

Company registration number: 235446

Correspondent: Eagle Way, Brentwood, Essex CM13 3BW (website: www.ford.co.uk/fbtrust)

Directors: Andrew Barratt; David Robinson; Graham Hoare; James Skerry; Kieran Cahill; Madeleine Hallwood; Monazza Khan; Peter Davies; Shaun Glanville; Timothy Holmes (female 20%; male 80%).

Nature of business: The Ford Motor Company Ltd is a wholly owned subsidiary of the Ford Motor Company of Dearborn, Michigan, USA.

The company's principal activity is the design, engineering and manufacture of low carbon technologies, commercial vehicles and automotive components and the sale of motor vehicles and automotive components.

The company and its subsidiaries operate principally in the UK and the Republic of Ireland. It is part of an integrated vehicle manufacturing group of Ford companies throughout Europe.

Year end	31/12/2017
Turnover	£12,863,000,000
Pre-tax profit	£698,000,000

UK employees: 8,784

Total employees: 8,893

Main locations: Ford have sites in the UK and Republic of Ireland.

Community involvement

Ford Motor Company Ltd operates the Ford Britain Trust (Charity Commission no. 269410), which makes grants for projects in communities close to Ford's locations, particularly those that focus on the areas of education, environment, children, people with disabilities, youth activities and projects working to benefit the community.

The company's 2016/17 annual report states: 'Our commitment to the community is built around the support and encouragement of various employee volunteering efforts, the backing and operating of the Ford Britain Trust and the on-going relationship and support of a range of charitable and altruistic activities.'

Ford's US foundation, the Ford Fund, runs STEM and educational projects with schools and universities in the UK.

Employee-led support

Employees are encouraged to contribute to their communities through Ford's Vibrant Volunteer Week and Global Caring Month.

Corporate charity

Ford Britain Trust (Charity Commission no. 269410) – see page 250.

Community contributions

Cash donations UK	£100,000

The annual report and accounts for 2017 did not declare a figure for charitable donations during the year. However, the Ford Britain Trust's 2016/17 accounts state that a donation of £100,000 was received from Ford Motor Company Ltd.

Freshfields Bruckhaus Deringer LLP

Education, enterprise and training

Company registration number: OC334789

Correspondent: CSR Team, 65 Fleet Street, London EC4Y 1HS (tel: 020 7936 4000; website: www.freshfields.com)

Directors: Colin Hargreaves; Edward Braham; Stephan Eilers (female 0%; male 100%).

Nature of business: Freshfields is an international law firm with offices in Europe, Asia, the Middle East and the USA.

Year end	30/04/2017
Turnover	£1,337,000,000
Pre-tax profit	£417,300,000

UK employees: 2,093

Total employees: 5,230

Main locations: In the UK, Freshfields has offices in London and Manchester.

Community involvement

The company aims to make a positive difference in the communities in which it operates through volunteering activities and pro bono work. The company's community investment programme focuses on access to opportunity with an emphasis on education and offering routes to work and access to the legal profession.

Scholarships

Determined to do something to address the disproportionally small numbers of black and black mixed race men in large commercial law firms, Freshfields and Doreen Lawrance launched the Freshfields Stephen Lawrence scholarship scheme in 2013. The scheme awards scholarships to exceptionally talented first year law undergraduates.

In-kind support

The company provides pro bono legal support to local charities and individuals. Pro bono clients can also benefit from free professional skills-based support such as IT, marketing and human resources. The company's UN Global Compact 2017 report states: 'Our pro bono and community efforts focus on minorities, refugees, women, children, people identifying as LGBT+, and the underprivileged and underrepresented.'

Employee-led support

In 2016/17 a total of 50% of staff took part in pro bono or volunteering activity contributing over 66,000 hours.

Employees are also able to support charities through payroll giving with 5% of employees donating through the scheme during the year.

Commercially led support

Through the Ready for Work programme in London the company supports people who face multiple barriers to work such as long-term unemployed, care leavers, ex-offenders and those who have been at risk of homelessness. Support includes mentoring, offering work experience placements, and making gifts in kind, such as lending rooms.

Applications

Contact the correspondent for further information.

Community contributions

The Responsible Business Update Report 2017 shows that £15.66 million was given in community contributions during the year. This figure includes management costs and we were unable to determine the amount given in cash and pro bono contributions in the UK.

Fujitsu Services Holdings plc

Children and young people, education (particularly STEM subjects), enterprise and training

Company registration number: 142200

Correspondent: CSR Team, 22 Baker Street, London, United Kingdom W1U 3BW (tel: 01235 797711; email: AskFujitsu@uk.fujitsu.com; website: www.fujitsu.com/uk/about/local/corporate-responsibility)

Directors: Duncan Tait; Hidehiro Tsukano; Rachel Hitching (female 33%; male 67%).

Nature of business: Fujitsu Services Holdings is the holding company of the IT services group Fujitsu.

Year end	31/03/2017
Turnover	£2,209,000,000
Pre-tax profit	(£46,900,000)

UK employees: 9,279

Total employees: 12,512

Main locations: The group's headquarters are in London.

Community involvement

The group supports charitable causes mainly through various partnerships and employee-led support. Regional Impact on Society groups, made up of employees, co-ordinate local charitable giving and volunteering.

The group focuses its community involvement on the following areas:

- Digital inclusion
- Social innovation
- Youth employment
- Volunteering to support society

Charity partners

From 2016 to 2018, the group was supporting Macmillan Cancer Support as its charity partner. The aim of the partnership was to raise money for the charity and improve the digital experience of Macmillan volunteers.

Young people and education

Led by the Impact on Society groups (see 'Employee-led support') the group works with schools and colleges to promote technology-related education and careers.

The group has a long standing relationship with The Prince's Trust, as a patron, running CV and interview workshops for young people on the Team programme.

The group also takes part in a number of schemes run by Business in the Community and holds events promoting STEM-related careers for young people.

Digital inclusion

The group works with local schools to run programmes that encourage more young people into the sector. It also works with its charity partners to identify and fill digital skills gaps.

Other partnerships

The group also takes part in a number of other schemes run by Business in the Community, such as Business Class and Business Connectors. There are also partnerships with Children in Need, Prince's Trust and the National Council for the Blind of Ireland.

In-kind support

As well as through employee fundraising, the group supports Children in Need by staffing one of its call centres to help process donations on appeal night.

Employee-led support

There are six regional Impact on Society (IOS) groups, made up of employees, each of which is allocated a budget and is responsible for: coordinating volunteering opportunities; liaising with charity partners, schools and colleges; supporting fundraising events; and dealing with requests for sponsorship or donations in the local area. According to the Responsible Business Report 2017, employees volunteered nearly 3,500 hours during the year for charities of their choice through the IOS group. Fujitsu hope to support ten charities per IOS region by 2020.

Employees fundraise for the group's partner charity, as well as other initiatives such as Children in Need and SSAFA.

Applications

Apply in writing to the correspondent. The group has a number of regional IOS groups, which coordinate charitable activities, including responding to requests. We would, therefore, suggest that local requests should be made in writing to the IOS group at the relevant site.

Community contributions

Cash donations worldwide	£115,000

According to its 2016/17 accounts, the group's charitable and educational donations during the year totalled £115,000.

G4S plc

Education, poverty and social exclusion, projects outside the UK

Company registration number: 4992207

Correspondent: CSR Team, 5th Floor, Southside, 105 Victoria Street, London SW1E 6QT (tel: 020 8770 7000; email: csr@g4s.com; website: www.g4s.com/en/social-responsibility)

Directors: Ashley Almanza; Barbara Thoralfsson; Elizabeth Fleuriot; John Connolly; John Daly; John Ramsay; Paul Spence; Steve Mogford; Tim Weller; Winnie Kin Wah Fok (female 30%; male 70%).

Nature of business: G4S provides a range of security services such as security personnel and prisoner transport.

Year end	31/12/2016
Turnover	£7,828,000,000
Pre-tax profit	£386,000,000

Total employees: 570,000

Main locations: The group works across the UK and internationally. Its UK offices are located in London; Sutton; and Belfast.

Community involvement

Support is mainly provided through cash and in-kind donations to community programmes worldwide.

Employee-led support

The group operates its matched funding scheme, Match-it, by which it matches employee fundraising efforts up to the value of £500 per application.

Applications

Contact the correspondent for further information.

Community contributions

Total contributions (cash and in kind)	£995,000

In 2016 the group contributed cash donations and provided goods and services worth a total of £945,000. There were 950 community programmes that benefitted from this support. The group also matched £50,000 of employee fundraising for local community causes across the world.

We were unable to determine a figure for cash or in-kind contributions given in the UK.

Galliford Try plc

General charitable purposes

Company registration number: 836539

Correspondent: Paul Kirkwood, PR Manager – Corporate Responsibility, Cowley Business Park, Cowley, Uxbridge, Middlesex UB8 2AL (tel: 01423 339941; email: paul.kirkwood@gallifordtry.co.uk; website: www.gallifordtry.co.uk/sustainability)

Directors: Andrew Hammond; Bill Hocking; Gavin Slark; Graham Prothero; Jeremy Townsend; Kevin Corbett; Peter Truscott; Peter Ventress; Stephen Teagle; Terry Miller; Tom Nicholson (female 25%; male 75%).

Nature of business: Galliford Try is a housebuilding and construction group operating in the UK.

Year end	30/06/2017
Turnover	£2,662,000,000
Pre-tax profit	£147,600,000

Main locations: The group has operations across the UK. See www.gallifordtry.co.uk/contacts for full details.

Community involvement

The group makes charitable contributions at a group, division, business unit and project level. The group donates time, money and materials and there is some focus on supporting the communities in which the group operates.

Linden Home Foundation

Linden Homes, one of the group's divisions, has set up a foundation to benefit the communities in which the company operates, with a focus on community initiatives and environmental schemes. Examples of support include: refurbishing a war memorial; raising money for local charities; volunteering for a community garden; and sponsoring a local school.

In-kind support

The group has a volunteering policy that entitles employees to two days' paid leave per year to volunteer for charitable causes.

Employee-led support

Employees volunteer for local charities and raise funds for various charities through events, such as the Land's End to John O'Groats cycle relay.

Applications

The foundation

For further information on the foundation visit: www.lindenhomes.co.uk/foundation.

For all other queries contact the correspondent or the division local to where your project is based.

Community contributions

Cash donations UK	£184,000
In-kind support UK	£324,000
Total contributions (cash and in kind)	£508,000

The group's 2016/17 annual report states that it made charitable contributions totalling £508,000. Contributions were broken down as follows:

Time	£263,000
Financial	£184,000
In-kind (materials)	£61,000

GKN Ltd

Children and young people, education (particularly STEM subjects)

Company registration number: 4191106

Correspondent: CSR Team, PO Box 55, Ipsley House, Ipsley Church Lane, Redditch, Worcestershire B98 0TL (tel: 01527 517715; email: cr@gkn.com; website: www.gkn.com/corporateresponsibility)

Directors: Christopher Miller; David Roper; Garry Barnes; Geoffrey Martin; Jonathon Crawford; Simon Peckham (female 0%; male 100%).

Nature of business: GKN is an international engineering group specialising in the automotive and aerospace industries.

Year end	31/12/2017
Turnover	£9,671,000,000
Pre-tax profit	£658,000,000

Total employees: 51,117

Main locations: The group has sites in Birmingham; Bristol; Filton; Isle of Wight; Leek; London; Luton; Redditch; Portsmouth; Telford; Yeovil.

Community involvement

GKN supports communities around the globe in which it operates. The group's companies and employees contribute to charitable work and community projects by fundraising and volunteering. Some causes are supported corporately by the group, who also offer a charitable giving scheme, but it appears that the majority are selected and supported by the employees themselves. There is some particular focus on: preparing young people for the world of work, particularly in relation to STEM subjects; and improving local communities through social projects and charitable donations.

Young Hearts

The group provides support to GKN employees who need financial support to help make a difference in youth and educational projects in which they are involved. In 2017/18 over £55,000 was granted to 30 applicants from 12 countries. Further information can be found on the 'Hearts of Gold' section of the group's website.

Employee-led support

Hearts of Gold

The group launched the Hearts of Gold awards to celebrate the charitable and community contributions made by its employees around the world. These contributions are mostly focused on supporting young people, particularly in the field of STEM subjects. This includes offering work experience and apprenticeships; sponsoring education; and technology institutions and events.

According to the Hearts of Gold website, some examples of employee contributions in the UK include: employees collecting for a local food bank; a team fundraising event for Unicef; and individual employees doing sponsored events. To see further examples of employee support for communities under this scheme, visit: www.gkn.com/heartsofgold.

Applications

Applications can be made in writing to the correspondent.

Community contributions

In 2017 the group made worldwide contributions totalling £1 million to 360 significant projects mostly supporting young people. Of this, over £500,000 was given to support the Hearts of Gold awards. We were unable to determine what form these contributions took, such as cash donations for example, and it is likely that the majority of these contributions were raised and/or delivered by the employees themselves at the group's various sites around the world. We were unable to determine how much the group itself actually donated to charitable causes or how much was contributed in the UK.

Glasgow Airport Ltd

Education, enterprise and training, the environment

Company registration number: SC096624

Correspondent: The FlightPath Committee, St Andrews Drive, Paisley PA3 2SW (email: flightpath@glasgowairport.com; website: www.glasgowairport.com/flightpath-fund)

Directors: Gonzalo Velasco; Iñaki García Bilbao; John Bruen; Juan Bullón; Martyn Booth; Simon Geere; Sir Peter Mason (female 0%; male 100%).

Nature of business: Glasgow Airport is owned by AGS Airports Ltd and is Scotland's principal long-haul airport as well as Scotland's largest charter hub. AGS was formed in September 2014 by Ferrovial and Macquire Group. The company acquired Aberdeen, Glasgow and Southampton Airports in December 2014 from Heathrow Airport Holdings.

Year end	31/12/2017
Turnover	£121,888,000
Pre-tax profit	£90,807,000

Main locations: The airport is in Glasgow.

Community involvement

Support is mainly provided through the company's FlightPath Fund.

FlightPath Fund

The fund supports local charities and community groups as well as the voluntary work and fundraising of employees. Funding is focused on three main areas: employment, environment and education. The fund makes donations to projects in areas most affected by the airport's operations. Projects are usually located in the relevant parts of Renfrewshire, East and West Dunbartonshire and Glasgow.

Exclusions

The FlightPath fund does not support running costs or provide funds for commercial sponsorship, to individuals, for third-party advertising or political campaigning.

Applications

Application forms and guidelines can be downloaded from the company's website.

Community contributions

We were unable to determine the company's charitable contributions for 2017.

GlaxoSmithKline plc

Health, STEM subjects

Company registration number: 1047315

Correspondent: Global Community Partnerships, GSK House, 980 Great West Road, Brentford, Middlesex TW6 9GS (email: community.partnerships@gsk.com; website: https://uk.gsk.com/en-gb/partnerships/charitable-partnerships)

Directors: Dr Hal Barron; Dr Jesse Goodman; Dr Laurie Glimcher; Dr Vivienne Cox; Emma Walmsley; Judy Lewent; Lyn Elsenhans; Mavinder Banga; Simon Dingemans; Sir Philip Hampton; Uhrs Rohner (female 45%; male 55%).

Nature of business: The group's principal activities are the creation and discovery, development, manufacture and marketing of pharmaceutical products, including vaccines, over-the-counter medicines and health-related consumer products.

Year end	31/12/2017
Turnover	£30,200,000,000
Pre-tax profit	£5,525,000,000

UK employees: 16,000

Main locations: The group's global headquarters are in Brentford. Other UK sites are located in County Durham; Harlow; Irvine; Maidenhead; Montrose; Slough; Stevenage; Ulverston; Uxbridge; Ware; Weybridge; and Worthing.

Community involvement

In the UK health charities and patient advocacy groups are supported through partnerships, donations and the GlaxoSmithKline (GSK) IMPACT Awards.

The website states:

> We are transparent about our charitable giving with data being published in our Annual Report and Corporate Responsibility Report in March each year. We are further increasing transparency by publishing details of our individual charitable grants over £10,000 ($15,000).

Details of GSK's grants awarded can be found on the Responsibility section of the company's website.

GlaxoSmithKline IMPACT Awards

The annual GSK IMPACT Awards are run in partnership with the King's Fund to recognise and promote excellence in community healthcare.

To be eligible for a GSK IMPACT Award, organisations must be registered, have an annual income of between £25,000 and £2 million, be working in a health-related field, and must have been operating in the UK for at least three years. The following applies:

- Up to ten winners receive £30,000 of unrestricted funding plus the overall winner will receive an extra £10,000
- Up to ten runners-up receive £3,000
- Organisations do not need to present a new project, and winners decide how to spend the award money
- Winning organisations will be offered free development and training up to the value of £6,000

For further details, visit the King's Fund's website: www.kingsfund.org.uk.

Partnerships

The company currently has nine charity partnerships that operate nationally. Details of partnerships in each region of the UK can be seen on the GSK's website.

UK Corporate Contributions Committee

The committee agrees charitable support for the UK. Support is given in the following areas: health and well-being; scientific education; and the environment. Criteria can be downloaded from the company's website.

STEM education

The company's Science Education website offers a range of free curriculum-based resources for 11–14-year-olds.

Patient Advocacy Group funding

Grants and donations are provided to help patient need and where there is mutual scientific interest.

In-kind support

GSK makes in-kind contributions in the form of product donations and staff time, particularly for financially developing countries. The group also provides vaccines and medicines at a not-for-profit price and shares its knowledge.

Employee-led support

The company supports employees' charitable and community involvement through two main volunteering programmes:

PULSE Volunteer Partnership – The programme gives GSK employees the opportunity to work with a non-profit organisation full time for three or six months. Since the initiative was launched in 2009, 770 employees have volunteered with 127 non-profit organisations around the world.

Orange Day volunteer programme – Through the Orange Day volunteer programme, employees are able to take one paid day's leave for volunteering purposes each year. Many employees volunteer for activities that promote STEM education to children and young people.

Employee fundraising

Most employees' fundraising efforts are focused on raising funds for the group's main global charity partner, Save the Children. Donations are then matched by the group.

Applications

For more information on funding requests and partnerships, contact the correspondent. However, note the following from the website:

> GSK supports community initiatives in both the developed and the developing world. Identifying the right projects is an important responsibility, and that's why the company takes a strategic, proactive approach and **does not generally support unsolicited requests for funding**.

GSK IMPACT Award

To apply for a GSK IMPACT Award, read the application guidelines and complete the online form available at: www.kingsfund.org.uk.

Patient Advocacy Group funding

Application forms can be downloaded from the company's website: https://uk.gsk.com/en-gb/partnerships/charitable-partnerships/patient-advocacy-group-funding.

Community contributions

Cash donations UK	£3,200,000
Cash donations worldwide	£80,000,000
In-kind support worldwide	£168,000,000
Total contributions (cash and in kind)	£251,200,000

In 2017 in the UK, GSK made donations of £10,000 or more directly to charitable organisations totalling £3.2 million. The company also makes smaller grants, although these are as yet unreported, so the figure we quote here is likely to be higher. No figure was available this year for in-kind support in the UK.

Note that the group do not generally accept unsolicited requests for funding, unless through an application made under the GSK IMPACT Awards.

Beneficiaries of grants in the UK during 2017 included: Tres Cantos Open Lab Foundation (£3 million); British Lung Foundation (£33,000 in three grants); Meningitis Now and The Adam Centre (£20,000 each); Scottish Centre for Simulation (£16,000).

Global contributions

Global contributions during the year totalled £248 million and were broken down as follows:

Product and in-kind donations	£165 million
Cash	£80 million
Time	£3 million

Global Media and Entertainment Ltd

Arts and culture, children and young people, health, poverty and social exclusion

Company registration number: 6251684

Correspondent: Stefanie Kha, Global Charities Correspondent, 30 Leicester Square, London WC2H 7LA (tel: 0345 606 0990; email: charities@global.com; website: www.thisisglobal.com/charities-and-communities)

Directors: Ashley Tabor; Darren Singer; Ian Hanson; Michael Gordon; Richard Park; Stephen Miron; The Lord Allen of Kensington; Will Harding (female 0%; male 100%).

Nature of business: The group operates several large commercial stations across the UK including Capital, Heart, Smooth, Classic FM, LBC, Radio X and Gold.

Year end	31/03/2017
Turnover	£302,634,000
Pre-tax profit	(£3,081,000)

Main locations: The group's head office is in London and it has around 22 broadcast stations across England, Scotland and Wales.

Community involvement

Global's charitable work focuses on supporting small charities working with disadvantaged children and young people across the UK. In addition, it helps to deliver The Big Music Project, an employability programme funded by the Big Lottery Fund. The charities it works with benefit from in-kind support and workshops delivered by Global employees.

Global Charities

Global Charities (Charity Commission no. 1091657) is the charitable arm of Global. The charity's flagship grant-giving programme, Global's Make Some Noise, raises money from Global Radio listeners, employees, and the entertainment and music industries. The charity then distributes the funds to support projects undertaken by small community charities, which will improve the lives of children and young people affected by disability, illness, or disadvantage in the UK.

All applicant charities must meet the following core criteria:

- Be a UK-registered charity
- Have an annual income of approximately £50,000 – £1.2 million
- Directly support children, young people and their families who are affected by illness, disability or lack of opportunity
- Be able to provide at least one year of filed accounts
- Be able to provide an up-to-date child protection and safeguarding policy for your charity
- Be able to identify a programme, service, role or capital project that Global's Make Some Noise could fund from April 2019 onwards

In 2016/17 the charity awarded 34 grants totalling £2.2 million. The grants were categorised as follows:

Disability	10	£601,000
Illness	6	£435,500
Lack of opportunity	6	£362,000
Mental health	5	£314,500
Bereavement	4	£278,000
Young carers	3	£218,000

Beneficiaries included: Momentum – London (£80,500); Once Upon A Smile – Manchester (£72,000); Suffolk Young People's Health Project – 4YP (£70,000); The Elizabeth Foundation – Hampshire (£68,000); Y Bont – Cardiff (£57,000); Action for Stammering Children – London (£32,000).

In-kind support

Global donated media time worth more than £2 million in 2016/17 to support its corporate charity's beneficiaries. Charities were profiled on air, on the website and across all of Global's brand and media platforms. Local broadcasting teams helped prepare and record the segments with the charities.

In addition Global provided eight tickets to Capital FM's Summertime Ball which were shared among three charities, and 29 tickets to Capital FM's Jingle Bell Ball which were shared between four charities. Over 300 beneficiaries attended events or took part in studio tours in London and the broadcast centres across the country. This enabled the charities to give their beneficiaries a special day out.

Employee-led support

Employees fundraise for Global Charities throughout the year and in October when there is a dedicated 'Make Some Noise' fundraising appeal. In addition, employees deliver masterclasses to help the staff at the beneficiary charities with marketing and communications skills.

Exclusions

The charity does not fund any of the following:

- Activities that do not directly contribute to the welfare or development of children, young people and their families affected by illness, disability or lack of opportunity
- Local government or NHS bodies

- Projects which promote religion, politics or other activity that is not for wider public benefit
- Trips or projects abroad
- Corporate or business activity
- Individuals
- Other grant-makers or projects where funds are to be redirected to other organisations or individuals
- Projects where the grant expenditure is due to start before the grant award date (retrospective funding)

For further details on Global's Make Some Noise grants and full criteria visit: www.makesomenoise.com.

Applications

The 2016/17 accounts describe the grant-making process as follows:

- Nomination through Global Radio's broadcast centres or Expression of Interest by prospective applicants on the Global Charities website: www.makesomenoise.com
- Assessment against minimum eligibility criteria by Global Charities' staff and subsequent shortlisting of prospective applicants
- Shortlist invited to apply within stated time frame
- Submission of application forms by those shortlisted. Rejection of all those not shortlisted, unless the trustees or delegated Grants Panel wish to review them
- Review and assessment of application forms by independent Grants Panel in line with approved grant-making criteria and risk management
- Recommendations by Grants Panel are submitted to the trustees for ratification

If an application is successful, Global will promote and advertise the charity to raise awareness for the project. Successful applicants will need to provide:

- A case study of one or more of the young people they support
- Photographs of the young people it supports and photos of current work and projects
- Site visits to the project/charity
- Interview opportunities with staff members
- Interview opportunities with young people and their families

Visit www.makesomenoise.com/whowehelp for further details.

Community contributions

Cash donations UK	£377,500
In-kind support UK	£2,000,000
Total contributions (cash and in kind)	£2,400,000

The 2016/17 accounts note the following:

> The Group is involved with a number of charities that are linked to its radio operations and during the course of the financial year, the Group's charities were involved in fundraising activities which generated £3.4 million for its own and many other third-party causes. The Group's donations to charities amounted to £377,500.

We have taken the group's cash donation to be £377,500, and its in-kind contributions of media time to be £2 million.

The Go-Ahead Group plc

Children and young people, community development, education, general charitable purposes

Company registration number: 2100855

Correspondent: Katy Taylor, Group Commercial and Customer Director, 4 Matthew Parker Street, Westminster, London SW1H 9NP (tel: 020 7799 8999; email: communications@go-ahead.com; website: www.go-ahead.com)

Directors: Adrian Ewer; Andrew Allner; Carolyn Ferguson; David Brown; Harry Holt; Katherine Innes Ker; Leanne Wood; Patrick Butcher (female 38%; male 63%).

Nature of business: The principal activity of the group is the provision of rail and bus public transport services.

Year end	30/06/2018
Turnover	£3,461,500,000
Pre-tax profit	£145,700,000

Total employees: 28,154

Main locations: The group has a head office in the City of Westminster, but has operating companies serving a broad geographical area within England. For more information on the group's companies and where they operate, see the operations map on the website (www.go-ahead.com/en/our-companies/our-operations.html).

Community involvement

At a corporate level, Go-Ahead supports two international but UK-based charities that have a transport focus and therefore have strong links to its business: Railway Children and Transaid. At a local level, each of its operating companies support local initiatives that reflect the concerns and priorities of the communities they serve.

In-kind support

Go-Ahead has an online education programme, Go-Learn, which is aimed at helping children and young people between the ages of 4 and 14 to improve their knowledge and confidence about public transport.

Employee-led support

The group's individual operating companies support their employees' charitable activities wherever possible.

Applications

The group's community involvement is co-ordinated at a local level by its operating companies. For more information about these operating companies and the areas they serve, see the operations map on the group's website (www.go-ahead.com/en/our-companies/our-operations.html).

Community contributions

Cash donations UK	£195,500
In-kind support UK	£283,000
Total contributions (cash and in kind)	£478,500

There is a document available to download from the website containing sustainability data for the group, which includes information on community contributions according to the London Benchmarking Group model.

In 2017/18 the group made community contributions totalling £478,500, which was given in the following forms:

Cash contributions	£195,500
Gifts in kind	£156,000
Value of employee time	£127,000

Management time contributed was valued at £78,000, although, as is our usual practice, we have not included this figure in our total for the group's contributions.

The sustainability data also provides a detailed breakdown of community contributions given by individual operating companies.

Goldman Sachs International

Education, enterprise and training, general charitable purposes, poverty and social exclusion

Company registration number: 2263951

Correspondent: Corporate Engagement Team, Peterborough Court, 133 Fleet Street, London EC4A 2BB (tel: 020 7774 1000; website: www.goldmansachs.com/citizenship/index.html)

Directors: Andreas Koernlein; Andrew Bagley; Anthony Grabiner; Carolyne Hodkin; Clare Richards; Daniel Parker; David Mackenzie; Dermot McDonogh; Eoghainn Calder; Esta Stecher; Faryar Shirzad; Jeremy Herman; Jonathan Cheatle; Jose Durao Barroso; Kostas Pantazopoulos; Kyle Williams; Marius Winkleman; Matthew Flett; Nigel Harman; Richard Buckingham; Richard Gnodde; Sally Boyle; Susan Kilsby; Therese Miller (female 25%; male 75%).

Nature of business: Goldman Sachs provides investment banking, trading, asset management and securities to corporations, financial institutions, governments and wealthy individuals.

Year end	31/12/2017
Turnover	£6,508,000,000
Pre-tax profit	£2,091,000,000

Main locations: The head office of Goldman Sachs is in London and it has various offices worldwide.

Community involvement

At a global level, the company's philanthropy includes four major initiatives: Goldman Sachs Gives, a donor-advised fund with which former and current senior employees have an input; Community Teamworks, a worldwide employee volunteering initiative; 10,000 Women, which looks to boost local economies by supporting females entrepreneurs; and 10,000 Small Businesses, which looks to create jobs and economic growth by investing in business education, opportunities and support services for entrepreneurs.

In the UK, Goldman Sachs has established two registered grant-making charities:

The Goldman Sachs Charitable Gift Fund (UK) (Charity Commission no. 1120148)

This fund was set up for the advancement of education, the relief of poverty, the advancement of religion and any other purposes charitable in both English and American law.

Goldman Sachs Gives (UK) (Charity Commission no. 1123956)

This is a grant-making charity, providing funds for a wide range of charitable projects.

Citizenship programmes

10,000 Women

This is a global initiative that fosters economic growth by providing women entrepreneurs around the world with a business and management education, mentoring and networking, and access to capital.

10,000 Small Businesses

This is an investment to help entrepreneurs create jobs and economic opportunity by providing greater access to education, capital and business support services. 10,000 Small Businesses is funded by Goldman Sachs and the Goldman Sachs Foundation.

Employee-led support

The volunteer programme is in operation for the company's employees around the globe. In 2017 employees from 51 offices in 21 countries took part in Community TeamWorks helping 700 organisations with 1,300 projects worldwide.

Commercially led support

Goldman Sachs has a long history of supporting arts and culture in the UK and sponsored the Serpentine Pavilion in 2017 and 2018.

Applications

Contact the Corporate Engagement Team for further information.

Corporate charity

Goldman Sachs Gives (UK) (Charity Commission no. 1123956) – see page 252. The Goldman Sachs Charitable Gift Fund (UK) (Charity Commission no. 1120148) – see page 251.

Community contributions

Cash donations worldwide	£18,460,000

In 2017 Goldman Sachs International made donations to charity totalling \$25 million (≈ £18.46 million as at October 2018) including a donation of \$22 million (≈ \$16.24 million as at October 2018) to Goldman Sachs Gives (UK). The Goldman Sachs Gives (UK) accounts covering the 2016/17 financial period state that £18.4 million was received from Goldman Sachs International.

Goodwin plc

General charitable purposes

Company registration number: 305907

Correspondent: John Goodwin, Chair, Ivy House Foundry, Hanley, Stoke-On-Trent ST1 3NR (tel: 01782 220000; email: jwgoodwin@goodwingroup.com; website: www.goodwin.co.uk)

Directors: Bernard Goodwin; Jennifer Kelly; John Conolly; John Goodwin; Matthew Goodwin; Richard Goodwin; Simon Goodwin; Steven Birks; Tim Goodwin (female 11%; male 89%).

Nature of business: Founded in 1883 as R. Goodwin and Sons Engineers, specialising in mechanical engineering The company remains under family management and control with over 51% of the voting shares still in the hands of the Goodwin family.

Year end	30/04/2017
Turnover	£124,811,000
Pre-tax profit	£13,300,000

UK employees: 1,042

Main locations: The group's head office is in Stoke-on-Trent.

Community involvement

The group's charitable support is mainly in the form of cash donations which are made to the local communities in which it operates.

Applications

Apply in writing to the correspondent.

Community contributions

Cash donations worldwide	£53,000

According to the 2017/18 annual report, donations by the group for charitable purposes amounted to £53,000. The majority of these were made to local communities within the group's operating environments.

Gowling WLG (UK) LLP

Education, housing and homelessness, poverty and social exclusion

Company registration number: OC304378

Correspondent: Lorna Gavin, Head of Corporate Responsibility, 4 More London Riverside, London SE1 2AU (tel: 020 7759 6963; email: lorna.gavin@gowlingwlg.com; website: gowlingwlg.com/en/corporate-responsibility/uk/community-investment)

Nature of business: Gowling WLG LLP is an international law firm, formed from the merger of Canadian law firm Gowling and UK-based firm Wragge Lawrence Graham & Co. LLP in 2016.

Year end	30/04/2017
Turnover	£190,149,000
Pre-tax profit	£60,936,000

Main locations: The firm has two offices in the UK – Birmingham and London. There are also offices in Belgium; Canada; China; France; Germany; Middle East; Monaco; Russia; and Singapore.

Community involvement

The firm provides support for a range of causes through its charitable trust, as well as providing volunteer and other support for issues such as homelessness, education and diversity. The firm nominates three Charity of the Year partners to support, and also provides pro bono legal advice to a range of charities.

Gowling WLG (UK) Charitable Trust (Charity Commission no. 803009)

Previously known as Wragge & Co. Charitable Trust, the group's corporate charity makes small grants to charities and also provides matched funding for employee fundraising initiatives. The trust supports a wide range of charitable purposes.

Charity of the Year

The firm's employees nominate three charities each year – one nationally, and two locally in the London and Birmingham offices. Employees fundraise for the charities and, where possible, pro bono and in-kind support is also provided. The Charity of the Year for 2018 was Dementia UK. Previous charities of the year have included: Young Minds, Bede House and Birmingham St Mary's Hospice, Beyond Food, Bliss, Help Harry Help Others, Dogs for the Good, KidsOut, Auditory Verbal UK, Macmillan, Alzheimer's Society, Friends of the Elderly and Make-a-Wish.

Partnerships

The firm is part of the Legal Social Mobility Partnership, providing work experience opportunities to disadvantaged young people. It also works in partnership with Enabling Enterprise, inviting schoolchildren to spend a day in the office and take part in enterprise activities. The 'Day in the Life of a Lawyer' programme offers a work placement, mentoring and skills development for young people, aiming to broaden access to the legal profession.

Employees in the firm volunteer with local primary schools in Birmingham and London to help with reading. Over 100 employees have also become school governors through the firm's partnership with the School Governors One Stop Shop.

The firm also sponsors a TeachFirst teacher in a school in Birmingham, and offers work placements to individuals through its homelessness support initiatives.

Suited for Success

The firm is one of the founding partners of the charity Suited for Success (Charity Commission no. 1165131), which provides interview clothing for people in Birmingham who are unemployed.

In-kind support

The firm provides pro bono legal advice to charities and community groups and through legal clinics, supporting local and national organisations including NSPCC, Oxfam, Roshni, SIFA Fireside, and The Big Issue Foundation.

Employees offer support through activities such as CV and interview workshops to help people who are homeless or disadvantaged to gain employability skills and confidence. Employees also provide support through delivering Christmas lunches, donating food and clothing and organising fundraising events. The firm also provides work placements for people in need of experience.

Employee-led support

Employee volunteering

The firm's volunteering programme focuses on homelessness, education and inner city needs. Employees volunteer in a range of activities to support these causes.

Inner city needs

Employees can donate to food and clothing banks in the firm's offices, supporting the Trussell Trust as well as local charities SIFA Fireside (in Birmingham) and Spitalfields Crypt Trust and St Giles Trust (in London).

Employee fundraising

Employees raise funds for partner charities and can also donate to charities through a payroll giving scheme. There is also a staff choir which raises money at concerts throughout the year.

Applications

Contact the correspondent for further information.

Pro bono

For further information on pro bono assistance contact Katie Rothwell (katie.rothwell@gowlingwlg.com) or Amy Tabari (amy.tabari@gowlingwlg.com).

Corporate charity

Gowling WLG (UK) Charitable Trust (Charity Commission no. 803009) – see page 252.

Community contributions

We were unable to determine a figure for the firm's total charitable contributions.

Greggs plc

Community development, children and young people, education

Company registration number: 502851

Correspondent: CSR Team, Greggs House, Quorum Business Park, Newcastle upon Tyne NE12 8BU (tel: 0191 281 7721; email: getintouch@greggs.co.uk; website: corporate.greggs.co.uk/social-responsibility)

Directors: Allison Kirkby; Helena Ganczakowski; Ian Durant; Jonathan Jowett; Jonathan Jowett; Peter McPhilips; Roger Whiteside; Sandra Turner (female 38%; male 63%).

Nature of business: The principal activity of the group is the retailing of sandwiches, savouries and other bakery related products with a particular focus on takeaway food and catering. The majority of products sold are manufactured in house.

Year end	30/12/2017
Turnover	£960,000,000
Pre-tax profit	£71,900,000

UK employees: 21,734

Main locations: Greggs' head office is located in Newcastle. The company operates stores nationwide.

Community involvement

Greggs looks to focus its community involvement in a number of ways, including through the Greggs Foundation, product and service donations, and employee involvement through volunteering and fundraising activities. The company and foundation tend to support charitable organisations that work with: children and young people, with a focus on education and nutrition; social and community welfare; and food banks/redistribution.

In-kind support

The company donates unsold food at the end of each working day to charitable organisations. There is now a dedicated page on the foundation's website which charities can use to apply for food donations. In 2017 the amount of food donated increased by 45% from the previous year. The company also assists the Greggs Foundation through the provision of free office space and management staff.

Managers in the company are entitled to one day per year to volunteer with local charitable organisations.

Employee-led support

Managers volunteer with local charitable organisations.

Commercially led support

In-store fundraising

The company encourages fundraising in its nationwide outlets and receives donations from customers for a variety of charitable purposes. In 2017 the charities supported this way included: BBC Children in Need; Disasters Emergency Committee (for the Nepal earthquake appeal); North of England Children's Cancer Research Fund; and the Poppy Appeal.

The company donates the proceeds from the carrier bag levy and sales of its Jammy Heart biscuit to the Greggs Foundation.

Sponsorship

The company is the main sponsor of the annual Children's Cancer Run, which is held in aid of the North of England Children's Cancer Research charity.

Applications

Contact the correspondent for further information.

Food donations
Applications can be made via the foundation's website.

Corporate charity

The Greggs Foundation (Charity Commission no. 296590) – see page 252.

Community contributions

Cash donations UK	£900,000

In 2017 the company donated £900,000 to the Greggs Foundation, which also benefitted from additional donations from the proceeds of carrier bag charges, and with funds raised in the company's shops and bakeries by employees and customers.

As is our usual practice, we have not included employee or customer-raised funds in our total. We were unable to determine the value of the in-kind or other support not given to the Greggs Foundation.

Grosvenor Group

Community development, health, poverty and social exclusion

Company registration number: 3219943

Correspondent: CSR Team, The Grosvenor Office, 70 Grosvenor Street, London W1K 3JP (email: Contact form on website; website: www.grosvenor.com)

Directors: Christopher Pratt; Dame Fiona Reynolds; Domenico Siniscalco; Mark Preston; Michael McLintock; Nicholas Scarles; Peter Vernon; Sir Philip Dilley (female 13%; male 88%).

Nature of business: The group's principal activities are property investment, financial services and general management in the UK and Ireland, the USA, Europe and Asia Pacific.

Year end	31/12/2017
Turnover	£378,500,000
Pre-tax profit	£233,100,000

Main locations: Grosvenor has UK offices in London and Liverpool.

Community involvement

The group provides support for health and welfare through its two foundations and The Living Cities Community Fund. It also supports community events, makes cash donations and provides employee matched funding.

The Westminster Foundation
Most of Grosvenor's community support is routed through the Westminster Foundation (Charity Commission no. 267618) which was established in 1974 as the Grosvenor family's charitable foundation. The foundation's grant-making is currently focused on the issue of poverty in the UK.

The foundation also runs events such as an Impact Assessment workshop attended by 80 charities as well as hosting major events for seven charities.

The Liverpool ONE Foundation
The group also established the Liverpool ONE Foundation in 2009, which is now managed by Community Foundation for Merseyside and awards funding for projects based around children and young people's mental well-being in Merseyside, and particularly Liverpool.

The Living Cities Community Fund
The fund was founded by Grosvenor in 2014 and is managed by the London Community Foundation. Grants of between £500 and £5,000 are available to organisations in South Westminster in the areas of health and community cohesion.

In-kind support

During the year the group supported 144 community events including 77 that were organised by the group itself.

Employee-led support

Matched funding for staff fundraising is supported through the Westminster Foundation.

Applications

The Westminster Foundation
Applications can be made through the foundation's website: www.westminsterfoundation.org.uk/how-to-apply/How-to-Apply.aspx.

The Liverpool One Foundation
Applications can be made through the Community Foundation for Merseyside website: www.cfmerseyside.org.uk/funds/liverpool-one.

The Living Communities Fund
Applications can be made through the London Community Foundation website: www.londoncf.org.uk.

For any other queries, contact the correspondent.

Corporate charity

The Westminster Foundation (Charity Commission no. 267618) – see page 287.

Community contributions

Cash donations worldwide	£4,200,000

In 2017 the group made a donation of £2.4 million to the Westminster Foundation. A further £1.7 million was given to other charitable causes by the group.

GVC Holdings plc

Sports and recreation

Company registration number: 4685V

Correspondent: CSR Team, 32 Athol Street, Douglas, Isle of Man IM1 1JB (tel: +350 200 78700; website: www.gvc-plc.com)

Directors: Jane Anscombe; Karl Diacono; Kenny Alexander; Lee Feldman; Paul Bowtell; Peter Isola; Pierre Bouchut; Stephen Morana; Virginia McDowell (female 22%; male 78%).

Nature of business: GVC Holdings owns several gaming and sports betting brands including bwin, Sportingbet and Foxy Bingo. In March 2018 it purchased Ladbrokes Coral. The group is headquartered and registered in the Isle of Man.

Year end	31/12/2017
Turnover	£896,100,000
Pre-tax profit	£25,600,000

Total employees: 26,000

Main locations: The group's head office is in the Isle of Man. It has over 7,000 betting shops and outlets in 20 countries worldwide.

Community involvement

The group's makes cash and in-kind contributions to responsible gambling charities as well as other causes. It has also pledged £2 million towards a new community fund which will support grassroots sport, women's sport and men's health.

Ladbrokes Coral Trust (Charity Commission no. 1101804)
The trust was established in 2003 and receives its income from Ladbrokes Coral's staff fundraising. It makes grants for community projects, education and healthcare. The trust also runs national campaigns with selected charity partners. In 2017 the trust partnered with Starlight Children's Foundation and raised £100,000 for the charity.

GVC Community Fund
The group has pledged £2 million towards a new fund which will support grassroots sport, women's sport and men's health. The fund will be managed in partnership with UK Community Foundations.

In-kind support

All office-based employees can spend up to two full working days per year helping with projects in their local communities.

Employee-led support

Ladbokes Coral staff raised £273,000 for the Ladbrokes Coral Trust in 2017.

Commercially led support

According to its 2017/18 CSR report, the group will be launching a new partnership with Sports Aid which will see at least £250,000 from retail scratchcards go towards supporting talented individuals within national sporting excellence programmes in the UK.

Applications

Contact the correspondent for further information.

Community contributions

Total contributions (cash and in kind)	£2,800,000

In 2017 the group's worldwide charitable contributions totalled £2.8 million. This figure includes contributions made by Ladbrokes Coral which was acquired by GVC Holdings plc in March 2018. Contributions were broken down as follows:

Contribution	GVC	Ladbrokes Coral
Cash and in-kind contributions towards responsible gambling charities	£227,500	£2.1 million
Cash and in-kind to charitable causes, excluding LCT and donations towards responsible gambling charities	£46,000	£393,000

Hammerson plc

Children and young people, enterprise and training, health

Company registration number: 360632

Correspondent: Charities Committee, Kings Place, 90 York Way, London N1 9GE (tel: 020 7887 1000; email: sustainability@hammerson.com; website: sustainability.hammerson.com/charity-partnerships.html)

Directors: Andrew Formica; David Atkins; David Tyler; Gwyn Burr; Jean-Philippe Mouton; Judy Gibbons; Peter Cole; Pierre Bouchut; Terry Duddy; Timom Drakesmith (female 20%; male 80%).

Nature of business: Hammerson is an owner-manager and developer of retail and office property in the UK and France.

Year end	31/12/2017
Turnover	£585,400,000
Pre-tax profit	£413,400,000

UK employees: 449

Total employees: 587

Main locations: Hammerson's UK office is located in London and it has properties throughout the UK. For details of the whereabouts of Hammerson properties see: www.hammerson.com/property.

Community involvement

Hammerson looks to develop relationships in the communities where it has a presence, both at a corporate level and through its locations in the UK and France. It does this through the Positive Places sustainability framework. Support is given to charities in the form of cash, in-kind and staff time contributions, and employees also play an active role in their communities through volunteering, fundraising and matched funding schemes.

Hammerson Positive Local Places Bursary Scheme

Every year, staff at Hammerson shopping centres choose a local charity to develop a relationship with and to donate a bursary of £5,000. Work is focused in four areas: health and well-being; young people; skills and employment; and regeneration.

Charity partners

Every two years the company selects a charity partner to work with via an employee nomination and vote. The charity receives a cash donation and employees are encouraged to fundraise for the charity. The current charity partner is The Outward Bound Trust. The partnership ends in June 2020.

In-kind support

Hammerson's volunteering policy allows staff to spend three paid days volunteering each year, including the annual Community Day.

Employee-led support

Employee volunteering

Employees are involved in a range of volunteering activities for local and national charities. Each year, Hammerson holds a Community Day, both in the UK and France, through which employees volunteer on their chosen activities.

The Butterfly Bank

The online platform (hammerson.thebutterflybank.co.uk) enables employees to create a profile and then sign up to volunteering opportunities. Employees who volunteer through the scheme can then 'bank' virtual butterflies as a reward. Those employees who bank the most butterflies as well as those who take up their full volunteering allowance are recognised.

Employee fundraising

Hammerson employees raise funds for charitable causes, including for the company's selected charity partners.

Matched funding

Hammerson matches funds raised by staff up to a value of £250 per employee.

Commercially led support

The Prosperity Programme

Hammerson works with partners at a national and local level to deliver employment, skills, training and enterprise schemes across its assets and developments. National partners include National Skills Academy, Retail Trust and LandAid. Partners at a local level include Young Enterprise, Job Centre Plus and Inspire.

Exclusions

Charities affiliated with religion or politics are not supported.

Applications

Positive Places

The company's website states: 'If you are interested in applying for funding under our Positive Places Bursary Scheme, please contact us at sustainability@hammerson.com. Our centre charity bursaries open for applications in Late Spring each year.'

Community contributions

Total contributions (cash and in kind)	£2,200,000

The Hammerson Annual Report 2017 states that during the year direct community contributions totalled £2.2 million. This figure includes cash donations and the value of in-kind support. We were unable to determine what proportion was given in the UK.

Heart of England Co-operative

General charitable purposes

Company registration number: IP02399R

Correspondent: Jo Dyke, Community & Membership Adviser, Whittle House, Foleshill Enterprise Park, Courtaulds Way, Coventry CV6 5NX (tel: 024 7638 2331; email: jo.dyke@heartofengland-coop.co.uk; website: www.heartofengland.coop)

Directors: Clive Miles; Paul Elverson; Ali Kurji; Colin Brown; Gary Haigh; Nick Matthews; Chris Newman; Andrew Tampion; Mark Alexander; Mark Rumsey (female 0%; male 100%).

Nature of business: The society is a food retailer and funeralcare provider.

Year end	20/01/2018
Turnover	£71,725,000
Pre-tax profit	£5,233,000

Main locations: The society has stores in Coventry, Warwickshire, south Leicestershire and Northamptonshire.

Community involvement

The society's Corporate Charity of the Year is decided by a staff vote each year. In 2017, £16,700 was raised for the Guide Dogs which was topped up to £25,000 with carrier bag sales. Zoe's Place was the nominated charity for 2018.

Helping Hands Awards scheme

The award scheme provides small grants to charities and groups in the regions of Coventry, Warwickshire, South Leicestershire and Northamptonshire.

Commercially led support

In 2017 the society donated £50,000 to charities from the sale of single-use carrier bags. A number of stores asked shoppers to vote for their favourite charity through a token scheme.

Applications

Application forms for the Helping Hearts Awards are available in all stores or can be requested from the correspondent.

Community contributions

Cash donations UK	£60,000

In 2017 the society donated £60,000 through its Helping Hands Awards scheme which represented 1.1% of pre-tax profit.

Heathrow Airport Holdings Ltd (formerly BAA Ltd)

Children and young people, education (particularly STEM subjects), enterprise and training, the environment

Company registration number: 5757208

Correspondent: Community Relations Team, The Compass Centre, Nelson Road, London Heathrow Airport, Hounslow TW6 2GW (email: communityrelations@heathrow.com; website: www.heathrow.com/company/community-and-environment/community)

Directors: Ahmed Ali Al-Hammadi; Akbar Al Baker; Benjamin Bao; Carol Hui; Chris Beale; Fidel López; Javier Echave; John Holland-Kaye; Jorge Gil; Lord Deighton; Mike Powell; Olivier Fortin; Prof. Dave Begg; Rachel Lomax; Stuart Baldwin (female 13%; male 87%).

Nature of business: Heathrow Airport Holdings Ltd (formerly BAA) owns and runs London Heathrow Airport.

Year end	31/12/2017
Turnover	£2,884,000,000
Pre-tax profit	£253,000,000

Total employees: 6,740

Main locations: The airport is based in London and supports the boroughs of Ealing, Hillingdon, Hounslow, Richmond, Runnymede, Slough, Spelthorne, South Buckinghamshire and Windsor and Maidenhead.

Community involvement

The group's charitable support is focused on the areas surrounding Heathrow Airport. The Heathrow Community Fund, which is part of the LHR Airport Communities Trust, makes grants to local projects supporting communities, environment, youth and education. Employees can also volunteer with local projects, and employees and customers contribute to fundraising for the group's partner charity.

Heathrow Community Fund

The community fund is part of the LHR Airport Communities Trust (Charity Commission no. 1058617), which receives funding from Heathrow (including funds raised through fines for breaching aircraft noise levels), as well as other airports in the same group, such as Aberdeen and Glasgow.

The trust also channels support for employee initiatives, including providing matched funding for staff donations.

The Heathrow Community Fund provides grants to community projects in areas local to Heathrow Airport, supporting youth, education and community.

Grants range from £2,000 to £25,000 and are made in the following categories: Communities for Youth – supporting young people's education and skills development; Communities for Tomorrow – projects protecting the environment or promoting environmental education and sustainable development; Communities Together – supporting smaller community-focused projects.

The fund can also offer volunteer support to projects in the local communities.

Further details on each of the grants schemes and what support currently available is given on the website: www.heathrowcommunityfund.com.

Charity partnership

The group has raised funds for its partner Oxfam since 2013. The group is also a partner of Step Up To Serve, a charity supporting Youth Social Action across the UK

Community investment

The group has a community investment programme which aims to support the economic prosperity of the areas surrounding the airport through skills development, careers support and engagement with educational institutions and businesses. The areas supported are Ealing, Hillingdon, Hounslow, Slough and Spelthorne. For example, in 2017, this included engagement with 52 local primary schools and 18 local secondary schools, running STEM-related challenges; as well as providing support for Duke of Edinburgh challenges and scout groups; and holding a careers fair. The group's Heathrow Academy supports local people with training and employment opportunities.

In-kind support

Through the Heathrow Community Fund, the group advertises local community projects looking for volunteer support to employees. Employees also volunteer with local schools.

Employee-led support

The group's employees have been fundraising for Oxfam, the group's partner charity, since 2013. The group provides matched funding for employees engaged in their own charitable fundraising initiatives.

Exclusions

For guidance notes and exclusions from each of the Heathrow Community Fund's grant schemes, refer to the website: www.heathrowcommunityfund.com.

Applications

Heathrow Community Fund

Information on how to apply to any of the fund's grants schemes is provided on the website, along with deadlines, application forms and guidance notes.

Volunteer support

Local organisations looking for volunteer support can advertise their project to employees by emailing communitiestrust@heathrow.com with the following information:

- Name of organisation
- Location of opportunity
- Dates/times volunteers needed
- What the volunteers are needed for
- How many volunteers are needed

Contact the correspondent for all other queries.

Corporate charity

LHR Airport Communities Trust (Charity Commission no. 1058617) – see page 258.

Community contributions

Cash donations UK	£1,700,000

The group's 2017 accounts state its total charitable donations during the year totalled £1.7 million.

Beneficiaries included: Hillingdon Community Trust (£1 million); LHR Airport Communities Trust (£700,000).

Customers and employees also raised a further £363,500 for the group's charity partner Oxfam.

Hiscox Ltd

Arts and culture, children and young people, education, poverty and social exclusion

Company registration number: 38877

Correspondent: CSR Team, 1 Great St Helen's, London EC3A 6HX (tel: 020 7448 6011; email: enquiries@hiscox.com; website: www.hiscoxgroup.com/responsibility)

Directors: Anne MacDonald; Caroline Foulger; Colin Keogh; Constantinos Mirtanthis; Lynn Pike; Michael Goodwin; Robert Childs; Robert Macmillan; Thomas Hurlimann (female 33%; male 67%).

Nature of business: Hiscox Ltd specialises in insurance and is registered in Bermuda. We have taken the figure for charitable donations from the annual report and accounts (for the year ending 31 December 2017) of Hiscox plc, a UK-registered holding company (registered company no. 02837811), and from the 2016/17 annual report and accounts of The Hiscox Foundation. Other financial and CSR information relates to Hiscox Ltd.

Year end	31/12/2017
Turnover	£2,549,279,000
Pre-tax profit	£30,798,000

Main locations: Hiscox has offices in Birmingham, Colchester, Glasgow, London, Maidenhead and Manchester.

Community involvement

Hiscox offices around the world play an active role in supporting their communities. In the UK, Hiscox makes an annual donation to The Hiscox Foundation (Charity Commission no. 327635) and works in partnership with other organisations to support programmes in the areas of business, arts, science and technology. Hiscox employees volunteer and fundraise for charitable causes, and are supported in their efforts by matched funding from the foundation.

Support for the arts, science and technology

In 2017 Hiscox supported the City of London's Sculpture in the City project and continued to be the insurance partner of the Whitechapel Gallery. Hiscox also became The National Gallery's first Contemporary Art Partner and supported Art Night – a free arts festival in London.

Employee-led support

Employees play an important role in choosing the charities Hiscox supports. In 2017 employees in Colchester raised £32,000 for Mid and North East Essex Mind and employees in York raised £6,000 for The Samaritans. Employees can also apply to the foundation to match funds raised or request support for a good cause.

Corporate charity

The Hiscox Foundation (Charity Commission no. 327635) – see page 254.

Community contributions

Cash donations worldwide	£694,000

The 2017 annual report and accounts for Hiscox Ltd did not include a figure for charitable donations, however the annual report and accounts for Hiscox plc, the UK-registered holding company, stated that during the year the company made donations totalling £694,000 to charitable organisations. We believe that £500,000 of this amount was given to The Hiscox Foundation.

C. Hoare and Co.

Animal welfare, the armed forces, arts and culture, community development, education, the environment, general charitable purposes, health, poverty and social exclusion

Company registration number: 240822

Correspondent: 37 Fleet Street, London EC40 4DQ (website: www.hoaresbank.co.uk)

Directors: Alexander Hoare; Alexander Hoare; Andrew McIntyre; Arabella Hoare; Dame Susan Rice; David Green; Johanna Waterous; Nicholas Macpherson; Simon Hoare; Venetia Hoare (female 40%; male 60%).

Nature of business: C. Hoare and Co. provides banking and ancillary services to a predominantly high net worth customer base.

Year end	31/03/2018
Turnover	£105,900,000
Pre-tax profit	£25,900,000

UK employees: 371

Main locations: The company's head office is in London.

Community involvement

The company makes donations to its corporate charity, The Golden Bottle Trust (Charity Commission no. 327026). The trust supports a wide range of general charitable purposes, including animal welfare, the arts, the environment, education and health.

Employee-led support

The company doubles charitable donations made by its employees through its payroll giving scheme.

Corporate charity

The Golden Bottle Trust (Charity Commission no. 327026) – see page 251.

Community contributions

Cash donations UK	£3,000,000

In 2017/18 the company donated £3 million to its corporate charity, The Golden Bottle Trust.

Holland and Barrett Retail Ltd

Education, the environment, health

Company registration number: 2758955

Correspondent: CSR Team, Samuel Ryder House, Barling Way, Nuneaton, Warwickshire CV10 7RH (tel: 01283 560011; email: customerservices@hollandandbarrett.com; website: www.hollandandbarrett.com)

Directors: Christian Keen; Hilary Leam; Lisa Garley-Evans; Steve Carson (female 50%; male 50%).

Nature of business: Holland and Barrett is a chain of health food shops.

Year end	30/09/2017
Turnover	£461,408,000
Pre-tax profit	£81,766,000

Total employees: 5,155

Main locations: The company's headquarters are in Nuneaton. There are 715 stores in the UK as well as stores in Holland, Belgium, Sweden and the Republic of Ireland.

Community involvement

The company makes donations to UK-based organisations. The company also has a charitable company, Healthy Hope Ltd, from which donations are made. Healthy Hope has a focus on: health and well-being; education relating to health; well-being and the environment; the protection and improvement of the environment. At the time of writing (November 2018), Healthy Hope Ltd was in the process of applying for charitable status.

Applications

Contact the correspondent for further information.

Community contributions

Cash donations UK	£189,500

In 2016/17 the company made charitable donations to UK-based organisations totalling £189,500.

Honda of the UK Manufacturing Ltd

Education, the environment, safety and crime prevention

Company registration number: 1887872

Correspondent: CSR Team, Highworth Road, South Marston, Swindon SN3 4TZ (website: www.hondamanufacturing.co.uk)

Directors: Ian Howells; Jun Nishimoto; Katsushi Inoue (female 0%; male 100%).

Nature of business: The principal activity of the company is the manufacture of motor vehicles, including the manufacture of motor engines and other vehicle parts.

Year end	31/03/2018
Turnover	£2,608,166,000
Pre-tax profit	£24,860,000

Main locations: The group's UK manufacturing facility is based in Swindon.

Community involvement

Honda of the UK Manufacturing Ltd invests in sustainability initiatives focusing on education, safety, environment and community. The company predominantly supports charitable and community initiatives in the area local to its Swindon base. The company also makes quarterly donations to charities voted for by employees.

In-kind support

The 2017/18 annual report states that Christmas hamper donations are made to local organisations.

Employee-led support

The group provides matched funding for fundraising events organised by employees.

Applications

Contact the correspondent for further information. There is an email enquiry form on the website.

Community contributions

Cash donations UK	£31,000

In 2017/18 the company made charitable donations of £31,000.

Howden Joinery Group plc

Disability, general charitable purposes

Company registration number: 2128710

Correspondent: CSR Team, 40 Portman Square, London W1H 6LT (website: www.howdenjoinerygroupplc.com/index.asp#Sustainability)

Directors: Andrew Livingston; Andy Gault; Andy Witts; Clive Cockburn; Gareth Hopkins; Kevin Barrett; Mark Robson; Rob Fenwick; Theresa Keating (female 11%; male 89%).

Nature of business: Howden supplies kitchens and joinery products to trade customers, principally small builders, in the UK.

Year end	26/12/2017
Turnover	£1,404,000,000
Pre-tax profit	£232,200,000

Total employees: 9,000+

Main locations: The company's head office is in London and there are 661 depots throughout the UK. There is a local depot search facility on the website.

Community involvement

Individual Howdens depots, manufacturing sites and distribution and support centres are involved in their immediate communities, contributing cash and stock donations. Employees take part in a wide range of fundraising initiatives.

Cash donations

As well as donating kitchens the company also makes small cash donations. The 2017 Sustainability Report states:

> We also support thousands of small local projects with cash donations. Typical donations may be just a few hundred pounds, but they will make a big difference. They might cover things like:
> - Buying new kit for a local children's sports team
> - Giving our staff's time and materials to help renovate facilities at a local community centre
> - Donating cash to a local hospital's appeal for vital equipment

Charity partner

Since 2004, Howdens has worked in partnership with Leonard Cheshire Disability. Its work with the charity has mainly focused on installing kitchens in its care homes, sponsoring the 'Can Do' volunteering initiative and offering support through skills training and employability workshops.

In-kind support

The 2017 Sustainability Report states that, during the year, Howdens 'supplied and fitted 62 complete kitchens in response to requests from local good causes'.

Employee-led support

Employees play an active role in supporting their local communities, principally through fundraising activities.

Applications

Direct requests to your local Howden depot, manufacturing site or distribution or support centre.

Community contributions

Total contributions (cash and in kind)	£1,500,000

The 2017 Sustainability Report states: 'In 2017, we've made 3,700 separate donations which have involved us giving cash or products worth £1.5m.'

HSBC Holdings plc

Disaster relief, education, enterprise and training, general charitable purposes

Company registration number: 617987

Correspondent: Community Investment Committee, 1 Centenary Square, Birmingham B1 1HQ (tel: 020 7991 8888; website: www.hsbc.com/our-approach/sustainability/communities)

Directors: Ben Matthews; David Nish; Heidi Miller; Henri de Castries; Iain Mackay; Irene Lee; Jackson Tai; John Flint; Jonathan Simmonds; Kathleen Casey; Laura Cha; Lord Evans of Weardale; Marc Moses; Mark Tucker; Pauline van de Meer Mohr (female 33%; male 67%).

Nature of business: HSBC is one of the largest banking and financial services organisations in the world, with businesses working in the areas of commercial banking, global banking and markets, global private banking and retail banking and wealth management.

Year end	31/12/2017
Turnover	£51,445,000,000
Pre-tax profit	£17,167,000,000

Main locations: HSBC's UK headquarters are in Birmingham. It has branches worldwide.

Community involvement

Globally most of the bank's community investment goes towards its themes of supporting responsible business and employability and financial capability. However, the bank also sets aside a quarter of its funding for causes that are important to local communities such as the environment and healthcare. Support is also provided to unforeseen events such as natural disasters and humanitarian crises.

Charity of the Year

The bank's six national charities are selected by employees every two years. The charities supported in 2018/19 are: Alzheimer's Society, Cancer Research UK, Dogs Trust, Macmillan Cancer Support, Mind and Shelter.

Young Enterprise

The bank has had a partnership with Young Enterprise for over 25 years. The bank supports the annual Innovation Awards and provides financial, pro bono, seconded and volunteering support to Young Enterprise across the UK.

In-kind support

Staff are given a day's paid leave each year to enable them to partake with community and charitable projects.

Employee-led support

Matched funding

Staff who volunteer with a registered charity can apply to HSBC for funding to support their cause.

Payroll giving

A payroll giving scheme is in operation.

Commercially led support

HSBC sponsors organisations in the areas of sport (mainly rugby and golf) and culture.

Applications

Contact the correspondent for further information.

Sponsorship

To apply for sponsorship, complete and submit the online form that can be found at: www.hsbc.com/about-hsbc/sponsorship.

Community contributions

Cash donations worldwide	£104,100,000
In-kind support worldwide	£7,100,000
Total contributions (cash and in kind)	£111,200,000

HSBC publishes a 'Key facts' document, which is available to download from the website and includes a breakdown of its worldwide cash and in-kind contributions according to geographical region. The following information was obtained from this document.

Worldwide contributions

During 2017 the group made cash donations totalling $136.1 million (≈ £104.1 million as at February 2019) to charities and non-profit organisations in support of projects benefitting communities around the world. These donations were broken down as follows:

Region	Amount*
Europe	£43.5 million
Asia Pacific	£40 million
North America	£14.5 million
Middle East	£4.7 million
Latin America	£1.5 million

*All values converted from US dollars in February 2019.

Worldwide, the cost of employees' volunteering in work time totalled $9.3 million (≈ £7.1 million as at February 2019).

An additional $10.12 million (≈ £7.8 million as at February 2019) was expended in management costs, although, as is our usual practice, we have not included this in the overall total for contributions.

Alan Hudson Ltd

Community development, older people

Company registration number: 613979

Correspondent: David Ball, Trustee, Bevis Lane, Wisbech St Mary, Wisbech, Cambridgeshire PE13 4RR (tel: 01945 583087)

Directors: David Ball; David Wheeler; Sarah Wheeler; Stephen Layton (female 25%; male 75%).

Nature of business: Alan Hudson is a fruit growing company. The company is wholly owned by the Hudson Foundation (Charity Commission no. 280332) and donates its taxable profits for the year to the charity by way of Gift Aid.

Year end	31/07/2017
Turnover	£1,200,000

UK employees: 19

Main locations: The company's head office is in Cambridgeshire.

Community involvement

Alan Hudson Ltd is the principal subsidiary of the Hudson Foundation and donates its profits to the foundation by way of Gift Aid. The foundation in turn awards grants to a range of charitable organisations and groups in the local area.

Corporate charity

The Hudson Foundation (Charity Commission no. 280332) – see page 255.

Community contributions

Cash donations UK	£314,000

The principal funding source of the foundation is its wholly owned trading subsidiary, Alan Hudson Ltd, which rents the foundation's investment property and donates its taxable profits by way of Gift Aid to the foundation. In 2016/17 this amounted to £314,000, which we have taken as the company's cash donation.

IBM United Kingdom Ltd

Education, particularly STEM subjects

Company registration number: 741598

Correspondent: Corporate Citizenship Team, PO Box 41, North Harbour, Portsmouth, Hampshire PO6 3AU (tel: 0239256 1000; email: ccruk@uk.ibm.com; website: www-05.ibm.com/uk/ondemandcommunity/index.html)

Directors: Flavio Sciuttu; Ian Ferguson; Timothy Eagle; William Kelleher (female 0%; male 100%).

Nature of business: IBM United Kingdom Ltd is the UK subsidiary of IBM Corporation. It is involved in the provision of information technology services and solutions, and the development, production and supply of advanced information technology products.

Year end	31/12/2017
Turnover	£3,713,300,000
Pre-tax profit	£109,200,000

UK employees: 12,047

Total employees: 366,000

Main locations: The company's head office is Portsmouth. Other locations include: Hounslow; Bristol; Cambridge; Edinburgh; Greenford; Greenock; Hursley; Manchester; Milton Keynes; Newcastle; Nottingham; South Bank; Warwick; Woking.

Community involvement

IBM provides charities with skills training and pro bono expertise. STEM training materials and programmes are also provided to schools. Support is usually focused in areas where the company has a presence.

Schools

The company has developed a number of free resources and community programmes for secondary and primary schools. The resources are designed to ensure students have the right STEM skills for the workplace.

IBM United Kingdom Trust

The company also makes contributions to its associated charity, IBM United Kingdom Trust (Charity Commission no. 290462), which derives most of its income from the IBM International Foundation and IBM subsidiaries.

The trust's primary focus areas are:

- To increase the scope, usage and understanding of information technology

- To enable disadvantaged people to acquire skills, particularly through the use of information technology
- To provide technology and technical support for disaster relief
- Promoting volunteering by IBM employees
- Providing support to universities and other research institutions

In-kind support

Impact Grants

Impact Grants provide software and pro bono expertise. Organisations should have a UK focus and have the resources necessary to implement the consultancy recommendations or software that is provided through the grant.

Charity Skills Masterclasses

IBM has partnered with the Small Charities Coalition to provide charities with an annual series of masterclasses. The masterclasses cover topics such selling techniques, product management, measuring impact, technology, website development, marketing and social media. Further information can be found on the Small Charities Coalition's website.

Employee-led support

The IBM Community Grants programme recognises the commitment of employees and retirees in their volunteering. Grants range in value depending on the number of volunteer hours undertaken and whether professional skills have been used. The scheme normally opens in April and closes in September/October or when the funds have been spent. Retirees and staff can apply for a grant on behalf of the charity or school at which they are volunteering. Applications are not accepted directly from organisations.

Applications

Impact Grants and the On Demand Community

Email ccruk@uk.ibm.com for further information on these initiatives.

Charity Skills Masterclasses

Further information can be found on the Small Charities Coalition's website.

Schools

Further information on STEM resources and programmes can be found on the UK Corporate Citizenship page of IBM's website.

Corporate charity

IBM United Kingdom Trust (Charity Commission no. 290462) – see page 255.

Community contributions

The company's annual report for 2017 did not declare a figure for charitable donations.

IGas Energy plc

Children and young people, education, the environment, health, poverty and social exclusion

Company registration number: 4981279

Correspondent: Sue Winch, Fund Administrator, 7 Down Street, London W1J 7AJ (email: contact@igascommunityfund.co.uk; website: www.igasplc.com)

Directors: Mike McTighe; Stephen Bowler; Cuth McDowell; Philip Jackson; Tushar Kumar (female 0%; male 100%).

Nature of business: Igas Energy operates onshore oil and gas fields.

Year end	31/12/2017
Turnover	£35,800,000
Pre-tax profit	(£3,249,000)

Main locations: The community fund supports projects near Igas Energy sites in Surrey, Hampshire, West Sussex, Cheshire, Lincolnshire and Nottinghamshire. There is a document on the fund's website with further information on locations.

Community involvement

The company makes grants to community and voluntary organisations near its sites in Surrey, Hampshire, West Sussex, Cheshire, Lincolnshire and Nottinghamshire.

IGas Energy Community Fund (not a registered charity)

The fund supports community and voluntary organisations that are charitable, educational or benevolent in purpose. Projects should be close to IGas sites.

The community fund's website states:

> We welcome applications from organisations that involve:
>
> - **A broad span of the community** – demonstrating support for a wide cross-section of people
> - **Children and young people** – especially projects focused on improving access to activities and services, and where young people play a key role in the decision-making
> - **Vulnerable people** – especially projects involving increased access to services and facilities for people with disabilities, the homeless and the elderly
> - **Community regeneration** – projects that improve health and education, reduce crime levels, regenerate employment, housing and the physical environment
> - **Energy** – projects that improve energy efficiency, employ green energy and reduce carbon
> - **Self-help groups** – community-based groups that deliver basic services
> - **Environmental and wildlife projects** – especially those involving improvements to communal land. Public access is essential
> - **Education and skills development** – group and community-based programmes, particularly for those who have had no previous access to training opportunities
> - **Health** – projects providing access to services that aim to improve the health and well-being of communities
> - **Heritage** – projects that celebrate and protect local heritage
> - **Sustainability** – projects that promote sustainable development

Applications

Applications can be made via the fund's website: www.igascommunityfund.co.uk/index.html.

Community contributions

We were unable to determine the company's charitable contributions for the year. However, the IGas Energy Community Fund's website states that it has distributed over £1 million in grants since it was established in 2008.

Informa plc

Children and young people, community development, education, enterprise and training, general charitable purposes, poverty and social exclusion

Company registration number: 8860726

Correspondent: The Sustainability Manager, 5 Howick Place, London SW1P 1WG, UK (email: sustainability@informa.com; website: informa.com/sustainability)

Directors: Cindy Rose; David Flaschen; David Wei; Derek Mapp; Gareth Bullock; Gareth Wright; Greg Lock; Helen Owers; John Rishton; Mary McDowell; Stephen Carter; Stephen Davidson (female 25%; male 75%).

Nature of business: Informa is an international provider of specialist information and services for academic, scientific, professional and commercial business communities across more than 40 countries.

Year end	31/12/2017
Turnover	£1,757,600,000
Pre-tax profit	£288,800,000

Main locations: Informa's head office is in London and it has other offices in Abingdon, Basingstoke, Chobham, Colchester, Macclesfield, Pathhead in Midlothian and Solihul. There is an office locator facility on the website.

Community involvement

Informa develops strategic relationships with community partners, both locally and internationally, by making cash and in-kind donations, and contributing skills and expertise through employee volunteering. Employees also take an active role in fundraising for charitable causes, including disaster appeals.

In-kind support

Informa builds relationships with various community partners, using human and other resources to help deliver on strategic objectives.

Employee-led support

In 2017 9% of Informa staff took part with various volunteering activities, including supporting the group's charity partners. During the year Informa employees also helped to raise £82,000 for charitable causes. The company organises an annual walk called Walk the World which in 2017 saw employees walk a combined 28,000 miles, raising over £155,000.

Exclusions

No support is given for political appeals.

Applications

The Informa website explains: 'Our businesses have their own sustainability budget to develop partnerships, so that our professional skills and resources can contribute to addressing local, regional and industry challenges.' In the first instance we recommend getting in touch with your local Informa business.

Community contributions

Cash donations worldwide	£411,000
In-kind support worldwide	£39,000
Total contributions (cash and in kind)	£739,000

According to the Informa Sustainability Report 2017, community contributions during the year totalled £763,000. We were unable to determine how much of this was given in the UK.

Innocent Ltd

Community development, poverty and social exclusion, projects outside the UK

Company registration number: 4007092

Correspondent: Kate Franks, Foundation Manager, Fruit Towers, 342 Ladbroke Grove, London W10 5BU (tel: 020 3235 0352; email: hello@innocentfoundation.org; website: www.innocentfoundation.org)

Directors: Douglas Lamont; James Davenport; Sandra Mori; Scott Roche (female 25%; male 75%).

Nature of business: The company develops, manufactures and distributes soft drinks.

Innocent Ltd's immediate parent company and immediate controlling company is Fresh Trading Ltd, a company incorporated in the UK. The ultimate parent company and ultimate controlling party is The Coca-Cola Company, a company incorporated in Delaware, USA.

Year end	31/12/2017
Turnover	£325,500,000
Pre-tax profit	£15,400,000

Main locations: Innocent's head office is in London.

Community involvement

Innocent donates 10% of its annual profits to charitable causes, primarily through its corporate charity The Innocent Foundation (Charity Commission no. 1104289) which makes grants to organisations working to alleviate food poverty.

Commercially led support

Innocent donate 25p to Age UK for every bottle of smoothie sold as part of the Big Knit Campaign (www.thebigknit.co.uk). People knit little woolly hats, which are sent to either Age UK or Innocent and then the hats are put on bottles of smoothies. Since 2013 people have knitted 7.5 million hats which has raised nearly £2.5 million for Age UK. In 2017 the Big Knit raised £1 million.

Applications

Contact the correspondent for further information.

Corporate charity

The Innocent Foundation (Charity Commission no. 1104289) – see page 256.

Community contributions

Cash donations UK	£1,700,000

In 2017 the company made contributions totalling to £1.7 million to charities. The majority of this (£950,000) was given to The Innocent Foundation. We were unable to identify any other beneficiaries.

Intercontinental Hotels Group plc

Disaster relief, enterprise and training, the environment

Company registration number: 5134420

Correspondent: Corporate Responsibility Team, Broadwater Park, North Orbital Road, Denham, near Uxbridge, Buckinghamshire UB9 5HR (tel: 01895 512000; email: companysecretariat@ihg.com; website: www.ihgplc.com)

Directors: Anne Busquet; Dale Morrison; Elie Maalouf; Ian Dyson; Jill McDonald; Jo Harlow; Keith Barr; Luke Mayhew; Malina Ngai; Patrick Cescau; Paul Edgecliffe-Johnson (female 40%; male 60%).

Nature of business: Intercontinental Hotels is a hospitality chain of hotels, soft drinks and public houses.

Year end	31/12/2017
Turnover	£1,784,000,000
Pre-tax profit	£678,000,000

Total employees: 12,213

Main locations: The group has hotels in nearly 100 countries. Its head office is in Denham, Buckinghamshire. There are also regional offices in China, Singapore and the USA.

Community involvement

The group provides support through monetary and in-kind donations, as well as partnerships. The group's corporate charity, the IHG Foundation (Charity Commission no. 1164791) was established in 2016.

Areas of focus

The group's community involvement activities, including partnerships and donations, are based on three areas of focus:

- The environment
- Local economic opportunity
- Disaster relief

Charitable donations

The group's charitable donations policy, detailed on its website, states that contributions are made to registered charities which support its areas of focus. The group can provide support through cash donations, in-kind support such as hotel rooms, and through partnerships.

Community partnerships

The following information has been taken from the group's website. It will only support organisations which:

- exhibit a clear purpose and defined need in one of IHG's three areas of focus
- recognise innovative approaches in addressing the defined need
- demonstrate an efficient organisation and detail the organisation's ability to follow through on its proposal
- explain clearly the benefits to IHG and our hotel communities

Local managers and employees are encouraged to use this list as a guide, along with its Code of Ethics, when deciding what is right for local community needs.

IHG Academy

This initiative focuses on skills, training and employment for local communities, working in partnership with local educational and community organisations. There are also initiatives to support people from low income backgrounds in China and Brazil to pursue education and career opportunities in the hospitality industry.

Disaster relief

The group works with CARE International to support disaster preparedness and relief in the areas where its hotels operate. There is a designated disaster relief fund which can offer immediate assistance to employees and local communities.

IHG Foundation

The group has established foundations in the UK, the USA and China to support its community involvement. The UK foundation focuses on the following four areas: providing skills for local people; supporting those impacted by disasters; protecting the environment; grassroots community support. Charities supported so far include British Red Cross; The Prince's Trust; and Unseen. Further information can be found on the foundation's website: www.ihgfoundation.org.

In-kind support

The group can provide hotel rooms to eligible charities under its donations policy.

Employee-led support

The group runs an annual Global Community Fundraising Week, where employees from across the group organise and take part in a range of fundraising events.

Exclusions

The group's website states the following:

> We do not support organisations that discriminate on the basis of race, religion, creed, gender, age, physical challenge or national origin. In addition, we will not generally provide contributions to:
>
> - Individuals
> - Religious organisations
> - General operating support for hospitals and health care institutions
> - Capital campaigns
> - Endowment funds
> - Conferences, workshops or seminars not directly related to our business interests
> - Multi-year grants; only the first year of multi-year requests will be assured, with support in subsequent years dependent upon annual evaluation
> - Political donations of any kind

Applications

The group

There is an online form for organisations to apply for cash donations, in-kind support or partnerships: www.ihgplc.com/responsible-business/corporate-responsibility/charitable-donations.

The foundation

The foundation's website states that it is focused on supporting a small number of organisations, and so does not accept unsolicited applications.

Community contributions

We were unable to determine the group's charitable contributions for the year.

International Personal Finance

Arts and culture, education, health, poverty and social exclusion

Company registration number: 6018973

Correspondent: UK Corporate Affairs Team, Number Three, Leeds City Office Park, Meadow Lane, Leeds LS11 5BD (tel: 0113 285 6700; website: www.ipfin.co.uk/en/sustainability)

Directors: Cathryn Riley; Dan O'Connor; Gerard Ryan; John Mangelaars; Justin Lockwood; Richard Moat; Tony Hales (female 14%; male 86%).

Nature of business: International Personal Finance is an international home credit business operating using the Provident brand.

Year end	31/12/2017
Turnover	£825,800,000
Pre-tax profit	£105,600,000

Total employees: 11,671

Main locations: The group's head office is in Leeds. There are also offices in Australia, Bulgaria, Czech Republic, Estonia, Finland, Hungary, Latvia, Lithuania, Mexico, Poland, Romania, Slovakia and Spain.

Community involvement

The group tends to support charitable causes in the areas where it operates, with a focus on financial education, as well as encouraging employee volunteering opportunities.

Financial education

The group works with a number of organisations internationally, such as schools, charities and universities, to deliver financial education programmes for communities and financially vulnerable groups.

Employee-led support

The 2017 annual report states that 3,056 hours were volunteered by employees in company time and a further 1,935 in their own time.

Applications

There is a Corporate Affairs Group, which discusses sustainability issues and new initiatives. However, many activities are organised at the level of each local branch – for contact details of each branch, refer to the website: www.ipfin.co.uk/en/contact-us.html

The head office is the only branch in the UK; this is based in Leeds.

Community contributions

Total contributions (cash and in kind)	£680,000

The 2017 annual report states that during the year, £680,000 was invested in local communities across the group. A further £114,000 was raised by employees for community investment purposes. It was not clear how much of this support was given in the UK.

Community donations were invested as follows:

Education	46%
Arts and culture	32%
Social welfare	8%
Other	8%
Health	6%

Interserve plc

General charitable purposes

Company registration number: 88456

Correspondent: The SustainAbilities Team, Interserve House, Ruscombe Park, Twyford, Reading RG10 9JU (email: Contact form on website; website: www.sustainabilities.interserve.com)

Directors: Anne Fahy; Debbie White; Dougie Sutherland; Gareth Edwards; Glyn Barker; Mark Whiteling; Nicholas Pollard; Nick Salmon; Russell King (female 11%; male 89%).

Nature of business: Interserve provides advice, design, construction, equipment, facilities management and frontline public services.

Year end	31/12/2016
Turnover	£3,244,600,000
Pre-tax profit	£106,500,000

Total employees: 33,157

Main locations: Interserve's head office is located in Twyford and it has operations throughout the UK. See the website for details (www.interserve.com/locations/uk-locations).

Community involvement

Interserve provides support to the communities in which it operates through cash donations, in-kind giving and employee volunteering. Employees are supported in their charitable involvement by the **Interserve Employee Foundation** (Charity Commission no. 1145338). Some Interserve subsidiaries also carry out their own community activities.

Interserve Employee Foundation (Charity Commission no. 1145338)
IEF exists to help connect employees with people living in the communities in which Interserve operates. The foundation receives donations from employee fundraising and from the group, suppliers and customers, which it uses to fund charitable projects run by employees. Foundation ambassadors working across the group promote its aims and help to get employees involved with local projects, particularly through the employee volunteering scheme 'Give A Day of Your Time'.

In-kind support

Through the Give a Day Of Your Time, employees can request up to two days' leave to assist a local community project or charity.

Gifts in kind
Interserve supports charities through donations of materials.

Employee-led support

Employee volunteering
During 2016, 12% of employees volunteered in their communities for a total of 7,400 days.

Employee fundraising
Employees fundraise for charities and causes supported by the Interserve Employee Foundation.

Applications

The Interserve Employee Foundation supports charities nominated by Interserve employees. More information is available from www.interserve.com/about-us/interserve-employee-foundation.

Contact the correspondent for all other queries.

Community contributions

Cash donations worldwide	£1,240,000
In-kind support worldwide	£1,117,000
Total contributions (cash and in kind)	£2,360,000

Based on information included in the SustainAbilities Progress Update for 2016, £2.36 million was given in charitable contributions by the group.

Donations to charitable causes	£1.24 million
Value of employee volunteering	£832,000
In-kind donations	£285,000

We believe, based on previous years, that a small proportion of cash donations (about £37,000) was given to the Interserve Employee Foundation.

A further £173,000 was contributed as 'Interserve leveraged fundraising'; we have taken this to refer to amounts raised by employees for example, and, as is our usual practice, we have not included this in the figure for the group's total contributions.

intu Properties plc

Children and young people, education, the environment, health, projects outside the UK, poverty and social exclusion

Company registration number: 3685527

Correspondent: Alexander Nicoll, Corporate Responsibility Manager, 40 Broadway, London SW1H 0BT (website: www.intugroup.co.uk/en/about-us/corporate-responsibility)

Directors: Adele Anderson; Andrew Huntley; Andrew Strang; David Fischel; John Strachan; John Whittaker; Lady Louise Patten; Matthew Roberts; Patrick Burgess; Rakhi Goss-Custard; Richard Gordon (female 27%; male 73%).

Nature of business: Intu Properties owns and manages shopping centres in the UK and Spain. The company was formerly known as Capital Shopping Centre Group plc and, before this, Liberty International plc.

Year end	31/12/2017
Turnover	£616,000,000
Pre-tax profit	£190,400,000

Total employees: 2,603

Main locations: Contact information for all Intu stores can be found at www.intugroup.co.uk/en/our-centres.

Community involvement

Intu Properties shopping centres develop partnerships with organisations in their local areas. Employees are also encouraged to take part with corporate responsibility and community initiatives.

Community partnerships
The company and its stores have partnerships with several charities. Intu has worked in partnership with The Conservation Volunteers to support its Green Gyms programme since 2007. The programme sees volunteers get involved in conservation sessions while also getting fit and active.

In-kind support

According to the company's 2017 annual report, in-kind donations totalled £513,000.

Employee-led support

Employee volunteering
According to the 2017 annual report, 28,000 hours were given to the community by intu staff.

Employee fundraising
In 2017 employees raised £45,000 for 30 charities. Matched funding from intu increased this figure to £55,000.

Applications

Approaches should be directed to the appropriate local intu-owned shopping centre.

Community contributions

Cash donations worldwide	£524,000
In-kind support worldwide	£1,217,000
Total contributions (cash and in kind)	£1,741,000

The 2017 annual report states that donations totalled £1.9 million and were broken down as follows:

Value of time	£704,000
Cash	£524,000
In-kind	£513,000
Facilitated	£179,000

Facilitated contributions have not been included in total charitable contributions as their status is not explained in the annual report. The 2017 corporate responsibility report states that the following causes were supported by the company and its customers:

Health	33%
Young people and education	32%
Other	20%
Emergency relief	5%
Arts and culture	3%
Economic development	3%
Environment	3%
Social welfare	1%

Investec plc

Education, enterprise and training, the environment

Company registration number: 3633621

Correspondent: Susie Steyn, Corporate Sustainability Manager, Corporate Sustainability – Community, 2 Gresham Street, London EC2V 7QP (tel: 020 7597 3713; email: CorporateSustainability@investec.co.uk; website: www.investec.com/en_gb/welcome-to-investec/corporate-responsibility/our-community.html)

Directors: Bernard Kantor; Charles Jacobs; Cheryl Carolus; David Frieland; Fani Titi; Glynn Burger; Hendrick du Toit; Ian Kantor; Khumo Shuenyane; Laurel Bowden; Lord Malloch-Brown; Perry Crosthwaite; Philip Hourquebie; Stephen Koseff; Zarina Bassa (female 20%; male 80%).

Nature of business: Investec is a specialist bank and asset management company.

Year end	31/03/2018
Turnover	£352,367,000
Pre-tax profit	£184,400,000

UK employees: 4,162

Total employees: 9,444

Main locations: Investec's head office is in London with offices located across the UK. See the 'Contact us' section website for the locations of individual offices.

Community involvement

Investec looks to contribute to the communities in which it has a presence in three core areas – education entrepreneurship, and the environment – by forging relationships with local charity partners, principally through employee volunteering, and by making small project grants.

Aside from their volunteering efforts, employees support charitable causes through Payroll Giving and various fundraising activities.

Partnerships

The sustainability report for 2018 provides numerous and detailed case studies of Investec's partnerships in the communities in which it has a presence. Examples of partnerships under the three areas of support, provided in the report are:

Education: Arrival Education

Investec has a partnership with Arrival Education, a social enterprise that focuses on talent management with young people from challenging backgrounds and minority ethnic groups. Investec staff volunteer on Arrival Educations programmes running workshops and becoming coaches to the students.

Entrepreneurship: Bromley by Bow Centre

The Bromley by Bow Centre works to promote economic regeneration in Tower Hamlets and, since 2008, has been a partner of Investec. Through the partnership, the Beyond Business programme is delivered and helps to support local people who want to set up their own social enterprise, providing successful applicants with funding and skills support. Volunteers from Investec sit on the selection panel and offer advice to shortlisted applicants. Each year, Investec also runs the Beyond Business College, providing specialist skills and expertise to entrepreneurs who have benefitted through the programme.

Project grants

As well as supporting its charity partners, Investec also provides grants (normally up to £6,000) to small and medium-sized charities that work in its focus areas – education, entrepreneurship and the environment.

The charity's grant guidelines state the following:

> **Criteria for charities we can support:**
>
> - Your charity's activities must fall within at least one of our broad focus areas. That is, education (beyond awareness of the charitable cause), entrepreneurship; and the environment
> - The charity must be UK-registered, and established for at least 12 months
> - It should not be politically affiliated or religious.
>
> We give preference to:
>
> - project funding, rather than requests for core funding
> - charities that are situated in and/or projects targeting communities close to one of Investec's offices
> - projects presented by small to medium sized charities (<£3m annual turnover)

Employee-led support

Employee fundraising

In 2017/18, £157,000 was raised by staff including funds raised at Investec sponsored events.

Payroll giving

In 2017/18 staff donated £544,000 to charity through payroll giving.

Applications

Project grants

Apply in writing to the correspondent including a completed summary sheet. Summary sheets which also contain details of what should be included in the application can be downloaded from the 'Our Communities' section of the company's website. Applications are reviewed in March and September and proposals should be received three weeks in advance.

Other support

Contact the correspondent for further information.

Community contributions

Total contributions (cash and in kind)	£7,200,000

The sustainability report 2018 states that 'CSI' (corporate social investment) spend across the group amounted to £7.2 million, of which £1.7 million was spent in the 'UK and other' and the remaining £5.5 million in Southern Africa. This spend equates to 1% of operating profit before tax.

We have taken the figure for 'UK and other' as our total for UK contributions. Although Investec also has operations in Ireland and Australia, we believe the vast majority of this CSI expenditure benefitted the UK. We believe the £1.7 million (of which £1.1 million was given at a group level) to include both cash donations and in-kind contributions. A breakdown of 'UK and other CSI spend' by percentage according to category was provided in the report:

Education	37%
Philanthropic and other	27%
Entrepreneurship	22%
Environment	13%

Isles of Scilly Steamship Company Ltd

Children and young people, education, the environment

Company registration number: 165746

Correspondent: The Community Fund Committee, Steamship House, Quay Street, Penzance TR18 4BZ (tel: 01736 334220; email: communityfund@issg.co.uk; website: www.islesofscilly-travel.co.uk)

Directors: Andrew May; Diccon Rogers; Gary Randall; Peter Hardaker; Sam Hicks; Stuart Reid (female 0%; male 100%).

Nature of business: The Isles of Scilly Steamship Company operates the principal shipping service from Penzance to the Isles of Scilly.

Year end	31/03/2018
Turnover	£17,450,000
Pre-tax profit	(£151,000)

Main locations: The company's head office is in Penzance. The Community Fund gives in the West Cornwall and Isles of Scilly region.

Community involvement

The company makes grants to organisations in West Cornwall and the Isles of Scilly through its Community Fund. Complimentary tickets are also provided to local good causes.

Isles of Scilly Steamship Group Community Fund (not a registered charity)

The fund provides around £30,000 per year for community projects in West Cornwall and the Isles of Scilly. Organisations and individuals can apply for grants of £500 to £3,000 per project and there are three application rounds per year. Projects are supported in the following categories:

- Education (all ages)
- Local projects and skills
- Young people
- Protection for the local environment
- Specific community projects

Applications for projects outside these areas can be considered by the committee if sufficient community or legacy benefits can be identified.

In-kind support

The company provides complimentary tickets for raffles, events, community groups and other good causes. It typically gives away £32,500 of tickets each year. It also provides free containers luggage containers and some free adult travel for school trips.

Exclusions

The fund's guidelines state:

> Grants will not be available for any large organisations such as:
> - Commercial organisations
> - Isles of Scilly Council, Cornwall Council or the Duchy of Cornwall
> - Projects that only benefit one individual
> - Projects that have already reached their conclusion regardless of their payment status
> - Projects that promote a specific religious, social or political positioning
> - Sponsorships or general fundraising that does not have a specific target or denied end result

Applications

Applications can be made via the fund's website. Alternatively, application forms can be downloaded from the company's website or collected from travel centres in Hugh Town or Penzance. The dates of committee meetings are shown on the company's website.

Community contributions

We were unable to determine the company's charitable contributions for the year. However, the company's 2017/18 Giving Back report states that the Community Fund usually gives around £30,000 per year.

Beneficiaries included: NCI Cape Cornwall (£3,000); Scilly Brownies and Guides (£1,500).

ITV plc

Disaster relief, health

Company registration number: 4967001

Correspondent: Corporate Responsiby Governance Board, ITV Responsibility, 11th Floor, The London Television Centre, Upper Ground, London SE1 9LT (email: responsibility@itv.com; website: itvresponsibility.com)

Directors: Anna Manz; Dame Carolyn McCall; Duncan Painter; Helen Tautz; Ian Griffiths; Margaret Ewing; Mary Harris; Roger Faxon; Salman Amin; Sir Peter Bazalgette (female 50%; male 50%).

Nature of business: ITV is an independent television company.

Year end	31/12/2017
Turnover	£3,132,000,000
Pre-tax profit	£800,000,000

Total employees: 6,390

Main locations: ITV have offices in Leeds, London and Salford.

Community involvement

ITV looks to make a positive social contribution by working in partnership with a range of organisations, charities, NGOs and government. The group has a dedicated 'Responsibility' website which explains that this approach allows it 'to deliver programmes and initiatives to empower our viewers and employees to make a positive difference, at regional, national and international scale'. The principal way in which ITV supports its partners is by contributing airtime for appeals and campaigns. Employees are also supported to take an active role in their local communities through paid volunteering time and pro bono work, and ITV viewers also contribute through fundraising appeals such as 'Text Santa'.

From 2017, ITV's on screen Cause Strategy is focusing on health and well-being by encouraging people to make a difference to their own or other people's health.

In-kind support

Employee time

Employees are able to take one day's paid leave per year for volunteering purposes. During 2017 staff contributed 10,880 hours, valued at £700,000.

Pro bono

ITV employees contribute their skills and expertise to benefit good causes. The company's legal team has provided pro bono legal support to the Body and Soul clinic for a number of years.

Airtime

ITV uses its position as an established commercial TV network to provide charitable causes with airtime. The Corporate Responsibility Summary Report explains: 'In 2017, we ran 10 campaigns onscreen, dedicating over 41 hours of airtime to charities and causes important to our viewers.'

Employee-led support

Employees take part in a range of volunteering activities. In previous years staff have worked in call centres on appeals such as Text Santa. Employees also take part in fundraising activities and in 2017 raised £51,500.

Applications

Organisations that are interested with partnering with ITV, should read the ITV Charities and Causes Policy guidelines. The guidelines are available to download from the ITV Responsibility website, where a link to the online application form can also be found.

Community contributions

Cash donations UK	£2,000,000
In-kind support UK	£28,800,000
Total contributions (cash and in kind)	£30,800,000

According to the ITV Corporate Responsibility Summary Report 2017, during the year charitable contributions totalled £30.8 million. Contributions were broken down as follows:

In-kind	£28.1 million
Cash	£2 million
Time	£705,500

The ITV website states:

> In-kind contributions include donations of ITV's product, services or resources e.g. commercial airtime, marketing airtime, meeting rooms. Cash contributions are donations to charities including celebrity prize money, auction prizes, merchandise sales and external promotional spend for campaigns and appeals.

Ivy Holdco Ltd (Gatwick Airport Ltd)

Children and young people, older people, enterprise and training

Company registration number: 7497036

Correspondent: CSR Team, 6th floor, Destinations Place, South Terminal, Gatwick Airport, West Sussex RH6 0NP (email: community@gatwickairport.com; website: www.gatwickairport.com/business-community/community-sustainability/local-community)

Directors: Andrew Gillespie; John McCarthy; Michael McGhee; William Woodburn (female 0%; male 100%).

Nature of business: Ivy Holdco Ltd is the ultimate parent company of Gatwick Airport.

Year end	31/03/2018
Turnover	£764,200,000
Pre-tax profit	£233,700,000

UK employees: 3,078

Main locations: The airport is near Crawley in West Sussex.

Community involvement

Support is mainly provided through The Gatwick Foundation Fund and the Gatwick Airport Community Trust (Charity Commission no. 1089683). The company also provides sponsorship and has several education programmes.

The Gatwick Foundation Fund (not a registered charity)

The fund distributes £300,000 per year in three grant rounds to projects in Kent, Surrey and Sussex. Support is focused on four main areas: employment, training and skills; families; widening horizons (projects which provide young people with opportunities); and older people.

Charity partners

The company has three charity partners which it works with on a longer term basis. These are St Catherine's Hospice, Kent, Surrey and Sussex Air Ambulance and Gatwick TravelCare Charity.

Education programmes

The company's Inform, Inspire, Invest programme helps young people develop job skills and has an emphasis on STEM subjects. Its Learn Live programme is broadcast live from the airport to classrooms and was viewed by over 20,000 students during the year.

Employee-led support

Employees fundraise for the company's charity partners.

Commercially led support

The company's 2017/18 annual report states:

> Gatwick has also supported a wide range of local and regional events throughout the year, including the Horley Carnival; Crawley High Street Live; South and South East in Bloom; Brighton Pride; the Brighton Marathon; as well as a range of business and economic programmes and events.

Applications

Sponsorship and partnerships

Contact the correspondent for further information.

The Gatwick Foundation Fund

Grants are distributed by Kent, Surrey and Sussex Community Foundations. Further information can be found on their websites.

Corporate charity

Gatwick Airport Community Trust (Charity Commission no. 1089683) – see page 250.

Community contributions

Cash donations UK	£512,000

In 2017/18 the company donated £300,000 through the Gatwick Community Fund and a further £212,000 to Gatwick Airport Community Trust.

William Jackson Food Group Ltd

Health, education, global food insecurity

Company registration number: 3974470

Correspondent: Community Giving Team, The Riverside Building, Livingstone Road, Hessle HU13 0DZ (tel: 01482 224939; email: info@wjfg.co.uk; website: www.wjfg.co.uk)

Directors: Adam Barraclough; Chris Gort; Gary Urmston; John Donovan; Katie Denyer; Nicholas Oughtred; Norman Soutar (female 14%; male 86%).

Nature of business: William Jackson Food Group is a food manufacturer.

Year end	29/04/2017
Turnover	£8,652,000
Pre-tax profit	£22,732,000

UK employees: 36

Main locations: The group operates across the UK. Its headquarters are in Hessle in Yorkshire.

Community involvement

The group supports charities which encourage health, well-being and education through cash donations, and employee volunteering and fundraising. The group also runs a community farming project in Malawi, which aims to reduce extreme poverty and food insecurity through permaculture. Twice a year company employees visit the project to volunteer. By 2020, the group aims to have worked with a total of 1,000 smallholder farmers.

WJFG Community Giving Programme

The group's community giving programme supports charities which encourage health, well-being and education. The programme is administered by the group's Community Giving Team. For details of projects recently supported, see the group's website.

Previous beneficiaries have included: Cash 4 Kids; Cat Zero; Mires Beck; The Freedom Festival and The Outward Bound Trust.

In-kind support

Employees can take one day's paid leave each year to support community projects local to where they work.

Employee-led support

Employees are encouraged to fundraise and volunteer for the group's charity partners.

Applications

Apply in writing to the correspondent.

Community contributions

The group's 2016/17 accounts did not give a figure for its overall community contributions.

Jaguar Land Rover Ltd

Community development, disability, education (particularly STEM subjects), enterprise and training, health, poverty and social exclusion, projects outside the UK

Company registration number: 1672070

Correspondent: See 'Applications', Abbey Road, Whitley, Coventry CV3 4LF (website: www.jaguar.co.uk/about-jaguar/responsibility/index.html)

Directors: Andrew Robb; Nasser Munjee; Natarajan Chandrasekaran; P. B. Balaji; Prof. Dr Ralf Speth (female 0%; male 100%).

Nature of business: Jaguar design, develop, manufacture and market high performance luxury saloons, specialist sports cars, four wheel drive off-road vehicles and related components.

The immediate parent undertaking is TML Holdings Pte. Ltd. (Singapore) and ultimate parent undertaking and controlling party is Tata Motors Ltd, India.

Year end	31/03/2018
Turnover	£25,786,000,000
Pre-tax profit	£1,536,000,000

Total employees: 34,533

Main locations: The group operates worldwide, but its headquarters and most of its employees are based in the UK, across eight sites – in West Midlands (Castle Bromwich; Coventry; Gaydon; Solihull; Wolverhampton; Warwick; Whitley) and in Liverpool.

Community involvement

The group's global CSR programme focuses on the following three areas:

- Education and talent – inspire the workforce of the future
- Design and technology – apply technological innovation for social good
- Wellbeing and health – support disadvantaged communities

The group supports a number of partner charities, through funding, fundraising and in-kind donations. Employees provide volunteer and pro bono support. The group's operating sites may also offer support to local charities and communities.

Partner charities

The group supports the charities International Federation of Red Cross and Red Crescent Societies (IFRC) and the Born Free Foundation.

The group also has a long-standing relationship with BEN, the automotive industry's benevolent fund. The group supports and organises fundraising initiatives in partnership with other car manufacturers and provides volunteer support.

The group also supports NSPCC, leading the Coventry NSPCC Business Group.

Local community support

Individual operating sites also support charities in their local areas, mainly focusing on employee-led fundraising and supporting charities nominated by employees. Further details are provided on the group's website.

Education

The group is a partner of Premiership Rugby, delivering the HITZ programme, which provides a programme of rugby, skills development, and mentoring for disadvantaged young people, particularly those not in education, employment or training.

A central part of the company's CSR programme involves the development of the next generation of engineers. One of the ways in which it does this is through the 'Inspiring Tomorrow's Engineers' (IET) programme. In collaboration with schools and colleges, the programme promotes 'learning and engagement on STEM subjects', with the aim of inspiring young people to take up careers in engineering or manufacturing.

In-kind support

In-kind support

The group provides in-kind support to charity partners – for example, it provides a fleet of Land Rover vehicles to the British Red Cross to help the charity's workers and volunteers to reach isolated or hard-to-reach areas in poor weather conditions. In the last year, more than 1.3 million people in the UK have visited a food bank. Through an employee volunteering initiative run from its manufacturing plant in Solihull, West Midlands, Jaguar Land Rover is working with social enterprise Gro-Organic to provide fresh food to people in need. As part of the initiative, employees took over a disused allotment plot close to the company's plant, completely transforming it to grow fruit and vegetables for people in need. The allotment is used by local schools and community groups, supporting education on sustainability, healthy eating and exercise.

Employee-led support

Employee volunteering

Employees are entitled to two days' paid volunteering leave a year on approved individual or team initiatives. In 2017/18, employees committed over 70,000 hours through the Volunteer Changemakers programme, supporting a diverse range of charity partners. 22% of these hours specifically supported the company's Technology for Good projects.

Commercially led support

Sponsorship

The group is the primary sponsor – or 'presenting partner' – of the Invictus Games.

Applications

Volunteer support

The website states that the group provides volunteering support for organisations, with a focus on education, young people or the environment, within a 30-mile radius of a Jaguar Land Rover facility. Requests from organisations meeting these criteria should be send to Dolores Evans, Community Relations Officer, at: devans31@jaguarlandrover.com or, for requests near the Halewood site in Liverpool, to Kate Birkenhead, CSR Communications Officer: kbirkenh@jaguarlandrover.com

Local charity support

The group's plants in the West Midlands and Liverpool can support charities in their local area – for further information, refer to the group's website: www.jaguarlandrover.com/gl/en/responsible-business/charity-fundraising.

Community contributions

The 2017/18 annual report did not state the group's total charitable contributions in the UK, however it did state that Jaguar Land Rover supported over 1.2 million people through its projects, volunteering hours and gifts in kind totalling over £10.5 million.

Jardine Lloyd Thompson Group plc

Education, health, disaster relief

Company registration number: 1679424

Correspondent: Group Charities Committee, The St Botolph Building, 138 Houndsditch, London EC3A 7AW (website: www.jlt.com/about-jlt/corporate-responsibility/social)

Directors: Adam Keswick; Andrew Didham; Annette Court; Charles Rozes; Dominic Burke; Geoffrey Howe; Lord Sasson; Lynne Peacock; Mark Brady; Nicholas Walsh; Richard Meddings (female 9%; male 91%).

Nature of business: Jardine Lloyd Thompson (JLT) is a provider of insurance, reinsurance and employee benefits-related advice, brokerage and associated services. It has offices in more than 40 countries and territories on six continents.

Year end	31/12/2017
Turnover	£1,386,000,000
Pre-tax profit	£191,500,000

Total employees: 10,000+

Main locations: JLT and its subsidiaries have offices in various locations across the UK. A helpful place to start is the 'Our locations' page on the website (www.jlt.com/our-locations/uk) which has links to the websites of JLT's principal UK businesses.

Community involvement

JLT aims to work with strategic charity partners in three areas that complement aspects of its business: sharing the social benefits of specialist knowledge (education); building resilience (disaster preparation); and well-being (healthcare).

According to the group's corporate responsibility report for 2017 (included in the annual report), the majority of its charitable giving is conducted on a 'business-by-business' basis, although the Group Charities Committee also manages a central budget, from which funding is allocated in support of strategic partners. A proportion of this budget is set aside to allow for matched funding of employees' fundraising efforts. JLT employees are encouraged to contribute to their communities in a number of ways, including through volunteering time and a payroll giving facility.

Charity partnerships

JLT partners with a charity for each of its strategic themes. Currently the company is partnered with Udaan Foundation (knowledge), Alzheimer's Society (well-being) and RedR (resilience).

In-kind support

The 2017 annual report states: 'We are sometimes able to offer our specialist expertise 'Pro Bono' for good causes, which we are pleased to do whenever our expert advisers can spare some capacity.' JLT staff are also entitled to take one day's paid leave per year to volunteer.

Employee-led support

Staff volunteer for a wide range of causes including partner charities. The company also engages its clients in fundraising events. All money raised is matched by the company.

Commercially led support

The community section of the website explains that a number of JLT businesses, including in Ireland and Australia, have developed 'specialised products that give lower-cost access to the benefits of risk management solutions to charities and volunteer/community groups, helping to keep community and volunteering sustainable in a risk-averse climate'.

Applications

Contact your local JLT office for further information.

Community contributions

Cash donations worldwide	£731,500

According to the annual report for 2017, during the year JLT contributed £731,500 to charitable causes, which we have taken to represent cash donations.

We were unable to determine how much of this was given in the UK.

Jewson Ltd

General charitable purposes

Company registration number: 348407

Correspondent: CSR Team, Saint-Gobain House, Binley Business Park, Coventry CV3 2TT (tel: 0800 197 8102; email: buildingbettercommunities@jewson.co.uk; website: www.buildingbettercommunities.co.uk)

Directors: Alun Oxenham; Kare Malo; Michael Chaldecott; Michael Newham; Nicholas Cammack (female 0%; male 100%).

Nature of business: Jewson is a builders' merchants.

Year end	31/12/2017
Turnover	£1,906,237,000
Pre-tax profit	£24,127,000

UK employees: 9,148

Main locations: Jewson has over 600 branches throughout the UK.

Community involvement

Jewson supports local projects through its Building Better Communities awards.

In-kind support

Building Better Communities

Jewson awards £250,000 of building materials to community projects and tradespeople who are in need or need materials for a community project they are working on.

Exclusions

Party political activities and activities that are a statutory obligation are not eligible. Religious organisations can apply but religious activities will not be funded. Employees of Jewson's parent company, Saint-Gobain, cannot apply.

Applications

Applications can be made via the Building Better Communities website. Projects are shortlisted based on the number of people it will help, how many people it will continue to help in the future and how detailed the entry is. Winners are chosen based on a combination of a judges' vote and a public vote.

Community contributions

In-kind support UK	£250,000

According to the Building Better Communities website, Jewson awarded £250,000 of building materials through the scheme in 2017. Examples of successful projects can be found on Jewson's website.

John Lewis Partnership plc

The environment, STEM subjects, general charitable purposes, projects outside the UK

Company registration number: 233462

Correspondent: CSR Team, 171 Victoria Street, London SW1E 5NN (email: Contact form on website; website: www.johnlewispartnership.co.uk/csr.html)

Directors: Andrew Mayfield; Berangere Michel; Patrick Lewis; Tracey Killen (female 25%; male 75%).

Nature of business: The company trades under the name of John Lewis (full line department stores and smaller 'at home' stores) and Waitrose (food shops, including supermarkets and convenience stores). The partnership is a retail business run on co-operative principles.

Year end	31/01/2018
Turnover	£10,200,000,000
Pre-tax profit	£289,000,000

Total employees: 85,500

Main locations: John Lewis and Waitrose have stores throughout the UK.

Community involvement

The partnership provides support through its volunteering scheme, in-kind donations of food and donations to charities via its foundations and Community Matters scheme.

The John Lewis Foundation (Charity Commission no. 1118162)

The John Lewis Foundation is designed to benefit the communities in the UK and overseas in which those who produce products for the partnership live and work. The foundation makes grants for projects that are focused on improving the local environment, employability and social inclusion. The trustees prioritise that support disadvantaged communities to gain skills for employment.

The John Spedan Lewis Foundation (Charity Commission no. 240473)

The foundation makes charitable contributions which reflect the interests of John Spedan Lewis, notably entomology, ornithology, horticulture and associated environmental and conservation projects.

Duchy Originals

In 2016/17 a total of £3.2 million was donated to the company's ultimate controlling party, The Prince of Wales's Charitable Foundation which trades as The Prince of Wales's Charitable Fund. The fund's main areas of interest are the built environment, responsible business and enterprise, young people and education, and global sustainability. Grants of up to £5,000 are awarded through its small grants programme.

In-kind support

In-kind donations of food to charities totalled £2.1 million.

The Golden Jubilee Trust (Charity Commission no. 1079195)

The Golden Jubilee Trust is the partnership's flagship volunteering programme. Partners are given the opportunity to volunteer full or part-time with a UK-registered charity for up to six months, on full pay. In 2017/18 over 21,000 hours were awarded to 40 charities.

Employee-led support

Partners have the opportunity to volunteer with charities through the Golden Jubilee Trust.

Commercially led support

In 2017/18 the partnership made a donation of £600,000 to The John Lewis Foundation received from carrier bag sales.

Community Matters

The Community Matters programme distributes money received from the carrier bag charge to good causes. Customers of Waitrose and John Lewis can vote for local charities in their local branches. National charities are also supported via online votes. In 2017/18 £3.9 million was donated to charities through Waitrose Community Matters and £500,000 through John Lewis Community Matters.

Applications

John Lewis Community Matters

Nomination forms can be downloaded from: www.johnlewis.com/our-services/helping-our-community.

Enquiries about charitable donations can also be made to the Community Liaison Co-ordinator at your local John Lewis branch.

Waitrose Community Matters

Nomination forms can be downloaded from: www.waitrose.com/content/waitrose/en/home/inspiration/community_matters.html.

Enquiries about charitable donations can also be made to the Community Liaison Co-ordinator at your local Waitrose branch.

The John Spedan Lewis Foundation

Further information can be found at: johnspedanlewisfoundation.wordpress.com.

Golden Jubilee Trust
For further information contact the Trust Manager at: Golden_Jubilee_Trust_ Enquiries@ johnlewis.co.uk. A brochure on the trust can also be downloaded from the corporate responsibility section of the John Lewis website.

The John Lewis Foundation
Application forms and guidance packs can be found on the foundation's website at: www.johnlewisfoundation.org.

The Prince of Wales's Charitable Fund
Applications can be made through the fund's website at: www.pwcf.org.uk/ apply-for-a-grant.

Community contributions

In-kind support UK	£2,100,000

In 2017/18 in-kind donations of food donated to charities totalled £2.1 million. We were unable to determine the partnership's cash donations.

S. C. Johnson Ltd

General charitable purposes

Company registration number: 4166155

Correspondent: CSR Team, Frimley Green, Camberley, Surrey GU16 7AJ (tel: 01276 852000; website: www.scjohnson.co.uk)

Directors: John Hayes; Luciana Abreu; Thomas Howard (female 33%; male 67%).

Nature of business: The company manufactures and markets waxes, polishes, air fresheners and cleaning products for the consumer and industrial markets.

Year end	30/06/2017
Turnover	£130,775,000
Pre-tax profit	£5,333,000

UK employees: 40

Main locations: The company's head office is in Frimley Green, Surrey.

Community involvement

In previous years the company has channelled its charitable support through its corporate foundation, The Johnson Wax Charitable Trust. According to the Charity Commission, the trust was removed from the Register on 18 August 2017. During the year, the trustees of the trust has awarded grants to UK-based charities such as The Prince's Trust and Age UK.

Employee-led support

Employees take part in various fundraising activities for charities in the UK.

Commercially led support

As part of its partnership with Age UK in 2016, Glade donated a proportion of its sales of certain Christmas products to the charity. Employees also fundraised for the charity and these two activities raised over £130,000.

Applications

Contact the correspondent for further information.

Community contributions

Cash donations UK	£419,000

In 2016/17 the company donated a total of £419,000 to the Johnson Wax Charitable Trust.

Previous beneficiaries have included: Abbots Hospital; Cancer Research UK; Johnson Wax Charitable Trust; Multiple Sclerosis; Surrey Heath Arts Council; Tongham Community Hall.

Johnson Matthey plc

Education (particularly STEM subjects), health, the environment, disaster relief,

Company registration number: 33774

Correspondent: Sustainability Department (Community and Charity), 5th Floor, 25 Farringdon Street, London EC4A 4AB (email: group.charity@ matthey.com; website: matthey.com/ sustainability/community)

Directors: Alan Ferguson; Anna Manz; Chris Mottershead; Jane Griffiths; John O'Higgins; John Walker; Odile Desforges; Patrick Thomas; Robert MacLeod; Simon Farrant (female 30%; male 70%).

Nature of business: Johnson Matthey is a speciality chemicals and sustainable technologies company that focuses on its core skills in catalysis, precious metals, fine chemicals and process technology.

Year end	31/03/2018
Turnover	£14,122,000,000
Pre-tax profit	£320,000,000

Total employees: 12,715

Main locations: In the UK the group has sites in: Annan, Billingham, Brimsdown, Cambridge, Clitheroe, Edinburgh, London, Reading, Royston, Stockton-on-Tees and Swindon.

Community involvement

Johnson Matthey looks to make a positive contribution in the areas in which it operates through charitable donations, the promotion of STEM education and employee volunteering and fundraising.

Charity of the Year
The group's partnership with Plan International ended in July 2018. At the time of writing (September 2018) its website stated: 'We shall continue to support Plan International UK and the important work they do. And before we partner again, we're developing our community investment strategy to align more closely to our business framework and goals.'

One-off donations
The group's website states:

> JM donates money each year on a one-off basis to charities or organisations that fall within our key giving themes; these are:
> - Science, technology, engineering and maths (STEM) education
> - Enhancing health and nutrition
> - Education of disadvantaged people
> - Environmental protection and repair
> - Development of local communities
> - Disaster and emergency relief

In-kind support

All employees are able to take two days annual leave for volunteering purposes.

Employee-led support

Employee volunteering
The group has a policy which entitles all permanent employees to two days' paid leave per year to support charities and projects in their local communities. During the year, employees took 678 paid volunteering days. The 2017/18 annual accounts state: '53% of volunteers' time was spent supporting STEM education in local schools, 14% was spent working on local community development and 12% on contributing to the education of disadvantaged people.'

Payroll giving
The group operates a payroll giving scheme.

Matched funding
Employees' fundraising efforts for the Johnson Matthey Charity of the Year or other registered charities of their choice, may be matched with central group funds up to £1,000 per individual employee per year. Matched funding is capped at £70,000 per year across the group as a whole. During the year employees raised £38,000 which was matched by the group.

Applications

Contact the correspondent for further information.

Community contributions

Cash donations worldwide	£680,000
In-kind support worldwide	£150,000
Total contributions (cash and in kind)	£830,000

In 2017/18 the group donated £830,000 worldwide, broken down as follows:

Donations by sites to local charities	£380,000
Other corporate donations	£272,000
Employee volunteering	£150,000
Donations to Plan International	£28,000

The 2017/18 annual report states 'The major elements of our spend were on STEM education and on health and nutrition.'

Jones Lang LaSalle Ltd

Community development, education, enterprise and training, equal opportunities, housing and homelessness

Company registration number: 1188567

Correspondent: Gemma Piggott, Community & Sustainability Manager, 30 Warwick Street, London W1B 5NH (tel: 020 7493 4933; email: BuildingAbetterTomorrow@eu.jll.com; website: jll.co.uk/ buildingabettertomorrow)

Directors: Alasdair Humphrey; Andrew Renshaw; Christopher Ireland; Christopher Macfarlane; James Gregory; Maria Grigorova; Richard Batten; Richard Howling; Thomas Smith (female 11%; male 89%).

Nature of business: Jones Lang LaSalle is a professional services and investment management company specializing in real estate. The company's immediate parent company is Jones Lang LaSalle Europe Ltd. The ultimate parent company is Jones Lang LaSalle Incorporated, a company incorporated in the USA.

Year end	31/12/2017
Turnover	£404,305,000
Pre-tax profit	£54,639,000

UK employees: 2,853

Total employees: 82,000

Main locations: The company has nearly 300 offices across 80 countries, including 28 offices in the UK.

Community involvement

The company works in partnership with a variety of organisations to help address issues related to urban regeneration, housing and homelessness, access to the property profession, and education and skills. Support is provided through pro bono advice and services, cash donations, employee volunteering and fundraising.

Partnerships

The company has an ongoing partnership with the national homeless charity Crisis, for which it fundraises and offers advice and volunteer support. Recent examples of the company's support includes, participating on grant panels to review business plans, helping with preparation for Christmas activities and assisting in sessions on maths, English language and employability. During the year, the company raised £274,500 for Crisis and provided pro bono services worth a total of £15,000. Previous charity partners have included Starlight Children's Foundation, Samaritans and the Alzheimer's Society.

According to its website, the company is also an active supporter of the following organisations: LandAid, Business in the Community, Ready for Work, Urban Land Institute, Enabling Enterprise.

JLL UK Foundation (Charity Commission no. 1170388)

In 2016 the company registered a new corporate charity, the JLL UK Foundation, with the Charity Commission. The charity's objects are to promote access to the property profession for people from underprivileged or challenging backgrounds. According to the foundation's Charity Commission record, this will be achieved by awarding scholarships and maintenance grants to individuals. The foundation also intends to provide support for charities, schools and universities.

At the time of writing (October 2018), the foundation was yet to submit its first set of accounts to the Charity Commission.

In-kind support

As part of its partnership with Crisis, JLL has developed a bespoke toolkit to help the charity identify potential retail markets and has provided advice on rental values and incentives.

Employee-led support

JLL hosts a number of annual sporting events to raise money for charity. Over the past few years, proceeds have gone to the company's national charity partners.

The company allows its employee to volunteer for charities during work time, and in 2017 employees volunteered for a total of 2,854 hours.

The company also has a payroll giving scheme, through which employees donated £56,500 in 2017.

Applications

Contact the correspondent for more information.

Community contributions

Cash donations UK	£840,000
In-kind support UK	£234,000
Total contributions (cash and in kind)	£1,074,000

The company's 2017 sustainability report states that in 2017 the company made cash donations of £840,000 including a significant donation to fund the creation of the JLL UK Foundation. The company also contributed £154,000 in staff time and £80,000 in pro bono services.

Kier Group plc

Enterprise and training

Company registration number: 2708030

Correspondent: Rebecca Staden, Foundation Manager, Tempsford Hall, Sandy, Bedfordshire SG19 2BD (email: Rebecca.Staden@kier.co.uk; website: www.kier.co.uk/corporate-responsibility/ the-kier-foundation.aspx)

Directors: Adam Walker; Bev Dew; Claudio Veritiero; Constance Baroudel; Haydn Mursell; Hugh Raven; Justin Atkinson; Kirsty Bashforth; Nick Winser; Philip Cox (female 20%; male 80%).

Nature of business: Kier is a building, civil engineering, opencast mining, facilities management, residential and commercial property investment and PFI project investment company. The group operates in England, Wales and Scotland, and also has locations in the Middle East, Asia and Australasia.

Year end	30/06/2017
Turnover	£4,100,000,000
Pre-tax profit	£126,100,000

Total employees: 16,233

Main locations: Kier Group has a presence across England, Scotland and Wales. For a map of specific locations see the website (www.kier.co.uk/get-in-touch/our-locations.aspx#/mapview).

Community involvement

Kier Group looks to contribute to communities in the areas where the group has a presence. Community contributions are principally made in the form of staff time.

The Kier Foundation (Charity Commission no. 1144803)

This independent foundation was established in 2012 to support Kier's charity partner and support causes close to the hearts of employees.

The foundation works to organise fundraising activities in support of Kier Group's corporate charity partner, which is chosen with the help of employees every two years. It also provides funding to assist with employees' fundraising activities, and supports Kier's local community engagement with donations of up to £5,000.

The foundation's regular source of income comes from an employee-only lottery – the Kier Winners' Club. Lottery members pay the equivalent of £1 per week and income is divided equally between charitable donations and employee prize money. The lottery raised £76,000 for the foundation during 2015/16.

The largest source of income for the foundation is the '£10k Board Challenge' through which each regional board of directors is challenged to raise £10,000 over the course of the year.

Corporate charity partner

Every two years Kier chooses a new charity partner from a list of charities employees have supported during the previous year. The British Heart Foundation was chosen as the group's partner charity for two years from July 2018.

Employee-led support

Employee fundraising

Employees take part in a wide range of fundraising activities for The Kier Foundation's charity partner. In 2017 over £200,000 was raised for the Alzheimer's Society.

Employee volunteering

The Corporate Responsibility Report 2017 notes that over 13,800 hours were given to support community projects in the Northern Powerhouse.

Matched funding

Employees are able to apply to the Kier Foundation for up to £200 twice a year to help support their own fundraising activities. The foundation will also match funds of up to £5,000.

Applications

The group's charity partner is chosen from a list of charities supported by employees over the previous year.

Community contributions

Cash donations UK	£689,000
In-kind support UK	£4,400,000
Total contributions (cash and in kind)	£5,100,000

According to the group's 2017 corporate responsibility report, Kier Group expended £5.1 million on community contributions, which were broken down as follows:

Value of community, employment and skills hours	£4.4 million
Cash donated and spent	£689,000

Kingfisher plc

Community development, poverty and social exclusion

Company registration number: 1664812

Correspondent: CSR Team, 3 Sheldon Square, Paddington, London W2 6PX (email: sustainability@kingfisher.com; website: www.kingfisher.com/sustainability)

Directors: Anders Dahlvig; Andy Cosslett; Clare Chapman; Jeff Carr; Karen Witts; Mark Seligman; Pascal Cagni; Rakhi Goss-Custard; Véronique Laury (female 44%; male 56%).

Nature of business: Kingfisher is a home improvement retail group with stores located in ten European countries. Kingfisher companies in the UK are B&Q and Screwfix.

Year end	31/01/2018
Turnover	£11,655,000,000
Pre-tax profit	£797,000,000

Total employees: 63,249

Main locations: Kingfisher is headquartered in London. See the Kingfisher website for a group directory. There are store finder searches on both the B&Q and Screwfix websites.

Community involvement

Kingfisher looks to make a positive impact in the communities in which it has a presence and in society more generally. Support is given in the form of in-kind contributions, cash contributions and employee time. Employees from across the group are actively involved in supporting local charities through volunteering, payroll giving and fundraising, which is supported by matched funding. Customers also contribute through fundraising appeals. Kingfisher companies (B&Q and Screwfix in the UK) are responsible for their own community and charitable policies.

The Screwfix Foundation

The foundation was established in 2013 and supports projects that will fix, repair, maintain and improve properties and community facilities for those in need throughout the UK.

In-kind support

Kingfisher companies donate products in support of good causes. The company's Kingfisher Corporate Centre employees are able to take one paid day per year for volunteering purposes.

Employee-led support

Employees are able to donate to charities through payroll giving schemes.

Employee fundraising

Employees working across the Kingfisher group take part in various fundraising activities. In 2017/18 staff and customers raised £1.4 million.

Employee volunteering

In 2017/18 employees spent more than 7,000 hours volunteering in their local communities.

Exclusions

B&Q

The company's website states:

> Please note that B&Q cannot support initiatives relating to:
>
> - Political parties or causes
> - Religious organisations whose principle aim is to propagate a particular faith or belief
> - Personal appeals by, or on behalf of individuals

Applications

B&Q

Contact your local store directly.

Screwfix

Contact the correspondent for further information.

Community contributions

Cash donations worldwide	£1,500,000
In-kind support worldwide	£882,000
Total contributions (cash and in kind)	£2,382,000

According to the Sustainability Report 2017/18, during the year community contributions in the form of cash, gifts in kind and employee time were given totalling £2.38 million. The report provided the following breakdown:

Cash	£1.5 million
Gifts in kind	£579,000
Time	£303,000

In 2017/18 employees and customers raised a further £1.38 million for good causes although this is not included in the total of contributions for the year.

The report further explains:

> We gave a total of £2.4 million through our community investment in 2017/18, an increase on the previous year (2016/17: £1.8 million), equivalent to 0.3% of underlying pre-tax profits (2016/17: 0.23%). This includes cash donations, employee time and gifts in kind, with product donations valued at cost price. We have supported 1,841 community projects since 2012/13. An estimated 62,000 people benefited from our community projects during 2017/18.

KPMG LLP

Education, particularly STEM subjects

Company registration number: OC301540

Correspondent: Rachel Hopcroft, Head of Corporate Affairs, 15 Canada Square, London E14 5GL (tel: 020 7311 1000; email: Contact form on website; website: home.kpmg.com/uk/en/home/about/corporate-responsibility.html)

Directors: Bernard Brown; Bill Michael; Christine Hewson; David Matthews;

James Stewart; Jane McCormick; Maggie Brereton; Mark Raddan; Melanie Richards; Paul Korolkiewicz; Philip Davidson; Ronnie McCombe; Sarah Willows; Sue Bonney; Tony Cates (female 40%; male 60%).

Nature of business: KPMG provides professional services including audit, tax and advisory.

Year end	30/09/2017
Turnover	£2,172,000,000
Pre-tax profit	£301,000,000

UK employees: 13,969

Main locations: KPMG's headquarters are in London. It has 22 offices throughout the UK.

Community involvement

The company's CSR activities are focused on improving literacy and numeracy skills and helping to develop opportunities for disadvantaged people across the UK. According to the company's website, it does this in four main ways:

- **Education:** Working with educational organisations to develop the next generation of talent for the jobs of the future
- **Employment:** Working across industry to broaden access to the profession
- **Engagement:** Working with clients, suppliers, government and civil society organisations to generate systemic change on the issues that matter
- **Strategic philanthropy:** Supporting the hardest to reach young people through our fundraising, skills and expertise

Support is also given through The KPMG Foundation (Charity Commission no. 1086518), which supports disadvantaged children and young adults.

Schools

KPMG works with over 30 primary and 100 secondary schools nationally. Partner schools are selected using an algorithm which allows the company to direct its support to areas that are most in need. The company also runs several work placement and school leaver programmes.

Numeracy and literacy

The foundation's Every Child Counts programme provides specialist numeracy teachers to schools and has so far reached over 30,000 children. KPMG has also supported research into numeracy and is a founding supporter of National Numeracy Day.

KPMG has worked with the National Literacy Forum to develop the Vision for Literacy Business Pledge. The pledge challenges businesses to improve literacy within their workforces and communities. Staff also work directly with young people to develop literacy skills. In 2016/17 over 150 staff gave almost 1,000 hours in support of activities aimed at improving literacy in less advantaged communities.

In-kind support

KPMG's volunteering and pro bono policy allows staff to spend six days per year volunteering for charities that promote social mobility. Over 80% of KPMG's volunteering and pro bono work is now connected with social mobility.

Applications

Contact the correspondent for further information.

Corporate charity

The KPMG Foundation (Charity Commission no. 1086518) – see page 256.

Community contributions

The 2016/17 annual report states that community contributions (including cash, in-kind and time donations, and management costs) during the year totalled £4.1 million. It also states that the group supported a total of 1,053 organisations during the year.

Lancashire Holdings Ltd

Children and young people, poverty and social exclusion, projects outside the UK

Company registration number: 1477482

Correspondent: 29th Floor, 20 Fenchurch Street, London EC3M 3BY (website: www.lancashiregroup.com/en/responsibility.html)

Directors: Alex Maloney; Elaine Whelan; Michael Dawson; Peter Clarke; Robert Lusardi; Samantha Hoe-Richardson; Simon Fraser (female 29%; male 71%).

Nature of business: Lancashire is a global provider of specialty insurance products operating in Bermuda and London.

Year end	31/12/2017
Turnover	£459,658,000
Pre-tax profit	(£56,641,400)

Total employees: 204

Main locations: Lancashire's head office is in the City of London.

Community involvement

Lancashire Holdings supports communities in the UK, Bermuda and around the world through The Lancashire Foundation (Charity Commission no. 1149184).

Employee-led support

All staff are encouraged to take part with volunteering days. Examples of staff volunteering include carrying out maintenance at Vauxhall City Farm and transforming the roof garden of St Giles Trust. The Lancashire Foundation matches funds raised by employees.

Corporate charity

The Lancashire Foundation (Charity Commission no. 1149184) – see page 257.

Community contributions

Cash donations UK	£545,500

In June 2017 the company made a donation of \$702,500 (≈ £545,500 as at August 2018) to the foundation.

Land Securities Group plc

Education, enterprise and training, general charitable purposes

Company registration number: 4369054

Correspondent: Caroline Hill, Head of Sustainability and Public Affairs, 5 Strand, London WC2N 5AF (website: www.landsecurities.com/sustainability/jobs-opportunities/activities/charity)

Directors: Chris Bartram; Colette O'Shea; Cressida Hogg; Edward Bonham Carter; Martin Greenslade; Nicholas Cadbury; Robert Noel; Scott Parsons; Simon Palley; Stacey Rauch (female 30%; male 70%).

Nature of business: Land Securities is the largest UK property group, involved in both property development and investment, and property outsourcing.

Year end	31/03/2018
Turnover	£852,000,000
Pre-tax profit	(£251,000,000)

UK employees: 615

Main locations: Land Securities owns properties across the UK. Details of its London and retail portfolios can be seen on the website (www.landsecurities.com/retail-portfolio).

Community involvement

Local and national charity partners are supported with fundraising, volunteering and pro bono work. The company also runs education and employment programmes.

Community Employment Programme

Since 2011 the company's Community Employment Programme has secured employment for over 1,000 people from disadvantaged backgrounds.

Charity partnerships

The company partners with both local and national charities to help people from disadvantaged backgrounds into work, educate young people and tackle local issues. Retail destinations and larger sites work with at least one local partner as well as the national charity partner, Barnardo's.

Education

The company runs a number of education programmes. Its 2017 annual report states:

> Many young people, especially those from disadvantaged backgrounds, face barriers that stop them accessing jobs in our industry. Through our education programmes we:
> - Inspire young people about career opportunities in property and construction
> - Give young people the skills they need to succeed
> - Enable our employees and partners to volunteer their expertise

In-kind support

The company provides pro bono support to partner charities as well as opening up spaces for community use.

Employee-led support

Land Securities employees are involved in a range of volunteering and fundraising activities for partner charities. In 2017/18 employees spent 2,399 hours volunteering.

Applications

For further information, contact the local Land Securities shopping centre or office in your area.

Community contributions

Total contributions (cash and in kind)	£1,900,000

The 2017/18 annual report states that the equivalent of £1.9 million was given in 'time, promotion and cash investment'.

Leeds Building Society

Community development, poverty and social exclusion, general charitable purposes

Company registration number: FCA 164992

Correspondent: Luke Wellock, Corporate Responsibility Manager, 105 Albion Street, Leeds LS1 5AS (tel: 0345 050 5075; website: www.leedsbuildingsociety.co.uk/your-society/charity-and-community/hub)

Directors: Andrew Greenwood; David Fisher; Gareth Hoskin; John Hunt; Karen Wint; Les Platts; Peter Hill; Peter Hill; Philip Jenks; Philippa Brown; Richard Fearon; Robin Ashton; Robin Litten (female 23%; male 77%).

Nature of business: Leeds Building Society is the fifth largest building society in the UK.

Year end	31/12/2017
Turnover	£233,100,000
Pre-tax profit	£133,000,000

Main locations: The building society is headquartered in Leeds and has branches across the UK.

Community involvement

Leeds Building Society makes donations to registered charities in the areas near its branches, principally through Leeds Building Society Charitable Foundation (Charity Commission no. 1074429).

Charity partner

From 2017 Samaritans will be the building society's charity partner.

Parkrun Community Reward Scheme

UK park runners can apply for funding for project which will make a difference to parkrun communities.

In-kind support

All employees are encouraged to take up to seven hours' paid leave each year to volunteer in their local communities. During 2017 over 50% of employees volunteered 4,700 hours to 160 projects.

Employee-led support

Employees are supported in their fundraising efforts through the matched funding scheme. In 2017 charitable contributions from employees totalled £67,000.

Commercially led support

The Your Interest in Theirs scheme enables members to donate up to 99p of interest each year to good causes. Each year, Leeds Building Society will make a donation equivalent to 1% of the average balance held in all Caring Saver accounts to named charities of the society's choice. In 2017 the Caring Saver Account and the Your Interest In Theirs scheme provided further donations of £18,000 and £107,500 respectively to specified charities. From 2018 donations will be made to Samaritans.

Applications

Contact the correspondent for further information.

Parkrun Community Reward Scheme

Applications can be made via the Leeds Building Society's website.

Corporate charity

Leeds Building Society Charitable Foundation (Charity Commission no. 1074429) – see page 258.

Community contributions

Cash donations UK	£90,000

In 2017 the society made a donation of £90,000 to the Leeds Building Society Charitable Foundation.

Legal & General plc

Children and young people, education, enterprise and training, health, housing and homelessness

Company registration number: 1417162

Correspondent: Sara Heald, Head of Community Involvement, One Coleman Street, London EC2R 5AA (website: csr.legalandgeneralgroup.com/csr)

Directors: Carolyn Bradley; Julia Wilson; Lesley Knox; Mark Gregory; Mark Zinkula; Nigel Wilson; Philip Broadley; Richard Meddings; Rudy Markham; Stuart Popham (female 30%; male 70%).

Nature of business: The group's principal activities are: the provision of long-term insurance, investment management and general insurance.

Year end	31/12/2017
Turnover	£40,491,000,000
Pre-tax profit	£2,061,000,000

Main locations: Legal & General have offices in Barnsley, Birmingham, Bracknell, Bristol, Cardiff, Edinburgh, Hove and London.

Community involvement

Legal & General supports a number of national charities through its strategic partnerships programme. Employees support local charities through volunteering and payroll giving initiatives.

Partnerships

Information on the company's partnership policy is contained in a helpful document available to download from the Legal & General website, titled 'Groupwide donations for charities, social enterprise and not-for-profit organisations'.

According to the document, at a group level, Legal & General seeks to develop strategic relationships and partnerships through three group-wide campaigns:

- Dealing with ill health the need to understand health trends and innovation
- Income in later life the need to support the retired who are living longer and typically on fixed incomes
- Access to housing the need to create housing opportunities for all

Community and social investment

Examples of the group's community and social investment initiatives include:

- **Financial education – Every Day Money Programme**: Legal & General delivers this programme, which is facilitated by Development Garden, within schools with the aim of encouraging children to consider the financial knowledge they already have, where they got it from and to explore how they can make informed financial decisions once they have the correct information. The programme is run in partnership with EdComms and aims to educate schoolchildren in Sussex about future responsibilities around money
- **Social enterprises – SE Assist**: In conjunction with Charities Aid Foundation (CAF), Legal & General provides funding to social enterprises in Greater Brighton, Croydon and Wales in the form of interest-free loans and mentoring

In-kind support

Legal & General encourages employees to take time to volunteer during their working day. During 2017 employees spent 1,504 hours volunteering.

Employee-led support

Employees fundraise for a wide range of charitable causes and are supported in their efforts by the group's matched funding scheme. The group also has a time matching scheme, which allows employees to turn the time they spend volunteering into cash for their chosen charities.

Payroll giving

Employees are able to donate to registered charities through the Give As You Earn scheme.

Exclusions

According to the donations policy document, Legal & General does not support:

- organisations that are not recognised as charitable in nature by regulating organisations such as the UK Charity Commission, Charities Aid Foundation or the IRS in the US
- religious organisations, except where it can be proven that the project to be undertaken will benefit the community as a whole
- personal appeals on behalf of individual people, including overseas trips
- any organisation, which is in conflict with our Bribery and Corruption policy i.e. Political organisations – direct or indirect donations are not permitted
- donations through Financial Intermediaries such as Independent Financial Advisors, Business Partners or Journalists
- benevolent Charity Funds
- events that involve gambling
- support sponsorship requests from individuals including our own employees

Applications

Decisions on strategic partnerships are made by the Charity Committee. Employees in each location choose which charities to support.

Community contributions

Total contributions (cash and in kind)	£985,500

In 2017 Legal & General contributed at least £985,000 through charitable investments in the UK. Expenditure on campaign projects and volunteering was broken down into the following categories:

Health	£298,000
Communities	£190,500
Education – Every Day Money	£169,500
Income in retirement	£125,500
SE Assist – social enterprises	£115,000
Housing and communities	£55,500
Volunteering	£31,500

A further £501,000 was expended in group costs, including governance. As is our usual practice, we have not included this in our figure for community contributions.

Employee fundraising in the UK amounted to an additional £1.4 million, however we were not able to determine how much of this came directly from the group in matched funding.

Leicester City Football Club Ltd

Sports and recreation, community development, children and young people, disability, education, health and medical research, older people

Company registration number: 4593477

Correspondent: Allison Tripney, Community Director, King Power Stadium, Filbert Way, Leicester, Leicestershire LE2 7FL (tel: 0116 291 5223; email: trust@lcfc.co.uk; website: www.lcfc.com)

Directors: Aiyawatt Srivaddhanaprabha; Apichet Srivaddhanaprabha; Shilai Liu; Susan Whelan; Vichai Srivaddhanaprabha (female 40%; male 60%).

Nature of business: Leicester City FC is a professional football club competing in the Premier League.

Year end	31/05/2017
Turnover	£233,013,000
Pre-tax profit	£98,487,000

UK employees: 252

Main locations: The football club is based in Leicester.

Community involvement

Leicester City FC's charitable support is primarily channelled through its two charities, the LCFC Foxes Foundation Ltd (Charity Commission no. 1144791) and the Leicester City Community Trust (Charity Commission no. 1126526). Support is provided through an education and sports programmes, fundraising, and cash and in-kind donations.

LCFC Foxes Foundation Ltd

Each year, the LCFC Foxes Foundation raises funds and awards grants to a selected number of local charities. In 2016/17 the foundation awarded grants of £187,000.

Leicester City Community Trust

The Leicester City Community Trust delivers the club's community activities. The trust works in partnership with the Premier League, Leicestershire Police, and local charities and businesses to provide a broad range of programmes for children, young people and adults in the areas of education; health; social inclusion; and sports participation, with a focus on football projects. Recent examples of the trusts programmes include:

- **Football Memories:** This programme offers older Leicester City fans the opportunity to attend regular coffee morning events at the club's King Power Stadium in order to prevent dementia, depression and loneliness
- **Looked-after Children:** This programme provides mentoring, support and signposting services to improve the self-esteem, confidence and educational attainment of children in care
- **Man vs Fat:** A six-a-side football league aimed at adult men 30 to 65 years with a BMI above 27, which allows participants to benefit from peer-to-peer support and encourages them to adopt healthier lifestyles through regular physical activity

For full details of all of the club's current community programmes see the website.

In-kind support

The club donates Stadium Tour vouchers to non-registered charities, which the charities can auction or used as raffle prizes to help raise funds.

Applications

Contact the correspondent for more information.

Corporate charity

LCFC Foxes Foundation Ltd (Charity Commission no. 1144791) – see page 257.

Community contributions

Cash donations UK	£1,280,000

According to its 2016/17 accounts, during the year the club made charitable donations of £1.28 million. This included a £1 million donation to the University of Leicester to establish a professorial position in children's medicine. The club also provides free administrative, accounting, and management support and in-kind donations to its two corporate charities; however, the total value of these contributions was not quantified in the club's accounts.

Eli Lilly and Company Ltd

Education, health

Company registration number: 284385

Correspondent: Community Engagement Team, Lilly House, Priestley Road, Basingstoke RG24 9NL (tel: 01256 315000; website: www.lilly.co.uk/en/responsibility/partnerships/index.aspx)

Directors: Ashley Diaz-Granados; Hamish Bennett; Karen Alexander; Nicholas Lemen; Peter Troutt; Susan Forda; Christopher Lewis (female 43%; male 57%).

Nature of business: The principal activity of the company is the production and supply of pharmaceuticals and animal health products to other subsidiaries and third parties in the UK and other areas of the world. It is a wholly owned subsidiary of Eli Lilly and Company, its US parent company. The UK company manufactures, promotes and supplies products from the global product portfolio, performs significant research and development in the UK as part of the global programme and acts as a regional office for certain specific activities such as strategic management.

Year end	31/12/2017
Turnover	£964,256,000
Pre-tax profit	£38,118,000

UK employees: 2,500

Total employees: 40,000

Main locations: There are sites in Basingstoke, Surrey and Speke.

Community involvement

In the UK Lilly partners with patient advocacy groups and provides grants to local charities through its Grants and Donations Programme.

At the Elanco site based in Speke, Liverpool, there is also a community engagement programme which 'complements the animal health division's commitment to end hunger for 100,000 families or 600,000 individuals globally by 2025 through a partnership with Heifer International'.

Partnerships and grants

In the UK Lilly partners with patient advocacy groups and provides grants through its Grants and Donations Programme. Grants are made to charities and public bodies for projects which support health and education projects near Lilly sites in Basingstoke and Erl Wood in Surrey.

In-kind support

According to the 2017 Integrated Summary Report, in that year Lilly celebrated its 10th annual Lilly Global Day of Service, on which Lilly and Elanco employees help neighbours and communities around the world. Since the programme launched, employees in over 65 countries have given more than one million hours and completed thousands of projects – from assembling cancer–care packages for patients to beautifying neighbourhoods by planting thousands of trees.

It also states:

> Lilly sponsors at least 100 employees each year to volunteer in impoverished communities through Connecting Hearts Abroad. They serve as health volunteers on community projects across Africa, Asia, Europe and Latin America. Challenged and inspired, they return with unique stories and insights that help us become a better, more globally aware company.

Employee-led support

Lilly and United Way (a US not-for-profit organisation that 'advances the common good in communities across the world'), are celebrating a 100-year relationship dating back to 1918. In 2017 contributions from Lilly US employees and retirees, plus a matching gift from the Lilly Foundation, totalled \$13.1 million dollars (≈ £9.9 million as at October 2018).

According to the UK website:

> Working with FareShare, an organisation committed to fighting hunger and preventing food waste, the Speke site 'aims to dedicate 3,500 hours of employee time and make a financial contribution'. Employees volunteer at the local Speke FareShare depot every fortnight and partner with the YMCA's Homeless Hostels Food Alliance, which uses urban green spaces and local volunteers to develop a local food network to support people across the city.

Applications

Grant applications can be made online through the Lilly website. Questions regarding applications should be directed to the Grants and Donations Committee at: UKgrants@lilly.com.

For all other queries, contact the correspondent.

Community contributions

No figures published for company contributions in the UK in 2017.

Lincolnshire Co-operative Ltd

General charitable purposes

Company registration number: 141R

Correspondent: Community Team, Stanley Bett House, 15/23 Tentercroft Street, Lincoln LN5 7DB (tel: 01522 544632; email: community@lincolnshire.coop; website: www.lincolnshire.coop)

Directors: Claudia Nel; David Maltby; Jane Moate; Julia Romney; Margaret Tranter; Peter Gault; Revd Barbara Hutchinson; Steve Hughes; Stuart Parker; Sue Neal (female 75%; male 25%).

Nature of business: The co-operative's businesses include supermarkets, pharmacies, funeral directors, florists and post offices.

Year end	01/09/2018
Turnover	£302,866,000

UK employees: 2,832

Main locations: The co-operative's head office is in Lincoln and it has stores throughout Lincolnshire.

Community involvement

Support is provided to organisations in Lincolnshire through donations and educational programmes.

Charity of the Year

Each year the co-operative fundraises for a charity which is nominated through a staff opinion survey.

Community Champions

Community Champions are selected by local members' groups in each area. Each time a member shops using their dividend card, a donation is made to the nominated Community Champion in that area. The Community Champions change on a quarterly basis and charities and good causes can register on a central list to be considered.

Education

There a number of staff members who are qualified and experienced in delivering lessons and information sessions in local schools. The co-operative has also developed a range of resources for schools.

In-kind support

Local charities can request smaller donations of goods or raffle prizes by taking a written request to a local store. Each year around £10,000 is given in smaller donations. Employees also receive two days' paid volunteering leave.

Employee-led support

Staff volunteer on practical projects as well as offering professional support and expertise.

Applications

Contact the correspondent for further information on Community Champions or Charity of the Year. Requests for smaller donations should be made in writing to a local store.

Enquiries about educational resources can be made to the correspondent or via an enquiry form on the website.

Community contributions

Cash donations UK	£334,000

In 2017/18 donations to charities and community groups totalled £334,000.

The Liverpool Football Club and Athletic Grounds Ltd

Sports and recreation, community development, disability, education, enterprise and training, health, older people, safety and crime prevention

Company registration number: 35668

Correspondent: Liverpool FC Foundation, Liverpool FC Foundation, Anfield Road, Liverpool L4 0TH (tel: 0151 432 5689; email: lfcfoundation@liverpoolfc.com; website: www.liverpoolfc.com)

Directors: Andrew Hughes; John Henry; Kenneth Dalglish; Michael Egan; Michael Gordon; Peter Moore; Thomas Werner (female 0%; male 100%).

Nature of business: Liverpool FC is a professional football club competing in the Premier League.

Year end	31/05/2017
Turnover	£364,246,000
Pre-tax profit	£39,797,000

UK employees: 735

Main locations: The football club is based in Liverpool.

Community involvement

The club provides support through in-kind donations and through its charity, the Liverpool FC Foundation (Charity Commission no. 1096572), which delivers a wide range of health, education and sport programmes in the local community.

Liverpool FC Foundation

The club's charity delivers a wide range of community programmes in areas of high-deprivation and need across Liverpool. The foundation also work internationally, supporting the work of charity partners and the Premier League.

The foundation's programmes focus on three key areas: well-being, skills, and communities. Recent examples of the foundation's programmes include:

- **Holiday Camps:** the foundation hosts school holiday camps across Liverpool, encouraging young people to stay active outside term time in a safe and supportive environment
- **Open Goals:** a multi-sport and physical activity project designed to support families to be more active together
- **Move:** a specialist-coaching project for Cystic Fibrosis patients, which helps to encourage young CF patient's physical activity levels, to improve lung function and quality of life

In 2017 the foundation held a 'Legends Charity Match' which raised over £1 million. 200 tickets for the game were donated to the foundation's charity partner, Alder Hey Children's Charity, to enable patients and their families to attend the match.

Full details of all of the foundation's current programmes can be found on its website: foundation.liverpoolfc.com.

Partnerships

In addition to delivering its own programmes, the foundation also works in partnership with local charities and non-profit organisations such as Alder Hey Children's Charity, Liverpool University and the Liverpool School of Tropical Medicine to improve the life and health chances of children and young people.

In-kind support

Each year, the club awards in-kind donations such as signed photographs, tickets for stadium and museum tours and other official merchandise to charities for fundraising purposes.

Exclusions

The club does not provide cash donations or sponsorship.

Applications

Requests for in-kind support can be submitted using an online form on the club's website (foundation.liverpoolfc.com/contact-us).

Community contributions

No figure was given for the club's total charitable contributions. The 2016/17 accounts for the Liverpool FC Foundation state that the club covered operating costs of £253,000 through in-kind and support for the foundation during the year.

Liverpool Victoria

Children and young people, general charitable purposes, health

Company registration number: FCA 110035

Correspondent: Regional Community Committee, County Gates, Bournemouth, Dorset BH1 2NF (tel: 01202 292333; website: www.lv.com/about-us/lv-cares)

Directors: Alan Cook; Alison Hutchinson; Andy Parsons; Colin Ledlie; David Barral; David Neave; Luke Savage; Richard Rowney (female 12%; male 88%).

Nature of business: Liverpool Victoria (LV=) is an insurance company offering a range of products, investment and retirement solutions.

Year end	31/12/2017
Turnover	£1,855,000,000
Pre-tax profit	£122,000,000

UK employees: 5,800+

Main locations: Liverpool Victoria has offices in Birmingham, Bournemouth, Brentwood, Bristol, Cardiff, Croydon, Exeter, Hitchin, Huddersfield, Ipswich, Leeds, London, Maidstone and Manchester.

Community involvement

Liverpool Victoria supports charities and communities in the locations in which it has a presence through donations, community partnerships and by supporting its employees' fundraising and volunteering efforts.

The company gives charitable support in various ways. These include:

Regional Community Committees

The company has Regional Community Committees made up of employee volunteers that help decide how best the company should lend its support. The committees are located in each of the company's 16 offices and donated £175,000 during the year, supporting 228 charities.

Partnerships

AutoRaise: Liverpool Victoria is working with AutoRaise, the vehicle repair industry's charity, helping to attract the next generation of apprentices and raise the profile of the benefits that a career in the industry can bring.

Age UK's telephone befriending service: 60 employee volunteers took part in Age UK's telephone befriending service, helping those who are lonely and marginalised in society.

Member Community Fund

The company has a Member Community Fund that donates to member-nominated charities. Nominations are assessed by a small committee of members.

Member Support Fund

The Member Support Fund was set up in 2001 to help members in financial hardship through awarding grants.

In-kind support

During the year, over 2,500 hours of employee time was spent directly supporting the local community.

Employee-led support

Volunteering

During the year, 60 employee volunteers took part in Age UK's telephone befriending service, making over 950 calls. Over 100 employees also volunteered for Children in Need during their telethon event, taking over 1,500 calls in one night.

Payroll giving

Employees raised over £244,000 for charities through payroll giving. Over half of the company's employees donate through the Pennies for Charity scheme, raising over £18,600 during the year which was then distributed to a local charity voted for by each office.

Employee fundraising

During the year, employees raised £33,000 for charities and community projects through fundraising. The company gave £70,000 in matched funding.

Commercially led support

Sponsorship

LV=KidZone: this is a scheme whereby the company works with RNLI and Bournemouth Council to reunite lost children with their parents on Bournemouth's beaches.

Applications

Apply in writing or via email to your nearest regional committee, locations and contact details of which are available from the website. Details of your project, charity or community initiative should be included, along with the type of support (funding or volunteering) you are looking for.

Community contributions

Cash donations UK	£175,000
In-kind support UK	£199,000
Total contributions (cash and in kind)	£373,000

According to its website, the company's total community contribution was worth over £373,000 during 2017. The company donated £175,000 to 228 charities during 2017 through its Regional Community Committees. We have taken this figure as its cash donations for the year.

Lloyd's

 General charitable purposes

Company registration number: FCA 202761

Correspondent: Community Affairs Team, One Lime Street, London EC3M 7HA (tel: 020 7327 6144; email: communityaffairs@lloyds.com; website: www.lloyds.com/lloyds/corporate-responsibility)

Directors: Andy Haste; Bruce Cargie-Brown; Dr Martin Read; Fiona Luck; Inga Beale; John Parry; Julian James; Michael Watson; Neil Maidment; Philip Swatman; Richard Pryce; Robert Childs; Simon Beale; Sir David Manning (female 21%; male 79%).

Nature of business: Lloyd's is a specialist insurance and reinsurance underwriter.

Year end	31/12/2017
Turnover	£476,000,000
Pre-tax profit	(£2,001,000,000)

UK employees: 797

Total employees: 994

Main locations: The group's head office is based in London, but it also has offices in: Africa and the Middle East; Asia and Pacific; Europe; Latin America; the USA.

Community involvement

Lloyd's focuses its community contributions primarily within the local communities in which it operates around the world. It gives support through its three grant-making charities and supports the community in East London through the Lloyd's Community Programme.

Lloyd's charities

Lloyd's Charities Trust (Charity Commission no. 207232)

The trust has supported local, national and international causes on Lloyd's behalf for more than 60 years.

The partner charities the trust was working with until 2019 were: Build Change; Mayor's Fund for London; RedR UK; Whizz-Kidz.

Lloyd's Patriotic Fund (Charity Commission no. 210173)

Lloyd's has a long history, over 200 years, of providing support to the UK armed forces community. This fund was established to make grants to serving and ex-service personnel and their families. It also provides support to a number of armed forces organisations with a particular focus on those working to help those in the military community who have disabilities or face poverty, illness and hardship.

Lloyd's Tercentenary Research Foundation (Charity Commission no. 298482)

This charity was established to mark the tercentenary of Lloyds in 1988. It funds research in the fields of medicine, science, safety, the environment, engineering and business.

Employee-led support

Lloyd's Together

In 2015 the group launched this new programme to provide support and encouragement for employees to take on community and charitable activities, with a focus on:

- Education and employability
- Environment and sustainability
- Social welfare and health
- Disaster preparedness and relief

Lloyd's Community Programme

Through the programme, employees are able to contribute their time and skills to community projects in East London.

- Employability skills – helping young people from Tower Hamlets secondary school and sixth form with mentoring and employability workshops
- Reading and numbers – helping local primary schoolchildren to develop their literacy and numeracy skills
- Neighbourhood games – helping to run sports tournaments for young people in Tower Hamlets
- Team challenges – practical team tasks such as giving a community centre a makeover or helping to cook breakfasts for homeless people

The group have more than 2,300 volunteers from over 60 companies who take part each year to help over 5,000 people through this programme.

Lloyd's Market Charity Awards

The Lloyd's website states that anyone who works in the Lloyd's market can apply for a donation to a charity or community organisation in which they are actively involved through the Lloyds Market Charity Awards scheme. Employees can win a donation of £4,000 for their chosen charity and winners are selected by the trustees of the Lloyd's Charities Trust.

Applications

All of Lloyd's charities can be contacted by emailing communityaffairs@lloyds.com. Any other corporate social responsibility enquiries can be sent to the Responsibility Team at: Responsiblebusiness@lloyds.com.

Lloyds Charities Trust – Lloyd's Charities Trust makes ad hoc donations and the majority of funds are committed to supporting the partner charities the trust works with. Current partner charities are being supported until October 2019.

Check the trust's website for further information on Lloyd's Charity Awards or contact Sarah Chamberlain at sarah.chamberlain@lloyds.com.

Lloyd's Patriotic Fund – Application forms are available from the correspondent and should be submitted along with your accounts and any other additional supporting information to the CSR Manager at: jo.taylor@lloyds.com. The application window is only open once a year and applications should be received by the end of March.

Lloyd's Tercentenary Research Foundation – For information on scholarships available, visit the Lloyd's website: www.lloyds.com/ltrf.

Corporate charity

Lloyd's Charities Trust (Charity Commission no. 207232) – see page 259.

Community contributions

Cash donations UK	£1,000,000

In its annual report and accounts for 2017, the group declared charitable donations of £1 million. Of this amount, £500,000 was given to the Lloyd's Charities Trust and £200,000 to Lloyd's Patriotic Fund.

Lloyds Banking Group

Education (particularly STEM subjects), enterprise and training, general charitable purposes

Company registration number: 2065

Correspondent: Responsible Business Team, 25 Gresham Street, London EC2V 7HN (tel: 020 7626 1500; website: www.lloydsbankinggroup.com/our-group/responsible-business)

Directors: Alan Dickson; Amanda Mackenzie; Anita Frew; António Horta-Osório; Deborah McWhinney; George Culmer; Juan Colombás; Lord Blackwell; Lord Lupton; Nick Prettejohn; Sara Weller; Simon Henry; Stuart Sinclair (female 31%; male 69%).

Nature of business: Lloyds Banking Group is one of the largest financial services companies in the UK, covering retail banking, commercial and corporate banking, mortgages, life assurance and pensions, general insurance, asset management, leasing, treasury and foreign exchange dealing.

Year end	31/12/2017
Turnover	£18,525,000,000
Pre-tax profit	£5,275,000,000

Main locations: The group's headquarters are in London and it has branches throughout the British Isles.

Community involvement

Lloyds Banking Group (Lloyds) has one of the largest community programmes in the UK. Through its Helping Britain Prosper Plan the group aims to help communities across the UK and does this through employee volunteering, support to community organisations, donations to the group's four foundations, and fundraising for its Charity of the Year. Lloyds also runs community investment programmes which fall under three key themes – education, employability and enterprise. These programmes are supported by employees, who are encouraged to dedicate their time and expertise.

Corporate foundations

Lloyds supports registered charities across the UK and the Channel Islands through its five corporate foundations – Lloyds Bank Foundation for England and Wales, the Corra Foundation (previously The Lloyd's TSB Foundation for Scotland), Bank of Scotland Foundation, Halifax Foundation for Northern Ireland and Lloyds Bank Foundation for the Channel Islands. As of 2018, the Corra Foundation will not be in receipt of any payments from Lloyds.

The foundations support charities that enable people, particularly those who are disadvantaged or who have disabilities, to play a fuller role in society. Applications are only accepted from registered charities that fit the grant-giving criteria.

Charity partners

Mental Health UK was chosen as the Charity of the Year for 2017 and 2018. The group also partners the Great Scottish Run in which 30,000 people take part.

Supporting credit unions

In 2014 the group launched a £4 million fund to support Credit Unions. Delivered in partnership with the Credit Union Foundation and the Association of British Credit Unions (ABCUL) it has so far helped 66 credit unions lend an additional £20 million to their members. The group announced that it will commit a further £1 million of funding in 2018.

Lloyds Scholars

This programme is a partnership with eight universities in the UK and is aimed at supporting students from lower income households with, according to the website, 'a unique combination of financial support, a Lloyds Banking Group mentor, sessions to develop their skills and the opportunity to gain valuable work experience through paid internships'. In return, the group asks that they volunteer for local causes which enhances their CV and gives back to the community.

The Lloyds Bank and Bank of Scotland Social Entrepreneurs Programme

Lloyds Banking Group and Bank of Scotland Social Entrepreneurs Programme is delivered through the group's partnership with the School for Social Entrepreneurs and the Big Lottery Fund. The School has supported 1,300 entrepreneurs to start and grow social business since its inception. The School has developed Match Trading, a new funding model for social entrepreneurs which matches their business's increase in income through trading pound to pound.

In-kind support

Employees are able to spend one paid day per year volunteering. In 2017 more than 258,000 was spent volunteering.

Employee-led support

Employee volunteering

Employees are able to volunteer with a charity or community project of their own choosing through the group's volunteering programme. In 2017 a total of 26,700 employees volunteered their time and expertise.

In 2017 a total of 5,000 employees took part with the UK's largest employee volunteering day, Give and Gain Day. Activities have included helping out with community sports events, running employability workshops and helping to rebuild flood-hit communities.

Employee fundraising

Employees raise funds for the Charity of the Year which, in 2017, was Mental Health UK. During the first 12 months of the two-year partnership, employees raised £4.8 million including matched funding.

Matched funding

Lloyds matches funds raised by employees for good causes.

Commercially led support

Sponsorship

In 2017 the group promoted digital skills in voluntary organisations, in line with the Digital Participation Charter. It sponsored 100 dedicated online centres in local communities and now has 100 digital connectors active in every nation in the UK.

Exclusions

Only UK-registered charities are supported. See the relevant foundation's website for further details of exclusions.

Applications

The website notes that queries or comments about Lloyds Banking Group's community programmes, environmental activities or approach to responsible business more generally can be directed to the correspondent in writing.

Corporate charity

Corra Foundation (OSCR no. SC009481) – see page 243. Halifax Foundation for Northern Ireland (NIC101763) – see page 253. Lloyds Bank Foundation for England and Wales (Charity Commission no. 327114) – see page 260. Lloyds Bank Foundation for the Channel Islands (Charity Commission no. 327113) – see page 261. The Bank of Scotland Foundation (OSCR No. SC032942) – see page 236.

Community contributions

Cash donations UK	£38,000,000
In-kind support UK	£4,900,000
Total contributions (cash and in kind)	£42,900,000

According to Lloyds Banking Group's annual report 2017, it gave a total of £58 million in community investment during the year. We have taken the group's cash donations, employee time and gift in-kind as its total contribution figure, provided in the Responsible Business Update 2017 as follows:

Cash donations	£38 million
Employee time	£4.8 million
Gifts in kind	£147,000

Over £14.7 million was given in management costs and leveraged support. The group uses the London Benchmarking Group (LBG) framework to calculate community investment. Of the total figure for cash donations, £20.7 million was awarded to the group's foundations.

Beneficiaries included: Wyre Forest Nightstop; Rural Women's Network; Autism Journey; Money for Life.

London Luton Airport Ltd (LLAL)

General charitable purposes

Company registration number: 2020381

Correspondent: Community Team, Hart House Business Centre, Kimpton Road, Luton LU2 0LA (tel: 01582 395305; email: communityupdate@ltn.aero; website: www.llal.org.uk/LLAL-CorporateSocialResponsibility.html)

Directors: Cllr Allan Skepelhorn; Cllr Amy O'Callaghan; Cllr Andrew Malcolm; Cllr David Franks; Cllr James Taylor; Cllr John Young; Cllr Tahir Khan; Cllr Waheed Akbar; Dr Romano Pagliari; Lord McKenzie of Luton (female 10%; male 90%).

Nature of business: London Luton Airport is an international airport located 1.5 miles east of Luton and 28 miles north of central London. The airport is owned by Luton Borough Council.

Year end	31/03/2017
Turnover	£41,467,000
Pre-tax profit	£52,603,000

Main locations: The airport is based in Luton.

Community involvement

London Luton Airport Ltd (LLAL) has a Community Funding Programme consisting of four separate funds through which it supports charitable organisations in Luton and its surrounding areas.

Partnership Fund

This fund aims to provide funding in the form of sponsorship and/or donations, to charitable organisations having a major and key role in contributing to the delivery of priority outcomes in the medium- to long-term. The fund is organised into seven funding themes: children, families and young people; citizen enablement; community involvement; community safety; environment and economy; health and wellbeing; and leisure and culture.

Luton Community Fund

This fund provides small one-off grants. The fund aims to support community and voluntary activity in Luton. Assistance can be given for project work, running costs, support with rent, rates or room hire, and capital investment. The company has expressed that the fund may not continue in the future and advises potential applicants to demonstrate that they have explored the potential for finding alternative funding. Applications may also be made to secure matched funding from other sources, to support capacity building, to encourage working in partnership with other organisations or to meet emerging or changing needs in the community.

Near Neighbour Fund

This fund provides small one-off grants. The fund aims to support community and voluntary organisations, activities and projects in communities outside the Borough of Luton, that are most affected by airport operations.

Enterprise Fund

This fund provides small one-off grants. The fund aims to support the start-up of small business, including social enterprises, in Luton with a particular focus being given to areas of significant deprivation.

Applications

Partnership Fund

For strategic and administrative purposes, LLAL's Partnership Fund is organised into seven funding themes. For more information on each funding theme, contact the following correspondents:

Children, Families and Young People

Theme Lead: Kelly O'Neill

T: 01582 548439

E: kelly.oneill@luton.gov.uk

Citizen Enablement

Theme Lead: Sue Nelson

T: 01582 547094

E: sue.nelson@luton.gov.uk

Community Involvement

Theme Lead: Sandra Hayes

T: 01582 548777

E: sandra.hayes@luton.gov.uk

Community Safety

Theme Lead: Vicky Hawkes

T: 01582 546159

E: vicky.hawkes@luton.gov.uk

Environment and Economy

Theme Lead: Lesley Nicholls

T: 01582 546271

E: lesley.nicholls@luton.gov.uk

Health and Wellbeing

Theme Lead: Michelle Granat

T: 01582 546201

E: michelle.granat@luton.gov.uk

Leisure and Culture

Theme Lead: Adam Divney

T: 01582 547850

E: adam.divney@luton.gov.uk

Luton Community Fund

This fund is administered by the Bedfordshire and Luton Community Foundation. Application forms can be downloaded at: www.blcf.org.uk/2017/09/20/london-luton-airport-operations-ltd-community-fund.

For more information, applicants can call 01234 834930

Near Neighbour Fund

This fund is administered by the Bedfordshire and Luton Community Foundation. Full guidelines and information on how to apply can be found at: www.blcf.org.uk.

Enterprise Fund

This fund is administered by Wenta. For more information email: marketing@wenta.co.uk.

Community contributions

Cash donations UK	£10,300,000

According to its 2016/17 accounts, the company donated a total of £10.3 million through its Community Funding Programme during the year. Donations can be broken down into the following funding themes:

Leisure and culture	£4.77 million
Children, families and young people	£2.2 million
Health and well-being	£929,000
Community involvement	£829,000
Community enablement	£783,000
Community safety	£578,000
Environment and economy	£217,000

Beneficiaries include: Luton Cultural Services Trust (£2.7 million); Active Luton (£1.4 million); Victim Support Bedfordshire (£310,000); Autism Bedfordshire (£280,000); Stepping Stones (£190,000); Luton All Women's Centre (£119,000); Luton Irish Forum (£31,000); Centre for Youth and Community Development (£25,000); Groundworks (£17,000).

London Stock Exchange Group plc

General charitable purposes

Company registration number: 5369106

Correspondent: Corporate Responsibility Team, 10 Paternoster Square, London EC4M 7LS (tel: 020 7797 1000; website: www.lseg.com/about-london-stock-exchange-group/london-stock-exchange-group-foundation)

Directors: Andrea Sironi; David Nish; David Schwimmer; David Warren; Donald Brydon; Jacques Aigrain; Marshall Bailey; Paul Heiden; Raffaele Jerusalmi; Stephen O'Connor; Val Rahmani (female 18%; male 82%).

Nature of business: London Stock Exchange Group (LSEG) is an international markets infrastructure business. The group has a presence in locations including the UK (London), France, Italy, Sri Lanka and the USA.

Year end	31/12/2017
Turnover	£1,768,000,000
Pre-tax profit	£564,000,000

Main locations: The group is headquartered in the City of London.

Community involvement

LSEG supports programmes making a positive difference in communities in which it has a presence. The majority of the group's charitable involvement is channelled through the London Stock Exchange Group Foundation, which was established in 2010 not as a registered charity but through the Charities Aid Foundation (CAF). Employees are also actively involved in their communities through the foundation's work.

London Stock Exchange Group (LSEG) Foundation

According to the LSEG Corporate Responsibility Report for 2017, the foundation has four main sources of income:

- Employee donations and fundraising events
- An annual charity trading day. The report explains: 'The Group donates the equivalent of all equity trading fees raised on London Stock Exchange, Turquoise and Borsa Italiana during their annual charity trading day.'
- Corporate donations from other companies in the group
- Money raised through fines levied by LSEG

The foundation's giving is based around the group's brand values and, according to the LSEG website, focuses on supporting 'significant endeavours' that help 'young and disadvantaged people to reach their full potential, through the development of life skills and business enterprise'. The foundation's beneficiaries are mainly based in the UK, however support is also given to charities in Italy, Australia, France, the USA and Sri Lanka.

Charity partners

Unicef: In 2015 the LSEG Foundation entered into partnership with Unicef as part of an effort to expand charitable involvement from only the communities in which LSEG has a presence to disadvantaged communities all over the world. The foundation supports a community investment programme in Zambia which work to develop the business skills of teenage girls over a period of three years.

Ellen McArthur Cancer Trust: Since 2012, the group have had a partnership with the Ellen McArthur Cancer Trust. The trust has benefitted from corporate donations, fundraising events and employee-led support. During 2017 the group raised over £6,000 for the trust through a pub quiz, bake sale, raffle and foreign exchange collection boxes.

School Home Support: In 2017 School Home Support was announced as the group's new UK charity partner for the next three years.

In-kind support

Venue hire

Charities in the UK and Italy can hire venues at the group's premises free of charge.

Pro bono

In Sri Lanka, MillenniumIT employees were involved in a number of activities; these included 'creating teaching content for IT syllabus development' and training workshops for teachers in collaboration with the Ministry of Education. A group of volunteers also 'built a technology platform to connect NGOs and the Government with the corporate sector with the aim of undertaking development projects'.

Employee-led support

Fundraising

Employees are involved with fundraising initiatives and provide one of the four principal sources of funding for the LSEG Foundation. In 2017 fundraising events included a mixed Touch Rugby Tournament organised in collaboration with the Rugby Football Union (RFU). The event helped to raise more than £34,500. LSEG employees also rode in the Tour of Cambridge Gran Fondo Cycling event on behalf of the Atlas Foundation, raising £16,000.

Volunteering

LSEG employees in the group's various global locations volunteer in their local communities. In the UK, employees took part in the Reading Buddies programme through Tower Hamlets Education Business Partners. Based in London, the programme sees LSEG employees partner with school pupils and provide them with one-to-one tuition once a week to help improve the students' reading skills and to raise their aspirations.

Applications

Email LSEGFoundation@lseg.com for further information about the foundation and how to apply.

Community contributions

Cash donations worldwide	£1,227,000
In-kind support worldwide	£136,000
Total contributions (cash and in kind)	£1,363,000

The London Stock Exchange Group's Corporate Responsibility Report for 2017 states that the group gave a total of £1.6 million during the year in community investment. We have excluded management costs from this total and taken £1.36 million as the group's figure for total contribution during the year. A breakdown of community investment was provided as follows:

Donations to LSEG Foundation	£1.12 million
Donations to charity	£107,000
In-kind donations	£136,000

We were not able to determine how much of the group's community investment was given in the UK. We have taken the group's donations to charity and its foundation as its cash donations worldwide.

LondonMetric Property plc

General charitable purposes

Company registration number: 7124797

Correspondent: Charities and Communities Working Group, One Curzon Street, London W1J 5HB (tel: 020 7484 9000; email: info@londonmetric.com; website: www.londonmetric.com/our-company/responsible-business)

Directors: Alec Pelmore; Andrew Jones; Andrew Livingston; James Dean; Mark Stirling; Martin McGann; Patrick Vaughan; Philip Watson; Rosalyn Wilton; Suzanne Avery; Valentine Beresford (female 27%; male 73%).

Nature of business: LondonMetric is a property development and investment company.

Year end	31/03/2018
Turnover	£82,881,000
Pre-tax profit	£186,050,000

UK employees: 31

Main locations: The company has an office in Mayfair, London, and properties in England, Scotland, Wales and the Isle of Man. For details of the whereabouts of properties, see the properties map on the website.

Community involvement

LondonMetric Property looks to make a positive contribution to communities in areas local to its properties. Support is given in the form of cash donations and gifts in kind. LondonMetric matches its employee charitable giving. The 2018 Responsible Business Report explains that, over the last few years, the company formed a Charities and Communities Working Group which formalised the company's approach to community activities and charitable giving.

In-kind support

The company's 2018 Responsible Business Report states that the company organised several community days in Leeds during the year and provided funding for a new local playground in Dagenham, the location of a new distribution warehouse construction.

Employee-led support

According to the group's 2017/18 annual report, it matches employee charitable giving.

Applications

Contact the correspondent for further information.

Community contributions

Cash donations UK	£25,000

In 2017/18 the group made charitable donations totalling £25,000. The group supported a number of local causes and other organisations such as LandAid through matched funding and events.

A full list of beneficiaries was not provided.

Lush Cosmetics Ltd

Human rights, animal welfare, the environment, community development, education, projects outside the UK

Company registration number: 4162033

Correspondent: Charity Pot Team, 29 High Street, Poole, Dorset BH15 1AB (tel: 01202 641001; email: charitypot@lush.co.uk; website: www.lush.co.uk/tag/our-policies)

Directors: Karl Bygrave; Margaret Constantine; Mark Constantine (female 33%; male 67%).

Nature of business: Lush produces a range of cosmetic products which it sells through its shops.

Year end	30/06/2017
Turnover	£497,788,000
Pre-tax profit	£73,482,000

Main locations: Lush is headquarted in Poole, Dorset and has stores throughout the UK.

Community involvement

Lush focuses its charitable giving on supporting small, grassroots organisations working in the areas of the environment, human rights and animal protection. Lush uses education, campaigns and activism as a way to address global issues. As well as supporting registered charities, Lush also supports political campaign groups and other organisations not registered with the Charity Commission. Lush prefers to support projects looking to create a long-term change, which address the root causes of social issues. Funding is also given to projects that provide aid and support, such as animal shelters or refugee support groups. The majority of Lush's funds that are distributed to good causes are raised from the sale of its Charity Pot lotion.

The Sustainable Lush (SLush) Fund

The SLush Fund was set up to fund permaculture and regenerative agriculture projects with the aim of supporting them until they could financially support themselves, and a few of the projects also provided ingredients for Lush products. At the time of writing (December 2018) the SLush Fund is undergoing a transformation, to become **'Re:Fund'.** The new fund will be fully dedicated to funding regenerative projects. According to its website, the Re:Fund will focus on the following three areas:

- Wildlife projects will be supported through rewilding and conservation
- The land and environment regenerated through permaculture and agroecology projects
- Work supporting people will be funded through responsive projects looking at displacement and disaster

Annual awards

Lush gives away around £200,000 each year to special groups it partners with, or it thinks are making a 'vital contribution to social change'. Additionally, the company gives away another £200,000 each year through its Lush Spring Prize to projects committed to regeneration.

Charity Pot

Charity Pot is a Lush hand and body cream where 100% of all sales (minus local taxes) are distributed as grants, to groups working in the areas of:

- Animal protection
- The environment
- Human rights (including social justice, peace and equality)

Charity Pot grants range from £100, up to a maximum of £10,000 per project/application. The average Charity Pot grant is between £2,000 and £4,000.

Through this initiative, Lush raised £9.8 million in 36 countries during 2016/17, going to a variety of good causes working in its focus area.

In-kind support

Individual Lush shops occasionally donate unwanted products to charities in their local areas.

Employee-led support

Staff volunteer their time to help the company's charity partners. Staff frequently participate in volunteer days with charity pot partners local to their shops or offices.

Lush's Carbon Tax Fund is a self-imposed tax charged on staff's international flights at a rate of £50 per tonne of carbon dioxide emitted with the raised funds being donated to environmental groups. A total of £318,000 was raised during the year.

Commercially led support

FunD

This fund supports children affected by the Fukushima disaster, and raises funds through global sales of Lush's FUN product. A total of £206,000 was raised during the year.

Limited edition products

Lush sells various limited edition products for specific charities and campaigns. Examples include the Error 404 bath bomb supporting the campaign to stop government enforced shut downs of internet services which raised £189,000 and its 'Buy One Set One Free' campaign which raised £61,000 to support Reprieve in their attempts to ensure the safe release of Andy Tsege who was kidnapped and held illegally on Ethiopia's death row.

Exclusions

According to the funding guidelines available on its website, Lush does not support organisations that:

- Deny the human rights of others
- Are involved in cruelty/subjugation of animals (incl. farming, testing or research)
- Coerces or forces others to change their beliefs or proselytizes
- Harbour racism or prejudice
- Prevents or impedes the free-speech of others
- Judge others on anything other than their actions
- Have not made every effort to be environmentally responsible
- Promote/support violence, aggression or oppression towards others (we will only support direct action groups if they are non-violent)

Applications

Charity Pot grants

Applicants are advised to read the full guidelines available at: uk.lush.com/article/charity-pot-funding-guidelines-0.

Applicants can then fill out the online application form available at: form.jotformeu.com/LushCharityPot/charity-pot-grant-application.

Applications are accepted at any time, and there are no cut-offs. However, you should allow at least three months from application to when you need the funds. Applications are assessed on a first-come-first-served basis; however, if your funding is exceptionally urgent, email: charitypot@lush.co.uk for advice.

Lush Spring Prize

The Lush Spring Prize accepts nominations from anywhere in the world. Full eligibility guidelines can be found at: springprize.org/regeneration.

Community contributions

Cash donations worldwide	£8,300,000

According to the 2016/17 annual report, Lush donated a total of £11.7 million to charities and other good causes, £8.3 million of this amount came directly from the group. Our research indicates that this amount includes funds raised from its Charity Pot sales, as 100% of this goes towards grants for charities, and the amount donated through the group's annual awards. We have taken £8.3 million as the group's cash donations worldwide. A breakdown by location was not provided.

The annual report also notes that in total £13.3 million was raised globally for good causes during the year, and funds that are not donated are carried forward for distribution in the following year.

Mactaggart and Mickel Group Ltd

Education, sports and recreation, general charitable purposes

Company registration number: SC326355

Correspondent: CSR Team, 1 Atlantic Quay, 1 Robertson Street, Glasgow G2 8JB (tel: 0141 332 0001; email: Contact form on website; website: www.macmic.co.uk/about/bcf)

Directors: Alan Hartley; Andrew Mickel; Edmund Monaghan; Keith Swinley; Paul McAnnich; Ross Mickel (female 0%; male 100%).

Nature of business: Mactaggart and Mickel Homes is a house builder.

Year end	30/04/2017
Turnover	£74,266,000
Pre-tax profit	£12,740,000

Main locations: The group's head office is in Glasgow. It mainly operates in Glasgow, Ayreshire, Edinburgh and the Lothians.

Community involvement

Charities, community groups, sports teams and schools can apply for a grant or in-kind support through the Building Communities Fund. Grants of up to £1,000 are available for equipment, refurbishment costs, travel expenses and revenue costs.

Recent beneficiaries included: Babes in the Wood Bishopbriggs, Dunipace FC, East Renfrewshire Disability Action and Recovery Across Mental Health (£1,000 each); South Western District Scout Council (£750); Interfaith Glasgow and Young Enterprise Scotland (£500 each); Craigmillar Community Arts (£250).

In-kind support

Occasionally employees undertake pro bono work through the Building Communities Fund, for example in 2018 a builder paved and painted Johnstone High School in preparation for the installation of outdoor equipment.

Applications

Applications to the Building Communities Fund can be made through the group's website.

Community contributions

Cash donations UK	£58,500

In 2016/17 the group declared cash donations of £58,500.

Man Group plc

Children and young people, education

Company registration number: 8172396

Correspondent: See 'Applications', Riverbank House, 2 Swan Lane, London EC4R 3AD (tel: 020 7144 1737; email: charitable.trust@man.com; website: www.man.com/GB/man-charitable-trust)

Directors: Andrew Horton; Dame Katherine Barker; Dev Sanyal; John Cryan; Jonathan Sorrell; Lord Livingston of Parkhead; Luke Ellis; Mark Jones; Matthew Lester; Richard Berliand; Zoe Cruz (female 10%; male 90%).

Nature of business: The company is a global provider of alternative investment products and solutions.

Year end	31/12/2017
Turnover	£842,500,000
Pre-tax profit	£214,600,000

Main locations: The group has two offices in London – its head office located in the City of London, and it has an office in Mayfair.

Community involvement

The majority of Man Group plc's community involvement is through its associated charity, Man Group plc Charitable Trust (Charity Commission no. 275386).

Man Group plc Charitable Trust

The trust has two main aims: to support organisations working to raise literacy and numeracy levels in the UK and to facilitate opportunities for Man Group employees to share their time and expertise for charitable causes. The trust supports small to medium-sized charities registered in the UK.

In-kind support

Through the group's community programme, 'ManKind', it offers employees two days' paid leave each year in volunteering time.

Employee-led support

Employees are actively involved in charitable initiatives and volunteering opportunities local to the firm's offices through its 'ManKind' programme. Employees volunteer throughout the year either with the group's charitable trust, or a charity of their choice. Employees also independently fundraise and donate through the group's Give As You Earn scheme. The group's matched funding for the year totalled $29,500 (≈ £23,500 as at January 2019).

Commercially led support

The company has sponsored the Man Booker Prize for Fiction since 2002 and also sponsors the Man Booker International Prize. It is explained on the website that 'sponsorship of the prizes underscores Man Group's charitable focus on literacy and education as well as the firm's commitment to excellence and entrepreneurship'.

Applications

Contact your local office for more information on the 'ManKind' programme.

Corporate charity

Man Group plc Charitable Trust (Charity Commission no. 275386) – see page 262. .

Community contributions

Cash donations UK	£50,000

Man Group's annual report and accounts for 2017 did not declare its donations. According to the trust's 2017 accounts, the group donated £50,000 to the trust. Its account also states that the group approved additional funding of £50,000 during the year to be paid to the trust in each 2018 and 2019, and £350,000 to be paid in 2020.

Manchester Airport Group plc

The environment, arts and culture, community development, animal welfare, education (particularly STEM subjects), children and young people, older people, enterprise and training

Company registration number: 4330721

Correspondent: Jack Carnell, CSR Manager, M.A.G Sustainability, 6th Floor, Olympic House, Manchester Airport, Manchester M90 1AA (tel: 0871 271 0711; website: www.magworld.co.uk)

Directors: Adrian Montague; Andrew Cowan; Cath Schefer; Charlie Cornish; Christian Seymour; David Molyneux; Jon Wragg; Ken O'Toole; Manoj Mehta; Neil Thompson; Richard Leese; Robert Napier; Vanda Murray (female 15%; male 85%).

Nature of business: The group is comprised of Manchester Airport, East Midlands Airport, Bournemouth Airport and London Stansted Airport.

Year end	31/03/2018
Turnover	£50,300,000
Pre-tax profit	£12,347,000

Main locations: The group's airports are in Bournemouth; East Midlands; Greater Manchester; London Stansted.

Community involvement

Each of the group's airports has a community fund through which grants are made to local causes. The group also sponsors arts initiatives and works with educational institutions in areas local to its airports.

Community funds

Each of the group's airports has a Community Fund, which provides grants to local charities and community groups. According to the group's annual report for 2016/17, the group donated £254,000 in grants through its community funds.

Manchester Airport Community Trust Fund (Charity Commission no. 1071703)

Grants of up to £3,000 are awarded to charitable organisations for projects which are 'community, socially or environmentally focused' and benefit communities within a ten-mile radius of Manchester Airport.

East Midlands Airport Community Fund (not a registered charity)

Grants are available to community organisations in the specified area of benefit (refer to the map provided on the airport's website) for projects which benefit the local community or environment.

Bournemouth Airport Community Fund (not a registered charity)

Grants of up to £2,000 are available to community organisations in the Borough of Christchurch for projects which are focused on: bringing the community together through sport, recreation or leisure activities; the environment or heritage conservation; environmental education; wildlife conservation.

Stansted Airport Community Trust (Charity Commission no. 1111200)

Grants are available for capital projects that benefit the local community within a ten-mile radius of Stansted Airport in a social, economic or environmental way.

We have included the Manchester Airport Community Trust Fund in our 'corporate charities' section, as it is the only community fund that meets our criteria. More information on each of the community funds, including guidelines and application forms, are available on their respective websites – see 'Applications'.

Partnerships

The group's national charity partner, chosen by employees in 2015/16 was CLIC Sargent. The group has set a goal of raising £1 million for the charity. During 2016/17 it raised £120,000.

Education

At Manchester, East Midlands and Stansted airports, the group has education centres called Aerozones, which work in collaboration with local educational institutions to offer STEM activities to young people.

The group also works in partnership with schools such as Manchester Enterprise Academy, where it provides opportunities such as shadowing placements to students. There is also a focus on promoting international cultures and languages through school partnerships.

Arts

The group also provides sponsorship for arts initiatives in the regions where it operates (North West; Essex; Bournemouth; East Midlands). This year MAG contributed £335,000 to supporting the 'vibrancy and culture of the cities' they operate in. Alongside numerous theatres, exhibitions and festivals, MAG continued to support the Hallé Orchestra, which runs workshops with local schools as part of sponsorship.

Employee-led support

In 2016/17 15% of employees volunteered in their local communities, a total of 11,787 hours equating to 1,473 working days.

Exclusions

Refer to the websites for exclusions from each of the community funds or from the group's arts sponsorship scheme.

Applications

Manchester Airport Community Trust Fund (Charity Commission no. 1071703)

Application forms can be found on the charity's website (www.manchesterairport.co.uk/communitytrustfund), along with guidelines.

East Midlands Airport Community Fund (not a registered charity)

Full application guidelines can be found at: www.eastmidlandsairport.com/community/supporting-the-local-community/charitable-giving.

Applications can be sent to:

Community Relations, Building 34, East Midlands Airport, Castle Donington, Derby DE74 2SA

Tel: 01332 818414

Email: community@eastmidlandsairport.com

Bournemouth Airport Community Fund (not a registered charity)

Contact the Consultative Committee at: Bournemouth Airport Consultative Committee; c/o Bournemouth Airport; Christchurch; Dorset; BH23 6SE.

Stansted Airport Community Trust (Charity Commission no. 1111200)

For further information and to request an application form, email Sandra_king@stanstedAirport.com.

Corporate charity

Manchester Airport Community Trust Fund (Charity Commission no. 1071703) – see page 263.

Community contributions

Cash donations UK	£1,000,000

The companies 2016/17 CSR report states that the group gave just over £1 million in charitable donations and sponsorships.

Manchester City Football Club Ltd

Sports and recreation, children and young people, disability, education, enterprise and training, community development, equal opportunities, health, poverty and social exclusion

Company registration number: 40946

Correspondent: City in the Community, Etihad Stadium, Etihad Campus, Manchester M11 3FF (tel: 0161 438 7712; email: citc@mcfc.co.uk; website: www.mancity.com/fans-and-community/community/manchester-community)

Directors: Abdulla Khouri; Alberto Galassi; John Macbeath; Khaldoon Al Mubarak; Martin Edelman; Mohamed Al Mazrouei; Ruigang Li; Simon Pearce (female 0%; male 100%).

Nature of business: Manchester City FC is a professional football club competing in the Premier League.

Year end	30/06/2018
Turnover	£500,456,000
Pre-tax profit	£10,438,000

UK employees: 449

Main locations: The football club is based in Manchester.

Community involvement

The club gives support through its charity, City in the Community (Charity Commission no. 1139229), which runs projects in the areas of education, health and inclusion. It also offers in-kind support to charities such as signed merchandise, tickets to matches and stadium tours, with a preference for charities in the East Manchester area.

City in the Community

The club's charity, City in the Community, focuses on the following areas, according to the website:

- **Education:** 'using football to promote increased educational access, engagement, attainment and progression for young people aged 11–24'
- **Health:** 'using football to promote improved health and wellbeing through increased physical activity and a healthier diet'
- **Inclusion:** 'using football to improve community integration and combat negative stereotypes'

The charity runs a number of projects to deliver these aims, in partnership with organisations such as charities, local educational institutions and local council. Recent examples of projects include:

- **City Pathways:** a sport and vocational course for young people
- **City Cooks:** a healthy eating programme for families
- **One City Disability:** a series of lessons in schools to raise awareness and understanding of disabilities

The club provides in-kind support to the charity including the use of facilities and promotion in match-day programmes. The club also covers administration costs and organises fundraising events for the charity.

Full details of all of the club's current programmes are available on its website.

International projects

Through City in the Community, the club delivers international projects through the Cityzens Giving Programme, which supports young leaders in 14 cities internationally to deliver football projects with a community purpose. Fans can vote to select which projects are supported. The Young Leaders programme provides training and support for 120 young people in Manchester and overseas to deliver community football projects tackling social issues.

In-kind support

The club provides in-kind support in the form of signed merchandise, tickets to matches and stadium tours upon request. Priority is given to charities in the east Manchester area. The club also supports local charities through bucket collections on matchdays.

Exclusions

The club does not provide monetary donations or sponsorship to charities upon request.

Applications

General enquiries can be submitted in writing to the correspondent.

Charity requests

Requests for in-kind donations such as signed merchandise, stadium tours and match tickets can be made using an online form on the club's website www.mancity.com/fans-and-community/community/charity-support.

Partnerships

Organisations interested in partnering with City in the Community should contact Michael Geary at Michael.geary@cityfootball.com.

Community contributions

Cash donations UK	£3,288,000

The club's 2017/18 financial report states donations to UK charities during the year amounted to £3.28 million. This amount included £3 million supporting Premier League led youth and community development programmes.

Manchester United Ltd

Sports and recreation, children and young people, community development, education, health, projects outside the UK

Company registration number: 2570509

Correspondent: Manchester United Foundation, Sir Matt Busby Way, Old Trafford, Manchester M16 0RA (tel: 0161 868 8600; email: enquiries@mufoundation.org; website: www.mufoundation.org/en/Charity)

Directors: Avram Glazer; Bryan Glazer; Cliff Baty; Darcie Glazer Kassewitz; Edward Glazer; Edward Woodward; Joel Glazer; John Hooks; Kevin Glazer; Manu Sawhney; Richard Arnold; Robert Leitão (female 8%; male 92%).

Nature of business: Manchester United is a professional football club competing in the English Premier League.

Year end	30/06/2018
Turnover	£590,022,000
Pre-tax profit	£26,097,000

Total employees: 922

Main locations: The club supports charitable causes worldwide. However, the majority of the foundation's community projects are delivered within Greater Manchester.

Community involvement

The club's community activities are mainly delivered through its corporate charity the Manchester United

Foundation, which works with locals and charity partners to deliver a wide-range of education and sport programmes. Support is also provided through fundraising and in-kind donations.

Manchester United Foundation (Charity Commission no. 1118310)
The Manchester United Foundation was established in 2006 as the charitable arm of Manchester United. According to its website, the foundation 'uses football to engage and inspire young people to build a better life for themselves and unite the communities in which they live'. To achieve its objectives, the foundation creates and develops strategic partnerships with local, regional and national organisations working in the areas of health, education and inclusion. Recent examples of the foundation's programmes include:

- **Volunteer Ninety-Nine:** This programme provides training, recognised qualifications and work experience to young people aged 16–21 who are interested in pursuing a career in sport
- **Inclusive Reds:** A disability sport initiative supported by BT Sport and the Premier League. Inclusive Reds aims for equal sport and physical activity opportunities for people with disabilities, their friends and family
- **Eat Well with Manchester United:** A ten-week programme that uses Manchester United to educate youngsters about being healthy in order to tackle rising obesity rates

Full details of all the foundation's current programmes are available on its website.

Charity partner
Since 1999, the club has been a partner of Unicef. Each year the club hosts the United for Unicef Gala Dinner, attended by the first-team players and management staff. In 2017 this event raised over £160,000 for the charity.

In-kind support

The club provides signed items such as shirts, pennants and photographs to charities and organisations for their own fundraising and events. Throughout the 2017/18 season, 1,473 items were donated raising over £200,000 for causes across the UK. The club also donates match tickets to its partner schools and projects, as well as to deserving fans in need of support at difficult times. Finally, each year the club's foundation hosts two 'Dream Days', giving fans with life-limiting and serious illnesses the chance to meet the Manchester United first team.

Applications

Charitable requests for signed shirts, football, pennants and photographs are managed by the foundation. Request can be made using an online form available on the foundation's website. Information about future 'Dream Days' can be requested from the foundation by email. Applicants must be aged seven years or older.

Community contributions

The annual report and accounts did not declare a figure for charitable donations.

The Mansfield Building Society

Arts and culture, community development, housing and homelessness, health, the environment, poverty and social exclusion, older people, disability, education

Company registration number: FCA 206049

Correspondent: Community Support Scheme, Regent House, Regent Street, Mansfield, Nottinghamshire NG18 1SS (tel: 01623 676300; email: enquiries@mansfieldbs.co.uk; website: mansfieldbs.co.uk)

Directors: Jeremy Cross; Gev Lynott; Paul Wheeler; Robert Hartley; Robert Clifford; Alison Chmiel; Colin Bradley; Nicholas Baxter (female 13%; male 88%).

Nature of business: The Mansfield Building Society is an independent mutual building society based in Nottinghamshire.

Year end	31/12/2017
Turnover	£6,283,000
Pre-tax profit	£1,914,000

UK employees: 75

Main locations: The society has branches in Nottinghamshire and Derbyshire.

Community involvement

The society supports communities in which it has a presence through its Community Support Scheme and employee volunteering. The group also partners with charities in the local area. The group have a corporate charity, the Mansfield Building Society Charitable Trust (Charity Commission no. 1177151).

The Mansfield Building Society Charitable Trust (Charity Commission no. 1177151)
The trust was set up by the society for the benefit of registered charities in its core operating area territory of Nottinghamshire, Derbyshire, Lincolnshire and South Yorkshire. During 2015, the society gifted an initial £50,000 to the trust with the intention that further contributions to be added.

Community Support Scheme
The society offers a Community Support Scheme which invites applications for funding of around £100–£500 from charitable groups in Nottinghamshire and Derbyshire that are in need of financial assistance to help with its objectives. The society considers applications in a number of different categories, including those that:

- Work in partnership with organisations assisting the disadvantaged
- Promote and encourage sporting activities
- Promote and encourage activities in the arts
- Support education and development
- Benefit the environment

Partnerships
According to the society's website, it has a 'special relationship' with a local charity called Jigsaw which helps people to remain independent at home. The society also announced Macmillan Cancer Support as its new official charity partner. Over the next two years the society will be co-ordinating a range of fundraising initiatives and volunteer work to support the charity in Mansfield, Ashfield and Chesterfield.

In-kind support

The society encourage staff to participate in the Work in the Community Scheme through granting two days' paid leave each year for employees to assist local causes.

Employee-led support

Employees chose Macmillan Cancer Support as the society's Charity of the Year, and have raised funds for the charity throughout the year. Employees participated in events including climbing Mount Snowdon, the Nottinghamshire 10k run, a quiz night, Branch to Branch walk, The Mansfield's own 'bake off', a 'biggest loser' sponsored diet and an exercise bike challenge in the Mansfield branch. In total employees, and their sponsors, raised £7,500.

Employee volunteering in 2017 included: supporting craft projects at a local school; clearing wasteland to create more useable space for a community garden; assisting with interview/CV practice and career evenings for local teenagers; supporting an initiative run by The Prince's Trust; and painting walls at a local school.

Commercially led support

In 2017 the society launched a range of Community Saver Accounts linked to the society's trust. Every year, the society will contribute to the trust based on balances held in the Community Saver account range.

In addition to the interest paid to savers, a donation equivalent to 0.1% of the average total balances invested in all Community Saver accounts is donated by the society to the trust each year.

Applications

To apply to the society's Community Support Scheme, applicants can fill out the application form available at: mansfieldbs.co.uk.

The scheme only accepts applications from groups in Nottinghamshire or Derbyshire.

Contact the correspondent for further information.

Corporate charity

The Mansfield Building Society Charitable Trust (Charity Commission no. 1177151) – see page 263.

Community contributions

Cash donations UK	£65,000

The society's Community Support Scheme contributions totalled £20,000 in 2017. The society also donated £45,000 to the Mansfield Building Society Charitable Trust. We have taken the total of £65,000 as our figure for the society's cash donations.

Marks and Spencer Group plc

Community development, general charitable purposes

Company registration number: 214436

Correspondent: Mike Barry, Director of Sustainable Business (Plan A), Waterside House, 35 North Wharf Street, London W2 1NW (tel: 020 7935 4422; website: corporate.marksandspencer.com/plan-a)

Directors: Alison Brittain; Amanda Mellor; Andrew Fisher; Andy Halford; Archie Norman; Humphrey Singer; Katie Bickerstaff; Pip McCrostie; Steve Rowe; Vindi Banga (female 40%; male 60%).

Nature of business: The principal activities of the group are retailing clothes, beauty products, home products, food and the provision of financial services.

Year end	31/03/2018
Turnover	£10,698,200,000
Pre-tax profit	£66,800,000

Main locations: The company's headquarters are in London. It has stores throughout the UK.

Community involvement

Marks and Spencer (M&S) supports charities in the areas local to its stores and, at a corporate level, builds strategic partnerships with a number of fundraising partners. M&S stores can select a Local Charity of the Year to raise funds for. Furthermore, 514 stores have donated surplus food to local charities. Employees and customers contribute to fundraising, and employees are supported in their community involvement through volunteering time, payroll giving and matched funding initiatives.

Partner charities

The company has a particular focus on fundraising for health and well-being charities and has a commitment to raising £20 million by 2020; £1.2 million was raised for local and national charities in the UK and Ireland during 2017/18. Having commissioned research during the year, the company plans to develop content focused on selected aspects of health and well-being, employability, and sustainability in schools and colleges. This content will be trialled in schools connected to the company's 'helping transform communities' commitment, and will be available to other schools and colleges in 2019/20.

Partners include: Collectively; Great Ormond Street Hospital; Marine Conservation Society; Newlife; Prostate Cancer UK; Shelter; The Royal British Legion; Unicef; Woodland Trust; WWF.

Community Energy Fund

M&S seeks to enable more communities in Great Britain to 'generate renewable energy and become environmentally and financially sustainable'. The website (www.mandsenergyfund.com) states that it accepts applications for not-for-profit projects that want to use renewable energy to provide community benefits. Community energy groups, sports clubs and community charitable organisations are all eligible to apply.

In-kind support

M&S donates unsold clothing, food and unwanted equipment to a range of charity partners. In 2015 the company introduced a nationwide 'food redistribution scheme' which connects its stores with local food charities.

Employee volunteering

In 2017/18 the company provided at least 30,534 hours of work-time volunteering, including the company's Making Every Moment Special community event, which was run across the UK and Ireland.

Employee-led support

The company operates a payroll giving scheme, and groups of employees (of five or more) who are fundraising can apply to have funds matched.

Commercially led support

'Sparks' card

On registering for the 'Sparks' loyalty card scheme, customers can choose a cause from a selected list of charities. Each time they make a transaction at M&S, their 'Sparks' card can be scanned and M&S makes a donation of 1p to their chosen charity. 'Sparks' members can also earn points by taking part in the Oxfam Shwopping scheme.

Exclusions

According to its website, M&S stores are not able to support:

- Personal appeals on behalf of individual people, including overseas trips
- Advertising or goodwill messages
- Political parties
- Third party fundraising on behalf of a charity
- Religious bodies, except where the project provides non-denominational, non-sectarian support for the benefit of the general project
- Supplying clothing, other than in exceptional circumstances, as we already give clothes to Newlife and Shelter

Applications

Small donations

Each store has a limited budget from which small donations of up to £50 can be made in support of local community causes. The M&S company website advises interested organisations to visit their local store and ask to speak with a manager.

Community Energy Fund

In the first instance, see the fund's website (www.mandsenergyfund.com).

Initial applications are usually made online and are then considered by a team of judges who produce a shortlist. The shortlist of projects is then voted on by the public and the project with the most validated votes in each region will secure the funding. According to the fund's website, prizes are also given to projects the judges feel were inspiring and 'went the extra mile for their community' but didn't win the public vote.

Community contributions

Cash donations UK	£5,900,000
In-kind support UK	£7,700,000
Total contributions (cash and in kind)	£13,600,000

According to the Plan A Report 2018, M&S made community contributions totalling £13.6 million. Based on previous years, we believe the majority of this was given in the UK. Contributions were distributed as follows:

In-kind	£6.5 million
Cash	£5.9 million
Time	£1.2 million

An additional £12.1 million was raised in leveraged funds, which are described in the report as being 'additional funds raised from other sources as a result of M&S activities'. We have taken this to represent funds raised by employees, customers and suppliers and so have not included this in our overall total for contributions.

Marsh Ltd

General charitable purposes

Company registration number: 1507274

Correspondent: CSR Team, 1 Tower Place West, Tower Place, London EC3R 5BU (tel: 020 7357 1000; website: www.marsh.com/uk/about-marsh/corporate-social-responsibility.html)

Directors: Alisa King; Christopher Lay; Claire Valentine; Colin Kiddie; James Nash; Jane Barker; John Hirst; Jospeh Grogan; Mark Chessher; Peter Box; Philip Barton; Roy White; Sally Williams (female 25%; male 75%).

Nature of business: Marsh is a global provider of insurance broking and risk management services with a presence in more than 130 countries.

The company is a wholly owned subsidiary of Marsh and McLennan Companies, Inc., incorporated in Delaware, USA.

Year end	31/12/2017
Turnover	£815,300,000
Pre-tax profit	£196,700,000

Main locations: The company has offices throughout the UK. Details of where they are located are available at www.marsh.com/uk/contact-us/office-locator.html.

Community involvement

The focus of the group's corporate social responsibility programmes is People and Communities at Risk. According to Marsh's UK website, philanthropy and employee volunteering are two of the central elements of its CSR programmes.

Donations policy

The company administers its charitable donations programme centrally. It establishes multi-year partnerships with six UK charities and agrees with each at the beginning of its involvement a specific project or activity that its donation will fund. Marsh then works with its charity to ensure the project or activity is achieved.

Charity partnership

MMC and the British Red Cross teamed up in 2016 for a five-year strategic partnership. The British Red Cross website states that the two organisations work together through fundraising, volunteering and business collaboration 'helping to build resilient communities'.

In-kind support

Through Marsh's volunteering policy, employees can take one day per year to spend on an activity or programme that supports their community.

Employee-led support

Volunteering

Employees are involved in a range of volunteering activities within their communities. The Marsh website also details that: 'In addition, Marsh colleagues in Bristol, Witham and London offices spend one lunchtime per week visiting local school children and helping them with their literacy and numeracy skills. In London, we have had a relationship with the Halley School since 1997.'

MAGIC (Matching and Giving for Involvement with Charities)

Through Marsh MAGIC (Matching and Giving for Involvement with Charities), the group matches employee fundraising efforts up to £300 per employee per year.

Payroll giving

Employees are able to contribute to charities of their choice through the Give As You Earn scheme. Payroll donations are topped up by 10% by Marsh.

Applications

Marsh's charitable donations programme is administered centrally. Contact the correspondent for further information.

Community contributions

Cash donations UK	£209,500

In 2017 the company made donations to charitable organisations in the UK totalling £209,500. We believe donations were received by the company's chosen national charities.

A figure for in-kind support was not provided.

National charity beneficiaries for 2016–19 were: Apps for Good; Business in the Community; Help Musicians UK; The Centre of Social Justice; The Silver Line and Tommy's.

Marshall of Cambridge (Holdings) Ltd

Community development, STEM subjects, general charitable purposes

Company registration number: 2051460

Correspondent: CSR Team, Airport House, The Airport, Newmarket Road, Cambridge CB5 8RY (tel: 01223 373737; website: www.marshall-group.co.uk)

Directors: Alex Dorrian; James Buxton; Julie Baddeley; Philip Yea; Robert Marshall; Sarah Moynihan; Sean Cummins (female 29%; male 71%).

Nature of business: Marshall of Cambridge is the private holding company of the Marshall family. The Marshall group operates in four business sectors; it has three wholly owned businesses – Marshall Aerospace and Defence Group, Marshall Fleet Solutions and Marshall Group Property – and is a majority shareholder of Marshall Motor Holdings plc, an independent public company.

Year end	31/12/2017
Turnover	£2,600,000,000
Pre-tax profit	£30,200,000

Total employees: 6,211

Main locations: The group is headquartered in Cambridge.

Community involvement

Marshall of Cambridge looks to make an active contribution in the communities in which it operates and principally in the area surrounding its group head office in Cambridge. Marshall's 'Code of Business Ethics' document explains that support in the form of cash and in-kind contributions is directed 'primarily to causes with educational, engineering and scientific objectives, as well as to social objectives connected with our business and our place in the wider community'.

The group has a fund with Cambridgeshire Community Foundation which makes grants to support small, local voluntary and community groups and charities in Cambridgeshire. A figure for how much was given to the fund by the group was not provided.

D. G. Marshall of Cambridge Trust (Charity Commission no. 286468)

Historically the trust received donations from the group, however in 2016/17 its income was derived from investments. The trust's primary objectives are to support:

- People who are in need, particularly those who are employees or ex-employees of 'the Company or any subsidiary or associated company' and their dependants
- Local charities
- Local educational institutions of a charitable nature

In 2016/17 the trust awarded grants totalling £99,500 to 39 organisations.

Beneficiaries included: Pembroke College (£51,000); Addenbrookes Charitable Trust (£5,000); National Literacy Trust (£2,000); Horizon Resource Centre (£1,500); Honourable Company of Air Pilots (£1,000); Child Brain Injury Trust (£500); Jimmy's (£120).

STEM – LaunchPad

In 2015 Marshall established LaunchPad, a programme aimed at encouraging young people between the ages of 8 and 18 to choose careers in engineering and related industries. The programme is delivered through local schools in the Cambridge area, and is led by a group of young engineers and apprentices from Marshall. Participants benefitted from talks from LaunchPad ambassadors, visits to Marshall and various engineering-themed activities and competitions. By 2016 the programme had doubled in size and was working with 15 schools, expecting to engage with more than 15,000 people.

Employee-led support

Employees at all levels are encouraged to be involved with their communities. The Group Strategic Report for 2017 explains:

> A large number of our employees are dedicated to local groups, organisations and charities, volunteering their time to undertake a whole host of activities. From parachuting out of an aircraft to raise money for Cancer, swimming the English Channel to raise money for BEN, to coaching a children's football team, our people make a real difference to the community in which they live.

Employees of Marshall and its subsidiary companies also raise funds for a wide range of charitable causes.

Applications

Contact the correspondent for further information.

Applications for the D. G. Marshall of Cambridge Trust should be submitted in writing to the trustees.

Community contributions

Cash donations UK	£32,000

In 2017 the group made charitable donations of £32,000.

Marston's plc

General charitable purposes

Company registration number: 31461

Correspondent: Corporate Social Responsibilty (CSR) Committee, Marston's House, Brewery Road, Wolverhampton WV1 4JT (tel: 01902 711811; website: www.marstons.co.uk/responsibility/charity)

Directors: Andrew Andrea; Anne-Marie Brennan; Carolyn Bradley; Catherine Glickman; Matthew Roberts; Ralph Findlay; Robin Rowland (female 43%; male 57%).

Nature of business: Marston's is a British brewery, pub and hotel operator. It operates over 1,500 pubs in the UK, and is the world's largest brewer of cask ale.

Year end	03/09/2017
Turnover	£840,900,000
Pre-tax profit	£100,300,000

Total employees: 14,500+

Main locations: Marston's is headquartered in Wolverhampton. There is a local pub finder facility on the Marston's website (www.marstons.co.uk/pubs/finder).

Community involvement

Marston's staff and customers support good causes in their local areas various ways, by taking part with fundraising activities. Marston's pubs assist by helping with collections, sponsored activities, the use of rooms, and publicity. Employees are supported in their fundraising activities by matched funding from the Marston's Inns and Taverns Charitable Trust (not a registered charity). There is also an employee charity fund, Marston's Employees Charity Fund (Charity Commission no. 513282) which is supported by donations from the company and makes grants for equipment to hospitals, schools for children with special educational needs and people with disabilities associated with Marston's.

In-kind support

The Marston's website states that its pubs 'assist by helping with collections, sponsored activities, the use of our rooms and publicity'.

Employee-led support

Employee fundraising

Marston's staff fundraise for a variety of local causes. According to the website, employees at Marston's Head Office take part with 'give back days' which feature activities such as cake sales and auctions.

Matched funding

Funds raised by Marston's employees are matched by the Marston's Inns and Taverns Charitable Trust.

Payroll giving

According to the website, employees give to the Marston's Inns and Taverns Charitable Trust voluntarily through their 'salary credit'.

Commercially led support

Cause-related marketing

In 2015 in association with Help for Heroes, Marston's has produced a blonde ale which is on sale in Tesco stores and in Marston's pubs. For each bottle sold in Tesco, five pence will be contributed to the charity and six pence will be donated from the sale of each pint of the ale in pubs. According to the Marston's website, sales of the ale have raised over £160,000 for the charity.

Sponsorship

Marston's sponsors Pub is the Hub, a not-for-profit organisation working to support rural pubs and communities.

Applications

Contact the correspondent for further information.

Community contributions

The annual report and accounts for 2016/17, did not declare a figure for charitable donations. We do know that the company makes contributions to support the employee charity fund, although we weren't able to determine a total for these.

Mazars LLP

Community development, poverty and social exclusion, projects outside the UK, general charitable purposes

Company registration number: OC308299

Correspondent: The Corporate Social Responsibility Team, Tower Bridge House, St Katherine's Way, London E1W 1DD (tel: 020 7063 4000; website: www.mazars.co.uk/Home/About-us/Corporate-Responsibility)

Directors: Antonio Bover; Christoph Regierer; Hervé Hélias; Phil Verity; Philippe Castagnac; Rudi Lang; Ton Tuinier; Victor Wahba; Wenxian Shi (female 0%; male 100%).

Nature of business: Mazars specialises in audit, tax and advisory services around the world.

Year end	31/08/2017
Turnover	£173,600,000
Pre-tax profit	£32,100,000

UK employees: 1,700

Total employees: 20,000

Main locations: Mazars operates in about 300 offices globally, 17 of which are based in the UK.

Community involvement

Mazars LLP donates a proportion its annual profits to various charities. The majority of its giving is through its corporate charity, the Mazars Charitable Trust (Charity Commission no. 1150459) which is funded by the firm. The charity makes grants to charities that have been nominated by teams of employees.

In-kind support

Mazars works closely with the third sector and is a member of organisations such as the Church of England Diocesan Accounting Group, the Charity Finance Group, the Charity Law Association and the Association of Chief Executives of Voluntary Organisations. It delivers free seminars for its charity clients every six months to consider issues affecting the sector.

Employees can take one day a year to volunteer for charities.

Employee-led support

Employees take part in 'Mazars Community Days', where employees can take a day away from the office to participate in community projects as a team. Employees also take part in fundraising events, for example in 2017 more than 200 employees raised over £100,000 for Sense by taking part in a national cycle relay, cycling 1,000 miles over 12 days.

Applications

Contact the correspondent for further information.

Corporate charity

Mazars Charitable Trust (Charity Commission no. 1150459) – see page 264.

Community contributions

Cash donations UK	£439,500

Mazars LLP did not declare its cash donations or total contributions for the year. The Mazars Charitable Trust's annual report 2016/17 notes that it received £439,500 from Mazars LLP. We have taken this figure to be the company's cash donations for the year.

Sir Robert McAlpine Ltd

Community development, education, children and young people, general charitable purposes

Company registration number: 566823

Correspondent: Gillian Bush, Charities Administrator, Eaton Court, Maylands Avenue, Hemel Hempstead, Hertfordshire HP2 7TR (tel: 0333 566 3444; email: sustainability@srm.com; website: www.sir-robert-mcalpine.com)

Directors: Boyd McFee; Gavin McAlpine; Hector McAlpine; James More; Karen Brookes; Martin Pitt; Paul Hamer; Robert McAlpine (female 13%; male 88%).

Nature of business: The company provides building construction, civil engineering, design and project development services.

Year end	31/10/2017
Turnover	£891,902,000
Pre-tax profit	(£23,083,000)

Main locations: The company has offices in Birmingham; Bristol; Cardiff; Edinburgh; Glasgow; Manchester; Newcastle; Leeds; London and Woking.

Community involvement

The company's charitable activities are mainly channelled through two charities, The Robert McAlpine Foundation (Charity Commission no. 226646), which awards grants to organisations, and The McAlpine Educational Endowment (Charity Commission no. 313156), which provides bursaries. The company invests in the communities within which it operates and seeks to establish links with local organisations, charities, schools, businesses and social enterprises.

The Robert McAlpine Foundation

The Robert McAlpine Foundation gives grants to support small UK-based charities with an income of less than £1 million. The foundation prefers to fund charities whose work falls within the following categories: children and young people; older people; social and medical research.

The McAlpine Educational Endowment

The McAlpine Educational Endowment provides bursaries to 13- to 18-year-olds who have sound academic ability, show leadership potential and are facing financial hardship.

Social value and place-making

The company regularly engages with local communities to maximise the social value of its construction projects. The company's 2016 sustainability report gives the recent example of its work on the City of Glasgow College. As part of the project, the company provided the local community with the opportunity to apply for funding via a Supported Futures Trust Fund for the betterment of both student life and educational experience. Successful applications included a project to develop a community garden. The garden is now being used as an outdoor leaning space for college students with learning disabilities.

Education

The company often engages with local schools and colleges to provide activities for students. In addition to employees visiting schools, students are regularly invited to company sites to gain first-hand experience of the construction industry.

Applications

Contact the correspondent for more information.

Community contributions

Cash donations UK	£112,000

The company's 2016/17 accounts do not provide a figure for its total community contributions. However, the company's 2016 sustainability report states that during the year the company donated a total of £112,000 to charity.

McCain Foods (GB) Ltd

General charitable purposes

Company registration number: 733218

Correspondent: Community Team, Havers Hill, Scarborough, North Yorkshire YO11 3BS (tel: 01723 584141; website: www.mccain.co.uk/about-mccain/our-community)

Directors: Alan Bridges; Allison McCain; Andrew Hoff; Daniel Metheringham; Mark Hodge; Mark McCain; Nicholas Vermont; Richard Jones; Richard Smelt; Ross Hunter; Saeeda Amin; Stuart Herd; William Bartlett (female 17%; male 83%).

Nature of business: McCain manufactures and supplies frozen and ambient food products principally in the UK.

Year end	15/11/2017
Turnover	£466,162,000
Pre-tax profit	£47,017,000

Main locations: McCain's has sites in Scarborough, Hull, Montrose, Peterborough and Wolverhampton.

Community involvement

The company's community support programme focuses resources on local issues concentrating on: encouraging healthy, active lifestyles and educating the next generation. The company operates a grant scheme that supports employees' voluntary work in the community.

Employee-led support

Employees' voluntary work is supported by McCain Community Stars grant scheme. No details as to how this scheme operates could be found.

Applications

Contact the correspondent for further information.

Community contributions

Cash donations UK	£52,000

According to the 2016/17 annual report, the company made charitable donations of £52,000. We have no information regarding the beneficiaries; however, the McCain global website states that its community involvement is 'mostly driven locally and managed by the individual regions'.

McDonald's Restaurants Ltd

Health, sports and recreation, children and young people, disability, education, the environment

Company registration number: 1002769

Correspondent: Corporate Affairs Manager, 11–59 High Road, East Finchley, London N2 8AW (website: www.mcdonalds.co.uk/ukhome/Ourworld.html)

Directors: Jason Clark; Douglas Goare; Malcolm Hicks; John Park; Paul Pomroy; Henry Trickey (female 0%; male 100%).

Nature of business: The principal activity of the company is the franchising and operation of a chain of limited menu quick service restaurants.

Year end	31/12/2017
Turnover	£1,593,000,000
Pre-tax profit	£314,000,000

Main locations: McDonald's has stores and franchises throughout the UK and worldwide. Its UK head office is in London.

Community involvement

McDonald's supports its corporate charity, the Ronald McDonald House Charities (UK) (Charity Commission no. 802047), which provides free 'home away from home' accommodation for families of children in hospital and hospices across the UK.

Commercially led support

The National Literacy Trust has worked in partnership with McDonald's since 2013 as part of McDonald's Happy Readers campaign, which strives to increase book ownership and make reading fun for kids by offering free book extracts in its Happy Meal products. Over 55 million books have been distributed through promotions with popular authors such as Roald Dahl and Jeff Kinney. McDonald's swaps out toys in the Happy Meal for books and includes a book offer on the Happy Meal box.

The group's Better Play initiative supports grassroots football. As a sponsorship partner of the four UK Football Associations, the group has a scheme to provide free kits to grassroots football teams and also runs community awards to recognise the contributions of volunteers.

Applications

McDonald's website states that it is fully committed to supporting Ronald McDonald House Charities so does not respond to unsolicited requests.

Community contributions

Cash donations UK	£437,500

The company's 2017 accounts state that it donated £899,000 to Ronald McDonald House Charities (UK) during the year. Of this, £437,500 came directly from the company, the rest was raised through the carrier bag levy in Wales and Scotland. We have taken £437,500 as the figure for the company's cash donation.

Medicash Health Benefits Ltd

Health

Company registration number: 258025

Correspondent: One Derby Square, Derby Square, Liverpool, England L2 1AB (tel: 0800 011 2222; website: www.medicash.org/charity)

Directors: Andrew Roberts; Rt Hon Frank Field; Paul Gambon; Robert Hodson; Susan Weir; William Tubey (female 17%; male 83%).

Nature of business: Medicash is a health insurance provider.

Year end	31/12/2017
Turnover	£25,660,000
Pre-tax profit	£3,467,000

Main locations: Medicash is based in Liverpool.

Community involvement

Support is provided through the company's corporate charity, the Medicash Charitable Trust (Charity Commission no. 257636) which supports health-related charities in the North West.

Corporate charity

Medicash Charitable Trust (Charity Commission no. 257636) – see page 264.

Community contributions

Cash donations UK	£102,000

In 2017 charitable donations to the company's corporate charity totalled £102,000.

Medtronic Ltd

Health

Company registration number: 1070807

Correspondent: CSR Team, Building 9, Croxley Park, Watford, Hertfordshire WD18 8WW (tel: 01923 212213; website: www.medtronic.co.uk)

Directors: Helen Brown; Jacqueline Fielding; Mark Elsey; Philip Albert (female 50%; male 50%).

Nature of business: Medtronic is a medical technology company that generates the majority of its sales and profits from the US healthcare system but is headquartered in Dublin, Ireland.

Year end	28/04/2017
Turnover	£460,844,000
Pre-tax profit	£16,687,000

Main locations: The company's headquarters are in Dublin and it has an office in Watford, Hertfordshire.

Community involvement

The company makes charitable donations predominantly to medical research causes.

Applications

Contact the company for further information.

Community contributions

Cash donations UK	£148,500

In 2016/17 the company made charitable donations totalling £148,500.

John Menzies plc

Education, projects outside the UK, general charitable purposes

Company registration number: SC34970

Correspondent: Charity Fund Administrator, 2 Lochside Avenue, Edinburgh Park EH12 9DJ (website: www.johnmenziesplc.com/responsibility.aspx)

Directors: David Garman; Dr Dermot Smurfit; Forsyth Black; Geoff Eaton; Giles Wilson; John Geddes; Paul Baines; Philip Joeinig; Silla Maizey (female 13%; male 88%).

Nature of business: John Menzies plc is the holding company of Menzies Aviation, an aviation and logistics support services business based in Edinburgh.

Year end	31/12/2017
Turnover	£2,517,700,000
Pre-tax profit	£67,100,000

Total employees: 36,205

Main locations: In the UK, the group has sites in Chester, Edinburgh, Kendal, Preston, Stockton-on-Tees and Wakefield.

Community involvement

The group looks to contribute to communities particularly where it has a presence. Apart from contributing 'skills and expertise' in its local areas, the group also makes charitable donations through its two funds, the Charities Fund and the John M. Menzies Community Fund. The group actively supports its employees' fundraising and volunteering activities.

Charities Fund

The group's Charities Fund supports a small number of charities which have been nominated by each operating division. Each division nominates charities based on their efficiency, integrity and effectiveness.

John Maxwell Menzies Fund

The fund makes cash donations of up to £350 per individual or £700 per team for employees who are involved with a charity or community project. During the year over £10,000 was donated through this fund.

Employee-led support

The group actively supports employees in their fundraising activities. During the year the Menzies Aviation Team completed a cycling challenge to raise money for the UK's first mobile All-Ability Cycling Club run by the charity Bikeworks.

Applications

Nominations are made by the group's divisions.

Community contributions

Cash donations UK	£100,000

In 2017 cash donations from the group totalled £100,000. Of this, £80,000 was allocated to the Main Charity Fund and £20,000 to the John Maxwell Menzies Fund.

Merck Sharp & Dohme Ltd

General charitable purposes

Company registration number: 820771

Correspondent: Corporate Responsibility Team, Hertford Road, Hoddesdon, Hertfordshire EN11 9BU (tel: 01992 467272; email: grantscommittee@merck.com; website: www.msd-uk.com/responsibility/ethics-and-transparency/home.xhtml)

Directors: Ebru Temucin; Louise Houson; Richard Robinski; Simon Nicholson (female 25%; male 75%).

Nature of business: MSD is the UK subsidiary of Merck and Co., Inc., which is headquartered in Kenilworth, New Jersey in the USA and specialises in discovering, developing, manufacturing and marketing pharmaceutical products for human and animal use.

Year end	31/12/2017
Turnover	£748,380,000
Pre-tax profit	£30,468,000

Main locations: There are four MSD sites in the UK: Hoddesdon, Hertfordshire (headquarters and pharmaceutical research and development laboratories); Cramlington, Northumberland (manufacturing); Milton Keynes, Buckinghamshire (animal health headquarters); and London (business development and licensing hub for Europe, the Middle East and Africa).

Community involvement

Merck Sharp & Dohme Ltd (MSD) supports academic, charitable and government organisations, with the aim of 'bringing about better health outcomes for patients'. The company also works with and supports patient organisations 'to enable people to make informed choices about their health'.

In-kind support

The group provides 40 hours of paid volunteering each year to its employees. Some projects include: Dementia Friends; Rennie Grove Hospice; the Scouts and FareShare.

Employee-led support

Employees are entitled to 40 hours of paid volunteering each year.

Applications

Contact the correspondent for further information.

Community contributions

Cash donations worldwide	£371,500

The company's annual report and accounts for 2017 did not declare charitable donations. However, there are two downloadable PDF. documents available from the website which provide a breakdown of payments and donations made during the year to patient organisations and to academic and other non-patient organisations. We have used the information in these documents to calculate the company's charitable contributions during the year.

Patient organisations

In 2017 the company gave financial support to patient organisations amounting to about £125,000. Note that this figure consists of payments given in GBP totalling around £36,000 and payments given in USD totalling $115,000 (≈ £89,000 as at October 2018). As our usual practice, we have not included expenditure such as membership fees or sponsorship in our total.

Beneficiaries included: Nam Publications (£35,000 for funding to support independent prevention and £30,000 to support the PrEP in Europe initiatives); Oral Health Foundation (£20,000 of funding for web-based development); Hepatitis C Trust (£10,000 grant to support peer to peer educations project in NHS Forth Valley).

Payments to academic and other non-patient organisations

In 2017 MSD gave support to academic and other non-patient organisations totalling around £246,500. Note that this figure includes payments given in GBP totalling around £61,500 and payments given in USD totalling $240,000 (≈ £185,000 as at October 2018). As our usual practice, we have not included expenditure such as membership fees or sponsorship in our total.

Beneficiaries included: Royal Society of Medicine (£147,000 in support for an 'expert meeting'); University of Liverpool (£41,000 in support for ongoing development and quality assurance of Hepatitis and HIV drug interaction resources); University of Liverpool (£20,000 in support for the 2017 Vaccinology in Africa); Nuffield Trust (£10,000 in supporter funding for Health Policy Summit); Royal Society of Chemistry (£2,600).

Merlin Entertainments

Health and disability, community development, marine conservation, children and young people

Company registration number: 5022287

Correspondent: CSR Team, 3 Market Close, Poole, Dorset BH15 1NQ (tel: 01202 666900; website: www.merlinentertainments.biz)

Directors: Anne-Francoise Nesmes; Fiona Eastwood; Fraser Montgomery; Hans Aksel Pedersen; John Jakobsen; Justin Platt; Mark Allsop; Mark Fisher; Matt Jowett; Natalie Bickford; Nick Mackenzie; Nick Varney (female 25%; male 75%).

Nature of business: Merlin is an entertainment company, running 115 attractions in 23 countries, in four continents. Examples of attractions in the UK include Alton Towers; Chessington World of Adventures; and Warwick Castle.

Year end	30/12/2017
Turnover	£1,595,000,000
Pre-tax profit	£271,000,000

Main locations: Attractions in the UK are based in Alton, Staffordshire; Birmingham; Blackpool; Brighton; Chertsey, Surrey; Chessington, Surrey; Edinburgh; Gweek, Cornwall; Great Yarmouth; Hunstanton; Loch Lomond; London; Manchester; Oban; Scarborough; Warwick; Weymouth; Windsor; York. There are also attractions in North America; Europe; and Asia Pacific locations.

Community involvement

The group's CSR strategy is called 'Being a Force for Good' and focuses mainly on support given through the group's two charities, Merlin's Magic Wand (Charity Commission no. 1124081), which provides days out and facilities for children in need, and the Sea Life Trust Ltd (Charity Commission no. 1175859), which focuses on marine conservation. The group's attractions also provide local community outreach through in-kind support.

Merlin's Magic Wand (Charity Commission no. 1124081)

The charity provides days out at the group's attractions for children who are seriously ill or disadvantaged or who have disabilities. The charity also creates 'Merlin's Magic Spaces' for organisations such as hospices and hospitals for children who cannot visit Merlin attractions.

In 2017 the charity provided days out for around 60,000 children; travel grants totalling £40,000; delivered eight 'Magic Spaces'; and undertook 38 community outreach visits.

Sea Life Trust Ltd (Charity Commission no. 1175859)

The trust supports conservation projects focusing on oceans and marine life. The trust's areas of focus include: increasing marine protection; reducing plastic litter; combating overfishing. In 2017 the trust committed donations of £68,000, making ten donations to projects and organisations.

Beneficiaries include: Team Turtle (£40,500); Olive Ridley Sea Turtle Projects (£25,000); Prodelphinus (£16,000); Marine Conservation Society (£7,100); Seal Signage Rescue (£5,000).

In-kind support

The company has various initiatives to involve its local communities. The company provides attraction tickets to its corporate charity 'Merlin's Magical Wands', so that disadvantaged children and their families can have a day out at a Merlin attraction.

Employee-led support

Employees support Merlin's Magic Wand through helping with outreach activities and organising fundraising initiatives.

Applications

Contact the correspondent for further information.

Community contributions

Cash donations UK	£617,000
In-kind support worldwide	£942,500
Total contributions (cash and in kind)	£1,560,000

No figure was provided for the group's total contribution. According to Sea Life Trust's 2017 accounts, the trust received a cash donation of £617,000 from Merlin Entertainments Group and gifts in kind of £17,500. Merlin Magic Wand's 2017 accounts also states that the group donated £942,500 in-kind donations and services.

We have taken £617,000 as the group's cash donations for the year, and £1.56 million as its total contribution.

Michelin Tyre plc

Community development, education, health, the environment

Company registration number: 84559

Correspondent: See 'applications', Campbell Road, Stoke-on-Trent, Staffordshire ST4 4EY (website: michelindevelopment.co.uk/support-community-organisations-charities)

Directors: Christopher Smith; Geoffrey Alderman; Gillian Duddy; John Reid; Juergen John; Keith Shepherd; Philippe Berther (female 14%; male 86%).

Nature of business: Michelin manufactures tyres, produces guides and provides mobility support services.

Year end	31/12/2017
Turnover	£685,912,000
Pre-tax profit	(£5,008,000)

Total employees: 2,125

Main locations: In the UK, Michelin have sites in Dundee, Stoke-on-Trent and Watford.

Community involvement

Through its Community Involvement Programme, Michelin looks to build relationships with charities, educational establishments and not-for-profit organisations that work to benefit the local communities in which it operates.

Priority is given to organisations working in Michelin's core focus areas, which are described on the website:

- **Education**: We are committed to developing creative thinkers for tomorrow's workplace. We foster and support programmes that build reading, literacy and numeracy skills within local schools. We also promote scientific and technical professions and encourage youth development through sport and culture. We believe these programmes nurture creativity and develop important life and work skills.
- **Mobility, safety and environment**: We are committed to support programmes that reduce the impact of our activities on the environment. In addition, we look to support programmes that sustain our natural environment and promote green mobility. We work to educate, raise awareness of and sustain better mobility through road safety initiatives.
- **Community enhancement – health and human**: We are committed to supporting programmes that enrich the quality of life for individuals and our communities as a whole. Providing support in Health & Human services should be considered and we also believe the Arts and our heritage are a powerful way to expose people to different cultures and celebrate the diversity of all people.

Support can be given in the form of cash donations, in-kind contributions or 'personnel resources'. It is further explained that 'support is generally awarded for specific activities, not general operating costs, however some operating costs may be allocated for the administration of a project'. Charities with a national presence or which work on a national basis can also be supported.

Commercially led support

Michelin Development

A subsidiary of the company is Michelin Development Ltd, which was established to support the creation of sustainable employment in the areas around Michelin's operations. Through Michelin Development, small and medium-sized businesses (SMEs) can apply for either financial assistance in the form of unsecured loans at subsidised interest rates, or business advice and expertise, or both. The Michelin Development website (michelindevelopment.co.uk) explains that 'support is available to viable projects that can demonstrate the potential to create quality sustainable jobs'.

Exclusions

According to the website, the Community Involvement Programme does not support requests which relate to:

- Organisations that do not have tax-exempt status
- Individuals
- Political organisations, candidates or lobby organisations
- Organisations with a limited constituency or membership
- Travel costs for groups or individuals
- Advertising
- Organisations outside the United Kingdom
- Activities that are not in line with Michelin's corporate values and image

Support is not given for general operating costs, although some operating costs may be given for the administration of a project.

Applications

All applications must be supported by a completed application form, which is available to download from the website. Organisations must make sure that they meet the eligibility criteria before submitting an application. Forms should be returned to the relevant correspondent by email, along with any supporting evidence

Each Michelin UK site has its own community involvement contact:

- Dundee: elaine.walker@michelin.com
- National: christine.reynolds@michelin.com
- Stoke-on-Trent: michelin.requests@michelin.com

The **'National'** contact should only be used for organisations that have a national presence or work on a national basis.

Applicants should allow 30 days for their request to be processed and responded to. Applications are acknowledged in writing. A new application must be submitted each year for ongoing projects.

Community contributions

A figure for charitable donations was not included in the annual report and accounts 2017.

Mick George Ltd

Community development, sports and recreation, general charitable purposes

Company registration number: 2417831

Correspondent: CSR Team, 6 Lancaster Way, Ermine Business Park, Huntingdon, Cambridgeshire PE29 6XU (tel: 0800 587 3329; email: sales@mickgeorge.co.uk; website: www.mickgeorge.co.uk/explore/community)

Directors: Geoffrey Craven; Jonathan Stump; Michael George; Neil Johnson; Peter Newman (female 0%; male 100%).

Nature of business: The company provides a wide range of services to the construction industry including excavation and earth moving, demolition and asbestos removal, skip hire, waste management services, aggregate and concrete supply and facility management.

Year end	31/05/2017
Turnover	£131,363,000
Pre-tax profit	£7,256,000

UK employees: 921

Main locations: The company headquarters are in Huntingdon.

Community involvement

The company supports local charities, sports clubs and community projects through grants, in-kind donations and sponsorship.

Mick George Sports Fund

Grants of £500 to £1,500 are available to sports projects in Peterborough and Cambridgeshire which are open to the general public. The fund is run in association with the charity Living Sport.

Mick George Community Fund

Grants of between £5,000 and £50,000 are available for community projects with a total cost of less than £100,000. Funding is provided by the company through the Landfill Communities Fund.

In-kind support

Local events, community projects and sports teams are supported with in-kind donations. Support is provided in a number of ways including time and resources, materials and specialist equipment.

Commercially led support

The company actively supports local sports clubs and associations within its operating area.

Applications

Sports sponsorship

Contact the correspondent for further information.

In-kind support

Applications can be made via the company's website: www.mickgeorge.co.uk/how-to-apply.

Mick George Sports Fund

Applications can be made via the Living Sport website: www.livingsport.co.uk/funding/mick-george-sports-fund.

Mick George Community Fund

Applications can be made via the Grantscape website: www.grantscape.org.uk/fund/mick-george-community-fund.

Community contributions

We were unable to determine the company's community contributions for the year.

Micro Focus International plc

Community development, children and young people, education

Company registration number: 5134647

Correspondent: Charity Committee, The Lawn, 22–30 Old Bath Road, Newbury, Berkshire RG14 1QN (tel: 01635 565200; website: www.microfocus.com/about/responsibility/index.aspx)

Directors: Amanda Brown; Chris Kennedy; Darren Roos; Karen Slatford; Kevin Loosemore; Lawton Fitt; Nils Braukmann; Richard Atkins; Silke Scheiber; Stephen Murdoch (female 20%; male 80%).

Nature of business: Micro Focus provides software that enables companies to develop, test, deploy, assess and modernize enterprise applications.

Year end	30/04/2017
Turnover	£1,064,000,000
Pre-tax profit	£151,370,500

Main locations: Micro Focus is based in Newbury, Berkshire.

Community involvement

Micro Focus supports its employees' participation in charitable activities through a matched-funding scheme, employee volunteering time and local sponsorships of sports, music clubs and school teams. All initiatives supported follow the 'core themes of education and local community support'.

The company has a local 'project grants' initiative through which 40 charity or community organisations 'with wide geographic spread across Micro Focus operations worldwide' benefitted during the year.

In-kind support

The company encourages employees to help local communities and support relevant charities by allocating a number of employee days per month to teams or individuals to directly benefit a chosen charity or community initiative.

Employee-led support

The company provides matched funding for selected employees charity initiatives.

Applications

Contact the correspondent for further information.

Community contributions

Cash donations worldwide	£62,500

In 2016/17 the group donated over \$80,000 (≈ £62,500 as at November 2018) to selected charities and community support projects across 11 countries in Australia, Bulgaria, China, Germany, India, Ireland, Singapore, South Africa, Spain, the UK and the USA.

In the UK, the following projects were supported:

- Funding equipment for a youth football team
- Supporting two projects providing recreational space for children
- Providing computing equipment to a local school in Newbury
- Helping to deliver a computer science project in Northern Ireland to children aged between 9 and 11

A breakdown by location was not provided.

Microsoft Ltd

General charitable purposes

Company registration number: 1624297

Correspondent: CSR Team, Microsoft Campus, Thames Valley Park, Reading RG6 1WG (email: ukprteam@microsoft.com; website: www.microsoft.com/en-gb/about/charities-communities/#)

Directors: Benjamin Orndorff; Cindy Rose; Keith Dolliver (female 33%; male 67%).

Nature of business: Microsoft Ltd is a subsidiary company of Microsoft Corporation – based in Redmond, Washington State, USA. It markets and supports systems, devices and applications software for business, professional and home use.

Year end	30/06/2017
Turnover	£1,121,000,000
Pre-tax profit	£106,269,000

Main locations: The group's UK head office is in Reading. There are also offices in Cambridge; Edinburgh; London; and Manchester.

Community involvement

The group provides in-kind technological support, matched funding and payroll giving, and has a focus on young people and education.

Education

The group has a number of initiatives to promote STEM education, working in partnership with schools, businesses and organisations such as Computing At School to provide resources for teachers and schools.

Young people

Microsoft runs a 'YouthSpark' initiative which aims to create opportunities for young people. The group also works in partnership with the charity UK Youth on its Generation Code programme, which teaches 14,000 'hard-to-reach' young people how to code, and gives them the opportunity to enter a national competition, The Generation Code Challenge, designing an app with a social action purpose in their community.

In-kind support

The company matches employee donations through its payroll giving scheme.

Software

Since 2006, Microsoft has been one of the companies working with the Technology Trust to provide software donations to eligible UK charities. The website states that it also offers charities and educational organisations subsidised refurbished PCs through the Microsoft Registered Refurbisher programme, and offers software design and development tools free of charge to students and educational organisations through Microsoft Imagine.

Office 365 for charities

Eligible UK charities may apply for Office 365 as a donation. A range of subscription plans are available, some of which donate the programme and others that offer the programme at a discounted price.

Humanitarian support

Globally, the group provides technological support, in-kind and cash donations to assist with humanitarian efforts.

Employee-led support

Employees are encouraged to volunteer in their communities through the group's employee volunteering policy. There is a worldwide corporate giving programme, through which employees donated $158 million (≈ £122.8 million as at November 2018), including the company's matched contribution.

Applications

Software donations

Microsoft makes its software donations through the Technology Trust. For more information see www.tt-exchange.org.

Office 365 options for charities

For more details of Office 365 donations or discounts see products.office.com/en-GB/non-profit/office-365-nonprofit.

Contact the correspondent for further information. Note that Microsoft is only able to donate cash to selected major charity projects.

Community contributions

Total contributions (cash and in kind)	£1,023,000,000

No figure was given for the group's UK charitable contributions.

The worldwide 2017 CSR report states that globally, the group donated more than $1.4 billion (≈ £1 billion as at October 2018) through in-kind technology donations to more than 96,000 charitable organisations. The group also gave $30 million (≈ £23.3 million as at October 2018) in 'technology and cash donations' to emergency response organisations and organisations serving refugees.

The Midcounties Co-operative

General charitable purposes

Company registration number: IP19025R

Correspondent: Community Team, Co-operative House, Warwick Technology Park, Gallows Hill, Warwick CV34 6DA (tel: 01926 516000; email: communityteam@midcounties.coop; website: www.midcounties.coop/community)

Directors: Clive Booker; Donald Morrison; Ellie Freeman; Gary Hayes; Heather Richardson; Helen Wiseman; Irene Kirkman; Jean Nunn-Price; Judith Feeney; Kathy Peterson; Martin Cook; Matthew Lane; Olivia Birch; Patrick Gray; Steve Allsopp; Vivian Woodell (female 50%; male 50%).

Nature of business: The Midcounties Co-operative is registered as an Industrial and Provident Society and has more than 500 trading sites.

Year end	27/01/2018
Turnover	£1,094,784,000
Pre-tax profit	£4,300,000

UK employees: 8,663

Main locations: The society's website describes its 'heartlands' as being Oxfordshire, Gloucestershire, Buckinghamshire, Shropshire, Staffordshire, the West Midlands, Wiltshire, and Worcestershire. It also trades in the surrounding counties and its energy, childcare, travel and flexible benefits businesses trade throughout the UK.

Community involvement

Support is mainly provided through community grants and charity partnerships.

Low level grants

Members can apply for up to £250 to support their local good cause and these grants are available throughout the year.

Co-operative Community Funding

Grants of up to £2,000 are available to groups working in a community where there is a Midcounties store.

Charity partners

The society has a charity partner in each regional community it works in. In 2017 almost £150,000 was raised for charity partners.

In-kind support

Every Midcounties Co-op employee is entitled to take up to three days' paid leave for volunteering purposes. In 2017 staff provided a total of 36,600 volunteering hours.

Employee-led support

The society's website explains that employees take part with a wide range of volunteering activities in their communities.

Applications

Volunteering

Contact the correspondent for further information.

Low level grants

Contact your nearest trading site for further information.

Community funding

Criteria and application forms can be downloaded from the society's website.

Community contributions

Cash donations UK	£262,000
In-kind support UK	£528,000
Total contributions (cash and in kind)	£790,000

In 2017/18 the society awarded £262,000 in grants. Volunteering by staff was equivalent to a financial value of £528,000.

Mills and Reeve LLP

Community development, health

Company registration number: OC326165

Correspondent: See 'Applications', 4th Floor, Monument Place, 24 Monument Street, London EC3R 8AJ (email: enquiry@mills-reeve.com; website: www.mills-reeve.com/csr)

Nature of business: Mills and Reeve are among the 50 largest law firms in the UK.

Year end	31/05/2017
Turnover	£93,300,000
Pre-tax profit	£35,700,000

UK employees: 1,000+

Main locations: Mills and Reeve have offices in Birmingham, Cambridge, Leeds, London, Manchester and Norwich.

Community involvement

Mills and Reeve's corporate responsibility programme focuses on the following areas:

- Giving cash donations through its corporate charity, the Mills and Reeves Charitable Trust (Charity Commission no. 326271), and through matched funding employees' fundraising efforts
- Pro bono work for community projects, charities and individuals
- Supporting local charities, schools and not-for-profit groups through employee volunteering and fundraising
- Improving the firm's environmental performance and supporting local environmental projects

Partnerships

The firm has a Charity of the Year programme and supported Dogs For Good in 2017. Employees also support IntoUniversity by volunteering to work with young people to develop their commercial awareness and career choices and coach them on interview techniques or time-management. Previously the firm has supported a wide range of charities including: Age Concern; Big Bus Project; Big C; Bloodwise; Macmillan Cancer Support; Teenage Cancer Trust; UK Community Foundations; WellChild.

Each of office also chooses a local charity to work with. Currently the offices support: Sifa Fireside – Birmingham; Blue Smile – Cambridge; St George's Crypt – Leeds; Toynbee Hall – London; Barnabus – Manchester; and The Priscilla Bacon Centre – Norwich.

In-kind support

Mills and Reeve is part of the LawWorks scheme and provides pro bono support to charities as well as to individuals who cannot afford legal representation. Examples of support include advising charities on amendments to their constitution, helping to set up and register new charities, and advising on the Stalham-with-Happing Partnership's conversion to charitable status.

Each employee is given one day's paid leave to volunteer each year.

Employee-led support

Employees volunteer and fundraise for the firm's Charity of the Year programme as well as for local charitable organisations. Recent examples on the firm's website include:

- Mentoring black and ethnic minority students in schools and universities in London and Birmingham
- Taking part in the Big Toy Count for Romsey Mill
- Exercising our green fingers to provide some TLC to the Age UK day centre garden in Norwich
- Donating suits to homeless people seeking jobs in Birmingham and Manchester

Applications

Contact your local office for further information on pro bono support and partnerships. Contact details can be found at https://www.mills-reeve.com/offices.

Corporate charity

Mills and Reeve Charitable Trust (Charity Commission no. 326271) – see page 264.

Community contributions

Cash donations UK	£70,000

In 2016/17 Mills and Reeve donated £70,000 to its corporate charity.

Moneysupermarket.com Group plc

Community development

Company registration number: 6160943

Correspondent: Community Team, Moneysupermarket House, St David's Park, Ewloe, Chester CH5 3UZ (tel: 01244 665700; website: corporate.moneysupermarket.com/company/csr.aspx)

Directors: Andrew Fisher; Bruce Carnegie-Brown; Darren Drabble; Genevieve Shore; Mark Lewis; Matthew Price; Robin Freestone; Sally James (female 25%; male 75%).

Nature of business: Moneysupermarket.com is a British price comparison website.

Year end	31/12/2017
Turnover	£329,700,000
Pre-tax profit	£96,100,000

Total employees: 631

Main locations: The group has three main offices in Ewloe (near Chester), London and Manchester.

Community involvement

Moneysupermarket.com and its employees supported more than 40 charities and community groups during 2017 through its 'Community Initiative' and a staff volunteering scheme. The group and its employees also select a Charity of the Year to support. The group tends to support charities within the areas of Flintshire and Cheshire.

Money Saving Expert (MSE) Charity (Charity Commission no. 1121320)

One of the group's subsidiaries, MoneySavingExpert, set up The MoneySavingExpert charity, which is a grant-making charity dedicated to improving information and education about debt, money and consumer issues with £60,000 donated in 2017. In addition to this, MoneySavingExpert supported a number of charities including ShelterBox, CAP UK and the Samaritans with donations totalling a further £30,000. We have not included this charity in our guide as its income is from public donations and proceeds from Martin Lewis's (the website's founder) publications.

Community Initiative

According to the group's 2017 annual report, £6,000 was given per quarter to the group's community initiative which was 'channelled via the Charities Aid Foundation, enabling the group to make gross donations to registered charities'. In addition to this, the group donated £31,000 to its Charity of the Year. Although no donations were made through the initiative in 2017, the annual report states that it will continue to develop its community involvement programme.

In-kind support

The group gives a total of 60 days a year through its staff volunteering scheme.

Employee-led support

Moneysupermarket.com employees play an active role in researching and finding local charitable causes for the group to help support. Each month, a volunteer group of employees meets to discuss requests for donations and to allocate funds in line with agreed guidelines.

Employee fundraising

During the year, the group's employees raised £41,500 for Shelter, the group's Charity of the Year.

Applications

Contact the correspondent for further information.

Community contributions

Cash donations UK	£138,000

According to the group's 2017 annual report, total donations to charitable causes during the year amounted to £138,000.

Costings for in-kind support were not provided.

Beneficiaries included: Allsorts Preschool; Citizens Advice; Flintshire Young Carers; Mold Community Hospital; Superkids and Whizz-Kidz.

Morgan Stanley and Co. International plc

Community development, general charitable purposes

Company registration number: 2068222

Correspondent: Community Affairs Team, 25 Cabot Square, Canary Wharf, London E14 4QA (tel: 020 7425 1302; email: communityaffairslondon@morganstanley.com; website: www.morganstanley.com/globalcitizen/community_affairs.html)

Directors: Alistair Darling; Dennia Nally; Elizabeth Corley; Hutham Olayan; James Gorman; Jami Miscik; Mary Schapiro; Nobuyuki Hirano; Perry Traquina; Rayford Wilkins; Robert Herz; Ryosuke Tamakoshi; Thomas Glocer (female 31%; male 69%).

Nature of business: The group's principal activity is the provision of financial services to corporations, governments and financial institutions.

Year end	31/12/2017
Pre-tax profit	£1,008,000,000

Main locations: In the UK, Morgan Stanley has offices in Glasgow and London.

Community involvement

Morgan Stanley supports organisations in regions where it has a presence through the Morgan Stanley International Foundation (Charity Commission no. 1042671). This includes the boroughs of Tower Hamlets and Newham in London, Glasgow, as well as continental Europe, the Middle East and Africa. Grants are made to organisations focusing on children's health and education.

In-kind support

The Strategy Challenge is Morgan Stanley's global pro bono programme. In 2017 five charities benefitted from pro bono work through the programme. A team worked with Save the Children helping to develop a strategy around the charity's vision to build an effective business model to grow its parental engagement programme in the UK.

Employee-led support

Global Volunteer Month is Morgan Stanley Group's annual global initiative focused on encouraging all employees to give their time to local communities. Through Global Volunteer Month and other campaigns, in 2017, employees logged 518,000 in volunteer hours for charities around the world.

According to the group's 2017 annual report, over '25,000 employees donated over $40 million to charities globally'.

Applications

Contact the correspondent for further information on Morgan Stanley's pro bono programme.

Corporate charity

Morgan Stanley International Foundation (Charity Commission no. 1042671) – see page 265.

Community contributions

Cash donations UK	£1,200,000
Cash donations worldwide	£1,600,000

According to the group's 2017 accounts, the group made donations to various charities totalling $2.1 million (≈ £1.6 million as at January 2019) worldwide, of which $1.5 million (≈ £1.2 million as at January 2019) was donated to the Morgan Stanley International Foundation.

We have taken the donation to the foundation to be the UK contribution.

Wm Morrison Supermarkets plc

General charitable purposes

Company registration number: 358949

Correspondent: CSR Team, Hillmore House, Gain Lane, Bradford BD3 7DL (email: cr@morrisonsplc.co.uk; website: www.morrisons-corporate.com/cr)

Directors: Andrew Higginson; Belinda Richards; David Potts; Kevin Havelock; Neil Davidson; Paula Vennells; Rooney Anand; Tony van Kralingen; Trevor Strain (female 22%; male 78%).

Nature of business: Wm Morrison Supermarkets operates a chain of retail supermarket stores under the Morrisons brand.

Year end	04/02/2018
Turnover	£17,262,000,000
Pre-tax profit	£374,000,000

UK employees: 105,487

Main locations: Morrisons operates stores throughout the UK.

Community involvement

Morrisons supports general charitable purposes through its grant-making corporate charity the Morrisons Foundation (Charity Commission no.1160224). The company also donates surplus food to local community groups and fundraises for its charity partners and other national charities.

The Morrisons Foundation

The foundation was set up in 2015 to provide financial support to registered charities in England, Scotland and Wales, with the aim of making positive difference in people's lives. Beneficiaries have included disability charities, educational projects, homeless shelters and hospices. Employees can also apply to the foundation for matched funding to support their fundraising activities.

The foundation receives its income from a number of sources and is the main beneficiary of funds raised through carrier bag sales in stores in England, Scotland and Wales. The foundation also benefits from some of the revenue generated by charity scratchcards and clothing banks at Morrisons.

According to the foundation's 2017/18 annual review, during the year the charity awarded £10 million in grants. This figure includes £550,000 in matched funding.

Partnerships

In 2017/18 Morrisons launched a new three-year national charity partnership with CLIC Sargent – the UK's leading charity for children and young people with cancer. During the year, the company raised over £3 million for the charity. Fundraising activities included static cycles, marathons, sponsored walks, coffee mornings and book sales.

In addition to its national charity partner, Morrisons helps to raise funds for other national charity campaigns such as Children in Need, the Poppy Appeal and Movember.

Morrisons also supports WRAP's 'Love Food Hate Waste' campaign to reduce food waste in the UK. Through its corporate social media channels, website and internal communications, the company provides employees and customers with information, hints and tips on how best to plan their food shopping, store food, and utilise leftovers to save money and reduce waste.

In-kind support

Through its unsold food programme Morrisons' partners with local community groups to donate any unsold food that is safe to eat. During the year, the company donated over three million unsold food products, working with over 420 community groups.

Employee-led support

Community Champions

Each Morrisons store has a Community Champion employee who manages engagement between the store and groups and charities in its local community. Community Champions organise activities to help raise funds for local causes, as well as for the Morrisons national charity partner. The Morrisons website explains that 'the Community Champion co-ordinates in store fundraising for our national charity partnership, organises community bag packs, school and community tours and looks to support local events – plus a whole host of other activity, bespoke to each store'.

Employee fundraising

Employees from Morrisons' stores, sites and head office raise funds through a varied range of activities – from individual running challenges to national in-store events such as 'Morrisons to the Moon' and 'Communi-Tea Parties'.

Matched funding

The Morrisons Foundation matches funds raised by employees for good causes (up to £1,000, two times per year).

Commercially led support

Morrisons donates money from the sales of certain products to charitable causes.

Applications

General enquiries can be submitted in writing to the correspondent.

The Morrisons Foundation

Applications must be made through the foundation's website. Matched funding applications are normally processed within six weeks and grant applications can take up to three months to review. Charities that have previously received a grant can apply for further funding after completing and submitting a post-grant report.

Local opportunities

Enquiries regarding local support or in-kind contributions can be directed to your local store's Community Champion.

Sponsorship

The Morrisons Foundation's website states: 'Unfortunately we're unable to support requests for sponsorship, although your local store may be able to provide a raffle prize, or food or drink for an event.'

Community contributions

The company's annual report and accounts for 2017/18 did not declare a figure for charitable donations, nor could we determine a figure for the value of in-kind support given by the group.

Mothercare plc

Education, health, children and young people

Company registration number: 1950509

Correspondent: Amy Whidburn, Global Head of Corporate Responsibility, Mothercare plc, Cherry Tree Road, Watford, Hertfordshire WD24 6SH (tel: 01923 241000; email: Corporate.Responsibility@Mothercare.com; website: www.mothercareplc.com/corporate-responsibility/communities.aspx)

Directors: Clive Whiley; David Wood; Gillian Kent; Glyn Hughes; Mark Newton-Jones; Nick Wharton (female 17%; male 83%).

Nature of business: Mothercare is a retailer specialising in products for mothers-to-be, babies and children up to the age of eight.

Year end	24/03/2018
Turnover	£654,500,000
Pre-tax profit	£7,100,000

UK employees: 4,567

Total employees: 4,727

Main locations: Mothercare operates stores across the UK. The group also has a presence in Asia.

Community involvement

The Mothercare Group Foundation (Charity Commission no. 1104386) aims to help parents in the UK and worldwide give their children the best chance of good health, education, well-being and a secure start in life.

According to the group's website, the foundation supports the following three areas:

- Ensuring the good health and well-being of mums-to-be, new mums and their children
- Special baby care needs and premature births; and
- Parenting initiatives (or charities) that support families on the parenting journey, uniting mums (and dads) to take on parenting together

Between 2004 and 2011, the foundation made donations in excess of £1 million to children's and parenting charities. At the time of writing (November 2018) the foundation was not accepting applications for grants. Instead, the foundation's funds have been used to support the group's Charity of the Year as well as its employee matched fundraising scheme.

The foundation receives donations from Mothercare's annual pre-tax profits. Funds are also generated from the proceeds of the group's staff shop, ad hoc donations and staff fundraising.

Partnerships

The group's official Charity of the Year for 2017/18 was Bliss, a UK charity working to provide care and support for premature and sick babies and their families. During the year, the group's foundation made donations of £40,000. In addition, many group employees engaged in fundraising activities, raising over £7,500 for the charity. Following a review by the foundation's trustees, it was decided to extend the partnership with Bliss until April 2019.

In-kind support

#giftabundle initiative

The group's #giftabundle initiative is run in partnership with the environmental charity Hubbub and encourages customers to donate bundles of good quality clothing for babies and children that are then distributed to other local families. In 2018 the initiative was extended to run in 42 stores across the UK. During the year, a total of 6,055 bundles were gifted by customers, amounting to approximately 52,000 items of clothing.

Store events

Mothercare's 'Expectant Parent' events run in around 130 stores across the UK, six times a year (usually in February, April, June, September, October and December). During these events employees give advice on in-car safety, sleep safety, pushchair choices and the best toys for baby's first year. Midwives, health visitors, first aid trainers and other experts also frequently attend the events to offer advice to parents-to-be. The group also provides advice to customers about relevant campaigns and events such as National Breastfeeding Week, World Prematurity Day and Child Safety Week.

Employee-led support

Mothercare runs a matched funding scheme, meaning that the group will match employees' own fundraising activities up to a maximum of £250. During 2017/18, £5,500 was donated to top-up employee fundraising efforts.

According to the group's 2017/18 annual report, the group intends to launch an employee-volunteering scheme in autumn 2018.

Commercially led support

In 2017/18 Mothercare donated all proceeds from the use of single-use carrier bags in England, Scotland and Wales to its chosen environmental charity, Trees for Cities, which works to create greener cities through volunteering, education and engagement with local communities. During the year, a total of £91,000 was donated to Trees for Cities, bringing the total donations to the charity since 2015 to £293,000.

Applications

General enquiries can be submitted in writing to the correspondent.

Mothercare Group Foundation

At the time of writing (October 2018), the group's website stated that 'regrettably, the foundation is not accepting funding applications at present, although this situation may change in the future'.

Community contributions

Mothercare's 2017/18 annual report does not provide a figure for its total community contributions.

Motorola Solutions UK Ltd

General charitable purposes

Company registration number: 912182

Correspondent: CSR Team, Nova South, 160 Victoria Street, London, United Kingdom SW1E 5LB (tel: 020 7019 0461; website: www.motorolasolutions.com)

Directors: Akash Raj; Ian McCullagh; Joanne Bamber; John Wozniak; Philip Jefferson; Simon Smith (female 17%; male 83%).

Nature of business: Motorola Solutions (Motorola) is a global provider of communication infrastructure, devices, accessories, software and services.

This record refers to Motorola Solutions UK Ltd, a UK-registered subsidiary whose ultimate parent company is Motorola Solutions, which is incorporated in the USA.

Year end	31/12/2016
Turnover	£78,500,000
Pre-tax profit	£10,500,000

Main locations: Motorola Solutions has offices worldwide. Its UK office is located in Basingstoke, Hampshire.

Community involvement

Motorola Solutions UK Ltd supports community causes in the form of cash and product donations, as well as employee volunteering and fundraising activities. The company's community involvement, which is supported by the work of the Motorola Solutions Foundation, is part of the commitment Motorola Solutions Inc. has in the communities in which it has a presence worldwide.

Motorola Solutions Foundation

According to Motorola's website, this US-based foundation was established in 1953 as the 'charitable and philanthropic arm' of Motorola. Each year, the foundation 'donates millions of dollars to science, technology, engineering and math education as well as public safety programs and disaster relief'. The foundation also facilitates employee matched giving programmes, both in the USA and around the globe.

The foundation operates several grants programmes across its chosen areas, including Innovation Generation (STEM) Grants and Public Safety Grants for organisations in the USA. Organisations based outside the USA are supported through the foundation's international grants programme.

The website explains:

> The International grant program supports programs that improve students' skills in science, technology, engineering and math (STEM) through hands-on activities or provide safety education and training to first responders, their families and the general public outside of North America.

More information on the international grants programme and the work carried out by the foundation can be found on the Motorola website.

According to the Motorola Solutions UK Ltd annual report, in 2016 the Motorola Solutions Foundation supported the following organisations in the UK:

- University of Bristol – support was given to the university's Enterprise Competition which helps find 'the newest technology entrepreneurs'
- University of Southampton – 'which received a grant to support robotics research among schoolchildren'
- The Blue Lamp Trust – 'which provides tangible support to vulnerable people in Hampshire'
- Greenpower Education Trust – 'a charity with the goal to advance education in the subjects of sustainable engineering and technology to young people and to change current views about engineering, presenting it as a fascinating, relevant and dynamic career choice for any young person'

In-kind support

Support is given in the form of product donations and employee volunteering.

Employee-led support

Volunteering

The company's 2016 annual report states that employee fundraising during the year contributed to over £2,000 to charities chosen by employees including Sport Relief, RNLI, Macmillan, The Tabitha Foundation and Child Victims of Crime.

According to the group's CSR report, 1,800 employees volunteered their time, contributing a total of 23,000 hours to charitable causes worldwide. It is unknown how any employees volunteered for causes in the UK.

Matched funding

According to the website, the Motorola Solutions Foundation provides 'employees with matching programs in the United States and globally'. We were unable to determine specific details of matched funding activities in the UK.

Applications

In the first instance, see the Motorola Solutions Foundation page on the company's website which gives more information about the foundation and its international grants programme, including guidelines and dates of application rounds.

For any further information, contact the correspondent.

Community contributions

Cash donations UK	£4,000
Total contributions (cash and in kind)	£8,800,000

According to the 2017 Corporate Responsibility Report, at a global level Motorola's and the Motorola Solutions Foundation's community contributions, including cash and in-kind donations, totalled \$11.5 million (≈ £8.8 million as at October 2018). This included 'employee matching gifts/volunteerism' which was valued at $1.4 million (≈ £1 million as at October 2018).

Of the total amount contributed by Motorola worldwide, $600,000 (≈ £462,500 as at October 2018) was given in Europe and Africa.

The annual report and accounts of Motorola Solutions UK Ltd 2016 declared donations to UK charities amounting to £4,000. We were unable to determine a value for in-kind donations given in the UK. It is therefore possible that the total amount contributed to charitable causes in the UK exceeded the figure declared in the annual report and accounts.

Music Sales Group Ltd

Arts and culture, education, health, disability, general charitable purposes

Company registration number: 884449

Correspondent: 14–15 Berners Street, London W1T 3LJ (website: www.musicsales.com)

Directors: Christopher Butler; Claude Duvivier; David Holley; David Rockberger; Ian Gilroy; James Rushton; Marcus Wise; Mildred Wise; Robert Wise; Tomas Wise (female 10%; male 90%).

Nature of business: The Music Sales Group of companies is engaged in the publishing, wholesaling and retailing of printed music and books, and is a publisher of standard and classical music copyright.

Year end	31/12/2017
Turnover	£66,600,000
Pre-tax profit	(£1,600,000)

Main locations: In the UK, the group has offices in London and Bury St Edmunds. Worldwide it has offices in Australia, Denmark, France, Germany, Hong Kong, Japan, Spain and the USA.

Community involvement

All of the group's charitable giving is directed through its corporate charity Music Sales Charitable Trust (Charity Commission no. 1014942).

Corporate charity

Music Sales Charitable Trust (Charity Commission no. 1014942) – see page 266.

Community contributions

Cash donations UK	£100,000

In 2017 the group donated £100,000 to its corporate charity.

N. Brown Group plc

Community development, education, health, older people, children and young people, projects outside the UK

Company registration number: 814103

Correspondent: CSR Team, Griffin House, 40 Lever Street, Manchester M60 6ES (tel: 0161 236 8256; email: ethicaltrading@nbrowngroup.co.uk; website: www.nbrown.co.uk/sustainability/charities)

Directors: Angela Spindler; Craig Lovelace; Gillian Barr; Lord David Alliance; Margaret Jones; Matthew Davies; Michael Ross; Richard Moross; Ron Macmillan; Stephen Johnson; Theresa Casey (female 36%; male 64%).

Nature of business: N. Brown provides internet and catalogue shopping, specialising in clothing, footwear, household and electrical goods.

Year end	03/03/2018
Turnover	£922,200,000
Pre-tax profit	£16,200,000

UK employees: 2,600+

Main locations: The group is headquartered in Manchester.

Community involvement

According to its website, the group is currently supporting three charities chosen by customers in the UK – Breast Cancer Now, Prostate Cancer UK and The Silver Line. It also supports Breaking The Cycle UK which provides further education opportunities for secondary school girls from financially disadvantaged families in Greater Sylhet, Bangladesh. The group sponsors 30 girls for five years through this programme.

Employee-led support

Employees volunteer and fundraise for local community causes.

Commercially led support

The group sponsors events in Manchester and the North West. In 2017 it sponsored the Manchester International Festival. Following the Manchester Arena bombing in 2017 the group designed a charity T-shirt and sweatshirt and raised £12,000 for the We Love Manchester Emergency Fund run by the British Red Cross.

Applications

Contact the correspondent for further information.

Community contributions

Cash donations UK	£93,500

In 2017/18 the group made donations of £93,500 to charities. A list of beneficiaries was not included.

National Express Group plc

General charitable purposes

Company registration number: 2590560

Correspondent: National Express House, Mill Lane, Digbeth, Birmingham B5 6DD (tel: 0845 013 0130; website: www.nationalexpressgroup.com/our-way)

Directors: Chris Davies; Chris Muntwyler; Dean Finch; Dr Ashley Steel; Jane Kingston; Joaquín Ayuso; Jorge Cosmen; Lee Sander; Matt Ashley; Matthew Crummack; Mike McKeon; Sir John Armitt (female 17%; male 83%).

Nature of business: National Express is a British multinational public transport company that operates bus, coach, train and tram services in the UK, the USA, Spain, Morocco and Germany.

Year end	31/12/2017
Turnover	£2,321,200,000
Pre-tax profit	£156,400,000

Main locations: National Express is headquartered in London.

Community involvement

The majority of the group's community support in the UK is carried out through its corporate charity, The National Express Foundation (Charity Commission no. 1148231). The charity makes grants to charitable and community groups working to 'support young people and promote cross-community cohesion'.

The group's companies also conduct their own community initiatives in their respective countries.

Partnerships

The group works with The Prince's Trust to deliver mentoring and volunteering programmes and host work experience placements.

Employee-led support

The group's employees play a central role in its community involvement through volunteering, fundraising activities and a payroll giving scheme. In 2009, the group launched the Employee Charity Panel, which meets quarterly to identify and allocate funds to charities in the UK.

Exclusions

The following information has been taken from the group's website:

> The focus for our charitable support is in areas aligned to our business and our employees. We are therefore unable to support financial requests from individuals outside the business, political or denominational groups, arts or sports

groups, medical and animal welfare organisations or building projects.

We don't support requests for advertising or sponsorship unless they are part of a project we are already involved with.

Because of the volume of requests we get, we are also unable to offer free travel for charity 'jailbreaks' and other external fundraising events.

Corporate charity

The National Express Foundation (Charity Commission no. 1148231) – see page 266.

Community contributions

Cash donations UK	£150,000

According to the group's 2017 annual report, it gave £150,000 in cash donations to The National Express Foundation.

The National Farmers Union Mutual Insurance Society Ltd (NFU)

Education, the environment, general charitable purposes

Company registration number: 111982

Correspondent: CSR Team, Tiddington Road, Stratford upon Avon, Warwickshire CV37 7BJ (email: doing_our_bit@nfumutual.co.uk; website: www.nfumutual.co.uk)

Directors: Ali Capper; Brian Duffin; Chris Stooke; Christine Kennedy; Eileen McCusker; Jim McLaren; Jon Bailie; Lindsay Sinclair; Nick Turner; Richard Percy; Steve Bower; Richard Morley (female 25%; male 75%).

Nature of business: The National Farmers Union Mutual Insurance Society Ltd, trading as NFU Mutual, is a UK-registered mutual insurance composite. It underwrites more than £1 billion in annual premium in life and general insurance lines for rural communities within the UK.

Year end	31/12/2017
Pre-tax profit	£640,000,000

UK employees: 3,756

Main locations: NFU's headquarters are in Warwickshire. There are over 300 local offices throughout the UK.

Community involvement

Support is provided charitable initiatives connected with agriculture, the countryside and the insurance industry through The NFU Mutual Charitable Trust (Charity Commission no. 1073064). Small grants are also made to community groups through the NFU Mutual Community Giving Fund.

The Community Giving Fund

The Community Giving Fund was set up in 2005 to support local initiatives and charitable events as well as boost staff fundraising initiatives. The fund makes grants of up to £250 and considers donations such as promotional items and prizes. In 2017 it helped 85 community groups and charities across the UK.

In-kind support

NFU gives employees one day a year to volunteer. In 2017 a total of 116 employees volunteered 812 hours.

Employee-led support

Each employee is offered the opportunity to volunteer one day a year to work on projects facilitated by one of NFU's volunteering partners or other community initiatives.

Exclusions

The NFU website states that the Community Giving Fund will not fund the following:

- Advertising
- Animal charities
- Charities overseas
- Political activity
- Our own products (i.e. insurance)
- Religious organisations
- Rent or property maintenance
- Requests for charity sponsorship (apart from our staff members)
- Retrospective requests
- Sponsorship and fundraising activities for the benefit of an individual
- Staffing costs
- Travel expenses

Applications

Community Giving Fund

Information on the fund can be found on the Community Giving Fund section of the NFU's website.

Application forms can be requested from the correspondent.

Corporate charity

The NFU Mutual Charitable Trust (Charity Commission no. 1073064) – see page 267.

Community contributions

Cash donations UK	£616,000

In 2017 charitable donations totalled £616,000 which included £300,000 to the NFU Mutual Charitable Trust, £300,000 to the Farm Safety Foundation and £16,000 to the Community Giving Fund.

National Grid plc

General charitable purposes

Company registration number: 4031152

Correspondent: The Responsibility and Sustainability Team, National Grid House, Warwick Technology Park, Gallows Hill, Warwick CV34 6DA (website: www2.nationalgrid.com/responsibility)

Directors: Alison Kay; Amanda Mesler; Dean Seavers; John Pettigrew; Jonathan Dawson; Mark Williamson; Nicola Shaw; Nora Mead Brownell; Paul Golby; Sir Peter Gershon; Therese Esperdy (female 45%; male 55%).

Nature of business: The principal operations of the group are the ownership and operation of regulated electricity and gas infrastructure networks in the UK and the US.

Year end	18/10/2018
Turnover	£15,250,000,000
Pre-tax profit	£2,708,000,000

Total employees: 23,023

Main locations: The group has sites in Castle Donnington, Hinckley, Leeds, London, Manchester, Newark, Solihull, Warwick and Wokingham.

Community involvement

National Grid focuses a large part of its community involvement, both in the UK and the USA, on education and skills development for young people in the form of cash donations, staff volunteering and sponsorship.

Community Grant Programme

Grants of up to £20,000 are available to charities and community organisations in areas where the work of National Grid impacts on communities.

Fuel poverty

Affordable Warmth Solutions CIC was set up by National Grid in 2009 and provides assistance to people experiencing fuel poverty in deprived areas. The CIC administrate The Warm Homes Fund, which is a £150 million fund provided by National Grid. The fund is designed to incentivise the installation of affordable heating solutions in fuel-poor households who do not use mains gas as their main heating fuel. The fund is split into the following three categories:

- Urban homes and communities
- Rural homes and communities
- Specific energy efficient/health related solutions

The fund has a series of bidding rounds and operates across Scotland, Wales and England. Local authorities and registered social landlords working with local partners are invited to apply. As of March 2018, £63 million has been allocated by the fund.

Charity of the Year

During the year, National Grid came to the end of an 18-month partnership with the Alzheimer's Society. At the time of writing (November 2018) the group had not selected a new charity partner.

In-kind support

National Grid employees delivered projects for young people to improve their STEM skills, and helped run a careers education and work experience programme.

The company also runs an employee-led internship programme for young people aged 17 to 25 with special educational needs and disabilities. In 2017/18 the company provided 14 placements at three UK offices for interns with 64% moving into employment.

Employee-led support

In 2017/18 over 22,390 hours of voluntary support was given to community projects across the UK. Employees also partook in various fundraising activities during the year. Over £270,000 was raised during the company's 18-month partnership with the Alzheimer's Society that ended in March 2018. The company also raised over £336,000 for other good causes.

Applications

Community Grant Programme

To apply to the Community Grant Programme the group asks applicants to read the 'who can apply' and 'what we fund' documents available at: betl.nationalgrid.co.uk. The group prefers to receive applications online but applicants can also call the Community Helpline (01285 841912) if they need assistance.

The Warm Homes Fund

Information on how to apply to The Warm Homes Fund can be found at: www.affordablewarmthsolutions.org.uk/warm-homes-fund/overview.

Community contributions

Cash donations UK	£242,000

The group's Strategic Report 2017/18 valued its 'volunteering, fundraising and community contributions' worldwide at £73 million. In the Annual Report 2017/18, it states that the group's overall contribution of its 'corporate responsibility work' in the UK was valued at just over £66 million. According to its website, the group awarded just over £242,000 worth of grants to a variety of community projects across in the UK through its Community Grant Programme during the year. We have taken this figure as the group's cash donations in the UK. A figure for the group's in-kind support was not provided.

Nationwide Building Society

Community development, housing and homelessness, social welfare

Company registration number: FCA 106078

Correspondent: See 'Applications', Nationwide House, Pipers Way, Swindon SN38 2SN (email: citizenship@nationwide.co.uk; website: your.nationwide.co.uk/your-news/articles/Pages/corporate-responsibility.aspx)

Directors: Chris Rhodes; David Roberts; Gunn Waersted; Joe Garner; Kevin Parry; Lynne Peacock; Mai Fyfield; Mark Rennison; Mitchel Lenson; Rita Clifton; Tim Tookey; Tony Prestedge; Usha Prasher (female 38%; male 62%).

Nature of business: The group provides a comprehensive range of personal financial services.

Year end	04/04/2017
Turnover	£3,351,000,000
Pre-tax profit	£1,054,000,000

UK employees: 18,761

Main locations: Nationwide's head office is in Swindon and it has a number of branches throughout the UK.

Community involvement

Nationwide's community involvement is mainly directed towards tackling the housing crisis and educating young people in numeracy and developing money skills. The majority of its charitable giving is funnelled through its corporate charity, The Nationwide Foundation (Charity Commission no. 1065552), and also through its community grants programme. Employees give time to charities through volunteering, and also fundraise for charitable causes.

Community grants programme

In order to help tackle the housing crisis Nationwide launched its community grants programme, which invites local organisations with housing solutions to apply for grants of up to £50,000. Applications get shortlisted and the society's Community Boards come together to award grants.

The society has formed regional Community Boards comprised of local Nationwide members, employees and housing experts who review and award grants to local charitable organisations. According to its website, the society has awarded over £1.25 million to 43 local housing projects to date (October 2018).

Charity partners

The society works with the housing and homelessness charity Shelter, and also supports the Elderly Accommodation Counsel's 'Live Safely and Well at Home' campaign. Recently, the society has set up a partnership with homeless charity St Mungo's to support rough sleepers across the country.

In-kind support

All employees are given up to 14 hours to volunteer during work time each year.

Employee-led support

According to the 2016/17 accounts, fundraising for national and local charities raised £1.7 million. During 2016/17, the value of employees volunteering their time was £1.2 million.

Nationwide also match employee fundraising.

Exclusions

No response to circular appeals. No support is given for advertising in charity brochures, animal welfare, appeals from individuals, medical research, overseas projects, political appeals, religious appeals, or for commercial sponsorship.

Applications

There are online forms through which charities can be nominated to receive funding or can request employee volunteers. They can be found on the 'Get involved' page on the 'Your Nationwide' section of the website: your.nationwide.co.uk/your-society/get-involved.

Corporate charity

The Nationwide Foundation (Charity Commission no. 1065552) – see page 267.

Community contributions

Cash donations UK	£5,500,000
In-kind support UK	£1,200,000
Total contributions (cash and in kind)	£6,700,000

According to the 2016/17 accounts, donations were made totalling £5.5 million, including £2.8 million to the Nationwide Foundation. Employee time for volunteering programmes was valued at a cost of £1.2 million, resulting in a total commitment to the community of £6.7 million.

NCC Group plc

General charitable purposes

Company registration number: 4627044

Correspondent: CSR Team, XYZ Building, 2 Hardman Boulevard, Spinningfields, Manchester M3 3AQ (tel: 0161 209 5200; website: www.nccgroup.trust/uk)

Directors: Adam Palser; Chris Batterham; Chris Stone; Jennifer Duvalier; Jonathan Brookes; Mike Ettling; Tim Kowalski (female 14%; male 86%).

Nature of business: NCC Group is an information assurance firm. Its service areas cover software verification, cyber security, website performance, software testing and domain services.

Year end	31/05/2018
Turnover	£233,200,000
Pre-tax profit	£11,900,000

Main locations: The group's head office is in Manchester. There are also offices in Cambridge, Cheltenham, Edinburgh, Glasgow, Leatherhead, Leeds, London, Milton Keynes, Reading and Slough.

Community involvement

The group makes donations to staff-nominated charities through its 12 Days of Christmas campaign.

12 Days of Christmas Campaign

During the year the group made donations of £5,000 to 12 charities through its 12 Days of Christmas Campaign. Donations are made in the run-up to Christmas and are chosen from a shortlist nominated by employees.

Beneficiaries included: Alder Hey Children's Hospital; Central Beacon's Mountain Rescue; Children's Hospice Association Scotland; Keep Smiling for Becky; Mary's Meals; MedEquip4Kids; South Tees Hospitals NHS Foundation Trust; Sunshine and Smiles; Rosie's Rainbow Fund; Willen Hospice; Woking and Sam Beare Hospices; Wood Street Mission.

Applications

Contact the correspondent for further information.

Community contributions

Cash donations UK	£70,000

In 2017/18 the group donated £60,000 through its 12 Days of Christmas Campaign and £10,000 through its charity raffle.

Newbury Building Society

Sports and recreation, arts and culture, education, the environment

Company registration number: 206077

Correspondent: CSR Team, 17 Bartholomew Street, Newbury, Berkshire RG14 5LY (tel: 01635 555700; website: www.newbury.co.uk/about-us/community-and-charity)

Directors: Erika Neves; Ian Wilson; John Parker; Lee Bambridge; Nigel Briggs; Peter Brickely; Phillippa Cardano; Piers Williamson; Roland Gardner; Ron Simms; Sarah Hordern; Tracy Morshead; William Roberts; Zoe Shaw (female 21%; male 79%).

Nature of business: Newbury Building Society is a building society based in Berkshire.

Year end	31/10/2017
Turnover	£15,869,000
Pre-tax profit	£7,343,000

Main locations: The society has branches in Abingdon, Alton, Andover, Basingstoke, Didcot, Hungerford, Newbury, Thatcham, Winchester and Wokingham.

Community involvement

The society makes donations to organisations in Berkshire and sponsors events and local sports teams.

Charity support scheme

The society makes donations, typically of between £100 to £500 to charities and community groups. Its website states:

> We consider applications for assistance in a number of different categories, including those that:
>
> - Promote and encourage sporting activities
> - Promote and encourage activities in the arts
> - Support education and development
> - Benefit the environment

Previous beneficiaries have included: Challengers; Didcot Smiles; Hungerford Rotary Club; Swings and Smiles; and Treloar School.

Charity partnership scheme

The society has long-term partnerships with eight charities which benefit from staff volunteering and fundraising. Information about the society's current partners can be found on their website.

Commercially led support

During the year the society sponsored a charity football tournament, the Winchester Hat Fair and a number of local sports teams.

Applications

Application forms for sponsorship and donations can be downloaded from the society's website. Applications are considered twice a year in May and November.

Community contributions

Cash donations UK	£26,000

In 2016/17 the society's charitable donations totalled £26,000.

Newcastle Building Society

Community development, education, enterprise and training, general charitable purposes

Company registration number: FCA 156058

Correspondent: Grants Team, Newcastle Building Society, FAO Corporate Social Responsibility, Portland House, New Bridge Street, Newcastle Upon Tyne NE1 8AL (tel: 0191 232 0505; email: csr@newcastle.co.uk; website: www.newcastle.co.uk)

Directors: Andrew Haigh; Anne Shiels; Bryce Glover; David Buffham; Ian Ward; John Morris; Karen Ingham; Patrick Ferguson; Phil Moorhouse; Stuart Miller (female 20%; male 80%).

Nature of business: Newcastle Building Society is a building society based in the North East of England.

Year end	31/12/2017
Turnover	£57,900,000
Pre-tax profit	£13,100,000

Total employees: 1,000+

Main locations: The group has branches across the North East and Cumbria; there is also a branch in Dumfries, Scotland and a branch in Gibraltar. The head office is in Newcastle.

Community involvement

The group supports charities and community groups in the areas where it operates, through its Community Fund. It also supports a group-wide partner charity and branches within the group support their own Charity of the Year. Employees provide support through volunteering and fundraising initiatives.

Newcastle Building Society Community Fund

Administered by Community Foundation Tyne and Wear and Northumberland (Charity Commission no. 700510), the Newcastle Building Society Community Fund awards grants to charities and community groups local to the group's branches. The fund's income is linked to one of the group's accounts products, the Newcastle Community Saver, receiving 0.1% of the total balances held in these accounts, in addition to income from employee fundraising. Customers can nominate projects to be considered for funding.

Financial education

The group has a number of initiatives to promote financial education in the local community.

The Boardroom Charity Challenge programme provides education about managing money for children in schools across the North East and Cumbria, along with a competition to develop a business idea. Each team is mentored by a Branch Manager. The winning team receives a £1,000 prize to put their idea into action, with proceeds going to a local charity.

The group also provides financial planning seminars for adults and young adults.

In-kind support

The group allocates two volunteer days each year to employees.

Employee-led support

During 2017, employees spent 2,600 hours of their time volunteering for local causes. Employees also fundraise to support charities chosen by their branch or for the group's Community Fund. Examples of fundraising initiatives include a racing night to support a local charity; a bake sale for Children in Need and a Coffee Morning for Macmillan Cancer Support; a 'Tour de Branch' fundraising cycle; employees taking part in the Great North Run. Staff can also nominate charities for support from the Community Fund. According to the 2016/17 annual report, employees raised in excess of £16,000 for important local causes.

Commercially led support

Market-led giving

The group has a long-standing relationship with the Sir Bobby Robson Foundation, which supports cancer research and facilities, particularly in the North East. Money is raised through the group's Sir Bobby Robson savings account, paying 0.1% of the total balance held in the accounts to the foundation. The Community Fund is funded in a similar way with its own savings account.

Sponsorship

The group sponsors The Chronicle Champions' Community Champion Award, recognising individuals who have made a significant contribution to their community.

Exclusions

The following information has been taken from the group's website:

We cannot fund requests to support:

- contributions to general appeals or circulars
- religious/political groups
- public bodies to carry out their statutory obligations
- activities which solely support animal welfare
- activities which have already taken place
- grant making by other organisations
- privately owned and profit-distributing companies or limited partnerships
- commercial/profit making ventures

Applications

Community Fund

For information on grants currently available, or details of the next funding round, refer to the group's website: https://www.newcastle.co.uk/about-us/community-and-charity

Applications are made using the online form. Customers, employees and members can nominate a charity or community group for support using the online form or by visiting their local branch.

According to the group's website, to make a nomination for funding organisations must meet the following criteria:

Groups must be nominated by at least one current customer of the Society

Recognised community groups/initiatives within the North East or branch area for out of area branches

Any funding provided must 'make a difference' and be the reason why the initiative would be able to start

Project must be at a stage where it can start within 3 months

The funding must be used for a specific project- not just a donation.

Community contributions

Cash donations UK	£770,000

The annual report and accounts for 2017 declared cash donations of £770,000 which equates to 6% of the group's profit before tax.

Beneficiaries included: Pelton Fell Community (£3,000); Annie Mawson's Sunbeams Music Trust (£2,800); Men In Sheds (£2,600); Tea Dancers Whitley Bay (£1,800); Tees Valley Wildlife Trust (£1,300).

Newsquest Media Group Ltd

Arts and culture, media and communications, disaster relief

Company registration number: 3165420

Correspondent: The Gannett Foundation, Gannett Foundation, Newsquest Media Group Ltd, 58 Church Street, Weybridge, Surrey KT13 8DP (tel: 01932 821212; email: foundation@gannett.com; website: www.newsquest.co.uk)

Directors: David Coates; Dawn Sweeney; Ewan Stark; Graham Morrison; Henry Faure Walker; Hussain Bayoomi; Jenny Thompson; Julia Lancett; Mike Harper; Nick Fellows; Paul Walker; Tim Potter; Toby Granville; Tony Portelli; Tracey Olaleye; Vincent Boni (female 19%; male 81%).

Nature of business: Newsquest Media Group owns local newspapers across the UK. It is a subsidiary of the Gannett Company, which is incorporated in the USA.

Year end	31/12/2017
Turnover	£130,461,000
Pre-tax profit	(£213,000,000)

Main locations: Newsquest's head office is in London. The group owns local newspapers throughout the UK.

Community involvement

Newsquest's parent company Gannett Company, Inc. funds the Gannett Foundation which provides grants to charities operating in the communities served by Newsquest's newspapers. In the UK grants are available through the foundation's Community Action Grants scheme.

The Gannett Foundation (not a registered charity)

The Gannett Foundation helps to improve lives in the communities where the group has a presence. In the UK, the Gannett Foundation makes grants to registered charities which bring benefits to the local communities served by Newsquest's news brands.

The group focuses on charities working in the areas of 'education and neighbourhood improvement, economic development, youth development, community problem-solving, assistance to disadvantaged people, environmental conservation and cultural enrichment'.

Some of the programmes funded by the foundation are as follows:

Gannett Match – Gannett employees' donations to eligible charities all across the country are matched by the Gannett Foundation.

VolunteerMatch – Support to employee volunteering by matching hours with a grant to the charitable organisation.

Community Action Grants – The Community Action Grants application process and cycle will change in 2019. In the UK, grants are available for arts, museums and libraries projects.

Media Grants – Grants for journalism education and training projects.

Disaster Relief Grants – Grants are made to communities affected by natural and other disasters, such as fire, flooding, tornadoes, and hurricanes. These grants are recommended by Gannett companies, and the foundation does not accept applications for this programme.

Executive Grants – This programme makes grants to eligible organisations in the US and the UK as recommended by senior Gannett executives (current and retired). The foundation does not accept applications for this programme.

During 2017 the foundation made charitable donations of £292,500 in the UK.

In-kind support

The company offers editorial support to local charitable initiatives, and also gives ten hours' paid leave to its employees for voluntary work in the local community.

Employee-led support

The Gannett Foundation has various employee-led programmes in place to support charities in the areas where the group has a presence; we assume that this includes UK communities where Newsquest has an office.

Employees are encouraged to use their ten hours' paid leave to participate in voluntary work in the local community. The group also run a VolunteerMatch scheme which awards $100 to the charities in which employees choose to volunteer.

The group has a payroll giving scheme and provides matched funding.

Exclusions

The following are not eligible for funding:

- Salaries, professional fees or day-to-day running or maintenance costs
- General appeals as opposed to specific projects
- Projects that do not bring benefits to local communities
- Political or religious objectives
- State or privately run schools (other than special needs)
- Hospitals (other than hospices)
- Individuals
- Private foundations
- Organisations which are not registered charities
- National or regional organisations, unless the programmes address specific local community needs
- Endowment funds
- Multiple-year pledge campaigns
- Medical or research organisations, including organisations funding single disease research
- Fraternal groups, athletic teams, bands, volunteer firefighters or similar groups

Applications

Community Action Grants

Applicants must be registered charities that have not received a Gannett Foundation grant within the last two years. The scheme is open to local registered charities within the circulation area of a Newsquest publication in Great Britain. The following link displays the complete list of local publications: www.newsquest.co.uk/portfolio/our-titles

Typically grants are made for substantial projects which require and merit awards of between £5,000 and £10,000. Small amounts will be considered but the foundation actively encourages imaginative and ambitious projects on a large scale.

Grants are made once a year, in the autumn. Promotions usually start in Newsquest regional newspapers from late July/early August onwards. The time is publicised in the local newspapers.

Applications must be made locally by downloading an application form from the newspaper website The completed form can be sent either by email or by post to the editor of the applicant's local paper. Note that the deadlines can vary according to the local newspaper.

Community contributions

Cash donations UK	£13,000

The annual report and accounts for 2017 declared charitable donations of £13,000 which we have taken as its cash donations for the year. Additionally, Newsquest's parent company, the Gannett Company, funds its foundation and awards grants in the UK on behalf of its subsidiary. The group's donations to the foundation were not listed.

Nex Group plc

General charitable purposes, projects outside the UK

Company registration number: 10013770

Correspondent: Giving Day Team, 2 Broadgate, London EC2M 7UR (tel: 020 7000 5000; website: www.nexgivingday.com)

Directors: Anna Ewing; Charles Gregson; Ivan Ritossa; John Sievwright; Ken Pigaga; Michael Spencer; Robert Standing; Samantha Wren (female 25%; male 75%).

Nature of business: The company is the world's largest interdealer broker and is active in the wholesale markets for over-the-counter derivatives, fixed income securities, money market products, foreign exchange, energy, credit and equity derivatives.

Year end	31/03/2018
Turnover	£591,000,000
Pre-tax profit	£127,000,000

Total employees: 1,800

Main locations: The company has headquarters in London and offices throughout the world.

Community involvement

Nex Group donates money raised during its annual Charity Day, launched in 1993, to charities across the globe. On this day each year, the group donates its entire revenue, and covers all costs, to various charities selected by local offices. Its brokers contribute 100% of their commission for the day.

Employee-led support

The company encourages employees' fundraising efforts by matching donations.

Applications

Contact the correspondent for further information.

Community contributions

Cash donations worldwide	£2,300,000

In 2018 Nex Group raised £2.3 million for charities around the world through its annual Giving Day.

UK beneficiaries included: Blue Marine Foundation; Juvenile Diabetes Research Fund; Missing People; Ovarian Cancer Action; Rooprai Spinal Trust; Spinal Research; West Ham United Foundation.

Next plc

Community development, health and medical research, disability, children and young people, older people

Company registration number: 4521150

Correspondent: Charity & Sponsorship Team, NEXT plc, Desford Road, Enderby, Leicester LE19 4AT (tel: 0333 777 4577; email: Charities_department@next.co.uk; website: www.nextplc.co.uk/corporate-responsibility/community)

Directors: Amanda James; Caroline Goodall; Dame Dianne Thompson; Francis Salway; Jane Shields; Jonathan Bewes; Lord Wolfson of Aspley Guise; Michael Roney; Richard Papp (female 44%; male 56%).

Nature of business: The principal activities of the group are high-street retailing, home shopping, customer services management and financial services.

Year end	01/01/2018
Turnover	£4,055,500,000
Pre-tax profit	£726,100,000

UK employees: 5,300

Main locations: Next has stores throughout the UK and Ireland.

FTSE4Good

Community involvement

Next worked with over 350 charities of various sizes during 2017/18. The group also provides support to organisations without charitable status and local sporting teams, especially where there is direct employee involvement. Resources are focused on projects that benefit communities in the UK and Ireland providing support in the areas of children and youth; people who are ill; people with disabilities; healthcare; medical research; and community support.

Next supports charitable organisations by providing cash donations and gifts in kind.

In-kind support

Next supports charities and community organisations through gifts in kind, mainly furniture and clothes which are unsellable or no longer needed. Next also host charity events, in which they gave £221,000 towards during the year.

Employee-led support

Employees have raised funds for a range of charities through various activities.

Commercially led support

Next offers commercial sponsorship to a small number of organisations. Local sporting teams are also supported, especially those with which an employee has a direct involvement.

Applications

All requests for charity donations and sponsorship are considered on an individual basis. To apply, charities should contact the company's Charity and Sponsorship team by email, fax or letter.

Community contributions

Cash donations UK	£1,000,000
In-kind support UK	£1,800,000
Total contributions (cash and in kind)	£2,800,000

During 2017/18 Next gave financial support to: registered charities amounting to £1 million; individual requests, local and national groups and organisations amounting to £13,000; and commercial support and sponsorship amounting to £92,000.

Financial support has been complemented with the following fundraising activities to generate additional funds for registered charities, individuals, groups or organisations:

Gifts in kind – product donations	£1.8 million
Charity linked sales	£372,000
NEXT charity events	£221,000
Employee fundraising	£52,000

The figure we use for the company's UK contributions includes donations given in Ireland. As is our usual practice, the figure does not include commercial sponsorship, charity-linked sales and employee fundraising; however, they are noted here to provide full information.

Beneficiaries included: Doncaster Refurnish.

Nisa Retail Ltd

General charitable purposes

Company registration number: 980790

Correspondent: CSR Team, Waldo Way, Normanby Enterprise Park, Scunthorpe, North Lincolnshire DN15 9GE (tel: 0845 604 4999; website: corporate.nisaretail.com)

Directors: Caroline Sellers; Kenneth Towle; Robin Brown; Steven Nuttall (female 25%; male 75%).

Nature of business: Nisa is a groceries wholesaler and wholly owned subsidiary of The Co-operative Group.

Year end	02/04/2017
Turnover	£1,280,239,000
Pre-tax profit	£4,284,000

Main locations: Nisa has stores throughout the UK.

Community involvement

Support is provided through the company's charity Making a Difference Locally Ltd (Charity Commission no. 1123800) which provides grants to charities in communities served by its retailers.

Commercially led support

Making a Difference Locally Ltd

The charity supports communities served by local independently-owned convenience stores that are members of Nisa, a buying organisation. The charity receives money from the sale of certain Making a Difference Locally (MADL) labelled products in store, including Nisa's own 'Heritage' range. Retailers nominate charities or good causes from their local communities to receive donations. The charity's administrative team verifies the charity or good cause to ensure it meets the requirements of MADL, then pass the request to the trustees who approve or decline the donation. The administrative team then processes the donation to the charity or good cause.

In 2016/17 MADL awarded 1,494 grants totalling £1.2 million.

Beneficiaries of grants over £10,000 were: Zoe's Place Baby Hospice (£54,000); DigiBete CIC (£30,000); Josies Dragonfly Trust (£25,000); Sweatpea Charity (£20,000); Ulster Barbarians (£15,000); Focus Leukaemia (£10,000).

Applications

Further information on Making a Difference Locally Ltd can be found on: www.makingadifferencelocally.com.

To find your nearest Nisa retailer visit: www.nisaretail.com.

Community contributions

In 2016/17 the company collected £546,500 from the sale of Making a Difference Locally products which was then transferred to its charity for distribution.

Nominet UK

General charitable purposes, STEM subjects

Company registration number: 3203859

Correspondent: Tech for Good Team, Minerva House, Edmund Halley Road, Oxford OX4 4DQ (tel: 01865 332244; email: nominet@nominet.uk; website: www.nominet.uk/tech-for-good)

Directors: James Bladel; Eleanor Bradley; Volker Greimann; Russell Haworth; Benjamin Hill; Simon McCalla; Stephen Page; Kelly Salter; David Thornton; Jane Tozer; Mark Wood (female 27%; male 73%).

Nature of business: Nominet UK is the .uk domain name registry in the UK.

Note: The financial information for this record is for the 18-month period to 31 March 2018.

Year end	31/03/2018
Turnover	£56,410,000
Pre-tax profit	£22,000,000

Main locations: In the UK, Nominet's head office is in Oxfordshire and it has an office in London.

Community involvement

The majority of the company's giving is through its corporate charity, the Social Tech Trust (Charity Commission no. 1125735). During the period, the trust supported over 30 organisations across two main areas, digital engagement and tech4good. The grants awarded have supported innovative start-ups such as Disrupt Disability and TapSOS, to more established organisations such as Action For Children and Carers Trust.

Nominet also runs its own initiatives to encourage and develop young people's digital skills. The main programme, Nominet Digital Neighbourhood, offers training and paid work experiences to young people with limited opportunities, and then pairs them with SMEs and charities. Nominet is also a founding patron of The Prince's Trust Online and a founding partner of the Micro:bit Foundation.

Partnerships

After partnering with BBC Children in Need in 2018, Nominet plans to fund projects that support disadvantaged children across the UK to access opportunities from a wide range of new advancements in technology and digital inclusion programmes. This is part of the company's wider strategy to highlight how digital technology can be used effectively by small charities and community groups across the UK.

Applications

Contact the correspondent for further information.

Corporate charity

Social Tech Trust (Charity Commission no. 1125735) – see page 278.

Community contributions

Cash donations UK	£5,400,000

In 2016/17 Nominet donated £5.4 million to its corporate charity.

Nomura International plc

Education, enterprise and training, children and young people

Company registration number: 1550505

Correspondent: 1 Angel Lane, London EC4R 3AB (website: www.nomura.com)

Directors: Anna Bentley; Christopher Barlow; David Godfrey; Hisato Miyashita; John Tierney; Jonathan Britton; Jonathan Lewis; Lewis O'Donald; Netta Atkar; Rosemary Murray; Yasou Kashiwagi (female 27%; male 73%).

Nature of business: Nomura Group is an Asian asset management company.

Year end	31/03/2017
Turnover	£1,142,970,000
Pre-tax profit	£230,370,000

Main locations: The company is headquartered in London.

Community involvement

The company's charitable giving is channelled through its corporate charity The Nomura Charitable Trust (UK) (Charity Commission no. 1130592).

Corporate charity

The Nomura Charitable Trust (Charity Commission no. 1130592) – see page 268.

Community contributions

Cash donations UK	£221,500

We were unable to determine the company's charitable contributions for the year. However, the Nomura Charitable trust's 2016/17 accounts state that it received £221,500 from Nomura Dormant Funds which we have taken as the figure for the company's cash donation.

Norse Group

Enterprise and training, health, the environment, children and young people, older people

Company registration number: 5694657

Correspondent: CSR Team, Lancaster House, 16 Central Avenue, St Andrews Business Park, Norwich NR7 0HR (tel: 01603 894100; email: info@ncsgrp.co.uk; website: www.ncsgrp.co.uk)

Directors: Andrew Jamieson; Dean Wetteland; Karen Knight; Thomas McCabe (female 25%; male 75%).

Nature of business: Norse Group is a holding company which brings together Facilities Management provider Norse Commercial Services, property consultancy NPS Group and care provider NorseCare.

Year end	31/03/2017
Turnover	£281,300,000
Pre-tax profit	£2,566,000

UK employees: 9,650

Main locations: Norse group have offices across England and Wales. The group's head office is based in Norwich.

Community involvement

The group supports charities and community groups in the areas in which it operates. Support is provided through cash and in-kind donations, sponsorship and volunteering. According to its website, the group's CSR strategy focuses on several key areas including: supporting older people; well-being and preventing obesity; local regeneration; employment and youth opportunities; skills and employee development; and environmental management.

Community Fund

The Nose Group Community Fund awards grants totalling around £50,000 each year to community groups and charities which are nominated by group employees. In order to be eligible the nominating employee must be actively involved in the charity. Grants are usually in the region of £750.

Partnerships

The group works with the Theatre Royal in Norwich to provide sponsorship which gives disadvantaged children and young people, aged 7 to 19, access to the theatre by providing subsidised tickets and travel via local schools. Since the partnership was launched five years ago, almost 21,000 children and young people have attended performances. The group also supports Norfolk County Council's campaign for a Dementia Friendly Norfolk. As part of the campaign, employees are encouraged to become 'Dementia Friends' and the group aims to have a Dementia Friends Champion in each of its key locations.

In-kind support

The group works with Norfolk ProHelp, a network of professional firms that offer pro bono services to community organisations in need of support. As part of the partnership Norse Group Ltd companies offer their expertise in a number of areas including business planning and HR. For more information visit the website, www.norfolkprohelp.com.

Employee-led support

Group employees are entitled to take up to eight hours' paid leave a year to volunteer for a good cause.

Applications

Contact the correspondent for more information.

Community contributions

The group's 2016/17 annual report did not provide a figure for its total community contribution.

Northern Gas Networks Ltd

The environment, STEM subjects

Company registration number: 5167070

Correspondent: Leeds Community Foundation Grants Team, 1100 Century Way, Thorpe Park Business Park, Colton, Leeds LS15 8TU (website: www.northerngasnetworks.co.uk)

Directors: Andrew Hunter; Chan Loi Sun; Duncan Macrae; John Burham; Kam Hing Lam; Mark Horsley; Neil McGee; Paul Rogerson; Tsai Chao Chung; Wan Chi Tin; Simon Beer (female 0%; male 100%).

Nature of business: Northern Gas Networks supplies gas to customers across the North of England.

Year end	31/03/2017
Turnover	£422,195,000
Pre-tax profit	£162,800,000

Main locations: The company's headquarters are in Leeds. It supplies gas to customers across the north of England.

Community involvement

The company's Community Promises Fund supports energy saving, fuel poverty, carbon monoxide awareness and STEM initiatives in the north of England.

Community Promises Fund

The fund provides grants of £1,000 to £10,000 to charities and community groups with innovative initiatives associated with energy saving, fuel poverty, carbon monoxide awareness and STEM across areas of the North of England served by Northern Gas. The fund makes grants totalling around £50,000 each year.

Beneficiaries have included: Age UK – Gateshead; Citizen Advice Newcastle; Community Voice FM Ltd – Cleveland; Hartlepower CIC; Highfield Food Co-op – Keighley; National Energy Action; Stockton and District Advice Information Service (SDAIS); The Canopy Housing Project – Leeds; Yorkshire Energy Doctor CIC.

Applications

Contact Leeds Community Foundation for further information on the Community Promises Fund.

Community contributions

Cash donations UK	£63,000

In 2016/17 the company donated £63,000 to Leeds Community Foundation in relation to its Community Promises Fund.

Northern Powergrid Holdings Company

General charitable purposes

Company registration number: 3476201

Correspondent: See 'Applications', Lloyds Court, 78 Grey Street, Newcastle Upon Tyne NE1 6AF (tel: 0800 011 3332; email: general.enquiries@northernpowergrid.com; website: www.northernpowergrid.com/about-us)

Directors: Andy Maclennan; Angie Patterson; Geoff Earl; John France; Mark Drye; Neil Applebee; Nick Gill; Patrick Erwin; Phil Jones; Tom Fielden (female 10%; male 90%).

Nature of business: Northern Powergrid Holdings Company is responsible for delivering electricity to properties across the North East of England, Yorkshire and northern Lincolnshire.

Year end	31/12/2017
Turnover	£781,500,000
Pre-tax profit	£257,000,000

Main locations: In the UK, the group's offices are located in Castleford; Houghton-le-Spring; Newcastle (two offices); and Stockton-on-Tees.

Community involvement

The group's most recent community investment strategy, developed in 2015/16 focuses on five areas: vulnerability to power cuts; public safety and education; energy affordability; employee engagement; and strengthening communities. The group works in partnerships with a range of charitable and voluntary organisations to deliver its activities, and also provides funding through the Community Foundation for Tyne and Wear and the Leeds Community Foundation.

Community Partnering Fund

The group have partnered with Northern Gas Networks and Leeds Community Foundation to provide funding for voluntary sector organisations and community groups with innovative approaches to delivering sustainable initiatives. The fund is administered by Leeds Community Foundation and will focus on the following objectives:

- Alleviating hardship associated with fuel poverty and promoting innovative energy-related environmental impact, energy efficiency or carbon reduction
- Educating and informing communities about safety in relation to domestic gas and power including the dangers from carbon monoxide (CO) poisoning and how to protect against it
- Encouraging interest in STEM subjects and related career opportunities
- Promoting use of the Priority Services Register, a free service provided by network operators and suppliers to customers in vulnerable circumstances within communities

Grants of between £1,000 and £10,000 are available.

Community Energy Seed Fund

The group has also awarded grants through its Community Energy Seed Fund with the Community Foundation for Tyne and Wear and Northumberland, supporting the development of community energy projects in the North East, North Lincolnshire and Yorkshire and the Humber. Grants awarded are between £1,000 and £10,000.

For information on what funds are currently available, refer to the Community Foundation's website: www.communityfoundation.org.uk.

Charity partnerships – vulnerable customers

The group works in partnership with a number of charities to support its vulnerable customers through the group's Priority Services Register. This initiative aims to support customers that are particularly vulnerable – for example, by providing 'winter warmer packs' and support services in the event of a power cut. It also runs a number of local, targeted initiatives in areas of deprivation to promote this support and reach those in need.

The group works in partnership organisations including the British Red Cross, Citizens Advice and National Energy Action to deliver this support.

Education

The group has a number of education programmes.

The group visits schools to promote safety around electricity, and has a website, the Fusebox (thefusebox.northernpowergrid.com), which provides activities and resources. According to its 2017 annual report, activities during the year included: Make the Grade in Energy, an education, skills and employability programme; Energy Heroes, targeted at primary school level pupils to promote awareness of energy costs and ways of saving energy; and attendance at the Big Bang Fair, which encourages young people to pursue STEM subjects.

The group also partnered with The Scout Association which to provide the 'Cub Home Safety Badge' which challenges scouts to pass various tasks surrounding home safety in order to obtain the badge. More information can be found at: fundraising.scouts.org.uk/northern-powergrid.

Employee-led support

Volunteering

Employees volunteer with the group's partners to support its community investment activities – for example, employees volunteer with partners The Trussell Trust and Ahead Partnership, supporting food banks and STEM activities in schools.

The group has previously run a Global Days of Service scheme, providing matched funding for employees to volunteer at local organisations of their choice.

Safety champions

The group's Safety Champions scheme rewards employees for delivering high safety standards by entering them into a draw to win a share of a £10,000 prize fund to donate to a charity chosen by the employee.

Commercially led support

The Hunslet Rugby Foundation announced a 'major sponsorship deal' with Northern Powergrid which will go towards an apprentice development officer position for 12 months. According to the foundation's website:

> The apprentice will deliver multi-skills activities in South Leeds primary schools under the supervision of our community development office, Darrell Robinson. A key part of these sessions will be delivering Northern Powergrid's safety message on the dangers of electricity and helping children recognise these dangers

Applications

Community Partnering Fund

Applicants can apply using the online application form available on the Leeds Community Foundation's website (www.leedscf.org.uk/community-partnering-fund). Applicants will also need to attach the following supporting documentation:

- List of names and addresses of management committee/board members/directors
- Audited accounts or approved management accounts that are no more than 15 months old
- Copy of governance document

Full criteria and information on how to apply is available on the Leeds Community Foundation's website.

Community Energy Seed Fund

Information on how to apply can be found on the Community Foundation serving Tyne and Wear's website: www.communityfoundation.org.uk.

Partnerships

The group provides a checklist of how it selects partners to work with to deliver its community investment activities. This can be found in the community investment strategy.

The group

Other enquiries can be submitted using the contact form on the group's website: www.northernpowergrid.com/contact-us.

Community contributions

No figure was given for the group's total charitable contributions.

Northumbrian Water Ltd

The environment, community development, education, health, sports and recreation

Company registration number: 4760441

Correspondent: Conservation, Boldon House, Wheatlands Way, Pity Me, Durham DH1 5FA (tel: 0870 608 4820; website: www.nwl.co.uk/your-home/community.aspx)

Directors: Andrew Hunter; Andrew Jones; Christopher Johns; Duncan MacRae; Frank Frame; Heidi Mottram; Hing Lam Kam; Loi Shun Chan; Margaret Fay; Martin Negre; Paul Rew; Simon Lyster; Wai Che Wendy Tong Barnes (female 23%; male 77%).

Nature of business: Northumbrian Water provides water and sewerage services in the North East and water services in the South East under the brand name Essex and Suffolk water.

Year end	31/03/2018
Turnover	£834,600,000
Pre-tax profit	£205,200,000

Main locations: The group supplies water to the North East, Essex and Suffolk. Its head office is in Durham.

Community involvement

Northumbrian Water contributes at least 1% of its annual pre-tax profits to benefit local communities. Funds are held with the following community foundations: Tyne, Wear and Northumberland; County Durham; Tees Valley. Northumbrian Water prefers to support projects with a focus on health, education, sport, community and the environment with priority being given to projects in areas where it has a company presence.

Branch Out

The Branch Out grant fund helps to deliver projects that benefit the natural environment and local communities within Northumbrian Water's operating area. Grants of up to £25,000 are available to organisations, community groups or individuals from the public, private, voluntary and education sectors. Branch Out grants have been used to secure funding from other sources for example Biffa, the Heritage Lottery and SITA.

> Any potential projects should be aiming to deliver benefits to the criteria listed below. Examples of how this might be achieved are provided:
>
> - Water in the natural environment – through projects that protect drinking water sources, enhance water quality or provide other benefits to wetland habitats
> - Wildlife – by linking up habitats, creating new areas for wildlife to use, or finding ways to reconnect people with the natural world around them
> - Community – encouraging local communities to enjoy the benefits of being outside and helping them to become more aware of the importance of the natural world, or providing opportunities for Northumbrian Water employees to volunteer to assist with projects in their operating area
> - Climate change – reducing the amount of water consumed or helping the natural world deliver vital services such as flood prevention
> - Sewerage and drainage – protecting vulnerable areas from diffuse pollution, or helping build capacity in the natural environment to help deal with storm events
> - Reputation – carrying out scientific research that would benefit Northumbrian Water, gaining positive exposure in the local and national media, or getting added value to the project through the other partners

In 2017, a total of 16 projects received a total of £60,000 which helped bring in an additional £350,000.

Partnerships

Northumbrian Water was one of the water companies that set up the international charity WaterAid in 1981 and continues to support the charity as one of its strategic partners. In 2015 Northumbrian Water launched a new five-year partnership with WaterAid and aims to raise £1 million to support the delivery of clean water and safe toilets to some of Madagascar's poorest communities. The group hosts fundraising events for the charity which raised £125,000 in 2017/18.

The group has a partnership with the national debt charity StepChange to help customers struggling to pay their bills.

Northumbrian Water delivers research projects with Durham University and has recently established the NE Water Hub, with the Environment Agency and Durham County Council. It also has a long-established collaboration with Newcastle University and formed a new partnership in 2017 to bring free tap-water refill points (Refill Stations) to the North East, Essex and Suffolk. The aim is to reduce the use of single-use plastic water bottles.

Education

Local schools can download and use free teaching resources about the water cycle and water conservation. Site tours of water treatment plants can also be arranged for schools and the group sponsors the Museum of Power in Essex, Ryhope Engines Museum and Tees Cottage Pumping Station.

In-kind support

Employees can take a minimum of 15 working hours a year to support community initiatives.

Employee-led support

Just an Hour is the group's employee volunteering programme. In 2017 52% of employees volunteered their time, giving support to 565 organisations.

Applications

Branch Out grants

In the first instance, consult the group's website – www.branchout-nw.co.uk.

Application guidance and forms can be found online as well as information on successful projects and upcoming deadlines. Forms should be returned via email to branchout@nwl.co.uk. Applicants will be informed in writing or via email within five working days of the bi-annual Branch Out board meeting.

Community Foundations

Applications should be made to the relevant community foundation. A panel of employees meet regularly to review and make decisions on grant applications.

Educational visits

To organise a visit, complete the online form available at www.nwl.co.uk/your-home/learn-about-water.

Community contributions

Cash donations UK	£624,000

In the 2017/18 'Our Contribution Report' states that direct financial contribution to environmental, community and charitable NGOs totalled £624,000 in 2017/18 which amounts to 1.22% of its profits. Of this, £23,500 was donated through the community foundations and £60,000 was awarded in Branch Out grants. The 2017/18 annual report notes that the group supported 1,145 organisations during the year.

Norton Rose Fulbright LLP

Education, sports and recreation, disability and health

Company registration number: OC328697

Correspondent: See 'Applications', 3 More London Riverside, London SE1 2AQ (website: www.nortonrosefulbright.com/uk/corporate-responsibility)

Nature of business: Norton Rose Fulbright LLP is a global law firm with over 50 offices in Africa, Asia, Australia, Canada, Europe, Latin America, the Middle East and the USA.

Year end	30/04/2017
Turnover	£458,000,000
Pre-tax profit	£114,000,000

Total employees: 5,000

Main locations: The firm has over 50 offices worldwide. In the UK there are offices in London and Newcastle.

Community involvement

Norton Rose Fulbright's community efforts focus on education, sports, disabilities and illnesses, volunteering at local schools, mentoring students, working in local hospitals and donating food, clothing and toys, as well as making grants to charities and not-for-profit organisations worldwide. The majority of charitable giving is through the firm's corporate charity, The Norton Rose Fulbright Charitable Foundation (Charity Commission no. 1102142).

In-kind support

The firm encourages employees to work pro bono for charities and local organisations. Lawyers regularly attend evening drop-in clinics organised by law centres in the London boroughs of Tower Hamlets and Croydon. Beyond legal pro bono work, the finance and marketing teams also provide pro bono support, for example assisting the Croydon Law Centre in implementing a more efficient billing system and helping to design and produce publicity materials.

Many offices offer leave for employees to spend on approved volunteer initiatives.

Employee-led support

Volunteering

Employees volunteer their legal and non-legal skills to charities and schools local to their office. Each month a team from the London office staffs the Liberty Public Advice Line to answer questions from callers on human rights and civil liberties. The London office also has a partnership with Smart Works, a charity that helps women start their careers or get back into work after a prolonged break. Employees donate interview clothing each month and volunteer to act as interview coaches. Norton Rose Fulbright also hosts an annual networking event with Smart Works' clients. As signatories of the National Literacy Trust, the firm works with local schools to provide assistance with reading and languages, as well as mathematics and sports.

Fundraising

Employees also support fundraising activities for the London Legal Support Trust, which provides assistance to local law centres. Each year, the firm hosts the start of its 'Walk the Thames' annual fundraiser in October, and enter a team in the 'London Legal Walk Fundraiser' in the spring.

Applications

For further information on pro bono support or potential partnerships, contact your local office.

Corporate charity

The Norton Rose Fulbright Charitable Foundation (Charity Commission no. 1102142) – see page 269.

Community contributions

Cash donations UK	£350,000

In 2016/17 the firm donated £350,000 to its corporate charity.

Nottingham Building Society

Education (particularly financial education), community development, enterprise and training, housing and homelessness, poverty and social exclusion, sports and recreation, children and young people

Company registration number: FCA 200785

Correspondent: Corporate Responsibility Team, Nottingham House, 3 Fulforth Street, Nottingham NG1 3DL (tel: 0344 481 4444; email: dgt@thenottingham.com; website: www.thenottingham.com)

Directors: Andrew Neden; Daniel Mundy; David Marlow; Jane Kibbey; John Edwards; Kavita Patel; Kerry Spooner; Simon Taylor (female 22%; male 78%).

Nature of business: Nottingham Building Society is a mutual society that provides mortgages, savings, estate agency services, home insurance and financial planning.

Year end	31/12/2017
Turnover	£48,300,000
Pre-tax profit	£14,500,000

Main locations: The group has offices across Cambridgeshire, Derbyshire, Hertfordshire, Leicestershire, Lincolnshire, Northamptonshire, Nottinghamshire and South Yorkshire. Its head office is in Nottingham.

Community involvement

The group's community programme, titled 'Doing Good Together', focuses on the following areas: education; financial capability; housing and homelessness; and employability. Support is given through a grants scheme, work with partner charities and employee fundraising and volunteering.

Partner charities

The group has a long-term partnership with Framework, a small homelessness charity in the East Midlands.

The group works with Young Enterprise, providing students at ten schools the opportunity for coaching, mentoring and experience with enterprise and employability skills through its Company Programme.

Grants scheme

The group's Grants for Good scheme is managed by Nottinghamshire Community Foundation and provides grants for charities and community groups running projects supporting the group's areas of focus: education, particularly numeracy and literacy; financial security and education; housing and homelessness; and employability. Grants of between £1,000 and £5,000 are provided to organisations within ten miles of one of the group's branches. During 2017, the group donated £37,000 to 14 local charities through this scheme.

Beneficiaries taken from the website included: Breaking Barriers Building Bridges; First Focus; High Peak Homeless Help; Niyo Enterprise; Rumbletums; Second Helpings Stamford; Speak-up Self Advocacy; TuffCycle CIC; The Zone Youth Project.

In-kind support

Pro bono

Ten local schools have benefitted from employees acting as Business Advisers as part of Young Enterprise's Company Programme. Employees have also provided financial education lessons to more than 300 pupils in the group's trading area through its 'Money Academy' sessions.

Employee-led support

Employee volunteering

In 2017 employees volunteered over 1,350 hours for local community projects.

Employee fundraising

Employees raised over £3,000 for Framework in 2017 by participating in the charity's fundraising events. During the year, employees raised an additional £3,000 for SportsAid.

Commercially led support

Sponsorship

Through its partnership with the charity SportsAid, the group sponsors aspiring athletes, raising funds for equipment, training and travel costs. The group also sponsors sports teams and events, including the AEGON Open Nottingham tennis competition and Leicester Tigers Rugby Club.

Each year a branch can sponsor a local football team up to £250. Since 2014, the group have sponsored 144 local football teams in the UK. Some branches have continued to sponsor the same club over the past three years. Other branches find different clubs within their vicinity each year to support.

Applications

Doing Good Together grants

For information on whether the grants scheme is currently open, refer to the Nottinghamshire Community Foundation website (www.nottscf.org.uk) where deadlines, criteria and application forms are provided.

Volunteer support

Requests for volunteer support from the group can be submitted to dgt@thenottingham.com

Sponsorship

For further information on sponsorship, visit your local branch.

Community contributions

Cash donations UK	£106,000

The 2017 annual report states that charitable donations during the year totalled £106,000.

Ocado Group plc

General charitable purposes

Company registration number: 7098618

Correspondent: Corporate Responsibility Team, Titan Court, 3 Bishop Square, Hatfield Business Park, Hatfield, Hertfordshire, AL10 9NE (tel: 01707 227800; website: www.ocadogroup.com/our-responsibilities.aspx)

Directors: Andrew Harrison; Douglas McCallum; Duncan Tatton-Brown; Emma Lloyd; Jörn Rausing; Julie Southern; Lord Rose; Luke Jensen; Mark Richardson; Neill Abrams; Ruth Anderson; Tim Steiner (female 25%; male 75%).

Nature of business: Ocado is a British online supermarket. In contrast to its main competitors, the company has no chain of stores and does all home deliveries from its warehouses.

Year end	29/01/2018
Turnover	£1,463,800,000
Pre-tax profit	£1,000,000

UK employees: 12,233

Main locations: Ocado's headquarters are in Hatfield, Hertfordshire.

Community involvement

The group's charitable support is mainly focused on in-kind donations of food and matching employee and customer fundraising efforts.

The Ocado Foundation (not a registered charity)

The foundation was established in 2015 and acts as a vehicle for all group and employee fundraising and charitable work.

Partnerships

Last year, 2017, marked the second of the group's five year partnership with WRAP, promoting recycling education projects to primary school children. In 2016/17 the company invested £100,000 in the partnership, along with an additional £30,000 to support Recycle Week, a social media campaign promoting the benefits of recycling with a reach of over 3.5 million people. The group also has a working partnership with HMP Northumberland which sees prisoners repurpose and sell old Ocado uniforms. The funds raised go to the Ocado Foundation.

In-kind support

In 2016/17 the group donated and distributed a total of 2,200 tonnes of food. The group also provided delivery vans to three of its Food Partners (food banks and food charities across the UK).

Employee-led support

During the year Ocado employees volunteered more than 2,000 hours for a variety of good causes and took part in fundraising activities through the foundation.

Fundraising

Money raised by employees during working hours is collected by the foundation and then proportionately distributed to Ocado sites. Each site then distributes the money to local or national charities determined by employees.

Matched funding

The group matches the fundraising efforts of employees up to £500 per person. In 2016/17 matched employee fundraising and volunteering activity resulted in donations of just over £22,000 being made to charities across the UK from the Ocado Foundation.

Commercially led support

Food donations

For every £1 customers give in Donate Food With Ocado vouchers, the group gives £2 worth of food to its Food Partners. In 2016/17 Ocado customers donated £142,500 in vouchers which was matched by the group and resulted in over 64 tonnes of food being given to local charities.

Carrier bags sales

The majority of the money generated by carrier bag sales goes to the Bag Buy Back Scheme which offers customers a financial incentive to return carrier bags.

The remaining funds are distributed by the Ocado Foundation to environmental, waste, and recycling projects.

Applications

Contact the correspondent for further information.

Community contributions

In-kind support worldwide	£142,500

In 2016/17 the group made in-kind donations of at least £142,500 through its Donate Food With Ocado scheme. We were unable to determine the value of the group's total contribution. A figure for cash donations was not provided.

OneFamily Advice Ltd

Education (particularly financial education), health, children and young people, general charitable purposes

Company registration number: 9188369

Correspondent: The Foundation Team, 16–17 West Street, Brighton, East Sussex BN1 2RL (tel: 08003730 10; email: foundation@onefamily.com; website: www.onefamily.com/your-foundation)

Directors: Christina McComb; Graham Lindsay; Ian Buckley; Peter Box; Simon Markey; Steve Colsell; Teddy Nyahasha (female 14%; male 86%).

Nature of business: OneFamily provides financial services (life assurance, savings and protection schemes).

In 2015 Family Investments merged with Engage Mutual to create OneFamily.

Year end	31/12/2017
Pre-tax profit	(£508,687,000)

UK employees: 521

Main locations: OneFamily's head office is in Brighton.

Community involvement

OneFamily channels its charitable giving through its foundation, the OneFamily Foundation (not a registered charity).

OneFamily Foundation

The foundation launched in 2015, following the merger between Family Investments and Engage Mutual, and the group aims to give £5 million to good causes chosen by customers over the following five years. Funded through a share of the profits, the foundation offers support in the following ways:

- **Community Grants** – OneFamily customers can apply for a Community Grant of up to £5,000 for a local group or cause. Grant recipients will be decided by a computerised draw at the end of each round
- **Charity Fund** - The Charity Fund is open to charities that are delivering a campaign to help combat and alleviate financial pressures of families across the UK. In 2017 the winning campaigns were Motor Neurone Disease Association, The Children's Society and Muscular Dystrophy UK
- **Community Awards** – There are three levels of award – £5,000, £10,000 and £25,000. Customers can nominate community projects to win funding with the foundation currently supporting projects in the following areas: active living; community groups; health, disability and social care; lifelong learning. In 2017 210 projects were selected for an award of which 32 were funded

Beneficiaries included: Hove Park School and St Tudy playing field (£25,000 each); Discover Wellbeing and Old Mill Cancer Foundation (£5,000 each).

Employee-led support

The group actively encourage employees to get involved in the local community and during 2017, ran a volunteer programme in Brighton where the group's head office is based. Employees worked with charities including Raysteade Animal Welfare Centre, Chestnut Tree House and the Martlets Hospice. The group plans to roll out this programme further in 2018.

The group also provides matched funding towards employees' fundraising efforts.

Commercially led support

During the year the group partnered with Brighton and Hove Pride in August and sponsored the family diversity area at the Pride festival. A number of employees took part in the parade on a OneFamily sponsored float.

Applications

Contact the correspondent for further information.

Community contributions

Cash donations UK	£124,000

The 2017 annual report states that £120,000 was allocated to the Charity Fund to share between three national charities. Information on how much the group gave through its Personal Grants and Community Award schemes was not provided. The 2017 annual report declared additional cash donations of £4,200, 'primarily through matching donations raised by staff for charities of their choice'. We have taken £124,000 as the society's cash donations during the year.

Ovo Energy Ltd

The environment, poverty and social exclusion, children and young people, education

Company registration number: 6890795

Correspondent: 1 Rivergate, Temple Quay, Bristol BS1 6ED (email: Contact form on website; website: www.ovoenergy.com)

Directors: Christopher Houghton; Niall Wass; Stephen Fitzpatrick; Stephen Murphy; Vincent Casey (female 0%; male 100%).

Nature of business: Ovo Energy is an energy supplier based in Bristol.

Year end	31/12/2017
Turnover	£762,521,000
Pre-tax profit	£4,510,000

Main locations: The company's headquarters are in Bristol. It also has offices in London.

Community involvement

Support is provided through the company's corporate charity The Ovo Charitable Foundation (Charity Commission no. 1155954).

Employee-led support

Employees volunteer over 1,000 hours per year with charities chosen for the foundation's Ovo Give Back Initiative.

Corporate charity

The Ovo Charitable Foundation (Charity Commission no. 1155954) – see page 270.

Community contributions

Cash donations UK	£684,000

In 2017 the company made a donation of £684,000 to The Ovo Charitable Foundation.

Paddy Power Betfair plc

Community development, sports and recreation, education, enterprise and training, the environment, disability, poverty and social exclusion, projects outside the UK

Company registration number: 16956

Correspondent: Corporate Responsibility Team, Waterfront, Hammersmith Embankment, Chancellors Road, London W6 9HP (tel: 020 8834 8000; website: corporate.betfair.com)

Directors: Alex Gersh; Emer Timmons; GaryMcGann; Ian Dyson; Jan Bolz; Michael Cawley; Peter Jackson; Peter

Rigby; Zillah Byng-Thorne (female 18%; male 82%).

Nature of business: Paddy Power Betfair provides betting services and online gaming products.

This record previously contained information about the community involvement of Betfair Group plc. In February 2016, the company merged with Paddy Power and its name was changed to Betfair Group Ltd. We have taken the information in this record from the annual report and accounts of Paddy Power Betfair plc, a company incorporated in Ireland, which is the immediate and ultimate parent company of Betfair Group Ltd.

Year end	31/12/2017
Turnover	£1,745,400,000
Pre-tax profit	£246,600,000

Total employees: 7,640

Main locations: Paddy Power Betfair's head office is in Dublin and it has an office in London.

FTSE4Good

Community involvement

According to the group's website, it focuses much of its support on grassroots sports clubs, organisations supporting responsible gambling and 'upskilling' organisations and projects across the UK, Ireland, Australia and Spain. The group supports organisations through cash donations and employee-led initiatives.

Cash4Clubs

Betfair has run the Cash4Clubs partnership in collaboration with Sports Aid since 2008. Cash4Clubs offers community sports clubs the chance to apply for grants of up to £1,000 to improve facilities, purchase new equipment or gain coaching qualifications. The scheme supports both mainstream sports and less popular sports.

Beneficiaries included: Hounslow Jets Swimming Club; Thorncliffe Junior Bowls.

Charity partners

Under the 'Upskilling' theme, the group partners with:

- **Tomorrow's People** – a charity that supports young adults aged 18–24 who face barriers to employment. The group provided funding for the charity to create youth hubs across London which give young adults the skills that they need to secure employment
- **New Entrepreneurs Foundation (NEF)** – a charity that encourages entrepreneurial spirit in the UK. The group's website states: 'We are a corporate donor of the programme and we also host several of NEF's entrepreneurs in different departments across our UK business.'
- **Jobcare Ireland** – a charity in Dublin that provides skills, training and work experience for adults that have either; suffered from third generation unemployment or have been unemployed for a significant amount of time. The group provides financial support to Jobcare Ireland and also support its networking events and mentor individuals from the Jobnet Programme

Under the Responsible Gambling theme, the group partners with:

- **Young Gamblers Education Trust (YGAM)** – a charity set up to help educate young people on the risks associated with gambling. The group's partnership with YGAM helps the charity to provide certified training to teachers, youth workers and community mental health workers so that they can educate young people on problem gambling. The partnership also helps the charity run peer education projects and research around attitudes, thinking and behaviours of young people towards gambling
- **Gambling Therapy** – a free online app that provides practical advice and emotional support to people affected by problem gambling in Europe. The group's donation to the charity helped to translate its online self-help website into a number of European languages

In-kind support

The group offers employees two days' paid leave each year to volunteer for a charity of their choice.

Employee-led support

Fundraising and matched giving

Employees take part in fundraising events throughout the year. The group's website states that employees can apply once a year for up to £500 in matched funding for money raised through a 'charity challenge'.

In 2017 the group launched a Community Investment Fund to encourage employees Paddy Power betting shops to donate to local causes. One of the initiatives supported by the fund in 2017 was Newham Giving, a place-based giving fund that delivers programmes for young people during the summer holidays and is administered by the East End Community Foundation.

Commercially led support

Sponsorship

Over the last number of years, the group has supported Special Olympics Ireland. This includes support in March 2017 to help send 24 athletes to the Special Olympics World Winter Games 2017 in Austria.

Applications

Contact the correspondent for further information.

Community contributions

According to its Annual Report 2017, the group commits over 0.1% of its 'gross gaming revenue' to the research, education and treatment of problem gambling through a variety of organisations, including Gamble Aware and the Young Gamblers Education Trust (YGAM).

A figure for the group's total contribution during 2017 was not provided.

LGBT+ charities and the World Cup 2018

In 2018 Paddy Power announced that during the World Cup the company would donate £10,000 to LGBT+ charities for every Russian goal scored. Paddy Power collaborated with Attitude magazine to decide which organisations should be supported. A total of £170,000 was donated through this initiative; however, we have not included this in our contributions as it took place after the end of the financial period reported on in this record.

Parabola Land Ltd

Arts and culture, medical research, projects outside the UK

Company registration number: 4298209

Correspondent: 101 George Street, Edinburgh EH2 3ES (tel: 0131 603 8300; email: info@parabola.com; website: www.parabola.com/philanthropy)

Directors: Kirsty MacGregor; Peter Millican; Tony Hordon (female 33%; male 67%).

Nature of business: Parabola is a privately-owned property group based in Edinburgh and Newcastle with built accommodation throughout the UK and a select number of sites in development.

Year end	31/03/2018
Turnover	£1,970,000
Pre-tax profit	£3,600,000

Main locations: The company has offices in Edinburgh and Newcastle.

Community involvement

All of the company's community involvement is directed through its corporate charity, the Parabola Foundation (Charity Commission no. 1156008).

Corporate charity

Parabola Foundation (Charity Commission no. 1156008) – see page 270.

Community contributions

Cash donations UK	£1,000,000

In 2017/18 the company gave £1 million to its corporate charity.

Paradigm Housing Group

General charitable purposes

Company registration number: IP28844R

Correspondent: Paradigm Housing Group, 1 Glory Park Avenue, Wooburn Green, Buckinghamshire HP10 0DF (tel: 0300 303 1010; email: enquiries@paradigmfoundation.org.uk; website: www.paradigmhousing.co.uk/about-paradigm/paradigm-foundation)

Directors: Eva Cullen; Janet Ogundele; John Cross; John Simpson; Julian Ashby; Mathew Bishop; Matthew Bailes; Pat Brandum; Peter Quinn; Phil Shepley; Philippa Lowe; Richard Archer (female 33%; male 67%).

Nature of business: Paradigm is one of the South East's largest housing providers, managing over 14,000 homes across 33 local authorities.

Year end	31/03/2017
Turnover	£136,700,000
Pre-tax profit	£33,800,000

Main locations: The group operates in over 33 local authorities, a map of which can be found at – www.paradigmhousing.co.uk/about-paradigm/where-we-work/areas-of-operation.

Community involvement

The majority of the group's community involvement is directed through its corporate charity, the Paradigm Foundation (Charity Commission no. 1156204).

Corporate charity

Paradigm Foundation (Charity Commission no. 1156204) – see page 270.

Community contributions

Cash donations UK	£350,500

In 2016/17 the group donated £350,500 to its corporate charity.

Paragon Banking Group plc

Children and young people

Company registration number: 2336032

Correspondent: CSR Team, 51 Homer Road, Solihull, West Midlands B91 3QJ (tel: 0345 849 4000; website: www.theparagongroup.co.uk/paragon-law/more-about-paragon-law/csr-and-community)

Directors: Alan Fletcher; Barbara Ridpath; Finlay Williamson; Fiona Clutterbuck; Graeme Yorston; Hugo Tudor; John Herron; Nigel Terrington; Patrick Newberry; Peter Hartill; Richard Woodman; Robert Dench (female 17%; male 83%).

Nature of business: Paragon is one of the UK's largest providers of mortgages and personal loans.

Year end	30/09/2017
Turnover	£252,900,000
Pre-tax profit	£144,800,000

UK employees: 1,318

Main locations: The group has offices in London and Solihull.

Community involvement

The group looks to contribute to registered charities 'relating to financial services or serving the local communities in which it operates'. It has a particular focus on children's and local charities and states in its annual report that 'no charity request is overlooked'.

Employee-led support

The group supports Paragon's Charity Committee, consisting of volunteer employees, which organises a variety of fundraising activities throughout the year. All employees are given the opportunity to nominate a charity each year and a vote is carried out to select the charity or charities to benefit from the following year's fundraising.

During 2016/17 employees delivered workshops in local schools and colleges focusing on financial awareness and employability skills, donated over 100 shoeboxes for local Samaritans project Operation Christmas Purse, and made regular contributions to local food banks.

Applications

Contact the correspondent for further information.

Community contributions

Cash donations UK	£1,900,000

In 2016/17 the group contributed almost £1.9 million to charitable causes. Of this amount, £1.8 million was donated in support of the Foundation for Credit Counselling, which operates StepChange. Other charity contributions during the year totalled £25,000.

Beneficiaries included: 3H Fund – Helping Hands for Holidays; British Heart Foundation; Down's Syndrome Association; Kids Cancer Charity; Kids in Action; Macmillan; Prostate Cancer UK; Renewable World; Soroptimist International Solihull and District; Strongbones Children's Charitable Trust; WellChild.

The Peel Group

The environment, poverty and social exclusion, children and young people

Company registration number: 004056V

Correspondent: CSR Team, The Trafford Centre, Stretford, Manchester M17 8PL (tel: 0161 629 8200; website: www.peel.co.uk)

Directors: Chris Eves; David Glover; Hani Lazkani; James Whittaker; John Peter Whittaker; John Whittaker; Louise Morrisey; Mark Whittaker; Mark Whitworth; Neil Lees; Peter Hosker; Peter Nears; Robert Hough; Stephen Wild; Steven Underwood; Tom Allison (female 6%; male 94%).

Nature of business: The Peel Group owns numerous businesses including ports, airports, retail parks, wind farms and media facilities.

Main locations: The group's headquarters are in Manchester. It has operations throughout the UK with many of its projects located in northern England.

Community involvement

At a group level Peel makes occasional large charitable donations and its employees fundraise for charity partners. Several of its subsidiaries also have their own giving programmes.

Peel Ports 500 Fund (not a registered charity)

The fund supports community projects in disadvantaged areas of Liverpool, Sefton, Halton and Wirral.

Mersey Docks and Harbour Company Fund (Charity Commission no. 206913)

The fund was established in 1963 and focuses on seafarers and social welfare within Liverpool.

Durham Tees Valley Airport

The airport supports two charities which are chosen by an employee vote. It also supports various local charities through the airport's community investment fund.

Doncaster Sheffield Airport

The airport's community investment fund provides grants of up to £1,000 in the Sheffield City region in the following categories:

- Youth projects related to education or sports
- Community development projects
- Small scale community regeneration projects
- Environmental conservation projects

Charity partnerships

Peel Group employees have identified cancer and young people as the two areas they wish to support. The group has selected three charity partners to benefit from its charitable initiatives: The Christie Charitable Fund, Once Upon a Smile and Child Action North West.

Employee-led support

Employees raise money for the group's partner charities through events including an annual fundraising day at the group's head office.

Applications

Peel Ports 500 Fund

Applications can be made through the Community Foundation for Merseyside website: www.cfmerseyside.org.uk/Funds.aspx.

Durham Tees Valley Airport

Further information can be found at: www.durhamteesvalleyairport.com/about-us/csr.

Doncaster Sheffield Airport

Further information can be found at: flydsa.co.uk/about-us/csr.

For all other queries contact the correspondent.

Corporate charity

The Mersey Docks and Harbour Company Charitable Fund (Charity Commission no. 206913) – see page 264.

Community contributions

We were unable to find financial information for the Peel Group as its ultimate parent company Tokenhouse Ltd is registered in the Isle of Man. The group's 2016 CSR report states that since 1996 charitable giving has totalled £18 million and gifts in kind have totalled £33 million. In this time the group has made several large donations including £12.5 million to the Imperial War Museum North and £1 million to the Royal Manchester Children's Hospital Charity.

Pennon Group plc

The environment, STEM subjects, children and young people

Company registration number: 2366640

Correspondent: Sustainability Committee, Peninsula House, Rydon Lane, Exeter EX2 7HR (tel: 01392 446677; website: www.pennon-group.co.uk/sustainability)

Directors: Christopher Loughlin; Gill Rider; Helen Barrett-Hague; Iain Evans; John Parker; Martin Angle; Neil Cooper; Susan Davy (female 43%; male 57%).

Nature of business: Pennon Group is a British water utility and waste management company that owns South West Water and Viridor, a recycling, renewable energy and waste management businesses.

Year end	31/03/2018
Turnover	£1,396,200,000
Pre-tax profit	£262,900,000

UK employees: 5,190

Main locations: Support is given throughout the South West of England.

Community involvement

Pennon Group and its subsidiaries support communities and charities in the areas in which they operate.

Our research indicates that South West Water's support focuses on water, the environment and youth education in the South West, while Viridor's business is UK wide and its community support focuses on environmental and science education.

The group's financial involvement in the community is channelled through a number of initiatives:

- Community support, sponsorship and donations (South West Water and Viridor)
- Landfill Tax Credit Scheme (Viridor Waste)

Both South West Water and Viridor fundraise for their preferred charities: Age UK Cornwall, Cornwall Air Ambulance Trust, Devon Air Ambulance Trust, Cornwall Food Action and the RNLI.

Employee-led support

Employees help to raise funds for the group's preferred charities. South West Water and Viridor both have active volunteering schemes.

Commercially led support

Viridor's community sponsorship programme focuses on educational initiatives and particularly those in the areas of STEM and the environment. This has included GO4SET, a Scottish flagship educational initiative with the Engineering Development Trust.

During the year, South West Water sponsorships included BeachCare with Keep Britain Tidy, Cornwall Wildlife Trust, Devon Wildlife Trust, South West Coast Path Association, Surf Life Saving GB and Beach Schools South West.

Applications

Contact the correspondent for further information.

Community contributions

Cash donations UK	£151,000

During 2017/18 the group as a whole provided a total of £151,000 in cash donations.

Viridor

According to the group's annual report 2017/18, Viridor provided £7.6 million to community support, sponsorship and charitable donations. Some £7.3 million of this was paid to Viridor Credits for distribution via the Landfill Communities Fund. Viridor's charitable donations helped 114 projects supporting STEM, environmental, resource and recycling education initiatives, communities coming together through sport and community events and communities focused on improving the quality of life for disadvantaged and priority groups.

South West Water

South West Water provided £97,000 of community sponsorship and supported a number of charities.

Beneficiaries included: Age UK Cornwall, Age UK Devon, Cornwall Air Ambulance Trust, Devon Air Ambulance Trust, Devon and Cornwall Food Action and the RNLI.

Pentland Group plc

Arts and culture, health and medical research, children and young people, religion, sports and recreation

Company registration number: 793577

Correspondent: CSR Team, The Pentland Centre, Lakeside, Squires Lane, London N3 2QL (tel: 020 8346 2600; email: corporateresponsibility@pentland.com; website: www.pentland.com)

Directors: Alison Mosheim; Andrew Rubin; Angela Rubin; Barry Mosheim; Carolyn Rubin; John Morgan; Robert Rubin; Tim Hockings (female 38%; male 63%).

Nature of business: The main activities of the subsidiary companies are footwear, clothing and sports, consumer products and international trading.

Year end	31/12/2017
Turnover	£3,638,900,000
Pre-tax profit	£295,200,000

Total employees: 32,290

Main locations: Pentland's head office is based in London.

Community involvement

The Pentland Group support charities within its area of operation through financial donations, in-kind support, and employee-led support. The group is a family-owned business founded by the Rubin Family, who are also the founders and trustees of The Rubin Foundation Charitable Trust (Charity Commission no. 327062). The group's subsidiary, JD Sports, also has a corporate charity, the JD Foundation (Charity Commission no. 1167090) through which it funnels its charitable giving.

Partnerships

In 2017 Pentland Brands completed its second year of three-year partnerships with global charity partners chosen by its employees. The group support projects relevant to its brands and those that 'mean the most' to employees:

British Red Cross – Improving access to clean water in Kenya for more than 65,000 people so far.

United Purposes - Empowering young girls in India to overcome gender inequality.

WWF – Protecting the endangered Javan rhino in Indonesia.

The Rubin Foundation Charitable Trust (Charity Commission no. 327062)

This foundation is closely connected with the Pentland Group; however, it is not the group's corporate charity. The foundation's income comes, in part, from donations from the company.

The foundation tends to support a select number of charities on an annual basis and there is a preference for supporting Jewish organisations and causes.

In 2016/17 the foundation awarded grants to organisations totalling £576,500.

In-kind support

Through the group's charity partner, In Kind Direct, it channels product donations to community organisations and people in need. In 2017 donations through In Kind Direct reached over 500 community projects focusing on youth, disability and family welfare. Over the past 17 years, more than 2,100 charities have benefitted from the group's product donations worth an estimated retail value of over £2.4 million.

Employee-led support

The group encourages employees to support their communities through its '28 Give Back Days'. During 2017, almost 400 employee took part in activities such as: clearing rubbish from beached and forests in China; gardening, cleaning and painting for community centres, historic houses and a wildlife rescue centre in the UK; and preparing food packages for families in need in Hong Kong and the UK.

Employees also helped to raise funds for the group's charity partners, which the group matches. In 2017 employees took part in charity challenge events, including the Great North Run, the Royal Parks Half Marathon and the London Marathon. The group also donated £5,000 to the World Land Trust, in support of an employee who left the business to row in the Atlantic in aid of the charity.

Commercially led support

JD Foundation (Charity Commission no. 1167090)

The foundation receives 100% of proceeds from the carrier bag charges from JD Sports with 50% of funds donated to Mountain Rescue and the other 50% donated to charities working with young people in the UK. In 2017 the foundation awarded grants of £549,500 to Mountain Rescue England and Wales and Scottish Mountain Rescue. An additional £461,500 was awarded to staff-nominated charities including: Cardiac Risk in the Young (C.R.Y); Once Upon A Smile; Rays of Sunshine; Salford Foundation; Street Games; Teenage Cancer Trust; The Factory Youth Zone; The London Sports Trust; The Retail Trust.

Exclusions

No support is given for local appeals not in areas of company presence.

Applications

Contact the correspondent for further information about in-kind donations.

The Rubin Foundation Charitable Trust (Charity Commission no. 327062)

The foundation has previously stated that 'grants are only given to people related to our businesses, such as charities known to members of the Rubin family and those associated with Pentland Group Ltd'. Unsolicited applications are unlikely to succeed.

JD Foundation (Charity Commission no. 1167090)

Applications can be made in writing to: Siobhan Mawdsley, Secretary; JD Sports Foundation; Edinburgh House; Hollins Brook Way; Bury; BL9 8RR.

Community contributions

Every year, Pentland Brands gives at least 1% of its net profit after tax to charitable causes through product donations and financial contributions. A figure was not provided.

Persimmon plc

General charitable purposes

Company registration number: 1818486

Correspondent: Corporate Responsibility Committee, Persimmon House, Fulford, York YO19 4FE (tel: 0370 703 0178; website: corporate.persimmonhomes.com/corporate-responsibility/our-community/supporting-community-and-charitable-initiatives)

Directors: Dave Jenkinson; Jeff Fairburn; Marion Sears; Milke Killoan; Nicholas Wrigley; Nigel Mills; Rachel Kentleton; Roger Devlin; Simon Litherland (female 22%; male 78%).

Nature of business: Persimmon Homes is a residential home builder and property developer.

Year end	31/12/2017
Turnover	£3,422,300,000
Pre-tax profit	£966,100,000

UK employees: 4,535

Main locations: Persimmon has offices throughout the UK, details of which can be found at www.persimmonhomes.com/corporate/about-us/national-presence.

Community involvement

The company carries out most of its charitable giving through The Persimmon Charitable Foundation (Charity Commission no. 1163608).

Employee-led support

Through fundraising activities, Persimmon employees raised some of the £156,000 which was donated to directly to charitable causes by the group during the year.

Applications

Contact the correspondent for further information.

Corporate charity

The Persimmon Charitable Foundation (Charity Commission no. 1163608) – see page 272.

Community contributions

Cash donations UK	£664,500

In 2017 the group made donations of £601,000 to its corporate charity and £63,500 to other good causes.

Personal Assurance plc

General charitable purposes

Company registration number: 1832067

Correspondent: John Ormond House, 899 Silbury Boulevard, Milton Keynes MK9 3XL (tel: 0800 542 5930; email: crm@personalgroup.com; website: www.personalgroup.com)

Directors: Michael Dugdale; Robert Head; Andrew Lothian; Deborah Rees-Frost; Kenneth Rooney; Mark Scanlon; Mark Winlow (female 14%; male 86%).

Nature of business: Personal Assurance is a provider of employee benefits and financial services.

Year end	31/12/2017
Turnover	£45,200,000
Pre-tax profit	£9,500,000

Main locations: The group has sites throughout the UK.

Community involvement

The company supports charities through its corporate charity The Personal Assurance Charitable Trust and has a partnership with the Memusi Foundation, an African education charity.

Charity partnership

The group has a partnership with the Memusi Foundation, an African education charity. The group provides financial support as well as assistance on projects from volunteers.

Corporate charity

Personal Assurance Charitable Trust (Charity Commission no. 1023274) – see page 272.

Community contributions

Cash donations UK	£100,000

In 2017 the company made a donation of £100,000 to its corporate charity The Personal Assurance Charitable Trust.

Pets at Home Ltd

Animal welfare

Company registration number: 1822577

Correspondent: Corporate Social Responsibility Committee, Epsom Avenue, Stanley Green Trading Estate, Handforth, Cheshire SK9 3RN (tel: 0800 328 4204; email: info@supportadoptionforpets.co.uk; website: www.supportadoptionforpets.co.uk)

Directors: Dennis Millard; Mike Iddon; Paul Moody; Peter Pritchard; Sharon Flood; Stanislas Laurent; Susan Dawson; Tony DeNunzio (female 25%; male 75%).

Nature of business: Pets at Home is a retailer of services and equipment for pets.

Year end	29/03/2018
Turnover	£898,924,000
Pre-tax profit	£79,596,000

Main locations: There are 430 Pets at Home stores in the UK.

Community involvement

The company's CSR strategy is focused on supporting animal charities. The company makes in-kind donations of food to charities as well as to Support Adoption for Pets (Charity Commission no. 110415). The company's employees and staff raise large amounts for a range of animal welfare charities each year.

Support Adoption for Pets

This charity was established by Pets at Home in 2006 to provide support for the re-homing of pets. Pets at Home hosts adoption centres in over 430 Pets at Home stores and customers who adopt through the centres are encouraged to donate to the charity. Financial support is provided to animal welfare charities and local re-homing organisations throughout the UK. According to the charity's website, the trustees will consider applications for the following:

- Running costs (limited to vet bills and/or boarding costs) to a maximum of 20% of a rescue's annual expenditure
- Trap, Neuter and Release schemes for feral or stray cats
- The purchase of capital items (for example, vehicles, UPVC pens for foster homes, field shelters) and equipment
- Low cost vaccination and/or neutering programmes made available to the public
- Building renovations and new building work on land which is either owned in the rescue's name, or is on a long-term (min. 25 year) lease to the rescue. We will not fund building work on land which is owned or leased by an individual

Eligible organisations include:

- National pet rescue charities
- Branches of national pet rescue organisations which receive minimal or no funding from central funds
- Independent pet rescue and rehoming centres
- Foster or boarding kennels/catteries

A full list of eligibility criteria is available to download from the charity's website.

Partnerships

Support Adoption for Pets operates a Partnership Scheme between local rescues and local Pets at Home stores to raise funds, build awareness and create opportunities for support. Eligible UK pet rescues are welcome to join the scheme, whether a registered charity or not, and get access to fundraising in store, donation bins and an invitation to join in the charity's national fundraising drives. Each store is able to partner with up to five local rescues and shelters that are within a 20-mile radius.

In-kind support

Dog food worth £475,500 was donated to the Dogs Trust.

Employee-led support

During the year employees raised more than £4.4 million for Support Adoption for Pets.

Commercially led support

VIP (Very Important Pets)

The company runs a VIP (Very Important Pets) loyalty scheme. Every time a member makes a purchase they receive points which can be converted into VIP Lifelines for a charity of their choice to purchase food and accessories from local stores. This year £2.2 million worth of lifelines were donated to support the rehoming of pets.

Santa Paws

The biggest fundraising event in the year is the annual Santa Paws Appeal, where customers are invited to donate 50p to buy a Christmas dinner for a pet in rescue, the company raised £1.4 million which was split between Support Adoption for Pets and locally partnered rescues.

Exclusions

Support Adoption for Pets cannot fund:

- Salaries, uniforms or expenses
- Education centres and programmes
- The purchase of food
- The cost of leasing a vehicle, road tax, insurance or petrol costs
- Loan or interest payments
- The purchase of land or buildings
- Charity shop fundraising costs
- Marketing materials

Wildlife charities are not supported. Grants cannot be made for retrospective projects or costs. For further details and restrictions, refer to the guidance on the charity's website.

Applications

Contact your local Pets At Home store for more information on in-kind donations.

Support Adoption for Pets

Prospective applicants are requested to check their eligibility against the charity's detailed online guidance. Eligible organisations can then complete and submit their applications via the charity's website.

Although the type of information requested varies depending on what applicants propose using the grant funding for. Broadly speaking, the charity requires that all applications include the following:

- 12 months of financial information
- Some evidence which demonstrates the total cost of the proposed project
- Contact details for two people who can provide a reference, one of whom must be the applicants main vet

The trustees note that stronger applications may also include:

- Photos and case studies showing examples of pets who would be helped by the grant
- For building projects, photos and even videos showing the current state of the facilities
- Ideas on how you will work with Support Adoption for Pets to promote a grant to their supporters and yours

Applications are considered approximately every five to six weeks for projects under £20,000, and quarterly for larger projects.

Partnerships

Details of how to apply for a partnership with your local Pets At Home store are posted on the Support Adoption for Pets website. The website also provides detailed eligibilty criteria and deadlines for applications to the scheme.

Community contributions

In-kind support UK	£475,500

In 2017/18 the company donated dog food worth £475,500 to the Dogs Trust. The company did not declare its cash donations.

Pfizer Ltd

Health, STEM subjects

Company registration number: 526209

Correspondent: Colleague and Community Engagement Team, Ramsgate Road, Sandwich, Kent CT13 9NJ (tel: 01304 616161; website: www.pfizer.co.uk/content/communities)

Directors: Ben Osborn; Colin Seller; Denise Harnett; Dr Berkeley Phillips; Edwin Pearson; Hendrikus Nordkamp; Ian Franklin; Julian Thompson; Susan Rienow (female 22%; male 78%).

Nature of business: The principal activities of the company are the discovery, development, manufacture, marketing and sale of pharmaceutical and animal health products.

Year end	30/11/2017
Turnover	£850,303,000
Pre-tax profit	£217,729,000

Main locations: The group's head office in the UK is in Walton Oaks, Surrey. There are also operations in Cambridge, Havant, Hurley, and Sandwich.

Community involvement

The group supports organisations in the field of healthcare, as well as organisations in areas where the company has a presence (Sandwich, Walton Oaks, Cambridge and Havant) and STEM education initiatives. The group provides support through financial and in-kind donations, as well as matched funding for employee donations. Employees offer support through volunteering and payroll giving.

Charitable donations

The group's website states that, when allocating its charitable donations, the group gives priority to donations which:

- Improve the quality and availability of healthcare, educate individuals and families about sound health practices in order to empower them to improve their health, and serve those most at risk of health problems, or
- Advance research and knowledge in medicine, healthcare and allied sciences and science education

The group states that it also supports small charitable organisations and projects, including academic, cultural and community organisations, in the areas surrounding its UK operating sites through financial support, in-kind donations and pro bono support from employees.

Strategic community investment initiatives

Regarding strategic community investment initiatives, the company's website states:

> We work in partnership with community organisations and other partners on social initiatives that can have a positive and lasting impact on the community, such as our contribution to STEM education around the UK.
>
> We also consider our Corporate Sponsorship of the Science Museum 'Superbugs, the fight for our life' exhibition to be part of our strategic community investments. The sponsorship and associated internal and external activities are run out of our Corporate Responsibility Team as part of our public health education approach.
>
> The management costs associated with running the charitable donations and strategic community investment programmes are also included within this category.

Medical and Educational Goods and Services (MEGS) donations

Financial and in-kind donations are made under this category by Pfizer to benefit patient care or the NHS. A full breakdown of these donations, along with the group's educational grants and studentships in 2017, can be found on the website.

STEM education

Pfizer is a member of the Science Industry Partnership, a group of companies working to promote education and careers in STEM. The group also provides science and medicine learning programmes for schools and colleges.

In-kind support

The group provides in-kind donations through the organisation International Health Partners (IHPs), which provides medical supplies to charities working in humanitarian and disaster relief. In 2017 Pfizer UK donated 110,000 packs of medicine for inclusion in IHP's Essential Health Packs which are given to doctors travelling to financially developing countries to support local health programmes and act as an immediate resource in emergency situations.

Employee volunteering

Employees receive five days' paid leave to volunteer. In 2017 employees in the UK volunteered for a total of 3,142 hours.

Employee-led support

Employees volunteer with local charities or schools through the company's Science Industry Partnerships and STEM programmes.

Employee fundraising

The group has a payroll giving scheme and also provides matched funding for employee fundraising.

Commercially led support

The group makes educational grants to areas in which the company has an interest, such as medical science or public health policy. It also funds studentships at academic institutions. Grants are provided to organisations, not individuals.

Applications

Contact the correspondent for further information. For local appeals in areas where the company has a presence, contact your local Pfizer site.

Community contributions

Total contributions (cash and in kind £1.4 million.

The group's website provides the following breakdown of its UK social investment in 2017:

Corporate donations and grants	£1.4 million
Strategic community investment initiatives	£262,000
Total volunteering time	£110,000
Total value of social investment	**£1.8 million**

The total value of social investment includes management costs and therefore has not been included in the financial information.

The company's website states:

> Corporate donations include cash and the value of benefits in kind donated by Pfizer UK. This includes donations made to national charity appeals, donations from each of our sites to local charities and community organisations, matched donations for colleague fundraising and payroll giving activities, as well as charitable donations provided to patient organisations

Phoenix Group Holdings plc

Financial education, older people

Company registration number: 11606773

Correspondent: Lucy Symonds, Corporate Responsibility Manager, Juxon House, 100 St Paul's Churchyard, London EC4M 8BU (tel: 020 3567 9100; website: www.thephoenixgroup.com)

Directors: Alastair Barbour; Belinda Richards; Clive Bannister; Henry Staunton; Ian Cormack; Jim McConville; John Pollock; Karen Green; Kory Sorenson; Nicholas Shott; Wendy Mayall (female 36%; male 64%).

Nature of business: The group is a closed life assurance fund consolidator that specialises in the management and acquisition of closed life and pension funds.

Year end	31/12/2017
Turnover	£6,084,000,000
Pre-tax profit	£125,000,000

UK employees: 1,249

Main locations: The group's headquarters are in Birmingham.

Community involvement

The group supports charities local to its offices through sponsorship, partnerships, employee fundraising and in-kind giving.

Charity partnerships

The Group has worked closely with 36 community partners across the year, providing time, skills and donations to their cause. Now into its fourth year of the six-year partnership with Midlands Air Ambulance Charity and London's Air Ambulance, the group is continuing to use this collaboration to engage staff in fundraising, volunteering and events for the cause. The annual report for 2017 states that: 'Since partnering in 2014 the group has donated in excess of £690,000 to the charities'.

In-kind support

The 2017 Responsibility Report provides detailed and useful information on the group's various types of in-kind giving.

Phoenix Group in Wythall donated carpet tiles and old furniture to help equip Citizens Advice Solihull Borough's new charity shop in Chelmsley Wood. In addition staff donated various items from home to help stock the new store in readiness for launch. Items included clothes, children's toys, books, DVDs and crockery. Staff also assisted behind the scenes helping to get the donated items ready for sale and adding creative flair with the displays.

The Wythall site's resources are frequently loaned to community partners. For example, Kings Norton Marching Band practise their routine in the grounds over the weekend, car parking facilities were made available to the Transport Museum, Wythall Radio Club and for the 2017 Mad March Hare Sportive. Meeting room facilities during the year have been donated to Ark Kings Academy for teacher inductions and Coppice Primary School for regional safeguarding training with other primary schools.

Phoenix sponsored 40 financial workshops in local secondary schools, reaching 1,100 pupils across the academic term 2016–2017. The workshops were designed to get young people thinking about real-life budgeting and how to make difficult decisions around the prioritisation of money.

Employee-led support

Employee volunteering

Employees are encouraged to take part in the group's volunteering initiative and in this financial year, gave a total of 3,163 volunteering hours. An example of structured volunteering activities taken from the 2017 Social Responsibility Report is that of 214 members of staff who attended an onsite Dementia Friend workshop, equipping them with the skills to better understand what living with dementia is like. The sessions have been run by staff members who were trained by Alzheimer's Society to become Dementia Friend Champions. According to the group's 2017 Social Responsibility Report 'their training has allowed them to conduct training sessions in the local community too – from parish councillors to local businesses they are making a difference'.

Staff have helped thin woodland at Millennium Wood, within Arrow Valley Country Park, in Redditch and subsequently used fallen branches to create a natural hedge-way and hibernaculum to house local wildlife onsite. In addition, at Sanders Park, Bromsgrove teams assisted with removing Himalayan balsam from the water-ways, an invasive weed which if left would overly consume the natural stream habitat. A third team assisted with removing overgrowth from the waterways at Lickey End Park, near Bromsgrove helping to protect the resident water vole.

Employee fundraising

Nearly £26,000 in matched funding was given by the group to selected charities and community groups.

Commercially led support

Sponsorship

During the year the group was the premier sponsor of the 'Wythall and Hollywood Fun Run' which included a 10km, 5km and 1.5km run through Wythall's community.

Exclusions

No political or religious causes are supported, and preference is given to those charities operating close to the group's offices.

Applications

Apply in writing to the correspondent.

Community contributions

Cash donations UK	£161,500

The group's website states that in 2017 the group donated £161,500 to various community initiatives.

Beneficiaries included: Birmingham St Mary's Hospice, Guide Dogs for the Blind, Macmillan Cancer Support, Ark Cancer Centre Charity, Dorset and Somerset Air Ambulance and Jessie May Trust.

Playtech plc

Poverty and social exclusion, education, children and young people

Correspondent: CSR Team, Ground Floor, St George's Court, Upper Church Street, Douglas, Isle of Man IM1 1EE (website: www.playtech.com)

Directors: Alan Jackson; Andrew Smith; Andrew Thomas; Claire Milne; John Jackson; Mor Weizer; Susan Ball (female 29%; male 71%).

Nature of business: Playtech is a gambling software development company. It is registered in the Isle of Man.

Year end	31/12/2017
Turnover	£670,000,000
Pre-tax profit	£231,000,000

Total employees: 5,000

Main locations: Support is given throughout the UK. The group has offices in London and Northern Ireland.

Community involvement

The group focuses on education and research into the treatment of problem gambling as well as providing donations to a range of charities.

Applications

Contact the correspondent for further information.

Community contributions

Cash donations worldwide	£363,000

According to the group's 2017 annual report donations totalling €407,000 (≈ £363,000 as at September 2018) were made 'primarily to charities that fund research into and treatment of problem gambling but also to a variety of charities operating in countries in which the Company's subsidiaries are based'.

We were unable to determine how much was given in the UK.

Premier Oil plc

The armed forces, housing and homelessness, health and medical research, disability, children and young people

Company registration number: SC234781

Correspondent: Corporate Services Team, 23 Lower Belgrave Street, London SW1W 0NR (tel: 020 7730 1111; email: premier@premier-oil.com; website: www.premier-oil.com)

Directors: Anne Cannon; Dave Blackwood; Iain Macdonald; Jane Hinkley; Mike Wheeler; Richard Rose; Robin Allen; Roy Franklin; Tony Durrant (female 22%; male 78%).

Nature of business: Premier Oil is an international gas and oil exploration and production company.

Year end	31/12/2017
Turnover	£1,063,600,000
Pre-tax profit	(£270,200,000)

Main locations: The group has offshore operations in the Falkland Islands, Indonesia, Pakistan, the UK and Vietnam. In the UK, the group's head office is London and it has offices in Aberdeen. There are also offices in Abu Dhabi and Brazil.

Community involvement

According to the 2017 corporate responsibility report, the group invest in community projects to help deliver sustainable, economic and environmental benefits for communities in the areas it has a presence.

UK community investment

According to the 2017 corporate responsibility report, the group supported a number of charities 'through the provision of funding', including:

- HorseBack UK, a charity that helps injured servicemen and others to regain their confidence and mobility by working with horses
- Charlie House, a charity that provides a range of support to babies, children and young people with life-limiting or life-threatening conditions as well as their families
- Aberdeen Seafarers Centre, which offers welfare services and advice to seafarers visiting the port of Aberdeen
- Archway, a charity that works across Aberdeen and throughout north east Scotland, helping people with learning disabilities develop their social and independent living skills and participate in community life
- The Passage, a charity close to the group's London office providing support to homeless and vulnerable people
- Macmillan Cancer Support

The group also provide bursaries for UK-based undergraduate students for participation in expeditions run by Operation Wallacea.

Applications

Contact the correspondent for further information.

Community contributions

Cash donations UK	£112,500
Cash donations overseas	£450,500
Total contributions (cash and in kind)	£563,000

According to the 2017 corporate responsibility report, community investment in the UK amounted to \$147,500 (≈ £112,500 as at October 2018). Community investment was also given in Indonesia, Pakistan and Vietnam totalling \$589,000 (≈ £450,500 as at October 2018). We have taken these figures as Premier Oil's cash donations for the year.

Beneficiaries included: Aberdeen Seafarers' Centre; Archway; Charlie House; HouseBack UK; Macmillan Cancer Support; The Passage.

Pret A Manger (Europe) Ltd

Homelessness

Company registration number: 1854213

Correspondent: Giovanna Pasini, Financial Donations Manager, 75b Verde, 10 Bressenden Place, London SW1E 5DH (email: Giovanna.Pasini@pret.com; website: www.pret.co.uk/en-gb/pret-foundation-trust)

Directors: Andrea Wareham; Clare Clough; Clive Schlee (female 67%; male 33%).

Nature of business: Pret A Manger (Pret) is an international sandwich shop chain based in the UK.

Year end	28/12/2017
Turnover	£637,000,000
Pre-tax profit	£65,000,000

Main locations: The company's head office is in London. At the end of 2017 there were 360 shops in the UK.

Community involvement

Pret's CSR strategy focuses on supporting homeless charities and people who are homeless in the UK. This is achieved through the distribution of unsold food at the end of each day from shops, employment programmes for homeless people, and financial donations to grassroots homeless partner charities.

Pret Foundation Trust (Charity Commission no. 1050195)

All of Pret's CSR activity is channelled through the trust. The trust operates a fleet of 'Charity Run' vans that collects food from shops and delivers them to charities. Grants are also made to homeless charities to support salaries, core costs and the delivery of services.

In 2017, 67 grants were awarded totalling £987,000, of which £111,000 was a one-off donation to the support people affected by the Grenfell Tower fire.

Beneficiaries included: Cardboard Citizens (£32,500); The Clock Tower Sanctuary (£24,500); Glasgow City Mission (£21,500); The Albert Kennedy Trust (£20,000); Manchester City Mission (£15,200); Create (Arts) Ltd (£12,600); Bridges Project (£8,400); The People's Kitchen (£5,000).

Rising Stars and Shooting Stars Programme

The Rising Stars Programme offers people who are homeless the opportunity of a three-month paid work experience programme, with the aim of helping them build a new future. The Shooting Stars Programme offers a cohort of eight graduated Rising Stars the opportunity to participate in a seven-month career development programme. It culminates in a STEC (Speke Training and Education Centre) level 2 in Work Skills and the opportunity to take GCSE English and Maths. The 'Shooting Stars' finish the programme with a clear Personal Development Plan should they wish to remain in Pret or follow a career elsewhere.

In-kind support

Pret arranges for charities to collect unsold food directly from shops or arranges a free delivery. It also donates kitchen equipment for small, grassroots homeless charities and shelters. In 2017 over 3.4 million main meal items were collected and distributed on behalf of charities.

Employee-led support

Employees fundraise for the Pret Foundation Trust and in 2017 they raised £16,000.

Commercially led support

The company donates 10p from every soup sold and 50p from Christmas sandwiches and baguettes to support the work of the trust. In 2017, £1.3 million was raised through commercially led support.

Applications

In order for charities to receive funding from the Pret Foundation Trust they must be:

- A registered charity
- Set up to support the homeless in some way
- Local to a Pret shop
- Receiving no more than 20% of income via statutory funding
- Solving a real problem in a practical way

The Financial Donations Manager, Giovanna Pasini, can be contacted prior to making an application to discuss how Pret can help. The manager can also help with requests for charity raffle prizes.

If you would like to know more about either the Rising Stars or Shooting Stars programme, contact the Pret Foundation Trust Employment Programme Managers, Giuseppe Finocchiaro (email: giuseppe.finocchiaro@pret.com) and Hind Meflah (email: Hind.Meflah@pret.com). They work closely with charities that work with the homeless, to identify those people ready to join the programme.

Community contributions

Although the 2017 accounts state that the company gave £1.5 million for charitable purposes, we have not included this in our overall figures as we believe this to be money raised through commercially led support and contributions to cover the support costs of the trust. It is evident that the company gives significantly in-kind donations to local homeless charities but the company does not quantify the amount given.

Pricewaterhouse-Coopers LLP

Poverty and social exclusion, health, enterprise and training

Company registration number: OC303525

Correspondent: David Adair, Head of Community Affairs, 1 Embankment Place, London WC2N 6RH (tel: 020 7212 7140; website: www.pwc.co.uk)

Directors: Dan Schwarzmann; Hemione Hudson; Jon Andrews; Kevin Burrowes; Kevin Ellis; Kevin Nicholson; Laura Hinton; Marco Amitrano; Margaret Cole; Marissa Thomas; Paul Terrington; Warwick Hunt (female 33%; male 67%).

Nature of business: PricewaterhouseCoopers (PwC) is a multinational professional services network providing assurance, tax and advisory services.

Year end	30/06/2018
Turnover	£3,764,000,000
Pre-tax profit	£987,000,000

Total employees: 22,305

Main locations: PricewaterhouseCoopers LLP has offices throughout the UK.

Community involvement

Note that PwC has offices all around the world and contributes to local causes in overseas operating areas. The information in our record relates to the UK site activities.

According to the group's website, its community strategy within the next five years will be focusing on social inclusion, health and well-being. The group also has a corporate charity, The PwC Foundation (Charity Commission no. 1144124) which was established to develop social inclusion and sustainable development in the UK.

Social mobility

The group has over 40 partner schools in socially deprived areas across the UK. Through its partnerships the group offers mentoring, work experience and employability workshops.

Mental health and well-being

Over the next five years the group will be supporting charities who are improving mental health and well-being across the UK through its foundation. The PwC Foundation has partnered with the Samaritans and Wellbeing for Women.

Social enterprise

The company's social enterprise hub, The Fire Station, houses several like-minded organisations working together to advance social and environmental change. The company's own social enterprise Brigade is a bar and bistro providing training and employment opportunities for people who are homeless or at risk of homelessness.

Employee-led support

Volunteering

The company works with several environmental charities to provide volunteering opportunities for its staff. The group's 2017/18 non-financial performance scorecard notes that 26% of staff volunteered a total of over 66,400 hours during the year.

Employee donations

Through payroll giving and donations to the PwC foundation staff gave a total of £700,000 during the year.

Applications

Contact the correspondent for further information.

Corporate charity

The PwC Foundation (Charity Commission no. 1144124) – see page 273.

Community contributions

According to the company's 2017/18 non-financial performance scorecard, the group's total contribution during the year was valued at £7.4 million. This figure includes 'cash, time, in-kind and management costs'. It is our usual practice not to include management costs in the group's total contribution and therefore we have not included a figure for contributions in the financial information.

Principality Building Society

Community development, children and young people, sports and recreation

Company registration number: FCA 155998

Correspondent: James Harper, Sponsorship and Events, PO Box 89, Principality Buildings, Queen Street, Cardiff CF10 1UA (website: www.principality.co.uk/about-us/our-community)

Directors: Claire Hafner; David Rigney; Derek Howell; Julie Haines; Laurence Adams; Nigel Annett; Robert Jones; Sally-Jones Evans; Steve Hughes; Thomas Denman (female 30%; male 70%).

Nature of business: The provision of housing finance and a range of insurance and financial services.

Year end	31/12/2017
Turnover	£116,600,000
Pre-tax profit	£37,500,000

UK employees: 1,129

Main locations: The company has branches throughout Wales.

Community involvement

The company supports employee-nominated charities every year as well as community projects where it has an office.

Charity partners

Employees nominate charity partners that they wish to support during the year. In 2017 the employees three chosen charity partners were Llamau, School of Hard Knocks and Cancer Research Wales.

Education

The company focuses on building the financial skills of young people and is involved in various initiatives that promote this. During the year, Principality branch employees participated in Financial Capability Week all around Wales.

The company works closely with Business in the Community (BITC), a business-led charity that supports young people, people who are unemployed, responsible enterprise and economic growth and helps boost workforce skills. The company partnered with BITC in support of community projects including volunteering-based action days and the Business Class school engagement programme.

In-kind support

In 2017 the company helped to deliver more than 40 lessons to more than 1,000 primary schoolchildren aged 5–11 in a week where they also partnered with Money Advice Service to launch their national research on financial education at Principality Stadium. The company also teamed up with Aspire 2Be to run innovative digital and broadcasting training camps for young people called i-Broadcast, including Principality Stadium and Zip World Stadium in Colwyn Bay.

Employee-led support

Throughout 2017 employees invested more than 1,000 hours of volunteer time, including volunteering at food banks and helping at the DIY SOS Big Build for Children in Need.

Staff members choose a charity partner they would like to support through their fundraising. The company also matches employees' fundraising efforts.

Commercially led support

There is a branch sponsorship scheme which aims to support sport, arts and culture. For more information on sponsorships, contact the correspondent.

Beneficiaries of sponsorships have included: the National Eisteddfod; Only Boys Aloud, Royal Welsh Show; Welsh Rugby Union.

Exclusions

According to the company's website, support is not given to:

- Political or religious causes
- Projects run on behalf of charities by companies for profit
- Projects outside the areas where the company has branches
- Development or running costs for projects
- Individuals

Applications

Sponsorship

Contact the correspondent for further information.

Community support

Enquiries can be made through Principality's website: www.principality.co.uk/about-us/our-community/community-request-form.

Community contributions

According to the company's 2017 annual report, £134,000 was fundraised for charity partners, which included a matched amount of £57,000. The annual report also states that 'over 130 community groups/projects have been supported with a combined investment of over £90,000'. We were unable to determine which of this amount was given in cash donations and how much was employee-led support.

Procter & Gamble UK

Health, disaster relief, children and young people, projects outside the UK

Company registration number: 83758

Correspondent: Janette Butler, Social Responsibility Programme Manager, The Heights, Brooklands, Weybridge, Surrey KT13 0XP (tel: 01932 896000; website: www.uk.pg.com)

Directors: Alexander Buckthorp; Anthony Appleton; Vijay Sitlani (female 0%; male 100%).

Nature of business: Procter & Gamble (P&G) UK, operating in the UK and Ireland, is a wholly owned subsidiary of The Procter & Gamble Company, incorporated in the USA. The principal activities of the company and its subsidiaries are the manufacture and marketing of innovative consumer products, with associated research and development services. We were unable to determine the financial figures for the company, as it only has investment subsidiaries registered in the UK.

Main locations: P&G has sites in London, Manchester, Newcastle, Reading, Seaton Delaval, Skelmersdale and Weybridge.

Community involvement

P&G supports local communities in the areas the company has a presence.

P&G Fund and P&G Grassroots Funds

The Community Foundation for Tyne and Wear and Northumberland manages the above funds on behalf of P&G to support the company's charitable giving. According to the Community Foundation's website, the fund concentrates on two areas:

- Creating the experience of home: turning houses into homes and providing the comforts of home to the people without them or who have been displaced
- Everyday health and confidence: enabling healthy lives through everyday healthy behaviours and hygiene education that enable confidence and self-esteem

The funds are open to charities in Tyne and Wear and Northumberland working with children in care; mental health; older people and other vulnerable/disadvantaged people; people experiencing, or at risk of experiencing, homelessness; and people in palliative care. Grants tend to be under £10,000 and applications should be made through the foundation. In May 2018, P&G announced that the fund had reached a £1 million milestone in grants to over 500 local communities.

Save the Children

Over the last three years the company has been working with Save the Children UK and have donated a total of £390,000 to help fund its Eat, Sleep, Learn, Play! programme. The programme supports children living in poverty by providing grants to families for household essentials such as beds, cookers, toys and books.

Disaster Relief

Globally P&G's disaster relief programmes provide daily essential products to victims of natural disasters as well as cash support.

Safe Drinking Water and Vaccination Programmes

The Children's Safe Drinking Water Programme helps provide clean drinking water to children and their families in financially developing countries. P&G

works with organisations such as CARE, ChildFund and Save the Children to deliver the programme. Pampers and Unicef have also been working together to vaccinate women and children against maternal and neonatal tetanus and have so far eliminated it from 17 countries.

In-kind support

In the UK, P&G partnered with In Kind Direct in 2002 and since then has donated an estimated £42 million worth of goods.

Applications

Company

More information on community support in the UK and Ireland can be obtained by contacting one of the regional co-ordinators or the correspondent.

P&G Community Fund

For more information on financial grants in Tyne and Wear and Northumberland only, contact Su Legg (email: sl@communityfoundation.org.uk, tel: 0191 222 0945). Applications should be made on the standard foundation form.

Community contributions

We were unable to determine a figure for P&G UK's community contributions.

Provident Financial plc

Community development, general charitable purposes

Company registration number: 668987

Correspondent: Corporate Responsibility Manager, No. 1 Godwin Street, Bradford BD1 2SU (tel: 01274 351135; email: corporateresponsibility@providentfinancial.com; website: www.providentfinancial.com)

Directors: Andrea Blance; Andrew Fisher; Angela Knight; John Straw; Libby Chambers; Malcolm Le May; Patrick Snowball; Paul Hewitt; Ron Anderson (female 25%; male 75%).

Nature of business: Provident Financial is a sub-prime lender specialising in credit cards, home-collected credit, online loans and consumer car finance.

Year end	31/12/2017
Turnover	£1,196,300,000
Pre-tax profit	(£123,000,000)

Total employees: 4,630

Main locations: The group's headquarters are in Bradford.

Community involvement

The group supports community projects that focus on helping people overcome issues that prevent financial inclusion. According to the group's 2017 Corporate Responsibility Report, the group delivers support in the following ways:

1. Supporting local projects which address social inclusion issues
2. Supporting accredited community intermediaries such as Community Foundations, to deliver programmes in the communities in which we operate
3. Providing employees with matched funding for fundraising and promoting volunteering activities
4. Encouraging our employees to take part in company-led volunteering initiatives
5. Supporting the money advice sector to address financial education issues, and carrying out research into broader, societal matters that relate to our customers

Community funds

The group have launched a total of five community funds, administered by community foundations in Leeds/Bradford, London, Kent and Hampshire Isle of Wright. The funds disburse grants to projects that address issues including mental health, food and nutrition, well-being, self-esteem, employability, family relationships and low educational attainment. In 2017 grants totalling £250,000 were awarded to 37 community organisations.

Charity partners

The group have a range of charity partners to address social inclusion and social mobility issues. Vanquis Bank (a subsidiary of Provident) has a partnership with Mencap and during the year provided funding to enable the charity to pilot the 'All In' award. The group also have a long-term partnership with Early Focus, a charity in Dublin addressing the needs of Children at St James' School in Basin – one of the most deprived areas in Dublin.

During 2017, the group had 43 'long-term community partnerships'.

Support for the money advice sector

The group has partnerships with several money advice organisations which enables them to provide better quality advice and help those who are having difficulty paying their debts. Money advice providers include: Advice UK, Citizens Advice, Step Change Debt Charity, Institute of Money Advisers, Money Advice Liaison Group, Money Advice Scotland, Money Advice Trust, and National Debtline.

In-kind support

Employee volunteering time was valued at £9,600.

Employee-led support

Volunteering

Employees are offered two days' paid leave to volunteer in their local communities through company-led challenges and skills-based volunteering. During 2017, employees volunteered 220 hours.

In 2017 the group launched an online employee volunteering portal to enable staff to identify individual volunteering activities. The group offers staff a volunteering grant for the organisation they give their time to.

Matched funding

Employees can apply for funding to match fundraising activities they undertake outside work. In 2017 Provident Financial Group provided £43,500 to support employees' fundraising.

Applications

Applications for grants can be made through the community foundations' websites:

- Leeds Community Foundation – www.leedscf.org.uk/open-grants
- Hampshire and Isle of Wright Community Foundation – www.hiwcf.com
- London Community Foundation – londoncf.org.uk
- Kent Community Foundation – kentcf.org.uk

Community contributions

Cash donations worldwide	£2,350,000
In-kind support UK	£9,600
Total contributions (cash and in kind)	£2,360,000

The 2017 CR Report states that the group's total community investment for the year totalled £2.59 million. Of this amount, £2.35 million was given in cash donations and management costs totalled £227,581 (which we have not included in our figures). The value of employee time was costed at £9,600 which we have included in the group's total contribution figure.

The 2017 CR Report states that each year the group aims to invest over 1% of pre-tax profit in community programmes.

PRS For Music Ltd

Music

Company registration number: 3444246

Correspondent: 2 Pancras Square, London N1C 4AG (website: www.prsformusic.com)

Directors: Charles Booth; Christopher Butler; Edward Gregson; Jacqueline Alway; John Minch; Julian Nott; Mark Poole; Nigel Elderton; Robert Ashcroft; Simon Darlow; Stephen Cooke; Stephen

Davidson; Stephen Levine; Thomas Toumazis (female 7%; male 93%).

Nature of business: PRS for Music is a collection society which undertakes collective rights management for musical works on behalf of its 130,000 members. It represents songwriter, composer and music publisher members' performing and mechanical rights, and collect royalties on their behalf whenever their music is player or performed publicly or reproduced as a physical product.

Year end	31/12/2017
Turnover	£100,160,000
Pre-tax profit	(£316,000)

UK employees: 450

Main locations: The company's headquarters are based in London.

Community involvement

The company's community involvement is channelled through its corporate charity, The Performing Right Society Foundation (Charity Commission no. 1080837).

Corporate charity

The Performing Right Society Foundation (Charity Commission no. 1080837) – see page 271.

Community contributions

Cash donations UK	£3,000,000

In 2017 the company gave £3 million to its corporate charity.

Prudential plc

Education, older people, disaster relief, projects outside the UK

Company registration number: 1397169

Correspondent: Corporate Responsibility Team, Laurence Pountney Hill, London EC4R 0HH (tel: 020 7220 7588; email: responsibility@prudential.co.uk; website: www.prudential.co.uk)

Directors: Paul Manduca; Mike Wells; Mark FitzPatrick; John Foley; Nic Nicandrou; Barry Stowe; James Turner; Philip Remnant; Howard Davies; David Law; Kai Nargolwala; Anthony Nitingale; Alice Schroeder; Lord Turner; Tom Watjen; Fields Wicker-Miurin (female 13%; male 88%).

Nature of business: Prudential provides retail financial services and insurance products in Europe, the USA, Asia and Africa.

Year end	31/12/2017
Turnover	£86,562,000,000
Pre-tax profit	£3,970,000,000

UK employees: 5,550

Total employees: 24,700+

Main locations: Prudential's main offices in the UK are in London, Reading and Stirling.

Community involvement

The company's community investment strategy is aimed at 'protecting and encouraging more sustainable and resilient communities' in the UK and overseas where it has offices. The company pursues partnerships with different charities aligned with its community investment strategy. The company focuses on these four principal areas through cash and in-kind support: social inclusion, financial education and life skills, disaster preparedness, and employee engagement. The group has a corporate charity, the Prudence Foundation, which supports projects in Asia.

Social inclusion

Age UK – in partnership with Age UK the company is financially supporting the 'Later Life Links' programme, providing long-term companionship, advice and practical help to older people.

In the UK, the company supports disadvantaged communities near its offices. During 2017, more than 190 charities received support through cash donations or employees volunteering. Grants typically focus on education, medical research, social welfare programmes, and children and youth projects.

Financial education and life skills

Young Enterprise – Working with Young Enterprise, the company developed an online educational resource for primary school students in England and Wales. The teaching resource has guidance on how to effectively integrate activities for home-learning. Since its launch in 2016, the resource has been downloaded over 20,000 times in more than 650 schools across the UK.

School partnerships – Through three secondary school partnerships in Paddington, Reading and Stirling, Prudential has supported over 3,700 young people since 2013, with 360 employees giving their time and sharing their knowledge and skills.

MyBank – The company's partnership with MyBank helped develop money skills for 5,000 young people in secondary schools in deprived areas in London.

Disaster readiness and relief

There is a fund to support communities which have suffered from natural disasters. The website suggests that both financial and in-kind support is mainly offered in Asia.

Save the Children

The group has been a partner of Save the Children's Emergency Fund for a number of years and in 2016 committed to the partnership for another three years.

In-kind support

A range of in-kind support is offered to organisations on a local basis. This includes employees' volunteering time and skills, as well as office space, meeting rooms, computers and office furniture.

Employee-led support

Employee volunteering

Employees are encouraged to get involved in their communities through volunteering and fundraising efforts. There are also local fundraising teams organising all fundraising activities on site and donating the money to select charities.

The website notes that in 2017, employees across the Prudential group volunteered a total of 96,493 hours.

The group also have a flagship international volunteering programme which helps support its global partners. Prudential donates £150 to its charity partners for every employee who registers with the programme. Charity partners use this money to seed-fund charitable projects for Prudential volunteers. Each year employees across the Group are involved in the voting process to decide on the most innovative projects, which receive extra funding towards their charitable objectives. During 2017, more than 8,000 employees around the world took part, volunteering over 27,000 hours to support 30 projects.

In the UK and Europe, employees supported Age UK's 'Call in Time' programme giving 414 hours of their time.

Payroll giving

Across the group £412,500 was donated by employees through the payroll giving scheme in 2017.

Commercially led support

In 2017 more than 846 charities benefitted from the Prudential RideLondon event which the company has sponsored since 2013.

Applications

Further information can be sought from the Corporate Responsibility Team.

Community contributions

Cash donations worldwide	£19,200,000

According to the group's 2017 annual report, cash donations to charitable organisations amounted to £19.2 million, of which approximately £4.9 million came from 'UK and EU operations'. Cash contributions from the group's UK and EU operations were distributed as follows:

Education	£2.9 million
Social/welfare/environment	£1.8 million
Cultural	£62,000

We are unable to tell how much was given in cash and in-kind support in the UK and Europe.

Rathbone Brothers plc

General charitable purposes

Company registration number: 1000403

Correspondent: CSR Team, 1 Curzon Street, Mayfair, London W1J 5HD (tel: 020 7399 0000; email: marketing@rathbones.com; website: www.rathbones.com)

Directors: Ali Johnson; James Dean; Jim Pettigrew; Mark Nicholls; Paul Stockton; Philip Howell; Sarah Gentleman; Terrie Duhon (female 25%; male 75%).

Nature of business: The group is an independent provider of investment and wealth management services for private investors, charities and trustees. It operates in the UK and Jersey.

Year end	31/12/2017
Turnover	£291,572,000
Pre-tax profit	£58,901,000

Total employees: 1,147

Main locations: Rathbones has 15 offices throughout the UK and Jersey. Office locations can be found on the group's website.

Community involvement

The group has a corporate charity, the Rathbone Brothers Foundation (Charity Commission no. 1150432) which makes grants to UK-based charities local to where it has an office.

Rathbones Financial Awareness Programme

This free scheme, aimed at 16- to 24-year-olds, forms a significant part of the company's youth development initiatives. It involves investment managers delivering presentations within the company's offices and at schools around the UK on financial matters, career routes and interview techniques in order to give young people the knowledge to manage their own finances at a young age.

Local communities

Regional offices are encouraged to get involved with local charity projects.

In-kind support

Employee skills and time are donated through educational initiatives, for example, the company's Financial Awareness Programme.

Employee-led support

Employees can support charities through the Give As You Earn (GAYE) scheme. In 2017 employees donated £225,000 through the scheme. The group will match staff donations of up to £200 per month made through the GAYE scheme. In 2017 a total of £161,000 was given to increase staff donations to their chosen causes.

Corporate charity

The Rathbone Brothers Foundation (Charity Commission no. 1150432) – see page 274.

Community contributions

Cash donations UK	£378,000

In 2017 the group made charitable donations totalling £378,000, including a £150,000 donation to The Rathbone Brothers Foundation.

Beneficiaries included: Cambridge Central Aid Society; Clearvision; The Connections Bus Project; Enabling Enterprise; Shepard's Down School; The Teapot Trust.

Reach plc

General charitable purposes

Company registration number: 82548

Correspondent: CSR Team, One Canada Square, Canary Wharf, London E14 5AP (tel: 020 7293 3000; website: www.reachplc.com)

Directors: Dr David Kelly; Helen Stevenson; Lee Ginsberg; Nicholas Prettejohn; Olivia Streatfeild; Simon Fox; Steve Hatch; Vijay Vaghela (female 25%; male 75%).

Nature of business: Formerly known as Trinity Mirror plc, Reach is a UK-based newspaper, magazine and digital publisher. It is one of the UK's largest newspaper groups, publishing 240 regional papers in addition to national papers such as the Daily Mirror, Sunday Mirror, and Daily Record.

Year end	31/12/2017
Turnover	£623,000,000
Pre-tax profit	£81,900,000

UK employees: 5,067

Main locations: The group operates across the UK.

Community involvement

The Corporate Social Responsibility section of the group's 2017 annual report explains that '[Reach] supports communities across the UK through its editorial work, raising awareness, publicising charities, running campaigns and organising fundraising appeals across all of its national and regional titles'. The report further explains that Reach 'makes direct cash donations to various charities connected with or associated with the newspaper, printing or advertising industries and to charities operating in the communities immediately surrounding the Group's offices and sites'. Previous research suggests that each of the group's regional newspaper companies has a small budget from which they can make donations to local charities working in their community. According to the group's annual report, donations are most likely to be awarded to 'smaller community-based charities where a modest donation will make a big impact'.

Awards ceremonies

The group runs a number of award events, both nationally and at regional level. The most widely known awards event is the Daily Mirror's Pride of Britain Awards, which has celebrated the nation's 'unsung heroes' since 1999 and is televised on ITV. At a national level, the group also runs the Pride of Sport and Animal Heroes Awards. At a regional level, the Sunday Mail Great Scot Awards has been honouring the achievements of ordinary Scottish people for more than 25 years and, as an extension of the 'Pride of...' series of awards, the group's regional news outlets also organise awards ceremonies.

Campaigns and fundraising

Reach's regional and national titles are involved with a range of issue-based campaigns. Recent examples include, a campaign to encourage organ donor registration, co-ordinating donations for starter packs for young people facing homelessness and partnering with Teach First to promote recruitment into teaching.

Following the May 2017 terrorist attack in Manchester, one of Reach's local publications the Manchester Evening News launched an appeal to support victims' families via JustGiving. In total the appeal raised over £2.5 million for victims of the attack.

In-kind support

Our previous research suggests that the group is willing to make office facilities and equipment available for use by charitable organisations. Staff volunteering time and expert skills are also offered.

Applications

Our previous research indicates that enquiries regarding donations should be addressed to the editor or manager of the newspaper/print site based in your community.

Community contributions

The annual report and accounts for 2017 did not include a figure for charitable donations.

Reckitt Benckiser Group plc

Health education and disease prevention, projects outside the UK

Company registration number: 527217

Correspondent: Sustainability Team, 103–105 Bath Road, Slough, Berkshire SL1 3UH (tel: 01753 217800; email: sustainability@rb.com; website: www.rb.com)

Directors: Rakesh Kapoor; Chris Sinclair; Andrew Bonfield; Nicandro Durante; Mary Harris; Adrien Hennah; Mehmood Khan; Pam Kirby; André Lacroix; Elane Stock; Warren Tucker (female 27%; male 73%).

Nature of business: The principal activities of the group are the manufacture and sale of household and healthcare products.

Year end	31/12/2017
Turnover	£11,512,000,000
Pre-tax profit	£2,499,000,000

UK employees: 3,431

Total employees: 40,000

Main locations: In the UK, the group is headquartered in London.

Community involvement

Reckitt Benckiser supports health education and disease prevention campaigns and initiatives in the UK and the rest of the world. According to its Social Investment Report 2017, it makes one-off or ad hoc donations in response to local needs in the community where the group has a presence.

Partnerships

Reckitt Benckiser has partnered with Save the Children since 2003 and in 2017 the group donated £900,000 to the charity. The main aim of the partnership is to deliver initiatives aimed at reducing the prevalence of diarrhoea among children. Reckitt Benckiser has a similar partnership with Plan International to stop diarrhoea in Pakistan.

Project Hope

Project Hope is Reckitt Benckiser's social enterprise model and aims to educate women regarding health and hygiene. It currently runs in India, Nigeria and Pakistan. Women are trained to earn a livelihood through selling Reckitt Benckiser's products to households within their villages and also to educate their neighbours on health and hygiene practices. The group contributed over £130,000 to Project Hope in Pakistan in 2017, which includes cash donations and employee time.

Health initiatives

The group runs other health and hygiene awareness programmes with its brands. For example, Dettol works with NGOs, healthcare professionals and governments to educate new mothers in hygiene habits that will protect their new babies and families. So far, the initiatives have reached 200 million people with the aim to reach a further 200 million people by 2020.

In-kind support

The group donates products (such as, handwashing bags, soaps and liquids) and educational material on health safety and hygiene. It also organises health-related awareness campaigns (for example, health camps and planting insect-repellent trees in India). Employees are given volunteering leave to deliver these campaigns. In-kind donations totalled around £1 million in 2017.

Employee-led support

Employees raised around £1 million for Save the Children in 2017 through various fundraising activities and gave an additional £30,000 through payroll giving. Over 3,000 employees volunteered during paid working time in 2017, contributing a total of 19,644 working hours.

Applications

Apply in writing to the correspondent, referenced 'Sustainability'. The Corporate Communications and Affairs Department handles requests for charitable giving.

Community contributions

Cash donations worldwide	£9,100,000
In-kind support worldwide	£1,400,000
Total contributions (cash and in kind)	£10,500,000

According to the group's 2017 Social Investment Report, its total social investment contribution worldwide totalled £10.1 million. The UK was one of 31 countries included in the 2017 assessment of social investment but a breakdown by location was not provided. The report states that the group's total contribution totalled £10.5 million in 2017 and it supported 11,778 organisations. The group use the London Benchmarking Group (LBG) model to calculate community involvement and notes that during the year, cash contributions totalled £9.1 million, in-kind product donations totalled £1 million and employee time was equivalent to £420,000.

Redrow Group plc

Community development, general charitable purposes

Company registration number: 2877315

Correspondent: Corporate Responsibility Committee, Redrow House, St David's Park, Ewloe, Flintshire CH5 3RX (tel: 01244 520044; email: groupservices@redrow.co.uk; website: www.redrowplc.co.uk)

Directors: Barbara Richmond; Debbie Hewitt; John Tutte; Michael Lyons; Nick Hewson; Steve Morgan; Vanda Murray (female 43%; male 57%).

Nature of business: Redrow is one of the largest British housebuilders with a network of 15 operational divisions across the UK.

Year end	30/06/2018
Turnover	£1,920,000,000
Pre-tax profit	£380,000,000

UK employees: 2,308

Main locations: Redrow has a network of 15 operational divisions across the UK. It is based in Ewloe, Flintshire.

Community involvement

The majority of the group's giving focuses on the improvement of local communities. It also makes cash donations, most of which go to The Steve Morgan Foundation (Charity Commission no. 1087056). Stephen Morgan is the chair and founder of Redrow and sits on the foundation's trustee board. The group is the founder of the Redrow Foundation (Charity Commission no. 1113073).

The Steve Morgan Foundation (Charity Commission no. 1087056)

The Steve Morgan Foundation was established in 2001 with an endowment of over £2 million from Stephen Morgan. The foundation supports projects that help children and families, people with physical or learning disabilities, older people, or those that are socially disadvantaged or isolated. The foundation typically provides funding for small to medium-sized organisations who are addressing a specific need and is particularly keen to support organisations 'who have already begun to make an impact, but need a helping hand to expand their work and increase their effectiveness'.

In 2017/18 grants totalled £7.3 million.

Previous beneficiaries have included: Neuro Therapy Centre (£75,000); Bridge Community Farm CIC (£65,000); Designs in Mind (£57,500); Chester

Sexual Abuse Support Service (£21,500); ADHD Foundation (£20,000); Birkenhead Youth Club Minibus (£15,000); Children's Trust (£10,000); Handicapped Children's Action Group (£2,000); Cancer Research (£250).

Redrow Foundation (Charity Commission no. 1113073)

The Redrow Foundation is a national charity that makes grants for the relief of poverty and sickness in the UK. It has a preference for supporting organisations that provide accommodation and related assistance to children, older people and those who are sick or infirm. As the foundation's income is so low we were unable to view its accounts or determine how much was awarded in the most recent financial period.

Employee-led support

The 2017/18 annual report states that 'the company and its employees are actively involved in fundraising activities for specific charities'.

Applications

Contact the correspondent for further information.

Community contributions

Cash donations UK	£400,000

According to its 2017/18 annual report, the group awarded £400,000 to national charities, of which the Steve Morgan Foundation received £300,000, with a further £100,000 awarded to local charities.

RELX plc

Poverty and social exclusion, education, enterprise and training, children and young people, projects outside the UK,

Company registration number: 2746616

Correspondent: Local RE Cares Champion, 1–3 Strand, London WC2N 5JR (tel: 020 7166 5500; email: corporate.responsibility@relx.com; website: www.relx.com/corporateresponsibility/community/Pages/Home.aspx)

Directors: Adrian Hennah; Ben van der Veer; Carol Mills; Dr Wolfhart Hauser; Erik Engstrom; Linda Sanford; Marike van Lier Lels; Nick Luff; Robert MacLeod; Sir Anthony Habgood; Suzanne Wood (female 36%; male 64%).

Nature of business: RELX is a global provider of information and analytics for professional business customers in four major industries: scientific; technical and medical; risk and business analytics; and legal. The group also organises exhibitions and events across 43 industry sectors.

Year end	31/12/2017
Turnover	£7,355,000,000
Pre-tax profit	£1,734,000,000

Total employees: 30,000+

Main locations: RELX's head office is in London.

Community involvement

RELX contributes to local and global communities through its RE Cares programme by making cash and in-kind donations to charities and by supporting employee-led initiatives.

RE Cares programme

This global programme is supported by a network of staff members – known as RE Cares Champions – from across the business who organise and promote community engagement. In 2017 there were over 220 RE Cares Champions, covering 72% of offices. The dedicated CR section of the group's website explains that, through the programme, the group prioritises 'education for disadvantaged young people that advances one or more of our unique contributions as a business'.

Each September, a dedicated RE Cares Month takes place, through which thousands of employees contribute time to volunteering and fundraising activities.

Central donations programme

The group's central donations programme is closely tied to RE Cares's priority of promoting the education of disadvantaged young people. RE Cares Champions vote on all applications, using decision criteria such as value to the beneficiary and opportunities for staff engagement.

In 2017 RE Cares Champions donated more than $366,800 (≈ £292,500 as at December 2018) to 34 charities including: educational support for Syrian refugee children in Greece, enabling them to attend local schools; funding for books, school materials, registration fees, uniforms, school shoes and transportation for orphaned and abandoned children in Baja, Mexico; providing access to education for at-risk street children in Cambodia; enabling young girls in India to complete their education; helping to prevent child marriage; and helping finance essential classroom materials in low-income schools in Ohio.

Charity partnerships

RELX's employee-nominated global fundraising partner during 2017 was SOS Children's Villages Netherlands (SOS), which supports girls' education in the Ivory Coast. During 2017, the group raised over $96,700 (≈ £77,000 as at December 2018) for the charity.

The group also has a longstanding partnership of more than 20 years with Book Aid International, having donated more than 666,000 books since 2004, as well as funding libraries and literary activities for young people in Uganda.

LexisNexis Legal and Professional UK, which is part of RELX Group, is a founding partner of the International Law Book Facility (ILBF), and has donated over 51,000 books to 190 organisations in 50 countries.

In-kind support

Staff are able to take up to two days for volunteering purposes in company time. In 2017 a total of 12,670 days were used as volunteering time.

Gifts in-kind

RELX has a product donations policy which is available to download from the website (www.relx.com/corporateresponsibility/policies/Pages/Home.aspx). Product donations are given to registered charities in the form of hardcopy products (e.g. books and educational materials), non-hardcopy products (e.g. free access to journals and investigative solutions), and unwanted IT equipment and office furnishings. It would appear that the majority of product donations are typically given to charities the group has a partnership with.

Employee-led support

Employees are encouraged to volunteer and fundraise for charities. During the year 45% of staff were engaged with volunteering activities through the RE Cares programme. The group also matches employees' fundraising efforts.

Fit2Win

RELX holds this annual competition which is designed to raise money for charity while promoting well-being among staff. Employees form teams to compete within four sports categories – walking, running, cycling and swimming – to win $1,000 for their chosen charities. In 2017 106 teams took part in the competition.

Applications

RELX's central donations programme, RE Cares, is employee-led, with donations received by charities nominated by staff.

Aside from the group's central CSR programme, many of the group's subsidiaries have developed their own CSR initiatives.

Contact the correspondent for further information.

Community contributions

Cash donations worldwide	£3,400,000
In-kind support worldwide	£4,100,000
Total contributions (cash and in kind)	£7,500,000

The corporate responsibility report for 2017 states that the group gave a total of £7.5 million in cash and in-kind donations worldwide. In-kind donations include the value of products, services and time. According to the 2017 annual report, £3.4 million was given in cash, including matched funding gifts.

A breakdown by location was not available.

Renishaw plc

Community development, education (particularly STEM subjects), health, sports and recreation, disability, children and young people, general charitable purposes

Company registration number: 1106260

Correspondent: Renishaw Charities Committee, New Mills, Wotton-under-Edge, Gloucestershire GL12 8JR (tel: 01453 524524; email: charities.committee@renishaw.com; website: www.renishaw.com/en)

Directors: Allen Roberts; Carol Chesney; Catherine Glickman; David Grant; David McMurtry; Geoff McFarland; John Deer; John Jeans; Mark Noble; William Lee (female 20%; male 80%).

Nature of business: Renishaw is a scientific technology company with expertise in measurement, motion control, spectroscopy and precision machining.

Year end	30/06/2018
Turnover	£612,000,000
Pre-tax profit	£155,000,000

UK employees: 2,934

Total employees: 4,639

Main locations: The company has headquarters in Stroud and operations at sites throughout the UK. A list of offices is available on the company website.

Community involvement

Renishaw's charitable work is focused through its charities committee and work in promoting STEM subjects to younger people.

Renishaw Charities Committee (RCC)

The committee is made up of employee representatives who meet bi-monthly to distribute funds made available by the company to support charitable and voluntary organisations local to the company's key UK locations. The RCC focuses on projects relating to the following areas:

- Children and young people
- People with disabilities
- Health and fitness
- Lifelong learning
- Community and social development
- Sport and leisure

A separate fund is administered by the RCC, which makes donations for disaster relief. The RCC also fully matches funds raised by employees for UK national fundraising events such as: Children in Need; Red Nose Day; and supports individual employee fundraising activities.

Education

Renishaw has been involved in several initiatives to encourage more young people to keeping studying STEM subjects as they get older. The company has tried to target influencers such as teachers, parents and careers advisors. The company encourages more girls to consider engineering as a career through its initiatives.

In-kind support

During the year, the company engaged with around 8,000 students through various outreach programmes in South Wales, Gloucestershire and Bristol.

The company gifted 800 of the new 'Little Miss Inventor' books to all primary schools within their key catchment areas and arranged for some of its female STEM ambassadors to read in selected schools during the week leading up to International Women in Engineering Day.

Commercially led support

During the year, the company worked with Brownies groups who earned 'Renishaw engineering' badges, and hosted activities for all of the Year 7 students from Stroud High School for Girls and ran a Girls only Rugby/Engineering camp with Gloucester Rugby.

Exclusions

According to the company's website, it will not fund the following:

- Prizes for raffles or draws
- Projects outside the geographical limitations
- Charities or organisations seeking funds to redistribute to other charities
- Political organisations and campaigns
- National or international organisations

Renishaw will not sponsor tables or purchase tickets for fundraising events.

Applications

Applications should be made in writing to the Renishaw Charities Committee via post or email. Applications can also be made online through the 'Charities Committee' section of the website.

According to the company's website, beneficiary organisations should be located within 30 miles of one of Renishaw's key operating sites in:

- Gloucestershire (Wotton-under-Edge, Woodchester, Stonehouse)
- Vale of Glamorgan (Miskin)
- Yorkshire (York)
- Staffordshire (Stone)

The committee meets in January, March, May, July, September and November to discuss applications.

Community contributions

Cash donations UK	£108,000

In 2017 the company made donations totalling £108,000 to over 269 organisations through its charity committee. A figure for in-kind support could not be determined.

Beneficiaries include: Cheltenham Hospital (£10,000); Thornbury Oasis and Ruskin Mill.

Rentokil Initial plc

Community development, the environment, health, disaster relief, education

Company registration number: 5393279

Correspondent: CSR Team, Riverbank, Meadows Business Park, Blackwater, Camberley GU17 9AB (tel: 020 7592 2700; website: www.rentokil-initial.com)

Directors: John McAdam; Andy Ransom; Richard Burrows; Sir Crispin Davis; John Pettigrew; Angela Seymour-Jackson; Julie Southern; Jeremy Townsend; Linda Yueh; Daragh Fagan (female 30%; male 70%).

Nature of business: Rentokil is an international company providing services to businesses, including: workwear; plants and landscaping; hygiene services; medical services; pest control; package delivery; catering; electronic security; cleaning.

Year end	31/12/2017
Turnover	£2,412,300,000
Pre-tax profit	£713,600,000

Total employees: 36,036

Main locations: Rentokil has branches throughout the UK. There is a list of branches on the company's website.

Community involvement

The company's social and community activities consist of three main areas:

Local community support

Local community support focuses on a country or region level. In the UK, the Helping Hands scheme matches employees' fundraising. The company has supported UK charity Malaria No More for five years, raising £180,000 to date.

Response to natural disasters

Following the hurricanes in the Caribbean, Puerto Rico and Florida in 2017, Rentokil management teams co-ordinated relief efforts for employees and their families who had been affected. Employees also fundraised and donated bottled water to relief efforts.

Global community support

The global health initiative, Better Futures, was launched in 2013 and gives health and safety training to children in India, Malaysia, Indonesia and South Africa.

In-kind support

In-kind support includes employee volunteering, pro bono services and product donations.

Employee-led support

Volunteering

According to the CSR report, employee volunteering plays an important role in the group's overall community support.

Matched funding

A Helping Hands scheme operates to allow Rentokil match any amount up to £1,000 raised by employees for charitable causes with an annual budget approved by the group board.

Fundraising

Employees have raised funds for Malaria No More by taking part in events such as bike rides, mountain climbs and bake sales. Over £180,000 has been raised in the last five years.

Applications

Contact the correspondent for further information.

Community contributions

Cash donations worldwide	£213,000

The 2017 Corporate Social Responsibility Report states that cash donations to charities worldwide amounted to £213,000. We could not determine the value of in-kind donations.

Beneficiaries included: Forest Row Sports Ground Association, London Legal Support Trust, Cystic Fibrosis Trust, Friends of Chernobyl Children, Dogs for good, Rockinghorse, The Children's Trust, Diabetes UK, CreateArts.org. uk, NSPCC, The Artemis Charitable Foundation, Wakefield Hospice, Cancer Research UK, Leukaemia Foundation of Australia, Macmillan Cancer Support and Movember.

Richer Sounds plc

Poverty and social exclusion, human rights, disability, animal welfare

Company registration number: 1402643

Correspondent: Teresa Chapman, PA to Julian Richer, Unit 3/4, Richer House, Gallery Court, Hankey Place, London SE1 4BB (tel: 020 7551 5343; email: teresac@richersounds.com; website: www.richersounds.com)

Directors: David Robinson; John Currier; Julian Richer (female 0%; male 100%).

Nature of business: Richer Sounds is a video and audio equipment retailer.

Year end	29/04/2017
Turnover	£156,000,000
Pre-tax profit	£7,642,000

Total employees: 497

Main locations: The foundation makes grants to charities throughout the UK.

Community involvement

The Persula Foundation (Charity Commission no. 1044174) was established in 1994 by Richer Sounds. The trust supports general charitable purposes, but its main aim is the relief and prevention of poverty. At present, the trust is focusing on providing funding for charities that are supporting the following causes:

- Homelessness
- People with disabilities
- Human rights
- Animal welfare

Commercially led support

The company established the Tapesense scheme which supplies blind and visually impaired people with subsidised audio products and accessories, such as audio cassettes, hi-fi accessories, interconnect cables, universal remote controls, headphones, microphones and digital (DAB) radios.

Applications

Contact the correspondent for further information.

Corporate charity

The Persula Foundation (Charity Commission no. 1044174) – see page 273.

Community contributions

Cash donations UK	£1,400,000

The company's 2016/17 annual report and accounts state that it made charitable donations of £1.4 million. Our research indicates that this was paid in full to the company's corporate charity, The Persula Foundation.

Roche Products Ltd

Education, health

Company registration number: 100674

Correspondent: Corporate Donations and Philanthropy Department, Medical Affairs Department, Roche Products Ltd, 6 Falcon Way, Shire Park, Welwyn Garden City, Hertfordshire AL7 1TW (email: welwyn.gd_requests_uk@roche.com; website: www.roche.co.uk/home/corporate-responsibility/grants-and-donations.html)

Directors: Beat Kraehenmann; Geoffrey Twist; Mandy Robertson; Richard Erwin; Timothy Kelly (female 20%; male 80%).

Nature of business: Roche manufactures pharmaceutical products.

Year end	31/12/2017
Turnover	£963,566,000
Pre-tax profit	£41,429,000

UK employees: 1,460

Total employees: 93,734

Main locations: The company has sites in Welwyn Garden City and Burgess Hill in West Sussex.

Community involvement

The company supports medical and educational activities of healthcare organisations and patient organisations through grants, donations and sponsorship.

Grants and donations

The company supports medical and educational activities organised by healthcare organisations/entities (grants) and by patient organisations (donations) to improve patient care and benefit research.

The guidance for applicants gives the following examples of work which may be supported:

- The promotion of excellence in patient care
- NHS Medical Education
- Activities organised by Healthcare Organisations, Patient Organisations or other Healthcare Entities which will benefit patient care
- Educational grant/donation applications including support for the organisation of meetings. Please note however, where there is an associated benefit to Roche Products Ltd (e.g. stand space) then the grants/donations process does not apply
- Externally sourced, contracted medical writing or data processing resource for peerreviewed publications, not otherwise included in any other Roche supported clinical research grant/donation

Employee-led support

Employees take part in skills-based volunteering and capacity-building projects. They also take part in fundraising activities such as the annual Roche Children's Walk. In 2017 a total of 145 company sites in 70 countries donated funds for children's education and health initiatives. Employees raise money individually and the company matches all funds raised for the campaign.

Commercially led support

The company provides sponsorship and its website states: 'Requests to support activities where Roche may receive return benefit (e.g. congress stands, etc.) are termed sponsorships.'

Exclusions

The following information is taken from the guidance documents. Roche cannot make grants or donations to:

- Political parties
- Healthcare organisations or patient organisations
- Healthcare events (e.g. charity balls, sports competitions)
- Individuals

Additionally, grants are not available for:

- Charity fundraising outside the UK
- Office equipment or capital spend (e.g. computer hardware, furniture, renovations)
- Commercial business activities
- Resources such as equipment or headcount funding where such resource is for Roche products only or where such resource is for an activity or purpose linked only to Roche products

Applications

Applications can be made in writing to the correspondent via email or post. Full details of the application process can be found in the Guidance for External Requestors document available to download from the Grants and Donations page of the company's website.

Community contributions

Cash donations UK	£444,000

In 2017 Roche declared donations totalling £444,000.

Rolls–Royce plc

Arts, culture and heritage, education (particularly STEM subjects), the environment

Company registration number: 1003142

Correspondent: Corporate Sustainability Team, 65 Buckingham Gate, London SW1E 6AT (tel: 020 7222 9020; website: www.rolls-royce.com)

Directors: Warren East; Ian Davis; Sir Kevin Smith; Stephen Daintith; Lewis Booth; Ruth Cairnie; Sir Frank Chapman; Irene Dorner; Beverly Goulet; Lee Hsien Yang; Nick Luff; Jasmin Staiblin; Bradley Singer; Pamela Coles (female 36%; male 64%).

Nature of business: Rolls-Royce is a global company providing power (gas turbines and reciprocating engines) on land, sea and air.

Year end	31/12/2017
Turnover	£16,307,000,000
Pre-tax profit	£4,897,000,000

UK employees: 22,500

Total employees: 50,000

Main locations: The group's has sites in Barnoldswick (Sunderland), Bristol and Derby. It has offices in London and Ansty in Warwickshire.

Community involvement

The group's website states that alongside STEM, its community support is particularly focused on: education and skills; environmental activities; social investment, with the intention of making a positive contribution; and arts, culture and heritage.

STEM Programmes

The group works closely with schools and universities to encourage interest and diversity in the STEM subjects. There are over 1,400 group ambassadors worldwide who are involved in promoting STEM programmes and activities.

Charity partnerships

The group has a partnership with Girlguiding UK, and together they have developed activities for the 'Brownie Science Investigator Badge', which helps girls discover science through different experiments such as making balloon-powered cars or making their own compass.

In-kind support

According to our research, the group can offer support in kind to local initiatives, including in-house training programmes, surplus computers, equipment and furniture, loans of engines and components, technical support, and free use of meeting rooms and premises.

Employee-led support

The group's Global Code of Conduct states that in most cases employees will be able to get support to work for voluntary organisations (for example, school communities or community groups). The group's 2017 annual report states: '1,400 Rolls-Royce employees volunteer their time as STEM ambassadors, helping us to reach 3.8 million 1 people since 2014. This includes one million people in 2017, 48% of whom were actively engaged in our programmes.'

Commercially led support

Sponsorship

Rolls-Royce sponsors the UK Female Undergraduate of the Year awards with the winner receiving a paid summer internship.

Rolls Royce Science Prize

Established in 2004, the Rolls-Royce Science Prize is part of the company's commitment to promote science and engineering in schools – 'It rewards excellent teaching of science as well as promoting innovative and sustainable strategies for teaching science.'

Exclusions

Rolls-Royce does not give donations to political parties or organisations that are closely associated with a political party or cause.

Applications

Apply in writing to the correspondent, referenced 'Corporate Sustainability Team'.

Community contributions

Cash donations worldwide	£4,300,000
Total contributions (cash and in kind)	£7,700,000

The 2017 annual report states that during the year, the group gave one-off donations to the Women in Tech Foundation and the Campaign for Science and Engineering. In total, the group invested £7.7 million in supporting communities in 2017 worldwide. This includes £4.3 million in cash contributions and 93,900 hours in employee time.

We have taken £7.7 million as the group's worldwide total contribution, and £4.3 million as its cash donations worldwide for 2017. We could not find information on how much of this was donated in the UK.

Rothschild & Co.

Community development, poverty and social exclusion, education (particularly STEM subjects), enterprise and training, children and young people,

Correspondent: Community Investment team, New Court, St Swithin's Lane, London EC4N 8AL (website: www.rothschild.com/en/who-we-are/community-investment)

Directors: Alain Massiera; Gary Powell; Grégoire Chertok; Helen Watson; Javed Khan; Jimmy Neissa; Jonathan Westcott; Laurent Gagnebin; Marc-Olivier Laurent;

Mark Crump; Martin Reitz; Paul Barry (female 17%; male 83%).

Nature of business: Rothschild & Co. is a global financial advisory group, with offices in more than 40 countries worldwide. Rothschild & Co. is a French partnership limited by shares and is listed on Euronext in Paris.

This record previously referred to N. M. Rothschild & Sons Ltd, which is a British division of Rothschild & Co. However, as the annual report and accounts for N. M. Rothschild & Sons Ltd no longer declare charitable donations, we have instead referred to its parent firm, which reports on CSR activities from across its divisions.

Year end	31/12/2017
Turnover	£1,422,943,000
Pre-tax profit	£353,838,000

Total employees: 3,500

Main locations: In the UK, Rothschild & Co. has offices in Birmingham, the City of London, Leeds and Manchester.

Community involvement

The company has a 'Community Investment Programme' through which it helps raise the aspirations of young people from disadvantaged backgrounds. The company offers a combination of skills-based employee volunteering and financial contributions to organisations. It also pursues long-term partnerships with charities, educational establishments and social enterprises.

The 'Rothschild & Co. Community Investment Strategy in the UK' (2016/17) document, which is available to download from the website, states that Rothschild & Co. focuses on 'helping young people to develop the skills that will help them to succeed at school and in the workplace, and on instilling in them the confidence to be more ambitious'.

Community partners

Through the company's employee volunteering initiatives and charitable giving programme, it partners with organisations. Examples include:

Ashoka – Through Ashoka the company partners with social enterprises that focus on raising the aspirations of young people. During 2016/17 employee volunteers gave their advisory skills in order to help social enterprises achieve greater financial stability.

Future First – The Employability Skills Project, funded through the Rothschild & Co. Charitable Giving programme and run by the national education charity Future First, equips students with the skills they need to succeed in work after leaving school and help them overcome barriers to achieving their potential.

The Access Project – The partnership between Rothschild & Co. and The Access Project provides support for students by providing a framework for tuition for A-level Maths.

Financial support for young people

In the UK, the Rothschild & Co. Bursary offers young people bursaries to help with living costs when they take up a place at a selective university outside London. The company's website notes that it can 'also offer charitable giving grants for projects that share our aims'.

In-kind support

Employee time

The Community Investment Strategy report notes that employee volunteering time was costed at £150,000 during 2016/17.

Employee-led support

Employee volunteering

During 2016/17, 43% of employees spent 2,441 hours volunteering.

Applications

Contact the correspondent for further information.

Community contributions

Cash donations worldwide	£577,500
In-kind support worldwide	£150,000
Total contributions (cash and in kind)	£727,500

The Community Investment Report for 2016/17 states that the company invested £577,500 towards charitable causes. The company's employees also spent 2,441 hours volunteering which was costed at £150,000. We have taken £727,500 to be the company's total contribution in the UK during 2016/17.

Rotork plc

General charitable purposes

Company registration number: 578327

Correspondent: Corporate Responsibility Committee, Brassmill Lane, Bath BA1 3JQ (tel: 01225 733200; website: www.rotork.com)

Directors: Gary Bullard; Jonathan Davis; Kevin Hostetler; Lucinda Ball; Martin Lamb; Peter Dilnot; Sally James; Sarah Parsons (female 38%; male 63%).

Nature of business: The company's activities include design and manufacture of actuators and flow control equipment.

Year end	31/12/2017
Turnover	£642,229,000
Pre-tax profit	£80,586,000

Total employees: 3,835

Main locations: The group has charity committees based in Leeds, Bath and Glasgow.

Community involvement

The group's CSR Committee and subcommittees donates to charities in the UK.

Employee-led support

The group's 2017 annual report states: 'Our employees also gave support to their local communities with the group contributing a further £175,000 to support these causes.'

Applications

Contact the Corporate Social Responsibility Committee for further information.

Community contributions

Cash donations worldwide	£265,000

According to the group's 2017 annual report, it donated a total of £265,000 to charities.

Beneficiaries included: WaterAid; Sightsavers; Forever Friends Appeal.

The Royal Bank of Scotland Group plc

Community development, arts and culture, disability, education, enterprise and training, health, sports and recreation, disaster relief, projects outside the UK,

Company registration number: SC045551

Correspondent: Sustainable Banking Committee, 1st Floor, House F, Gogarburn, Edinburgh EH12 1HQ (tel: 0131 556 8555; website: www.rbs.com/community)

Directors: Aileen Taylor; Alison Davis; Baroness Noakes; Brendan Nelson; Dr Lena Wilson; Frank Dangeard; Howard Davies; Mark Seligman; Mike Rogers; Morten Friis; Patrick Flynn; Robert Gillespie; Ross McEwan (female 31%; male 69%).

Nature of business: RBS is a UK-based banking and financial services group.

Year end	31/12/2017
Turnover	£13,133,000,000
Pre-tax profit	£2,239,000,000

Total employees: 71,200

Main locations: RBS operates in the United Kingdom, Europe, the Middle East, the Americas and Asia, serving over 24 million customers worldwide. Its principal offices in the UK are based in Edinburgh, East Belfast, Jersey Channel Islands, and London.

Community involvement

RBS supports a wide range of charitable purposes through the delivery of strategic programmes, cash and in-kind donations, and through employee fundraising and volunteering.

Skills and Opportunities Fund

Launched in 2015, the Skills and Opportunities Fund provided grants to local charities, social enterprises, state-funded schools and colleges, and community groups to enable people in disadvantaged communities to develop or access the skills and opportunities they need to build their financial capability skills or to start or develop a new business. In 2017 a total of £2.5 million was distributed to 110 organisations. Applications for the fund's final round have now closed. To stay updated on any future funding opportunities visit the fund's website www.skillsandopportunitiesfund.rbs.com.

RBS Social and Community Capital (Charity Commission no. 1079626)

The group's charity, RBS Social and Community Capital provides loans to social enterprises, charities, not-for-profit organisations and social businesses, particularly for those unable to access mainstream finance. To apply for a loan, organisations must be based in the UK, be an established third sector organisation with social or environmental aims, and not eligible for mainstream funding from banks.

Enterprise

The group has a number of ongoing initiatives aimed at inspiring people to start businesses and providing the support and resources they need to help them succeed.

- **Entrepreneurial Spark:** This programme offers free workspaces, mentoring, funding clinics, and workshops for start-up and scale-up businesses
- **The Prince's Trust Enterprise Programme:** The group is the largest corporate sponsor of The Prince's Trust Enterprise Programme which supports young entrepreneurs by providing start-up help to 18- to 30-year-olds who are unemployed or working fewer than 16 hours a week. During the year, the group donated £1 million to the trust. RBS employees also raised £97,000 for the charity and helped to deliver workshops and provide business mentoring

Emergency Appeals

In addition to its strategic giving, the group also responds to emergency appeal. In 2017 for example, the group supported the Disasters and Emergency Committee (DEC) East Africa Crisis Appeal raising over £211,000 from employees and customers. The group also supported the Appeal for People Fleeing Myanmar and worked with the British Red Cross in support of the UK Solidarity Fund for people who have been affected by terror attacks in the UK.

In-kind support

The group provides charities and not-for-profit organisations with free and reduced fee banking services. According to the group's website, the total value of these services in 2017 was £13.7 million.

Employee-led support

Employee volunteering

There is a well-established employee volunteering and giving programme at RBS. Employees are entitled to three days' paid leave to volunteer in their local communities. In 2017 employees devoted 86,093 hours to volunteering.

Employee fundraising

Employees and interns are encouraged to fundraise for charitable causes in their local communities and can benefit from the group's Community Cashback programme, which recognises employee fundraising and volunteering efforts with a £250 grant to their chosen charity. In 2017, 3,049 employees claimed cashback, with £762,500 being donated to charities.

The group also operates a payroll giving scheme. In 2017, 8,449 employees in the UK, Ireland and India participated in the scheme raising a total of £2.73 million.

Commercially led support

Customer fundraising

The group's Reward Accounts help to facilitate customer donations to ten different charities: Alzheimer's Society, Barnardo's, British Heart Foundation, Cancer Research UK, Macmillan, NSPCC, The Prince's Trust, RNIB, Disaster and Emergency Committee and Sport Relief. In 2017 Reward Account customers donated a total of £239,000.

The group is a founding partner of #Giving Tuesday, an international social media campaign which encourages consumers to make donations to charity following Black Friday and Cyber Monday. For #GivingTuesday 2017, the group invited its Reward Account customers to donate their MyRewards to charity. This initiative led to an uplift in customer donations during the months of November and December.

The group also offers a scheme in which its customers can donate to select charities through the group's ATM machines. A total of 26 charities benefit from this scheme, including RNIB, Oxfam, RSPCA and Cancer Research UK. In 2017 a total of £173,000 was donated through this scheme.

Applications

General enquiries should be submitted in writing to the correspondent.

RBS Social and Community Capital

To apply for a loan from the group's corporate charity visit www.business.rbs.co.uk/business/social-community-capital or contact by email: rbsscc@rbs.co.uk.

Community contributions

According to its website, in 2017 the group made worldwide community investments totalling £29.3 million. This figure includes cash donations, in-kind, employee time and fundraising.

The Royal London Mutual Insurance Society Ltd

Health, general charitable purposes

Company registration number: 99064

Correspondent: CSR Team, Royal London House, Alderley Road, Wilmslow SK9 1PF (tel: 0345 050 2020; website: www.royallondon.com)

Directors: Andrew Palmer; David Weymouth; Ian Dilks; Jon Macdonald; Olivia Dickson; Phil Loney; Rupert Pennant-Lea; Sally Bridgeland; Tim Harris; Tracey Graham (female 30%; male 70%).

Nature of business: Principal activities of the group's businesses are provision of pensions, life assurance, savings and investment products, protection insurance and investment management services.

The group comprises The Royal London Mutual Insurance Society Ltd and its subsidiaries.

Year end	31/12/2017
Turnover	£7,366,000,000
Pre-tax profit	£455,000,000

Main locations: The group has offices in the following locations: Bath; Dublin; Edinburgh; Glasgow; London; Reading; and Wilmslow.

Community involvement

The group's community involvement focuses on its partner charities and The Royal London Foundation (not a registered charity).

Charity partners

The theme of the group's CSR programme is 'to support people with a chronic or long-term condition'. Each office has partnered with a charity aligned with this theme. The partnerships are due to end in December 2019.

Partner charities include: Butterfly Trust; The Joshua Tree; Lambeth and Southwark Mind.

The group also partners with Business in the Community (BITC) and with The Silver Line.

The Royal London Foundation

The foundation re-launched in 2017 and makes grants to small, local organisations nominated by its members. In 2017 the foundation awarded a total of £185,000 to 37 non-profit organisations throughout the UK.

In-kind support

The group's volunteering programme gives employees two days a year to volunteer.

Employee-led support

The group matches a proportion of staff fundraising. In 2017 through this scheme the group and its staff donated £144,000 to charities. Staff also volunteer for local charities and in 2017 volunteered for a total of 3,281 hours.

Commercially led support

The group sponsors cricket-related initiatives, including one-day international and domestic cricket, as well as grassroots cricket internationally through the Gilbert Cup for children. The group also sponsors the Professional Cricketers' Association Benevolent Fund for current and former players in need.

Applications

Further information on the Royal London foundation can be found at: members.royallondon.com/foundation

All other enquiries should be made to the correspondent.

Community contributions

Cash donations UK	£185,000

In 2017 the group made grants totalling £185,000 through its Royal London Foundation. A figure for the group's matched funding was not available.

Royal Mail plc

General charitable purposes

Company registration number: 8680755

Correspondent: Corporate Respnsibility Team, 100 Victoria Embankment, London EC4Y 0HQ (tel: 0345 774 0740; website: www.royalmailgroup.com)

Directors: Keith Williams; Les Owen; Oran Ni-Chionna; Rico Back; Rita Griffin; Simon Thompson; Stuart Simpson; Sue Whalley (female 38%; male 63%).

Nature of business: Royal Mail plc is the ultimate parent company of the Royal Mail Group, which operates through two core divisions UK Parcels, International and Letters (UKPIL) and GLS (operating in continental Europe and Ireland). The group's main activities include letter and parcel services, and design and manufacture of UK stamps and philatelic products.

Year end	26/03/2018
Turnover	£10,172,000,000
Pre-tax profit	£212,000,000

UK employees: 141,000

Total employees: 159,000

Main locations: The group's headquarters are in London.

Community involvement

The group gives both in-kind and financial support to charities across the UK. The group has many charity partners, and also chooses one main corporate charity partner which in 2017/18 was Action for Children. According to its Corporate Social Responsibility Report 2017/18, the group's community strategy is to:

- **Leverage our national scale:** our charity partner programme focuses our national scale around a single cause chosen by our people, to which we can make a measurable difference
- **Use our local presence:** our Missing People partnership uses our presence in communities to help find vulnerable people of all ages; our Community Support and payroll giving schemes support the causes our people feel passionate about
- **Unlock potential through education:** our online magazine, Teacher's Post, provides classroom resources, and our partnership with The Prince's Trust enables the Trust to support young people with mental health problems

Mental health awareness

The group has launched a multi-year campaign for mental health. In May 2017, the group announced a new charity partnership with Action for Children, focused on addressing mental health issues in young people. The charity was selected by almost 36,000 Royal Mail employees out of a shortlist which included Mind and Mental Health UK. The group will also work with Mind, Mental Health UK and The Prince's Trust to deliver a 'wide-reaching campaign' for mental health.

The partnerships cover mental health training, awareness-raising, communications, pro bono support, work placements and fundraising. The group aims to raise £2 million for Action for Children, its lead charity partner, to fund a preventative mental health programme in schools.

Sports Foundation

The group's Sports Foundation supports local sports clubs. Grants given to employees to provide funds for equipment, trophies and training. During 2017/18, the group supported 50 sports clubs and individual sporting events by providing a total of almost £30,000 in grant funding.

Rowland Hill Fund

The Rowland Hill Fund provides support to current and former Royal Mail employees who fall on hard times. Royal Mail makes an annual contribution of £50,000 to the fund, plus an additional £60,000 a year in in-kind donations. During 2017/18, employees donated a further £68,500 through payroll giving.

Post Office Orphans Benevolent Institution

Each year, the Post Office Orphans Benevolent Institution provides £250,000 in grants to children of Royal Mail employees facing hardship. The institution provides university bursaries and awards for children with special vocational talent. It also assists families in need.

Disaster relief

During 2017/18, Royal Mail made donations to the British Red Cross following the Manchester bombing, London terror attacks and the Grenfell Tower fire. The group gave £15,000 to support the victims of these events.

GSL activities

GSL is the group's European parcel delivery service. It supports local charities that address key issues in communities.

In-kind support

Education

The group's online resource library, Teacher's Post, offers a wide range of educational resources that are aligned to the National Curriculum. Teacher's Post is available to view online at www.teacherspost.co.uk.

Articles for the Blind

The group's Articles for the Blind service delivers items free of charge to blind and partially-sighted people across the UK. Charities working with blind and partially sighted people can also use this scheme.

Disaster relief

The group set up a PO Box at its Mount Pleasant Delivery Office, to support those wishing to make postal donations to DEC appeals. The central location allows donations to be sorted quickly and transferred to the DEC, so that funds can be put to use as soon as possible. In 2017/18 the PO Box received donations for three major international appeals: the East Africa Crisis Appeal, the Yemen Cholera Appeal, and the Emergency Appeal for People Fleeing Myanmar. As a result, £4 million was raised through over 40,000 donations during 2017/18.

Employee-led support

The group encourage employees to support causes important to them through a range of fundraising and volunteering initiatives.

Payroll giving

Employees have the opportunity to make donations directly from their pay to charities of their choice through 'Pennies from Pay' and payroll giving. Pennies from Pay enables employees to have their pay rounded down to the nearest £1, with the difference going to the group's charity partner. During the year, almost 30,000 employees raised around £2.3 million for 800 charities through both schemes. Donations made to the charity partner through payroll giving are matched penny-for-penny by the business. By year end, nearly 900 employees had signed up to give £28,000 to Action for Children through this scheme.

Charity partner matched giving

The group matches amounts raised by employees for its main corporate charity partner up to £2,500 per employee per year, and up to £1 million in total.

Matched funding

The group matches funds raised by employees for all other charities and good causes, up to £200 per employee per year. It also offers employees the ability to apply for a grant of up to £200 to cover the cost of fundraising activities. This year, employees supported around 300 charities through matched giving and fundraising grants. The group also offers retired employees £50 per person per year in matched giving for money they raise for good causes.

Volunteering

The group offers grants of up to £400 per employee per year to help cover the cost of materials used at volunteering events. In 2017/18 the group distributed 67 grants totalling nearly £18,000.

Applications

Contact the correspondent for further information. It appears that local organisations can also apply directly to their regional office for support.

Community contributions

Cash donations UK	£2,020,000
In-kind support UK	£4,820,000
Total contributions (cash and in kind)	£6,840,000

According to its 2017/18 Corporate Social Responsibility Report, Royal Mail contributed £7 million 'directly to good causes and schemes for disadvantaged groups'. Cash donations totalled £2.02 million and in-kind donations and the cost of employee time totalled £4.82 million. Included in the in-kind total is the cost of the Articles for the Blind service, which totalled £4.5 million.

Management costs and funds raised by employees have been excluded from our figures, as is our usual practice.

Beneficiaries included: Action for Children; British Red Cross; Mental Health UK; Mind; Missing People; The Prince's Trust; The Rowland Hill Fund.

RPS Group plc

The environment, education, projects outside the UK

Company registration number: 2087786

Correspondent: Corporate Governance Committee, Centurion Court, 85 Milton Park, Abingdon, Oxfordshire OX14 4RY (tel: 01235 438000; email: rpsmp@rpsgroup.com; website: www.rpsgroup.com/Group/About-Us/Corporate-Social-Responsibility.aspx)

Directors: Dr Alan Hearne; Gary Young; John Bennett; Ken Lever; Louise Charlton; Nicholas Rowe; Robert Bakewell (female 14%; male 86%).

Nature of business: RPS in the UK provides multi-disciplinary consultancies advising on all aspects of: built and natural environment; oil, gas and other natural resources; renewable energy; and energy infrastructure.

Year end	31/12/2017
Turnover	£630,600,000
Pre-tax profit	(£1,600,000)

Main locations: The group has offices throughout the UK.

Community involvement

The group is a largest corporate sponsor and partner of TREE AID, a UK-based development charity that focuses on planting trees as a way of reducing poverty and protecting the environment. As well as financial support, RPS also provides multidisciplinary technical support and training.

Education

RPS group also provides funding for academic bursaries and educational initiatives. In 2017 this totalled £276,000.

Employee-led support

The group's employees contribute to charitable causes supported by the group, through cash contributions and volunteering time.

Applications

Contact the correspondent for further information.

Community contributions

The group's 2017 annual report notes that a total of £973,000 was awarded, which includes both the group and staff contributions and an additional £276,000 spent on academic bursaries and educational initiatives. A further £66,000 was given to support Tree Aid. We were unable to separate the money donated by the company from the employee contributions nor could we determine the amount awarded in cash in the UK. Using the figure spent on academic bursaries and the support give to Tree Aid we estimate that the group contributions totalled at least around £276,000.

RSA Insurance Group plc

Community development, education, enterprise and training, general charitable purposes

Company registration number: 2339826

Correspondent: Natalie Tickle, Group and UK Charity and Communities CR Manager, 20 Fenchurch Street, London EC3M 3AU (tel: 01403 232323; website: www.rsagroup.com)

Directors: Alaister Barbour; Charlotte Jones; Enrico Cucchiani; Isabel Hudson; Joseph Streppel; Kath Cates; Martin Scicluna; Martin Strobel; Scott Egan; Stephen Hester (female 30%; male 70%).

Nature of business: The group's principal activity is the transaction of personal and commercial general insurance business.

Year end	31/12/2017
Turnover	£7,105,000,000
Pre-tax profit	£448,000,000

Total employees: 13,363

Main locations: RSA works throughout the UK and has main offices in Liverpool, Birmingham, Horsham and London.

Community involvement

The group's Thriving Communities scheme helps communities in the following three ways:

- **Supporting education and employability** – the group encourages employees to share their experience with young people to help build their confidence required for the workplace
- **Working with enterprise and social entrepreneurs** – the group has a partnership with the School for Social Entrepreneurs and provides skilled guidance, mentorship and training to leaders of social businesses in the UK and Canada
- **Facilitating employees to support local causes that they are passionate about** – the group encourages employees to support causes they are connected with in some way

According to the RSA Community and Charity Policy Statement, the group supports priority focus areas which all have a link with insurance, namely: safety, social inclusion and the environment.

In-kind support

The group gives all employees two days to volunteer for charitable causes.

Pro bono

In the UK, the group's 'Ready, Set, Achieve' programme helped young people develop the skills, knowledge and confidence they need to secure employment, through bespoke workshops hosted by employees. In 2017 employees from London, Sunderland and Manchester spent 180 hours running employability workshops to help 100 people.

Employee-led support

Employees take part in volunteering, and fundraise for charities and good causes. In 2017 employees donated almost 9,000 hours of time volunteering for causes of their choice. Employees also raised £266,000 for charities through their fundraising efforts.

Payroll giving

RSA operates local payroll giving schemes for current employees.

Matched funding

RSA will provide capped matched funding for employee fundraising initiatives each year (nationally set amount).

Exclusions

The group is unable to support any organisation which supports one specific religious faith, political parties, sports teams (unless there is a compelling community justification), arts organisations (unless supporting disadvantaged groups) or individual sponsorships.

Applications

Contact the correspondent for further information.

The group's Community and Charity Policy Statement states the following:

> RSA will provide direct financial support only if one or all of the following conditions is satisfied:
>
> - The scope falls under one of the priority focus areas or regional variations
> - Actively involves RSA employees volunteering
> - Part of wider active partnership

Community contributions

Cash donations worldwide	£1,400,000
In-kind support worldwide	£204,300
Total contributions (cash and in kind)	£1,600,000

In 2017 the group's total contributions was valued at £1.6 million. The group's total community investment was provided on the website as follows:

Payments to charities	£1.4 million
Employee raised	£266,000
Volunteering value	£197,500
Gifts in kind	£6,800

As is our usual practice, we have not included the figure for 'employee raised' funds in the group's total contributions. We have taken £1.4 million as our figure for cash donations.

Beneficiaries included: Hope Family Trust; Farliegh Hospice; Hackney Caribbean Elderly Organisation; Stepney City Farm; Core Landscapes Community gardens; Nene Valley Railway; Thorpe Hall Hospice.

Saga plc

Community development, older people, projects outside the UK, education, health, disability, children and young people

Company registration number: 8804263

Correspondent: John Billingham, Trust Manager, Enbrook Park, Sandgate, Folkestone, Kent CT20 3SE (website: www.saga.co.uk/saga-charitable-foundation.aspx)

Directors: Bridget McIntyre; Gareth Williams; Lance Batchelor; Orna NiChionna; Patrick O'Sullivan; Ray King (female 22%; male 78%).

Nature of business: The group provides travel, financial, insurance, health and lifestyle products and services for people aged 50 and over.

Year end	31/01/2018
Turnover	£860,100,000
Pre-tax profit	£178,700,000

Main locations: Saga works throughout the UK and has headquarters in Kent.

Community involvement

This group supports charities that are local to its office sites. All of the group's charitable giving is administered by its corporate charity, The Saga Charitable Trust (Charity Commission no. 291991).

Saga Charitable Trust (Charity Commission no. 291991)

The trust is supported and sponsored by the Saga group of companies and acts as an umbrella for Saga's charitable activities. This includes the funding of sustainable projects in financially developing countries visited by Saga holidaymakers and supporting Saga's national charity partner, The Silver Line. According to its 2017 annual report, the group gave the charity £228,000 which was given through 'the support of customers, employees and the business'.

Local giving programme

In 2017 the company launched its local giving programme, which assists registered charities based within a 20-mile radius of its office sites.

The Saga Respite for Carers Trust

The Saga Respite for Carers Trust provided 28 holidays for unpaid carers during 2017, utilising remaining trust funds before closing on 2 February 2018.

Armed forces

The group is a signatory of the Armed Forces Covenant. On Armed Forces Day, representatives from the armed services were invited to Saga's headquarters. Donations were made to Help for Heroes, The Royal British Legion, The Royal Navy and Royal Marines Charity, and SSAFA.

Employee-led support

Fundraising and matched funding

Employees taking part in fundraising activities for registered charities can receive matched funding. The group also launched an employee lottery in aid of charity during the year.

Exclusions

Our research indicates that support is not normally given for advertising in charity brochures, animal welfare, the arts, enterprise/training, fundraising events, medical research, political or religious appeals, science/technology; or sport.

Applications

Further information can be obtained by writing to the correspondent.

The Saga Charitable Trust (Charity Commission no. 291991)
Apply in writing to the correspondent. Applications are accepted at any time throughout the year. Grants are decided at regular meetings by the trustees where applications are considered for various types of funding.

Funding proposals should include the following information: outline and objectives of the project; who will benefit and how; resources required and timeframe; management and sustainability of the project; how funds will be managed and accounted for; and three years of the organisation's financial accounts.

Community contributions

According its 2017/18 accounts, The Saga Charitable Trust received £60,000 from the group during the year.

Although the group's 2017/18 annual report states that it gave a total of £371,000 in charitable donations it is unclear which support came directly from the group, its employees and customers.

The Sage Group plc

Community development, poverty and social exclusion, women, children and young people, projects outside the UK

Company registration number: 2231246

Correspondent: CSR Team, North Park, Newcastle Upon Tyne NE13 9AA (tel: 0191 294 3000; website: www.sage.com/company/sage-foundation)

Directors: Cath Keers; Donald Brydon; Drummond Hall; Jonathan Howell; Neil Berkett; Soni Jiandani; Stephen Kelly; Steve Hare (female 25%; male 75%).

Nature of business: Sage is a global technology company, providing automated business solutions for accounting and HR.

Year end	30/09/2017
Turnover	£1,715,000,000
Pre-tax profit	£342,000,000

Total employees: 13,795

Main locations: The company is based in Newcastle and operates worldwide.

Community involvement

The group makes contributions to community and charitable organisations worldwide through its foundation, which is not a registered charity. Preference tends to be given to organisations that work with women, young people and military veterans. In the UK, there may be some preference towards organisations in North East England as the group are very active in the community where its head office is based.

Sage Foundation
According to its website, the Sage Foundation was launched in June 2015, with the aim of 'transforming lives by investing time, money, expertise and technology to create sustainable social, economic and entrepreneurial opportunity in our local communities around the world'. The foundation follows a so-called '2+2+2 model', through which employees are encouraged to donate 2% of their time to charitable causes, 2% of the group's free cash flow is donated to charities, and the charities and non-profits are offered up to two free licenses for Sage products.

At the time of writing (August 2018), the foundation administered two grant programmes.

Grants for Change: develops partnerships with non-profit organisations that support young people, women and military veterans. Applications to this grant programme are by invitation only.

The Enterprise Fund: supports new or piloted entrepreneurial programmes or initiatives that may go no further due to funding challenges. Projects should help improve the lives of either: military veterans, young people or women and girls in the 21 countries where Sage operates around the world. According to the group's website, the fund has four main areas of focus:

- Education
- Enterprise and Employment
- Diversity and Inclusion
- Health and Wellbeing

Grants are awarded for between $10,000-$25,000 (≈ £7,800–£19,600 as at November 2018). Full details including eligibility criteria can be found on the foundation section of the group's website.

In-kind support

The Sage Foundation provides donated licenses to eligible charities, social enterprises and non-profit organisations through its software donation programme.

Employee-led support

Volunteering
The company's employees are entitled to five days per year to volunteer for charitable causes. There are no restrictions on the charities that employees can support, although volunteering is usually focused on young people; working with socially and economically deprived communities; and the development of entrepreneurism and social enterprise.

Fundraising
In 2016 Sage's CFO Steve Hare pledged to run 500 km for his chosen charity–CVY P. This original pledge has since turned into the 'Million Dollar Challenge', a fundraising initiative designed to mobilise Sage's employees, customers and partners to raise a total $1 million (≈ £781,000 as at November 2018) for their chosen causes and a range of activities. At the time of writing (September 2018) the initiative had raised just over $289,000 (≈ £226,000 as at November 2018).

Applications

Applications to the Sage Foundation's Enterprise Fund can be submitted online at: www.sage.com/company/sage-foundation/the-enterprise-fund. To apply for a donation of a product licence, visit: www.sage.com/company/sage_foundation/products.

Community contributions

Cash donations worldwide	£1,800,000

The company aims to give 2% of its free cash flow to its foundation and to charities around the world. During the 2016/17 financial year, the group awarded a total of £1.8 million in grants. The group also donated software licenses to charities and non-profits; however, the value of these donations was not quantified in its annual report.

J. Sainsbury plc

Poverty and social exclusion, health, general charitable purposes, sports and recreation, children and young people

Company registration number: 185647

Correspondent: CSR Team, 33 Holborn, London EC1N 2HT (website: j-sainsbury.co.uk/responsibility)

Directors: Brian Cassin; David Keens; David Tyler; Jean Tomlin; Jo Harlow; John Rogers; Kevin O'Byrne; Matt Brittin; Mike Coupe; Susan Rice (female 30%; male 70%).

Nature of business: Sainsbury's is the second largest chain of supermarkets in the UK. Banking and financial services products are offered through the wholly owned subsidiary, Sainsbury's Bank, and the group has a number of joint ventures, including property development.

Year end	11/03/2018
Turnover	£31,735,000,000
Pre-tax profit	£539,000,000

Total employees: 189,200

Main locations: The company headquarters are based in London. There are Sainsbury's stores throughout the UK.

Community involvement

At a local level, charities and community groups are supported by individual Sainsbury's stores. At a national level, support is given through its partnerships and community schemes such as Active Kids.

Charity partners

Sainsbury's has several partnerships with national charities that benefit from commercial support and employee and customer fundraising. These include: Comic Relief; Macmillan Cancer Support; The Irish Cancer Charity; The Royal British Legion; The Woodland Trust.

Sainsbury Family Charitable Trusts

The Sainsbury Family Charitable Trusts is the operating office of a group of 17 grant-making charities affiliated with the Sainsbury family. Each trust is operated independently with separate boards of trustees each led by a member of the family.

Community fridges

The company has funded over 30 community fridges over the past year. These reduce food waste and provide local people with nutritious food.

Local Charity of the Year

Each year the local stores draw up a shortlist of charities which the public votes for. The winning charity then receives support from the store such as awareness-raising and fundraising in store, volunteering and donations.

In-kind support

Surplus food fit for human consumption is donated from Sainsbury's stores to charities such as FoodCycle.

Employee-led support

Employee fundraising

Sainsbury's employees fundraise for various partner charities and causes. Though the Local Charity of the Year employees fundraise for a customer-nominated charity and also take part with national appeals such as Comic Relief.

Matched funding

Through the Local Heroes scheme, employees who volunteer in their own time for their community are acknowledged and rewarded. Sainsbury's donate £5 per hour spent volunteering to the employees' chosen charity or community group, up to a value of £200 per employee.

Payroll giving

Over 11,500 employees contribute through payroll giving.

Commercially led support

The Active Kids scheme provides children's holiday clubs with funding and equipment. Money is raised through customers collecting vouchers.

Applications

Local Charity of the Year

Charity representatives should complete a form available from their local store. Each store then creates a shortlist of three local charities, which are then invited to present to the store. One is then selected to receive fundraising and volunteering support over the next 12 months.

Active Kids

Further information about Active Kids can be found on the website: activekids.sainsburys.co.uk.

Food donations

Arrangements for food donations are made at store level.

Sainsbury Family Charitable Trusts

The trusts vary in their approach to grant-making and applications. Some have their own application forms, whereas others do not accept unsolicited proposals. More details are available from the Sainsbury Family Charitable Trusts website: www.sfct.org.uk.

Community fridges

For more information on community fridges visit: www.hubbub.org.uk/the-community-fridge.

Community contributions

We were unable to determine the company's corporate donations for the year. However, the company's 2018 annual report states:

> In 2017/18, our colleagues and customers have helped to generate over £35 million for charities, communities and good causes...This includes all our corporate donations, volunteering, fundraising, awareness-raising and investment in community programmes such as Active Kids.

Samworth Brothers (Holdings) Ltd

Sports and recreation

Company registration number: 409738

Correspondent: CSR Team, 1 Samworth Way, Leicester Road, Melton Mowbray, Leicestershire LE13 1GA (email: sportsopportunityfund@samworthbrothers.co.uk; website: www.samworthbrothers.co.uk)

Directors: Aileen Richards; Flor Healy; Hannu Ryopponen; Jeffrey Van Der Eems; Mark Samworth; Nicholas Linney; Timothy Barker; William Kendall (female 13%; male 88%).

Nature of business: Samworth Brothers is a British food manufacturer and owner of brands such as Ginsters, Soreen and West Cornwall Pasty Co.

Year end	30/12/2017
Turnover	£1,079,544,000
Pre-tax profit	£4,190,000

UK employees: 9,273

Main locations: The company's headquarters are in Melton Mowbray, Leicestershire. It has operations in Leicestershire and Cornwall.

Community involvement

Support is provided to youth sport projects in areas in which Samworth Brothers businesses are located.

Sports Opportunity Fund

The fund has two grant funds:

- A small grant fund that provides grants of up to £1,000 for projects nominated by Samworth Brothers employees
- A large grants fund for larger projects. Multi-year funding is considered and does not require an employee nomination

Projects should be located in areas in which Samworth Brothers businesses play an important role in the community. Projects should help young people, particularly from disadvantaged backgrounds, develop life skills, confidence and self-esteem through sport.

Employee-led support

Every two years the company holds a triathlon-style event called the Samworth Brothers Charity Challenge. Over £1.9 million has been raised since it was launched ten years ago.

Applications

Further information and application forms for the Sports Opportunity Fund can be requested from the correspondent.

Community contributions

Cash donations UK	£231,000

In 2017 charitable donations totalled £231,000.

Santander UK plc

Community development and education

Company registration number: 2294747

Correspondent: CSR Team, 2 Triton Square, Regent's Place, London NW1 3AN (tel: 0870 607 6000; email: community@santander.co.uk; website: www.santander.co.uk/uk/about-santander-uk/csr)

Directors: Alain Dromer; Ana Botín; Annemarie Durbin; Antonio Roman; Chris Jones; Ed Giera; Genenieve Shore; Gerry Byrne; Javier San Felix; Juan Rodríguez Inciarte; Lindsey Argalas; Nathan Bostock; Scott Wheway; Shriti Vadera (female 36%; male 64%).

Nature of business: Santander UK provides personal and corporate financial products and services and is an autonomous unit and forms part of the Banco Santander group, which operates internationally with headquarters in Spain.

Year end	31/12/2017
Turnover	£4,912,000,000
Pre-tax profit	£1,817,000,000

UK employees: 20,000

Main locations: Santander UK operates throughout the UK. Its head office is in London. It is owned by Santander Group, which is based in Spain.

Community involvement

Santander has an extensive programme of support for charitable causes, mainly focusing on education, employment, enterprise and communities, particularly through the Santander UK Foundation Ltd (Charity Commission no. 803655), which launched its Discovery Grants scheme in 2016. It also provides support for these causes through the Santander Universities scheme and other educational activities. Santander employees volunteer with local charities and educational initiatives and fundraise for a nominated charity partners, as well as donating to other charities through payroll giving and matched funding from the group.

The Santander UK Foundation Ltd (Charity Commission no. 803655)

The foundation is the main channel of the company's corporate donations and provides grants to small, local UK-registered charities, CICs or Credit Unions helping disadvantaged people through knowledge, skills and innovation to reach new opportunities. In 2016 the foundation amalgamated its three previous grants programmes into one scheme, Discovery Grants, as part of its refreshed community investment strategy.

The Changemaker Fund

In October 2016, Santander launched a partnership with Crowdfunder UK to raise funds for entrepreneurs and community groups tackling social challenges and creating positive local impact. Eligible projects seeking funds of up to £20,000 that get the crowd's backing receive 50% of their funding requirement from Santander to ensure the enterprise reaches its target. In 2018 Santander announced that the Changemaker Fund had surpassed £1 million in matched funding and support from the crowd for charities, social enterprises and community projects across the UK.

Santander Universities

Santander Universities is the group's global programme which aims to support and advance higher education. Santander partnered with 83 universities in the UK. Money that has been donated by the company helps provide scholarships, travel grants, support for special projects, academic and non-academic awards to university students.

In-kind support

Employee volunteering

In 2017 almost 9,000 employees took part in volunteering which was valued by the company at £1.9 million.

Employee-led support

Employees volunteer for various charities in the local area, as well as take part in various fundraising activities.

Charity partners

In 2016 employees voted to support Age UK and Barnardo's as the group's three-year charity partners. Employees organised a wide range of fundraising events and activities, raising over £1 million in 2017.

Matched funding

In 2017 the Santander Foundation donated a total of £2.3 million through its employee Matched Donation Scheme to support employees' fundraising activities for charities of their choice.

Applications

The company

Any enquiries, other than those relating to the foundation, should be directed to the CSR team on: community@santander.co.uk.

Corporate charity

Santander UK Foundation Ltd (Charity Commission no. 803655) – see page 275.

Community contributions

Total contributions (cash and in kind)	£20,300,000

According to the group's 2017 Sustainability Report, UK community investment in 2017 totalled £20.3 million. This figure includes the value of employee volunteering time, £1.9 million, and donations to the Santander Universities programme, £10 million.

Investment was broken down into the following categories:

Education	£11 million
Communities	£5.6 million
Other	£2 million
Employment	£901,000
Enterprise/changemaker	£677,500

Beneficiaries included: British Heart Foundation (£190,000); Mayor's Fund for London (£85,000); Access to Business, Headway, MS Society, Sight Cymru, Small Charities Coalition, Citizens Advice South Gloucestershire and Tees Valley Women's Centre (£10,000 each).

Schroders plc

General charitable purposes, enterprise and training, young people

Company registration number: 3909886

Correspondent: Corporate Responsibility Manager, 31 Gresham Street, London EC2V 7QA (tel: 020 7658 6000; email: cr@schroders.com; website: www.schroders.com)

Directors: Bruno Schroder; Damon Buffini; Ian King; Michael Dobson; Nichola Pease; Peter Harrison; Philip Mallinckrodt; Rakhi Goss-Custard; Rhian Davies; Richard Keers; Robin Buchanan (female 27%; male 73%).

Nature of business: Schroders is an international asset management provider.

The group's work is divided into wealth management and asset management, which has two divisions: investment and distribution.

Year end	31/12/2017
Turnover	£2,010,200,000
Pre-tax profit	£760,200,000

UK employees: 2,494

Total employees: 4,619

Main locations: The group's offices in the UK are located in: London; Chester; Edinburgh; and Oxford. The group also has offices in a number of countries worldwide.

Community involvement

The charity focuses on employee-led giving, through matched-funded payroll giving and volunteering. It has a partnership with the Social Mobility Foundation and Action for Kids, to provide work placements for students from low income backgrounds and young adults with learning disabilities.

In-kind support

According to its 2017 annual report, the company offers 'time matching' for volunteering hours employees complete outside working hours, and up to 15 hours of volunteering leave a year.

Employee-led support

Payroll-giving schemes operate in a number of its offices. In the UK, 29% of employees chose to give in this way during 2017.

Applications

Contact the correspondent for further information.

Community contributions

In 2017 the company donated £2 million to charitable causes worldwide, of this amount £1.2 million was given in the UK. As the majority of the company's donations was through employee-led payroll giving and matched funding, we were unable to determine how much was given by the company. A list of beneficiaries was not included.

Scott Bader Company Ltd

Education (particularly STEM subjects), the environment, health, community development, sustainable livelihoods, disability, women

Company registration number: 189141

Correspondent: Hayley Sutherland, Commonwealth Secretary, Wollaston Hall, Wollaston, Wellingborough, Northamptonshire NN29 7RL (tel: 01933 666755; email: enquiries@scottbader.com; website: www.scottbader.com)

Directors: Calvin O'Connor; David Rossouw; Jean-Claude Pierre; Karl-Heinz Funke; Malcolm Forsyth; Matthew Collins; Peter Harthill; Ruzica Geceg; Steven Brown (female 0%; male 100%).

Nature of business: The company is an internationally operating manufacturer and distributor of synthetic resins and chemical intermediates.

The annual report and accounts for 2017 state:

> Scott Bader Company Ltd is wholly owned as a financial and social investment by The Scott Bader Commonwealth Ltd, a company limited by guarantee and a registered charity. ... Everyone working for Scott Bader may become a member of The Commonwealth and, by this mean, become a trustee holding, in common with other members, the shares of Scott Bader Company Ltd.

Year end	31/12/2017
Turnover	£202,000,000
Pre-tax profit	£5,770,000

Main locations: There are 16 companies within the group. The group's headquarters are based in Wellingborough, Northamptonshire. Its other companies are based in Brazil; Canada; China; Croatia; Czech Republic; Dubai; France; Germany; India; Ireland; South Africa; Spain; Sweden; the USA.

Community involvement

The group's charitable giving is mainly channelled through its charity and parent company, Scott Bader Commonwealth Ltd, which makes grants to charities worldwide. The charity receives income equal to the group staff bonus, or 1% of salary costs – whichever is greater. The charity is also the parent company and holds the shares of Scott Bader Company Ltd in trust on behalf of its employees.

The group supports the following causes: education; the environment; health; community; sustainable livelihoods; disability. Companies within the group also make donations to charities locally.

The Scott Bader Commonwealth Ltd (Charity Commission no. 206391)

The charity fulfils its objectives by making grants to charitable organisations around the world whose purposes are to help young or disadvantaged people, especially anyone suffering deprivation and discrimination, such as poor, homeless and vulnerable women and children or minority communities, particularly where people are affected by poverty, a lack of education, malnutrition and disease.

Funds are divided into four categories:

Local funds

Funds are made available to all the companies in the Scott Bader Group for them to submit applications to the commonwealth for charities they wish to support. Each supports the work of charities associated with them or situated nearby.

Large project funding

Each year funding is allocated to support between two and four large community-based environmental or educational projects that benefit young or disadvantaged people to the value of £25,000 each. These projects can be located anywhere in the world.

Small international fund

This fund awards small grants of £500–£2,000 to support international projects that do not fit the local fund or large fund criteria.

Life President's Fund

The group's Life President, Godric Bader, distributes funding to charities of his choice. In 2017 a total of £7,500 was distributed to nine charities.

In-kind support

The group offers its facilities as in-kind support for local charitable organisations to host fundraising events and by allowing community groups to use the Scott Bader minibus.

The group's employees are entitled to one day of paid leave for volunteering, which was taken up by 100 employees across the group during the year.

Employee-led support

The group provides matched funding (up to £1,000 per employee) for employee fundraising initiatives, which is managed by the Commonwealth charity. Employees are also encouraged to volunteer for local organisation.

Exclusions

Local grants are not usually given for projects or large capital appeals where a significant amount of money still needs to be raised.

Applications

The Scott Bader Commonwealth Ltd

Assessment criteria are available to download from the website. Deadlines for large project funding are available on the website. Applications for the small international fund are accepted all year round and are only accepted from charities that are either registered in the UK or already known to Scott Bader. Applications for local funds should be made to the local office – company addresses can be found on the website, and application forms can be obtained from hayley_sutherland@scottbader.com.

General enquiries regarding the group's giving or charitable policies can be addressed to the company at: enquiries@scottbader.com.

Community contributions

Cash donations worldwide	£308,000

In 2017 the company donated £257,000 to Scott Bader Commonwealth Ltd and a further £31,000 to other charities. In addition to the donation to the charity the company also provided £20,000 under the Group Matched Funding Scheme.

Scottish Midland Co-operative Society Ltd

Community development, health, poverty and social exclusion, arts and culture, the environment, sports and recreation, disability

Company registration number: SP2059RS

Correspondent: Membership and Community Team, Hillwood House, 2 Harvest Drive, Newbridge, Edinburgh EH28 8QJ (tel: 0131 335 4400; email: membership@scotmid.co.uk; website: www.scotmid.coop)

Directors: Alexandra Williamson; Andy Simm; David Paterson; Eddie Thorn; Grace Smallman; Harry Cairney; Iain Gilchrist; Jim Watson; John Anderson; John Miller; Michael Ross; Sheila Downie; Tom McKnight (female 23%; male 77%).

Nature of business: The Scottish Midland Co-operative Society, trading as Scotmid, is an independent retail consumers' co-operative.

Year end	27/01/2018
Turnover	£373,712,000
Pre-tax profit	£5,958,000

UK employees: 4,081

Main locations: Scotmid's headquarters are in Edinburgh and the group has stores throughout the UK.

Community involvement

The group supports local charities and groups by making cash donations and supporting employee-led initiatives.

Community Connect

Through this initiative, members of the society can vote for 'Good Cause Groups' using a 'Community Connect' card each time they shop. The three groups with the most votes can receive awards of up to £15,000, depending on how many votes they receive. Charities in the local community centred around Scotmid or Semichem stores are able to apply to become Good Cause Groups.

Community grants

Charities can apply for grants of up to £500 through the group's Community Grant programme. The group focuses on projects that fall into one of the following categories:

- Children and young people
- Social inclusion
- Active lifestyles
- Environment
- Health and well-being
- Older people
- Fairtrade
- Arts and culture

Charity of the Year

The group picks a charity partner each year to support through various fundraising initiatives. The group's charity partner for 2018/19 is Scottish SPCA. The partnership between Scotland's animal welfare charity and the group aims to raise £300,000 and also increase awareness of the vital work the charity carries out in local communities across Scotland, with a particular focus on educating primary schoolchildren and adults on animal welfare.

Samaritans was chosen as the charity partner of the year for 2017/18 and the group raised £121,000 during the year.

Clothes recycling

The group has 54 Salvation Army clothes banks at Scotmid and Lakes and Dales Co-operative stores all over Scotland and the North of England. When people donate clothes the money raised is split between the Salvation Army, Scotmid and Lakes and Dales for investment in its communities. The group raised so much through this initiative that is was able to make a separate grant fund which will exclusively benefit community projects near stores with an environmental focus.

Employee-led support

Employees take part in various fundraising initiatives on behalf of the group's Charity of the Year.

Applications

Community Connect

Local groups and charities can apply to become a 'Good Cause Group' if they:

- Benefit the local community centred around Scotmid or Semichem stores
- Have the greatest possible benefit to their community
- Are scheduled to be completed within 24 months of the award date

The full terms and conditions for groups thinking of applying can be found at: www.scotmid.coop/community-connect-terms-and-conditions.

Community grants

Groups or individuals applying for a community grant must apply via an online form available at: www.scotmid.coop/community-and-charity/supporting-local-communities/community-grant-form.

Applications are welcome from: local community, self-help or voluntary groups and charities (including local branches of national charities) or individuals acting for the benefit of the local community.

Charity partners

For information on applying for the group's 'Charity of the Year', contact the correspondent.

Community contributions

We were unable to determine how much the group gave in charitable donations.

ScottishPower UK plc

The environment, enterprise and training, STEM subjects, arts, culture and heritage, community development

Company registration number: SC117120

Correspondent: The CSR & Reputation Committee in the UK, 1 Atlantic Quay, Glasgow G2 8SP (tel: 0141 248 8200; website: www.scottishpower.com)

Directors: Ignacio Sánchez Galán; Jim McDonald; José Sáinz Armada; Juan Carlos Rebollo; Keith Anderson; Lord Kerr of Kinlochard; Nicola Brewer (female 14%; male 86%).

Nature of business: ScottishPower has been part of the Iberdrola Group since April 2007, and is one of the UK's largest energy companies employing more than eight thousand people across Generation; Transmission; Distribution and Retail sectors.

Year end	31/12/2017
Turnover	£5,239,100,000
Pre-tax profit	£517,000,000

UK employees: 8,000+

Main locations: The group has sites in Cheshire, Merseyside, North Wales, North Shropshire and Scotland.

Community involvement

The majority of the group's giving is through its long-term partnership with Cancer Research and its corporate charity, the ScottishPower Foundation (OSCR no. SC043862) which makes grants to registered charities for general charitable purposes.

Cancer Research UK

Since 2012, ScottishPower has raised over £15 million for its long-term charity partner, Cancer Research UK. To show its support ScottishPower has developed its 'Help Beat Cancer Energy tariff', which the company makes a donation to for every month a customer stays on the tariff. The company also distributes health information and advice to customers, and encourages employees to fundraise.

In-kind support

ScottishPower employees can take one day's paid leave for volunteering each year.

Employee-led support

STEM Ambassadors

ScottishPower has STEM Ambassadors who are dedicated employee volunteers who encourage young people to study STEM subjects.

Iberdrola International Volunteering Day

Iberdrola International Volunteering Day was launched in 2010 and channels the charitable spirit of employees in Spain, the USA, Brazil, Mexico and the UK who join forces to complete a variety of projects across the five countries on the same day.

International Volunteering Holidays

Iberdrola offers employees the opportunity to take part in an international volunteering project in Sao Paulo, Brazil each year. 'Sao Paulo 2.0' aims to train young people aged 12–16 in computing and presentation skills to help them develop new skills and gain confidence to change their lives and aspire for a better future.

Matched funding

Employee fundraising efforts are matched up to a maximum of £200 per application.

Payroll giving

The company operates the Give As You Earn scheme in the UK.

Commercially led support

Sponsorships

ScottishPower has sponsored the Race for Life for the past six years. The group is also a sponsor of the Glasgow Warriors.

The ScottishPower Green Energy Trust (OSCR no. SC030104)

The trust was established in 1998 as an independent charity and is funded by ScottishPower Green tariff customers who make an annual donation to the trust. It aims to supports the development of new renewable sources in the UK, helping to reduce the reliance on fossil fuels and combat climate change.

Applications

General enquiries regarding company giving can be directed to the correspondent or for local requests, addressed to regional offices.

Corporate charity

ScottishPower Foundation (OSCR no. SC043862) – see page 275.

Community contributions

Total contributions (cash and in kind)	£5,200,000

According to the group's annual report and accounts for 2017, it gave a total of £5.2 million in cash, employee time and in-kind donations, of which £3.6 million was awarded in voluntary community benefit payments to the communities neighbouring its wind farms. It is unclear how much of this amount was given in cash; however, we do know that the group gave at least £1.87 million in cash to the ScottishPower Foundation, according to the foundation's accounts. The group also stated that it contributed £6.6 million in community investment, which we believe went towards community consultations.

SDC Builders Ltd

General charitable purposes

Company registration number: 1251716

Correspondent: Community Fund Team, Limegrove House, Caxton Road, Bedford MK4 10QQ (tel: 01234 363155; email: See 'applications'; website: www.sdc.co.uk)

Directors: Adam Knaggs; Craig Millar; Francis Shiner; Gary Wykes; Martin Lowndes (female 0%; male 100%).

Nature of business: SDC Builders provides construction services across a diverse range of sectors including commercial, manufacturing, automotive, healthcare, and education.

The company operates under the umbrella of an Employee Benefit Trust. This means instead of being owned by shareholders, the company is governed by a Board of Trustees who are responsible for safeguarding SDC's long-term prosperity and sharing any profits among members of staff and the wider community.

Year end	30/09/2017
Turnover	£164,630,000
Pre-tax profit	£1,433,000

Total employees: 369

Main locations: The company is based in Bedford. It also has an office in Oxfordshire.

Community involvement

The company supports general charitable purposes through cash-donations and employee volunteering. While the company does support some national charities, preference is given for charities and community groups which are local to the company's area of operation.

Community Fund

SDC's Community Fund was created in 2014 using contributions from the Employee Benefit Trust. According to the company's website, 'the fund was established to provide a mechanism for supporting the communities in which SDC operates, adding social value to causes that are close to both staff and clients, as well as leaving a positive legacy for future generations'.

The fund can support a wide range of organisations and projects including charities, sports clubs, community groups, renovation projects, scout groups, and schools. Preference is given to organisations that intend to use the money towards a specific project, item or event.

Previous beneficiaries have included: Bedfordshire County Scouts, Beds Garden Carers, Bedford Hospitals Charity, Cancer Research UK, Help for Heroes, Multiple Sclerosis Society, NSPCC, Road Victims Trust, Sportstrade.

Employee-led support

In addition to offering cash-donations, the company also encourages its employees to volunteer their time to the charities and community groups which it supports.

Applications

Contact Phil Janes or Sam Woolston on phil.janes@sdc.co.uk or sam.woolston@sdc.co.uk for further information about how to apply to the Community Fund.

Community contributions

The company's account for 2016/17 did not provide a figure for its total community contribution.

SEGRO plc

The environment, education, enterprise and training, health and medical research, poverty and social exclusion, sports and recreation, animal welfare, arts and culture

Company registration number: 167591

Correspondent: Charity Committee, Cunard House, 15 Regent Street, London SW1Y 4LR (tel: 020 7451 9100; email: uk@SEGRO.com; website: www.segro.com)

Directors: Gerald Corbett; Sue Calyton; Soumen Das; Carol Fairweather; Christopher Fisher; Andy Gulliford; Martin Moore; Phil Redding; David Sleath; Doug Webb (female 20%; male 80%).

Nature of business: Industrial and commercial property development, construction and investment, supply of utility services and the provision of services associated with such activities.

Year end	31/12/2017
Turnover	£334,700,000
Pre-tax profit	£976,300,000

Total employees: 300

Main locations: In the UK, the group has offices in London and Slough. There are also offices in the Czech Republic; France; Germany; Italy; Luxembourg; Poland; Spain; and the Netherlands.

Community involvement

This group supports local charities, social enterprises and grassroot community groups that help local vulnerable people return to employment. The group offers support in the form of direct donations, in-kind donations and employee volunteering time. The group manage their charitable work through a Central Charity Committee with four specific subcommittees for its business units, that decide independently which charities to support.

Partnerships

The company has a long-standing relationship with the charity LandAid, which aims to improve the lives of children and young people in disadvantaged circumstances. In 2017 SEGRO donated £40,000 to LandAid's Habitat for Humanity GB Homes, which will help bring an empty property in East London back into use as a shared house for young people leaving care.

Thames Valley Community Fund

In 2017 the group launched the Thames Valley Community Fund to help local charities in the Slough, Reading and Bracknell area. The fund is administered by The Berkshire Community Foundation, and invites community groups who focus on education and training to apply for grants of up to £5,000. A total of £25,000 will be available through this fund.

London Community Fund

This fund is available to community projects in the areas of London in which the company operates. Since 2015, SEGRO has contributed over £150,000 to grassroots community groups and charities through this fund. The fund helps to provide training and volunteering opportunities to the local community to help people into employment or education.

In-kind support

Volunteering

In 2017 the equivalent of £107,500 was given in the form of employee volunteering time. In June 2017, 190 employees across seven different countries took part in the group's 'Day of Giving' to help a number of local charities.

Employee-led support

Fundraising

According to the company's website, 'in 2018 seven employees completed the LandAid sleepout which raised funds to rebuild an old property into LandAid house'.

Applications

A 'charitable donation request form' is available on the group's website. Once completed, the form must be signed, scanned and posted to the correspondence address. Decisions are made by the Central Charity Committee or its subcommittees within each of the company's four Business Units.

Community contributions

Cash donations worldwide	£240,500
In-kind support worldwide	£877,500
Total contributions (cash and in kind)	£1,180,000

According to the 2017 Annual Report, the group contributed a total of £1.18 million to charities. Of this amount, £240,500 was giving in the form of 'direct donations', £107,500 through employee volunteering and £770,000 through in-kind support.

A breakdown by location was not provided.

Severn Trent plc

The environment, general charitable purposes

Company registration number: 2366619

Correspondent: Corporate Responsibility Team, Seven Trent Centre, PO Box 5309, Coventry CV3 9FH (tel: 024 7771 5000; email: corporate.responsibility@severntrent.co.uk; website: www.severn-trent.com)

Directors: Andrew Duff; Dame Angela Strank; Dominique Reiniche; James Bowling; John Coghlan; Kevin Beeston; Liv Garfield; Philip Remnant (female 38%; male 63%).

Nature of business: The group's principal activities are the supply of water and sewerage services, waste management and the provision of environmental services in the UK and internationally.

Year end	31/03/2018
Turnover	£1,694,100,000
Pre-tax profit	£503,800,000

Total employees: 5,660

Main locations: The group operates in the Midlands and mid-Wales. It also has operations in Ireland, Italy, and the USA.

Community involvement

The group supports charities through its community programme – Community Champions. Support is given through employee volunteering, fundraising and financial support through its corporate charity, the Severn Trent Charitable Water Trust Fund (Charity Commission no. 1108278).

Severn Trent Water Charitable Trust Fund (Charity Commission no. 1108278)

The group's corporate charity, the Severn Trent Water Charitable Trust Fund (Charity Commission no. 1108278) provides support to those living in poverty or with debt who are struggling to pay their water charges. Individual customers are provided with assistance to meet water charges.

Partnerships

The group has a long-term partnership with WaterAid (Charity Commission no.288701), and supports Children in Need and Comic Relief with their national call centres and fundraising activities.

Environmental partners

The group works with a number of environmental charities and other organisations to deliver its environmental objectives – including Wye and Usk Foundation, Trent Rivers Trust and Nottinghamshire Wildlife Trust.

In-kind support

The group's employee volunteering programme gives all employees two paid days per year to participate in voluntary work in the community. Most volunteering is done through the group's Community Champions programme. During the year, over 40% of employees volunteered, working alongside The Wildlife Trust, Comic Relief, Sport Relief and Children in need.

Employee-led support

Employees raised nearly £300,000 for charity partners during the year.

Exclusions

The group does not make donations for political purposes, or to EU political parties or expenditure.

Applications

The website states that enquiries about the group's corporate responsibility activities should be directed to the CR team at: corporate.responsibility@severntrent.co.uk.

Severn Trent Charitable Water Trust Fund

To apply for an organisation grant from the Severn Trent Trust Fund, email office@sttf.org.uk or call 0121 321 1324 to discuss criteria and funding opportunities. More information is provided on the charity's website: www.sttf.org.uk.

Corporate charity

The Severn Trent Water Charitable Trust Fund (Charity Commission no. 1108278) – see page 276.

Community contributions

Cash donations worldwide	£82,000

According to the 2017/18 annual report, donations to charitable organisations during the year totalled almost £82,000. Its report states that donations were awarded to 'employee-nominated charities through a matched funding scheme and health and safety reward schemes'.

Beneficiaries included: WaterAid; Comic Relief; Children in Need.

Shaftesbury plc

Children and young people, health and disability, education, sports and recreation, arts and culture, community development

Company registration number: 1999238

Correspondent: Penny Thomas, Company Secretary, 22 Ganton Street, Carnaby, London, W1f 7FD (tel: 020 7333 8118; email: penny.thomas@shaftesbury.co.uk; website: www.shaftesbury.co.uk)

Directors: Brian Bickell; Chris Ward; Dermot Mathias; Hilary Riva; Jill Little; Jonathan Nicholls; Richard Akers; Sally Waldon; Simon Quayle; Tom Welton (female 30%; male 70%).

Nature of business: Shaftesbury is a property investor and developer. It owns a portfolio properties in London's West End (Carnaby, Charlotte Street, Chinatown, Covent Garden, Soho).

Year end	30/09/2017
Turnover	£111,500,000
Pre-tax profit	£301,600,000

UK employees: 29

Main locations: The group operates in the West End of London.

Community involvement

The company owns properties in the West End of London and focuses its community involvement activities on this area, supporting schools and charities for purposes including arts, sustainability and community. The company has key community partners which have been nominated by employees. The company supports its community through cash donations, in-kind support and employee time.

The company's 2017 Sustainability Report states that the company is establishing a community investment committee to oversee the strategic direction and effectiveness of its community giving.

Partnerships

The company partners with employee-nominated charities. The company's key community partners include the following organisations: LandAid; Phoenix Gardens; ENO Community Choir; House of St Barnarbas; Pathway to Property; Westminster Tea Dance; The Connection at St Martin's-in-the-field; Trekstock; ZSL; Soho Food Feast; Chinese Community Centre and Pride.

Applications

The website states that CSR queries should be addressed to the Company Secretary, Penny Thomas at: penny.thomas@shaftesbury.co.uk.

Community contributions

Cash donations UK	£292,000
In-kind support UK	£225,000
Total contributions (cash and in kind)	£517,000

The 2017 Sustainability Report states that the company's overall contribution to communities equated to £517,000, which has been measured in accordance the London Benchmarking Group (LGB). As our usual practice, we have not included management costs in the company's total contribution figure.

An additional £513,000 was given to the local councils in 106 planning contributions. Contributions can be broken down as follows:

Cash	£292,000
In-kind	£107,000
Employee time	£118,000

Arts and culture	29%
Other	23%
Social welfare	18%
Education	14%
Health	10%
Environment	6%

In addition to the company's key community partners, they also supported Seven Dials Trust, St Anne's Church, Westminster Kingsway College, London Chinatown Chinese Association, China Exchange Book Fair, The Samaritans (Central London), London College of Fashion, Sir Simon Milton Foundation, Sustainable Restaurant Association Food Made Good Awards, Dragon Hall and many others.

Shawbrook Group plc

General charitable purposes

Company registration number: 7240248

Correspondent: CSR Team, Lutea House, Warley Hill Business Park, The Drive, Great Warley, Brentwood, Essex CM13 3BE (email: companysecretary@shawbrook.co.uk; website: www.shawbrook.co.uk)

Directors: Andrew Didham; Cedric Dubourdieu; David Gagie; Dylan Minto; Ian Cowie; John Callender; Lindsey McMurray; Paul Lawrence; Robin Ashton; Roger Lovering; Sally-Ann Hibberd (female 18%; male 82%).

Nature of business: Shawbrook is a specialist UK lending and savings bank founded in 2011 to serve the needs of SMEs, trusts and charities in the UK with a range of lending and saving products.

Year end	31/12/2017
Turnover	£237,300,000
Pre-tax profit	£86,500,000

UK employees: 671

Main locations: The company has offices based in the following areas: Birmingham; Brentwood; Croydon; Dorking; Glasgow; Leeds; London; Manchester; West Malling; Wisbech.

Community involvement

Shawbrook supports charities nominated by employees mainly through employee-led fundraising initiatives, volunteering and 'gift matching'. The group is committed to supporting Contact the Elderly, Little Havens and Future First.

In 2017 donations were made to over 50 causes.

In-kind support

In order to encourage employees to support their local communities and charities the group launched its 'Making a Difference Days'. This allows every employee up to one volunteer day per year so they can gift their time to a cause they're keen to support.

Employee-led support

Each month the group hosts a charity day to encourage donations and awareness for a cause nominated by a member of its team. In 2017 over £5,000 was raised from charity collections.

Matched funding

According to its annual report, the group supports employees and their families that gift their time and fundraise for charities they want to help and in 2017, a contribution of over £42,000 was made to employee-nominated causes.

Applications

Contact the correspondent for further information.

Community contributions

The company's Corporate Responsibility Report 2017 states: 'We have been able to contribute over £42,000 to staff nominated causes.' However, it is not clear whether this figure is employee-raised funds or matched funding by the company, or both.

A figure for in-kind support was not provided.

Beneficiaries included: Contact the Elderly; Little Havens; Future First.

Shell (UK Ltd)

Education (particluarly STEM subjects), enterprise and training, disaster relief, community development

Company registration number: 140141

Correspondent: Head of Shell UK Social Investment, Shell Centre, York Road, London SE1 7NA (tel: 020 7934 1234; website: www.shell.co.uk)

Directors: Nigel Hobson; Sarah Judd; Jonathan Kohn; Sinead Lynch; Steven Phimister; Bernadette Williamson (female 29%; male 71%).

Nature of business: Shell is a global group of energy and petrochemicals companies. Its activities in the UK correspond to those of the group and include the exploration, production and sale of oil and natural gas and marketing of petroleum products. Shell activities also include: generating electricity (including wind power); providing oil products for industrial uses; producing petrochemicals used for plastics, coatings and detergents; and developing technology for hydrogen vehicles.

Shell UK Ltd forms part of the Shell Group controlled by Royal Dutch Shell plc.

Year end	31/12/2017
Turnover	£5,344,000,000
Pre-tax profit	(£162,000,000)

UK employees: 2,123

Main locations: Shell operates throughout the UK and globally. The group has operations or offices in Aberdeen; Fife; London; Manchester; Norfolk; Peterhead; Warwickshire.

Community involvement

Shell UK supports sustainable energy and enterprise, STEM education and community initiatives. Support is offered internationally through the Shell Foundation, through grants for local community projects near its sites in the UK, educational programmes, and employee volunteering.

The Shell Group also has various worldwide initiatives, detailed examples of which can be found on the website or the global Sustainability Report.

Grants for community projects

The group's website states that in the UK, the group's sites work with local charities and projects to support local communities. In Aberdeen, Bacton, Mossmorron and St Fergus, the group offers grants for community projects or events.

Shell Foundation (Charity Commission no. 1080999)

The group has a corporate charity, the Shell Foundation. The foundation's website states that it focuses on entrepreneurial solutions to global development challenges – particularly on the following issues: sustainable job creation; access to energy; sustainable mobility; new technology and innovation. The foundation was established with a $250 million (around £203 million) endowment from the Shell Group and is registered in the UK but operates internationally, particularly in Africa, South America and Asia.

The Shell Centenary Scholarship Fund (Charity Commission no. 1071178)

The fund provides money for Shell Centenary Scholarships to support educational development and provide opportunities for graduate students from overseas to study in the UK. It provides at least 65 full cost scholarships (to cover tuition, accommodation, maintenance costs and return airfare) to international students on one year taught postgraduate courses at seven universities in the UK (Cambridge, Durham, Edinburgh, Imperial College London, Oxford and University College London) and also a number universities in the Netherlands.

Partnerships

Shell works in partnership with charitable organisations in many of the countries it operates in. For example, the group has a partnership with Mercy Corps, an international charity that provides humanitarian relief in areas affected by disaster. The group has also partnered with the government's Cashback for Communities scheme to provide 'Shell Twilight Basketball', a free basketball coaching for young people aged 10–19 in Scotland.

STEM education

Various initiatives are undertaken in support of STEM subjects:

- This is Engineering – Shell is a principle partner of this campaign which aims to transform perceptions of engineering among 13- to 18-year-olds
- Girls in Energy – this programme promotes STEM career opportunities to young women
- Shell Engineering Scheme – a two-year programme giving young adults the skills they need to secure jobs in the energy sector
- QEPrize for engineering – the group is a founding donor of the Queen Elizabeth Prize for Engineering
- Geobus – an educational outreach programme focusing on Earth Science, in partnership with The University of St Andrews, NERC and other organisations and businesses
- SCDI Engineers and Science Clubs – designed to give primary and secondary school students in Scotland the chance to engage in fun, hands-on STEM activities
- Bright Ideas Challenge – the group runs a STEM-focused competition on the topic of future energy solutions for cities, offering prizes of up to £50,000 for schools
- Tomorrow's Engineers – Shell has invested more than £1 million in the national programme run by EngineeringUK in 2017. It seeks to give every 11- to 14-year-old a first-hand engineering experience with local employers, and helps students connect what they learn in the classroom with the world around them and the opportunities of a career in engineering. The priority of the project is to increase the number of girls studying STEM subjects and going into engineering

Employee-led support

Employee volunteering

The group provides Employee Action Grants to Shell UK employees and pensioners who volunteer for at least 20 hours a year with a UK-based charity or community group.

Commercially led support

Sponsorship

The group works in partnership with Scottish Sports Futures, sponsoring Twilight Basketball, which provides free sports, arts and business activities for young people in Scotland.

Exclusions

Community grants are not given outside the company's operation area.

Applications

UK community grants and sponsorship

An application form for the UK community grants and sponsorship application form are available online at: www.shell.co.uk/sustainability/society/working-with-communities/sponsorship-and-donations.html.

Other enquiries about local support should be directed at the community relations teams at Shell plants or offices.

Shell does not award grants outside neighbourhoods surrounding Shell plants and offices, but if you have an enquiry not appropriate for local sites, you should address it to the UK Social Investment Department at the company's address.

Note: Unsolicited applications for community grants outside the communities in which Shell operates (Aberdeen, Bacton, Mossmorron and St Fergus) are not supported.

The foundation

The principal contact person for the foundation is Sam Parker (email: shell-foundation@shell.com) at the company's address.

Community contributions

The group's global sustainability report states that 'estimated voluntary and social investment (equity share)' in 2017 totalled $111 million, of which $57 million was in line with the group's global themes. The remaining $54 million was spent on local programmes for community development, disaster relief, education, road safety, health and biodiversity. The group gave 6% of its social investment in Europe/CIS, no further breakdown was available.

Shoe Zone Ltd

Community development, education, poverty and social exclusion, children and young people

Company registration number: 148038

Correspondent: CSR Team, Haramead Business Centre, Humberstone Road, Leicester LE1 2LH (tel: 0116 222 3000; website: www.shoezone.com)

Directors: Anthony Smith; Charles Smith; Charlie Caminada; Clare Howes; Jeremy Sharman; Jonathan Fearn; Malcolm Collins; Naomi Shefford; Nick Davis; Richard Bower (female 17%; male 83%).

Nature of business: The company is a footwear retailer in the UK and Ireland. It is a wholly owned subsidiary of Shoe Zone Group Ltd.

Year end	30/09/2017
Turnover	£157,777,000
Pre-tax profit	£9,503,000

UK employees: 3,750

Main locations: The group's head office is based in Leicester. It has stores throughout the UK.

Community involvement

According to its website, the group has previously supported a range of charities, locally and nationally. Support appears to be given through the group's corporate charity The Shoe Zone Trust (Charity Commission no. 1112972), which supports causes such as children, education and relief of poverty, as well as through employee-led fundraising. The group has supported Children in Need for the last five years through employee-led fundraising.

Employee-led support

The 2017 annual report states that employees have raised over £600,000 for BBC Children in need during the last five years.

Applications

Contact the correspondent for further information.

Community contributions

During 2017, Shoe Zone donated over £100,000 to charitable causes. Our research indicates that the majority of the amount donated went to The Shoe Zone Trust, and was raised through the carrier bag levy.

Shoosmiths LLP

General charitable purposes

Company registration number: OC374987

Correspondent: CSR Team, Witan Gate House, 500–600 Witan Gate West, Milton Keynes, Buckinghamshire MK9 1SH (tel: 0370 086 8788; email: corporate.responsibility@shoosmiths.co.uk; website: www.shoosmiths.co.uk)

Nature of business: Shoosmiths LLP is a full service national law firm.

Year end	30/04/2017
Turnover	£116,739,000
Pre-tax profit	£29,379,000

UK employees: 1,295

Main locations: The firm has offices in Southampton, Basingstoke, Reading, London, Northampton, Milton Keynes, Birmingham, Manchester, Nottingham, Leeds, Edinburgh and Belfast.

Community involvement

According to its 2016/17 corporate responsibility report, the firm's community investment programme for 2016–19 focuses on the following:

- provision of pro bono advice to individuals, charities and groups unable to afford to pay
- developing and maintaining enduring relationships with community partners rather than responding to approaches for donations
- seeking out innovative opportunities for wider community investment for charities, community groups and social enterprises
- staff volunteering through provision of good quality, skills-based volunteering

The firm recently moved away from national charity funding partnerships, and now concentrates on supporting local charity partners and investing staff volunteering time in the local communities where its offices are based.

Partnerships

Each year the firm supports designated charities local to its offices, undertaking staff fundraising and providing a range of in-kind resources. Charities further benefit from 'Pennies from Heaven' contributions, an annual firm-wide silent auction and cash donations.

Previous beneficiaries have included: St Michael's Hospice in Basingstoke, SIFA Fireside in Birmingham, Scottish Association for Mental Health, The Smile of Arran Trust and the Multiple Sclerosis Trust in Edinburgh, Brain Tumour Research in Manchester, Milton Keynes Community Foundation in Milton Keynes, Northampton Hope Centre in Northampton, Nottingham Women's Centre in Nottingham, Motiv8 South in Southampton and Guide Dogs in Thames Valley.

In-kind support

Pro bono

The firm provides legal advice on a pro bono basis in all areas of law that are practised across the business. In 2016/17 1,119 pro bono hours were recorded.

Access Legal helpline

The firm's Access Legal Solicitors helpline was established in 2010 and provides free advice to individuals. In 2016/17 the helpline passed on over 2,000 enquiries to the business. Consumers can contact the helpline on 03700 868686 or via email at helpline@shoosmiths.co.uk

Employee-led support

Shoosmiths employees are entitled to one day of paid leave to volunteer. In 2016/17 employees volunteered for a total of 2,064 hours.

Exclusions

The firm's community investment policy states that support is not given for any of the following:

- Political parties or groups of any kind
- Religious organisations
- Personal appeals by, or on behalf of individuals

Applications

Contact the correspondent for more information.

Community contributions

In 2016/17 the firm supported 105 organisations via national or office fundraising donations, volunteering and in-kind support. The firm's corporate responsibility report states that £97,000 was raised for these organisations through staff fundraising and firm donations. However, it was not possible to determine what proportion of this figure was donated by the firm itself. This figure does not include the value of pro bono services which was not quantified in the firm's annual report.

Shop Direct Ltd

General charitable purposes, homelessness

Company registration number: 4730752

Correspondent: Matt Dixon, CSR Board Chair, Skyways House, Speke Road, Speke, Liverpool L70 1AB (tel: 0844 292 1000; website: www.shopdirect.com/corporate-responsibility-page/chary-community)

Directors: Aiden Barclay; David Kershaw; Howard Barclay; Michael Seal; Philip Peters; Stuart Winton (female 0%; male 100%).

Nature of business: The principal activities of the group are online and home shopping retail and financial services, customer relationship management solutions and property management.

Year end	30/06/2018
Turnover	£1,958,800,000
Pre-tax profit	(£24,700,000)

UK employees: 3,500

Main locations: The group has offices in Merseyside (Liverpool and Bootle), Greater Manchester (Bolton, Manchester and Oldham) and Wrexham.

Community involvement

The company supports employee-led giving through matched funding, payroll giving and online fundraising platforms. Every year, employees choose a local, digitally focused charitable project to support through their fundraising efforts.

Charity partners

In 2016 the company completed its year-long partnership with Claire House, raising £440,000 which enabled the charity to open its new hospice 18 months ahead of schedule. In 2017 employees voted to support Booth Centre and Whitechapel Centre, the leading homelessness charities in Liverpool and Greater Manchester for two years. The company have committed to raising £600,000 to support the charities in delivering a multi-faceted approach to improve digital inclusion and employment for people who are homeless.

In-kind support

According to the company's CSR Report, it donates all of its sample clothing to its chosen charity partner.

Employee-led support

Shop Direct's website explains that employees are 'given opportunities to volunteer their time and expertise to charities and community groups'. Employees fundraise for a range of causes, either the Shop Direct chosen charity or a charity of their own choosing. They also donate to charities through payroll giving, and through the 'Helping Hands' online portal, employees can have their fundraising matched up to a value of £200 per activity.

Commercially led support

Shop Direct fundraises through a themed charity ball held on a biennial basis, the proceeds are donated to its nominated Charity of the Year.

Exclusions

Shop Direct does not support any charities which have religious or political connections.

Applications

Contact the correspondent for further information.

Community contributions

The annual report and accounts for 2017/18 did not provide a figure for charitable donations.

Siemens plc

Education (particularly STEM subjects), community development, the environment, disaster relief

Company registration number: 727817

Correspondent: Corporate Citizenship Manager, Sir William Siemens Square, Frimley, Camberley, Surrey GU16 8QD (tel: 01276 696000; email: info.cc.uk@siemens.com; website: www.siemens.co.uk)

Directors: Joe Kaeser; Dr Roland Busch; Lisa Davis; Klaus Helmrich; Janina Kugel; Cedrik Neike; Michael Sen; Ralf Thomas (female 25%; male 75%).

Nature of business: The principal activities of Siemens in the UK cover manufacture and sale of products in the areas of: electricity generation and distribution, transportation systems, industrial and building automation, metallurgical engineering and healthcare equipment and services. The company are also provides IT and other business infrastructure services.

The company is a subsidiary of the Siemens Group AG.

Year end	30/09/2017
Turnover	£1,939,000,000

UK employees: 15,000

Total employees: 372,000

Main locations: The group has offices worldwide. In the UK, its head office is in Frimley, Surrey, but it also has offices in a number of locations across England, Scotland and Wales – a full list can be found online at: www.siemens.co.uk/en/about_us/index/uk-locations-text.htm.

Community involvement

Siemens invests in education programmes, strategic partnerships with charities and local organisations, fundraising and volunteering in the UK. The group also supports charities through its charity fund.

Education programmes

The group launched its 'Curiosity Project' in 2015 to bring STEM to life for children, teachers and adults. This three-year programme aims to inspire the next generation of engineers and address the growing skills gap in the UK.

The Curiosity Project runs alongside the Siemens education website, which provides resources for teachers, parents and young people.

Partnerships and sponsorships

The group works with a number of charitable organisations. An example of this is its partnership with the Wildlife Trusts. Teams of employees volunteer to help manage the reserves close to its operating sites.

Corporate charities

The group has corporate charities in Argentina; Brazil; Columbia; Denmark; France; Germany; United States. The charities, which are part of the Global Alliance of Siemens Foundations, support sustainable social development projects and education initiatives.

In-kind support

According to the Business to Society UK Report, the company contributed 77 hours' paid volunteering time towards the Manchester Museum of Science and Industry's 'Science Busking with Siemens' workshops.

Employee-led support

Employee volunteering

According to the group's 'corporate citizenship focus areas' on its website, employee-volunteering time was identified as a 'strategic priority'. The group will be rolling out a volunteering platform and guidelines in fiscal 2018 – goals will include 'creating a more structured approach, encouraging volunteerism, raising awareness, and broadening the impact on our communities and business'. According to the group's 2017 Business to Society UK Report, employees took part in a volunteer-led partnership with the Wildlife Trusts to help manage the reserves close to operating sites.

Payroll giving

The group's 2017 Business to Society UK report states that 10% of employees donate to charities through payroll giving.

Applications

Contact the correspondent for further information.

Community contributions

Total contributions (cash and in kind)	£3,000,000

The 2017 Business to Society UK Report states that Siemens plc donated £3 million during the year, including cash, volunteering time and in-kind support.

Beneficiaries included: Kings High School; St Edwards School; Parkstone Christian Centre; Dorset Association for the Blind; Cancer Research UK.

SIG plc

Community development, education, general charitable purposes

Company registration number: 998314

Correspondent: Corporate Responsibility Team, 3 Sheldon Square, Paddington, London W2 6HY (tel: 020 3204 5418; email: groupcommunications@sigplc.com; website: www.sigplc.co.uk)

Directors: Alan Lovell; Andrea Abt; Andrew Allner; Cyrille Ragoucy; Ian Duncan; Janet Ashdown; Meinie Oldersma; Nick Maddock (female 25%; male 75%).

Nature of business: The principal activity of the group is the supply of specialist products to construction and related markets in the UK, Ireland and Mainland Europe. The main products distributed are Insulation and Energy Management, Exteriors and Interiors.

Year end	31/12/2017
Turnover	£2,878,400,000
Pre-tax profit	(£51,200,000)

Total employees: 9,674

Main locations: The group has 312 branches in the UK. There are also businesses in Austria; Belgium; France; Germany; Ireland; Luxembourg; Poland; the Netherlands.

Community involvement

The group mainly focuses on organisations and projects which enhance its engagement in the community, assist in managing the sustainability of the local environment, educate young people and assist disadvantaged groups. Support is given in the form of donations, employee-led fundraising and matched funding. The group also works closely with local universities and social enterprise groups, as well as participating in community construction projects and sponsoring local and professional sports teams.

Partners

In the UK, the group has been working with business students at Sheffield Hallam University as they study for a course module on strategy.

Employee-led support

Employee fundraising

The group offers support to employees undertaking their own fundraising efforts, particularly through its matched funding scheme, which matches up to £500 for employees' charitable efforts. Employees' individual activities have ranged from running in the London Marathon to raise funds for charities like Cancer Research UK and the Alzheimer's Society; to taking part in a 12k Iron Run race for Macmillan Cancer Support; to supporting the Teenage Cancer Trust and the Rainy Day Trust by driving through ten countries in the Pavestone Rally.

Payroll giving scheme

In 2017 employees raised £14,000 through payroll giving.

Exclusions

The group has a policy not to support political parties.

Applications

Contact the correspondent for further information. Activities may also be organised by local divisions of the group.

Community contributions

Cash donations worldwide	£63,500

In 2017 the group donated £63,500 to charity, including donations made through its matched funding scheme. It was not clear how much of this was given in the UK.

Simmons & Simmons LLP

Social inclusion and legal access, human rights, arts and culture

Company registration number: OC352713

Correspondent: Corporate Responsibility Team, CityPoint, One Ropemaker Street, London EC2Y 9SS (tel: 020 7825 3814; email: corporate.responsibility@simmons-simmons.com; website: www.simmons-simmons.com)

Directors: Andrea Accornero; Arthur Stewart; Chris Horton; Colin Passmore; Fiona Loughrey; Jeremy Hoyland; Kathryn Greaves; Laurence Renard; Michael Woodford; Rob Turner; Rodger Hughes (female 27%; male 73%).

Nature of business: Simmons & Simmons LLP is a limited liability partnership providing legal services and international tax advice.

Year end	30/04/2017
Turnover	£316,636,000
Pre-tax profit	£95,389,000

Total employees: 1,900

Main locations: The group has 22 offices worldwide. UK offices are located in Bristol and London.

Community involvement

The firm primarily provides support for communities through its extensive pro bono programme, which offers free legal advice to individuals and organisations. Support is also provided through sponsorship, mentoring and training schemes as well as through its corporate charity The Simmons & Simmons Charitable Foundation (Charity Commission no. 1129643) which awards grants to smaller charities working to promote social inclusion and legal access.

The Simmons & Simmons Charitable Foundation

The foundation provides grants mainly to smaller charities local to the group's offices that support social inclusion. The group also funds pro bono work and makes international donations (usually relating to the charitable work of the group's branches outside the UK).

Young Talent programme

The firm's young talent programme is designed to raise aspirations and access to the legal profession. Each year, 12 Year 10 students are selected to participate in the seven-year programme, which includes activities such as work experience, skills sessions, presentation work, and a paid internship.

In-kind support

Pro bono

According to its latest corporate responsibility report, the firm's pro bono programme focuses on providing advice to individuals and organisations in the following areas:

Access to Justice and advice to individuals:

- Disability benefits appeals
- At clinics including the Battersea Legal advice centre and the Queen Mary Legal Advice Centre
- To prisoners through the Prisoner's Advice Centre letter writing scheme

Social and environmental responsibility:

- Ongoing corporate advice to charities and NGOs, which are approved by our Pro Bono Committee, including our 15 strategic partners

Alleviate poverty through the Rule of Law. We advise:

- NGOs on areas such as microfinance and social impact bonds
- NGOs in relation to international human rights including land rights, children's rights, migrant worker's rights, human rights defenders and international humanitarian law
- Least developed and climate vulnerable counties in the UK Climate Change negotiations through the Legal Response Initiative

A total of 18 of the firm's 22 offices are currently involved in pro bono work and in 2016/17 carried out 14,123 pro bono hours. Recent examples of the firm's pro bono work include:

- **Access to Justice:** Launched in 2015, this scheme delivers end-to-end casework for welfare benefit appeals at the First Tier Tribunal. So far, the firm has taken on 150 cases, with a success rate of 92%
- **Shelter:** In Bristol, the firm has advised the national housing charity Shelter in relation to proposed amendments to legislation that could incentivise the provision of housing especially affordable housing in the UK
- **Child Soldiers International (CSI):** The firm has provided legal support in relation to an online global report relating to the application of international laws pertaining to the recruitment of child soldiers
- **RNIB:** The firm's ICT team provided legal advice on the launch of RNIB's In Your Pocket service – a mobile-based application that delivers spoken-word news and magazine content to blind and partially sighted individuals via a smart phone

The firm's pro bono work is governed by an International Pro Bono Committee, which meets monthly to set the direction of the Pro Bono Programme and approve new pro bono clients.

Employee-led support

Mentoring

The firm co-ordinates a number of mentoring schemes ranging from reading with young children to advising students about careers and university application processes. The firm's Bristol office works with Envision and supports Redland Green School on the annual city-wide Community Apprentice programme under which employees support 20 local students from disadvantaged backgrounds to develop community-focused projects.

Big Issue Vendor Development Programme

As part of its participation in the Big Issue's Vendor Development Programme, firm employees provide training for Big Issue vendors to enhance their job prospects.

Commercially led support

The firm supports arts organisations through sponsorship. Recent organisations supported include; Donmar Warehouse, the English National Ballet, and the Frieze London Art Show.

Applications

Contact the correspondent for more information.

Corporate charity

The Simmons & Simmons Charitable Foundation (Charity Commission no. 1129643) – see page 276.

Community contributions

Cash donations UK	£132,000

No figure was given for the firm's total charitable contributions for 2016/17. However, during the year £132,000 was donated by the group to The Simmons & Simmons Charitable Foundation.

Simplyhealth Group Ltd

Health, disability, older people

Company registration number: 5445654

Correspondent: Wendy Cummins, Corporate Giving Manager, Hambleden House, Waterloo Court, Andover, Hampshire SP10 1LQ (tel: 0300 100 1030; email: wendy.cummins@simplyhealth.co.uk; website: www.simplyhealth.co.uk/about-us/charitable-giving)

Directors: Alexandra Pike; Gil Baldwin; John Maltby; Kenneth Piggott; Michael Hall; Richard Harris; Romana Abdin (female 29%; male 71%).

Nature of business: Simplyhealth provides health cash, dental, accident, and personal health plans for individuals; and private medical insurance, health cash, and dental plans for businesses in the UK.

Year end	31/12/2017
Turnover	£238,100,000
Pre-tax profit	£5,200,000

Total employees: 1,301

Main locations: Simplyhealth has offices in Andover and Winchester.

Community involvement

The company supports health-related projects and charities across the UK with a preference for Andover and Winchester in Hampshire. Support is given through cash and in-kind donations, sponsorship, and employee fundraising and volunteering.

Charitable giving

The company prefers to support small, local charities who focus on specific local issues, although it will also fund larger national charities who need support for projects on a local level. The company's website, lists the following areas of focus for its charitable giving:

- An ageing population – this has a serious impact on how sustainable health and social care can be
- Carers – we aim to support carers directly so that they can support those they care for and still make the most of their lives
- Ability/mobility – improving or preventing both physical and mental wellbeing issues
- Dental health – more than just good teeth, early action means long-term oral health
- Professional partners – supporting dental and animal health specialists as they support you

At a local level, the company administers two Community Funds in Andover and Winchester where its offices are based. The funds are used to support projects which address one or more of the following health and care issues:

- Isolation of older people
- Youth Mental Health
- Physical activity of older people

Applications are welcomed from charities and groups within a 15-mile radius of the company's offices.

In-kind support

In addition to providing financial support, the website states that the company also offers its charity partners support with tasks such as website development, data protection, surveys and analysis.

Employee-led support

The company has a Give As Your Earn scheme and matches employee contributions. The company also matches any funds raised by its employees in their own time.

All Simplyhealth employees are entitled to three days each year to volunteer. Staff members who serve their local communities as school governors get an extra three days per year to do so. In 2017 Simplyhealth employees volunteered for a total of 2,496 hours.

Commercially led support

Simplyhealth is the main sponsor of the Great Run series of event held across the UK. Mind is the official charity partner for the series. All runners without a chosen charity are encouraged to run for Mind. In 2018 the company hopes to raise in excess of £1 million for the charity.

Exclusions

Community Fund applications are not accepted from projects in Basingstoke or Southampton. The website explains that, 'these towns are [already] well-serviced by a wealth of large businesses who are as committed to giving as we are'.

In addition, the Community Fund application form details the following list of exclusions:

- Support outside the local area, major towns or cities or groups that supply support on a national or international basis
- General appeals for non targeted funding and disaster appeals e.g. DEC
- Research projects
- Promoting religious or political causes
- Organisations solely supporting animals e.g. rescue centres
- Heritage, building restoration projects or more general building works including maintenance
- Marketing or promotional funding that will solely be used for marketing or promotional activity
- Money to pay salaries

Applications

For general corporate giving requests email the correspondent.

Winchester Community Fund

Applications forms can be downloaded from the website. Applications can be submitted by email to: CommunityFund@denplan.co.uk or by post to: Debby Edwards, Winchester Community Fund Co-ordinator, Simplyhealth Professionals, Simplyhealth House, Victoria Road, Winchester SO23 7RG.

Andover Community Fund

Applications forms can be downloaded from the website. Applications can be submitted by email to: CommunityFund-Andover@simplyhealth.co.uk or by post to: Debbie Clarke Andover Community Fund Co-ordinator Simplyhealth, Hambleden House, Waterloo Court, Andover Hants SP10 1LQ.

Community contributions

Cash donations UK	£800,000

The company's CSR report for 2017 states that during the year the Simplyhealth made community contributions of £1.13 million. This figure includes £800,000 in cash-donations to 19 charities.

Sirius Minerals plc

STEM subjects, the environment, community development, general charitable purposes

Company registration number: 4948435

Correspondent: CSR Team, Resolution House, Lake View, Scarborough YO11 3ZB (tel: 01723 470010; email: info@siriusminerals.com; website: siriusminerals.com/corporate-responsibility)

Directors: Chris Fraser; Jane Lodge; John Hutton; Keith Clarke; Louise Hardy; Noel Harwerth; Russell Scrimshaw; Thomas Staley (female 38%; male 63%).

Nature of business: Sirius Minerals is a mining company.

Year end	31/12/2017
Turnover	£23,981,000
Pre-tax profit	£79,249,000

Main locations: The company has offices in Scarborough and London. Support is focused around the Woodsmith Mine in The North York Moors National Park.

Community involvement

Sirius plans to contribute an annual royalty of 0.5% of revenue to its corporate charity, the Sirius Minerals Foundation Ltd (Charity Commission no. 1163127) which funds community projects in the North York Moors National Park, Scarborough and Redcar.

Education

The company's educational outreach programme encourages pupils to take up STEM subjects and careers in primary and secondary schools. The company took part in 35 education events in 2017. Employees deliver this programme in schools.

Environment

As part of the company's Section 106 agreements, it has committed £130 million to improving and safeguarding the environment in the areas the company has a presence. During 2017, first payments of £122,500 were made to the North York Moors National Park Authority for landscaping and ecology, and an additional £85,000 was granted for tree planting.

Commercially led support

Since 2011 the company has been the headline sponsor of Scarborough Engineering Week.

Applications

Contact the correspondent for further information.

Corporate charity

Sirius Minerals Foundation Ltd (Charity Commission no. 1163127) – see page 277.

Community contributions

Cash donations UK	£2,000,000

In 2017 the company made a donation of £2 million to its corporate charity.

Skipton Building Society

Poverty and social exclusion, older people, children and young people

Company registration number: 153706

Correspondent: Grassroots Giving Team, The Bailey, Skipton, North Yorkshire BD23 1DN (email: grgapply@skipton.co.uk; website: www.skiptongrg.co.uk)

Directors: Amanda Burton; Andrew Bottomley; Bobby Ndawula; David Cutter; Denise Cockrem; Dennis Hall; Helen Stevenson; Ian Cornelius; Marisa Cassoni; Mark Lund; Richard Coates; Robert East (female 33%; male 67%).

Nature of business: Skipton Building Society is the fourth largest in the UK. The society has several subsidiary companies, including Connells Group, one of the largest estate agency networks in the UK. In 2010 it merged with Chesham Building Society, based in Buckinghamshire. All branches now operate under the 'Skipton' name.

Year end	31/12/2017
Turnover	£735,600,000
Pre-tax profit	£200,100,000

UK employees: 2,147

Main locations: The head office is in Skipton. The foundation and the society make grants throughout the UK.

Community involvement

Support is provided through the society's Grassroots Giving programme and the Skipton Building Society Foundation (Charity Commission no. 1079538).

Grassroots Giving programme

The Grassroots Giving programme makes grants of £500 to community groups that are not registered charities.

Groups should consist entirely of volunteers and the donation should benefit vulnerable people such as older people and people who are homeless.

Exclusions

Grassroots Giving

According to the society's website, the following will not be eligible for funding:

- Rent and/or maintenance of a property
- Expeditions, holidays or travel programmes
- UK centres for overseas projects
- Projects which are normally the responsibility of other organisations such as the NHS or local government
- Medical research and medical equipment
- Animal welfare
- Party political activities
- Promotion of religious causes
- Running costs including: rent, insurance, employee wages, expenses and training of volunteers
- Direct costs of fundraising events, including: paying for food, drink, room hire, promotional goods or other direct elements of a fundraising event or activities
- Loans or business finance
- Requests to cover the costs of travel expenses or sponsorship of events
- Individuals and students not part of a wider group
- Groups that have an annual net profit of more than £10,000
- Activities taking place outside of the UK

Applications

Details of how to apply for a Grassroots Giving grant can be found on the society's website.

Corporate charity

Skipton Building Society Foundation (Charity Commission no. 1079538) – see page 277.

Community contributions

Cash donations UK	£150,000

In 2017 the society donated £150,000 to the Skipton Building Society Foundation. We were unable to determine how much was given through Grassroots Giving.

Sky plc

Sports and recreation, children and young people, the environment, community development

Company registration number: 2247735

Correspondent: Bigger Picture Team, Grant Way, Isleworth, Middlesex TW7 5QD (tel: 0333 100 0333; email: biggerpicture@bskyb.com; website: www.skygroup.sky/corporate/bigger-picture)

Directors: Adine Grate Axen; Andrew Griffith; David Darroch; James Conyers; Matthieu Pigasse (female 20%; male 80%).

Nature of business: Sky is a Europe-wide entertainment company. In the UK and Ireland the group provides paid television, broadband and streaming services. BSkyB launched its digital television services in the UK on 1 October 1998.

Year end	30/06/2017
Turnover	£12,916,000,000
Pre-tax profit	£803,000,000

Total employees: 31,000+

Main locations: The group has offices in Dublin, London, Milan, Munich and Vienna.

Community involvement

The Bigger Picture is Sky's CSR programme and focuses on education, the environment, sport and health. Sky continues to align its community investment to the wider goals of the business and its customers, by utilising its brand, platform and technology in community investment.

Sky Academy and the MAMA Youth Project

The MAMA Youth Project provides media and television industry training for young people from under-represented groups, and those with limited educational or employment opportunities. Sky has worked with the charity since 2011, and every year provides financial support to put 24 trainees through the programme, as well as work experience placements with Sky and several of its production company partners.

The Sky Academy provides training in news journalism and media technology skills. Since opening in 2012, 85,000 young people have visited Sky Academy Studios in London and Livingston.

Sky Ocean Rescue

Following the success of Sky's previous campaign to protect Rainforests, the group has partnered with WWF to protect and restore oceans. Sky has made three commitments for the campaign:

- To eliminate all single-use plastics from its operations, products and supply chain by 2020
- To commit a total of £25 million, over five years, to fund new ways to improve ocean health
- To partner with WWF to safeguard over 400,000km^2 of Marine Protected Areas across Europe's oceans

The following information is taken from the programme's website (www.skyoceanrescue.com):

> Sky Ocean Ventures is an impact investment vehicle that will invest in new ideas and businesses who can help solve the oceans plastic crisis. With Sky's cornerstone commitment of £25m and the ambition to quickly scale up to £100m with the support of other businesses, Sky Ocean Ventures will seek to find solutions to everyday plastic problems.
>
> Sky Ocean Ventures is encouraging, among others, businesses and innovators who are developing plastic packaging alternatives, new tech for the home that will help assist recycling and those developing alternative fibres for clothing to share their ideas and seek support. Ideas could include alternatives to coffee cups, plastic bottles and plastic bags as well as tech that foster a virtuous recycling circle between consumers, retailers and local authorities.

Employee-led support

In 2016/17 in the UK and Ireland 7% of Sky employees gave to charity through payroll giving or matched funding and 10% volunteered with Sky Academy Studios and Sky Sports Living for Sport.

Commercially led support

Over the past 20 years Sky has contributed more than £10 billion to British and Irish sports organisations. Cycling is one of the main group's sponsorships and the group has a collaboration with British Cycling.

Exclusions

Our research suggests that support is not generally given for animal welfare charities, appeals from individuals, older people, heritage, medical research, overseas projects, political or religious appeals.

Applications

Apply in writing to the correspondent.

Community contributions

Cash donations worldwide	£13,200,000
In-kind support worldwide	£3,300,000
Total contributions (cash and in kind)	£16,500,000

In 2016/17 the group valued its 'community contribution' (based on London Benchmarking Group model) at almost £19.8 million. We are unable to determine the amount given for charitable purposes both in the UK and worldwide. A further breakdown is given on the group's website which details the following information:

Cash	£13.2 million
Management*	£3 million
In-kind	£2.3 million
Time	£1.1 million

*We do not include management costs in our overall figures for community contributions.

We have taken £16.5 million to be the group's total figure for worldwide contributions.

Slaughter and May (Trust Ltd)

Education, health, community development, children and young people, older people

Company registration number: 335458

Correspondent: Kate Hursthouse, Senior Corporate Responsibility Manager, 2 Lambs Passage, London EC1Y 8BB (tel: 020 7600 1200; email: corporateresponsibility@slaughterandmay.com; website: www.slaughterandmay.com)

Directors: Cathy Connolly; David Wittmann; Dominic Robertson; Ewan Brown; Gareth Miles; Isabel Taylor; John Nevin; John Nevin; Paul Stacey; Richard Smith; Robert Byk (female 18%; male 82%).

Nature of business: Slaughter and May is a multinational law firm.

Year end	30/04/2017

Total employees: 1,164

Main locations: The firm's UK office is located in Islington, London. There are also offices in Beijing; Brussels; and Hong Kong.

Community involvement

The firm supports general charitable purposes with a focus on education, employability, and young people. Support is provided through cash donations, pro bono legal advice, matched funding, employee volunteering and fundraising. Much of the firm's community outreach is concentrated in the London borough of Islington where its UK office is based. The firm's charitable donations are made through its corporate charity The Slaughter and May Charitable Trust (Charity Commission no. 1082765), which awards grants to a range of legal, educational, health and community projects, with a particular interest in children and young people and older people.

Partnerships

At a local level, the firm works with St Luke's Community Centre in Islington to deliver projects for the local community, such as Firm Futures, where employees volunteer as business mentors for local unemployed people wanting to set up their own businesses, and PC Pals, supporting older people using the internet.

The firm also works in partnership with Macquarie to deliver the Community Resourcing (CoRe) programme, which supports charities in Islington. Teams of employee volunteers are matched with local charities and provide strategic support over a six-month period.

Education and employability

Working together with national charity partners and local schools, the firm delivers a wide range of programmes aimed at promoting educational attainment and literacy. Recent highlights of the firm's education initiatives include:

- **Tutoring:** The firm works in partnership with educational charity The Access Project, and the Central Foundation Boys' School to help students achieve places at top universities. Since its launch in 2012, five times more students are now going to the most selective universities
- **Mentoring:** Volunteers help students make decisions about university progression and write their personal statements for their university applications
- **Careers and employability:** Volunteers share their advice and career experience to provide students with an opportunity to learn about the diverse range of roles available in the City
- **Literacy:** The firm funds the National Literacy Trust's annual literacy survey and provides reading support at local primary schools
- **Work experience:** In 2013 the firm developed a joint legal work experience initiative with ITV, which has since developed the Social Mobility Business Partnership (SMBP), a charity that engages with over 90 organisations and 300 young people across the country. The firm is also a founding member of PRIME, an initiative to promote access to work experience in the legal sector

In-kind support

Pro bono

The firm has partnered with Legal Advice Centre (University House) in East London to provide pro bono advocacy to individuals making disability benefit appeals to the First Tier Tribunal.

The group also has pro bono champions in each of its divisions, and receives referrals of charities and community groups locally and globally from a number of organisations including LawWorks and TrustLaw. The group also provides a 'Legal Toolkit for Charities', available online, designed to answer common questions for charity professionals, and also delivers masterclasses to complement this.

Employee-led support

Employee fundraising

The firm has an employee charity committee, which allows staff to vote for charities to support, and organises fundraising activities such as a quiz, baking competitions and physical challenges. The charity selected for 2017/18 is Dementia UK. The firm also has a Payroll Giving scheme, and provides matched funding for employees who fundraise in their own time for charities and schools through its 'Funds for Fundraisers' scheme.

Employee volunteering

The firm's employees volunteer through a range of initiatives with its charity partners, such as helping with the Job Club at St Luke's Community Centre in Islington, or offering support with reading for children at local primary schools.

Applications

The firm's website states that its is 'unable to accept unsolicited funding applications from schools, charities or individuals'. Contact the correspondent for more information.

Corporate charity

The Slaughter and May Charitable Trust (Charity Commission no. 1082765) – see page 277.

Community contributions

Cash donations UK	£80,000

No figure was given for the group's overall charitable contribution during the year.

The Slaughter and May Charitable Trust's 2016/17 accounts state that it received donations from partners of the firm totalling £320,500 and an advance from Slaughter and May of £80,000 was outstanding at the year end. We have taken the latter figure as the cash donation from the company.

Smith & Nephew plc

Disaster relief, health and medical research, education

Company registration number: 324357

Correspondent: Local CSR Team, 15 Adam Street, London WC2R 6LA (tel: 020 7401 7646; website: www.smith-nephew.com)

Directors: Angie Risley; Erik Engstrom; Graham Baker; Ian Barlow; Joseph Papa; Marc Owen; Michael Friedman; Olivier Bohuon; Roberto Quarta; Robin Freestone; Roland Diggelmann; Susan Swabey; The Rt Hon. Baroness Virginia Bottomley; Vinita Bali (female 29%; male 71%).

Nature of business: Smith & Nephew is a global medical technology business established in 1856.

Year end	31/12/2017
Turnover	£4,765,000,000
Pre-tax profit	£879,000,000

Total employees: 15,933

Main locations: In the UK, Smith & Nephew have offices in Hull, London, Watford.

FTSE4Good

Community involvement

Each location's site operates a local programme that is designed and run to best engage its employees and meet local needs.

The company values its close links with Hull where it was founded some 160 years ago. As a major partner of 'Hull City of Culture 2017', employees at this UK site have been participating in a year of cultural activity through volunteering, ticketing opportunities and onsite events. Initiatives included 'Culture Clubs' in areas such as photography, art, language and walking, all run by volunteers within the company.

In-kind support

Each full-time employee is entitled to one day's paid leave a year to volunteer for charities or non-profit organisations. In the UK, a team from the Croxley Park site helped clean up the Grand Union Canal, improving the environment for the local community.

The company donates products to charitable or not-for-profit organisations, medical institutions, accredited educational programmes, medical foundations or professional societies as governed by its Global Policy and Procedure.

Employee-led support

In 2017 Smith & Nephew launched a city-wide charity initiative, More Together. Bringing together companies from Hull and the surrounding region in a three-event challenge, the initiative consisted of three sponsored events; walking the Yorkshire Three Peaks, taking part in 'Total Warrior', a challenging obstacle race, and a Humber Bridge Family Fun Walk. The challenge raised almost £75,000 for local charities.

Globally, the company matches employees' eligible charitable donations up to $500 per employee on an annual basis.

Commercially led support

The 2017 corporate sustainability report states that, in addition to its philanthropic giving, the company provided '$12.5 million (≈ £970,000 as at October 2018) in educational grants and sponsorships aimed at supporting and improving the skills of surgeons in the application of our products and technologies, thereby expanding access to world-class healthcare solutions'.

Applications

Apply in writing to your local site referencing your communication 'Local Community Giving Programme'.

Community contributions

Total contributions (cash and in kind)	£3,510,000

According to the 2017 corporate sustainability report, 'philanthropic activities' totalled $4.53 million altogether (≈ £3.51 million as at October 2018), of which $4.41 million (≈ £3.41 million as at October 2018) consisted of cash and product donations and $118,000 (≈ £91,500 as at October 2018) arose from the matching of employee gifts to charities. We were unable to determine what amounts were given in the UK.

DS Smith Holdings plc

Education, the environment

Company registration number: 1377658

Correspondent: 7th Floor, 350 Euston Road, Regent's Place, London NW1 3AX (tel: 020 7756 1800; email: sustainability@dssmith.com; website: www.dssmith.com)

Directors: Adrian Marsh; Chris Britton; Gareth Davis; Jonathan Nicholls; Kathleen O'Donovan; Louise Smalley; Miles Roberts (female 29%; male 71%).

Nature of business: DS Smith produces corrugated and plastic packaging, primarily from recycled waste, and the distribution of office products.

Year end	30/04/2018
Turnover	£4,781,000,000
Pre-tax profit	£326,000,000

UK employees: 4,900

Main locations: The company has headquarters in London and operations in 37 countries around the world.

Community involvement

Most of the group's charitable activities in the UK are co-ordinated through its corporate charity, The DS Smith Charitable Foundation. However, individual businesses within the group also run their own initiatives, and there are also group-wide partnerships.

Employee-led support

Employees volunteer and fundraise as part of the group's sponsorship of the Green Flag Award Scheme. The scheme recognises and rewards well managed parks and green spaces throughout the UK and worldwide.

Corporate charity

The DS Smith Charitable Foundation (Charity Commission no. 1142817) – see page 246.

Community contributions

Cash donations UK	£44,500

In 2017/18 The DS Smith Charitable Foundation received £44,500 in dividends from the company.

Smiths Group plc

Community development, the environment, health and medical research, education (particularly STEM subjects)

Company registration number: 137013

Correspondent: Corporate Responsibility Team, 4th Floor, 11–12 St James's Square, London, England SW1Y 4LB (tel: 020 7004 1600; email: cr@smiths.com; website: www.smiths.com)

Directors: Andy Reynolds Smith; Bill Seeger; Bruno Angelici; George Buckley; John Shipsey; Kevin Tebbit; Mark Seligman; Noel Tata; Oliver Bohuon; Tanya Fratto (female 10%; male 90%).

Nature of business: The group has several divisions: medical; industrial; energy; aerospace; communication; engineered components; and threat and contraband detection markets. Its customers include governments, hospitals, petrochemical companies, equipment manufacturers and service providers in other sectors.

Year end	31/07/2017
Turnover	£3,280,000,000
Pre-tax profit	£528,000,000

UK employees: 1,400

Total employees: 22,000

Main locations: The group has operations in over 50 countries. The group's UK operations are based in London.

Community involvement

The Smiths Group supports the communities in which it works through charitable giving and educational initiatives. The group's charitable activities are primarily managed at a divisional level, focusing on projects local to the group's operational facilities or connected to the industries in which the group works. However, the group does also offer some support to community and charitable organisations through a central charitable donations fund. According to the group's website, preference is given to charities and organisations which work to 'enhance the well-being of people through improved education, health and welfare or environment'.

Smiths Group Corporate Charitable Donations Fund

This fund provides funding to small grants to charitable organisations that:

- Work in the community close to the group's head office in London
- Have connections to the industries in which the group operates

To be eligible for a grant, organisations must demonstrate how a donation will improve the well-being of people through education, health, welfare or environmental activities. Grants are generally of under £1,000.

Employee-led support

The 2016/17 corporate responsibility report provides a number of examples of charitable initiatives undertaken by the group's employees. For example, during the year, the team at Smiths Interconnect, ran a wide-ranging community programme which included the provision of food, clothing and baby supplies for at-risk teenagers and young mothers. Outstanding contributions to local communities by Smiths employees are celebrated at the annual Smiths Excellence Awards, where winning teams each receive $1,000 to donate to a charity of their choice.

Exclusions

According to its website, the group will not fund:

- Individuals for sponsorship for fundraising activities
- Initiatives involving people engaging in dangerous activities such as bungee jumping or parachuting
- Political organisations and campaigns
- Any initiative that does not meet the specified funding criteria

Applications

For grants from the corporate charitable donations fund, organisations that meet the eligibility criteria outlined by the group should complete an application form, which can be downloaded from the website, and send it to: cr@smiths.com. Applications sent via post will not be considered. Applications are reviewed twice a year.

For applications to a local division, apply in writing to the relevant division, details of which can be found on the group's website.

Community contributions

Cash donations worldwide	£348,000

According to its 2016/17 annual report, during the year the group made charitable donations amounting to £348,000. The proportion of this total which was given in the UK could not be determined.

Sony Europe Ltd

STEM subjects

Company registration number: 2422874

Correspondent: CSR Committee, Sony UK Technology Centre, Pencoed Technology Park, Pencoed, Bridgend CF35 5HZ (tel: 01656 860666; email: CSRPCD@eu.sony.com; website: www.sonypencoed.co.uk/community)

Directors: Masaki Kurebayashi; Ricky Lodema; Shigeru Kumekawa (female 0%; male 100%).

Nature of business: The company is the distributor of Sony branded products.

Year end	31/03/2018
Turnover	£3,409,690,000
Pre-tax profit	(£2,001,000)

Total employees: 2,730

Main locations: Support is primarily given to organisations and schools within a 30-mile radius of the Sony UK Technology Centre in Bridgend.

Community involvement

Each year the Sony UK Technology Centre selects one organisation to partner with as its annual adopted charity. Adopted charities are the primary beneficiaries of the centre's fundraising initiatives. For the past five years, The Children's Ward at the Princess of Wales Hospital in Bridgend has been selected by the company as its adopted charity.

Educational visits and programmes

Sony host regular visits from schools, colleges and universities. The Sony UK Technology Environmental Centre is also used by schoolchildren for environmental field trips.

Sony supports several of the programmes run by The Engineering Education Scheme Wales (EESW), which encourage young people to choose a career in one of the STEM subjects. The company also supports the schools programme of the charity Ospreys in the Community, by providing pupils with the opportunity to learn about local engineering prospects and see the latest technology as it is built.

In-kind support

The company supports local organisations through the donation of Sony products, which can be used for fundraising or raffles.

Exclusions

The following information was taken from the website.

> Sony will not support the following:
>
> - The promotion of religious ideas
> - Sexist or racist groups
> - Political groups, private or secret societies
> - Profit-making bodies

Applications

In-kind support

To be eligible for in-kind support organisations should be located within 30-miles of its UK Technology Centre in Bridgend. Application forms can be requested from the website: www.sonypencoed.co.uk/community-support. The CSR Committee meet approximately every four weeks. to discuss donations.

Educational visits

Enquiries about educational visits to the Sony UK Technology Park can be made using an online form on the company's website at: www.sonypencoed.co.uk/contact/educational-visits.

Community contributions

We were unable to determine the company's community contributions for 2017/18.

Sopra Steria Ltd

Education, enterprise and training, children and young people

Company registration number: 4077975

Correspondent: CSR Team, Three Cherry Trees Lane, Hemel Hempstead, Hertfordshire HP2 7AH (tel: 0370 600 4466; website: www.soprasteria.co.uk/en)

Directors: Davinder Ahluwalia; John Moran; John Torrie; Kathleen Clark-Bracco; Pierre-Yves Commanay (female 20%; male 80%).

Nature of business: Sopra Steria provides IT support services in the UK and Europe.

Year end	31/12/2017
Turnover	£445,424,000
Pre-tax profit	£11,884,000

Main locations: The company's headquarters are in Hemel Hemstead. There are offices in: Belfast, Birmingham, Bristol, Catham, Chester, Dunstable, Edinburgh, Glasgow, Hemel Hemstead, Horsham, London, Manchester, Oxford, Reading, Stockton and Warrington.

Community involvement

The company's charitable support is mainly focused on education and skills development, digital inclusion and entrepreneurship. In 2017 the company supported educational initiatives and schools, mental health and medical research, homelessness, animal welfare, and hospices and hospitals.

Charity partnerships

The company is a digital technology partner of Widnes Viking's Game Changer project which promotes health lifestyles to schoolchildren in the North West. It also has a partnership with The Prince's Trust and several employees have volunteered to help run and lead programmes that inspire and empower young people to realise their potential.

In-kind support

The company refurbishes computer equipment for community groups and employees are also given one day to volunteer in the community.

Employee-led support

Employees can take paid leave to volunteer and Sopra Steria match individual fundraising efforts.

Applications

Contact the correspondent for further information.

Community contributions

Cash donations UK	£150,000

During 2017, more than 139 community projects and UK-registered charities were supported by employees and the company invested over £150,000 in donations, grants and sponsorship.

The Southern Co-operative Ltd

General charitable purposes

Company registration number: IP01591R

Correspondent: Community Support/ Donations, 1000 Lakeside, Western Road, Portsmouth, Hampshire PO6 3FE (tel: 023 9222 2500; email: community@ southerncoops.co.uk; website: www. thesouthernco-operative.co.uk)

Directors: Amber Prior; Beth Rogers; Bev Wyatt; Gareth Lewis; Helen Jackson; Jason Crouch; Joanne Gray; John Harrington; Mark Ralf; Neil Blanchard; Silena Dominy (female 55%; male 45%).

Nature of business: The Southern Co-operative (TSC) is an independent consumer co-operative society. It operates over 250 community stores and funeral homes across 11 counties in southern England. In addition, the co-operative operates a home shopping business and a portfolio of rental properties.

Year end	27/01/2018
Turnover	£431,190,000
Pre-tax profit	£2,431,000

Main locations: TSC has various stores and funeral homes across the south of England, including West and South Outer London. There is also a store in Gwent, South East Wales.

Community involvement

TSC's Love your Neighbour programme provides funding, in-kind donations and partnership opportunities.

Love Your Neighbourhood

This is a new programme launched by TSC in 2016 with its activities funded by its community fund and the proceeds of the carrier bag charge. It focuses on four community themes: to create greener, safer, healthier and more inclusive communities; and features the following:

- In-kind product donations
- Local fundraising (giving out cash donations of between £50 to £1,000)
- Local partnerships
- Employee volunteering

Support is focused on local charitable or not-for-profit organisations in areas where the co-operative operates. Local branches of national charities are welcome to apply if there is a TSC store in the locality.

In-kind support

The company provides donations for community/fundraising events such as prizes, hampers or refreshments.

Employee-led support

As part of TSC's community involvement, employees and members are encouraged to volunteer their time for local good causes or environmental projects. Employees and customers actively fundraise for the society's local charity partners.

Exclusions

Exclusions for local funding, in-kind donations and local partnerships can be downloaded from the TSC website.

Applications

Food banks

If you believe that there is a need for a collection point to be installed in your local store, contact TSC via the Contact Us page on its website.

In-kind donations and local funding

Application forms are available to download from the TSC website.

Local partnerships

Application forms can be downloaded from the TSC website and should be returned to your local store.

Volunteering

Charities with volunteering opportunities should contact their local store.

Community contributions

Total contributions (cash and in kind)	£407,500

According to its 2017/18 annual review, TSC invested £407,500 in local charities and community groups. A further £857,000 was raised through staff fundraising, member donations from their share of the profits, supplier donations and customer donations raised through funeral tributes.

Southern Water Services Ltd

The environment, education, health, general charitable purposes, children and young people

Company registration number: 2366670

Correspondent: Community Engagement Team, Southern Water, PO Box 41, Worthing BN13 3NZ (tel: 0330 303 1263; email: community@ southernwater.co.uk; website: www. southernwater.co.uk/community)

Directors: Bill Tame; Ian Francis; Ian McAulay; Mike Putnam; Paul Sheffield; Richard Manning; Rosemary Boot; Sara Sulaiman; Wendy Barnes; William Lambe (female 30%; male 70%).

Nature of business: Southern Water provides water supply and wastewater services in the south east of England.

Year end	31/03/2018
Turnover	£829,700,000
Pre-tax profit	£176,200,000

Total employees: 2,289

Main locations: The company provides services in the south east of England.

Community involvement

Southern Water support charities and community groups in Hampshire, Sussex, Kent and the Isle of Wight with a focus on the environment, young people, education and health. Support is provided through charity partnerships, a community grant programme, employee volunteering, and road shows and customer events.

Community grants

The company awards grants to local community groups and charities in areas which have been affected by its activities. According to its website, the company is keen to support projects which focus on:

healthy lifestyles; the environment; and education and opportunities.

Previous beneficiaries have included: Empty Plate Café, Keep Lancing Lovely, Men in Sheds, Sholing Village Study Centre, Weston Church Youth Project, Worthing D and D Basketball, Yellow Door Solent, YMCA Fairthorne Group.

Partnerships

Each year the company's employees vote for regional charity partners, who receive £10,000 to complete a project within 12 months that benefits their local community. Recent regional charity partners have included, Off the Fence, The Aldingbourne Trust, Battersea, Naomi House and Jacksplace.

Every two years the company also selects a single charity to be its company-wide partner. The company's current charity partner is the Alzheimer's Society.

Learn to Swim

The company works in partnership with Swim England to deliver its Learn to Swim programme aimed at helping youngsters to become more confident swimmers.

As part of the programme the company supports pools and swimming instructors with:

- Equipment for swimming lessons
- Organising Achiever Awards
- Providing instructors' seminars

In 2017/18 a total of 14,000 children signed up for a Learn to Swim session.

Education

The company works with schools and other groups to deliver a range of educational programmes focused on saving water, water safety and healthy lifestyles.

Community events

The Southern Water Roadshow team attends community events across South East England. At the events employees offer advice and give free giveaways to help customers save water and prevent fat, oil and grease from blocking the pipes.

In-kind support

The company provides water bottles for schools and other youth groups at a discounted rate.

Employee-led support

Volunteering

The company has a community volunteering programme which allows employees to spend two days' paid leave working individually or in a team for their chosen charity or community project each year. Recent examples of employee volunteering have included, helping at the hedgehog hospital at Brent Wildlife Lodge, hamper packing for the Salvation Army, and clearing the grounds at the Countryside Education Trust. In 2017/18 employees volunteered for a total of 4,676 hours.

Fundraising

Southern Water employees engage in a range of activities to raise funds for the company's chosen charity partners.

Applications

Community grants

New community grant schemes are advertised on the company's website as they become available. Check the website for the latest information.

Volunteering

To request volunteering support from Southern Water employees, organisations should email the company at: volunteer@southernwater.co.uk.

Community contributions

Cash donations UK	£147,000

According to its 2017/18 Community Engagement report, during the year the company awarded grants of over £147,000. This figure includes grants of £10,000 awarded to each of the company's four new charity partners.

Spar (UK) Ltd

Health, disaster relief, general charitable purposes

Company registration number: 634226

Correspondent: CSR Team, Mezzanine Floor, Hygeia Building, 66–68 College Road, Harrow, Middlesex HA1 1BE (tel: 020 8426 3700; email: customer.relations@spar.co.uk; website: www.spar.co.uk)

Directors: Christopher Lewis; Deborah Robinson; Ian Taylor; Jacqueline Mackenzie; Mark Keeley (female 40%; male 60%).

Nature of business: Spar (UK) Ltd is a voluntary, independently owned trading group operating convenience and grocery stores under the SPAR banner throughout the UK.

The company's accounts state: 'Spar (UK) Ltd is the Central Office of the Spar retail organisation owned 100% by Spar Food Distributors Ltd whose shareholders are five regional distribution companies.' The companies are: A. F. Blakemore and Son Ltd; Appleby Westward Group Ltd; C. J. Lang and Son Ltd; Henderson Wholesale Ltd; and James Hall and Company (Holdings) Ltd.

Year end	29/04/2017
Turnover	£61,620,000
Pre-tax profit	£420,500

Main locations: The company operates across the UK.

Community involvement

SPAR provides support to its national partners through employee fundraising as well as through donations granted from the income received from the sale of certain SPAR products. The company also provides more general charitable support through its corporate charity the Spar Charitable Fund (Charity Commission no. 236252), which supports employees in need and makes grants to organisations in response to emergency appeals.

Partnerships

The majority of SPAR (UK) Ltd's charitable activities are carried out in partnership with various national charities. Between 2006 and 2016, the company supported the NSPCC as a partner charity but in 2016/17 announced a new partnership with Marie Curie. SPAR provides support to its partner through employee fundraising as well as through donations from the income received from the sale of certain SPAR products.

Spar Charitable Fund

The company provides more general charitable support through its corporate charity the Spar Charitable Fund, which supports employees in need and makes grants to organisations in response to emergency appeals.

Employee-led support

Employees regularly organise fundraising activities to raise money for the company's partner charity. In 2016/17 these activities included treks to the top of Ben Nevis and Scafell Pike.

Commercially led support

In 2016/17 the company supported Marie Curie's 'Blooming Great Tea Party' fundraising initiative, by donating income received from the sale of a certain range of cakes to charity. During the year, the company also sold Marie Curie Daffodil badges in store to support Marie Curie's Great Daffodil Appeal and donated revenue from the sale of Christmas sandwiches to its charity partner.

Applications

General queries regarding the company's CSR policies can be submitted in writing to the correspondent or via email to: customer.relations@spar.co.uk. Enquiries regarding local initiatives should be addressed to the local store manager.

Corporate charity

Spar Charitable Fund (Charity Commission no. 236252) – see page 278.

Community contributions

The company's accounts did not provide an overall figure for the company's 2016/17 charitable contribution.

Spirax-Sarco Engineering plc

Community development, education (particularly STEM subjects), disability and health, arts and culture, the environment, disaster relief

Company registration number: 596337

Correspondent: Sustainability Commitee, Charlton House, Cirencester Road, Cheltenham, Gloucestershire GL53 8ER (tel: 01242 521361; website: www.spiraxsarcoengineering.com)

Directors: Clive Watson; Jamie Pike; Jane Kingston; Jay Whalen; Kevin Boyd; Neil Daws; Nicholas Anderson; Peter France; Trudy Schoolenberg (female 22%; male 78%).

Nature of business: Spirax-Sarco is a British manufacturer of steam management systems and peristaltic pumps and associated fluid path technologies.

Year end	31/12/2017
Turnover	£998,700,000
Pre-tax profit	£229,100,000

UK employees: 1,546

Main locations: In the UK, the group is based in Cheltenham, Cornwall and Hampshire. It also has operations in 57 countries worldwide.

Community involvement

The group supports local community initiatives, education (particularly STEM), social welfare, disability, healthcare, arts, the environment and disaster relief. Assistance is provided through cash and in-kind donations as well as employee volunteering. Much of the company's charitable support is channelled through the Spirax Sarco Group Charitable Trust (not a registered charity).

Spirax Sarco Group Charitable Trust

Larger group-sponsored charitable contributions, including those made to major UK and international charitable organisations, are reviewed and administered by the Spirax-Sarco Group Charitable Trust. The trust's primary focus is education (particularly in the sciences and engineering), but it also seeks to identify and respond to local needs and so will make donations and organise activities in support of underprivileged young people, individuals with disabilities, or older people. The trust also contributes to natural disaster relief efforts.

During 2017, the trust made 56 donations ranging in size from £150 to £20,000 with a total value of £231,000.

Community Engagement Awards

In 2017 the group launched its first Community Engagement Awards to celebrate high quality community engagement activities from across the business. Winners were selected by the group's Sustainability Committee and each received £5,000 to be spent on community engagement activities locally.

Examples of community engagement in 2017 included, sponsorship of the annual Cheltenham Science Festival. During the year the group also hosted STEMnet (Science, Technology, Engineering and Mathematics Network) events at its Cheltenham manufacturing and R&D site.

In-kind support

The group provides in-kind donations such as products and office equipment. In 2017 the group donated the equivalent of £33,000 in in-kind donations.

Exclusions

According to its charitable donations policy, the group will not provide funding for any of the following:

- Commercial organisations
- Political parties, organisations, or political events
- Religious organisations where the donation is used to promote a particular faith or belief (note: donations to religious organisations could be acceptable if the organisation is undertaking charitable work, such as disaster relief, where receipt of aid is not conditional upon religious affiliation)
- Organisations that discriminate in the allocation of their support according to race, sexual
- orientation, gender, religion, or disability
- Organisations that are involved in human rights abuses, are subject to UN, EU, UK or US
- Sanctions, or violate the Group Sanctions, Embargoes & Restrictions Policy
- Organisations whose activities contribute to environmental damage
- Organisations that cause harm to animals
- Individuals or private pursuits
- Research projects such as books, research papers or articles in professional journals
- Activities that contravene the Group Anti-Bribery and Corruption Policy, the Group Human
- Rights Policy or the Group Management Code
- Activities prohibited by law or regulation or that are deemed offensive or inappropriate; or
- Activities that encourage a relationship of dependence

Applications

Enquiries can be submitted using an online form in the 'Contact us' section of the group's website.

Group charitable donations are managed locally and are made at the discretion of the company's general manager. As such, applications for funding should be submitted in writing to your local company. Contact details are available on the group's website.

Community contributions

Cash donations worldwide	£381,000
In-kind support worldwide	£494,000
Total contributions (cash and in kind)	£875,000

In 2017 the Spirax Sarco Group Charitable Trust made 56 grants totalling £231,000. A further £150,000 was donated to charitable causes by companies within the group. In addition to financial donations, the group's operating companies donated the equivalent of £33,000 in in-kind donations and contributed over 1,900 hours of working time to community engagement activities. Using an average hourly salary to estimate the cost to the company of employee volunteering, the group's 2017 annual report estimates that the total value of the group's operating companies' community engagement activities in 2017 was approximately £230,000, taking the group's total community contributions to £875,000. It was not possible to determine what proportion of this figure was given in the UK.

Beneficiaries included: National Star College in Cheltenham and American Red Cross's Hurricane Irma and Hurricane Harvey relief funds (£20,000 each).

Sports Direct International plc

Sports and recreation, children and young people

Company registration number: 6035106

Correspondent: CSR Team, Unit A, Brook Park East, Shirebrook, Derbyshire NG20 8RY (tel: 0344 245 9200; email: investor.relations@sportsdirect.com; website: www.sports-direct-international.com)

Directors: David Brayshaw; David Daly; Dr Keith Hellawell; John Kempster; Mike Ashley; Simon Bentley (female 0%; male 100%).

Nature of business: Sports Direct is one of the UK's largest sports-goods retailer.

Year end	29/04/2018
Turnover	£3,360,000,000
Pre-tax profit	£77,500,000

UK employees: 14,100

Total employees: 26,500

Main locations: The group's headquarters are based in Shirebrook, Derbyshire. The group operates stores in the UK, Europe, the USA and Malaysia.

Community involvement

The primary focus of the group's community engagement is participation in sport. According to the group's 2017/18 annual report, the company 'believe[s] that everyone should have a chance to participate in sports and enjoy the health and lifestyle benefits it brings'. To achieve this the group, 'provide[s] a wide range of equipment and clothing to promote sports participation amongst people of all abilities, including those who would not normally have access to equipment and facilities'. In addition, the group also makes occasional cash donations to charitable causes and works closely with the Shirebrook Forward NG20 Working Group, which aims 'to help Shirebrook retain its breadth of services, local support functions and community spirit'.

In-kind support

Most of the group's support for charitable causes is through in-kind donations. In 2017/18 for example, the group provided sporting equipment to organisations near its headquarters in Shirebrook. The group also offered local community groups the opportunity to hold events at its 500-seat Shirebrook campus auditorium free of charge.

Applications

Contact the correspondent for more information.

Community contributions

Cash donations UK	£66,000

According to the group's 2017/18 annual report, cash donations to charities totalled £66,000. Further donations of sporting equipment were made by the group and its brands; however, the value of these contributions was not quantified in the group's accounts.

Previous beneficiaries have included: Salvation Army; The Breast Cancer Research Foundation; The Jerry Colangelo Prostate Cancer Event; Comic Relief; Dr Theodore A Atlas Foundation.

SSE plc

Community development, education, the environment, sports and recreation, general charitable purposes

Company registration number: SC117119

Correspondent: Morven Smith, Head of Community Investment, Inveralmond House, 200 Dunkeld Road, Perth, Perthshire PH1 3AQ (tel: 01738 456000; email: sustainability@sse.com; website: sse.com/communities)

Directors: Alistair Phillips-Davies; Crawford Gillies; Dame Susan Bruce; Gregor Alexander; Helen Mahy; Martin Pibworth; Peter Lynas; Richard Gillingwater; Tony Cocker (female 22%; male 78%).

Nature of business: SSE produces, distributes and supplies electricity and gas and provides other energy-related services.

Year end	31/03/2018
Turnover	£3,226,400,000
Pre-tax profit	£1,418,900,000

UK employees: 20,786

Main locations: The group operates across the UK and Ireland.

FTSE4Good

Community involvement

The group supports communities within its areas of operation through a range of community investment funds and employee volunteering.

Community investment funds

Through its community investment programme, SSE delivers financial support to a diverse range of community projects near to its renewable developments in the UK and Ireland. The group currently manages 32 funds, which have supported over 2,500 community projects with grants of £22.1 million since 2008. In 2017/18 these funds awarded £5.12 million and €667,000 in the UK and Ireland respectively to help support over 700 projects.

For full details of all of the group's community funds including beneficial areas, eligibility criteria and deadlines see the website.

Sustainable Development Fund

In addition to its community funds, SSE also provides grants to support strategic projects in the following regions: Dumfries and Galloway; Highlands; North Lincolnshire; Perth and Kinross; Scottish Borders; South Lanarkshire.

According to the group's website, the funds support projects that help to achieve the following objectives:

- Creating opportunities – increase opportunities for education and employment
- Empowering communities – build resilience and protect vulnerable residents
- Building sustainable places – stimulate meaningful community regeneration

Further information about eligibility criteria and deadlines is provided on the company's website, along with a full list of beneficiaries.

Resilient Communities Fund

The Resilient Communities Fund offers support for communities to prepare for extreme weather events. In 2017 SSE confirmed its continued support for the fund until at least 2023. In addition, following a stakeholder consultation, the fund was enhanced to include support for building community capacity to cope with an emergency incident or event, and to prioritise the resilience of vulnerable people. In 2017/18 the fund invested nearly £510,000 across 77 different projects within SSE's network area.

The Scottish Hydro Electric Community Trust (OSCR No: SC027243)

The Scottish Hydro Electric Community Trust is an independent charitable trust, which was established by SSE to provide help to individual customers in the north of Scotland (Dunblane northwards), faced with high charges for an electricity connection.

For more details and to apply, check the trust's website at: www.shect.org.

Employee-led support

Volunteering

The company's employee volunteering programme, Be the Difference, allows each employee one day each year to volunteer at a community project of their choice. In 2017/18 SSE employees volunteered 2,387 days, supporting over 850 projects across the UK and Ireland. Charities can request volunteer support using a form available on the website.

Matched funding

According to the 2017/18 sustainability report, the company matches employees' fundraising efforts up to £150. In 2017/18 the group provided £44,500 in charitable donations through its matched funding initiative.

Commercially led support

SSE has a diverse sponsorship portfolio, which includes sport and entertainment venues, national sporting events and the UK's largest independent music therapy charity, Nordoff Robbins. SSE also supports women's football through its sponsorship of The SSE Women's FA Cup and The SSE Scottish Women's Cup.

Exclusions

According to the website, grants from the company's local community funds cannot be awarded for political or religious causes, to subsidise the cost of energy consumption, for purposes 'adverse to SSE's interests', to replace statutory funding, or to individuals. Grants from the Sustainable

Development Fund are not awarded for individuals, or groups without a constitution.

For further details on all exclusions from the group's community, investment funds refer to the website.

Applications

Community investment funds

Application forms for each of the local community investment funds, as well as the Sustainable Development Fund, are available on the SSE website, along with guidance, deadlines and contact details for each fund.

Be the Difference

To apply for volunteer support from employees through the Be the Difference scheme, download a volunteer request form from the SSE website (sse.com/communities/bethedifference) and send via email (bethedifference@sse.com) or post (SSE, Be the difference, Corporate Affairs, 1 Waterloo Street, Glasgow G2 6AY).

Resilient Communities Fund

To apply to the Resilient Communities Fund, visit: www.ssen.co.uk/resiliencefund, where applications can be downloaded, along with guidance notes and deadlines.

Community contributions

Total contributions (cash and in kind)	£6,500,000

In 2017/18 SSE provided over £6.5 million to communities across the UK and Ireland. This contribution includes SSE's Community Investment Funds, Resilient Communities Fund, charitable donations as well as the financial value of employee volunteering.

St James's Place plc

Financial awareness and employability, general charitable purposes

Company registration number: 3183415

Correspondent: Alex Davies, Head of Corporate Responsibility, St James's Place House, 1 Tetbury Road, Cirencester, Gloucestershire GL7 1FP (tel: 01285 640302; email: cr@sjp.co.uk; website: www.sjp.co.uk/about-st-james-place/our-responsibilities)

Directors: Andrew Croft; Baroness Wheatcroft; Craig Gentle; David Lamb; Iain Cornish; Ian Gascoigne; Roger Yates; Sarah Bates; Simon Jeffreys (female 22%; male 78%).

Nature of business: St James's Place is a financial services group involved in the provision of wealth management services.

Year end	31/12/2017
Turnover	£9,080,000,000
Pre-tax profit	£186,100,000

UK employees: 1,965

Total employees: 2,155

Main locations: The group has offices in: Aberdeen; Belfast; Bristol; Cirencester; Edinburgh; Essex; Glasgow; Leeds; Liverpool; London; Manchester; Newbury; Newcastle; Nottingham; Solent; Solihull; Westerham.

Community involvement

The company supports a wide range of charitable causes with a particular focus on financial awareness and employability. Support is provided through local community partnerships, cash and in-kind donations, and employee volunteering. Support is also given through the company's corporate charity the St James's Place Charitable Foundation (Charity Commission no. 1144606) which makes grants to registered charities under the following themes: cherishing the children; combating cancer; supporting hospices; mental health.

Partnerships

At a local level, the company looks to build long-term relationships with community groups and charities, which are local to its offices, especially its head office in Cirencester. According to the company's annual report, this support is not targeted at specific projects, but rather 'to the heart of the charity with a view to improving efficiency and sustainability'. These partnerships usually last for between three to five years. Recently, the company has partnered with the Cirencester Opportunity Group, an independent pre-school charity enabling children with additional needs to play and learn with other children; and Cirencester Signpost, a local charity that works to support people in need, focusing on hunger, homelessness, isolation, and financial hardship.

Employability and Financial Education

The company works with local schools and colleges to provide a variety of financial education programmes for students. These employee-led events give students the opportunity to learn about a range of topics related to personal finance and become self-confident in their ability to manage their own money.

In addition to its programmes promoting financial awareness, the company also offers career workshops and supports a range of skill-focused events including CV workshops, networking days, assemblies, and interview training.

As part of its focus on employability and financial awareness the company has recently increased its grant support for youth development organisations like Young Enterprise, Employability UK, and Urban Stars, and has worked closely with The Duke of Edinburgh's Award, to support their work to bridge the gap between education and work for disadvantaged young people.

The 2017/18 annual report states that this aspect of the company's corporate responsibility is an area, which the company will look to develop further in 2018.

Employee-led support

Each year employees are entitled to take two days to volunteer for a local community group or charity. In 2017/18 employees volunteered a total of 14,300 hours of their time. According to the 2017/18 annual report, this contribution had a total value of approximately, £672,500.

In addition to offering employees, time to volunteer during working hours, the company also supports volunteering which employees undertake in their own time by awarding grants of £300 to the charities, which they support. In 2017 118 of these grants were awarded.

Every year the company arranges a number of 'community team challenges', whereby groups of employees work together to deliver projects which benefit their local community. In 2017/18 the company delivered 34 projects involving 353 employees. As part of this initiative, in 2017, company employees volunteered in support of WellChild's Helping Hands programme, which transforms gardens to give access to the outdoors for children with life-limiting illnesses. In 2018 the company has committed to provide volunteers for 12 two-day projects.

The company runs a payroll giving scheme. Funds donated by employees to the St James Place Charitable Foundation are matched by the company. In 2017 the company donated a total of £11 million to its foundation in matched funding.

Applications

General queries can be submitted using an online form on the group's website, at https://www.sjp.co.uk/contact-us.

Corporate charity

St James's Place Charitable Foundation (Charity Commission no. 1144606) – see page 278.

Community contributions

Cash donations UK	£13,100,000

According to its 2017 corporate responsibility report, during the year the company provided approximately

£13.1 million in charitable contributions. This figure included around £11 million given in matched funds to the St James's Place Charitable Foundation.

St Mary's Football Group Ltd (Southampton Football Club)

Sports and recreation, community development, education, health and disability

Company registration number: 6951765

Correspondent: Saints Foundation, St Mary's Stadium, Britannia Road, Southampton SO14 5FP (tel: 0845 688 9370; email: charities@saintsfc.co.uk; website: saintsfoundation.co.uk)

Directors: Leslie Arnold Reed; Martin Semmens; Ralph Krueger (female 0%; male 100%).

Nature of business: St Mary's Football Group Ltd is the ultimate parent company of Southampton Football Club, a professional football club competing in the English Premier League.

Year end	30/06/2017
Turnover	£182,252,000
Pre-tax profit	£43,713,000

UK employees: 380

Main locations: The club is based in Southampton.

Community involvement

Southampton's community involvement is channelled through the Saints Foundation (Charity Commission no. 1090916) which delivers targeted programmes across several areas of social concern, including Employability and Learning, Education, Health and Well-Being, and Community. The foundation also provides in-kind support for charities in Southampton and the surrounding areas.

Saints Foundation (SFC)

The Saints Foundation is the official charity of Southampton Football Club. The foundation supports disadvantaged young people and adults at risk within the following six core themes: football and sports participation; schools and community; Saints4All (accessible sport); education; health and well-being; employability and learning.

According to its 2016/17 accounts, during the year the foundation had a charitable expenditure of £1.17 million. This included £23,000 which was donated in the form of grants to local charities.

Recent examples of the foundation's programmes include:

- **Generation Gains:** A wide-ranging health and well-being programme for isolated older people, which combines core stability exercise sessions, reminiscence groups that use football and sport as a vehicle to tackle early signs of dementia and a programme of social and physical activities
- **Saints Connect:** A referral based project, targeting young men and women aged 13–16 who have been identified as being in need of additional support. The project provides participants the opportunity to engage in sport and a range of creative activities, and to achieve accredited outcomes
- **SaintsAbility:** Offers regular football sessions for people of all ages with physical and cognitive impairments

For full details of all of the foundation's current programmes, see the website.

Bucket Collections

Charities can apply to hold bucket collections at the St Mary Stadium on matchdays.

Saints Giving

The foundation's 2016/17 annual report notes that it intends to launch an initiative called Saints Giving, which will see the charity make grants to like-minded charities across Hampshire and the surrounding area. See the foundation's website for announcements and updates.

In-kind support

Charities can apply to receive a signed pennant for a fundraising event.

Exclusions

Requests from organisations located outside Hampshire cannot be considered. All requests must come from the charity itself using the online application.

Applications

General enquiries can be submitted using the online contact form on the Get in Touch section of the foundation's website.

Fundraising support

Applications for signed pennants can be submitted using an online form on the club's website (https://southamptonfc.com/saints-foundation/fundraising-support). Schools and local youth football teams are requested to submit their applications directly to charities@saintsfc.co.uk.

Bucket Collections

Applications to hold a bucket collection at St Mary's on a matchday can be submitted using an online form on the club's website (southamptonfc.com/saints-foundation/charity-bucket-collection).

Community contributions

Cash donations UK	£55,000

The club's annual report and accounts for 2016/17 did not declare a figure for its charitable contributions. However, according to the Saints Foundation's 2016/17 accounts, the club made a donation of £55,000 to the charity.

St Modwen Properties plc

Economic generation, community development

Company registration number: 349201

Correspondent: CSR Team, Park Point, 17 High Street, Longbridge, Birmingham B31 2UQ (tel: 0121 222 9400; email: info@stmodwen.co.uk; website: www.stmodwen-csr.co.uk)

Directors: Bill Shannon; Ian Bull; Jamie Hopkins; Jenefer Greenwood; Lesley James; Mark Allen; Rob Hudson; Simon Clarke (female 25%; male 75%).

Nature of business: St Modwen Properties is a residential and commercial property development group specialising in urban regeneration and brownfield land renewal.

Year end	30/11/2017
Turnover	£318,600,000
Pre-tax profit	£70,300,000

UK employees: 481

Main locations: The group has operations across England and South Wales.

Community involvement

The company provides support for projects which promote economic generation and community development. Support is offered through a variety of means including, employee volunteering, in-kind donations, partnerships and sponsorship.

On its website, the company provides the following description of its approach to charitable giving: 'Due to the variety of projects across our portfolio, we have chosen not to focus on a single national charity. Instead, we support a number of local charities linked or in close proximity to our development sites.'

To enable its staff to take an active role in local activities, the St Modwen's website also explains that the company 'will continue to adopt a practical approach to charitable giving, seeking to provide equipment, time and expertise as well as funding'.

Recent examples of the kinds of support offered by St Modwen include:

- Donating an adapted minibus for the Ysgol Bae Baglan School
- Sponsoring a local youth football team
- Visiting local schools to educate pupils about Health and Safety
- Hosting a 10k race to raise money to tackle youth homelessness

Further case studies of the company's charitable activities are available to view on its website.

Employee-led support

Company employees regularly volunteer their time and skills to support local charities and community projects.

Commercially led support

The company offers sponsorship opportunities for local sports clubs.

Applications

Contact the correspondent for more information.

Community contributions

No figure for total contributions was provided in the 2016/17 annual report or the February 2018 CSR report (the latest available at the time of writing).

Stagecoach Group plc

Education, health, the armed forces, children and young people

Company registration number: SC100764

Correspondent: Steven Stewart, Director of Communications, 10 Dunkeld Road, Perth, Perthshire PH1 5TW (tel: 01738 442111; email: charity@stagecoachgroup.com; website: www.stagecoachgroup.com)

Directors: Ann Gloag; Gregor Alexander; James Bilefield; Julie Southern; Karen Thomson; Martin Griffiths; Ray O'Toole; Ross Paterson; Sir Brian Souter; Sir Ewan Brown; Will Whitehorn (female 27%; male 73%).

Nature of business: Stagecoach is an international transport group, operating public transport services in the UK and the USA.

Year end	28/04/2018
Turnover	£3,226,800,000
Pre-tax profit	£95,300,000

UK employees: 30,000

Total employees: 34,000

Main locations: The group has operations in the UK, Canada, Europe and the USA.

Community involvement

Stagecoach supports a wide range of charitable causes, including children and young people, education, health, and the armed forces. The group also supports a number of bus and rail industry charities and events each year. Support is provided through various means including, charitable donations, in-kind support, sponsorship, employee fundraising and volunteering. The group supports activities across the UK. Group companies in USA and Canada also support a number of charitable causes locally through fundraising and volunteering.

Stagecoach Group Community Fund

Charities can apply for grants from the Stagecoach Group Community Fund which supports local, national and international charities. Much of the fund's support is focused on young people, health, education and local community projects. Funding is also provided to match the fundraising efforts of Stagecoach employees.

Partnerships

Stagecoach has an ongoing partnership with the Diana Award, with whom it collaborates on the #BeNiceBus project – an anti-bullying campaign in the UK and Ireland which gives young people the skills, confidence and training to become ambassadors to tackle the problem of bullying. As part of the project, a bus donated by Stagecoach undertakes an educational tour of schools across England, Scotland and Wales.

In 2018 Stagecoach also launched a two-year partnership with the Royal Manchester Children's Hospital Charity, whose nurses were involved in treating children injured in the Manchester Arena terrorist attack in 2017. The Stagecoach group also has several ongoing partnerships with veterans' groups in the UK and the USA.

Many of the local companies within the Stagecoach group support a Charity of the Year. For more information, refer to the websites of the individual companies.

In-kind support

Many Stagecoach employees carry out their own fundraising activities in their spare time, and the company often offers matched funding to complement their efforts. The group has also contributed significant in-kind support by seconding staff to good causes overseas as well as getting involved with local events in the UK and the USA.

Applications

To apply for support from the Stagecoach Group Community Fund, download the application form and email the completed document to: charity@stagecoachgroup.com. Applications can also be submitted by post.

General queries regarding the company's CSR policies should be directed to the correspondent.

Community contributions

Total contributions (cash and in kind)	£900,000

According to its website, each year Stagecoach invests between 0.5% and 1% of the profits from its transport operations in the UK and the USA in good causes and community projects. In 2017/18, £900,000 was donated by Stagecoach to help a number of charities and to support fundraising events and services. In addition, the group also provides substantial in-kind support, such as complimentary bus and rail travel. However, the value of this in-kind support was not quantified in the group's annual report.

Previous beneficiaries have included: The Duke of Edinburgh Award, Enterprise Education Trust, The Prince's Trust, Save the Children, Scottish Air Ambulance, and Whizz-Kidz.

Standard Chartered plc

Health, financial inclusion and education, projects outside the UK

Company registration number: 966425

Correspondent: Sustainability Team, 1 Basinghall Avenue, London EC2V 5DD (tel: 020 7885 8888; website: www.sc.com/sustainability)

Directors: Andy Halford; Bill Winters; Christine Hodgson; David Conner; Dr Byron Grote; Dr Han Seung-Soo; Dr Louis Cheung; Dr Ngozi Okonjo-Iweala; Gay Huey Evans; Jasmine Whitbread; Jose Vinals; Naguib Kheraj; Om Bhatt (female 33%; male 67%).

Nature of business: Standard Chartered is a multinational banking and financial services company.

Year end	31/12/2017
Turnover	£10,921,000,000
Pre-tax profit	£1,828,000,000

UK employees: 2,030

Total employees: 86,724

Main locations: The group operates globally in 63 countries. In the UK, the group is headquartered in London.

Community involvement

Standard Chartered works with local partners to deliver programmes that improve people's health and educational opportunities. Support is also provided through in-kind donations and employee volunteering.

Seeing is Believing

Seeing is Believing is a partnership set up between Standard Chartered and the International Agency for the Prevention of Blindness in 2003. The programme aims to prevent and treat avoidable blindness and provide eye care in countries in Asia, Africa and the Middle East where there is a lack of quality, affordable eye care. In 2018 the group achieved its goal of raising $100 million for the programme two years ahead of schedule. More information is available at: www.seeingisbelieving.org.

Goal

Goal is an education programme set up by Standard Chartered. The programme is aimed at girls aged 12–18 from urban communities across the world who are educationally disadvantaged and living on a low income. The programme's curriculum was developed in partnership with the Population Council and focuses on four key areas: communication; health and hygiene; rights; and financial literacy. The programme is delivered by organisations locally across the world. Between 2006 and 2017, Goal reached more than 381,000 girls across over 20 countries.

In-kind support

All employees are offered three days of paid volunteering each year. In 2017 employees volunteered for more than 66,000 days.

Employee-led support

Employees volunteer and fundraise for partner and local charitable organisations. In 2017 employees raised $5 million (≈ £3.79 million as at October 2018).

Financial education

The company provides financial education programmes which aim to build financial awareness among young people and micro and small businesses. Programmes are delivered on a voluntary basis by the company's employees. In 2017 the group trained more than 117,000 young people and 1,500 entrepreneurs.

Applications

Contact the correspondent for more information.

Community contributions

Cash donations worldwide	£16,730,000
In-kind support worldwide	£13,776,000
Total contributions (cash and in kind)	£30,496,000

The 2017 annual report states that total community investment by the group amounted to $40.3 million (≈ £31.9 million as at October 2018), of which cash contributions totalled $22.1 million (≈ £16.73 million as at October 2018), employee time was valued at $18.1 million (≈ £13.7 million as at October 2018), and gifts in kind totalled $100,000 (≈ £76,000 as at October 2018). As is our practice management costs and employee donations have been excluded from the total. It was not specified how much was given in the UK.

Standard Life Aberdeen plc

General charitable purposes

Company registration number: SC286832

Correspondent: Frances Horsburgh, 1 George Street, Edinburgh, United Kingdom EH2 2LL (tel: 01224 211666; email: sustainability@aberdeenstandard.com; website: www.standardlifeaberdeen.com/who-we-are)

Directors: Bill Rattray; Cathi Raffaeli; Gerhard Fusenig; John Devine; Jutta af Rosenborg; Keith Skeoch; Kevin Parry; Martin Gilbert; Martin Pike; Melanie Gee; Richard Mully; Rod Paris; Simon Troughton; Sir Douglas Flint; Sir Gerry Grimestone (female 20%; male 80%).

Nature of business: The group is a leading investment company.

Year end	31/12/2017
Turnover	£16,980,000,000
Pre-tax profit	£964,000,000

Total employees: 2,700

Main locations: The group has operations in 46 locations across Europe, the Americas, Asia, the Middle East and Australia.

Community involvement

In August 2017, Standard Life and Aberdeen Asset Management merged to become Standard Life Aberdeen. Previously, Standard Life funnelled its charitable giving through its corporate charity, the Standard Life Foundation (OSCR no. SC040877), and Aberdeen Asset Management through the Aberdeen Standard Investments Charitable Foundation (OSCR no. SC042597). The merged company continues to funnel its charitable giving through its charities. The company also run its Standard Life Charity Fund (OSCR no. SC030702) which aims to support charities chosen by its employees.

Aberdeen Standard Investments Charitable Foundation (OSCR no. SC042597)

The foundation's two core focuses – emerging markets and local communities – reflect the business's desire to give back to areas which are a key strategic focus and to build on its pattern of giving to communities in which employees of Aberdeen Standard Investments (Aberdeen) live and work.

The criteria for each focus are outlined on the foundation's website as follows:

Emerging markets

Each year the foundation will select an emerging market and focus its investment in that area. The emerging markets allocation will be focused on a small number of long-term partnerships (average duration of three years). All charities must meet the following criteria to be considered for an emerging market grant:

- UK registered
- Small to medium in size or, if a larger charity, must have an identifiable project that Aberdeen can support
- Clear focus on the promotion of education and providing wider opportunities for underprivileged young people

Local communities

All charities applying for local community grants must meet the following criteria:

- UK registered
- Clear connection to a community local to one of Aberdeen's offices
- Investment should be capable of having a clear and meaningful impact, for example:
  - Small charities where the contribution amount is significant relative to the charity's size
  - Larger charities with identifiable project opportunities that Aberdeen could put its name to
  - Projects which include the opportunity for Aberdeen employee involvement through volunteering
  - Local organisations where Aberdeen can have a visible impact
- Governance structure in place to allow Aberdeen to monitor the impact of the investment

In 2016/17 the foundation had assets of £1.16 million and an income of £7,200. Donations were made amounting to £1.04 million, of which £307,500 was awarded to 'emerging markets' projects and £731,500 awarded to local community support.

Beneficiaries included: ChildHope UK (£208,500); AbleChild Africa (£146,000); Karen Hilltribes Trust (£146,000).

Standard Life Foundation (OSCR no. SC040877)

As of 2017, the foundation's main focus is financial well-being and financial education. At the time of writing (November 2018) the foundation was conducting a review of research into spending and financial well-being. Its website states:

> Following a careful process of evaluation, the Foundation will be commissioning a systematic review of research into the topic of financial well-being.
>
> This independent review will form the key focus of the Foundation's activity in 2018. It will provide the building blocks for the Foundation to make a real and lasting impact to improving financial well-being and resilience across the UK.

In 2017 the foundation had assets of £85.3 million and an income of £81.3 million, nearly all of which was a donation from Standard Life Aberdeen. During the year, the foundation gave a total of £24,000 in one grant to the Edinburgh University Business School for its research review into financial well-being.

Beneficiaries included: Edinburgh University Business School (£24,000).

In-kind support

The group provides three days' paid volunteering leave for employees.

Employee-led support

The group encourages all employees to volunteer and fundraise for charitable projects. Each office has a charity committee which supports local causes.

Standard Life Charity Fund (OSCR no. SC030702)

This fund aims to raise money through various Standard Life Aberdeen UK employee fundraising activities, including a monthly 'Slotto' lottery, local challenges, company-wide initiatives, Give As You Earn scheme and charity raffles. The company also matches employees' fundraising efforts. The fund's income is disbursed to charities chosen by employees. The fund tends to support charities that work in the areas of education and training, health care and disabilities.

In 2017 the total income raised was £319,500 from donations and charitable activities. A grant totalling £229,500 was given to Place2Be, as voted for by employees.

Applications

Aberdeen Standard Investments Charitable Foundation (OSCR no. SC042597)

Application forms are available – along with full criteria and terms and conditions – from the company's website. Completed forms should be returned to the foundation by email (foundation.uk@aberdeen-asset.com), and be accompanied by a PDF copy of your latest annual review. Successful applicants will be notified within three months of their application being submitted. The foundation notes that, due to the volume of applications it receives, it cannot respond to all unsuccessful applicants. Recipients of grants will be required to complete an annual impact assessment form.

Standard Life Foundation (OSCR no. SC040877)

At the time of writing (November 2018) the foundation was not accepting applications. Its website states:

> At the moment we are not taking unsolicited bids for funding or research projects. However, we do aim to undertake a systematic research review in the future and will be asking for expressions of interests on this project in advance. Please contact the Foundation on enquiries@standardlifefoundation.org.uk if you would like to be informed about this project when it is launched.

Corporate charity

Aberdeen Standard Investments Charitable Foundation (OSCR no. SC042597) – see page 229. Standard Life Foundation (OSCR no. SC040877) – see page 279.

Community contributions

Cash donations UK	£81,300,000

The Standard Life Foundation's 2017 accounts state that Standard Life Aberdeen donated a total of £81.3 million in cash during the year. The company also gives support in the form of employee time, matched funding and donations of equipment and services; however, these donations have not been costed.

Stewarts Law LLP

Community development, education, poverty and social exclusion, disability

Company registration number: OC329883

Correspondent: See 'Applications', 5 New Street Square, London EC4A 3BF (tel: 020 7822 8000; website: www.stewartslaw.com/about/social-impact)

Nature of business: Stewarts Law LLP (Stewarts) is a litigation-only law firm in the UK.

Year end	30/04/2017
Turnover	£79,200,000

UK employees: 350

Main locations: The firm has offices in Leeds and London.

Community involvement

The firm awards grants to charities through its corporate charity, The Stewarts Law Foundation (Charity Commission no. 1136714) and has committed £1 million over four years to the Access for Justice Foundation. For the first time in 2017, employees had the opportunity to vote for the firm's Charity of the Year and chose to support CHICKS (Country Holidays for Inner City Kids), a national charity that provides free respite breaks to disadvantaged children. The firm also provides pro bono support.

In-kind support

The firm's website states that its employees provide around 10,000 of pro bono support each year. The firm has partnered with The Legal Service, LawWorks, the National Pro Bono Centre and Justice. Stewarts also accepts pro bono work from Advocates for International Development, a charity that empowers lawyers to use their skills to fight world poverty.

Employee-led support

Employees fundraise and volunteer for their chosen charities, as well as for the firm's Charity of the Year.

Applications

Contact your local office for further information.

Corporate charity

The Stewarts Law Foundation (Charity Commission no. 1136714) – see page 279.

Community contributions

Cash donations UK	£658,000

In 2016/17 the firm donated £658,000 to its corporate charity.

STV Group plc

Children and young people, poverty and social exclusion

Company registration number: SC042391

Correspondent: STV Appeal Team, Pacific Quay, Glasgow G51 1PQ (tel: 0141 300 3000; email: enquiries@stv.tv; website: www.stvplc.tv)

Directors: Anne Cannon; Baroness Ford of Cunninghame; Christian Woolfenden; George Watt; Ian Steele; Simon Pitts; Simon Miller; David Bergg (female 25%; male 75%).

Nature of business: STV Group is a Scottish media company.

Year end	31/12/2017
Turnover	£117,000,000
Pre-tax profit	£13,900,000

Main locations: STV is based in Glasgow but support is given throughout Scotland.

Community involvement

The group's major initiative is the STV Appeal (OCSR no. SC042429), mainly funded by individual donations from STV viewers and fundraising from corporate partners. The appeal was launched in 2011 in partnership with The Hunter Foundation and aims to address child poverty Scotland. It is funded through individual donations from STV viewers and fundraising from corporate partners. The group's employees take part through fundraising and volunteering. The Scottish Government provides matched funding for the first £1 million raised, an arrangement which has been in place since the appeal started.

The money raised goes towards the provision of food and clothing, opportunities for training and employability, also practical, social and emotional support. The STV Appeal's annual report for 2017 notes that from January to December 2017, it invested a total of £2.2 million to support 22 large projects and 234 small projects in every local authority across Scotland.

Employee-led support

The group's employees contribute their time and fundraising efforts to the STV Appeal and raised £113,500 which was matched by the group.

Applications

Applications to the charity are not accepted. Instead, it works with specialists in the field of child poverty and social deprivation who advise the STV Children's Appeal on where it should invest and on which projects require support.

Community contributions

Cash donations UK	£144,500
In-kind support UK	£505,500
Total contributions (cash and in kind)	£650,000

In 2017 STV Group made cash donations of £144,500 and in-kind donations of £505,500 to the STV Appeal.

SuperGroup plc

Education, children and young people

Company registration number: 7063562

Correspondent: CSR Team, Unit 60, The Runnings, Cheltenham, Gloucestershire GL51 9NW (tel: 01242 578376; website: corporate.superdry.com)

Directors: Dennis Millard; Ed Barker; Euan Sutherland; John Smith; Minnow Powell; Penny Hughes; Peter Bamford; Simon Callander (female 13%; male 88%).

Nature of business: Supergroup is a UK clothing company, and owner of the Superdry label.

Year end	28/04/2018
Turnover	£872,000,000
Pre-tax profit	£65,300,000

UK employees: 2,750

Total employees: 4,814

Main locations: The group's head office is based in Cheltenham, but it has retail operations worldwide.

Community involvement

SuperGroup supports education and young people through cash and in-kind donations, work placements, matched funding, and fundraising.

Work experience and placements

Through its 'Superdry School Days programme', the group works with local schools to provide opportunities for students to experience working for the retailer. As part of the programme students are given the opportunity to participate in focus groups, shadow staff members and discuss their future careers with Superdry employees.

The group also has an ongoing partnership with the University of Gloucestershire, providing placements, materials, and support to undergraduates on fashion, graphic design and photography courses.

In-kind support

As part of its partnership with the charity for children with disabilities, Newlife, the group donates its unsellable products, which the charity de-brands and sells to raise funds. To date, garments with a resale value of approximately £126,000 have been donated.

Employee-led support

The group provides matched funding for employee fundraising initiatives internationally. In 2017/18 this totalled £7,200.

Applications

Contact the correspondent for more information.

Community contributions

In 2017/18 SuperGroup raised or donated approximately £451,000. However it was not possible to determine what proportion of this figure came from the company itself.

John Swire & Sons Ltd

Education, health and medical research, general charitable purposes

Company registration number: 133143

Correspondent: Swire House, 59 Buckingham Gate, London SW1E 6AJ (website: www.swire.com/en/sustainability)

Directors: Barnaby Swire; Baroness Lydia Dunn; Gordon McCallum; James Edward Hughes-Hallet; James Wyndham Hughes-Hallet; John Swire; Martin Cubbon; Merlin Swire; Nicholas Fenwick; Samuel Swire; William Wemyss (female 9%; male 91%).

Nature of business: The principal activities of the group are transport, particularly aviation, shipping, cold storage and road transport, industrial and trading activities, and property.

Year end	31/12/2016
Turnover	£7,961,000,000
Pre-tax profit	£291,000,000

Main locations: The company's head office is in London.

Community involvement

John Swire & Sons Ltd appears to direct its charitable contributions through several charities connected to the company.

Corporate charity

The Adrian Swire Charitable Trust (Charity Commission no. 800493) – see page 280. The John Swire (1989) Charitable Trust (Charity Commission no. 802142) – see page 280. The Swire Charitable Trust (Charity Commission no. 270726) – see page 280.

Community contributions

Although the charities listed above all have connections to the company, it is only The Swire Charitable Trust that receives almost all of its income from the company and it is to this charity that we refer.

In 2016 The Swire Charitable Trust received a donation of £1.7 million from John Swire & Sons Ltd.

Syncona Ltd

Health

Correspondent: PO Box 255, Trafalgar Court, Les Banques, St Peter Port, Guernsey GY1 3QL (website: www.synconaltd.com/about-us/charities)

Directors: Ellen Strahlman; Gian Piero Reverberi; Jeremy Tigue; Nick Moss; Nigel Keen; Rob Hutchinson; Thomas Henderson (female 14%; male 86%).

Nature of business: Syncona is an investment company focused on healthcare. It is incorporated in Guernsey as a registered closed-ended investment company.

Year end	31/03/2017

Main locations: The company has an office in Guernsey.

Community involvement

Support is provided through the Syncona Foundation which funds research into cancer and associated diseases.

Corporate charity

The Syncona Foundation (Charity Commission no. 1149202) – see page 281.

Community contributions

Cash donations UK	£4,750,000

The company donates 0.3% of its Net Asset Value to charity each year. In 2016/17 the company's charitable contribution was £4.75 million. Half of the donation goes to The Institute of Cancer Research and half goes to the Syncona Foundation.

TalkTalk Group

Digital skills, safety and security

Company registration number: 7105891

Correspondent: CSR Team, 11 Evesham Street, London W11 4AR (tel: 020 3417 1000; email: concerns@talktalkplc.com; website: www.talktalkgroup.com)

Directors: Cath Keers; Ian West; John Allwood; John Gildersleeve; Kate Ferry; Nigel Langstaff; Phil Jordan; Roger Taylor; Sir Charles Dunstone; Sir Howard Stringer; Tim Morris; Tristia Harrison (female 25%; male 75%).

Nature of business: TalkTalk provides television, telecommunications, Internet access, and mobile network services to businesses and consumers in the United Kingdom.

Year end	31/03/2017
Turnover	£1,783,000,000
Pre-tax profit	£133,000,000

UK employees: 2,226

Main locations: The group operates across the UK.

Community involvement

The group works to improve digital skills, safety and security through financial and in-kind donations to organisations. The group mainly partners with charitable organisations that focus on its priority areas, and it also donates to charities that matter most to employees.

Digital skills

The group works with the Good Things Foundation. The foundation works with a number of partners that come together to create the Online Centres Network, a place where people across the UK can gain support and skills to overcome social challenges.

Digital safety and security

The group supports Get Safe Online, an organisation that provides practical advice on how to protect people, devices and businesses against fraud. The group also launched 'Beat the Scammers', an education and awareness campaign, designed to protect people against scams. To help keep children safe online, the group partnered with BT, Sky and Virgin Media to create Internet Matters, an independent not-for-profit organisation that provides information, support and advice for parents and carers.

The group also joined the Royal Foundation Taskforce on the prevention of cyberbullying, working with industry partners and advisers to ensure families are supported and have the confidence to find appropriate help and resources.

Employee-led support

The group has a scheme called Give Something Back, which allows employees paid time out of work to volunteer and fundraise for charitable causes.

Many TalkTalk employees are trained as Digital Champions, volunteering at the Good Things Foundation's online centres near to TalkTalk offices, helping learners to improve their digital skills. According to the group's website, 'Hundreds of TalkTalk employees also continue to volunteer as digital champions at their local Online Centre, helping learners gain the vital digital skills needed in today's world.'

In the last ten years, the group have raised £3 million on behalf of Ambitious about Autism, the national charity for children and young people with autism. In November 2016, the group raised £403,000 for the charity through hosting a gala dinner.

Employees are also given the opportunity to nominate a registered charity to receive £50 every year from the group.

Applications

Contact the correspondent for further information.

Community contributions

Cash donations UK	£725,000

According to the group's Annual Report 2017, the group donated a total of £725,000.

Beneficiaries included: Internet Matters (£500,000); Internet Watch Foundation (£104,000); Good Things Foundation (£80,000); Get Safe Online (£25,000).

In addition, the group also donated £16,200 to 106 charities across the UK to causes that 'matter most to employees'.

Tata Steel Europe Ltd

Education, the environment, health

Company registration number: 5957565

Correspondent: Nia Singleton, Community Liaison Manager, 30 Millbank, London SW1P 4WY (tel: 020 7717 4444; email: community.support@tatasteel.com; website: www.tatasteeleurope.com)

Directors: Andrew Robb; Bimlendra Jha; Dr Hans Fischer; Koushik Chatterjee; N. K. Misra; Petrus Blauwhoff; T. V. Narendran (female 0%; male 100%).

Nature of business: Tata Steel is involved in the manufacture and sale of steel products. The company is a wholly owned subsidiary of Tata Steel Global Holdings Pte Ltd, an unlisted company based in Singapore. The ultimate parent company is Tata Steel Ltd, incorporated in India.

Year end	31/03/2018
Turnover	£6,988,000,000
Pre-tax profit	£1,382,000,000

Total employees: 1,681

Main locations: Tata Steel has operations throughout the UK, details of which can be found here: www.tatasteeleurope.com/en/careers/locations/locations

Community involvement

The company supports the communities in which it operates through its Community Partnership Programme, which awards donations to organisations under the themes of education, the environment and health and well-being. Support is also offered through education programmes, partnerships and sponsorship.

Community Partnership Programme

The company's Community Partnership Programme supports charitable and non-profit organisations in the communities in which it operates. The main theme of the programme is Future Generations. All funded projects should support Future Generations and align with one of the following sub-themes:

- Education
- Environment
- Health and well-being

Education

Tata Steel proactively supports learning and education with programmes in the UK and Netherlands, particularly in the areas of science and technology. For example, in Wales the company runs interactive sessions with primary and secondary schools and offers advice on careers and skills development. In South Yorkshire meanwhile, the company has partnered with the Titans Community Foundation to deliver an annual event which uses sport as a way of encouraging young people to take an interest in maths and science.

UK Steel Enterprise

UK Steel Enterprise is a subsidiary of Tata Steel. It aims to help the economic regeneration of communities affected by changes in the steel industry through supporting small and medium sized businesses with finance and business premises. In addition, the company also offers in-kind and financial support to various community initiatives. For more information, see the website at: www.uksteelenterprise.co.uk/in-the-community.

Commercially led support

Tata Steel sponsors the Kids of Steel triathlon series, which it launched in partnership with the British Triathlon Federation in 2007, with the aim of introducing young people to the sport. The company also sponsors the annual Tata Steel Chess Tournament, which brings together the world's leading chess players and the most passionate amateurs with its grandmaster groups and amateur events.

Exclusions

The website notes that: 'Tata Steel is not able to offer support to commercial or profit-making organisations. The company is not able to offer donations to individuals, or to cover participation fees, expeditions or trips performed by individuals in the context of fundraising.'

Applications

Applications to the Community Partnership Programme can be made through the company's website: www.tatasteeleurope.com/en/sustainability/communities/community-partnership-programme. Applications are assessed by a panel of representatives from Tata Steel and the communities in which they operate.

Community contributions

The company's 2017/18 accounts did not provide a figure for its community contribution.

Tate & Lyle plc

Health, education (particularly STEM subjects), food poverty

Company registration number: 76535

Correspondent: Community Relations Manager, 1 Kingsway, London WC2B 6AT (tel: 020 7257 2100; email: sustainability@tateandlyle.com; website: www.tateandlyle.com)

Directors: Anne Minto; Douglas Hurt; Dr Ajai Puri; Gerry Murphy; Imran Nawaz; Lars Frederiksen; Nick Hampton; Paul Forman; Sybella Stanley (female 22%; male 78%).

Nature of business: The group is a global provider of ingredients and solutions for the food and beverage industry. The company's UK sugar refinery is in London.

Year end	31/03/2018
Turnover	£2,710,000,000
Pre-tax profit	£286,000,000

Total employees: 4,192

Main locations: The group has operations worldwide; its head office is based in London.

Community involvement

The group's community involvement strategy focuses on the following three areas: health; education (particularly STEM); and food poverty. The group's annual report states that particular emphasis is given to supporting children and young people in these areas.

In addition to its strategic areas of focus, the group has previously also supported organisations working to address environmental issues and homelessness, and has made donations for emergency relief following natural disasters. Support is typically provided through partnerships, cash donations, scholarships, and employee volunteering.

Locally, businesses within the group support community initiatives near to their facilities and offices. At a global level, the group works with a range of partners including, registered charities, educational institutions and non-governmental agencies. In recent years the group has partnered with the homeless charity Crisis in the UK, with universities in Vietnam and America, and with the environment charity Earthwatch.

STEM-focused grants

Each year, the group awards grants to teachers in order to support STEM-focused educational projects, which allow their students to explore careers in science, technology, engineering and mathematics. In addition to funding the projects, group employees are also encouraged to volunteer their time and expertise to help make the projects a success. Projects previously supported include, a project to send weather balloons into space and a project to help students create their own 'how to' YouTube videos to teach others about mathematical formulas

Employee-led support

Employees from businesses across the group are encouraged to volunteer for projects with partner charities as well as with local community initiatives.

Applications

Queries regarding the group's CSR policies or charitable activities can be submitted using an online form on its website: www.tateandlyle.com/contact-us.

Community contributions

Cash donations worldwide	£479,000

In 2017/18 the group's community contributions totalled £479,000. It was not possible to determine from the group's annual accounts what proportion of this figure was given in the UK. Funds were distributed in the following areas: education (33%); Health (32%); Hunger (12%); Environment (10%); other (13%).

Taylor Wimpey plc

Homelessness, poverty and social exclusion, community development, education

Company registration number: 296805

Correspondent: Charity Committee, Gate House, Turnpike Road, High Wycombe, Buckinghamshire HP12 3NR (tel: 01494 558323; website: www.taylorwimpey.co.uk/about-us/who-we-are/charity-and-local-support)

Directors: Angela Knight; Chris Carney; Gwynn Burr; Humphrey Singer; James Jordan; Jennie Daly; Kate Barker; Kevin Beeston; Pete Redfern (female 44%; male 56%).

Nature of business: Taylor Wimpey is one of the UK's largest house-building companies.

Year end	31/12/2017
Turnover	£3,965,200,000
Pre-tax profit	£682,000,000

UK employees: 5,183

Main locations: The group has 24 regional businesses across the UK, divided into North, Central and South West, London and South East divisions, with a head office in High Wycombe. The group also has operations in Spain.

Community involvement

The group supports local, regional and smaller national charities, particularly those local to its development sites, as well as smaller community groups in local areas. It also works with a network of homelessness charities, and supports an annually selected national charity with employee fundraising.

The group's Charity and Community Support Policy outlines the following priorities for its charitable activities.

- Projects which promote aspiration and education in disadvantaged areas
- Intervening and improving homeless situations for seriously economically disadvantaged groups in the UK
- Local projects that have a direct link with our regional businesses and developments

The policy also states that contributions will not be limited to financial support alone, but will also include employee volunteering time.

Partnerships

Taylor Wimpey has several partnerships with national charities as well as local charity partners across the UK. The group's six national charities partners are the Youth Adventure Trust, End Youth Homelessness, Crisis, CRASH (the construction and property industry's charity for the homeless), St Mungo's and Foundations Independent Living Trust. National charity partners are selected by the group's Charity Committee, with regional charities selected by its regional businesses.

Community Development

At sites where the company will be working over a long time period, they may set up Community Development Trusts to support long-term activities or fund community development workers. They also provide sponsorship for community events, local clubs and other community initiatives.

In-kind support

Regional divisions in the company often provide in-kind support such as materials and volunteers for local projects.

Employee-led support

Volunteering

Taylor Wimpey's volunteering policy allows employees to take up to four half-days' (or two full days') paid leave per year to volunteer at one of its national charity partners.

Fundraising

During 2017, employees participated in fundraising events for charitable causes including St Mungo's; The Youth Adventure Trust; CRASH; Crisis UK and Centrepoint. Collectively these efforts raised over £295,000. A notable example of employee fundraising in 2017 was the fourth annual Taylor Wimpey Challenge, organised in partnership with the Youth Adventure Trust (YAT), a charity which provides adventure camps and day activities for disadvantaged young people. The company-wide fundraising event saw 400 staff members attempt to climb 24 Lake District peaks in 24 hours. The event raised £171,000, which was donated to the YAT as well as a selection of charities local to Taylor Wimpey's regional businesses.

Exclusions

Support is generally not given to larger national charities, major events that are able to attract large corporate donors or elicit a national response, or political parties. The company prefers to select causes where employees can be directly involved, rather than simply providing financial assistance. The company's 'Donations Policy' and 'Charity and Community Support Policy' are both available to view on its website.

Applications

Queries regarding support for charities and local community groups can be submitted using an electronic form on the company's website at: www.taylorwimpey.co.uk/about-us/who-we-are/charity-and-local-support.

Community contributions

Cash donations worldwide	£816,000

In 2017 the group donated £816,000 to various charities and community groups, the majority of which were in the UK. This figure does not include funds raised by Taylor Wimpey employees which totalled £295,000 in 2017.

Tesco plc

Community development, health, the environment, general charitable purposes

Company registration number: 445790

Correspondent: Group Corporate Responsibility Team, Tesco Stores Ltd, Tesco House, Shire Park, Kestrel Way, Welwyn Garden City AL7 1GA (tel: 0800 505555; email: cr.enquiries@uk.tesco.com; website: www.tescoplc.com)

Directors: Alan Stewart; Alison Platt; Byron Grote; Dave Lewis; Deanna Oppenheimer; John Allan; Lindsey Pownall; Mark Armour; Mikael Olsson; Robert Welch; Simon Patterson; Steve Golsby; Stewart Gilliland (female 23%; male 77%).

Nature of business: The principal activity of the group is retailing and associated activities in the UK and around the world, including China, the Czech Republic, Hungary, the Republic of Ireland, India, Japan, Malaysia, Poland, Slovakia, South Korea, Thailand and Turkey. The group also provides retail banking and insurance services through its subsidiary, Tesco Bank, mobile services through Tesco Mobile, and petrol station services.

Year end	24/02/2018
Turnover	£57,500,000,000
Pre-tax profit	£1,298,000,000

Total employees: 440,000

Main locations: Tesco operates in the UK and around the world, including China, the Czech Republic, Hungary, the Republic of Ireland, India, Japan, Malaysia, Poland, Slovakia, South Korea, Thailand and Turkey.

Community involvement

The group supports causes including health, children and young people, poverty, social welfare and the environment, through financial donations and in-kind support. The group works with a number of charity partners on different initiatives, and its Community Champions coordinate local charitable and community activities. Further examples of the group's charitable activities, in the UK and internationally, can be found on Tesco's corporate website.

Community Champions

Tesco Community Champions are employees who are responsible for engagement with their local community. They are responsible for co-ordinating activities such as local community events and promoting the group's charitable activities. Community Champions work with local charities to organise in-store activities, including bag packing and store collections. Each store has a budget for community donations, which can be used to respond to requests from local charities.

The store collections scheme allows charities to collect money or food at the front of Tesco stores. (www.tasteattesco.com/Charity.aspx).

Partnerships

Between 2015 and 2017 Tesco ran a national charity partnership with Diabetes UK and British Heart Foundation. During this time, Tesco customers and employees raised over £25 million for the charities. In January 2018, Tesco launched a new charity partnership with Cancer Research UK, Diabetes UK and British Heart Foundation with the aim of promoting healthier living, as well as supporting the prevention and cure of cancer, diabetes and heart disease.

Since 2007, the group has also worked with the charity British Red Cross, supporting them through both financial and in-kind donations, bucket collections and employee fundraising. Through this partnership, Tesco is also a member of the Disaster Relief Alliance which aims to provide preventative support before emergencies occur.

Tesco Charity Trust (Charity Commission no. 297126)

The group previously had a corporate charity, the Tesco Charity Trust. However, in order to enable Tesco to link its community giving to its company strategy and to 'concentrate on maximising communication to customers and colleagues', in July 2015 the trust was collapsed and the funds transferred under the remit of Tesco Stores Ltd. At the time, the trustees stated that the group will 'continue to support charitable activities on a local, national and international basis and to support Tesco colleagues with their charitable activities by providing them with a discretionary 20% top up on their fundraising for their chosen charity'.

In-kind support

Surplus food donation scheme

Tesco has recently partnered with FareShare and the Irish social enterprise FoodCloud to redistribute surplus food from its stores to charities and community groups. Using the FareShare FoodCloud app, stores alert charities to the amount of surplus food they have at the end of each day. This food can then be collected by the charities free of charge and turned into meals for those in need. According to the group's website, in 2016/17 11,424 tonnes of surplus food donations, equivalent to 28.5 million meals, were donated to community organisations. Tesco has set a target to halve its own operational food waste by 2030. In addition, across the UK Tesco has 56 community rooms on its premises, which it makes available for various community classes and activities, including mother and baby groups, dance classes, and digital literacy classes.

Food collection programme

Through its food collection programme run in partnership with the Trussell Trust and FareShare, Tesco encourages customers to donate long-life food to charity using its in-store food collection points. According to the group's website, the December 2016 collection contributed 3.4 million meals to people in need. Following each food collection, Tesco tops-up its customers' donations by 20%.

Employee-led support

Tesco employees can apply for a 20% top-up on their personal fundraising. Tesco automatically tops-up employee fundraising for its charity partners and Cancer Research UK's Race for Life.

Commercially led support

Bags of Help

Tesco distributes funds received through the 5p carrier bag levy through its Bags of Help scheme, a grants programme administered by the charity Groundwork UK. Grants are available for community groups and charities in England, Scotland and Wales. Projects range from improving community buildings and outdoor spaces, to new equipment, training coaches and volunteers, and hosting community events. Customers can vote for the projects they want Tesco to support. Every two months the group awards grants of up to £4,000, £2,000 and £1,000 in 566 regions across the UK. Similar grant schemes are also run in Ireland and Central Europe. Through these schemes the group has to date distributed over £51 million and supported more than 24,000 local projects.

Exclusions

Tesco stores are unable to sponsor events or individuals.

Applications

To request support from a local store, charities should contact their local Community Champion. A list of contact details can be found on the website: www.tescoplc.com/tesco-and-society/supporting-local-communities/supporting-at-a-local-store-level.

Applications for donations of surplus food from Tesco should be made through FareShare FoodCloud – charities can register their interest here: www.FareShare.org.uk/FareShare-foodcloud.

To request permission to do a store collection, register online through the Taste At Tesco website: www.tasteattesco.com/charity-registration.aspx.

For requests for donations and charity-related enquiries, email: customer.service@uk.tesco.com.

For any other enquiries, contact the Group Corporate Responsibility Team at: cr.enquiries@uk.tesco.com.

Community contributions

No overall figure for the group's community contributions was provided.

Thales UK Ltd

Education (particularly STEM subjects), humanitarian aid and disaster relief

Company registration number: 868273

Correspondent: Ethics & Corporate Responsibility Department, 350 Longwater Avenue, Green Park, Reading, Berkshire, United Kingdom RG2 6GF (tel: 0118 943 4500; email: ethics.cr@thalesgroup.com; website: www.thalesgroup.co.uk)

Directors: Alexander Beatty; Denis Plantier; Edwin Awang; Ewen McCrorie; Gareth Williams; Ian Waite; Lynne Watson; Paul Gosling; Philip Naybour; Shaun Jones; Stephen McCann; Stuart Boulton; Suzanne Stratton; Victor Chavez; William Wilby (female 13%; male 87%).

Nature of business: The company is involved in the fields of aerospace, defence, security and transportation. Its activities include the design, manufacture and sale of defence electronic products, encompassing electronic warfare, radar, displays, defence radio and command information systems.

The company's immediate parent company is Thales Holdings UK plc and the ultimate parent company is Thales SA, incorporated in France.

Year end	31/12/2017
Turnover	£1,065,292,000
Pre-tax profit	£125,087,000

UK employees: 5,173

Main locations: In the UK, the group's main locations are: Basingstoke; Belfast; Crawley; Cheadle Heath; Glasgow; Leicester; London; Reading; Templecombe; Wells. The group has operations in 56 countries and is based in France.

Community involvement

The group's 2017 corporate responsibility report states that its community involvement focuses on education, particularly STEM subjects and humanitarian action, particularly 'natural and environmental risk protection and disaster preparedness'. Thales sites tend to support local organisations. The Thales Foundation supports projects nominated by employees globally, while the Thales Charitable Trust (Charity Commission no. 1000162) supports a range of charities in the UK, particularly those focusing on child health and education.

The Thales Charitable Trust

In the UK, the group's corporate charity is The Thales Charitable Trust. The trust makes grants to a range of charitable organisations for purposes such as education, youth, technology, and health. It also supports charities working in sectors relevant to Thales's activities, such as armed services, civil service and rail transport services benevolence funds, those providing medical care for permanent or terminal conditions, those providing humanitarian and crisis support and those working with veterans. In 2017 the trust awarded donations of £110,000.

Thales Foundation

The group also has corporate charities in other countries; the main one being the Thales Foundation in France, which supports projects proposed by employees in any country. The call for projects is held annually in September and projects are centred on the group's two areas of focus: education and prevention of humanitarian crises or natural disasters. In 2017 the foundation supported six education projects and two humanitarian risk reduction projects.

Education

The group works in partnership with Teach First and Women in Science and Engineering (WISE) as well as with schools and universities to encourage engagement with STEM subjects.

Employee-led support

The Thales Foundation supports projects proposed by employees and has a network of employee ambassadors who promote its activities and lead employee involvement in the foundation's community projects.

Commercially led support

In the UK, the company sponsors a number of charity events each year, including The Railway Children charity's annual ball and Military Mind Corporate Symposium organised by Combat Stress.

Applications

Contact the correspondent for more information.

Corporate charity

The Thales Charitable Trust (Charity Commission no. 1000162) – see page 281.

Community contributions

Cash donations UK	£175,000

The company's accounts for 2017 did not provide a figure for its community contribution. However, according to the accounts of The Thales Charitable Trust, during the year the company made a donation of £175,000.

Thames Water Ltd

The environment, health

Company registration number: 2366623

Correspondent: The Community Investment Team, Clearwater Court, Vastern Road, Reading RG1 8DB (email: community.investment@thameswater.co.uk; website: www.thameswater.co.uk)

Directors: Brandon Rennet; Christopher Deacon; Ed Richards; Greg Pestrak; Ian Marchant; Ian Pearson; Kenton Bradbury; Lorraine Baldry; Nick Fincham; Nick Land; Steve Robertson (female 9%; male 91%).

Nature of business: Thames Water is responsible for public water supply and waste water treatment.

Year end	31/03/2018
Turnover	£2,044,900,000
Pre-tax profit	£150,800,000

UK employees: 6,245

Main locations: The company's head office is in Reading. The Thames Water area covers parts of: London, Surrey, Berkshire, Gloucestershire and Wiltshire.

Community involvement

Support is mainly provided through funding to charities in the Thames Water area which have a link to water and the environment or water and healthy living.

Charitable support

Charities within the Thames Water supply area can apply for charitable support from the company. The Charities Committee guidelines state the following:

> Whilst we are a large organisation, we do not have unlimited funds. The Charities Committee has therefore agreed to support organisations or projects where there is a good link to our core business of water supply and wastewater treatment which falls under the following criteria:
>
> **Water and the environment –** Our focus is on enhancing the quality of life within urban areas by improving open spaces, especially natural environments that are adjacent to water – for example rivers or canals. By 'environment' we mean the environment in which people live as well as the natural environment.
>
> **Water and healthy living –** We support projects that encourage individuals to look after their own health and encourage a healthy lifestyle through the benefits of water.

Community speakers

The company has several community speakers which are available to speak to community groups on what the company does and how to be more water efficient.

Charity partnership

The company has a long-term partnership with WaterAid which has seen over £35 million donated to the charity through customer and employee fundraising since 1981.

Schools

There is a schools education programme which includes education centres, talks in schools and online resources.

In-kind support

The company gives employees two volunteering days per year.

Employee-led support

Employees are encouraged to fundraise and volunteer for charitable organisations. The company's matched funding scheme matches employee's fundraising efforts up to a maximum of £2,000 for registered charities. There is also a payroll giving scheme in place. The company adds an extra 10% to employee donations.

Exclusions

According to the grant guidelines, the following are not supported:

- Advertisements, sponsorship or tickets for fundraising events
- Political and sectarian activities
- Organisations with a racial or religious bias
- Individuals fundraising for national charities
- Individuals fundraising for personal challenges (non-charitable)
- Salaries/project management fees, etc
- Overseas charities other than our principal charity, WaterAid
- Projects outside of the Thames Water region

Applications

Application forms can be downloaded from the company's website. Speaker request forms can also be downloaded from the website.

Community contributions

We were unable to determine the company's charitable contributions.

the7stars UK Ltd

Children and young people

Company registration number: 5387218

Correspondent: Alexandra Taliodoros, Foundation Director, Floor 6–8, Melbourne House, 46 Aldwych, London WC2B 4LL (website: www.the7starsfoundation.co.uk)

Directors: Anuschka Clarke; Gareth Jones; Henry Dalglish; Jennifer Biggam; Liam Mullins; Nicholas Maddison; Rhiannon Murphy (female 43%; male 57%).

Nature of business: the7stars is an independent media agency.

Year end	31/03/2017
Turnover	£245,500,000
Pre-tax profit	£2,500,000

Main locations: The company's head office is in London.

Community involvement

the7stars' community contributions are made through its corporate charity, the7stars Foundation (Charity Commission no. 1168240), which supports children in the priority areas of homelessness, abuse, addiction and child carers.

Applications

Applicants are directed to the7stars foundation's website, where application forms are available to download. Completed forms can be returned to the Foundation Director by email. The Foundation Director can be contacted with any questions about your application, the application form or the application process.

Corporate charity

the7stars Foundation (Charity Commission no. 1168240) – see page 282.

Community contributions

Cash donations UK	£141,000

In 2016/17 the company made a donation of £141,000 to its corporate charity the7stars Foundation.

Thomson Reuters

Human rights, education, women's rights, journalism

Company registration number: 145516

Correspondent: Corporate Responsibility Team, The Thomson Reuters Building, 30 South Colonnade, Canary Wharf, London E14 5EP (tel: 020 7542 7015; email: foundation@thomsonreuters.com; website: www.thomsonreuters.com)

Directors: Giray Erol; Justin Scott; Peter Thorn; Timothy Knowland (female 0%; male 100%).

Nature of business: Thomson Reuters is an international news agency headquartered in London. It is a division of the Thomson Reuters Corporation a Canadian multinational mass media and information firm.

Year end	31/12/2017
Turnover	£1,401,000,000
Pre-tax profit	(£24,000,000)

Total employees: 4,565

Main locations: In the UK, the company's head office is in London. Thomson Reuters has around 110 offices worldwide.

Community involvement

The company's charitable giving is mainly directed through its corporate charity, the Thomson Reuters Foundation (Charity Commission no. 1082139) which supports human rights, education, women's rights, journalism and legal aid. Support is also provided through employee volunteering, fundraising and matched funding.

Thomson Reuters Foundation

The foundation was established in 2000 to promote socio-economic progress and the rule of law worldwide. It acts as an impact multiplier, leveraging the skills, expertise and values of the Thomson Reuters enterprise to run programmes that inform, connect and ultimately empower people around the world. Thomson Reuters delivers its pro bono programme through the foundation.

There are four main programmes:

- **TrustLaw** – TrustLaw is the foundation's pro bono legal programme which connects legal firms and NGOs around the world
- **World's under-reported stories** – the foundation covers stories related to human rights, human trafficking and women's rights that are often overlooked by the mainstream media
- **Media development and training** – the foundation promotes high standards in journalism globally
- **Trust women** – the foundation takes action to put the rule of law behind women's rights and to fight modern day slavery

In-kind support

In-kind support is given to the Thomas Reuters Foundation, including office space, communications, computer equipment, also marketing services, licences, staff time and trainers, lending of tools, advertising platform and legal collateral.

The foundation's accounts note that employees' pro bono work was valued at \$24 million (≈ £19 million as at December 2018).

Employee-led support

Community Champion Awards

The annual Community Champion Awards program celebrates the volunteering efforts of Reuters' employees. Winners of the award receive a substantial donation for a cause of their choice.

Matched funding

The company operates a 'matching gifts programme', whereby employees' charitable donations to registered charities are matched up to \$1,000 (≈ £774 as at October 2018) a year.

Volunteering

Employee volunteering is coordinated by the company's 'Global Volunteer Networks' – employee-led groups which drive volunteering efforts across the company's office locations, by arranging volunteering activities, supporting local projects and developing long-lasting relationships with community partners.

Each year employees are given two days to volunteer in their local communities. In addition, through the company's 'Volunteer Grants' programme, employees that volunteer for more than 20 hours can receive a charitable grant of up to \$1,000 (≈ £774 as at October 2018) per year. In 2017 employees volunteered over 177,000 hours to charitable organisations and causes across the world.

Applications

Thomson Reuters Foundation does not consider unsolicited requests for support.

Other enquiries relating to the company's CSR policies should be directed to the CSR Team.

Community contributions

Cash donations worldwide	£5,000,000

In 2017 the company awarded charitable donations of £5 million. This primarily consisted of donations to Thomson Reuters Foundation.

TI Media Ltd (formerly Time Inc. UK Ltd)

General charitable purposes

Company registration number: 53626

Correspondent: Jane Mortimore, Corporate Responsiblity Manager, Blue Fin Building, 110 Southwark Street, London SE1 0SU (tel: 020 3148 5404; email: jane.mortimore@ti-media.com; website: www.ti-media.com)

Directors: Adrian Hughes; Andrea Davies; Angela O'Farrell; Marcus Rich; Neil Robinson; Samuel Finlay (female 33%; male 67%).

Nature of business: TI Media specialises in the publication of print and digital magazines.

Year end	31/12/2017
Turnover	£221,055,000
Pre-tax profit	(£13,681,000)

Main locations: The company has offices in London, Birmingham and Farnborough.

Community involvement

TI Media supports communities through charity partnerships, pro bono work, employee fundraising and volunteering. Ad hoc support is also given to organisations local to the company's offices in the form of cash or in-kind donations.

Partnerships

Every two years TI Media employees nominate a charity partner for which employees fundraise and lend their time and skills. In 2017 TI Media launched a new partnership with Rainbow Trust which supports families who have a child aged up to 18 years of age with a life threatening or terminal illness. During the year, the company donated a total of £28,500 to the charity through fundraising, in-kind support and volunteering time.

In support of its CSR programme, the company is also a member of the Responsible Media Forum, The Heart of the City and the Professional Publishers Association's Sustainability Action Group. For more information, see the company's website.

Other charitable support

According to its website, the company also leverages support for charities through its brands. Recent examples include, woman&home which has a long-standing partnership with Breast Cancer Care, and Decanter which has raised more than £500,000 for the charity WaterAid from its readers and website users.

Support in the form of financial or in-kind donations is also given on an ad hoc basis to charities whose work is aligned to the company's key corporate responsibility priorities.

Educational Initiatives

TI Media works with local schools, colleges, universities and charities to give young people aged 16 to 24, the opportunity to learn about careers in the creative sector. Working with the charity A New Direction, the company provides career advice, hosts workshops, and invites students to attend creative masterclasses.

In-kind support

Staff are encouraged to contribute their skills and expertise to local causes and partner charities, as well as through the company's own educational initiatives. According to the website, in 2017 employees provided editorial and advertising support to 25 UK charities.

Employee-led support

Employee volunteering

According to the company's website, staff are offered the opportunity to contribute to their communities through skilled volunteering, which uses their media skills and expertise, as well as more general activities such as primary school reading activities or by taking part in a team challenge. Employees can request up to two days' paid time per year for volunteering purposes. In 2017 employees volunteered for a total of 600 hours.

Employee fundraising

Employees take part in various fundraising activities, including for the company's chosen charity partner. Examples of fundraising challenges mentioned on the website include, charity runs, walks and skydives. Fundraising events and activities within the company's offices are arranged by the company's charity champions.

Payroll giving

Employees are able to donate to charities through a payroll giving scheme.

Applications

Apply in writing to the correspondent.

Community contributions

The company's accounts for 2017 did not declare a figure for its charitable donations. The company's website states that it made corporate responsibility contributions of £3.1 million. However, it was not possible to determine what proportion of this figure came from the company itself.

Timpson Group plc

Looked-after children, homelessness, poverty and social exclusion, offenders and ex-offenders

Company registration number: 2339274

Correspondent: See 'Applications', Timpson House, Claverton Road, Wythenshawe, Manchester M23 9TT (tel: 0161 946 6228; website: www.timpson-group.co.uk)

Directors: James Timpson OBE; Paresh Majithia; Roger Lane-Smith; Sir John Timpson; Stephen Robertson (female 0%; male 100%).

Nature of business: Timpson specialises in shoe repairs, key cutting and engraving, as well as dry cleaning and photo processing.

Year end	30/09/2017
Turnover	£260,103,000
Pre-tax profit	£12,629,000

UK employees: 4,944

Main locations: The group operates stores across the UK.

Community involvement

The group's charitable activities are delivered through the Timpson Foundation, which supports the training and employment of ex-offenders and the Alex Timpson Trust, which supports foster families and promotes excellence among small schools.

The Alex Timpson Trust (Charity Commission no. 1174098)

In October 2017, the Alex Timpson Trust became the official company charity of the Timpson Group. The trust was founded in tribute to Alex Timpson MBE who died in January 2016. The charity's main aim is to help schools better respond to the emotional needs of looked after (fostered and adopted) children. To achieve this aim the trust supports the development of training courses on attachment awareness. The trust has also made three books on attachment awareness written by John Timpson freely available from Timpson Group stores. A donation of £750,000 from the trust will be used to fund a new research programme at the Rees Centre for Research in Fostering and Education at Oxford University. The donation will be released over the course of a five-year period, and will be used to establish the Timpson Attachment Programme, a research initiative focused on attachment awareness.

In addition, the trust also provides free holidays for foster families in three holiday lodges purchased exclusively for this purpose. Nominations can be made at any Timpson, Max Photo, Johnsons or Timpson at Morrisons store.

The Timpson Foundation

The Timpson Foundation focuses on the rehabilitation and recruitment of prisoners and other marginalised groups within society. As part of its work, the foundation runs training workshops in prisons and offers prisoners eligible for release on temporary license (ROTL) to gain work experience in its stores.

Free Jobs scheme

Through Timpson's Free Jobs scheme, employees are encouraged to provide services (such as punching a hole for a belt or stitching a shoe) free of charge but request that customers make an in-store charitable contribution. The scheme has previously helped to raise over £4 million for children's charities. In future, funds raised by the scheme will be used to support the work of the Alex Timpson Trust.

Applications

Apply in writing to the trustees of either the Timpson Foundation or the Alex Timpson Trust.

Community contributions

Cash donations UK	£299,000

According to the group's 2016/17 annual report, during the year the group made donations of £299,000 for charitable purposes. In addition, a £583,000 was spent on Timpson Foundation programmes to assist with the rehabilitation and training of ex-offenders.

TJX UK

Education, children and young people, health and medical research, general charitable purposes

Company registration number: 3094828

Correspondent: Local TK Maxx Stores, 50 Clarendon Road, Watford, Hertfordshire WD17 1TX (tel: 01923 473561; website: www.tkmaxx.com/page/community)

Directors: David Averill; John Klinger; Mary Reynolds (female 33%; male 67%).

Nature of business: The main activity of TJX UK is the retail of brand name merchandise through TK Maxx and HomeSense stores, as well as the TKMaxx.com website.

TJX UK's immediate parent company is TJX Europe Ltd and its ultimate parent company and controlling party is The TJX Companies, Inc., incorporated in Delaware, USA.

Year end	03/02/2018
Turnover	£2,968,600,000
Pre-tax profit	£87,100,000

Main locations: There are TK Maxx stores nationwide and HomeSense stores in England, Scotland and Wales. See the store search facility for details of TK Maxx and HomeSense locations (www.tkmaxx.com/store-locator/page/storelocator).

Community involvement

Globally, TJX's community strategy focuses on the following areas:

- Fulfilling critical basic needs for disadvantaged children and young people
- Providing education and training
- Supporting research and care for life-threatening illnesses
- Preventing domestic violence in the US and Canada
- Disaster relief in the areas where TJX has a presence

It does this in three ways:

- Giving through its foundations in the US, Canada and the UK
- Cause marketing and in-store fundraising
- Employee volunteering, fundraising and giving

In the UK, TJX supports its long-term charity partners through customer and employee fundraising and supports local and national children charities through its corporate charity, the TJX UK Foundation (Charity Commission no. 1162073).

Partnerships

The group has a number of long-term partnerships. In the UK, TK Maxx has long-term partnerships with:

- **Cancer Research UK** – support is given through cause-related marketing, in-store fundraising and the clothing donation programme, Give Up Clothes For Good. Through the programme, people drop off their high-quality, used clothes, accessories, and homeware at TK Maxx stores for donation to Cancer Research UK. The items are then sold at Cancer Research UK charity shops to raise funds
- **Comic Relief** – in 2017 it was the official t-shirt retailer for the charity
- **The Prince's Trust** – it supports the trust's Get Into Retail programme and delivered 15 programmes to over 200 young people in 2017
- **The Woodland Trust** – teams of employees plant trees to help preserve native woodland
- **Enable Ireland** – in the Republic of Ireland TK Maxx raises money for the charity via the Give Up Clothes For Good programme

Commercially led support

Christmas Sock Day

TK Maxx celebrated Christmas Sock Day on 6 December to help raise funds for its partner charity Cancer Research UK. Official Christmas Socks were sold at TK Maxx stores with a proportion of the proceeds from the sale of each pack donated to the charity. Children's designs were priced from £2.99 and adults' from £4.99, with at least 99p donated from children's sales and £2 from adults'. The socks were sold alongside other 'socking fillers' including chocolate lollipops and Christmas cards.

People were encouraged to take a photo of them wearing their Christmas socks and show their support for the event on social media using the hashtag #socksie. For each #socksie photo uploaded on Twitter, Facebook or Instagram, TK Maxx donated £1 to Cancer Research UK.

The Sport Relief apron

Ltd edition aprons created by the designer Orla Kiely were sold at TK Maxx and HomeSense stores, as well as online, to raise funds for Sport Relief 2016. The apron, which featured on The Great Sport Relief Bake Off, was available for £12.99, with £5.25 from the sale of each product donated to Sport Relief, which benefits some of the most disadvantaged people in the UK and around the world.

Comic Relief T-shirts

In aid of Comic Relief, TK Maxx stores sell specially designed t-shirts from which all net profits are donated. According to the website, 'the T-shirts are wholly manufactured in Africa, with 100% of the cotton sourced from Fair Trade certified organic cotton co-operatives in Mali. This ensures good quality, pesticide and GM free cotton and a fair price for the farmers.'

Bags for life and carrier bag sales

As part of TK Maxx's support for Cancer Research UK, the charity has received donations from the profits generated by sales of bags for life.

The Woodland Trust receives all money raised from sales of carrier bags in Welsh stores.

Clothes collections

The public can donate unwanted items of clothing at TK Maxx stores which host permanent donation points. The clothing is then sold by Cancer Research UK, with each bag generating as much as £25.

Applications

In reference to the major charities supported by TJX UK, the annual report 2015/16 states that 'All charity initiatives within the business were directed towards these organisations'. Support from The Community Fund is given to charities which are important to TJX employees and customers.

For more information regarding the global community involvement activities of The TJX Companies, Inc., see the 'Communities' section of the website (www.tjx.com/corporate/communities.html).

Corporate charity

TJX UK Foundation (Charity Commission no. 1162073) – see page 282.

Community contributions

Cash donations UK	£2,100,000

The 2017/18 annual report states that 'Company, community fund donations and fundraising activities came to the value of £9.4 million'. We were unable to determine how much of this came from TJX and how much was raised through customer and employee donations. The 2017/18 accounts for the foundation state that it received £2.1 million from TJX UK during the year. We have taken this figure as the TJX UK's total cash contribution.

Beneficiaries included: Cancer Research UK, Comic Relief and The Prince's Trust.

TLT LLP

General charitable purposes

Company registration number: OC308658

Correspondent: CSR Team, One Redcliff Street, Bristol BS1 6TP, United Kingdom (tel: 0333 006 0000; website: www.tltsolicitors.com)

Nature of business: TLT LLP is a law firm with expertise in financial services, clean energy, retail, digital, real estate and the public sector.

Year end	30/04/2017
Turnover	£73,500,000

Total employees: 849

Main locations: The company's UK offices are in Bristol, London, Manchester, Glasgow, Edinburgh, and Belfast. The company also has an office in Piraeus, Greece.

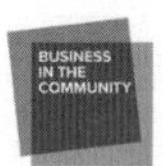

Community involvement

The company supports a wide range of charitable purposes across the UK. The company offers pro bono legal advice and supports charities and community groups through cash donations and employee-led volunteering and fundraising.

In-kind support

The company offers pro bono support for organisations and people that might not otherwise be able to get the legal advice they need. The company's pro bono work recently included support for the Island Trust, a charity that provides sailing opportunities for disadvantaged young people. In addition to legal advice, the company also provided cash donations to the charity and hosted a launch event at its offices.

Employee-led support

TLT employees are given three hours paid leave every month to volunteer for a charity, school or other community enterprise of their choice. Recent projects supported include, a Bristol-based reading and mentoring scheme for young people and reading, listening and speaking workshops for 4- to 11-year-olds in Tower Hamlets.

Each year employees in each of the company's UK offices vote for a dedicated charity to support for the financial year. The charities chosen for 2018/19 include: Northern Ireland Hospice, Children's Hospice South West, Solidarity Sports, Mustard Tree, and the Scottish Association of Mental Health.

Applications

Apply in writing to the correspondent.

Community contributions

The company's accounts did not provide a figure for its total community contributions.

Tottenham Hotspur Ltd

Health and well-being, community cohesion, education, equalities and inclusion

Company registration number: 1706358

Correspondent: Tottenham Hotspur Foundation, Percy House, 796 High Road, Tottenham, London N17 0DH (tel: 020 8365 5138; email: foundation@tottenhamhotspur.com; website: www.tottenhamhotspur.com/the-club/charities)

Directors: Daniel Levy; Donna-Maria Cullen; Kevan Watts; Matthew Collecott; Rebecca Caplehorn; Ron Robson (female 33%; male 67%).

Nature of business: Tottenham Hotspur FC is a professional football club competing in the Premier League.

Year end	30/06/2017
Turnover	£306,321,000
Pre-tax profit	£57,866,000

UK employees: 439

Main locations: The club's community activities are mainly delivered in North London especially in the Haringey and Enfield districts.

Community involvement

The club's charitable activities are mostly directed through the club's charity the Tottenham Hotspur Foundation (Charity Commission no. 1113725) which delivers a wide range of education, sport and employability programmes across North London.

Tottenham Hotspur Foundation

The Tottenham Hotspur Foundation works with a variety of partners to deliver a wide range of themed programmes in communities across North London. The foundation's community work is intended to impact four key areas of focus:

- Health and well-being
- Community cohesion
- Education
- Equalities and inclusion

Recent examples of the foundation's programmes include:

- **Your Future:** A programme aimed at engaging and helping young people who have experienced injury or trauma through violence via a sport-based mentoring project
- **Premier League International:** Delivered in partnership with charity Slum Soccer, this programme helps children in India to improve their football skills, develop positive behaviour, build their self-esteem and steer them away from potential unemployment or crime
- **Get up and go:** A free exercise class for residents of Green Towers Community Centre run in partnership with the Metropolitan Housing Association in Wood Green

Full details of all the foundations current programmes can be found on the club's website.

Partnerships

The club has an official charity partner on a two-year cycle. The club's current partner is Noah's Ark Children's Hospice – North London's only hospice-at-home service offering support to children and young people with life-limiting or life-threatening illnesses and their families. The partnership aims to raise awareness of the charity's work and drive recruitment of volunteers.

Spurs Wishes

The Spurs Wishes initiative was launched in 2011 and exists separately from the club's foundation. It brings together the club's staff, management and players to assist terminally ill fans by giving them memorable experiences.

Tottenham Tribute Trust (Charity Commission no. 1094092)

The Tottenham Tribute Trust was set up in 2002 to help individuals connected with the football club who have fallen on difficult times. The trust was created as a joint initiative between the club and its supporters and, although run by a board of trustees independent of the club, it continues to work closely with the club. For more information see: www.tottenhamtt.org.

Exclusions

The club's website notes that national charitable initiatives, for example disaster appeals, Sport Relief or Children in Need, are responded to centrally by the club so individual applications for such causes are not accepted.

Applications

General enquiries can be submitted in writing to the correspondent.

Spurs Wishes

Appeals to Spurs Wishes should be sent via email to: spurs.wishes@tottenhamhotspur.com.

Community contributions

Cash donations worldwide	£112,500

According to the company's annual report and accounts for 2016/17, the group made cash donations totalling

£112,500 to international, UK-based and local charities during the year. The accounts also note that 'the group continues to make contributions with a value in excess of £0.5m per annum' to the foundation and 'continues to underwrite the ongoing good works of the charity'.

Town Centre Securities plc

General charitable purposes

Company registration number: 623364

Correspondent: Charlotte Daisy Ziff, CSR Co-ordinator, Town Centre House, The Merrion Centre, Leeds LS2 8LY (tel: 0113 222 1234; email: info@tcs-plc.co.uk; website: tcs-plc.co.uk)

Directors: Ben Ziff; Edward Ziff; Ian Marcus; Jeremy Collins; Mark Dilley; Michael Ziff; Paul Huberman; Richard Lewis (female 0%; male 100%).

Nature of business: Town Centre Securities is a property development group.

Year end	30/06/2017
Turnover	£27,540,000
Pre-tax profit	£6,275,000

UK employees: 116

Main locations: The company owns properties across the UK, including in transport hubs such as Leeds, London, Manchester, Edinburgh and Glasgow. The company's offices are in Leeds and London.

Community involvement

The company supports a wide range of charitable organisations, with some preference given to those operating in the area close to its head office in Leeds. Support is provided through cash donations and fundraising initiatives. In 2016/17 the company partnered with a number of charities including, Candlelighters, The Leeds Jewish Welfare Board, Variety The Children's Charity, LionHeart, The British Legion and Autism Angels. The company also has ongoing partnerships with a number of schools in Leeds. According to its website, the company is currently 'actively seeking further partnerships and opportunities'.

Applications

Contact the correspondent for more information.

Community contributions

Cash donations UK	£78,000

In 2016/17 the company made charitable donations totalling £78,000.

Beneficiaries included: Autism Angels; The British Legion; Candlelighters; Leeds Jewish Welfare Board; Lion Heart.

Toyota Motor Manufacturing (UK) Ltd

Social inclusion, road safety, health, the environment

Company registration number: 2352348

Correspondent: CSR Team, Burnaston, Derbyshire, East Midlands DE1 9TA (tel: 01332 282121; email: external.affairs@toyotauk.com; website: www.toyotauk.com)

Directors: Akito Takami; Dr Johanes Van Zyl; Hiroyuki Hatakeyama; James Crosbie; Marvin Cooke; Shigeru Teramoto (female 0%; male 100%).

Nature of business: Toyota Motor Manufacturing (UK) is a car and engine manufacturer.

Year end	31/03/2017
Turnover	£2,499,000,000
Pre-tax profit	£37,966,000

UK employees: 3,000

Main locations: The company has plants in Deeside (North Wales) and Burnston (Derbyshire).

Community involvement

Toyota supports community groups, charities and schools in the areas surrounding its plants in Deeside (North Wales) and Burnston (Derbyshire). Support is provided through cash and in-kind donations, employee volunteering and fundraising, and educational programmes. According to its website, the company's main charitable areas of focus are social deprivation/inclusion, road safety and health, although the company does also support some environmental causes.

In addition, assistance is provided through the company's corporate charity the Toyota Manufacturing UK Charitable Trust (Charity Commission no. 1124678) which awards grants to organisations that support one or more of the company's charitable areas of focus.

Public visit programme

Toyota runs a public visit programme that allows members of the local community, businesses and schools to visit the company's plants to learn more about their operations and company culture. The programme typically runs between April and November each year.

School programme

As part of its school programme, Toyota offers a range of educational programmes from primary, secondary and sixth form students. These programmes are designed to inspire young people to achieve their full potential and choose STEM-based subjects and careers. Full details of all of the company's current education programmes are provided on its website.

Toyota Fund for Europe

The Toyota Fund for Europe (TFfE) operates at a pan-European level to support a wide range of projects in European countries in which Toyota has operations. The fund supports projects in the areas of the environment, road safety and education. Each local Toyota company operates its own funding to support local projects. Your proposal will be evaluated by the local Toyota company, following its own selection criteria. Further details about the fund can be found on the company's website.

Employee-led support

Employee involvement in the community is encouraged and, where suitable, supported financially through the company's corporate charity. The company is a member of Business in the Community and participates in its 'Give and Gain' programme – a nationwide day of volunteering.

Applications

Public visits

Community groups can register their interest in visiting a site on the company's website. Primary or secondary schools wishing to arrange a visit should email the company's Learning and Development Team at: schoolprogrammes@toyotauk.com.

General enquiries

General enquiries regarding the company's corporate responsibility should be submitted in writing to the correspondent.

Corporate charity

Toyota Manufacturing UK Charitable Trust (Charity Commission no. 1124678) – see page 282.

Community contributions

Total contributions (cash and in kind)	£750,000

In 2016/17 the company made charitable donations amounting to a total of €845,000 (≈ £750,000 as at September 2018). These donations comprised: €4,000 (≈ £3,600 as at September 2018) donated to charities involved in conserving the environment and promoting environmental awareness; €180,000 (≈ £160,000 as at September 2018) donated to charities involved in medical, health and human service research; and €661,000 (≈ £587,500 as at September 2018) donated to local charities and community groups in Burnaston and Deeside. It is unclear if these figures include the value of in-kind donations.

Trailfinders Ltd

Medical research, youth community projects, the armed forces

Company registration number: 1004502

Correspondent: 48 Earls Court Road, London W8 6FT (email: trailfinders@trailfinders.com; website: www.trailfinders.com)

Directors: Anthony Russell; David Ness; Edwin Lee; Fiona Gooley; Gareth Dyer; Mark West; Matthew Raymond; Michael Gooley; Nikki Davies; Ross Simpson; Russell McHardy; Toby Kelly; Tristan Gooley (female 15%; male 85%).

Nature of business: Trailfinders is a travel company based in the UK and Ireland.

Year end	28/02/2018
Turnover	£719,000,000
Pre-tax profit	£35,800,000

UK employees: 990

Main locations: The company operates from 31 travel centres in the UK and three in Ireland.

Community involvement

The majority of Trailfinders' community involvement is directed through its corporate charity, The Mike Gooley Trailfinders Charity (Charity Commission no. 1048993) which makes grants to charities. Occasionally, the company makes cash donations directly to charities.

Corporate charity

The Mike Gooley Trailfinders Charity (Charity Commission no. 1048993) – see page 283.

Community contributions

Cash donations UK	£10,000,000

In 2017/18 the company donated £10 million to charity, of which £9 million was awarded to its corporate charity. A further £75,000 was awarded to Great Ormond Street Hospital and £1,500 was awarded to SSAFA.

Travis Perkins plc

Disability and health, poverty and social exclusion

Company registration number: 824821

Correspondent: CSR Team, Lodge Way House, Harlestone Road, Northampton NN5 7UG (tel: 01604 752424; email: communications@travisperkins.co.uk; website: www.travisperkinsplc.co.uk)

Directors: Alan Williams; Christopher Rogers; Coline McConville; John Carter; John Rogers; Pete Redfern; Ruth Anderson; Stuart Chambers; Tony Buffin (female 22%; male 78%).

Nature of business: Travis Perkins group is involved in marketing and distribution of timber, building and plumbing materials and the hiring of tools to the building trade and industry generally.

Year end	31/12/2017
Turnover	£6,433,000,000
Pre-tax profit	£290,000,000

Total employees: 29,776

Main locations: The group has operations throughout the UK. Its head office is in Northampton.

Community involvement

Charitable activities are generally organised by each of the businesses within the group. Each one has a partnership with a different national charity selected by employees. Most recently, poverty, disability and health charities have been supported.

Corporate partnerships

Each of the group's 20+ businesses support a charity chosen by its employees. The charities chosen usually support children and/or adults affected by poverty, disability or ill health in the UK.

Current partnerships include: Alzheimer's Research UK (partner of Wickes); Anthony Nolan (partner of Tile Giant); Prostate Cancer UK (partner of Keyline and Travis Perkins Masters Golf); and RNLI (partner of Toolstation).

Local support

Support for assistance for a local community project or charity may also be provided by individual stores or branches.

Employee-led support

Employee fundraising activities include a Colleague Lottery, as well as payroll giving and other employee-led initiatives. Fundraising and volunteering activities are generally organised by each business individually.

Applications

Corporate charity partnerships

At the time of writing (October 2018) the group's website states:

> We've a number of long standing corporate charity partnerships across our businesses. **At this moment in time, we are not looking for any new corporate sponsors or partners.** However, if you would like to flag your interest in becoming a corporate charity partner in the future, please email: communications@travisperkins.co.uk

Local support

The group's website states: 'If you would like to request support or assistance for a local community project or charity, please contact your local branch or store direct.'

Community contributions

The annual report states that the group's fundraising activities totalled over £1 million in 2017. It was not specified how much of this was from the company and how much was from employee fundraising.

Tullis Russell Group Ltd

General charitable purposes

Company registration number: SC150075

Correspondent: Rothersfield, Markinch, Fife KY7 6PB (tel: 01592 753311; website: www.trg.co.uk)

Directors: Frederick Bowden; Geoffrey Miller; Michael Arrowsmith; Michael Thompson; Stephen Dorgan (female 0%; male 100%).

Nature of business: Tullis Russell Group is an employee-owned industrial holding company, providing management services. The principal subsidiary companies are involved in the manufacture of papers, boards and other paper products for clients worldwide.

Year end	01/04/2017
Turnover	£35,009,000
Pre-tax profit	£2,491,000

Main locations: Historically the company had a site in Fife. It has since moved operations to Bollington in Cheshire.

Community involvement

The 2016/17 annual report and accounts state that donations were all made to local charitable organisations in order to support the community. The majority of the company's giving is through its corporate charity, the Russell Trust (OSCR no. SC004424) which makes grants to organisations in Fife.

Corporate charity

Russell Trust (OSCR no. SC004424) – see page 275.

Community contributions

Cash donations UK	£251,000

The group declared cash donations of £251,000 in 2016/17, of which £250,000 was donated to the Russell Trust.

Turner and Townsend Ltd

Social mobility, education (particularly STEM subjects and literacy)

Company registration number: 6468643

Correspondent: CSR Team, Low Hall, Calverley Lane/Low Hall Road, Horsforth, Leeds LS18 4GH (tel: 0113 258 4400; email: csr@turntown.com; website: www.turnerandtownsend.com)

Directors: James Dand; Jeremy Lathom-Sharp; Jon White; Murray Rowden; Patricia Moore; Sean Christie; Vincent Clancy (female 14%; male 86%).

Nature of business: Turner and Townsend is a professional services company specialising in project management, cost management and consulting across the property, infrastructure and natural resources sectors.

Year end	30/04/2018
Turnover	£548,667,000
Pre-tax profit	£54,672,000

UK employees: 2,554

Total employees: 5,209

Main locations: The group operates globally with 108 offices in 45 countries. In the UK, the group works from 17 offices across England, Scotland, and Northern Ireland.

Community involvement

Turner and Townsend support a wide range of charitable purposes with a focus on education and social mobility. Support is offered in the form of cash donations, pro bono services, partnerships and employee fundraising and volunteering.

Education fund

The group works in partnership with the charity Action for Children to provide grants of £50 for disadvantaged children and families to pay for school supplies. In 2017/18 a total of 1,888 grants were awarded.

Social mobility and education programmes

To help achieve its goal of promoting social mobility the group has established a wide range of education and employability programmes for young people.

In the UK the group works with the National Literacy Trust to improve literacy skills, raise aspirations and increase awareness of careers in STEM. During the year, over 50 group employees volunteered with five primary schools in disadvantaged areas where they helped to deliver activities designed to promote a love of reading. As part of the programme, the group also gifted a number of library books which promote STEM subjects and show women in construction roles.

Through its Career Ready programme meanwhile, group employees mentored 92 young people preparing them for the transition from education to the workplace.

In-kind support

The group offers pro bono support to its charity partners including mentorship for senior leadership as well as advice about organisational management. In 2017/18 the group provided a total of 440 hours of pro bono support.

Employee-led support

Group employees are encouraged to volunteer their time to assist with the delivery of the group's programmes. In 2017/18 group employees volunteered for a total of 7,629 hours.

Applications

Apply in writing to the correspondent.

Community contributions

According to its 2017/18 Corporate Responsibility Report, during the year the group's corporate charitable and employee fundraising donations totalled £433,000. However, it was not possible to determine what proportion of this figure came from the group itself. The value of pro bono and employee volunteering hours was not quantified.

UBM plc

General charitable purposes, disaster relief, homelessness

Correspondent: CSR Team, 240 Blackfriars Road, London SE1 8BF (tel: 020 7921 5000; website: www.ubm.com)

Directors: David Wei; Greg Lock; John McConnell; Marina Wyatt; Mary McDowell; Terry Neill; Tim Cobbold; Trynka Shineman; Warren Finegold (female 33%; male 67%).

Nature of business: UBM is a global business-to-business events organiser. In June 2018 it was acquired by Informa plc.

Year end	31/12/2017
Turnover	£1,002,900,000
Pre-tax profit	£268,800,000

Total employees: 3,933

Main locations: The group has operations worldwide. Within the UK, the group has offices in Cheshire, Kent, Manchester and London.

Community involvement

The group mainly supports general charitable purposes in the communities local to either its offices or events, although support is also occasionally provided for disaster relief. Support is provided through partnerships, cash and in-kind donations, matched funding, employee fundraising and volunteering. The group has supported CRASH (the construction and property industry's charity for homeless people) since 2013.

In-kind support

The group offers charity partners the opportunity to have a presence at its events. In the past this form of in-kind support has included, the provision of complementary stands and promotional materials as well as the facilitation of workshops for charities to raise awareness of their cause among delegates.

Employee-led support

Volunteering

UBM provides employees with up to 32 hours per year to volunteer with charities and non-profits. In 2017 19% of employees used their volunteering allowance, spending over 3,000 hours supporting community groups. In addition to their time allocations, employees who volunteer for a charity on a regular basis are also eligible to receive a volunteer grant of £750 for their charity.

Fundraising

Each year the group provides up to £500 of matched funding to support employee fundraising initiatives. In 2017 UBM employees raised a total of £73,000.

In addition to their own fundraising efforts, employees are also able to donate points earnt as part of an employee reward scheme to one of three selected charities, which are also Event Charity partners. In 2017 these were: Orbis, a global charity fighting avoidable blindness; e-NABLE, a charity that creates 3D printed prosthetic hands and arms; and International Medical Corps, which provides disaster relief and delivers healthcare around the world. During the year, UBM employees donated points worth a total of £25,000.

Applications

Most activities are organised by individual businesses within the company. For contact details, refer to the website.

Community contributions

Cash donations worldwide	£419,500
In-kind support worldwide	£1,500,000
Total contributions (cash and in kind)	£1,920,000

In 2017 UBM made total charitable donations of £1.92 million. This included £419,500 in matched funding and grants, and almost £1.5 million in in-kind donations. It was not specified how much of this was given in the UK.

UIA (Insurance) Ltd

Human rights, poverty and social inclusion, rehabilitation initiatives for marginalised people

Company registration number: 3400457

Correspondent: CSR Team, Kings Court, London Road, Stevenage, Hertfordshire SG1 2TP (tel: 01438 761761; website: www.uia.co.uk)

Directors: Bob Abberley; Eithne McManus; Jon Craven; Lucia McKeever; Marion Saunders; Oliver Peterken; Peter Dodd; Tim Holliday; Tony Woodley (female 33%; male 67%).

Nature of business: UIA (Insurance) is a mutual insurance company providing household insurance to trade union members and their families.

Note: We used the figure defined as 'Gross premiums written' as the company's annual turnover.

Year end	31/12/2017
Turnover	£23,949,000
Pre-tax profit	(£492,000)

Main locations: The company's head office is in Stevenage.

Community involvement

The majority of the company's support is directed through its corporate charity the UIA Charitable Foundation (Charity Commission no. 1079982) which awards grants to a wide range of charitable organisations both in the UK and overseas. The foundation is entirely funded by donations from the company.

Applications

For general enquiries regarding the company's CSR contact the correspondent.

Corporate charity

UIA Charitable Foundation (Charity Commission no. 1079982) – see page 283.

Community contributions

Cash donations UK	£49,500

According to its 2017 annual report, the company made charitable donations of £49,500 during the year. This figure included a £37,500 donation to the UIA Charitable Foundation.

Ulster Carpet Mills (Holdings) Ltd

Mental health, medical research, general charitable purposes

Company registration number: NI001207

Correspondent: David Acheson, Trustee, The John Wilson Memorial Trust, Castleisland Factory, Craigavon BT62 1EE, Northern Ireland (tel: 028 3833 4433; email: jwmt@ulstercarpets.com; website: johnwilsontrust.com)

Directors: Caroline Somerville; David Acheson; Edward Wilson; Jeremy Wilson; Jesper Jensen; John Wilson; Lydia Inglis; Mary Montgomery; Nicholas Coburn; Raymond McKeown; Richard Wilson (female 27%; male 73%).

Nature of business: Ulster Carpet Mills is a luxury carpet manufacturer.

Year end	31/03/2018
Turnover	£76,284,000
Pre-tax profit	£10,702,000

Total employees: 666

Main locations: The company operates in the UK and the USA. Its head office is in Craigavon, Northern Ireland.

Community involvement

The company's community activities are primarily channelled through its corporate charity The John Wilson Memorial Trust (NIC No. 105836). The company also provides sponsorship for sporting events and fundraises for charities local to its Craigavon office.

The John Wilson Memorial Trust

The John Wilson Memorial Trust is the corporate charity of Ulster Carpet Mills and was set up in memory of the late John Wilson, son of Ulster Carpet Mills' founder, George Walter Wilson.

The trust provides grants to charities in the area of mental health. In addition, the trust also offers funding for local SMEs (small and medium enterprises) as well as bursaries and scholarships to support medical research. The trust primarily supports organisations in the area surround the company's head office in Craigavon. Full information about the trust's recent projects can be found on its website.

In the past three years, the trust has awarded grants to Action Mental Health (AMH MensSana) to support mental health counselling among young people across Northern Ireland. Grants have also been awarded to the East Belfast Independent Advice Centre to help advocacy efforts with young people, people with an intellectual disability, and those who are vulnerable. A project to investigate the links between eating and health has also been funded.

As the trust has recently registered with the Northern Irish Charity Commission, no financial information was available.

Employee-led support

Company employees are encouraged to participate in fundraising activities for local charities.

Commercially led support

The company seeks to promote participation in sport by sponsoring various sporting events. Most notable is its ongoing partnership with Ulster Youth Rugby to sponsor their Youth and High School competitions.

Applications

Apply in writing to the correspondent.

Community contributions

A figure for the company's total community contribution was not included in its 2017/18 accounts.

Unilever plc

Sustainability, health, the environment, equality, projects outside the UK

Company registration number: 41424

Correspondent: Sustainability Team, Unilever House, Springfield Drive, Leatherhead KT22 7GR (tel: 01372 945000; website: www.unilever.co.uk)

Directors: Andrea Jung; Dr Judith Hartmann; Dr Marijn Dekkers; Feike Sijbesma; Graeme Pitkethly; John Rishton; Laura Cha; Mary Ma; Nils Andersen; Paul Polman; Prof. Youngme Moon; Strive Masiyiwa; Vittorio Colao (female 38%; male 62%).

Nature of business: Unilever is one of the world's leading suppliers of fast moving consumer goods in foods, household and personal care products.

Year end	31/12/2017
Turnover	£47,460,000,000
Pre-tax profit	£7,203,600,000

Total employees: 161,000

Main locations: The group has operations worldwide. In the UK, Unilever has its head office in London, research facilities in Port Sunlight (Wirral), Colworth (Bedfordshire) and Leeds as well as manufacturing and distribution centres across the UK.

Community involvement

Unilever delivers an extensive range of charitable activities, focusing particularly on sustainability; health and well-being; environment; equality; and improving livelihoods. The company works in partnership with organisations in the UK and worldwide to deliver its sustainability plans. Unilever has a group-wide sustainability strategy, but activities such as employee volunteering, charitable donations and sponsorship are coordinated by local companies.

Unilever Sustainable Living Plan

Unilever has an extensive Sustainable Living strategy, encompassing many different initiatives, partnerships and projects throughout the world. The group's sustainable living plan focuses on the following areas:

Improving health and well-being

- Health and hygiene
- Nutrition

Enhancing livelihoods

- Fairness in the workplace
- Opportunities for women
- Inclusive business

Reducing environmental impact

- Greenhouse gases
- Water use
- Waste and packaging
- Sustainable sourcing

Recent examples of the group's sustainable living initiatives include the following:

- The Dove Self Esteem project aims to improve the self-esteem of young people by delivering sessions and workshops in schools, as well as providing online. Unilever's employees volunteer to deliver these workshops on Dove Day, an annual event
- The group's laundry brand Dirt is Good works in partnership with Unicef to deliver the Learning for Tomorrow Initiative, which helps children in Brazil, India and Vietnam to gain access to learning opportunities by: training teachers; enhancing education standards; and creating campaigns designed to increase demand for good quality education
- The group has a long-term relationship with Oxfam, supporting its UK Poverty programme, providing emergency food through food banks and supporting other opportunities
- The group has worked with Save the Children in Myanmar to help prepare and respond to disasters rapidly and effectively, through pre-positioning of 3,000 household and hygiene kits, which will be deployed in the event of a disaster
- The group's Vaseline brand has an ongoing partnership with Direct Relief, a humanitarian aid organisation dedicated to improving the health and lives of people affected by poverty and emergency situations. Through this partnership, over one million Vaseline products have been donated to a network of partner clinics and hospitals worldwide

For details of all of the group's current Sustainable Living initiatives see the website.

Employee-led support

Many of Unilever's partnerships and programmes involve employee volunteering. Examples in the UK include volunteering for the Dove Self Esteem campaign, helping food banks, and handing out goodie bags at the Pride in London parade.

Applications

The website states that donations and sponsorship decisions are made by local companies, and so any charity wishing to enquire about this should contact their local company using the contact form on the website: www.unilever.co.uk/contact.

Community contributions

Unilever's 2017 annual report did not provide a figure for its total community contributions.

Unite Group plc

Education, equal opportunities, children and young people

Company registration number: 3199160

Correspondent: CSR Team, South Quay House, Temple Back, Bristol BS1 6FL (tel: 0117 302 7000; email: info@unite-students.com; website: www.unite-group.co.uk)

Directors: Andrew Jones; Elizabeth McMeikan; Joe Lister; Phil White; Prof. Sir Tim Wilson; Richard Smith; Ross Paterson (female 14%; male 86%).

Nature of business: United Group is a developer and operator of student accommodation across the UK.

Year end	31/12/2017
Turnover	£119,300,000
Pre-tax profit	£229,400,000

Total employees: 1,262

Main locations: The group has accommodation in major university cities across the UK. The head office is in London.

Community involvement

The group works with charity partners and offers support through employee volunteering and in-kind donations. Support is also offered through the group's corporate charity, The Unite Foundation.

The Unite Foundation (Charity Commission/OSCR no. 1147344/ SC043324)

The company's corporate charity, The Unite Foundation focuses on social mobility and educational inequality. It works to enable individuals from disadvantaged backgrounds to access higher education, encourages students to engage with their local communities and helps young people develop skills and access employment. Its main area of activity is the provision of scholarships, including free accommodation, to undergraduate students from disadvantaged backgrounds, particularly those who have been in care. The foundation currently works in partnership with 28 universities to deliver this scheme and the company's 2017 annual report states that during the academic year, around 170 scholarships were provided. More information can be found on the foundation's website: www.unitefoundation.co.uk.

Life Skills

In 2017 the group launched a pilot Life Skills programme offering 100 16- to 17-year-olds the chance to visit group properties and attend a workshop focused on the potential pitfalls of shared living.

Partnerships

At the start of 2017, the group selected the British Heart Foundation as its new national Charity of the Year. As part of the partnership, the group operates a stock donation program, whereby students and employees were encouraged to donate unwanted goods to charity. In the first year of the partnership, £272,000 was raised for the charity. A further 22 City Charities of the Year are selected annually by local teams.

In addition to support for its selected charities of the year, the group also has an ongoing partnership with Into University, a charity focused on raising aspirations of young people to go onto university or other further learning after leaving school.

In-kind support

The group supports local charities through the provision of commercial premises at nominal rates. In 2017 the group provided premises to two organisations, the London-based charity MahaDevi Yoga and the Bristol-based charity 16–25 Independent People.

Employee-led support

Employees are entitled to a day of paid volunteering with a local charitable cause. In 2017, around 19% of employees volunteered more than 5,000 hours. The company also provides matched funding for employees' fundraising initiatives.

Applications

For general enquiries, apply in writing to the correspondent.

To apply to the Unite Foundation, or to get more information about the foundation, contact: info@unitefoundation.co.uk or call 0117 302 7073.

Community contributions

Cash donations worldwide	£1,600,000

According to its 2017 annual report, during the year the group donated £1.6 million to charities. This figure includes support for the Unite Foundation as well as its Charity of the Year, the British Heart Foundation.

United Utilities Group plc

Poverty and social inclusion, education, the environment, health

Company registration number: 6559020

Correspondent: Corporate Responsibility Committee, Haweswater House, Lingley Mere Business Park, Lingey Green Avenue, Great Sankey, Warrington WA5 3LP (tel: 01925 234000; website: www.unitedutilities.com)

Directors: Alison Goligher; Brian May; Dr John McAdam; Mark Clare; Paulette Rowe; Russ Houlden; Sara Weller; Stephen Carter; Steve Fraser; Steve Mogford (female 30%; male 70%).

Nature of business: United Utilities Group is the intermediate holding company of the UK's largest listed water business. The group owns and manages the regulated water and wastewater network in the North West of England, through its subsidiary United Utilities Water (UUW).

Year end	31/03/2018
Turnover	£1,736,000,000
Pre-tax profit	£432,000,000

Total employees: 5,223

Main locations: The group has a head office based in Lingley Mere, Warrington. The group also has a main office in Whitehaven, Cumbria, 575 wastewater treatment works and 96 water treatment works located in various North West locations from Crewe to Carlisle.

Community involvement

The group supports community groups and charities across the North West, and particularly in areas where it is delivering long-running or disruptive engineering works. Contributions include cash donations, employee volunteering, matched funding, and in-kind support. Support is given for a wide range of charitable causes including, social welfare, education, the environment, and health and well-being. The group also helps its customers who are struggling financially.

According to its website, the group measures its own corporate responsibility performance against the following five 'Business Principle Commitments':

- Invest in community partnerships for mutual benefit with particular focus on current social issues
- Encourage [the company's] employees to get involved and make a positive contribution to local communities
- Invest in education programmes both in schools and the wider community
- Recognise the effect that [the company's] operations have upon the community and invest in programmes that support those affected
- Provide access and recreation at [the company's] sites where it is appropriate

Lancashire Community Fund

Following a water quality incident in Lancashire in August 2015, the group created the Lancashire Community Fund, to support community groups and charities that work to address issues: relating to social and economic deprivation and isolation; debt; health and well-being; and the environment.

Grants of between £2,500 and £20,000 are available over a period of one to two years. The fund is currently entering its final round. Funding is still available in the Fylde, South Ribble, Wyre and Preston North parliamentary constituencies. In 2016/17 the group distributed almost £700,000 worth of grants.

The scheme is administered by the Community Foundation for Lancashire. Full details including eligibility criteria are available on the foundation's website at: www.lancsfoundation.org.uk/funds/united-utilities-lancashire-community-fund.

Access and recreation

The group owns and manages over 57,000 hectares of land around its reservoirs in Cheshire, Cumbria, Greater Manchester, Lancashire, and the Peak District. It has initiated the following activities to encourage and develop public access:

- Produced an interactive map
- Resurfaced bridleways and footpaths and maintained public access infrastructure
- Runs an ongoing campaign to educate people of the dangers of swimming in reservoirs

Education

The group runs a varied education programme, aimed at primary and secondary schoolchildren, which includes water efficiency workshops, online resources, a campaign to protect and enhance beaches and bathing waters, and career advice (for STEM subjects).

Partnerships

The group has a long-standing community investment partnership with Groundwork UK called United Futures, which helps to regenerate neighbourhoods following mains and sewer improvement works. In 2016/17 the group supported a range of local environmental projects around its Davyhulme treatment works in Greater Manchester, including the creation of a community orchard at Broadway Park.

Between 2011 and 2017, the group supported its charity partner North West Air Ambulance through matched funded employee fundraising, raising a total of £330,000. In 2017 The group announced a new Charity of the Year partnership with the cancer charity Macmillan.

Rivington Heritage Trust (Charity Commission no. 1064700)

The trust was established by United Utilities to preserve and take care of Rivington Terraced Gardens. In 2016/17 the group donated £51,500 to the charity. For further information on the charity visit: www.rivingtonheritagetrust.co.uk.

United Utilities Trust Fund (Charity Commission no. 1108296)

This grant-making charity was established in 2005 to help people out of poverty and debt and to provide grants to debt and money advice services. The trust is funded partly by United Utilities and partly by contribution from customers through their water bills. The group's website states it invests £5 million per year into the trust.

Employee-led support

Volunteering

The group's employees are allowed three days per year to volunteer in the local community. According to the group's 2017/18 accounts, during the year employees spent a total of 3,577 hours volunteering. Activities included, delivering talks and workshops in schools to promote careers in STEM subjects and participating in various environmental projects (such as tree planting, beach cleaning and scrub clearance).

Matched funding

The group also supports employee fundraising efforts by providing matched funding of up to £250 per person per year, and by covering the administration fees associated with payroll giving.

Commercially led support

The group has a number of schemes and tariffs designed to support vulnerable customers. See the website for full details.

Exclusions

According to the Community Foundation for Lancashire's website, the Lancashire Community Fund will not support the following:

- Statutory organisations or work that is their responsibility
- National organisations that cannot demonstrate local governance and control of local finances
- Commercial ventures
- Purchase/maintenance of vehicles
- Activities that will have already taken place before [you are offered] a grant
- Politically connected or exclusively religious activities
- Projects for personal profit
- Organisations that are set up for the benefit of animals or plants: environmental groups that work with animals or the environment (such as city farms) are acceptable
- Groups comprising just one family or organisations that have less than 3 unrelated management committee members/Directors/Trustees
- Debts and other liabilities
- Reclaimable VAT
- Travel outside UK

Applications

General enquiries can be submitted in writing to the correspondent.

Lancashire Community Fund

Applications for grants can be submitted using an online form on the Community Foundation for Lancashire's website: www.lancsfoundation.org.uk.

Corporate charity

United Utilities Trust Fund (Charity Commission no. 1108296) – see page 284.

Community contributions

Cash donations UK	£3,400,000
In-kind support UK	£69,000
Total contributions (cash and in kind)	£3,469,000

According to the 2017/18 accounts, during the year the group made community contributions worth a total of £3.47 million. This included employee time and cash donations and was broken down as follows:

Cash	£3.4 million
Time	£69,000

This figure does not include the group's annual contribution of around £5 million to its corporate charity the United Utilities Trust Fund.

Unum Ltd

Arts and culture, education, health

Company registration number: 983768

Correspondent: Susan Sanderson, CSR Manager, Milton Court, Dorking, Surrey RH4 3LZ (tel: 01306 887766; email: susan.sanderson@unum.co.uk; website: www.unum.co.uk/csr)

Directors: Cheryl Black; Clifton Melvin; Jon Fletcher; Malcolm McCraig; Peter O'Donnell; Rick McKenney; Samantha Hoe-Richardson (female 29%; male 71%).

Nature of business: Unum is an employee benefits provider offering financial protection through the workplace including income protection, life insurance, critical illness and dental cover. The company is a member of the Unum Group of Companies.

Year end	31/12/2017
Turnover	£477,600,000
Pre-tax profit	£81,050,000

UK employees: 750+

Main locations: The group's UK head office is based in Dorking, Surrey. The other two main offices are in Basingstoke and Bristol, and there are also regional sales offices in Birmingham, Glasgow and London.

Community involvement

The group has a grants scheme for charities working in the areas of education; health and well-being; and arts, culture and sport. It also supports charities through partnerships, employee volunteering, and matched funding.

Charitable donations scheme

The group's charitable donations scheme provides grants of up to £10,000 to registered charities working in the following areas: education; health and well-being (including disability); arts, culture and sport. There is some preference given to organisations with which employees are involved.

Partnerships

As part of the company's charity partnerships programmes, employees choose national and regional charities to support. For 2018 and 2019 the chosen charity partners are: Ark Cancer Centre Charity (Basingstoke), Child Bereavement UK (national), and Halow (Dorking).

In addition, the company also has an ongoing partnership with Maggie's – a charity that offers free emotional, practical and social support to people with cancer and their families and friends.

As part of the partnership, Unum has commissioned research to better understand the barriers preventing people with cancer from working. In addition, the company will also be running educational events and has created a range of resources to help employers and employees address the challenges faced as a result of cancer in the workplace. These resources are available to download from the company's website.

Through the Unum Access to University Fund created in partnership with Birkbeck University, the company has pledged funding for bursaries of £1,000 to 15 students over the next two academic years. Bursaries will support students with a disability or those whose financial circumstances present barriers to study.

In-kind support

The company organises an annual food drive for community projects and food banks. In 2017 company employees donated 1,770 kg of food and toiletries.

In 2017 the company also arranged its first children's book drive. Working with the charity Delight, employees were asked to donate children's books for disadvantaged primary schoolchildren. In total 1,650 books were donated.

Employee-led support

Volunteering

Employees are entitled to up to two working days per year to volunteer for a local charity or community project. In 2017 staff volunteered 4,510 hours (622 working days) on projects ranging from painting and decorating, landscaping and conservation team challenges to longer-term mentoring partnerships with local schools.

Fundraising

In addition to volunteering, Unum Ltd employees organise and participate in fundraising events for the company's chosen national and regional charity partners. In 2017 employee fundraising initiatives raised over £100,000.

Payroll giving

The company operates a payroll giving scheme and provides matched funding for employee donations that fall under any of the three focus areas that the group supports. According to the company's CSR report, on average around £45,000 is donated through payroll giving each year.

Exclusions

The group does not provides support for: admin, staff or other general running costs; organisations that have a political or religious affiliation; and medical research.

Grants are only awarded to registered charities supporting at least one of the specified areas of focus (education; health and well-being; arts, culture and sport).

Applications

Application forms for the company's charitable grants scheme are available on the website, along with guidance about what should be included. Applications are considered four times a year by the charitable donations committee and should be submitted in writing to the Corporate Social Responsibility Manager. Only one application per organisation will be considered in a 12-month period.

All other queries should be directed to the company's CSR team.

Community contributions

Total contributions (cash and in kind)	£246,000

According to its 2017 annual report, during the financial year the company provided a total of £246,000 in charitable contributions. This figure includes the value of 622 volunteering days undertaken by company employees during the year. The company's CSR report for 2016/17 states that during this period a total of £228,000 was awarded in charitable grants. However, it was not possible to determine the total awarded in charitable grants during the 2017 financial year.

Beneficiaries included: St Michael's Hospice, Rainbow Trust Children's Charity, Envision, Challengers, The Halow Project, National Opera Studio.

UPP Group Ltd

Education

Company registration number: 6218832

Correspondent: 40 Gracechurch Street, London EC3V 0BT (tel: 020 7398 7200; email: info@upp-ltd.com; website: www.upp-ltd.com)

Directors: Julian Benkel; Richard Bienfait; Michael Eady; Dr Paul Marshall; Paul Milner; Sean O'Shea; Andrew Percival; Kelly Stafford; Mark Swindlehurst; Jonathan Wakeford (female 10%; male 90%).

Nature of business: The group's principal activity is the development, funding, construction and operation (including facilities management) of student accommodation under the University Partnerships Programme (UPP).

Year end	31/08/2017
Turnover	£178,900,000
Pre-tax profit	£73,900,000

UK employees: 789

Main locations: The group's head office is in London. It owns and manages property at 16 universities across England and Wales, a list of which can be found at: www.upp-ltd.com/contact.

Community involvement

The majority of UPP's giving is channelled through its corporate charity, the UPP Foundation (Charity Commission no. 1166323).

Employee-led support

In 2017 the group established UPP Gives, an employee fundraising committee that organises UPP-wide charitable initiatives, the first of which was The Prince's Trust Step Challenge in February 2018.

Corporate charity

UPP Foundation (Charity Commission no. 1166323) – see page 284.

Community contributions

Cash donations UK	£468,000

In 2016/17 UPP donated £413,000 to its corporate charity. The annual report notes that in 2017/18 the group donated £55,000 to leading mental health charity Student Minds to train UPP employees and students at Nottingham Trent University on mental health issues. We have taken £468,000 to be the group's total charitable contribution for the year.

Victrex plc

Education, particularly STEM subjects

Company registration number: 2793780

Correspondent: Community Investment Team, Victrex Technology Centre, Hillhouse International, Thornton Cleveleys, Lancashire FY5 4QD (tel: 01253 897700; email: ir@victrex.com; website: www.victrexplc.com)

Directors: Brendan Connolly; David Thomas; Jacob Sigurdsson; Jane Toogood; Janet Ashdown; Larry Pentz; Martin Court; Pamela Kirby; Richard Armitage; Tim Cooper (female 30%; male 70%).

Nature of business: Victrex, is a leading global manufacturer of high performance polymers.

Year end	30/09/2017
Turnover	£290,200,000
Pre-tax profit	£111,000,000

Total employees: 763

Main locations: The group has operations in the UK and internationally. Its head office is based in Thornton Cleveleys, Lancashire.

Community involvement

The group's social responsibility activities focus on the promotion of STEM subjects in education and inspiring young people through educational activities.

The group has set three objectives in relation to its corporate social responsibility which it hopes to achieve by 2023:

- 10,000 employee hours (cumulative) supporting community activity by 2023
- 1,000 young people reached through education activities
- 50% of employees engaged on sustainability

Charitable donations

In 2017 Victrex established a Community Investment Team to manage the distribution of the group's charitable donations in the UK. During the year, charitable donations totalling £115,500 were made to charities nominated by Victrex employees.

Partnerships

The group has a partnership with Catalyst Discovery Centre in the UK, which teaches school-age children about chemistry and how polymers are made. The group is also actively involved in the Science Industry Partnership ('SIP'). As part of Business in the Community's Business Class scheme, Victrex also supports Fleetwood High School – which is located near to the head office – to achieve improved STEM academic results.

Employee-led support

The 2016/17 sustainability report states that during the year, Victrex employees spent a total of 600 hours in total volunteering in local communities.

Applications

Contact the correspondent for more information.

Community contributions

Cash donations UK	£115,500

According to its 2016/17 annual report, during the year the group made charitable donations of £115,500 in the UK.

Virgin Money Group

Financial education, enterprise and training, community development, medical research

Company registration number: 3087587

Correspondent: Culture and Community Team, Virgin Money, Discovery House, Whiting Road, Norwich NR4 6E (email: community@virginmoney.com; website: uk.virginmoney.com)

Directors: Amy Stirling; Colin Keogh; Darren Pope; Eva Eisenschimmel; Geeta Gopalan; Irene Dorner; Jayne-Anne Gadhia; Norman McLuskie; Patrick McCall; Peter Bole (female 50%; male 50%).

Nature of business: Virgin Money is a bank and financial services company owned by the Virgin Group and based in the UK.

Year end	31/12/2017
Turnover	£662,700,000
Pre-tax profit	£262,600,000

Total employees: 3,447

Main locations: The group has four main offices in the UK – in Edinburgh, London, Newcastle and Norwich. It also has stores across the UK.

Community involvement

Virgin Money's corporate responsibility focuses on four areas: fundraising; investing in education; employability and enterprise; and supporting employee engagement in local communities. Support is provided through partnerships, education programmes, employee volunteering and fundraising as well as through the Virgin Money Foundation (Charity Commission no. 1161290), which awards grants to charities and community groups. The group also sponsors the London Marathon and has an online donation platform, Virgin Money Giving.

Virgin Money Foundation

Established in 2015, the Virgin Money Foundation supports disadvantaged communities, across the UK with a preference for the North East, Glasgow, Sheffield and Norfolk. Funding is given for youth education and employment, homelessness support, social enterprise and feasibility studies for large capital projects. In 2017 the foundation awarded grants totalling nearly £3 million.

Virgin Money Giving

Virgin Money Giving is an online platform created by Virgin Money to enable online fundraising and donations. The website operates on a not-for-profit basis, with running costs covered by a start-up fee and 2% of donations from each charity. In 2017, £95 million was donated to charities through Virgin Money Giving.

Partnerships

The group's Charity of the Year for 2018/19 is Alzheimer's Research UK, which will be the official charity for the 2019 Virgin Money London Marathon. Previous Charity of the Year partners have included the NSPCC and the Heads Together campaign. According to the group's annual report, the Heads Together campaign raised £1.94 million through its partnership with Virgin Money, including £250,000 raised by group employees.

Education

The group works with a variety of organisations to deliver a range of educational programmes related to financial awareness, employability and enterprise. Current initiatives include:

- **Make £5 Grow:** An annual competition for primary schools across the UK, which encourages enterprise and related skills, by providing pupils aged 9–11 with a loan of £5 each to start small business initiatives. Further information can be found at: make-5-grow.co.uk
- **LifeSavers:** A financial education programme for primary schools, giving children the knowledge, skills and attitudes to manage money well
- **Virgin StartUp:** A support and mentoring programme for young entrepreneurs
- **Strive to Thrive:** A programme designed to help young people aged 14–19 increase their chances of finding employment through improving their confidence and self-awareness and giving them employability and life skills

In-kind support

The group offers use of its Virgin Money Lounges free of charge to community groups and charities for running events.

Employee-led support

Employees of Virgin Money are entitled to a few days' paid volunteering leave each year. In 2017 employees spent a total of 1,555 days volunteering. Examples of employee community activities included, taking part in fundraising initiatives, volunteering with local charities or in charity appeal call centres, and acting as ambassadors for the Make £5 Grow scheme in schools.

Commercially led support

The group sponsors the Virgin Money London Marathon and provides the official fundraising site for the marathon, Virgin Money Giving (www.virginmoneygiving.com). Runners in the 2017 Virgin Money London Marathon raised £62 million for charity, setting a new world record for an annual, single day charity fundraising event.

Virgin Money also sponsors events at the Edinburgh Festival Fringe (Virgin Money Fringe on the Royal Mile and the Virgin Money Fringe on the Mound), as well as the Fireworks Concert which concludes the Edinburgh International Festival.

Applications

Contact the correspondent for more information.

Corporate charity

Virgin Money Foundation (Charity Commission no. 1161290) – see page 285.

Community contributions

Cash donations UK	£1,400,000

There was no overall figure for the group's community contributions. However, the group's 2017 accounts state that during the year it made donations of £1.4 million to the Virgin Money Foundation. We have taken this figure as the group's cash donations total for the year.

Virgin Rail Group Holdings Ltd

General charitable purposes

Company registration number: 4196341

Correspondent: Joanna Buckley, Community Manager, The Battleship Building, 179 Harrow Road, London W2 6NB (email: joanna.buckley@virgintrains.co.uk; website: www.virgintrains.co.uk/about/social-responsibility/community)

Directors: John Sullivan; Mark Whitehouse; Natasha Grice; Peter Broadley; Phil Whittingham; Richard Scott; Sarah Copley (female 29%; male 71%).

Nature of business: Virgin Rail is a UK-based train operating company.

Year end	31/03/2018
Turnover	£1,165,991,000
Pre-tax profit	£64,264,000

Total employees: 3,289

Main locations: The group operates train services across the UK.

Community involvement

The group supports general charitable purposes across the UK. Support is provided through partnerships, in-kind donations, and employee fundraising and volunteering.

Partnerships

In 2017 Virgin Trains formed a new partnership with the mental health charity Rethink Mental Illness. As part of the partnership, the group has delivered a programme of fundraising activities in and around its stations.

In-kind support

The group offers complimentary train tickets for mental health charities travelling on its West Coast services. The group also offers complimentary tickets for parents or guardians travelling with their children to receive specialist hospital treatment.

More generally, Virgin Trains offers a 20% discount on Advance tickets for all registered charities. Charities can register their interest on the Trainline website at: www.thetrainline.com/about-us/business/charity-account.

Employee-led support

The group's engagement with local communities is coordinated by a network of 'Community Champions' who work with local groups and organisations to discover the best ways for the company and its employees to support local causes, including through volunteering and hosting events at stations.

Exclusions

The group's website states that it cannot provide free train travel for school trips.

Applications

Train tickets

Charities and individuals can make requests for complimentary train tickets using an online form of the group's website: forms1.thrive-csr.com/virgin_trains/apply_for_tickets.html.

Community Champions

Details about your local community champion can be found on the Community Board at Virgin train stations.

Community contributions

The group's 2017/18 annual report did not provide a figure for its total community contributions.

Viridian Group Investments Ltd

Financial education, general charitable purposes

Company registration number: NI33250

Correspondent: CSR Team, Greenwood House, 64 Newforge Lane, Belfast BT9 5NF (email: contact@viridiangroup.co.uk; website: www.viridiangroup.co.uk)

Directors: Ian Thorn; Roy Foreman; Siobhan Bailey; Stephen McCully; Tom Gillen (female 20%; male 80%).

Nature of business: Viridian is an independent energy company supplying Northern Ireland and Republic of Ireland.

Year end	31/03/2018
Turnover	£1,561,000,000
Pre-tax profit	(£97,400,000)

UK employees: 579

Total employees: 702

Main locations: The group's head office is in Belfast. The group covers Northern Ireland and Republic of Ireland.

Community involvement

The group provides support in Northern Ireland and Republic of Ireland through its community benefit funds and direct donations.

Energia Community Benefit Funds

During the year over £297,000 was distributed by Energia via its community funds across the island of Ireland. The community funds cover areas in which Energia operate wind farms. In Northern Ireland, this includes Thornog, Long Mountain and Rathsherry which are operated by the Community Foundation for Northern Ireland and managed by the Teiges Mountain.

During the year Energia donated a further €120,000 (≈ £105,000 as at November 2018) to Grow It Yourself, Seachtain na Gaeilge, Christmassy Homes and donations to local charities.

Charity of the Year

During the year Power NI supported Action Mental Health and Energia sponsored Foyle Down Syndrome Trust and Down Syndrome Ireland.

Employee-led support

Power NI's Helping Hands in the Community Scheme

Power NI employees are able to apply for support of up to £250 for an organisation/charity that they are involved with. During the year Power NI raised £7,000 for Action Mental Health and Energia staff contributed over £11,000 to its chosen charities. Energia also partially matches its staff's own fundraising.

Applications

Energia Community Benefit Funds

Visit www.fermanaghtrust.org or www.communityfoundationni.org for further information on the grant schemes.

All other queries should be made to the correspondent.

Community contributions

Total contributions (cash and in kind)	£477,000

In 2017/18 the group's charitable contributions totalled £477,000.

Viridian International Ltd

The environment, children and young people

Company registration number: 3750310

Correspondent: CSR Team, 15 High March, Daventry, Northamptonshire NN11 4HB UK (tel: 01327 878050; website: www.viridian-nutrition.com/charity.aspx)

Directors: Cheryl Thallon; Clare Longdon (female 100%; male 0%).

Nature of business: Viridian International is a producer and distributor of vitamins and health supplements.

Year end	30/04/2017

UK employees: 35

Main locations: The company supplies its products in over 20 countries worldwide.

Community involvement

The company supports environmental and children's charities through its charity donation programme.

Viridian Nutrition Charity Donation programme

Through the Viridian Nutrition Charity Donation programme, the company provides cash donations to a wide range of registered charities. Beneficiary charities are nominated on an annual basis by the company's stockists. The only restriction is that 40% is donated to children's charities and 40% is donated to environmental charities. The remaining 20% is then donated to other charitable causes. Since the programme was established, the company has donated over £350,000.

Previous beneficiaries have included: Friends of the Earth, NSPCC, Woodland Trust, Unicef, The Prince's Trust, Comic Relief, RSPB, Terrence Higgins Trust, Shelter, Save the Children.

In-kind support

The company has an ongoing partnership with the Monkey Sanctuary, a project of the charity Wild Futures, which cares for rescued primates from the UK primate pet trade. As part of the partnership Viridian Nutrition donates a range of nutritional supplements to help support the primates' health and well-being.

Applications

Apply in writing to the correspondent.

Community contributions

A figure for the company's total community contribution was not provided in its 2016/17 annual report.

Vodafone Group plc

Health, education, disaster relief, women, projects outside the UK

Company registration number: 1833679

Correspondent: CSR Team, Vodafone House, The Connection, Newbury, Berkshire RG14 2FN (tel: 01635 33251; website: www.vodafone.com)

Directors: Dame Clara Furse; David Nish; Gerard Kleisterlee; Margherita Della Valle; Maria Amparo Moraleda Martinez; Michel Demare; Nick Read; Renee James; Samuel Jonah; Sir Crispin Davis; Valerie Gooding (female 45%; male 55%).

Nature of business: Vodafone is a mobile telecommunications provider operating worldwide.

Year end	31/03/2018
Turnover	£41,355,000,000
Pre-tax profit	£3,443,000,000

Total employees: 104,000

Main locations: The group operates in 25 countries worldwide.

Community involvement

Much of the group's charitable activities are channelled through its corporate charity, The Vodafone Foundation (Charity Commission no. 1089625), which supports projects that are focused on delivering public benefit through the application of technology across the areas of health, education and disaster relief. Globally the group runs a variety of programmes designed to promote women's empowerment, energy innovation and youth employment.

The Vodafone Foundation

The group has 27 foundations around the world. The UK-registered foundation encompasses both UK and wider activities, and supports a wide range of projects in the areas of health, education and disaster relief. Recent initiatives have included the development of the JustTextGiving platform, and TecSOS an initiative that provides victims of domestic abuse with an immediate connection to the police via a specially adapted mobile handset.

Sustainable Business Strategy

At a global level, the group's sustainability activities are focused around three goals:

- Women's empowerment
- Energy innovation
- Youth skills and jobs

The group runs a variety of projects and initiatives internationally to achieve these goals. Examples include:

- Funding for girls to attend school in India
- Providing mobile banking services for women entrepreneurs in low- and middle-income countries
- Supporting the UN's HeForShe campaign
- Supporting the Paris Pledge for Action on climate change
- Working with Enactus to support social entrepreneurs in Egypt
- Providing mentoring, apprenticeships and internships, as well as bursaries for STEM education

Further details of the group's international activities can be found in the 2018 sustainability report, available on the website.

Employee-led support

Employee volunteering

Vodafone UK gives employees 24 hours paid volunteering leave every year, which can be taken either as individuals or in teams.

Employee fundraising

Vodafone UK provides matched funding of up to £350 for employee fundraising initiatives, and runs a payroll giving scheme.

Applications

Contact the correspondent for more information.

Corporate charity

The Vodafone Foundation (Charity Commission no. 1089625) – see page 285.

Community contributions

Cash donations UK	£16,300,000

No figure was provided for the group's charitable contributions; however, the foundation's accounts note that the group donated £16.3 million to the charity, which we have taken as its cash donation.

Warburtons Ltd

General charitable purposes, health, education, employability

Company registration number: 178711

Correspondent: Nichola Atkinson, Community and Communications Co-ordinator, Back o'th' Bank House, Hereford Street, Bolton, Lancashire BL1 8JB (tel: 01204 556600; website: www.warburtons.co.uk)

Directors: Andrew Campbell; Brett Warburton; David Light; Jonathan Warburton; Mark Allen; Nigel Dunlop; Ross Warburton (female 0%; male 100%).

Nature of business: Warburtons is a family-owned bakery producer and distributor.

Year end	30/09/2017
Turnover	£524,500,000
Pre-tax profit	£38,700,000

UK employees: 4,500+

Main locations: The company operates across the UK.

Community involvement

Warburtons supports a wide range of charitable causes throughout the UK with a particular focus on health, employability, and education. The company provides support in a variety of ways including through grants, its national school visitors programme, product donations, volunteering, matched funding, fundraising and payroll giving.

Financial giving programme

The company's financial giving programme is aimed at supporting projects, activities and organisations that have charitable aims and will be of real direct benefit to families. The support provided is intended to reach charities and organisations delivering work that aligns with the following priorities as outlined in its 'Family Matters' report:

- **Health:** Help families lead healthier lifestyles
- **Financial stability:** Help families manage their finances
- **Worklessness:** Help families recognise the economic and social benefits of employment
- **Health Education:** Help educate families about healthy lifestyles. (No Project Grants)
- **Aspiration:** Help raise career aspirations to improve prospects for them and their families

- **Employability and skills:** Help raise employment prospects for family members seeking employment

Warburton's can support charities and organisations financially in two ways:

- **Community Grants:** Grants of up to £250 to support charitable organisations that require funding to help them deliver a broader activity. Applications for Community Grants are reviewed on a quarterly basis
- **Project Grants:** Grants of £1,000–£10,000 for projects Within 15 miles of a Warburton bakery or depot site. Project Grants are managed through a closed process. As such, unsolicited applications for this programme are not currently accepted

Over the last four years, Warburtons has given £969,000 in Project Grants and £162,500 in Community Grants.

Partnerships

The company's national charity partner is Cancer Research UK. Employees regularly participate in various activities and initiatives to raise funds for the charity and in 2016/17 raised nearly £315,000.

In-kind support

School visits

Warburtons National School Visitor Programme has been running for over 20 years. It enables the company's 'school visitors' to pay annual visits to primary schools to introduce pupils to bread making and educate them about leading healthy lifestyles. In 2016/17 Warburtons arranged 1,402 workshops reaching over 40,000 children across the UK.

Product donations

Warburtons regularly donates food to support local organisations including breakfast clubs and food banks. In 2016/17 the company donated a total of 523,500 products.

Employee-led support

Payroll giving

A payroll giving scheme operates to enable monthly deductions from salaries in support of charitable causes. During 2016/17, Warburtons employees donated nearly £47,000 through payroll giving.

Matched funding

The company matches employee fundraising up to £250 per person or £375 for funds raised for Cancer Research UK. In 2016/17 the company provided over £30,000 in matched funding.

Skills exchange

The company has a skills exchange programme, which enables employees to volunteer with local organisations. In 2016/17, 310 employees volunteered a total of 1,639 hours of their time.

Exclusions

The company's Financial Giving Policy provides a comprehensive list of exclusions which apply to Warburton's Community Grant and Project Grant programmes. The policy is available to download from the company's website.

Applications

Product donations

Applications for product donations can be submitted using an online form at: www.warburtons.co.uk/corporate/sustainability/product-donation.

Community Grants

Applications for Community Grants can be submitted online at: www.warburtons.co.uk/corporate/sustainability/community/grant.

Community contributions

Cash donations UK	£368,000

The company's 2016/17 sustainability report states that during the year, Warburtons awarded a total of £338,000 in Community Grants and Project Grants. In addition, the company also provided just over £30,000 in matched funding. A numerical value for the company's in-kind donations was not provided. As such, we have taken the figure of £368,000 to be the company's total community contributions for the financial year.

Waterstones Booksellers Ltd

Literacy and reading projects for children and young people

Company registration number: 610095

Correspondent: CSR Team, 203–206 Piccadilly, London W1J 9HD (tel: 0808 118 8787; website: www.waterstones.com)

Directors: James Daunt; Jane Molloy; Paul Best (female 33%; male 67%).

Nature of business: Waterstones is a British book retailer.

Year end	29/04/2017
Turnover	£387,973,000
Pre-tax profit	£19,157,000

UK employees: 3,195

Main locations: The company operates stores across the UK.

Community involvement

The company supports a range of charitable causes with a particular focus on literacy and reading especially among children. Support is provided through partnerships, donations, fundraising and sponsorship.

Partnerships

Since 2013, Waterstones has worked closely with the BookTrust, a charity which works to ensure that children and young people do not miss out on the life-changing benefits that reading can bring.

The company's stores and booksellers regularly participate in fundraising and awareness raising initiatives and have raised over £200,000 to support BookTrust's programmes, including the Letterbox Club to help improve the educational outlook for children in care.

Commercially led support

Waterstones is the main sponsor of the Waterstones Children's Laureate, awarded every two years to celebrate outstanding achievement by a children's writer or illustrator.

Applications

Contact the correspondent for further information.

Community contributions

Cash donations UK	£280,000

According to its 2016/17 annual report, during the year the company donated a total of £280,000 to charitable causes.

Wates Group Ltd

Community development, education, the environment, general charitable purposes

Company registration number: 1824828

Correspondent: Group Sustainability Team, Wates House, Station Approach, Leatherhead, Surrey KT22 7SW (tel: 01372 861000; website: www.wates.co.uk)

Directors: Andrew Wates; Charles Wates; David Allen; David Barclay; Deena Mattar; James Wates; Joe Oatley; Jonathan Wates; Timothy Wates (female 11%; male 89%).

Nature of business: The Wates Group is a family-owned construction, property services and development company.

Year end	31/12/2017
Turnover	£1,621,973,000
Pre-tax profit	£35,706,000

Total employees: 3,863

Main locations: The group has offices throughout the UK.

Community involvement

The Wates Family Enterprise Trust (Charity Commission no. 1126007) was established in 2008 by the Wates family. Through the Wates Giving programme, the trust provides grants for community projects where the group works. The trust also provides financial support for employee volunteering and matches employee fundraising. In 2017 the trust awarded grants of £1.25 million to support 231 charitable causes across the UK.

The Wates Foundation (Charity Commission no. 247941)

The Wates Group also runs an independent grant-making family trust supporting the charitable and voluntary sector. It was established in 1966 and since then has made grants totalling over £100 million. Its grant-making strategy is organised around five themes, building family values, community health, life transitions, safer communities, and strengthening the voluntary sector. Recently the foundation adopted a new proactive grant-making approach in which members of the Wates family seek out charities to support. As such, unsolicited applications are not accepted.

Building Futures

Building Futures is a two-week programme for job seekers. It offers adults the chance to visit active construction sites, trains them in key skills, awards them an industry-recognised skills certificate and opens routes for a potential employment in the construction industry. To date, over 1,100 people have participated in over 100 Building Futures Programmes, with over half of these moving into education, employment or training thereafter.

Partnerships

The group has a number of strategic partnerships in place to support its charitable activities. Current partners include, Social Enterprise UK, Business in the Community, Prince's Trust, Ixion Holdings and Career Read. In 2017 the group awarded a grant of £65,000 to The Prince's Trust.

Employee-led support

Volunteering

The annual Reshaping Tomorrow week brings together employees, customers and supply chain partners to carry out a wide range of projects. In 2017 Wates employees donated over 10,700 hours to help 93 community projects across the UK. In addition to the time volunteered, Wates Giving donated £23,000 to a range of local community projects.

Matched funding

During the year, 162 awards were made to match funds for employees' own fundraising including sponsored climbs, runs and raffles. Wates Giving provided £148,000 of matched funding which brought the total raised by employees during the year to £337,000.

Payroll giving

The group operates a Give As You Earn scheme that allows regular salary deductions to support good causes. In 2017 Give As You Earn donations totalled almost £16,000.

Employee community involvement

During the year, Wates Giving awarded 30 grants to support employees who work in their community in roles such as trustees, sports coaches and fundraisers. The group also supports its employees' community work by providing 16 hours paid time for them to volunteer locally.

Applications

Contact the correspondent for more information.

Corporate charity

Wates Family Enterprise Trust (Charity Commission no. 1126007) – see page 286.

Community contributions

Cash donations worldwide	£1,280,000

According to the group's 2017 accounts, during the year the group made charitable donations amounting to £1.28 million.

The Watford Association Football Club Ltd

Children and young people, sports and recreation, equal opportunities, health

Company registration number: 104194

Correspondent: Anne-Marie Burn, Trust Administrator, Watford FC, Vicarage Road Stadium, Watford WD18 0ER (tel: 01923 496362; email: community@watfordfc.com; website: www.watfordfccsetrust.com)

Directors: David Fransen; Scott Duxbury; Stuart Timperley (female 0%; male 100%).

Nature of business: Watford FC is a professional football club competing in the Premier League.

Year end	30/06/2017
Turnover	£123,907,000
Pre-tax profit	£4,028,000

UK employees: 254

Main locations: The trust works in Hertfordshire and the boroughs of Harrow and Hillingdon.

Community involvement

The club delivers most of its charitable activities through its associated registered charity Watford FC's Community Sports and Education Trust (Charity Commission no. 1102239), which delivers a range of programmes focused on sport, inclusion, health, education and community in Hertfordshire and the London boroughs of Harrow and Hillingdon. The club also supports local charities through in-kind and cash donations.

Watford Community Sports and Education Trust

The trust works in partnership with other organisations to deliver a range of programmes in Hertfordshire and surrounding areas as well as the boroughs of Harrow and Hillingdon. The website notes that even though the trust 'may traditionally be seen as purely a football provider, this is certainly no longer the case'. The trust's current five key themes are: sports participation, social inclusion, health, education and community facilities. It focuses on promoting the welfare of children and young people and vulnerable adults. The trust is self-financing and has a secured loan from the company totalling £669,000. For detailed information on all of the trust's current programmes, see the website.

In-kind support

The club can arrange for items of merchandise to be signed for fundraising purposes. Given the large number of requests that the club receives it requests that charities purchase or supply the shirt/footballs in the first instance. The club also requests that a donation be made to the Watford FC Community Sports and Education Trust for any item that Watford FC have agreed to be signed by the Watford FC squad. Once payment has been received, the club will organise for the item to be signed by individual players or as many members of the first team squad as possible, within a maximum of six weeks.

Applications

Signed items

For enquiries about signed items contact Alex Ashby (alex.ashby@watfordfc.com) or Dave Messenger (dave.messenger@watfordfc.com).

Donations

The club's website notes that donation requests to the club are not accepted via email. You should write your request on a headed paper, provide full details of the event you are seeking support for and, if appropriate, include a letter of authorization from the charity the event would benefit (giving their registered charity number). Appeals should be addressed to the Charities Department.

The club's charity can be reached at the same address. Any requests or queries to the trust may also be directed at the Trust Administrator, Anne-Marie Burn (email: annemarie.burn@watfordfc.com).

Community contributions

The company's accounts for 2016/17 do not provide a figure for the club's community contributions during the year.

Watkin Jones Group plc

General charitable purposes

Company registration number: 4084303

Correspondent: Watkin Jones Community Fund, 55 Ffordd William Morgan, St Asaph Business Park, St Asaph, Denbighshire LL17 0JG (tel: 01745 538200; email: communityfund@watkinjones.com; website: www.watkinjones.com)

Directors: Andrew McDonough; Berwyn Evans; Geraint Morgan; Graham Davies; Ian Pease; Jim Davies; Mark Watkin Jones; Phillip Byrom; Rebecca Hopewell (female 11%; male 89%).

Nature of business: Watkin Jones Group is a construction and property development company.

Year end	30/09/2017
Turnover	£301,900,000
Pre-tax profit	£43,300,000

UK employees: 680

Main locations: The group's head office is in Bangnor, Wales. The group also has offices in London, Preston, Cardiff and St Asaph.

Community involvement

The group supports general charitable purposes through cash donations and employee volunteering.

Watkin Jones Community Fund

Through its Community Fund, the group awards grants to support projects which benefit local communities. The fund aims to provide financial assistance to a wide range of projects with a particular emphasis on enhancing the physical environment and improving quality of life for local people. Applications are welcomed from all community-based groups and not-for-profit organisations. Grants are typically for up to £1,000 but in exceptional circumstances, the group may consider applications for larger amounts.

Employee-led support

Employees often visit local schools and colleges to discuss careers options and invite students to tour current developments to gain an insight into the construction sector.

Exclusions

Community grants will not be awarded to individuals or companies who aim to distribute a profit.

Applications

Application forms are available to download from the website or by emailing: communityfund@watkinjones.com. All completed applications should submitted by post. Applications will be considered every three months.

Community contributions

The group's 2016/17 accounts did not provide a figure for its total community contribution.

The Weir Group plc

Community development, health, education (particularly STEM subjects)

Company registration number: SC002934

Correspondent: CSR Team, 1 West Regent Street, Glasgow, Scotland G2 1RW (tel: 0141 637 7111; email: philanthropy@mail.weir; website: www.weir.co.uk)

Directors: Barbara Jeremiah; Cal Collins; Charles Berry; Clare Chapman; Graham Vanhegan; Jim McDonald; John Heasley; Jon Stanton; Mary Jo Jacobi; Richard Menell; Stephen Young (female 27%; male 73%).

Nature of business: The Weir Group provides specialist engineering services and products.

Year end	31/12/2017
Turnover	£2,356,000,000
Pre-tax profit	£250,000,000

Total employees: 14,906

Main locations: The group has operations worldwide. In the UK, it has offices and facilities in Aberdeen; Alloa; Barton on Humber; Bedford; Cardiff; Derby; East Kilbride; Hampshire; Teesside; and Todmorden. The group's head office is in Glasgow.

Community involvement

The group supports charities involved in community development; health; and education, (particularly STEM). The group provides financial donations, in-kind support and employee volunteering. Community activities are mainly organised by individual businesses within the group.

Partnerships

In 2017 the group continued its support for the Arkwright Scholarships programme which identifies and nurtures high-potential students in UK schools and encourages them to pursue engineering or technical design at university or through higher-level apprenticeships.

Other examples of charitable partnerships included: support for Primary Engineer, a charity which encourages young people to engage with STEM education; and a £100,000 donation to Newlands Junior College, a vocational school that provides career opportunities to young people who have become disengaged from the traditional education system.

Employee-led support

Each business within the group operates its own policies for supporting employees to engage in charitable work.

Applications

The website states that all enquiries regarding charitable donations or partnerships should be forwarded to: philanthropy@mail.weir.

Community contributions

Total contributions (cash and in kind)	£533,000

The 2017 annual report states that during the year, the group donated £533,000 to charitable causes. This figure includes both financial donations as well as in-kind support, such as products, the use of group's facilities and employee volunteer time. Charitable support was given for the following causes: Education (56%); Community (29%); Health (12%).

Wellington Management International Ltd

Arts and culture, children and young people, education, projects outside the UK

Company registration number: 4283513

Correspondent: Cardinal Place, 80 Victoria Street, London SW1E 5JL (tel: 020 7126 6000; website: www.wellington.com)

Directors: Susanne Ballauff; Natasha Brook-Walters; Cynthia Clarke; Carl Enderlein; Stefan Haselwandter; Ray Helfer Jr; Lucinda Marrs; John Parsons; Phillip Perelmuter; Mary Pryshlak; Edward Steinborn; Luke Stellini (female 42%; male 58%).

Nature of business: Wellington Management is a global investment management firm. We have taken the information for this record from the company registered in the UK. The ultimate parent company, Wellington Management Global, is registered in Bermuda.

Year end	31/12/2017
Turnover	£318,600,000
Pre-tax profit	£58,800,000

Total employees: 300

Main locations: In Europe, Wellington have offices in London, Frankfurt, Luxembourg and Zurich.

Community involvement

Wellington Management CSR strategy focuses on supporting the communities in which its employees live and work. The group has two corporate charities, one in the UK and one in the US. Both make grants to support educational opportunities for disadvantaged young people, including arts-based programmes. In the UK, the group's charitable giving is channelled through the Wellington Management UK Foundation (Charity Commission no. 1167369).

In-kind support

Employees are given two paid days leave each year to volunteer for non-profit organisations.

Employee-led support

The group matches employee donations to registered non-profit organisations. It also runs an 'Annual Appeal' to allow employees to fundraise and donate to global and regional non-profit organisations.

Corporate charity

Wellington Management UK Foundation (Charity Commission no. 1167369) – see page 286.

Community contributions

Cash donations UK	£227,000

In 2017 the group donated £227,000 to its UK corporate charity.

Wesleyan Assurance Society

Education, health, poverty and social exclusion

Company registration number: ZC000145

Correspondent: Colmore Circus, Birmingham B4 6AR (email: www.wesleyan.co.uk/foundation; website: www.wesleyan.co.uk/foundation)

Directors: Ahmed Farooq; Andrew Neden; Chris Brinsmead; Dr Craig Errington; Martin Bryant; Nathan Moss; Nigel Masters; Phil Green (female 0%; male 100%).

Nature of business: Wesleyan is a financial services mutual that provides specialist advice and solutions to professionals such as doctors, dentists, teachers and lawyers.

Year end	31/12/2017
Turnover	£857,700,000
Pre-tax profit	£14,600,000

UK employees: 1,596

Main locations: The society's head office is in Birmingham.

Community involvement

The society provides most of its support through its foundation which makes grants for education, health, innovation and social development. Staff also volunteer and fundraise for its charity partners.

Wesleyan Foundation (not a registered charity)

The foundation was launched in May 2017 and supports projects involving the promotion and/or development of education, health, innovation and social development. Registered charities as well as constituted voluntary and community groups are supported. Organisations should be based within the United Kingdom and have an income of under £250,000. Grants are available through the following community foundations:

- Heart of England Community Foundation (Coventry and Warwickshire)
- Birmingham and Black Country Community Foundation
- Quartet Community Foundation (Bristol)
- Leeds Community Foundation
- Leicester and Rutland
- Nottinghamshire Community Foundation
- Northern Ireland Community Foundation
- Foundation Scotland
- South Yorkshire Community Foundation
- The Community Foundation in Wales

Charity partnerships

In 2017 a four year partnership with Birmingham Children's Hospital came to an end. During the four years Wesleyan staff raised over £1 million towards Magnolia House. The society started a new two year partnership with Partnership for Children, a national charity that promotes the mental health and emotional well-being of children in schools across the UK.

In-kind support

In 2017 the society supported LoveBrum's Bags for Brummies event by donating essential items for 70 bags which were distributed to homeless people in December.

Each member of staff receives a day's leave to offer practical support to charities. In 2017 over 2,000 hours of support were given.

Employee-led support

In 2017 staff raised over £250,000 for Magnolia House at Birmingham Children's Hospital and £25,000 for Partnership for Children. A number of charitable events were supported by employees where their personal contribution was matched by the society. In 2017 over 120 staff used their volunteering days to help local charities.

Applications

Wesleyan Foundation

Applicants should visit the relevant community foundation website where further information on the grant schemes can be found. Any queries should be directed to your local community foundation.

Community contributions

According to the society's 2017 annual report, charitable donations totalled £768,000. We were unable to determine the breakdown between company donations and employee fundraising.

Wessex Water Services Ltd

The environment, education (particularly STEM subjects), older people, children and young people

Company registration number: 2366648

Correspondent: CSR Committee, Claverton Down Road, Claverton Down, Bath BA2 7WW (tel: 01225 526000; website: www.wessexwater.co.uk)

Directors: Andy Pymer; Colin Skellett; David Barclay; Fiona Reynolds; Francis Yeoh; Gillian Camm; Hann Yeoh; Hong Yeoh; Huw Davies; James Rider; Mark Watts; Mark Yeoh; Richard Keys (female 15%; male 85%).

Nature of business: Wessex Water is a regional water and sewage treatment business serving the south west of England. The ultimate parent company of Wessex Water Services Ltd is YTL Corporation Berhad (incorporated in Malaysia).

Year end	31/03/2018
Turnover	£540,600,000
Pre-tax profit	£151,300,000

UK employees: 2,370

Main locations: The company operates in various locations across the south west of England, including: Avon; Dorset; Gloucestershire; Hampshire; Somerset; and Wiltshire.

Community involvement

The company focuses most of its charitable support within the region where it operates and contributes to environmental and educational projects. The company also works closely with NGOs working elsewhere in the world, such as WaterAid. Support is provided through grants, in-kind support, volunteering and fundraising.

Community Fund

The Wessex Water Community fund offers grants of up to £1,500 to groups working to build cohesion and bring communities together. According to the company's website, priority will be given to 'applications from groups working in areas of financial deprivation or rural isolation and/or raising awareness of drinking water for healthy living or promoting water saving initiatives'.

To deliver the scheme, the company works in partnership with four of the region's community foundations (see 'Applications' section).

Watermark awards

The Watermark scheme supports environmental projects based in the Wessex Water region. It is organised by the Conservation Foundation (Charity Commission no. 284656) and applications are reviewed by a panel of experts chaired by one of the foundation's co-founders, TV presenter David Bellamy.

Grants of up to £1,500 are available to schools, parish councils, youth groups and community organisations. A special project receives the Wessex Watermark gold award worth £2,500, which is awarded every quarter. To mark the scheme's 25th anniversary, the company will be providing some additional funding to address the need to reduce single-use plastics.

The awards are open to research projects identified in local authority biodiversity action plans (BAP) or Wessex Water's own BAP (see below).

BAP (biodiversity action plan) Partners Programme

Now in its fifth phase, the BAP partners programme funds projects that will conserve and enhance biodiversity in the region where the company operates. Partnerships and grants are made to wildlife conservation organisations. The programme generally funds projects that focus on: habitat creation; species or survey work; restoration work; or more strategic work to enhance biodiversity or water quality.

From 2015 to 2020 the company is supporting the following four projects: Avon Wildlife Trust; Cranborne Chase Area of Outstanding Natural Beauty; Dorset Wiltshire Trust; Wiltshire Wildlife Trust.

Small grants scheme

The Partners Programme is offering grants of between £2,500 and £5,000 every six months until October 2019. The grants are aimed at short-term, small scale practical projects that address catchment, ecosystems and science and research issues, such as: habitat creation and restoration; ancillary conservation works (such as fencing and support services for grazing); land management actions to improve water quality; provision of land management advice; dissemination and communication of information; or to meet immediate research or monitoring needs.

Money Matters awards scheme

Under this scheme, organisations which run community-based projects to improve financial literacy and money management skills among young people and vulnerable customers can apply for a grant of up to £5,000 towards specific projects.

WaterAid

Since its creation Wessex Water has supported the international water and sanitation charity WaterAid by organising fundraising events, corporate support and raising money and awareness through customers and staff. In 2018 employees and contractors raised a total of £201,000 for WaterAid, of which £100,000 was dedicated to a three-year project in Faratsiho, central Madagascar, to help provide access to clean water, sanitation and to deliver some hygiene education.

In-kind support

In 2018 the company launched an employee volunteering programme, Wessex Water Force. As part of the programme, employees are given one working day a year to volunteer for a local community group or charity.

The company offers a free education service to schools and colleges in the region in which it operates. This includes visits to primary and secondary schools to deliver a range of services including school assemblies and classroom learning. In 2017 over 29,000 students benefitted from school visits and trips to water and sewage treatment works.

Commercially led support

The company works with debt advisers and other community-based organisations to support vulnerable customers to afford their ongoing water bills and repay their debt.

Applications

Community Fund

For more details about the Community Fund, contact the relevant community foundation:

- Somerset Community Foundation – 01749 344949
- Wiltshire Community Foundation – 01380 729284
- Quartet Community Foundation – 0117 989 7700
- Dorset Community Foundation – 01202 670815

Watermark awards

Applications for the Watermark awards can be directed to the company on 01225 526327 or by contacting the Conservation Foundation on 020 7591 3111 or by email at: info@conservationfoundation.co.uk. More information can be found on the website: www.conservationfoundation.co.uk.

BAP Partners Programme

Applications for the BAP Partners Programme small grants scheme can be made using the application form on the company's website. The scheme is open to applications from 1 to 30 April and 1 to 31 October each year until 2019.

Money Matters award scheme

Grants for the Money Matters awards scheme are awarded in January and July each year. The scheme is administered by the Quartet Community Foundation. Applications can be submitted via the foundation's website: quartetcf.org.uk/grant-programmes/wessex-water-money-matters.

Schools

Schools can apply for an education service site or school visit using the company's online form, available under the 'Community' section of the website.

All other enquiries can be directed at the company's head office. Board member, Gillian Camm, is Chair of the Customer and Communities panel and CSR committee.

Community contributions

Cash donations UK	£335,000

During the year £335,000 was donated to UK charities of which £224,500 was donated to local debt advice agencies to help provide debt and financial advice to customers in the company's area of operation who are struggling to pay their water bills.

Western Power Distribution Group

Education, the environment, fuel poverty

Company registration number: 9223384

Correspondent: see 'Applications', Avonbank, Feeder Road, Bristol BS2 0TB (tel: 0800 096 3080; email: info@westernpower.co.uk; website: www.westernpower.co.uk)

Directors: Alexander Torok; Alison Sleightholm; Gregory Dunkin; Ian Williams; Joanne Raphael; Philip Swift; Robert Symons; Vincent Sorgi (female 25%; male 75%).

Nature of business: Western Power Distribution is the trading identity of four electricity distribution companies – Western Power Distribution (East Midlands) plc (registered no. 2366923); Western Power Distribution (West Midlands) plc (registered no. 3600574); Western Power Distribution (South West) plc (registered no. 2366894); and Western Power Distribution (South Wales) plc (registered no. 2366985).

Year end	31/03/2018
Turnover	£1,620,900,000
Pre-tax profit	£705,300,000

UK employees: 6,646

Total employees: 6,646

Main locations: The company operates across the Midlands, South West and Wales.

Community involvement

Western Power Distribution supports local causes in the areas where it operates. The three main strands of support are education, safety and the environment. Support is provided through cash and in-kind donations, education programmes and bursaries, sponsorship and partnerships.

Keen to be Green

Keen to be Green is a core element of the company's community support with the aim of focusing on projects that have an environmental link.

As part of the initiative, the company partners with the various Wildlife Trusts in its network area, providing schoolchildren with hands-on nature experiences, and helping them understand the importance of protecting vulnerable wildlife like bats and hedgehogs. The company also plants native trees in public open spaces with conservation groups like The Conservation Volunteers and Groundwork Wales. Charities, community groups and schools are encouraged to apply.

Education

During the year, the group delivered 3,200 educational safety sessions, reaching over 81,000 schoolchildren. These included school visits and life skill initiatives. The group also provided bursary support for underprivileged students in South Wales involved in the Duke of Edinburgh Award.

Fuel poverty

The group also provides signposting and referral services for customers who are at risk of fuel poverty.

In-kind support

During the year, the group continued to partner with Age Cymru to deliver its Winter Warmth campaign. As part of the campaign the group distributed thermometers to the over 65s in South Wales. The group also supported a British Heart Foundation initiative to provide CPR kits in Bristol schools.

Employee-led support

Staff members take part in the safety and educational initiatives organised by the group and volunteer to support their local communities.

Exclusions

To qualify for support organisations must fall within the group's distribution area.

Applications

For further information about the group's community support, call the number that relates to your distribution area.

Keen to be Green

For further details about the company's Keen to be Green initiative, contact Tracy Carr, Keen to be Green Co-ordinator, by post at: Western Power Distribution, Feeder Road, Bristol or by phone at: 0117 933 2376.

Community contributions

Total contributions (cash and in kind)	£265,000

According to its 2017/18 report, during the year the group assisted 318 charitable and non-charitable organisations as part of a commitment of £265,000.

Westmorland Ltd

General charitable purposes, community development

Company registration number: 5357857

Correspondent: Community Team, Westmorland Place, Orton, Penrith, Cumbria CA10 3SB (tel: 01539 624511; website: www.westmorlandfamily.com)

Directors: Katherine Davis; Laurence King; Nick Candler; Sarah Dunning (female 50%; male 50%).

Nature of business: Westmorland operates a range of hospitality services, including motorway service stations, hotels, and visitor centres.

Year end	02/07/2017
Turnover	£88,293,000
Pre-tax profit	£5,813,000

UK employees: 912

Main locations: The company operates services in Cumbria, Gloucestershire and Lanarkshire.

Community involvement

Westmorland supports a wide range of local charities and community groups in the areas that it operates. Support is provided through a community fund, charity partnerships, in-kind and cash donations, and fundraising.

The Westmorland Family Community Fund

The Westmorland Family Community Fund provides grants of £500 or more to charities and community groups in the Eden area of Cumbria. According to the Cumbria Community Foundation's website (which administers the fund), the purpose of the fund is as follows:

- To support community projects in the travel to work area for Westmorland Ltd. Priority areas for the fund are Appleby, Kirkby Stephen, Brough, Tebay, Shap & Penrith
- To support the development of young people by enabling them to maximise their skills, knowledge, incomes, self-confidence and employability
- To promote learning, personal development, innovation and enterprise
- To support activities that promote enterprise and local food

Gloucestershire Gateway Trust

As part an ongoing partnership with the Gloucestershire Gateway Trust the company has agreed to donate a proportion of the annual turnover from its Gloucester Services' to the charity which is then distributed to a range of partner charities, located primarily into the local communities of Matson, Tuffley, Podsmead and White City and the Stonehouse/GL10 area.

The Gloucestershire Gateway Trust has already committed to support four local registered charities and three community-based organisations through to 2022, but states on its website that it continues to support and work with a wide range of other community organisations within its target communities. Current partners include: Together in Matson, The Nelson Trust, The Gloucestershire Wildlife Trusts and All Pulling Together.

In 2016/17 the company donated a total of £500,000 to the trust. Over the next twenty years, it is estimated that the company will contribute around £10 million.

Partnerships

Every five years, the company chooses a long-term charity partner, which it supports through fundraising and employee volunteering. In 2012 the company started a new five-year partnership with The Calvert Trust, which enables people with disabilities to achieve their potential through outdoor activities. In 2016/17 the company raised a total of £46,000 for the charity.

In-kind support

The company's website notes that in addition to cash donations, the company's business also looks to support community projects in more direct ways. Examples of alternative forms of support given include: donations of food hampers, business coaching and mentoring, and some practical hands-on help, for example, reading with local, primary schoolchildren.

Exclusions

The community fund will not support the direct replacement of statutory obligations or retrospective grants.

Applications

Westmorland Family Community Fund

The Westmorland Family Community Fund is administered by the Cumbria Community Foundation. For further information about the fund including details of how to apply contact Ellen Clements on 01900 825760 or email: ellen@cumbriafoundation.org.

Community contributions

Cash donations UK	£500,000

The company's 2016/17 accounts do not provide an overall figure for its community contributions. However, the accounts do state that during the year a total of £500,000 was donated to the Gloucestershire Gateway Trust as part of its ongoing partnership.

WH Holding Ltd (West Ham United)

Health, education, poverty and social exclusion, children and young people, sports and recreation

Company registration number: 5993863

Correspondent: West Ham United Foundation, 60A Albatross Close, Off Woolwich Manor Way, London E6 5NX (tel: 020 7473 7720; email: foundation@westhamunited.co.uk; website: www.whufc.com/club-foundation/foundation)

Directors: Albert Smith; Andy Mollett; Daniel Harris; David Gold; David Sullivan; Karren Brady (female 17%; male 83%).

Nature of business: West Ham United is a professional football club competing in the Premier League.

Year end	31/05/2017
Turnover	£183,340,000
Pre-tax profit	£43,479,000

UK employees: 399

Main locations: The football club is based in East London.

Community involvement

The club's community support is principally channelled through its charity the West Ham Foundation (Charity Commission no. 1114458) which delivers a wide range of programmes focusing on health and well-being, education, social welfare, inclusion, and children and young people. The club also provides ongoing support for its two principal charity partners, Moore Family Foundation and DT38 Foundation.

West Ham Foundation

The West Ham Foundation works with partners to deliver a broad range of community outreach programmes in East London and Essex. Following the club's move to the London Stadium in 2017, the foundation has committed to invest around £2.5 million each year for the next ten years. Recent examples of the foundation's programmes include.

- **Any Old Irons:** Delivered in partnership with the Premier League, the Professional Footballers' Association (PFA) and Friends of the Elderly, this programme gives participants the opportunity to connect with other fans and locals in their community, bringing them together for fun and friendship
- **150Club:** This 24-week programme is delivered in partnership with NHS Newham CCG, Newham Council and the 150Club partnership and offers local residents at risk of diabetes or cardiovascular disease a range of tailored physical activities to help combat the diseases. It aims to empower local people and enable them to take greater control of their own health
- **MOPAC Project:** Established in 2014, the MOPAC (The Mayor's Office for Policing And Crime) project targets hard-to-reach and vulnerable adolescents between the ages of 12 and 19 through engagement in sport

Full details of all of the foundation's current programmes is available on the club's website.

Partnerships

The club has two principal charity partners, Moore Family Foundation and DT38 Foundation.

- **Moore Family Foundation:** Established in memory of West Ham and England player Bobby Moore, the Moore Family Foundation provides life-changing opportunities for Year 6 students in Newham, Tower Hamlets, Barking and Dagenham, Thurrock, Brentwood and Basildon. As part of the partnership, the West Ham United Foundation provides literacy and numeracy support for pupils. The foundation also arranges matchday tours of the club's stadium
- **DT38 Foundation:** This charity was set up in memory of club academy player Dylan Tombides and exists to raise awareness and change the stigma associated with men's health issues with a focus on testicular cancer

The club's other charity partners include Richard House Children's Hospice, The Bobby Moore Fund for Cancer Research UK, Blesma, Ambition Aspire Achieve.

Applications

Contact the correspondent for more information.

Community contributions

The club's 2016/17 accounts do not provide a figure for its overall community contribution.

In 2016/17 the foundation had a charitable expenditure of £2.41 million, however it was not possible to determine what proportion of this figure came directly from the football club.

Wheatley Housing Group Ltd

Employability, education, digital inclusion, poverty and social exclusion, sport and art

Company registration number: SC426094

Correspondent: The Foundation Team, Wheatley House, 25 Cochrane Street, Glasgow G1 1HL (tel: 0800 479 7979; email: foundation@wheatley-group.com; website: www.wheatley-group.com)

Directors: Alastair Macnish; Bernadette Hewitt; James Muir; John Hill; Josephine Armstrong; Margaret Mulligan; Martin Armstrong; Martin Kelso; Peter Kelly; Prof. Patrick Gray; Ronnie Jacobs; Shelia Gunn; William Blyth (female 31%; male 69%).

Nature of business: Wheatley Housing is a housing, care and property management group.

Year end	31/03/2018
Turnover	£304,551,000
Pre-tax profit	£6,962,000

UK employees: 2,600

Main locations: The group operates across Scotland.

Community involvement

The group mainly offers community support through its corporate charity The Wheatley Foundation Ltd (OSCR no. SC046607), which delivers a wide range of programmes focusing on the issues of employability, education, digital inclusion, poverty, sport and art, within Wheatley communities across Scotland. Programmes are delivered directly as well as in collaboration with a wide range of local and national partners.

According to the group's website, the foundation's five key areas of interest are as follows:

- Poverty: tackling social exclusion and taking people out of poverty
- Employability: Wheatley Works is creating job, career, training and apprenticeship opportunities
- Education: providing access to Higher and Further Education
- Digital Inclusion increasing and expanding digital and online access and capability
- Sport and Art: helping people, old and young, to lead more vibrant, active lives

Recent examples of the foundation's programmes include:

- **My Money:** A £4.2 million service, funded by Big Lottery and the European Social Fund, providing financial advice and support to disadvantaged people in Glasgow through a team of specialist mentors recruited from the third sector
- **Wheatley Bursaries:** A programme offering full-time students up to £1,500 a year for two years, and part-time students £750 a year.
- **Home Comforts:** a programme to provide tenants in financial difficulty, with free, good-quality recycled white goods and furniture
- **Click and Connect:** A network of 38 centres offering free access to computers and tuition helping tenants get online

Full details of all of the foundation's current programmes is available on the group's website.

Partnerships

In addition to the programmes delivered through its foundation, the group also works with partners to 'improve communities and people's life chances'. In 2017/18 the group partnered with the charity Social Bite on the Housing First programme which aims to support people sleeping rough to move into a home and sustain their tenancy. As part of the project, the group pledged more than 200 homes over two years.

Applications

General enquiries can be submitted in writing to the correspondent.

The Wheatley Foundation (OSCR no. SC046607)

The group's website states the following about applications to its foundation: 'The Foundation was set up by Wheatley Group, and is funded by the Group and its subsidiaries, to benefit our customers'. As a result, we are not open to receiving unsolicited proposals and applications.'

Community contributions

Cash donations UK	£121,000

A figure for the group's total community contributions was not provided in its 2017/18 accounts. However, the Wheatley Foundation accounts for the same period reveal that during the year, the group donated around £121,000.

WHSmith plc

Literacy and reading projects for children and young people, general charitable purposes

Company registration number: 5202036

Correspondent: CSR Team, Greenbridge Road, Swindon, Wiltshire SN3 3LD (tel: 01793 616161; email: corporate.responsibility@whsmith.co.uk; website: www.whsmithplc.co.uk)

Directors: Annemarie Durbin; Drummond Hall; Henry Staunton; Ian Houghton; Robert Moorhead; Stephen Clarke; Suzanne Baxter (female 29%; male 71%).

Nature of business: WHSmith is a convenience, book and stationery retailer.

Year end	31/08/2017
Turnover	£610,000,000
Pre-tax profit	£140,000,000

UK employees: 14,000

Main locations: The group has operations throughout the UK, as well as international units in China; Middle East; Australia; South-East Asia; India; and Europe. Its main offices are in London and Swindon.

Community involvement

According to its website, WHSmith is 'committed to making a positive impact' wherever its stores operate. The company supports a wide range of causes, although the promotion of literacy remains the primary focus of its community involvement.

The company raises funds through the carrier bag levy, sale of charity products as well as employee and customer fundraising. The company also actively supports employee volunteering and provides in-kind support for projects that support literacy. In addition, through its charity The WHSmith Group Charitable Trust (Charity Commission no. 1013782), the company awards 'community grants' to a wide range of charitable organisations in which members of staff are involved.

According to its website, WHSmith has set the following targets for its community involvement up to 2020:

- In the decade to 2020, we will have invested £10m in local communities through donations of cash, employee time and gifts in kind
- In the decade to 2020, staff and customer fundraising initiatives will have raised over £1.25m to support partner charities
- In the decade to 2020, we will have worked in partnership with the WHSmith Trust to help over 20,000 children discover the joy of reading

Charity partners

Each year company employees select a number of charity partners to support through fundraising. The company's corporate responsibility report states that it works closely with partners to identify projects, which will make a long-lasting difference to the work they do. In 2016/17 WHSmith's charity partners were Cancer Research UK, Mind and the National Literacy Trust. During the year, WHSmith Australia also established a partnership with Save the Children.

Community grants

Through its charity The WHSmith Group Charitable Trust (Charity Commission no. 1013782) WHSmith distributes the proceeds of the carrier bag levy to customer-nominated charities, schools and community organisations.

WHSmith Community Awards

The company's annual WHSmith Community Awards aim to share good practice and encourage stores to engage with their local communities. The awards recognise those stores which have successfully built strong links with their local community. Each winning store receives a cash prize to donate to a local school or charity.

In-kind support

WHSmith has worked closely with National Literacy Trust's to support the Young Readers Programme since 2005.

The Young Readers Programme motivates children and young people to read for enjoyment through a series of events that celebrate the fun of reading. As part of the partnership, WHSmith hosted school visits to local stores and donated books to school and classroom libraries.

To celebrate World Book Day, in 2016/17 WHSmith partnered with the WHSmith Trust to donate book vouchers to 225 schools across the UK, helping them to increase their school library resources.

Employee-led support

WHSmith actively supports employee volunteering and fundraising efforts. In 2016/17 for example, WHSmith employees raised over £175,000 for Save the Children's Christmas Jumper Day. Employees across the UK also took part in Race for Life events to raise money for Cancer Research UK and held raffles, dress up days and bake sales to mark World Cancer Day.

Commercially led support

WHSmith supports a broad range of charities through the products it sells in store. To mark World Cancer Day for example, over 45,000 Unity Bands were sold in store, raising a total of £63,900. In support of Save the Children meanwhile, stores sold special Christmas cards, Christmas gift wrap and teddy bears.

Applications

General queries about corporate responsibility should be made by email to: corporate.responsibility@whsmith.co.uk or by telephone on: 01793 616161.

Corporate charity

The WHSmith Group Charitable Trust (Charity Commission no. 1013782) – see page 288.

Community contributions

Cash donations worldwide	£1,240,000
In-kind support worldwide	£372,000
Total contributions (cash and in kind)	£1,610,000

The company's 2016/17 CSR report provides the following helpful breakdown of its community contributions:

Cash donated	£1.24 million
Gifts in kind	£279,000
Management costs	£251,000
Staff time donated	£93,000

We take the figure of £1.61 million (excluding management costs) to represent the company's total community contributions. It would appear that charitable giving is mainly concentrated in the UK.

Wilkinson Hardware Stores Ltd

Health and disability, animal welfare, children and young people, domestic violence

Company registration number: 8856837

Correspondent: CSR Team, J. K. House, Roebuck Way, Manton Wood, Worksop, Nottinghamshire S80 3EG (tel: 01909 505505; email: charity@wilko.com; website: corporate.wilko.com)

Directors: Dalton Phillips; John Jackson; Lisa Wilkinson; Robin Terrell; Sean Toal (female 20%; male 80%).

Nature of business: Wilkinson Hardware Stores is a high-street chain which sells homewares and household goods under the name Wilkinsons.

Year end	28/01/2017
Turnover	£1,512,800,000
Pre-tax profit	£5,198,000

UK employees: 11,243

Main locations: The company has outlets throughout the UK. The company's headquarters are in Worksop, Nottinghamshire.

Community involvement

The company awards small donations to various local causes in the areas where its stores operate. The company also supports local organisations through corporate partnerships and helps national charities through staff fundraising. A range of causes are supported including: health and disability; animals; children; and domestic violence.

Helping Hands

As part of the company's Helping Hands initiative, every Wilko store is given a small budget to be distributed in the form of cash donations or in-kind support to local groups and community projects. Organisations previously supported include, local schools, playgroups and nurseries, parent or family groups, disability groups, youth clubs, groups for older people, luncheon clubs, community and tenants' associations plus appeals from the local police, fire service and local councils.

In-kind support

As part of the Helping Hands initiative, the company's various stores donate Wilko gift cards or products to community groups.

Employee-led support

Together for Families programme

In March 2018, the company launched its Together for Families programme, designed to support families in times of need. As part of the programme, Wilko employees will be raising money to support three partner charities which work to tackle social issues which affect family life, namely: Alzheimer's Society, Save the Children and Teenage Cancer Trust. The company has set a target to raise £5 million for the charities over the next three years.

Volunteering

Wilko employees are entitled to one day per year to volunteer in their local communities.

Commercially led support

The company donates funds received from the 5p carrier bag levy to charities across the UK. In 2017 a total of £1.39 million was distributed. In England, the money raised from the carrier bag charge is split between: In Kind Direct, The Prince's Trust, WRAP and The Woodland Trust. In Wales, the money is donated to: Keep Wales Tidy, Ty Hafan, Wales Air Ambulance, Alzheimer's Research UK and Cancer Research Wales. In Scotland, funds from the carrier bag charge are donated to National Trust Scotland and The Scottish Wildlife Trust.

Exclusions

No support is given for local appeals not in areas of company presence.

The Helping Hands scheme cannot support the following:

- Expeditions
- Political parties
- Private or fee-paying schools
- Branches of national charities
- Profitable organisations
- Third-party private fundraising groups

Applications

Applications for small donations through the **Helping Hands** scheme should be directed to your local Wilko store. The application forms can be picked up from the store or downloaded from the website. Once completed they should be returned to the store.

Any other enquiries can be made in writing to the correspondent at the company's address.

Community contributions

Cash donations UK	£131,000

According to the 2016/17 annual report, during the year Wilko made charitable cash donations of £131,000.

William Hill plc

Sports and recreation, general charitable purposes

Company registration number: 4212563

Correspondent: CSR Team, Greenside House, 50 Station Road, Wood Green, London N22 7TP (tel: 020 8918 3600; website: www.williamhillplc.com)

Directors: David Lowden; Georgina Harvey; Luke Thomas; Mark Brooker; Philip Bowcock; Robin Terrell; Roger Devlin; Roy Gardner; Ruth Prior (female 22%; male 78%).

Nature of business: William Hill is a UK-based bookmaker. The principal activities of the company include the operation of licensed betting shops and the provision of telephone, online and interactive television betting services.

Year end	26/12/2017
Turnover	£1,711,000,000
Pre-tax profit	(£78,600,000)

Total employees: 16,000+

Main locations: The company operates worldwide. Its headquarters are based in London.

Community involvement

William Hill seeks to support the communities in which it operates through charitable donations, partnerships with national charities and other charitable initiatives, including the promotion of responsible gambling. The company also provides ongoing support for sport in the UK and overseas through sponsorship.

The William Hill Foundation (Charity Commission no. 1146270)

Much of the company's charitable activities are carried out through its charitable foundation. The foundation was created in 2011 and registered with the Charity Commission in 2012. It was initially designed as a hardship fund to support William Hill employees and their families but for the past five years has also acted as an umbrella organisation for 'Project Africa' – a project to help the remote community of Ol Maisor in Kenya become more self-sufficient. In 2016/17 the foundation awarded a total of 25 grants through its Hardship Fund totalling £28,000.

Close to Home

Close to Home is William Hill's community commitment launched in 2015. Through the scheme William Hill supports its employees to give their time and skills to make a positive contribution to the communities where we live and work. The scheme focuses on three areas:

- Creating opportunities through sport
- Promoting skills and opportunity
- Improving the local environment

Partnerships

As part of its CSR strategy William Hill develops partnerships with a range of organisations. Recently, these have included a partnership with the Scottish Football Association to help tackle mental health problems in sport, and a partnership with Everton in the Community to create a Youth Zone evening programme to engage young people in sport. Through its partnerships, with social enterprise Our Club and the Tottenham Hotspur Foundation meanwhile, William Hill has helped to provide employment to 106 individuals, many of whom were previously long-term unemployed. Other recent partners have included the Chelsea Foundation and the Bobby Moore Fund. CLIC Sargent, the UK's largest children's cancer charity, was the company's Retail Charity of the Year for 2017.

Responsible Gambling

The one of the main focuses of the company's CSR approach is addressing the negative impacts of gambling. In 2017 the company donated £1 million to GambleAware to fund research, education and treatment of problem gambling.

Employee-led support

During the year, William Hill employees participated in 108 charity fundraising events raising £56,000. This total was matched by donations made by William Hill.

As part of the Close to Home scheme William Hill employees volunteered nearly 7000 hours of staff time to charitable causes.

Commercially led support

William Hill is the main sponsor of the Haringey Box Cup, the largest international amateur boxing competition. Through its sponsorship, William Hill helps to provide an opportunity for young boxers from across the world to compete in the three-day annual event at Alexandra Palace in London. At the event, William Hill also offers boxing clubs and members of the public the chance to win a volunteering project for their community on behalf of William Hill.

Applications

CSR queries should be made in writing to the correspondent. Employees can obtain an application form to apply for a grant form the William Hill Foundation Hardship Fund by emailing: williamhillfoundation@williamhill.co.uk.

Community contributions

Cash donations worldwide	£1,900,000

In 2016/17 the company's charitable donations amounted to £1.9 million, including a £1 million donation to GambleAware and £56,000 in matched funding.

Willmott Dixon Holdings Ltd

Community development, social exclusion, offenders and ex-offenders, homelessness, disability, education

Company registration number: 198032

Correspondent: Sarah Fraser, Head of the Willmott Dixon Foundation, Spirella 2, Icknield Way, Letchworth Garden City, Hertfordshire SG6 4GY (tel: 01462 671852; email: sarah.fraser@willmottdixon.co.uk; website: www.willmottdixon.co.uk/our-approach/social-value-and-sustainable-futures)

Directors: Christopher Sheridan; Colin Enticknap; Graham Dundas; Jonathon Porritt; Rick Willmott; Wendy McWilliams (female 17%; male 83%).

Nature of business: Willmott Dixon specialises in construction, residential development and property support services.

Year end	31/12/2017
Turnover	£1,296,414,000
Pre-tax profit	£33,510,000

Total employees: 2,062

Main locations: Willmott Dixon has offices across England and Wales. A map showing specific locations is available from: www.willmottdixon.co.uk/contact.

Community involvement

The company delivers most of its community activities through its corporate charity, The Willmott Dixon Foundation (Charity Commission no. 326530) which supports projects and causes which promote the training of young people and the welfare of people with special needs. Support is provided through cash and in-kind donations, employee fundraising and volunteering.

The Willmott Dixon Foundation

The Willmott Dixon Foundation was set up in 1984 and is chaired by the Group Chief Executive, Rick Willmott.Through its foundation the company delivers a wide range of community investment activities, focused on the following three areas:

Youth unemployment and inspiring young people: The company's employees provide training, mentoring and other forms of support for young people who are at risk of becoming NEET (not in education, employment or training).

Social exclusion: The company delivers a range of projects aimed at supporting people living in poverty, ex-offenders, those who are homeless or those living with a disability. This includes, for example, working with prisons and young offender institutes to help steer those in custody away from re-offending.

Community transformation: The company seeks to employ local people and deliver social value in the communities within which it works. The company also delivers a wide range of community transformation projects from litter clearing activities to large-scale renovation projects.

In 2013 the company set itself a target: 'to enhance the life-chances of 3,000 young people by 2015'. After successfully meeting this target, the company then extended the target to 10,000 by 2020. In 2017 the company's residential and property maintenance businesses became separate companies. The target was therefore split between Willmott Dixon and sister companies, Fortem and Be. Willmott Dixon's share of the target is to enhance the life chances of 6,185 young people. By the end of 2017 the company had enhanced the life-chances of a total of 5,112 young people. As part of its work towards meeting its target, the company delivered a wide range of projects which included:

- Providing nearly 900 work experience opportunities
- Attending 63 school and college careers events
- Delivering over 1,000 mock interviews
- Visiting over 60 schools and other organisations

Management Trainee Challenge

The company's Management Trainee Challenge brings trainees from across the business together to identify, plan and deliver local community projects on behalf of the foundation. In 2017, 11 trainees entered the challenge. They were supported by 339 other employees and 107 supply chain partners. As a result, local communities benefitted from time, gifts and donations worth over £243,000. The winning challenge for the year brought together company employees, supply chain partners, a charity and long-term homeless and socially-excluded people to refurbish Age UK's Healthy Living Centre in Bermondsey.

Employee-led support

In 2017 company employees helped to raise a total of almost £200,000 for charity. During the year, 80% of employees took part in community projects, completing nearly 47,000 hours of volunteering.

Applications

Contact the correspondent for more information.

Corporate charity

The Willmott Dixon Foundation (Charity Commission no. 326530) – see page 288.

Community contributions

Total contributions (cash and in kind)	£1,950,000

According to its 2017 annual report, the value of the company's community investment for the year was £1.95 million.

WPP plc

Human rights, health, community development, education, arts and culture, the environment

Company registration number: 111714

Correspondent: Vanessa Edwards, Head of Sustainability, 27 Farm Street, London W1J 5RJ (tel: 020 7408 2204; email: sustainability@wpp.com; website: www.wpp.com)

Directors: Daniela Riccardi; Jacques Aigrain; John Hood; Mark Read; Nicole Seligman; Paul Richardson; Roberto Quarta; Ruigang Li; Sally Susman; Sol Trujillo; Tarek Farahat (female 27%; male 73%).

Nature of business: WPP Group is an international group of companies providing a wide range of communications, management, advertising and public relations services.

Year end	31/12/2017
Turnover	£15,265,400,000
Pre-tax profit	£2,109,300,000

Total employees: 203,000

Main locations: The group operates in 112 countries and has over 4,000 offices, with more than 200 in the UK. Details of where each of its businesses and their offices are located can be found on the WPP website.

Community involvement

The group and its businesses support various causes, particularly human rights, health, local communities, education, the arts, and the environment. Support is provided through cash donations as well as pro bono services and media space.

Individual projects are generally managed by the group's local operating companies, but the parent company WPP coordinates some pro bono initiatives involving multiple companies and makes donations to organisations working in the areas of education, the arts and young people.

Common Ground

In 2016 WPP launched Common Ground – a collaboration between the world's six biggest advertising and marketing services groups and the United Nations – which aims to use the power of communication to accelerate progress towards achieving the UN's 17 Sustainable Development Goals by 2030. The primary focus of WPP is gender equality. So far, more than 26 of WPP's companies have participated, developing over 33 projects.

International

In India, the group has established WPP India CSR Foundation, which makes grants to organisations supporting children, particularly through education, and will also work in partnership with charities to deliver projects.

In-kind support

The group offers extensive pro bono support in areas such as communications, media, advertising, public relations and research, to charitable organisations supporting a range of causes such as health, education, human rights and arts. This support amounted to the value of £12.7 million in 2017 (worldwide). During the year, the group also negotiated free media space for pro bono clients, which was worth a total of £29 million.

Beneficiaries of pro bono support have included: Age UK; British Stammering Organisation; Care International; Operation Smile; Plan UK; Pride in London; StreetSmart; Start Network; The Prince's Trust; Tusk Trust; Unicef; UNHCR.

Examples of the group's pro bono campaigns are included in its 'Pro bono book', which is available to download from WPP's website.

Employee-led support

Employees at businesses in the group worldwide offer time to charities and communities through fundraising and volunteering. Examples of employee-led support in the UK in 2017 included employees of m/SIX volunteering for the homelessness and drug abuse charity The Mix. According to the group's website: 'Staff from m/SIX and The Mix spent the day together coming up with creative ideas to engage with young people including a gamification app enabling young people to get help with mental health issues in a more informal way.'

Applications

Many charitable and pro bono activities are organised by individual businesses within the group; for the contact details of each of the businesses in the group, see the WPP website: www.wpp.com/wpp/companies.

Community contributions

Cash donations worldwide	£7,700,000
In-kind support worldwide	£41,700,000
Total contributions (cash and in kind)	£49,400,000

According to the 2017 sustainability report, the group's cash charitable donations (worldwide) totalled £7.7 million during the year. The group also gave £12.7 million in direct pro bono support and negotiated free media space worth £29 million for pro bono clients. This brings the group's total worldwide charitable contributions to £49.4 million. The causes supported were broken down as follows:

Cause	Pro bono support	Cash donations
Local community	42%	51%
Education	21%	19%
Health	16%	15%
Human rights	13%	11%
Arts	6%	3%
Environment	2%	1%

Beneficiaries included: Action for Children; Chai Cancer Care; Farms for City Children; Jewish Blind and Disabled; Listening Books; National Portrait Gallery; Royal Star and Garter Homes; The Food Chain; Tower Hamlets Mission; Wellbeing of Women; Wheelchair Rugby.

Xerox (UK) Ltd

Education, equal opportunities, health, children and young people

Company registration number: 330754

Correspondent: CSR Team, Bridge House, Oxford Road, Uxbridge UB8 1HS (tel: 01895 251133; website: www.xerox.com)

Directors: Julie Hesselgrove Ward; Oliver Dehon (female 50%; male 50%).

Nature of business: The principal activity of the group is marketing and financing of xerographic and electronic printing equipment, document managing systems and ancillary supplies in the UK. The ultimate parent company of Xerox (UK) Ltd is Xerox Corporation, incorporated in the USA.

Year end	31/12/2016
Turnover	£272,100,000
Pre-tax profit	£32,500,000

Total employees: 1,688

Main locations: The group's UK headquarters are based in Uxbridge.

Community involvement

The company's giving is channelled through its associated charitable trust – The Xerox (UK) Trust (Charity Commission no. 284698). It is also a patron of The Prince's Trust, which is supported through employee-led initiatives.

The Xerox (UK) Trust

The group's corporate charity, The Xerox (UK) Trust, makes grants to a wide range of causes, including education; health and well-being; children and young people. The trust receives income from its investments as well as from donations from the group. The trust also makes use of the group's office space and receives support from group employees.

Charity partners

The group is a patron supporter of The Prince's Trust and provides support through employee-led fundraising activities. The group has also previously provided in-kind support, donating printing equipment for the charity's office. Globally, the group also has a number of charitable programmes, as well as an American corporate charity, The Xerox Foundation, which supports STEM education, local communities, employee volunteering, and other charitable initiatives.

Employee-led support

In the UK, the company's employees participate in fundraising events to support The Prince's Trust. Examples in 2016 included taking part in the trust's Million Makers competition and participating in the trust's Palace-to-Palace Cycle Ride.

Applications

Contact the correspondent for more information.

Community contributions

The company's 2016 accounts state that no charitable donations were made during the year. In previous years, the company has made donations to the Xerox (UK) Trust, but the 2016 accounts state that 'the directors deemed there to be sufficient funds for charitable purposes in respect of the year ended 31 December 2016'.

Yattendon Group plc

General charitable purposes

Company registration number: 288238

Correspondent: Catherine Fleming, Trustee of the The Iliffe Family Charitable Trust, Barn Close, Burnt Hill, Yattendon, Newbury, Berkshire RG18 0UX (tel: 01635 203929; email: info@yattendongroup.co.uk; website: www.yattendongroup.co.uk)

Directors: Edward Iliffe; Francois Austin; Lord Iliffe; Michael Spencer; Stephen Sadler (female 0%; male 100%).

Nature of business: Yattendon Group is a private company owned by the Iliffe family. The principal activities of the group include; marina operations, farming, printing and property management.

Year end	31/03/2018
Turnover	£56,600,000
Pre-tax profit	£24,200,000

Total employees: 371

Main locations: The group has operations in the UK, Europe and the USA.

Community involvement

The group gives through its corporate charity, The Iliffe Family Charitable Trust (Charity Commission no. 273437) which makes grants to UK-registered charities in the areas of: education; health and disability; welfare; religion; conservation and heritage; children and young people; and older people. Both Lord Iliffe and Edward Iliffe are trustees of the charity. The 2017/18 annual report and accounts for The Iliffe Family Charitable Trust were not available at the time of writing (October 2018). The 2016/17 annual report notes that the trust made grants totalling £86,500. It appears that the company made no donations to the trust in 2016/17.

Applications

Contact the correspondent for more information.

Corporate charity

The Iliffe Family Charitable Trust (Charity Commission no. 273437).

Community contributions

The group did not declare its charitable donations in its annual report and accounts for 2017/18.

Yorkshire Building Society

General charitable purposes, community development, animal welfare, older people, disability, health

Company registration number: FCA 106085

Correspondent: Pauline Giroux, Corporate Responsibility Manager, Yorkshire House, Yorkshire Drive, Bradford BD5 8LJ (tel: 0345 166 9271; email: corporateresponsibility@ybs.co.uk; website: www.ybs.co.uk)

Directors: Alasdair Lenman; Alison Hutchinson; Gordon Ireland; Guy Parsons; John Heaps; Mark Pain; Mike Regnier; Neeta Atkar; Stephen White (female 22%; male 78%).

Nature of business: Yorkshire Building Society is the third largest building society in the UK and provides financial services, including mortgages, insurance products and financial advice.

Year end	31/12/2017
Turnover	£535,800,000
Pre-tax profit	£166,000,000

Total employees: 4,220

Main locations: The building society is headquartered in Bradford and has branches throughout the UK.

Community involvement

The group offers support for communities through its charitable foundation, charity partnerships, fundraising activities, and by encouraging employee volunteering. Support is given for general charitable purposes, with some preference for causes relating to: older people; health and disability; community welfare; and animal welfare.

Yorkshire Building Society Charitable Foundation (Charity Commission no. 1069082)

The group's charitable foundation supports registered charities providing help to vulnerable individuals (particularly: older people; people suffering hardship such as isolation; children or adults with disabilities, including learning disabilities; and people who are seriously or terminally ill) as well as organisations working in the field of animal welfare. In 2017 the charity awarded grants totalling £203,000 to 203 charities.

The foundation receives some funding and administrative support from the group. However, the majority of the charity's funding comes from the Small Change Big Difference (SCBD) scheme which encourages customers to donate the annual pence interest on savings and mortgage accounts.

Partnerships

In 2017 the group launched a three-year partnership with the charity End Youth Homelessness. Over the duration of the partnership, the group aims to help 700 homeless young people aged 16 to 25 move into their own homes. Through employee and customer fundraising, the group raised more than £293,000 in 2017. Fundraising activities included a walk and abseil event in the Peak district and a 'Sleep Out' challenge. In addition to fundraising, during the year group employees contributed 659 hours of extra volunteering time to support End Youth Homelessness member charities, and together with customers collected warm clothing and toiletries for young homeless people worth £18,500.

In addition to its work with End Youth Homelessness, the group has continued to support the charity Silver Line, which works to reduce loneliness and isolation among older people. During the year, 27 employees made weekly calls to Silver Line friends.

Employee-led support

All group employees are entitled to 31 hours of paid leave to take part in voluntary or charitable activities annually. In 2017, 56% of employees volunteered, contributing over 22,000 hours in the community. Examples of previous volunteering activities have included, mentoring and befriending, financial literacy sessions, employability workshops, and redecorating community centres.

Applications

General enquiries can be submitted via email. Alternatively speak to a staff member in your local branch.

Corporate charity

Yorkshire Building Society Charitable Foundation (Charity Commission no. 1069082) – see page 289.

Community contributions

Cash donations UK	£1,230,000
In-kind support UK	£378,000
Total contributions (cash and in kind)	£1,610,000

According to its 2017 annual report, during the year the group made charitable donations of almost £1.2 million, which included donations of £293,500 to End Youth Homelessness. In addition, employees contributed time for volunteering worth a total of £378,000. The group also donated £30,000 to the Yorkshire Building Society Charitable foundation.

ZPG Ltd

Health, children and young people, community development

Company registration number: 9005884

Correspondent: CSR Team, The Cooperage, 5 Copper Row, London, England SE1 2LH (tel: 020 3544 1000; website: www.zpg.co.uk)

Directors: Alex Chesterman; Andy Botha; Charlie Bryant; Gareth Helm; Lorraine Metcalf; Matthew Cohan; Mike Blakemore; Paul Whitehead; Tariq Syed (female 20%; male 80%).

Nature of business: The group runs property and price comparison websites Zoopla, uSwitch and PrimeLocation, as well as supplying software and workflow solutions to the property industry.

Year end	30/09/2017
Turnover	£244,500,000
Pre-tax profit	£48,100,000

Total employees: 882

Main locations: The group's head office is based in Southwark, London.

Community involvement

The group provides support through payroll giving, matched funding, employee volunteering, donations and partnerships, with a particular focus on health, young people and communities.

Partnerships

The group's charity partner for 2017 and 2018 is Cancer Research UK, as nominated and voted for by ZPG Ltd employees. Employees raise money for the charity through a range of activities including, sporting challenges, quiz nights, cake sales and raffles.

In-kind support

In 2017 the group arranged an in-house volunteering event in partnership with Age UK. As part of the event a dozen older local residents visited ZPG's offices for the day, where they were offered practical guidance on internet safety, how to stay in touch online and how to compare service providers online to save money on their household bills. The group states in its annual report that it hopes to replicate this event and host similar ones in all of its regional offices in 2018.

Employee-led support

Matched funding

The group provides matched funding of up to £500 per employee per year for fundraising events in aid of CRUK, and up to £250 for any other charity.

Payroll giving

The group has a payroll giving scheme and encourages regular donations by matching up to £20 per month for donations to CRUK and up to £10 per month to any other charity. In 2017 the group raised a total of £24,000 for CRUK through its payroll giving programme.

Volunteering

Employees are entitled to one day of paid volunteering each year.

Applications

Contact the correspondent for further information.

Community contributions

Cash donations UK	£64,000

According to its 2016/17 annual report, during the year the group made donations to registered charities totalling £64,000.

Zurich Insurance Group

Poverty and social exclusion, projects outside the UK, general charitable purposes

Company registration number: BR7985

Correspondent: Corporate Responsibility Team, Zurich Community Trust Ltd, PO Box 1288, Swindon SN1 1FL (email: CRZurichUK@uk.zurich.com; website: www.zurich.co.uk/en/about-us/corporate-responsibility)

Directors: Catherine Bessant; Christoph Franz; Dame Alison Carnwath; David Nish; Jeffrey Hayman; Joan Amble; Kishore Mahbubani; Monica Mächler; Fred Kindle; Susan Bies; Tom de Swaan (female 45%; male 55%).

Nature of business: Zurich is an insurance company headquartered in Zurich, Switzerland which, according to its website, has over 50,000 employees working in over 170 countries. The group's UK branch provides a range of personal, business, public sector, and charity and community insurance products.

Year end	31/12/2017
Turnover	£63,961,000,000
Pre-tax profit	£5,125,000,000

Total employees: 51,633

Main locations: Zurich has offices located throughout the UK. For details of specific locations, see the website (www.zurich.co.uk/en/about-us/our-offices). Zurich Community Trust's website explains:

> Most of our funds that are open to apply to are designated in areas around our main office locations in Gloucestershire, Fareham and Farnborough in Hampshire, London and Wiltshire. There are smaller budgets for Birmingham, Bristol, Cardiff, Glasgow, Manchester and Leeds.

Community involvement

Zurich's UK community involvement is channelled through the Zurich Community Trust (Charity Commission no. 266983). The trust manages Zurich's grant-making, employee volunteering and pro bono activities in the UK. Internationally the group's community involvement is supported by the Z Zurich Foundation. The foundation's Local Programs initiative gives Zurich offices the opportunity to apply for funding to support local long-term community investment initiatives to address issues such as health and well-being, youth empowerment and disaster resilience.

In-kind support

Zurich employees are encouraged to share their knowledge and skills through programmes involving national and local partners managed by the Zurich Community Trust. Opportunities include the following:

Skillshare projects – The purpose of these projects is to allow employees to use their skills to make an important contribution to a community organisation in a short space of time. They are usually one-off projects and can cover a wide range of areas (from marketing to business and strategic planning to social media training) and range in length from two hours to 20, either in one go or over a period of a few months.

Business to charity mentoring – The trust's website explains that 'Zurich already runs a successful in-house mentoring scheme, and now Zurich Community Trust is starting to develop external mentoring between a staff member and the CEO or senior manager of a local or national charity'. Mentors and mentees currently meet three or four times each year, with support also given via telephone, email or Skype.

Employee-led support

Zurich employees in the UK gave 4,690 days of volunteering time in 2017. The group is currently working to make volunteering opportunities accessible to retirees as well as current employees.

Challenge – Challenge is Zurich's biggest annual team volunteer event, bringing together employee teams from Zurich, Endsleigh, Capita and Openwork to complete a one-off project which benefits a local voluntary organisation. In 2017 employee volunteer teams completed 208 challenges for charities and organisations across the UK.

Trusteeship and school governors – Employees volunteer as governors or trustees and can apply for an annual grant of £200 for the school or charity which they support.

Call in Time – Employees volunteer to call an older person supported by Age UK to have a chat and check on their well-being.

Lunchtime volunteering – Employees use their lunchtime to help children with their reading and writing.

Evolving – The programme gives people in the last six months of employment one half day a week to volunteer in their local community.

Employee fundraising

In 2017, Zurich employees raised over £400,000 for Zurich cares and other nominated charities.

Payroll giving – More than 23% of Zurich's UK employees are enrolled in the payroll giving scheme, helping to earn Zurich a Platinum Quality Mark Award. Contributions help to support the work of the Zurich Community Trust. Zurich retirees can also support the trust through tax payments on their pensions.

Matched funding – The Zurich Cares initiative is half funded by employees and is matched by the Zurich Community Trust using the annual donation it receives from Zurich UK businesses.

'Round Pound' scheme – Zurich employees can contribute odd pennies from their monthly wages to Zurich Cares.

Zurich Cares Lottery – Employees can take part in a monthly lottery, the proceeds from which are contributed to the Zurich Cares initiative.

Applications

General enquiries regarding Zurich's Corporate Responsibility Programme can be directed to the Corporate Responsibility team by email (CRZurichUK@uk.zurich.com).

Skillshare applications can be made via the trust's website.

Corporate charity

Zurich Community Trust (UK) Ltd (Charity Commission no. 266983) – see page 290.

Community contributions

Cash donations worldwide	£19,500,000

According to its 2017 corporate social responsibility report, during the year the group awarded a total of $25.5 million (≈ £19.5 million as at January 2019) in cash donations. This figure included $2.4 million (≈ £1.83 million as at January 2019) in matched contributions from Zurich business units worldwide. The 2017 annual report for Zurich Community Trust (UK) Ltd states that it received a donation of £2.5 million from Zurich businesses in the UK during the year. We have taken this as the company's UK cash donation.

Corporate charities in alphabetical order

This edition of the guide provides a section containing information on 128 corporate charities (compared to 132 in the eleventh edition), all of which have a close association with the company to which they are linked. Typically, the corporate charities rely on their companies for a substantial part of their income.

Each entry provides an overview of charitable activities as well as details on grant-making such as the number of grants made, the total value of those grants, the beneficiaries and beneficial areas. This information can provide a useful starting point for any organisation considering applying to a corporate charity for funding.

Aberdeen Standard Investments Charitable Foundation

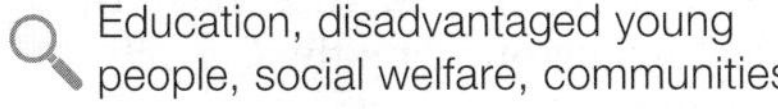

Education, disadvantaged young people, social welfare, communities

UK and overseas where the company has a presence

£1.04 million (2016/17)

OSCR number: SC042597

Trustees: P. B. Aggett; A. A. Laing; H. Young; S. Walker; B. Hendry.

Correspondent: The Trustees, 10 Queen's Terrace, Aberdeen AB10 1YG (email: foundation.uk@aberdeen-asset.com)

aboutus.aberdeen-asset.com/en/aboutus/responsible-business/aberdeen-charitable

Registered in 2011, this is the charitable foundation of Aberdeen Asset Management plc, a global investment management group, managing assets for both institutional and retail clients from some 37 offices in 25 countries. The foundation looks to work in partnership with smaller charities across the globe and, since 2012, has supported more than 400 charities. It is explained on the foundation's webpage that it seeks to give funds where they 'can be seen to have a meaningful and measurable impact'. Employees of Aberdeen Asset Management are also encouraged to contribute their time and skills in support of the foundation's charitable projects.

The foundation's two core focuses – emerging markets and local communities – reflect the business' desire to give back to areas which are a key strategic focus and to build on its pattern of giving to communities in which its employees live and work.

The criteria for each focus are outlined on the foundation's website as follows:

> *Emerging Markets*
>
> Each year the Foundation will select an emerging market and focus its investment in that area. The emerging markets allocation will be focused on a small number of long-term partnerships (average duration of three years). All charities must meet the following criteria to be considered for an emerging market grant:
>
> - UK registered
> - Small to medium in size or, if a larger charity, must have an identifiable project that Aberdeen can support
> - Clear focus on the promotion of education and providing wider opportunities for underprivileged young people
>
> *Local Communities*
>
> All charities applying for local community grants must meet the following criteria:
>
> - Be a registered charity
> - Clear connection to a community local to one of Aberdeen's offices
> - The investment should be capable of having a clear and meaningful impact, for example: – Small charities where the contribution amount is significant relative to the charity's size – Larger charities with identifiable project opportunities that Aberdeen could put its name to – Projects which include the opportunity for Aberdeen employee involvement through volunteering – Local organisations where Aberdeen can have a visible impact
> - A governance structure in place to allow Aberdeen to monitor the impact of the investment

Financial information

In 2016/17 the foundation had assets of £1.16 million and an income of £7,200. Donations were made amounting to £1.04 million, of which £307,500 was awarded to 'emerging markets' projects and £731,500 awarded to local community support.

Beneficiaries included: ChildHope UK (£208,500); AbleChild Africa and Karen Hilltribes Trust (£146,000 each).

Exclusions

The foundation does not support political causes, parties or organisations or charities with a religious focus.

Applications

Application forms are available – along with full criteria and terms and conditions – from the company's website. Completed forms should be returned to the foundation by email (foundation.uk@aberdeen-asset.com), and be accompanied by a PDF copy of your latest annual review. Successful applicants will be notified within three months of their application being submitted. The foundation notes that, due to the volume of applications it receives, it cannot respond to all unsuccessful applicants. Recipients of grants will be required to complete an annual impact assessment form.

The Addleshaw Goddard Charitable Trust

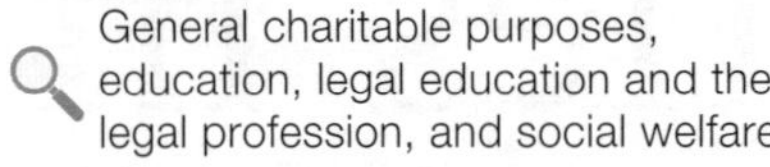

General charitable purposes, education, legal education and the legal profession, and social welfare

Greater London, Manchester and Leeds

£45,000 (2016/17)

CC number: 286887

Trustees: Bruce Lightbody; Jonathan Cheney; Lisa Rodgers; Pervinder Kaur; Christopher Noel; Therese Ryan.

Correspondent: Christopher Noel, Trustee, Addleshaw Goddard LLP, One St Peter's Square, Manchester M2 3DE (tel: 0161 934 6000; email: christopher.noel@addleshawgoddard.com)

Registered in 1983, this is the charitable trust of Addleshaw Goddard LLP, a law firm with UK offices in London, Leeds and Manchester. The objects of the trust are as follows:

- Promote any charitable purpose for the benefit of the communities in any city (whether in England or any other jurisdiction) in which Addleshaw Goddard LLP (or any of its successor firms) operates an office, and in particular the advancement of education, the furtherance of health and the relief of poverty, distress and sickness
- Promote any charitable object or purpose connected with the legal profession and in particular to assist the persons engaged in that profession and the wives, widows, children and other dependants of such persons being in conditions of need, hardship or distress
- To advance legal education in all its aspects insofar as such advancement may be charitable

Financial information

In 2016/17 the trust had assets of £129,500 and an income of £31,500, the majority of which was received from Addleshaw Goddard LLP. Grants were made totalling £45,000, and a further £28,500 was paid in matched staff funding.

A full list of beneficiaries was not provided in the accounts.

Applications

Apply in writing to the correspondent.

The Adnams Community Trust

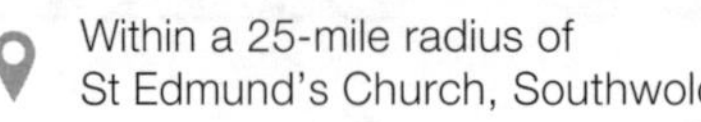

Education, health, social welfare, the arts, recreation, the environment, buildings/community facilities

Within a 25-mile radius of St Edmund's Church, Southwold

£79,500 (2016/17)

CC number: 1000203

Trustees: Melvyn Horn; Simon Loftus; Andy Wood; Jonathan Adnams; Emma Hibbert; Guy Heald; Ann-Marie Cross; Tracey Clark; Sarah Churchyard.

Correspondent: Rebecca Abrahall, Adnams Community Trust Administrator, Adnams plc, Sole Bay Brewery, East Green, Southwold, Suffolk IP18 6JW (tel: 01502 727200; email: communitytrust@adnams.co.uk)

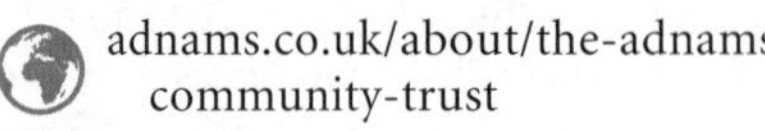

adnams.co.uk/about/the-adnams-community-trust

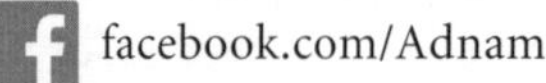

facebook.com/Adnams

@adnams

@Adnams

The Adnams Charity was founded in 1990 to mark the centenary of the Adnams brewing company and is funded mainly by the annual donation from the profits of Adnams plc. It supports a wide variety of organisations within a 25-mile radius of Southwold.

Applications from national charities which operate within a 25-mile area of Southwold may be considered if assurances can be given that the money will be used for a specific purpose within the area.

The trustees prefer to make one-off grants for specific items which normally range from £100 to £2,500. They expect to see the result of their donations within 12 months.

Areas of work

According to the charity's website, most grants are made in the following areas:

- Education
- Health and social welfare
- The arts
- Recreation
- Buildings/community facilities
- The environment/conservation

Financial information

In 2016/17 the trust had assets totalling £3,900 and an income of £74,000, most of which came from Adnams plc. During the year, the trustees awarded £79,500 in grants to 84 organisations.

Beneficiaries included: Over the Rainbow Children's Charity (£2,100); North East Suffolk Citizens Advice (£1,700); Cancer Campaign in Suffolk (£1,800); 1st Eye Scouts (£768); Metfield Parish Council (£500); Sole Bay Arts CIO (£470).

Exclusions

The trust will not support:

- Individuals
- Religious organisations or private clubs unless they can demonstrate that the purpose of the grant is for something of clear public benefit, accessible to all
- Sponsorship, raffle prizes or the fundraising efforts of individuals
- Hardware associated with solar panels (although educational equipment linked to 'green energy' and energy conservation may be considered)

Grants are only made for specific purposes (ongoing running costs are rarely supported) and are not usually made to the same organisation two years in succession.

Applications

Application forms are available on request to the Charity Administrator. Grants are considered at quarterly meetings, in January, April, July and October. Application deadlines usually fall in the previous month and are listed on the charity's website.

Allchurches Trust Ltd

Churches, social welfare, education

UK and Ireland

£15.6 million (2017)

CC number: 263960

Trustees: Archdeacon Annette Cooper; Sir Philip Mawer; Christopher Smith; Denise Wilson; Sir Lawrence Maguns; Michael Arlington; Timothy Carroll; Steven Hudson.

Correspondent: Iain Hearn, Beaufort House, Brunswick Road, Gloucester GL1 1JZ (tel: 01452 873184; email: atl@allchurches.co.uk)

www.allchurches.co.uk

Allchurches Trust Ltd was established in 1972. Its income is derived from its wholly owned subsidiary company Ecclesiastical Insurance Group. Its aims are 'to promote the Christian religion, to contribute to the funds of any charitable institutions, associations, funds or objects and to carry out any charitable purpose'.

Grant-making

The trust likes to fund organisations 'addressing real social need with clear vision, strong local support and a sustainable future'. The trust tends to give a large number of small grants and a limited number of larger grants.

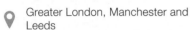

Charities and educational establishments applying for funding should be UK registered or have exempt status and have a Christian foundation or links. Churches seeking funding should belong to denominations which are members of Churches Together in England (CTE), Action of Churches Together in Scotland (ACTS), Churches Together in Wales (Cytun) or the Irish Council of Churches.

According to its website, the trust likes to fund:

> **Churches and cathedrals of all denominations**:
>
> - Mission and ministry
> - Church halls
> - Community and outreach
> - Repairs
> - Conservation
> - Reordering and new works
> - Bells, organs and music
> - Heating, lighting, amenities and building security
> - Churchyards and cemeteries
>
> **Charities with Christian links:**
>
> - Counselling and trauma recovery
> - Homelessness and social exclusion
> - Community healthcare
> - Refugee and asylum-seeker support
> - Women's projects
> - Youth work
> - Ex-offender support
>
> **Schools, colleges, hostels, care homes and other communities:**
>
> - Apprenticeships and bursary schemes
> - Leadership development
> - Quiet rooms, prayer rooms, sibling support rooms
> - Chapels and chaplaincy projects

Financial information

In 2017 the trust had assets of £582.6 million an income of £32.6 million, of which £26 million was donated by Ecclesiastical Insurance Group. Grants awarded to organisations totalled £15.6 million and were distributed as follows:

England	£13 million
National bodies	£1.3 million
Wales	£492,000
Ireland	£475,000
Other	£83,000

Beneficiaries included: Methodist Connexion, London (£910,000); The Diocese of London (£448,000); The Representative Body of the Church of Wales (£182,000); Church Planting Initiative, London (£150,000); Trustees of the Methodist Church in Ireland (£55,000).

Exclusions

The trust's website states that it will not normally fund the following:

> - Overseas charities
> - Charities with a political association
> - Individuals or causes that will benefit only one person such as student grants
> - Running costs
> - Healthcare projects, although hospices can apply for funding towards the provision of chapel and chaplaincy space
> - Work that is primarily the responsibility of statutory authorities including residential, respite, day care and housing provision
> - Animal welfare or rescue
> - Retrospective grants, although we may be prepared to consider applications for work already done which was urgent (such as essential emergency roof repairs) or for major capital projects (where work has started before all funding has been raised)
> - More than one application from the same organisation within a 24 month period
> - One-off events that benefit only a few people – we prefer to support projects that have a long-term benefit for more people

Applications

Applications should be submitted online via the trust's website, where the grants policy and terms and conditions can also be found. The website advises:

> To make your application stand out from the crowd follow our tips and advice.
>
> When describing your project make sure it includes:
>
> - The work you want to do
> - Who will benefit
> - How you will achieve on-going viability
>
> Your applications will catch the attention of our Trustees if:
>
> - It has vision and illustrates enthusiastic support
> - It aims to bring improvements in areas of greatest need
> - It demonstrates financial sustainability, and how you plan to keep up the good work

The Allen & Overy Foundation

Disaster relief, access to justice, access to education, employment and training

London; Northern Ireland; India; Nepal; Syria; Tanzania; Uganda

£1.5 million (2016/17)

CC number: 1153738

Trustees: Mark Mansell; Andrew Wedderburn-Day; Jane Finlayson-Brown; Jane Townsend; Philip Mansfield; Annelies van der Pauw; Christopher Mainwaring-Taylor.

Correspondent: The Trustees, One Bishops Square, London E1 6AD (tel: 020 3088 0000; email: allenoveryfoundation@allenovery.com)

www.allenovery.com/corporate-responsibility/charitable-giving/Pages/Local-charitable-giving.aspx

Allen & Overy is a large international law firm with its headquarters in London. Its foundation is funded by contributions from all Allen & Overy partners around the world. The foundation supports organisations in London, the North of Ireland, India, Nepal, Syria, Tanzania and Uganda that address the following core themes:

- Access to justice
- Access to education and employment

Grant programmes

The following information about the two grant programmes has been taken from the foundation's website:

> **Global Grants Programme**
>
> The Global Grants Programme supports three or four charities each year under the core themes, as well as providing seed funding to our Global Charity Partner and responding to disaster relief efforts.
>
> The Foundation is funded by contributions from all of A&O's partners worldwide and supports:
>
> - Our global charity partnership
> - Disaster relief efforts
> - Three or four charities a year through a global grants programme
>
> The remainder of the foundation['s income] is distributed via local communities to ensure we are addressing the priority issues in the area local to us.
>
> Charities may ring-fence 20% of the grant core funding (not necessarily related to the project funded).
>
> **Local Charitable Giving (London)**
>
> The Foundation in London is administered by the London Grants Committee, which is made up of partners within the London office and a member of the Pro Bono and Community Investment team. The London Grants Committee makes donations to charities that meet one or more of the following criteria:
>
> - Charities which work to promote access to justice in the UK
> - Charities which support and develop projects focusing on issues of education, employment and training based in or benefiting those in Tower Hamlets or Hackney
> - Charities to which Allen & Overy volunteers have made a significant contribution by participating in their activities or providing pro bono and volunteering support

The average grant size is £5,000–£10,000 which may be given for projects or core costs.

Financial information

In 2016/17 the foundation held assets of £599,500 and had an income of almost £1.6 million. Grants awarded to organisations totalled £1.5 million.

Beneficiaries included: War Child (£453,000); Charities Aid Foundation (£100,000); East End Community Foundation (£28,500); British Red Cross and Justice without Borders (£25,000 each); London Legal Support Trust (£10,000); Mind (£5,000).

Applications

The Allen & Overy Foundation (London) – Application forms are available from the correspondent by email. Application guidelines are on the foundation's website, along with the next deadline. The committee meets to consider grants in March and October.

Global Grants Programme – Applications should be made in a letter of no more than two pages. Details of what to include and information on when the next round of funding will open, are given on the website.

Anglo American Group Foundation

Community development, education and training, environment, health (particularly HIV/AIDS) and welfare, international development

UK (Westminster, Southwark and Lambeth) and overseas (Brazil; Chile; Colombia; Peru; China; India; Zimbabwe)

£2.16 million (2017)

CC number: 1111719

Trustees: Duncan Wanblad; Jon Samuel; Angela Bromfield.

Correspondent: Laura Dunne, Foundation Manager, Anglo American House, 20 Carlton House Terrace, London SW1Y 5AN (tel: 020 7968 8888; email: aagf@angloamerican.com)

www.angloamericangroup foundation.org

The foundation was established in 2005 by Anglo American plc, a multinational mining company. The foundation's website states that: 'Anglo American seeks to ensure that its impacts contribute to sustainable livelihoods in the communities in which it operates and the Foundation was founded on the same principles.'

The foundation receives donations from Anglo American plc and supports development initiatives in the areas where the company has operations, projects or representative offices, these include: UK (London, in the City of Westminster, Southwark and Lambeth); Brazil; Chile; Colombia; Peru; China; India; Zimbabwe.

Grant-making policy

As explained on its website, the foundation 'prefers to fund specific projects or components of projects within the overall activities of an organisation that are a priority area in need of support' and that 'have clearly defined objectives with quantifiable outcomes'.

The foundation's website states:

> The Foundation's main objective is to promote sustainable livelihoods and its main areas of interest are:
>
> - Community development
> - Education and training
> - Environment
> - HIV/AIDS and welfare

Support is also provided for community development projects near the group's London offices in Westminster, Southwark and Lambeth.

The foundation's 2017 accounts provide the following information on its giving structure:

> The Foundation seeks to develop continuing relationships with a small number of charitable organisations which contribute to its identified priority objectives. These will then be augmented from time to time by applications which come within the Foundation's priorities and relate to those parts of the world where the AA plc Group does business. Resources are also allocated by way of matching funds raised for charities by employees who work in the Anglo American London office.

Financial information

In 2017 the foundation held assets of £83,500 and had an income of £2.1 million, almost all of which came from Anglo American plc. Grants totalled £2.16 million.

Beneficiaries included: International Youth Foundation (£1.2 million); Engineers Without Borders UK (£540,000).

A full list of beneficiaries was not given in the accounts; however, further case studies are provided on the foundation's website.

Exclusions

According to its website, the foundation only funds registered charities and does not support:

- Animal charities
- Armed forces charities
- Community Interest Companies (CICs)
- Educational fees
- Expeditions overseas
- General health charities
- Hospital trusts
- Individuals
- Music festivals and choirs
- Political or quasi-political bodies
- Religious organisations (other than community outreach)
- Trade unions

Applications

Apply in writing to the correspondent. The trustees meet quarterly.

The Apax Foundation

Social entrepreneurship, social welfare, education

UK and overseas, with a focus on disadvantaged communities

£1.16 million (2016/17)

CC number: 1112845

Trustees: Sir Ronald Cohen; Peter Englander; Rohan Haldea; Simon Cresswell; David Marks; John Megrue; Shasshank Singh; Mitch Truwit; Jason Wright.

Correspondent: Kate Albert, Foundation Manager, c/o Apax Partners LLP, 33 Jermyn Street, London SW1Y 6DN (tel: 020 7872 6300; email: foundation@apax.com)

www.apax.com/responsibility/apax-foundation

The Apax Foundation is the corporate charity for Apax Partners LLP. The foundation channels the firm's charitable giving and receives a percentage of the firm's profits.

The charity's objects are, according to the foundation's annual report:

> - The relief of financial hardship, either generally or individually, of people living in socially and economically deprived areas in the UK and overseas through the provision of grants, goods or services
> - The advancement of education
> - To further such other purposes which are charitable in accordance with the law of England and Wales as the trustees think fit

According to the foundation's website, its main focus is social entrepreneurship:

> Social entrepreneurship was chosen as the focus for the Apax Foundation's major grant giving as it is the natural extension of what Apax does commercially and builds on the firm's history of support in that area, most notably as one of the founders of Bridges Ventures. It is also an area where some of the Foundation's Trustees have significant experience. This provides us with a steady flow of introductions to leading charities in the field, both from within the firm and from our wider network.

Most grants tend to be of £10,000 or less, although a few major grants are awarded each year.

As well as making grants, the foundation also runs a matched giving scheme for Apax employees who are fundraising for charitable causes.

Financial information

In 2016/17 the foundation had assets of £25.8 million and an income of £1.8 million, £783,000 of which was donated by Apax Partners LLP. Grants were made totalling almost £1.16 million and were distributed as follows:

Social enterprise and relief of hardship	£470,000
Other charitable purposes	£436,500
Education	£256,00

Beneficiaries included: Opportunity Network (£291,000); Impetus – The Private Equity Foundation (£215,000); Mosaic (£87,000); Grameen America (£74,000); StreetSquash (£20,500); Aga Khan Foundation (£20,000); Pilotlight (£10,800).

Applications

Apply in writing to the correspondent. The trustees review grant applications which meet the criteria and evaluate the following:

- How effective the charity is at achieving its aims
- The number of beneficiaries reached
- The sustainability of the charity's programmes
- The strength and stability of the charity's management team and internal processes
- The long-term public benefits that would arise from a grant being made

Any further enquiries can be directed to Kate Albert, the foundation's manager.

The Arsenal Foundation Ltd

Education, sport, health, medical, disability, social welfare

Islington; Camden; Hackney; Barnet; Walthamstow; Hertsmere

£1.2 million (2016/17)

CC number: 1145668

Trustees: David Miles; Alan Sefton; Kenneth Friar; Ivan Gazidid; Svenja Geissmar; Andrew Jolly.

Correspondent: Svenja Geissmar, Trustee, Highbury House, 75 Drayton Park, London N5 1BU (email: thearsenalfoundation@arsenal.co.uk)

www.arsenal.com/thearsenalfoundation

facebook.com/TheArsenalFoundation

@AFC_Foundation

@arsenal_foundation

The Arsenal Foundation was established in 2012 as 'the club's grant-giving organisation'. The foundation aims to help young people in North London and around the world fulfil their potential.

Guidelines

The following information was taken from the foundation's website:

> Priority is given to the following areas of need:
>
> - Education (including academic, social, physical education and skills training)
> - Sports capable of improving health
> - Medical
> - Sickness and the relief of suffering
> - Disability
> - Poverty
> - Individual misfortune
>
> The following is a non-exhaustive list of potential beneficiaries or groups of beneficiaries:
>
> - Organisations connected to Arsenal FC
> - Charity or community projects connected to Arsenal FC
> - Projects that have been developed by Arsenal FC's community team
> - Staff-initiated projects
> - Supporter-initiated projects
> - Projects where The Foundation's donation, even though relatively small, will make a difference
> - Projects where the gesture of support from a charity associated with Arsenal FC can have a greater effect than the money itself
> - Football-linked campaigns or public bodies
> - Projects where the person requesting a donation is doing something active to raise money for the cause
> - Projects where the person is playing a significant and voluntary role in raising money for the charity
> - Awards to reward success or achievement in areas of endeavour that fall within the objectives of The Foundation
> - Where funds are donated to The Foundation for a specific project or purpose and The Foundation acts as a partner and makes an additional contribution

The Gunners Fund

The aim of The Gunners Fund is to support charities in the boroughs of Islington, Camden and Hackney by offering smaller grants of up to £2,500 that can make a big difference to the community. The priorities and objectives of the fund are the same as those of the foundation.

Financial information

In 2016/17 the foundation held assets of £1.7 million and had an income of £1.9 million. Grants awarded to organisations totalled £1.2 million and were broken down as follows:

Save the Children	£565,500
Other grants	£452,500
Local pitch projects	£88,000
Manchester Emergency appeal	£50,000
Willow	£50,000
Islington Giving	£1,800

Exclusions

Charities based outside the UK.

Applications

Application forms are available to download from the foundation's website, along with grant-making guidelines. The foundation states that it is unable to respond to all of the applications it receives, due to the high volume, so if you do not receive a response within one month, you should assume that you have been unsuccessful.

The Artemis Charitable Foundation

Health, poverty, education, disaster appeals and the environment

UK and overseas

£1.15 million (2017)

OSCR number: SC037857

Trustee: The Trustees.

Correspondent: The Trustees, 42 Melville Street, Edinburgh EH3 7HA (tel: 0131 225 7300)

www.artemisfunds.com/en/about-artemis/artemis-charitable-foundation

The Artemis Charitable Foundation was founded in 2007, and acts as Artemis Investment Management LLP's charitable arm. According to the foundation's website, the foundation awards one-off grants to 'core' charities in the UK and internationally in the following areas:

- Health
- Poverty
- Education
- Environment

The foundation also makes donations to global disasters and emergencies when they occur.

Financial information

In 2017 the foundation had assets of £711,500 and an income of £1.3 million, of which £1 million was from Artemis Investment Management LLP. During the year, the foundation awarded a total of £1.15 million in grants to organisations.

Beneficiaries included: Mercy Corps (£193,000); Mary's Meals (£74,500); The Rock Trust (£41,000); Robbie's Rally (£30,000); Crisis (£20,000); Mind (£500).

Applications

Apply in writing to the correspondent. The foundation's 2017 accounts state that 'applications for donations are considered from all sources, although greater consideration is placed on requests from staff, in particular where they are actively involved in the charity, through fundraising or volunteering'.

The Ove Arup Foundation

The built environment, engineering, architecture, education

UK and overseas

£187,000 (2016/17)

CC number: 328138

Trustees: Joanna Kennedy; Caroline Cole; Terry Hill; Gregory Hodkinson; Dr Andrew Chan; Faith Wainwright; Tim Chapman.

Correspondent: John Ward, Secretary, c/o Ove Arup & Partners, 13 Fitzroy Street, London W1T 4BQ (email: ovarfound@arup.com)

www.ovearupfoundation.org

facebook.com/Ove-Arup-Foundation-178993628799895

@arupfoundation

This foundation was established in 1989 in memory of Sir Ove Arup, who was an engineer, designer and philosopher. The trustees of the foundation are appointed by the board of Arup Group Ltd. The foundation's 2016/17 annual report explains that its 'principal objective is the advancement of education of the public, directed towards the promotion, furtherance and dissemination of knowledge of matters associated with the built environment'. The foundation also has 'subsidiary powers' to support academic research and any other charitable activity with similar purposes.

As part of its work to achieve its objective, the foundation has worked with partner organisations from across the sector. Partners have included The Royal Academy of Arts, The Royal Institute of British Architects and The Institution of Civil Engineers.

Grant-making

Every year, the foundation's trustees set aside a proportion of its budget to support projects that fall within the foundation's education purposes in relation to the built environment. The website explains:

> Each initiative awarded a grant by the Foundation will be assigned a Trustee, who will liaise with the organisation or individual to offer advice and encouragement. At the end of the grant-period, the sponsored organisation is required to produce a report on how its initiative has progressed, the outcomes and how the grant aided this. The Foundation may post notice of the grant or project outcome on this website.
>
> Small, one-off donations are occasionally considered for a purpose or activity that the Foundation views as worthwhile in itself.

Financial information

In 2016/17 the foundation held assets of £4.4 million and had an income of £319,500 which included a donation of £175,000 from Ove Arup Partnership Charitable Trust. Grants were made to nine organisations and totalled £187,000.

Beneficiaries included: Hong Kong Polytechnic University (£51,500); The University of Edinburgh (£49,000); Useful Simple Projects Ltd (£39,000); Institution of Civil Engineers and Project H Design (£15,000 each); Midlands Architecture and Designed Environment (£10,200); Design Education CIC (£4,200); The Anglo Danish Society (£2,000).

Exclusions

No grants are made to individuals.

Applications

Application forms are available to download from the website.

Ove Arup Partnership Charitable Trust

General charitable purposes

UK

£435,500 (2016/17)

CC number: 1038737

Trustee: Ove Arup Partnership Trust Corporation Ltd.

Correspondent: Stephanie Wilde, Ove Arup & Partners, 13 Fitzroy Street, London W1T 4BQ (email: stephanie.wilde@arup.com)

This trust was established by a trust deed in January 1978. The annual report for 2016/17 explains that the trust 'is not in receipt of a regular income and relies on gifts from Arup Group Ltd'.

Income from the company is used to make charitable donations to charities. Donations are made for a wide range of purposes and particularly education, social care, health, welfare, disaster relief, poverty alleviation, local community development, sustainability, the environment and technology.

Grant-making policy

As the annual report explains, grants are made for causes and charities 'that operate in areas related to Arup's skills and business activities where these are aligned with Arup's values, as expressed in Ove Arup's 'Key Speech', of doing socially useful work and of being engaged in activities for the benefit of society at large'.

When making a decision, the trustee takes into account the size and structure of the recipient organisation in relation to the size of the donation 'in order to maximise the impact and effectiveness of that donation'.

Financial information

In 2016/17 the trust had assets of £17,700 and an income of £438,000, almost all of which was received in the form of a donation from Arup Group Ltd. During the year, donations were made totalling £435,500.

Beneficiaries included: The Prince's Trust (£23,500); Engineers for Overseas Development (£20,000); Architecture Sans Frontieres; British Heart Foundation; Habitat for Humanity Great Britain (£10,000 each); Borders Children's Charity (£500).

Grants of less than £500 totalled £7,700.

Applications

Apply in writing to the correspondent.

The Asda Foundation

Sport and recreation, community development, general charitable purposes

England and Wales

£6.37 million (2017)

CC number: 1124268

Trustees: Gerald Oppenheim; John Cookman; Ann Rocks; Carolyn Heaney; Alison Seabrook; Jane Earnshaw; Jason Martin; Andrew Murray.

Correspondent: Julie Ward, Foundation Manager, Asda House, Great Wilson Street, Leeds LS11 5AD (tel: 0113 243 5435)

www.asdafoundation.org

@asdafoundation

The Asda Foundation is the corporate charity of Asda Stores Ltd. It supplements the good causes that employees support locally, as well as a number of bigger ad-hoc projects in local communities. It also manages all funds raised for national charities and monies raised in its headquarters, Asda House.

The foundation's main objective is to make donations to local good causes. It funds a wide range of causes supported by staff, including everything from local charities and playgroups to football teams.

According to the foundation's website: 'The Foundation works in partnership with other charities tackling issues within local communities and supporting charities made a real difference to thousands of people across the UK.'

Financial information

In 2017 the foundation had assets of £8.98 million and an income of £5.1 million including £4 million from Asda Stores Ltd. Grants totalled £6.37 million with £941,000 awarded to Asda's national campaigns.

Beneficiaries included: Silver Line (£375,000); Young Minds Trust (£197,000); University of Leeds (£115,000); Leeds Rhinos (£41,500); The Salvation Army (£17,000).

Applications

There is an eligibility checker and 'store locator' on the website. To apply, contact your local store or depot and speak to the Community Champion.

Autonomous Research Charitable Trust (ARCT)

People who are disadvantaged, empowering people to improve their quality of life, general charitable purposes

Mainly London and overseas

£397,500 (2016/17)

CC number: 1137503

Trustees: Jonathan Firkins; Andrew Crean; Donald Betson; Rif Huque-Iverson.

Correspondent: Nicki Fletcher, Trust Administrator, c/o Moore Stephens, 150 Aldersgate Street, London EC1A 4AB (tel: 020 7334 9191; email: nicki.fletcher@moorestephens.com)

This trust was established in 2010 for general charitable purposes. It is the charitable trust of Autonomous Research LLP, a company that provides intelligence on banking and insurance companies. The company donates a share of its profits to charitable causes through this trust, as well as through its US foundation, Autonomous Research Foundation US (ARFUS).

The 2016/17 annual report states that the trust's core aims are:

- To help disadvantaged people get a step up in life
- To empower people to improve the quality of their lives
- To focus our resources upon a small number of key partner charities, both in London and abroad, where we feel we can make a difference and establish long-term relationships

It is further explained that the charity works towards these aims and objectives by:

- Providing funding to other recognised charitable institutions
- Providing mentoring, business and career advice and a variety of other hands-on roles which the Trustees believe would ultimately be a benefit to the public

Grant-making policy

The trust's 2016/17 annual report provides the following information about the grant-making process:

> At the beginning of each year, the Trustees will consider and agree a short list of charities that are to be Core Partner Charities for that year. Specific support will be directed to these organisations, with meetings and other feedback being sought, as well as considering other worthy causes that fall within the criteria and aims of the trustees. Alongside the core charity partners the charity maintains discretional funds for ad hoc distributions'.
>
> Unsolicited applications are accepted, but the trustees do receive a high number of grant applications which, in line with the Trustees' grant making policy, are mostly unsuccessful. The trustees prefer to support donations to charities whose work they have researched and which is in accordance with the aims and objectives of the charity for the year. Financial circumstances will be relevant only in determining the amount of an award

Financial information

In 2016/17 the trust held assets of £161,500 and had an income of £402,000. Grants were made to 32 organisations and totalled £397,500.

Beneficiaries included: Five Talents (£200,000); Food Cycle (£107,000); The October Club (£35,000); Facing the World and Renewable World (£10,000 each); Miss Isle School of Sailing (£2,500); Bloodwise (£1,500); The Parish of St Michael's Cornhill (£1,300); Cancer Research, NSPCC and Plan International UK (£1,000 each).

Grants for less than £1,000 were awarded to six organisations and totalled £3,200.

Applications

Applications may be made in writing to the correspondent. Unsolicited applications are accepted but are unlikely to be successful; the trustees prefer to take a proactive approach to their grant-making.

Axis Foundation

Social welfare

London, the South East and the West Midlands

£179,000 (2016/17)

CC number: 1126117

Trustees:

Correspondent: The Trustees, 145–149 Vauxhall Street, London SE11 5RH (tel: 020 7564 2100; email: info@axisfoundation.com)

 www.axisfoundation.org

The foundation is the corporate charity of Axis Europe, a contractor active in social housing, education, commercial and retail sectors. Each year the company donates a percentage of its profits to the foundation.

The foundation's website states that it funds 'projects dedicated to helping improve lives, from the underprivileged, vulnerable and disabled to those who just need a hand to realise their potential'. It funds projects in areas in which the company operates – primarily London, the South East and the West Midlands.

Financial information

In 2016/17 the foundation held assets of £116,500 and had an income of £247,500. Grants awarded to organisations totalled £179,000.

Beneficiaries included: Demelza House (£53,500); Sparks (£53,000); Maypole Trust (£9,000); Swale Gloves (£5,000); Friends of Mapledown School (£3,000).

Applications

Applications can be made via the foundation's website.

The Balfour Beatty Charitable Trust

Disadvantaged young people

UK

£148,500 (2017)

CC number: 1127453

Trustees: Peter Varney; John Hayes; Michael Hayes; Timothy Hayes; Maurice Gertsky; Sandra Ryan; Yusef Ibrahim.

Correspondent: Paul Raby, Trustee, The Curve, Axis Business Park, Hurricane Way, Langley, Slough SL3 8AG (tel: 01753 211121; email: bbfutures@balfourbeatty.com or sustainability@balfourbeatty.com)

 https://www.balfourbeatty.com/sustainability

Balfour Beatty plc is a multinational infrastructure group with capabilities in construction services, support services and infrastructure investments. The trust was founded by the company to support its corporate and social responsibility provision and to act as a focus for employee fundraising as well as to develop into a significant grant funder.

The website states that the trust is part of the group's Building Better Futures programme which focuses on the following three themes:

- Young people's employability and employment
- Helping the most disadvantaged young people in society
- Health, sport and wellbeing

The trust's work in this area has focused on three partners: Barnardo's (£6,700); and The Prince's Trust; Coram.

Financial information

In 2016 the trust had assets of £133,000 and an income of £121,000, of which £100,000 was donated by Balfour Beatty plc. Grants during the year totalled £148,500.

Beneficiaries included: The Prince's Trust (£49,800); Barnardo's (£6,700); and The Thomas Coram Foundation (£6,400).

Applications

The trustees work together with the Balfour Beatty Community Engagement Working Group (CEWG) to identify suitable charities to support. Apply to the correspondent for further information.

The Bank of Scotland Foundation

Community development, financial literacy and inclusion

Scotland

£1.3 million (2017)

OSCR number: SC032942

Trustees: Philip Grant; Robin Bulloch; Sarah Deas; Sir Paul Grice; Martin Fleming.

Correspondent: Lorraine O'Neill, Finance and Grants Manager, The Mound, Edinburgh EH1 1YZ (tel: 0131 300 9006; email: enquiries@bankofscotlandfoundation.co.uk)

www.bankofscotlandfoundation.org

The Bank of Scotland Foundation is an independent charity providing grants to local, regional and national charities across Scotland, supporting people and their local communities. The foundation receives a £2 million donation from Lloyds Banking Group each year, which is used to fund its funding programmes.

Areas of support

The foundation gives support in two core areas, details of which have been taken from the foundation's website.

The development and improvement of local communities

Within any community, there will be a diverse collection of individuals and charities tackling local issues. Some issues will be unique to the local area, others will be replicated across the country or parts of it. We feel it is important to help individuals and groups work together to ensure a better quality of life within their community. Practical ways of making this happen may include:

- Initiatives designed to encourage the involvement in the community of those too often excluded
- Working with people on low incomes, at risk from poverty or with problems finding accommodation
- Improving the standard of local facilities

Financial literacy and financial inclusion

Making informed judgements and taking effective decisions regarding money are important skills – skills which some people can find to be beyond their grasp. Building the confidence and competence of everyone about finance is a particular priority for the Bank of Scotland Foundation. In order to achieve this, we're committed to supporting financial literacy and financial inclusion right across Scotland. We aim to help make these essential skills both easy and accessible for all.

Initiatives that we are particularly interested in supporting are:

- Promoting financial awareness and money advice
- Enhancing debt counselling services within the community
- Supporting life-skills in all age groups and sections of the community

Funding programmes

The foundation has three grants programmes through which charities registered in Scotland can apply:

- **Small Grants Programme:** Grants are made to support the development and improvement of local communities. Applications are accepted for amounts between £1,000 and £10,000 and grants are awarded for one year only
- **Medium Grants Programme:** Grants are made to support the development and improvement of local communities and financial literacy and inclusion. Applications are accepted for amounts between £10,001 and £25,000 and grants are awarded for one year only
- **Large Grants Programme:** Grants are made to support the development and improvement of local communities and financial literacy and inclusion. Applications are accepted for amounts between £50,000 and £100,000 and grants can be awarded over one or two years

The foundation also runs Lloyds Banking Group's Matched Giving Programme, through which employees of the group can apply for up to £1,000 for charities of their choice (up to £500 for fundraising activities and up to £500 for voluntary time given).

All funding programmes run by the foundation are subject to their own eligibility criteria and guidelines. Full information can be found on the website.

Financial information

In 2017 the foundation held assets of £428,500 and had an income of £2.4 million. Grants totalled £1.3 million and were broken down as follows:

Developing and improving local communities	81	£922,500
Money advice and financial literacy	15	£380,000

Beneficiaries included: Govan Law Centre (£100,000); Edinburgh Rape Crisis Centre (£19,000); The Preshal Trust (£13,500); Ignite Theatre, Linnvale Community Bus and Epilepsy Scotland (£5,000 each); Music in Hospitals (£3,000).

Exclusions

The foundation does not support/fund:

- Discriminatory or political organisations
- The promotion of religion
- Animal charities or medical research
- Organisations that redistribute funding for grant-making to other organisations and/or individuals
- Individuals
- Advertising or sponsorship

Applications

Applications can be made via the online form on the foundation's website, where eligibility criteria and guidelines are also available. Appeals for small and medium grants can be made once every 12 months and for large grants can be submitted only after two years have passed from the receipt of an award. Unsuccessful organisations should wait one year before trying again. The submission deadlines for each programme vary – see the website for the most up-to-date information.

BC Partners Foundation

Community development, environmental conservation, arts, education

UK; USA; France; Germany

£428,000 (2017)

CC number: 1136956

Trustees: Nikos Stathopolous; Richard Kunzer; Cedric Dubourdieu; Francesco Loredan; Jan Kengelbach.

Correspondent: The Trustees, BC Partners LLP, 40 Portman Square, London W1H 6DA (tel: 020 7009 4800; email: bcpfoundation@bcpartners.com)

www.bcpartners.com/about-us/bcp-foundation.aspx

Established in 2010 for general charitable purposes, this is the foundation of private equity firm BC Partners.

The firm's website states that the foundation provides matched funding for employee fundraising initiatives and supports charities nominated by employees of BC Partners or trustees of the foundation. Employees in each office also nominate two charities each year to receive donations and volunteer support from staff.

The foundation's website states:

> The Foundation is not restricted in relation to the beneficiaries of its charitable giving, but focuses on the following areas:
>
> - Community development including infrastructure advancements, development aid, health care improvements
> - Conservation of the environment including endeavours related to pollution reduction, natural preservation, clean technologies
> - Arts and Education including support for educational, scholastic, or artistic programs

The foundation is principally funded by the firm and by employee donations. Apply to the correspondent for further information.

Financial information

In 2017 the foundation held assets of £613,000 and had an income of £415,000, largely in donations from the firm. Grants were made to 77 organisations totalling £428,000.

Beneficiaries included: Private Equity Foundation (£100,000); Dr Challoner's School Educational Trust (£20,000); Over the Wall (£17,600); Serious Fun Children's Network (£9,800); Music as Therapy (£7,500); Dolphin Society and Fine Cell Work (£5,000 each); Guernsey Sports Association for the Disabled (£2,900); Disasters Emergency Committee (£300); Diabetes UK (£100).

Applications

The foundation does not accept unsolicited applications – charities must be nominated by BC Partners employees or trustees of the foundation.

The Berkeley Charitable Foundation

Housing, employment, education and training, care

Greater London, Berkshire, Birmingham, Buckinghamshire, Hertfordshire, Oxfordshire, Surrey, Kent, Hampshire, West Sussex and Warwickshire

£2.3 million (2016/17)

CC number: 1152596

Trustees: Anthony Pidgley; Robert Perrins; Wendy Pritchard; Elaine Driver.

Correspondent: Sally Dickinson, Head of the Berkeley Foundation, Berkeley House, 19 Portsmouth Road, Cobham, Surrey KT11 1JG (tel: 01932 584555; email: info@berkeleyfoundation.org.uk)

 www.berkeleyfoundation.org.uk

 @berkeleyfoundation/?hl=en

The Berkeley Foundation was established by the British property developer Berkeley Group Holdings plc in March 2011 and became a registered charity in 2013. According to the foundation's annual report 2016/17, funding for the foundation comes from money raised by staff which the Berkeley Group matches. The Berkeley Group also provides the foundation's core funding, paying its overheads and covering the cost of specific events. Finally, the trustees also note that they also receive a number of direct donations from individuals and companies who support the foundation's work.

The foundation aims to help young people and their communities across London, Birmingham and the south of England. It invests its funds in three ways:

- **Strategic partnerships** with seven national charities like Crisis and The Lord's Taverners
- **Designated charities** chosen by staff and local to the Berkeley Group's sites and offices
- **A Community Investment Fund** which makes grants to projects in line with the foundation's strategy

Grant programmes

The foundation's Community Investment Fund aims to support small-medium sized charitable organisations address social issues. Through this fund, the foundation works in partnership with the voluntary sector across four key areas:

- A safe place to call home – ensuring young people have secure, stable accommodation
- Health and wellbeing – supporting young people to live happy, healthy lives
- The skills to succeed – helping young people develop the skills and capabilities they need to thrive
- Access to employment – enabling young people to overcome barriers to work and kick-start their careers

New funding programmes are regularly announced on the foundation's website. Each funding programme focuses on a specific theme within one of the four areas list above. Funding of up to £250,000 is available for each programme over a period of two years.

The foundation contacted DSC with information of a new programme:

> The Berkeley Foundation is launching Empowering Young Women into work, a funding programme which will support young women aged 16–30 years to access decent and sustainable employment. There is £250,000 of funding available through the programme and the foundation is aiming to support voluntary organisations working to empower young women who are unemployed and for whom there is existing provision, to access decent and sustainable employment.
>
> The Foundation particularly encourages applications from smaller organisations with a turnover of less than £1m.

According to its website, the foundation has launched a Capacity Building Fund, which is open to all of its existing charity partners. The fund aims to help the foundation's charity partners build resilience and operate more effectively.

Financial information

In 2016/17 the foundation had assets of £544,000 and an income of £2.7 million, which includes funding from The Berkeley Group and Give As You Earn contributions. During the year, the foundation gave around £2.3 million in grants to organisations, this figure includes commitments and grants given to strategic and designated partners, and grants and donations to other charities within the foundation's core focus areas.

Beneficiaries included: The Change Foundation (£495,000); Crisis and Imperial College (£450,000); Richard House Hospice and Multiple Sclerosis Trials Collaboration (£200,000 each).

Grants made under £50,000 to other charities totalled £241,000.

Applications

Applicants must complete and submit the foundation's online application form. Applications or proposals submitted by email will not be considered. The application period for funding programmes under the Community Investment Fund are generally open for one month. Deadlines for each grant programmes will be displayed on the foundation's website.

The Bestway Foundation

Education and training, social welfare, health, medical causes, overseas aid

UK and overseas

£415,000 (2016/17)

CC number: 297178

Trustees: Mohammed Younus Sheikh; Sirr Anwar Pervez; Zameer Choudrey; Dawood Pervez; Rizwan Pervez.

Correspondent: Mohammed Younus Sheikh, Trustee, Abbey Road, London NW10 7BW (tel: 020 8453 1234; email: zulfikaur.wajid-hasan@bestway.co.uk)

 www.bestwaygroup.co.uk/responsibility/bestway-foundation

Registered with the Charity Commission in 1987, the Bestway Foundation is the corporate charity of the Bestway Group, an independent food wholesale group in the UK. Each year the group contributes approximately 2.5% of its post-tax profits to the foundation. All of the foundation's trustees are directors and shareholders of their Bestway Group.

The foundation's page on the Bestway Group website describes its mission statement as follows:

- The advancement of education for public benefit in both the UK and overseas by providing assistance through promotion of local schools; provision of scholarships to university students; supporting education initiatives and endowing universities
- The relief of sickness and the preservation of health for public benefit in both the UK and overseas by way of grants and endowments to existing hospitals, clinics, medical research establishments; and by establishing new health facilities
- The provision of financial and material support to victims of natural disasters
- To have a significant impact on poverty reduction in Pakistan through strategic investments in affordable financial and social services catering to the poor
- The development of technical skills within the local communities in which we operate through structured apprenticeship and training programmes

Grants are made to registered and non-registered charities in the UK as well as overseas. Academic institutions are also supported.

Financial information

In 2016/17 the foundation had assets of £6.2 million and an income of £363,000. During the year the foundation awarded grants of £415,000, of which £240,500 was awarded to 15 UK organisations.

Beneficiaries included: Duke of Edinburgh Awards (£100,000); British Asian Trust (£42,500); Crimestoppers (£40,000); Grocery Aid (£10,000); Springboard Charity (£8,000); Ella Foundation and SOS Children's Villages (£5,000 each).

Applications

Applications may be made in writing to the correspondent, enclosing an sae. The foundation has previously noted that telephone calls are not invited.

The Birmingham International Airport Community Trust Fund

Community, environment, heritage, sport, health and well-being

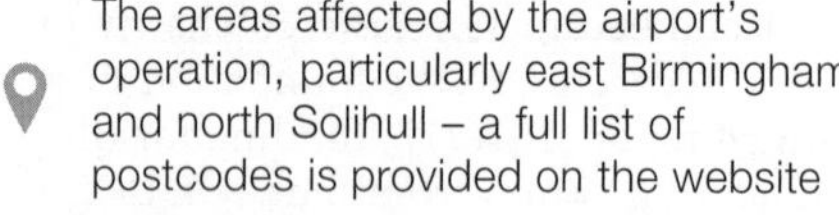

The areas affected by the airport's operation, particularly east Birmingham and north Solihull – a full list of postcodes is provided on the website

£78,500 (2016/17)

CC number: 1071176

Trustees: Cllr Michael Ward; Paul Orton; Andrew Holding; Edward Richards; Margaret Kennet; Cllr Majid Mahmood; David Cuthbert; Cllr Robert Grinsell.

Correspondent: The Community Trust Fund Administrator, Birmingham Airport, Birmingham B26 3QJ (tel: 0121 767 7448; email: andy.holding@birminghamairport.co.uk)

www.birminghamairport.co.uk/about-us/community-and-environment/community-investment/community-trust-fund

Established in 1998, the trust aims to compensate those communities most affected by Birmingham International Airport. The airport company donates £75,000 each year to the trust, which is topped up by fines imposed on airlines for exceeding the airport's noise violation levels.

A full list of postcode areas eligible for support is provided on the website.

According to its guidelines, the trust will support projects in any of the following areas:

- Heritage conservation
- Environment improvement, improving awareness of environmental issues, environmental education and training, encouraging and protecting wildlife
- Bringing the Community closer together through facilities for sport, recreation and other leisure time activities
- Improving health and wellbeing through the promotion of healthy lifestyles and employment opportunities

Work should benefit a substantial section of the community rather than less inclusive groups, although work with older people or people with special needs is positively encouraged.

The maximum grant made is for £3,000. Grants may be for capital or revenue projects, although the trust will not commit to recurrent or running costs, such as salaries.

Financial information

In 2016/17 the trust had assets of £25,000 and an income of £79,500. Grants were made totalling £78,500.

Previous beneficiaries have included: John Taylor Hospice – Men's Shed and Training Ship Stirling (£3,000 each); Spotlight Stage School (£2,000); Coleshill Parish Church (£1,000).

Exclusions

The trust will not support:

- Running costs, such as salaries or expenses
- Individuals
- Medical treatment
- Organisations with statutory responsibilities, unless the project is clearly above their obligations
- Purchase of land and buildings, or general repair and maintenance (adaptions for disability or security may be supported)
- Sports kits or uniforms
- Short-term projects, such as events or trips
- Projects which have already taken place
- Branches of national or international organisations are not usually supported

Applications

Applicants should first read the trust's guidelines, available to download from the website, and then use the online form to request an application pack. Grants are made twice a year, in April and October, and deadlines are posted on the website.

Blakemore Foundation

General charitable purposes

England and Wales excluding parts of the North and Southwest. There is a map on the foundation's website

£135,000 (2016/17)

CC number: 1015938

Trustees: Peter Blakemore; Ita McCauley.

Correspondent: Kate Senter, Community Affairs Officer, A. F. Blakemore & Sons Ltd, Longacre, Willenhall WV13 2JP (tel: 0121 568 2910; email: ksenter@afblakemore.com)

www.afblakemore.com/our-community/the-blakemore-foundation

The Blakemore Foundation is a charitable trust established by the Blakemore family to support good causes across its trading area. A.F. Blakemore and Son Ltd is a food retail, wholesale and distribution company located in the West Midlands.

According to the foundation's website, it offers four types of support:

- **Match fund donations** – donations for causes supported by employees of A.F. Blakemore & Son Ltd up to the value of £200

- **In-kind donations** - donations which are given in the form of food, drink or supplies from our Blakemore Wholesale depots or Blakemore Retail SPAR stores
- **Monetary donations** – donations given to good causes up to the value of £200 to help towards projects, events, workshops and ongoing charitable work
- **Independent retail donations** - grants which allow SPAR retailers to apply for a donation for a good cause of their choice

Organisations eligible for support include:

- Social clubs/community groups
- Sports clubs
- Schools/education
- Medical/research/hospitals/health
- Hospices
- Emergency services/armed forces
- Environmental organisations

Financial information

In 2016/17 the foundation had assets of £52,500 and an income of £356,500 which was donated by the company. Grants awarded to organisations totalled £135,000 and other charitable contributions totalled £164,000.

Previous beneficiaries have included: Foundation for Conductive Education; St Andrew's Church – Biggleswade and Wenlock Poetry Festival.

Exclusions

The foundation's guidelines state that the following requests are not eligible for support:

- Salaries
- National charities (unless directly linked to an A.F. Blakemore employee or local branch)
- Grants for an individual
- Good causes that fall outside of A.F. Blakemore's trading area
- Overseas appeals
- Expeditions or overseas travel
- Sponsorship and marketing promotions
- Endowment and hardship funds
- Political causes

Applications

Applications can be made through the foundation's website. Applications are decided upon on the last Friday of every month.

The Boodle & Dunthorne Charitable Trust

General charitable purposes

UK and overseas

£123,000 (2016/17)

CC number: 1077748

Trustees: Nicholas Wainwright; Michael Wainwright.

Correspondent: Nicholas Wainwright, Trustee, Boodle & Dunthorne, 35 Lord Street, Liverpool L2 9SQ (tel: 0151 224 0580)

Established in 1999, the Boodle & Dunthorne Charitable Trust is the corporate charity of Boodles, a family jewellers based in North West England. The trust supports general charitable purposes. It provides an annual donation to Shining Faces in India which the Wainwright family administer.

Financial information

In 2016/17 the trust had assets of £774,000 and an income of £213,500 which included a donation of £200,000 from Boodle & Dunthorne Ltd. Grants were made to four charities and totalled £123,000.

Beneficiaries were: Shining Faces in India (£55,000); Hope and Homes for Children (£25,000); The Prince's Trust (£15,000); Rainbow Trust (£1,750).

Applications

Apply in writing to the correspondent. The 2016/17 annual report states: 'The Trustees have discretion over where and when grants made. Grants will be made by the Trustees as and when they identify a suitable and deserving cause.'

Boots Charitable Trust

Health, social care, education and training, community development, general charitable purposes

Nottingham and Nottinghamshire

£187,500 (2016/17)

CC number: 1045927

Trustees: Lavina Moxley; Adrian Bremner; Una Kent.

Correspondent: James Kirkpatrick, Boots UK Ltd D90E S09, 1 Thane Road West, Nottingham NG90 1BS (tel: 07739 835909; email: james@fundingsupport.co.uk)

www.boots-uk.com/corporate-social-responsibility/what-we-do/community/boots-charitable-trust

Registered with the Charity Commission in 1995, Boots Charitable Trust is wholly funded by Boots UK Ltd. Boots UK is part of the Retail Pharmacy International Division of Walgreens Boots Alliance, Inc. Boots became a subsidiary of the new company, Walgreens Boots Alliance, on 31 December 2014.

The trust gives to charities and voluntary organisations that benefit Nottingham and Nottinghamshire. It is explained on the Boots website that: 'Supporting the Nottinghamshire community has always been important to Boots. Jesse Boot opened the very first Boots store in the mid-19th century in Nottingham, and we continue to give to local causes that are important to our colleagues and customers.'

Areas of support

The trust considers support for a wide range of charities and voluntary organisations although its main focus is on four areas which are very close to the 'heart and heritage' of Boots. These areas are outlined on the website:

- **Health**: Both community healthcare such as homecare or support for sufferers of medical conditions as well as health education and prevention
- **Lifelong learning**: For example literacy and numeracy projects
- **Community development**: Such as supporting councils in providing voluntary services
- **Social care**: Be it personal, social or community activities or schemes

The website states that it also funds 'smaller voluntary organisations in Nottinghamshire which are too small to qualify for charitable status, but who still desperately need some financial support for their projects'.

Funding types

The trust's charitable giving policy states:

> The Trust will consider applications for funding for most expenditure items, including salary and running costs. Where a general overhead allocation is part of the funding requested, the method of calculation must be included. Generally, large building or construction projects will not be funded although minor structural improvements and refurbishments would be considered.

Financial information

In 2016/17 the trust had assets of £73,000 and an income of £274,500. Grants to 24 organisations totalled £187,500 and were distributed as follows:

Health	7	£57,000
Social care	6	£49,000
Lifelong learning	7	£44,000
Community development	4	£37,500

Beneficiaries included: Stonebridge City Farm (£10,000); The Friary (£9,000); Nottingham Health and Education Support (£6,900); First Story (£5,600); Cornwater Clubs and Pintsize Theatre (£5,000 each).

Exclusions

The trust's charitable giving policy states that it will not fund the following:

- Projects benefitting those people outside of Nottinghamshire
- Individuals
- Organisations which are NOT registered charities and have an income or expenditure of more than £5,000 per year
- Charities seeking funds to re-distribute to other charities

- Projects for which there is a legal statutory obligation or which replace statutory funding

Applications

There is an online application form on the website, alongside guidance on eligibility. Paper application forms can also be requested on: james@fundingsupport.co.uk or 07739 835909.

The trustees review applications on a bi-monthly basis. Applications should be received by the 7th day of February; April; June; August; October; and December. The website explains that the application process can take between two and four months.

BRIT Trust

Music, performing arts, young people

UK

£2.3 million (2017)

CC number: 1000413

Trustees: John Deacon; John Craig; Andy Cleary; Jonathan Morrish; Rob Dickins; Tony Wadsworth; David Kassner; Geoff Taylor; Korda Marshall; David Sharpe; William Rowe; David Munns; Margaret Crowe; Angela Watts; Simon Presswell; Melanie Fox; Gerald Doherty; Rita Broe; Max Hole; Henry Semmence.

Correspondent: Maggie Crowe, Trustee, c/o BPI, Riverside Building, County Hall, Westminster Bridge Road, London SE1 7JA (tel: 020 7803 1351; email: maggie.crowe@bpi.co.uk)

 www.brittrust.co.uk

 facebook.com/The-BRIT-Trust-100825950530180

 @thebrittrust

Established in 1989, the BRIT Trust is entirely funded by the British music industry, and receives a large part of its income from the profits of the annual BRIT Awards. Its mission is 'to encourage young people in the exploration and pursuit of educational, cultural or therapeutic benefits emanating from music', which it does principally through its commitments to the BRIT School in Croydon – the UK's only non-fee paying performing arts school – and to Nordoff-Robbins, which is the UK's leading independent provider of music therapy. The trust also makes small contributions to other registered charities in line with its mission statement.

Financial information

In 2017 the trust held assets of almost £11 million and had an income of £1.77 million, of which £1.6 million was received in donations from BPI, the company that organises the BRIT awards. Grants were made to 12 organisations and totalled £2.3 million. The majority of funds awarded were given to BRIT School for the Performing Arts and Technology and Nordoff-Robbins Music Therapy, which received £1.67 million and £360,000 respectively.

Beneficiaries included: East London Arts and Music (ELAM) (£60,000); Key4Life and Music Support (£30,000 each); Heart n Soul (£10,000); Abram Wilson Foundation, Nathan Timothy Foundation, Royal Opera House, Tarbent Youth Group and Urban Development (£5,000 each).

Exclusions

The trust only supports UK-registered charities. It does not consider applications for grants to individuals, scholarships, capital grants or grant donations outside the UK.

Applications

Applicants are requested to complete the application form available to download from the trust's website and submit it by post or email. Applications are considered at trustee meetings.

British Gas (Scottish Gas) Energy Trust

 Fuel poverty, financial education (in relation to debt awareness and prevention)

 England, Scotland and Wales

 £2.3 million (2016/17)

CC number: 1106218

Trustees: Imelda Redmond; Andrew Brown; Daksha Piparia; Colin Trend; Peter Smith; Steven McClenaghan.

Correspondent: The Trustees, 3rd Floor, Trinity Court, Trinity Street, Peterborough PE1 1DA (tel: 01733 421021; email: britishgasenergytrust@lets-talk.online)

 www.britishgasenergytrust.org.uk

The British Gas Energy Trust was established in 2004. The trust's website describes the aims of the charity as follows:

- The relief of poverty among those who are unable to meet or pay charges for the supply of energy to premises used or occupied by them
- The education of the public in relation to debt awareness and prevention
- To work with other UK trust funds and organisations to encourage good practice and consistency for the public good

Organisational Grants Programme

The trust's 2016/17 annual report provides the following information on its Organisational Grants Programme:

> Grants are awarded to increase specialist fuel debt advice, providing one-to-one assistance including:
>
> - Resolving energy debt problems and negotiating with energy suppliers
> - Completing applications to the British Gas Energy Trust and other grant giving schemes
> - Referrals to other grant making trusts or schemes or alternative specialist advice agencies for resolution of other debt issues
>
> A range of other energy related advice such as:
>
> - Energy efficiency advice
> - How to read energy meters
> - Setting up payment plans and monthly direct debits

The trust also makes grants to vulnerable individuals and families to clear energy and other priority household debts (such as bankruptcy fees or funeral arrears) and to purchase energy efficient white goods.

Financial information

In 2016/17 the trust had assets of £1.5 million and an income of £12.7 million. Grants totalled £12 million with £2.3 million given to organisations.

The Chair's Report 2016/17 provides the following information:

> During 2016/17, the Charity's Organisational Grants Programme continued to fund 27 organisations (including 13 Shelter locations and their national helpline) across Great Britain. Total grants of £2.3 million funded 66 specialist advisors within 36 individual projects. Twenty three advisors worked within the Charity's 'Debt via Health' (DVH) projects, seeking to tackle fuel poverty and promote energy efficiency via the local health sector.

Beneficiaries included: Shelter (£407,000); St Helen's Citizens Advice (£90,000); Energy Project Plus (£75,000); Zinthyia (£64,000); Speakeasy (£62,500); Preston Citizens Advice and Bromley by Bow Centre (£52,500 each); Local Solutions Liverpool (£52,000); St Ann's Advice Group (£51,500).

Applications

Contact the trust for further information on organisational grants.

Individuals can apply via the trust's online application form. Alternatively, an application form can be downloaded and submitted via the trust's freepost address (Freepost BRITISH GAS ENERGY TRUST).

See the website for full guidelines.

Bupa UK Foundation

Health and well-being, mental health, carers

UK

£379,000 (2017)

CC number: 1162759

Trustees: Andrea Spyropoulos; Dr Paula Franklin; Ruth Owen; Catherine Barton; Helen Cliffe; Sally Pain; Charles Richardson.

Correspondent: Tina Gwynne-Evans, Head of Bupa UK Foundation, Battle Bridge House, 300–306 Gray's Inn Road, London WC1X 8DU (email: bupaukfoundation@bupa.com)

 www.bupaukfoundation.org

This is the corporate charity of the healthcare group Bupa Ltd and is entirely funded by the group. It was established in 2015 to replace the group's previous charity, The Bupa Foundation.

According to the website, the foundation's purpose is 'to help people live healthier, happier lives' by funding 'practical projects to tackle critical challenges in health and social care and make a direct impact on people's health and wellbeing'.

Grant programmes

The website states that the foundation's funding programmes focus on specific themes, each with their own criteria which are released on the website as the programme is announced, along with application deadlines. Grants are made to support specific projects, rather than general core costs, but the foundation awards an additional 15% of grant funding to successful applicants for core costs. Social enterprises, CICs and for-profit organisations are also eligible to apply if they are running a charitable project.

The foundation has three main grant programmes, details of which have been taken from its website:

Mid-life Mental Health

This fund focuses on the mental health needs of people in middle age, focusing on the following priorities:

- Piloting new interventions and services
- Supporting people in crisis
- Breaking down barriers and taboos
- Developing skills and employment opportunities
- Creating communities for mutual support

Caring for Carers

This programmes focuses on the health and well-being needs of unpaid adult carers, focusing in particular on the following priorities:

- Piloting and extending new interventions and services
- Supporting the health and wellbeing of carers through exercise, diet and nutrition
- Creating communities for mutual support
- Improving support for carers in the workplace

Healthy Futures

Our Healthy Futures funding programme focuses on supporting and empowering young adults aged 18 to 25 living with ongoing health challenges. Young adults are particularly vulnerable as they leave secondary education and move towards becoming independent. For young adults with health concerns this period can be even more difficult. Poor transitions, changing support networks and gaps in provision, along with new responsibilities all have the potential to lead to poorer outcomes and experiences.

Financial information

In 2017 the foundation held assets of £5.06 million and had an income of £505,500. Grants to 16 organisations totalled £379,000.

Beneficiaries included: CLIC Sargent (£42,000); Bike for Good (£34,500); Asthma UK and Soundabout (£23,000 each); Cumbria Youth Alliance (£18,400); Royal Brompton and Harefield Hospitals Charity (£15,500).

Exclusions

The website states that the following will not be funded by the foundation:

- Work that does not fall within the scope of the Bupa UK Foundation's charitable purposes
- Work that is not clearly aligned with the stated funding priorities of a specific funding programme
- Projects delivered outside of the UK
- Long-term projects and initiatives – we expect the vast majority of projects funded to be delivered within 12 to 18 months
- Work being delivered by local authorities and housing associations
- Work which might reasonably be eligible for funding from statutory bodies
- General awareness and information campaigns
- Sponsorship of or attendance at meetings, events and conferences
- Fundraising appeals, including requests for contributions to capital or equipment costs
- Unrestricted funding for charities or other organisations
- Educational bursaries or grants for university or postgraduate education, school trips or projects, gap year or elective year projects
- Academic research, including funding for educational or research posts

Applications

Applicants should first refer to the website to see which grants programmes are currently open for application, along with eligibility criteria and deadlines.

The Burberry Foundation

 General charitable purposes

 Worldwide, with a strong preference for communities where Burberry employees live and work

£125,000 (2016/17)

CC number: 1154468

Trustees: Christopher Baily; Leanne Wood; Lord Christopher Holmes.

Correspondent: Pamela Batty, Secretary, Burberry Ltd, Horseferry House, Horseferry Road, London SW1P 2AW (email: enquiries@burberryfoundation.com)

 www.burberryfoundation.org

The Burberry Foundation was established as an independent charity in 2008 by the luxury fashion house Burberry Group plc. The foundation board is comprised of two Burberry representatives and an independent trustee.

According to its website, the foundation is 'conscious of the varied social environmental and economic impacts of the luxury industry on communities worldwide'. As such, the foundation states that it is, 'dedicated to using the power of creativity to drive positive change in these communities and build a more sustainable future through innovation'.

Following a recent strategic review of its objectives, the trustees decided to focus the foundation's future grant-making in the following areas:

- Science, Technology, Engineering, Arts and Mathematics (STEAM) subjects
- Tackling educational inequality
- Reducing waste
- Supporting social and economic development

According to the foundation's 2016/17 annual report, in considering requests for support the foundation will consider projects that:

- Are managed competently through accountability, cost effectiveness, strong leadership and creativity
- Provide a significant and measurable impact
- Are located in a community where Burberry Group employees live and work
- Have the potential to offer volunteering opportunities for Burberry Group employees

As part of its grant-making agenda, during 2017/18 the foundation launched five-year partnerships with the following organisations: Teach First and The Careers and Enterprise Company, the Royal College of Art, Oxfam, Pur Project and Elvis and Kresse.

Financial information

In 2016/17 the foundation had assets of £7.7 million and an income of £1.36 million including a donation of £1.1 million from Burberry Group plc. During the year, in anticipation of a new focus the foundation began to phase out existing partners and programmes that were not aligned with its future charitable ambitions. As a result, the foundation's grant-making was almost completely paused during 2016/17, with only a single grant of £125,000 made to The Beautiful Foundation in Korea.

Applications

Apply in writing to the correspondent. The trustees meet four times a year.

The Cadbury Foundation

Education, training and employment, sport, sustainable environment, general charitable purposes

UK and overseas

£599,000 (2017)

CC number: 1050482

Trustees: Jonathan Horrell; Eoin Kellett; Glenn Caton; Michael Taylor; Lisa Crane.

Correspondent: Kelly Farrell, Community Affairs Manager, PO BOX 12, Bourneville, Birmingham B30 2LU (tel: 0121 787 2421; email: kelly.farrell@mdlz.com)

www.cadbury.co.uk/cadbury-foundation

The Cadbury Foundation was established in 1935 in recognition of the founders of the Cadbury's chocolate company George and Richard Cadbury. In 2010 Kraft Foods Inc. gained control of Cadbury plc, and two years later divided the corporation into Kraft Food Group plc and Mondelēz, the latter of which now funds the Cadbury Foundation.

The foundation tends to focus much of its funding on larger projects, although it also contributes to local communities near the Company's operations, so that where possible donations can be backed up with employee volunteering work and gifts in kind.

Grants are made under the following four pillars:

- **Skill Development** – giving an awareness of the world of work and enhancing the ability of young people and disadvantaged adults to gain and sustain employment
- **Olympic and Paralympic Legacy** – to build stronger, healthier communities through sport
- **Source Projects** – supporting the development of sustainable cocoa growing communities where Mondelēz International sources its cocoa and coffee beans
- **Employee Passions** – some funds are reserved for employee-related grants and cash match where the company's volunteers can either have their fundraising efforts matched, or where they can bid for a grant to support the work of a chosen charity

In its 2017 accounts, the foundation provides the following information regarding its grant-making policy:

> In considering projects for support, the Foundation considers value-for-money in terms of attaining maximum community benefit. The Foundation is guided in making its selections for grant-giving by the demonstration of factors such as genuine community need, benefit for 'at risk' client groups or areas of social deprivation and those who will obtain the maximum community benefit from an association with the charity.
>
> The Foundation also works with major community partners to develop clear objectives and assess outcomes. Outcome measurements might include: number of people reached by the project, improvement in performance levels, evaluation rating by recipients, impact of the charity's involvement and community partner efficiency.

Financial information

In 2017 the foundation had assets of £150,500 and an income of £639,50 which included £600,000 from Mondelēz UK Holdings and Services Ltd. Grants to 29 organisations totalled £599,000.

Beneficiaries included: British Paralympic Association (£100,000); Cashmatch (£70,000); Health for Life in the Community (£50,000); Abacus and Cancerfondon (£5,000 each).

Applications

The trustees actively seek out projects to support and therefore cannot accept any unsolicited requests for funding. The 2016 annual report explains that the trustees prefer to provide more substantial assistance in their chosen areas rather than providing 'token' grants in response to regular applications.

The Cadogan Charity

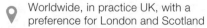

General charitable purposes, in particular, social welfare, medical research, service charities, animal welfare, education and conservation and the environment

Worldwide, in practice UK, with a preference for London and Scotland

£2.3 million (2016/17)

CC number: 247773

Trustees: Rt. Hon. The Earl Cadogan; Countess Cadogan; Viscount Chelsea; Lady Anna Thomson; The Hon. William Cadogan.

Correspondent: Paul Loutit, Secretary, The Cadogan Group, 10 Duke of York Sqaure, London SW3 4LY (tel: 020 7730 4567; email: paul.loutit@cadogan.co.uk)

The charity was established in 1966 for general charitable purposes. The charity currently operates two funds, the general fund and the rectors' fund. The rectors' fund was created with a gift from Cadogan Holdings Company in 1985 to pay an annual amount to one or any of the rectors of Holy Trinity Church – Sloane Street, St Luke's Church and Chelsea Old Church. The general fund provides support for registered charities in a wide range of areas (see below).

Financial information

In 2016/17 the charity had assets of £69.5 million and an income of £2.2 million, including around £1.4 million in dividends from investments in Cadogan Group Ltd. During the year, the charity gave a total of £2.3 million in grants. Grants were distributed as follows:

Education	13	£900,000
Military charities	10	£554,500
Social welfare in the community	17	£458,500
Medical research	32	£320,500
Conservation and the environment	4	£45,000
Animal welfare	8	£34,000

Beneficiaries included: Natural History Museum (£500,000); National Army Museum (£350,000); Royal Academy of Arts (£250,000); Alzheimer's Research UK and Barts Charity (£50,000 each); Prostate Cancer UK (£20,000); St Mary's Birnam (£15,000); YMCA England (£5,000); British Exploring Society (£2,500); Erskine (£2,000).

Exclusions

No grants are given to individuals.

Applications

Apply in writing to the correspondent.

Corra Foundation

 Social welfare

Scotland; Malawi; Zambia; Rwanda

£17.96 million (2017)

OSCR number: SC009481

Trustee: Trevor Civval, Timothy Hall, Henry Abram, Joy Barlow, Elizabeth Carmichael, Claire Gibson, David Johnson, Richard Martin, Luke McCullough, Elaine McKean, Fiona Sandford, Dr Judith Turbyne, David Urch.

Correspondent: Connie Williamson, Grants Manager, Riverside House, 502 Gorgie Road, Edinburgh EH11 3AF (tel: 0131 444 4020; email: hello@corra.scot)

 www.corra.scot

 facebook.com/CorraFoundation

 @corrascot

The foundation was previously known as Lloyds TSB Foundation for Scotland until it rebranded in August 2017. It is one of five Lloyds Banking Group charities, covering England and Wales, Scotland, Northern Ireland and the Channel Islands. The foundation is an independent grant-maker; its relationship with Lloyd Banking Group is outlined on the website:

> A covenant was agreed between Trustee Savings Bank and Trustee Savings Bank (TSB) Foundation for Scotland in 1985, making provision for Scottish communities to benefit from their share of 1% of the Group's pre-tax profits (Scotland's share being 19.46% of the total). In 1997 Lloyds Bank and TSB Group merged. This significantly increased our income and the foundation became the largest Scottish independent grant making trust. In early 2010 Lloyds Banking Group gave notice on the agreement and the final payment will be received in February 2018.

What the foundation does

The foundation works to improve the lives of disadvantaged individuals and communities with the following mission: 'to make a difference to the lives of individuals and communities in Scotland, by encouraging positive change, opportunities, fairness and growth of aspirations, which improve quality of life'. It has three strategic objectives, details of which have been taken from the foundation's website:

- To be the best grant maker we can be – Grant making is at the heart of what we do and we want to do it as well as possible, with an open and accessible approach
- To get alongside communities – We are working differently, including with communities we don't historically reach, and others with a big appetite for change
- To share expertise – We will use our 30+ years experience in grant making to support others
- Partnership – We want to make a bigger difference to people by working together with others

Foundation programmes

The following programmes are available from the foundation, as stated on the website:

Henry Duncan Awards

The foundation's main grants programme was renamed in 2010 in honour of the Rev. Henry Duncan, the founder of the first Trustee Savings Bank.

In order to be eligible to apply for a grant, charities must have an annual income of less than £500,000 and be working to deliver programmes or services which are clearly aimed at improving quality of life for people in their community who are facing disadvantage. According to the website, awards of up to £7,000 are made on a one-off basis to charities working with people 'who may typically be experiencing challenging family circumstances, disability, mental ill health, abuse or poverty'. Grants are awarded for projects addressing a wide range of issues, a list of which can be found in the guidance notes on the foundation's website.

The foundation's website explains that trustees are particularly interested in projects supporting:

- Vulnerable children and young people
- Isolated older people
- Carers
- Families in poverty
- People affected by disability or mental health issues

Funding can be awarded for core costs, such as salaries or running costs, or project funds. The trustees will also consider applications for small capital costs such as equipment.

Partnership Drugs Initiative

The Partnership Drugs Initiative (PDI) was established in 2001 to support work carried out by the voluntary sectors with children and young people who are affected by issues associated with substance abuse. The initiative is delivered in partnership with the Scottish Government and The Robertson Trust. According to the foundation's website, the initiative specifically looks to:

- Increase the wellbeing of children and young people (0 to 25) in Scotland affected by alcohol and other drugs
- Help develop and influence both local and national policy

In 2014 the PDI adopted a new strategic direction addressing four specific areas, which are: identifying and addressing geographical gaps; identifying and addressing thematic gaps; disseminating learning; and optimising funding.

The PDI is based around building relationships between 'policy makers, local partners and projects to ensure collectively we can make a positive difference to children and young people affected by drugs and alcohol'. It is further explained that 'PDI works closely with all potential and supported groups to help us improve our approach and understanding of what it takes to make a difference to children and young people. Support for groups is offered by sharing our learning and knowledge from other groups and partners.'

The initiative targets three areas, which are outlined on the website:

- Children and young people affected by parental substance issues (alcohol and other drugs)
- Pre-teen children who are at higher risk of developing issues relating to alcohol and other drugs
- Young people in need of support due to their own alcohol or drug issue

It is further explained that: 'PDI provides funding support and will contribute up to a maximum of 50% towards the overall costs of delivering a project/service that will help improve outcomes for children and young people. You can apply for up to three years'.

Full information, including how to make an initial application, is provided on the website.

Managed programmes

The foundation also administers and manages programmes on behalf of other organisations. At the time of writing (October 2018) these included:

Scottish Government International Development Small Grants Programme

The aim of the programme is to build capacity and upscale small international development organisations so they have the ability to bid for funding through its International Development Fund (IDF) and also those of other funders. Project grants of £60,000 over three years and feasibility grants of up to £10,000 are available. Projects should be based in one of the Scottish Government's partners countries – Malawi, Zambia or Rwanda.

The Children, Young People, Families, Early Intervention and Adult Learning and Empowering Communities Fund

The foundation is working in partnership with the Scottish Government to deliver this fund.

The core elements of the CYPFEIF (Children, Young People, Families, Early Intervention Fund) aspect of the fund, which the website states 'aims to improve outcomes for children, young people and their families', are:

- Promote the GIRFEC wellbeing indicators and the implementation of UNCRC
- Delivery of prevention and early intervention activities
- Improving parenting capacity and family support

The website further explains that the ALEC (Adult Learning and Empowering Communities) element of the fund 'supports third sector organisations to deliver outcomes that improve opportunities for adult learning and building community capacity'. This fund has the following objectives:

- Prevention and early intervention through adult learning and community capacity building
- Supporting the delivery of lifelong, learner-centred adult learning as outlined in the Adult Learning in Scotland Statement of Ambition
- Using asset based approaches to work with adult learners or with communities to plan and co-design learning or capacity building opportunities

Both core funding and project funding are available through the CYPFEIF and ALEC Fund. See the website for full information.

Financial information

In 2017 the foundation had assets of £19.7 million and an income of £22.4 million. Grants were awarded totalling £17.96 million.

Previous beneficiaries have included: Relationships Scotland (£1.1 million); Action for Children (£880,000); Barnardo's (£150,000); Sleep Scotland (£38,000); Circle (£35,000); Woodcraft Folk Scotland (£8,500); People First (£3,500); Fairfield Sports and Leisure Club (£1,500); Forth and Tay Disabled Ramblers (£750).

Exclusions

Each programme has its own criteria. Refer to the foundation's website for more information.

Applications

Application forms for all programmes, complete with comprehensive guidance notes and application deadlines, are available from the foundation. Foundation staff are always willing to provide additional help.

Coutts Charitable Foundation

Women and girls

UK

£568,500 (2016/17)

CC number: 1150784

Trustees: Lenka Setkova; Sir Christopher Geidt; Dr Linda Yeuh; Lord Waldegrave of North Hill; Leslie Gent; Ali Hammad; Alison Rose-Slade; Thomas Kenrick; Peter Flavel; Camilla Stowell.

Correspondent: Anna Hudson, Foundation Administrator, Coutts & Co., 440 Strand, London WC2R 0QS (tel: 020 7957 2822; email: coutts.foundation@coutts.com)

https://www.coutts.com/coutts-foundation.html

Coutts & Co. is a private bank and wealth manager. It is one of the world's oldest banks (founded 1692) and is wholly owned by the Royal Bank of Scotland Group. Headquartered in London, Coutts is the wealth division of the Royal Bank of Scotland Group, with clients from over 40 offices in financial centres in the UK, Switzerland, the Middle East and Asia.

Areas of work

Coutts Charitable Foundation was established in February 2013 and registered with the Charity Commission in the same month. The following information is taken from the Coutts website:

> The mission of the Coutts Foundation is to support sustainable approaches to tackle the causes and consequences of poverty, focusing on the communities where Coutts has a presence. This mission builds on the legacy of Angela Burdett-Coutts, the grand-daughter of Thomas Coutts, who was a progressive 19th-century philanthropist concerned with breaking cycles of poverty and providing basic human needs. At this time the core focus of the Foundation is supporting women and girls in the UK.
>
> The Coutts Foundation makes significant commitments to a small number of organisations that reflect its mission. At this time the core focus of the foundation is supporting women and girls in the UK.

Financial information

In 2016/17 the foundation had assets of £4.3 million and an income of £1.06 million. Grants were made to 13 organisations totalling £568,500.

Beneficiaries included: Mother's Choice (£100,000); water.org (£83,500); Toynbee Hall (£60,000); Working Chance Ltd (£35,000); City Gateway (£30,000); Women for Refugee Women (£25,000).

Applications

The following information is provided on the foundation's website:

> The Foundation does not accept unsolicited proposals for funding. However, if you wish to bring information about your organisation or programmes that fit with our funding priorities to our attention, please complete the information submission form and either email it to us or post it.
>
> Coutts Foundation, 440 Strand, London WC2R 0QS
>
> The Coutts Foundation will be in touch if we would like to learn more about your organisation.

The information submission form is available to download on the foundation's website.

Coventry Building Society Charitable Foundation

Education and training, social welfare

Areas within the building society's branch network

£70,000 (2017)

CC number: 1072244

Trustees: Darin Landon; Thomas Crane.

Correspondent: Contact the relevant community foundation, Coventry Building Society, Oak Tree Court, Harry Weston Road, Coventry CV3 2UN (tel: 024 7643 5229)

www.coventrybuildingsociety.co.uk/consumer/who-we-are/charities/charitable-foundation.html

The foundation was launched in 1998 and is entirely funded by the Coventry Building Society.

Grants of up to £2,000 are provided to charities and community groups with an income under £250,000. Priority is given to projects aimed at improving the quality of life and opportunities in communities affected by disadvantage, deprivation and social exclusion.

The building society's grants are administered by the following various community foundations which operate within the area of its branch network:

- Birmingham and Black Country Community Foundation
- Gloucestershire Community Foundation
- Heart of England Community Foundation
- Leicestershire and Rutland Community Foundation
- Milton Keynes Community Foundation
- Northamptonshire Community Foundation

- Nottinghamshire Community Foundation
- Oxfordshire Community Foundation
- Quartet Community Foundation
- Somerset Community Foundation
- South Yorkshire Community Foundation
- Staffordshire Community Foundation
- The Community Foundation in Wales
- Wiltshire and Swindon Community Foundation

Financial information

In 2017 the foundation held assets of £5,300 and had an income of £70,000. Grants to community foundations totalled £70,000.

A list of beneficiaries was not available.

Applications

Applications can be made online through the community foundation for your area. In order to do this choose the area closest to where your charity operates from the table at the bottom of the foundation's website and click on the relevant link. This will take you to the relevant community foundation's website. There you will be able to find out more about your local community foundation and all of the information that you need to apply for a grant.

The foundation asks: 'If you have any queries about the application process please contact your local Community Foundation directly.'

The grants panel from each Community Foundation meet on a bi-monthly or quarterly basis to consider applications. All applications are acknowledged.

Credit Suisse EMEA Foundation

 Youth education

 Countries where Credit Suisse has offices, in Europe, the Middle East and Africa

£1.66 million (2017)

CC number: 1122472

Trustees: Stefano Toffolo; Patrick Flaherty; Michelle Mendelsson; Colin Hely-Hutchinson; Mark Ellis; Marisa Drew; Marc Pereira-Mendoza; Angus Kidd; Guy Varney; Natalia Nicolaidis.

Correspondent: Kate Butchart, Corporate Citizenship Team, Credit Suisse, 1 Cabot Square, London E14 4QJ (email: emea.corporatecitizenship@credit-suisse.com)

The foundation was established by Credit Suisse AG and channels the group's corporate citizenship activities in Europe, the Middle East and Africa. It supports general charitable purposes in the areas where the company has a presence, but has a preference for supporting organisations that improve the educational attainment, employability and aspirations of young, disadvantaged people.

The foundation makes grants to registered charities (although other charitable organisations may be considered occasionally). The foundation looks to provide funding for two to five years if possible and further funding may be offered to charities which meet the foundation's priorities effectively. Grants may be given for specific projects or for core costs and salaries.

The foundation also makes grants for the Credit Suisse group's Charity of the Year programme, and occasionally for other charities nominated by employees.

Financial information

In 2017 the foundation held assets of £1.9 million and had an income of £1.77 million, of which £1.7 million was donated by Credit Suisse AG. Grants were made to 17 organisations and totalled £1.66 million.

Beneficiaries included: Institute for Teaching (£252,000); The Young Foundation (£205,000); The Polish Children and Youth Foundation (£164,000); Global Teachers Institute (£100,000); The Royal Springboard Foundation (£50,000); Social Mobility Foundation (£30,000); Teach First (£25,500).

Exclusions

According to the foundation's 2017 accounts, it will not support applications:

- that directly replace or subsidise statutory funding
- that are the primary responsibility of statutory funders such as local and central government and health authorities
- for administration and costs not directly associated with the application
- from individuals, or which are for the benefit of one individual
- for the promotion of religious or political causes
- for holidays
- for work that has already taken place
- for general appeals
- for animal welfare
- for festivals, sports and leisure activities

Applications

Apply in writing to the correspondent.

Cumberland Building Society Charitable Foundation

 General charitable purposes

 Cumbria, South-West Scotland, North Lancashire (Preston area) and Northumberland (Haltwhistle area)

£25,500 (2017/18)

CC number: 1072435

Trustees: Richard Atkinson; Louise Brown; David Edwards; Linda Christine Slinger; Nick Utting; Sheelagh O'Brien; Michael Pearson.

Correspondent: Cumberland Building Society Charitable Foundation, Cumberland House, Cooper Way, Parkhouse, Carlisle, Cumbria CA3 0JF (tel: 01228 541341; email: charitablefoundation@cumberland.co.uk)

 www.cumberland.co.uk

The Cumberland Building Society Charitable Foundation is a registered charity set up by Cumberland Building Society in November 1998. Although the foundation was established by the society, they are separate organisations.

The foundation supports general charitable purposes in Cumbria, Dumfries and Galloway, Lancashire and Northumberland. The current policy of the foundation is to make a relatively large number of small grants in the beneficial areas. Grants are normally in the region of £250 to £750; however, in exceptional circumstances a donation of £1,000 may be awarded.

Applications are welcomed from any of the following:

- Registered charities, charitable voluntary organisations and self-help groups, particularly those assisting vulnerable members of the community
- National charities, providing donations help to support initiatives in Cumbria, South-West Scotland (all DG postcodes and TD9), West Northumberland (NE45–49), or the Preston area of North Lancashire (all PR, FY, LA AND BB1–3 and BB5–7)
- Community services, for example community centres, village halls, youth clubs (the trustees prefer to provide funding for the purchase of specific items, such as equipment)
- Individuals via a charity
- Local heritage preservers

Financial information

In 2017/18 the foundation had assets of £2,800 and an income of £28,000. There were 49 grants made totalling £25,500.

No donation of over £1,000 was made during this period.

Previous beneficiaries have included: Children's Heart Federation, Community Action Furness, Community Transport South Lakeland, Currock House Association, DEBRA, the Food Train, the Genesis Appeal, Hospice at Home, L'Arche Preston and St John Ambulance.

Applications

Applications can be submitted using an online form which can be accessed via the Cumberland Building Society website: www.cumberland.co.uk/charitable-foundation.

Dentons UKMEA LLP Charitable Trust

General charitable purposes, with a preference for children and young people, arts and culture, medical

UK, primarily City of London and Milton Keynes

£110,000 (2016/17)

CC number: 1041204

Trustees: Virginia Glastonbury; Brandon Ransley; Daniel Bodle; Alexis Graham.

Correspondent: Bernadette O'Sullivan, One Fleet Place, London EC4M 7WS (tel: 020 7246 4843)

Established in 1994, the Dentons UKMEA LLP Charitable Trust administered and funded by the law firm Dentons UKMEA LLP. The trust supports general charitable purposes and has a preference for organisations which have a connection with Dentons or are local to the firm's offices. In 2016/17 grants ranged from £75 to £6,000 although the majority of awards were between £500 and £1,000.

Financial information

In 2016/17 the trust held assets of £49,000 and had an income of £129,000, of which £103,000 was donated by the company. There were 96 grants made totalling £110,000.

Beneficiaries included: Worktree Milton Keynes and Prisoner's Advice and Care Trust (£3,900 each); London Legal Walk (£2,000); Red Lions Boy's Club and Wireless for the Bedridden (£1,500 each); Asylum Support Appeals Project, Contact the Elderly, Embrace Child Victims of Crime and Single Homeless Project (£750 each); WWF UK (£500); Teach First (£250); Macmillan Cancer Support (£150); Alzheimer's Society (£75).

Exclusions

No grants are given to individuals. Scholarships are not funded.

Applications

Apply in writing to the correspondent.

The Laduma Dhamecha Charitable Trust

General charitable purposes including: medical equipment for hospitals and education

UK and overseas

£305,500 (2016/17)

CC number: 328678

Trustees: K R. Dhamecha; Shantilal Dhamecha; Pradip Dhamecha.

Correspondent: Pradip Dhamecha, Trustee, The Dhamecha Group, 2 Hathaway Close, Stanmore, Middlesex HA7 3NR (tel: 020 8903 8181; email: info@dhamecha.com)

The trust was founded by the Dhamecha family who founded and operate the Dhamecha cash and carry group based in Greater London. The trust supports a wide range of organisations in the UK and overseas. The aims of the trust are listed in the annual report as being:

- To provide relief of sickness by the provision of medical equipment and the establishing or improvement of facilities at hospitals
- To provide for the advancement of education and/or an educational establishment in rural areas to make children self-sufficient in the long term
- Other general charitable purposes

Financial information

In 2016/17 the trust had assets of £2.5 million and an income of £629,500 mainly from donations including £513,000 from Dhamecha Foods Ltd. Grants totalled £1.5 million. Grants were made to UK organisations totalling £284,500 and to organisations and projects outside the UK totalling £20,500.

No list of beneficiaries was available.

Applications

Apply in writing to the correspondent.

The DLA Piper Charitable Trust

Medical research, social welfare

UK

£54,000 (2016/17)

CC number: 327280

Trustees: Philip Rooney; Sean Mahon; Sandra Wallace.

Correspondent: Godfrey Smallman, Secretary, c/o Wrigleys Solicitors LLP, Fountain Precinct, Balm Green, Sheffield S1 2JA (email: godfrey.smallman@wrigleys.co.uk)

The DLA Piper Charitable Trust is the corporate charity of the law firm DLA Piper.

Its 2015/16 accounts state that its grants policy aims to support registered charities through grants which:

- to encourage and support the fundraising efforts of members and employees of DLA Piper UK LLP
- to support, for instance, a charity project selected by a DLA Piper office for fundraising activities throughout a financial or calendar year
- to give significant support to a charity or charities offering service to particular communities or needy groups (for example, people who are ill or are facing other disadvantage)

The trust was registered with general charitable purposes, although it appears to give in two main areas – medical research and social welfare. Grants are usually for less than £1,000, although larger grants can be made.

Financial information

In 2016/17 the trust had an income of £167 and a total expenditure of £54,500. The trust's annual accounts were not available to view on the Charity Commission website due to its low income. We estimate that grants totalled around £54,000.

Previous beneficiaries have included: Unicef (£10,500 in two grants); Net4Kids, The Save the Children Fund and United Way Romania (£5,000 each); Bloodwise (£7,500 in two grants); Leeds Teaching Hospitals Charitable Foundation (£2,100 in three grants); Refugee Action, Scottish Association for Mental Health and Walthew House (£1,000 each).

Exclusions

No grants are given to individuals.

Applications

Apply in writing to the correspondent. The trustees meet four times a year to discuss applications. Applications from members, partners and employees of DLA Piper for grants in support of charities are encouraged.

The DS Smith Charitable Foundation

Education and training, environmental conservation

England and Wales

£310,500 (2016/17)

CC number: 1142817

Trustees: Anne Steele; Rachel Stevens; Emma Ciechan; Mark Reeve; Catriona O'Grady.

Correspondent: Rachel Stevens, Trustee, 7th Floor, 350 Euston Road, London NW1 3AX (tel: 020 7756 1823; email: charitablefoundation@dssmith.com)

 www.dssmith.com/company/sustainability/our-people/community-involvement/charitable-foundation

The DS Smith Charitable Foundation is the charity of the British-based international packaging business DS Smith plc. Registered in 2011, the foundation supports charities engaged in conservation of the environment and training or education.

The following information was taken from the foundation's website:

> Please note that only charities in the fields of environmental improvement and of education and training, will be considered, so please ensure that any application fulfils this criteria. The charity aims to make a combination of small donations (£1,000 or less) and larger donations each year. We particularly welcome opportunities to develop multi-year partnerships with key selected charities.

Financial information

In 2016/17 the foundation held assets of £2.2 million and had an income of £48,000. Grants totalling £310,500 were made to 41 organisations. Grants were distributed as follows:

Education	24	£161,500
Environment	11	£158,500
Other	6	£12,000

Beneficiaries included: Keep Britain Tidy (£100,000); Unicef (£44,000); Museum of Brands (£40,000); AT Bristol and In Kind Direct (£30,000 each); Arkwright Scholarship Trust (£20,000); Durham University and Edinburgh Science Festival (£5,000 each); Contains Art CIC (£2,500); Action for Kids (£2,000).

Applications

Applications can be submitted via the foundation's website.

The James Dyson Foundation

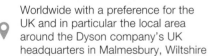

Medical research, engineering education

Worldwide with a preference for the UK and in particular the local area around the Dyson company's UK headquarters in Malmesbury, Wiltshire

£83,000 to organisations (2017)

CC number: 1099709

Trustees: Sir James Dyson; Lady Deirdre Dyson; Valerie West; Dr Fenella Dyson.

Correspondent: Lydia Beaton, Foundation Manager, Dyson Group plc, Tetbury Hill, Malmesbury, Wiltshire SN16 0RP (tel: 01666 828416; email: jamesdysonfoundation@dyson.com)

 www.jamesdysonfoundation.com

 facebook.com/JamesDysonFoundation

 @JDF

 @jamesdysonfoundation

The James Dyson Foundation is the charitable foundation of the British technology company Dyson Ltd. The foundation was established in 2002 to promote charitable giving, especially to charities working in the fields of science, design, engineering education and medical research. The foundation is almost exclusively funded by donations from Dyson Ltd.

The 2017 annual report defines the foundation's charitable objects as follows:

- To advance education and training, particularly in the fields of design and technology. This work can take a number of forms including the free provision of support resources for teachers of design and technology in schools, the running of design engineering workshops and lectures in schools and universities, as well as bursary schemes and collaborative projects
- To support medical and scientific research
- To support charitable and educational projects in the region in which The James Dyson Foundation operates

In addition to the provision of grants and bursaries, each year, the foundation also donates a number of Dyson vacuum cleaners (for raffle prizes) to charitable causes which fall within its objectives. Furthermore, the foundation also works with schools and universities, offering a range of educational resources, activities, and events (the cost of these in-kind contributions have been excluded from the grant total).

Financial information

In 2017 the foundation had liabilities of £49,500 and an income of £1.52 million. During the year, the foundation awarded grants and bursaries worth a total of £239,000 including £83,000 to organisations.

Beneficiaries included: Malmesbury School Project (£36,000); Alzheimer's Research UK (£15,000).

Exclusions

According to its website, the foundation will not fund any of the following:

- Animal welfare
- Loans or funding for individuals or companies
- Sports team sponsorship

Applications

Organisations can apply for funding by completing the online form, accessed via the 'Contact' section of the foundation's website.

The Economist Charitable Trust

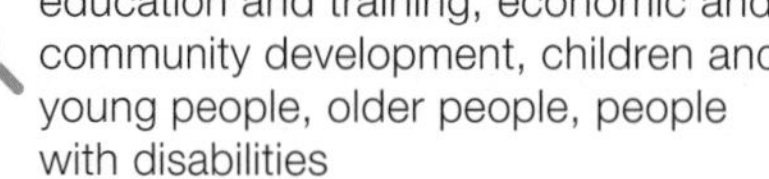

General charitable purposes, education and training, economic and community development, children and young people, older people, people with disabilities

 UK

£150,500 (2016/17)

CC number: 293709

Trustees: Ada Simkins; Kiran Malik; Cecelia Block; Susan Clark; Jamie Credland; Ursula Esling; Tasmin Anastasi-Pace.

Correspondent: The Trustees, The Adelphi, 1–11 John Adam Street, London WC2N 6HT (tel: 020 7576 8000)

 www.economist.com

The Economist Charitable Trust is the charity of The Economist Newspaper Ltd, a multinational media company specialising in international business and world affairs.

The trust was established in 1985 to distribute funds received from the Economist Newspaper Ltd to various charities. Around 60–70% of the trust's donations go to charities in the fields of communication, education, literacy and re-training for individuals and groups who are disadvantaged in some way. Approximately 30–40% of funds are used to match donations made by employees of the Economist Group. The remaining funds are utilised to make small donations to small and local charities.

Financial information

In 2016/17 the trust had assets of £1,600 and an income of £133,000, mostly from the Economist Newspaper Ltd. Grants made totalling £150,500. A list of beneficiaries was not available.

Applications

The trust does not accept unsolicited applications.

EDF Energy Trust (EDFET)

Fuel poverty, money/debt advice, fuel debt prevention

UK

£179,500 to organisations (2017)

CC number: 1099446

Trustees: Denise Fennell; Tim Cole; David Hawkes; Vic Szewczyk.

Correspondent: The Trustees, 3rd Floor, Trinity Court, Trinity Street, Peterborough PE1 1DA (tel: 01733 421060; email: edfet@charisgrants.com)

 www.edfenergytrust.org.uk

EDF Energy Trust, established in October 2003, makes grants to support individuals and families who are in 'need, poverty, suffering and distress who are struggling to pay their gas and/ or electricity debts'. The trust's grants scheme is administered by Charis Grants Ltd.

Organisational Grants Programme

The majority of grant funding is provided to individuals to assist with gas and electricity. However, some funding is also available to organisations to support the trust's purposes. The 2017 annual report states grants are given to organisations for the following purposes:

- Provision of specialist money/debt advice and resolving energy debt problems for all clients
- Supporting EDF Energy customers to apply to the charity where appropriate
- Promoting the Charity to local organisations, developing partnerships for referrals
- Promotion of energy debt awareness and prevention

Financial information

In 2017 the trust had assets of almost £2.3 million and an income of £2.67 million, the majority of which came from EDF Energy. Grants were made to two organisations totalling £179,500. Grants were also made to individuals and families totalling £2.6 million.

Beneficiaries were: Plymouth Citizens Advice (£99,000); Talking Money – Bristol (£80,500).

Applications

Contact the trust for further information.

Esh Foundation

General charitable purposes

 Cumbria; Durham; North Yorkshire; Northumberland

£101,500 (2017)

CC number: 1112040

Trustees: Michael Hogan; John Flynn; Jack Lumsden; Ron Batty; Tony Carroll; Brian Manning; Paul Brooks; Geoffrey Parkin.

Correspondent: Andrew Radcliffe, Secretary, Esh House, Bowburn North Industrial Estate, Bowburn, Durham DH6 5PF (tel: 07976 077621; email: enquiries@esh.uk.com)

 www.eshgroup.co.uk/added-value/community/esh-communities

The foundation was set up in 2005. It is the charitable foundation of the Esh Group, a civil engineering, construction and house building company based in Durham. The company makes an annual grant to the foundation.

Its website states:

> Esh Communities is Esh Group's community funding programme, which accepts grant applications from any community group charitable organisation or social enterprise which can demonstrate the aptitude and ability to make a real difference to their service users.

Financial information

In 2017 the foundation had assets of £38,000 and an income of £42,500 majority of which came from the company. Grants were made to 58 organisations totalling £101,500.

Beneficiaries included: Eagles Community Foundation (£20,000); St Cuthbert's Hospice (£5,000); Artists Collective Gallery (£1,000).

Applications

Applicants need to have a relationship with one of the group's clients. The company provides its clients with unique application codes which can then be used to access the application form on the company's website.

The Fidelity UK Foundation

 Arts, culture and heritage, community, development, education, health, environment

 UK with a strong preference for London, Kent and Surrey

£7.7 million (2017)

CC number: 327899

Trustees: Barry Bateman; Anthony Bolton; Richard Millar; John Owen; Sally Walden; Abigail Johnson; Elizabeth Bishop Johnson; Malcolm Austin Rogers.

Correspondent: Sian Parry, Head of Foundations, Oakhill House, 130 Tonbridge Road, Hildenborough, Tonbridge, Kent TN11 9DZ (tel: 01732 777364; email: foundation@fil.com)

 www.fidelityukfoundation.org

The Fidelity UK Foundation is the charitable foundation of the financial services company Fidelity Worldwide Investments. The foundation was established in 1988 and primarily supports UK-registered charities based in areas where Fidelity Worldwide Investment has corporate offices: London; Kent and Surrey. Applications are also considered from elsewhere in the UK, provided the organisation is a nationally recognised centre of excellence with national coverage. Grants are generally made to organisations with an annual operating budget in excess of £250,000.

According to its website, the foundation's charitable giving is mainly in the areas of:

- **Arts, culture and heritage** – Including nationally significant heritage sites, internationally recognised museums and class leading organisations in the visual and performing arts
- **Community** - Particularly early interventions and charities which help young and/or disadvantaged people achieve their potential
- **Education** - Particularly initiatives which improve education outcomes for the disadvantaged, from early years through to transition to work
- **Health** – Including disability, palliative care and centres of excellence involved in ground-breaking research and treatments to address chronic illness (with a particular focus on investment in specialist equipment)
- **Environment** - Particularly preservation and sustainable initiatives that have a positive impact on the natural world

Types of projects

Grants are typically directed to specific projects in the following categories:

> **Capital improvements** – Large-scale projects central to the overall growth and sustainability of the applicant, such as new construction, renovations, expansions, equipment and other initiatives that support the organisation's strategic vision.
>
> **Technology projects** - High-impact technology projects that can substantially increase an organisations efficiency, effectiveness and sustainability.
>
> **Organisational development** - Projects which seek to establish a new, transformational strategic path. This could include support for an initiative that helps a growing organisation achieve scale efficiencies, the development of a

franchise model or helping charities to yield consolidation efficiencies through mergers

Planning initiatives - Funding for expert/external consultants to develop strategic, business, technology and other types of plans.

Grant size

Grant size depends upon the impact and scope of the project. The majority of grants are for between £25,000–£150,000, although in exceptional circumstances trustees may choose to exceed this amount. Grants are not normally intended to cover the entire cost of a project.

The Fidelity International Foundation

Fidelity also has an international foundation which makes grants to organisations in countries where the company has operations and which serve beneficiaries in Continental Europe, Australia, Bermuda, China, Hong Kong, India, Japan, Korea, Singapore and Taiwan. Enquiry forms can be found on the UK foundation's website.

Financial information

In 2017 the foundation held assets of almost £259 million and had an income of £11.5 million. During the year, 64 grants were made totalling £7.7 million. Grants were broken down as follows:

Education	22	£3.04 million
Arts, culture and heritage	19	£2.38 million
Health	7	£1.81 million
Community Development	16	£1.46 million

Beneficiaries included: Royal College of Music (£500,000); Canterbury Cathedral and National Maritime Museum (£350,000 each); Raspberry Pi Foundation (£328,000); Royal Airforce Museum (£200,000); National Youth Orchestra of Great Britain (£35,500); The Grange Festival (£20,000).

Exclusions

Grants are not generally made to:

- Start-up, political or sectarian organisations
- Organisations which have been running for less than three years
- Individuals
- Private schools

Grants are not generally made for:

- Sponsorships
- Scholarships
- Corporate membership
- Advertising and promotional projects
- Exhibitions
- General running costs
- Replacement of dated IT hardware, routine system upgrades or ongoing website content
- Grants will not normally cover costs incurred prior to application and/or the grant being awarded

Applications

Applicants should submit an initial enquiry via the foundation's website. The review process takes six to eight weeks. If you are invited to make a full application the foundation staff will request further information and possibly a site visit. Initial enquiries can be submitted at any time.

The Sir John Fisher Foundation

General charitable purposes with a preference for maritime causes, medicine, people with disabilities, education, music, the arts, community projects

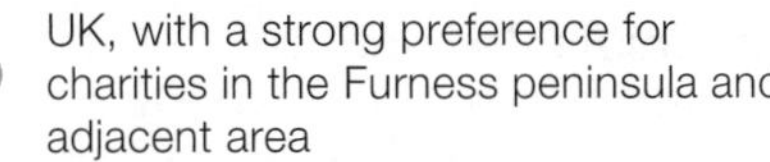

UK, with a strong preference for charities in the Furness peninsula and adjacent area

£1.9 million (2016/17)

CC number: 277844

Trustees: Diane Meacock; Daniel Tindall; Rowland Hart Jackson; Michael Shields; Thomas Meacock; Christine Tomlinson; Christopher Batten.

Correspondent: Dr David Jackson, Secretary, Heaning Wood, Ulverston, Cumbria LA12 7NZ (tel: 01229 580349; email: info@sirjohnfisherfoundation.org.uk)

www.sirjohnfisherfoundation.org.uk

The foundation registered with the Charity Commission in 1979 and was established by the founders, Sir John and Lady Maria Fisher. The foundation is closely associated with James Fisher and Sons plc which provides marine engineering services.

Areas of support

The foundation's website states that it supports charitable causes particularly in the six following categories:

- Maritime
- Medical and disability
- Education
- Music
- Arts
- Community projects in and around Barrow-in-Furness

Capital and revenue funding is available for up to three years. Most grants are for less than £10,000.

The trustees have a preference for supporting community projects in the Barrow-in-Furness area to meet the needs of the community and in particular the vulnerable and disadvantaged.

The foundation's website notes that:

> The Trustees are likely to favour those local organisations who have sound and stable governance, and who have a strategy and considered plans for the future. In the local area community projects involving sick, disabled, children, education, family support, maritime, arts and music will receive priority.
>
> Outside the Barrow-in-Furness area, a very much more limited number of community causes will be supported in Cumbria and North Lancashire.

Some projects are supported nationally, particularly projects that fall under the maritime, music and arts categories. The trustees are also willing to fund a limited amount of medical research.

Financial information

In 2016/17 the foundation held assets of £125 million and had an income of £2.5 million, of which £1.8 million was dividend income from James Fisher and Sons plc. During the year there were 164 grants made totalling £1.9 million. Grants to 143 local organisations totalled £1.14 million. A further 21 national organisations were awarded £755,500, of which £500,000 was granted to the RNLI.

Local beneficiaries included: Lancaster University (£58,000); St John's Hospice (£29,000); Furness Homeless Support Group (£20,000); Families Matter Counselling and Support Services Ltd (£14,000); Barrow Food Bank (£10,000); Kendal Brewery Arts Centre Trust (£8,000); The Owl Sanctuary (£5,000); Opus Music CIC (£3,100); Barrow Amateur Swimming Club (£2,000); South Walney Infant and Nursery School (£1,000); Ulverston Pantomime Society (£500).

Exclusions

According to the foundation's website, it will not make grants for:

- Sponsorship
- Expeditions
- The promotion of religion or places of worship
- Animal welfare
- Activities or projects that have already taken place
- Community projects outside Barrow-in-Furness and surrounding area (except occasional projects in Cumbria or North Lancashire or if they fall within one of the other categories supported by the foundation)

Individuals and pressure groups are also ineligible for funding.

Applications

Application forms are available from the correspondent or to download from the website, where guidelines can also be found. Completed forms should be returned to the Secretary, along with your organisation's most recent set of audited accounts, at least six weeks before the trustees' meetings at the beginning of May and November each year. The closing dates for applications are 1 March and 21 September, respectively. The Secretary can be contacted for an informal discussion before an application for funding is submitted.

Ford Britain Trust

Communities, children and young people, education, special educational needs, disability

UK with a preference for locations near Ford Motor Company Ltd or FCE Bank plc UK operations. These are: Essex (including East London), Bridgend, Southampton, Daventry, Manchester and Liverpool

£116,000 (2016/17)

CC number: 269410

Trustees: Michael Callaghan; David Russell; Michael Brophy; Dr June-Alison Sealy; Wendy James; Jane Skerry; Paul Bailey; Lara Nicoll.

Correspondent: Deborah Chennels, Trust Director, Room 1/623, c/o Ford Motor Company Ltd, Eagle Way, Brentwood, Essex CM13 3BW (email: fbtrust@ford.com)

www.ford.co.uk/experience-ford/about-ford/ford-britain-trust

The Ford Britain Trust serves the communities in which Ford Motor Company Ltd and its employees are located. The trust provides grants mainly to registered charities and schools that are in support of youth development; schools and education, with particular emphasis on special educational needs; disabilities; and community related services.

The trust particularly encourages applications from Ford employees, but is open to all, provided that applicants meet the selection criteria.

Grants

The website states that grants are typically one-off, provided for specific capital projects or parts of a project, and fall into two categories:

- Small grants – for amounts up to £250, available four times a year
- Large grants – for amounts over £250 and usually up to £3,000, available twice a year

Grants can be made to registered charities, schools or PTAs, and other non-profit organisations. Support is given in the following categories:

- Local community or environment
- Young people and children
- Education and schools
- Special education needs
- People with disabilities

Grants can be given for the following purposes:

- Contributions towards capital projects, such as refurbishments
- Capital expenditure items, such as equipment or furniture
- Contributions towards the purchase of new Ford vehicles (only up to £3,000, and when two-thirds of the purchase price can be raised from other sources)

Guidelines on applications for IT equipment, such as the maximum grant available, can be requested from the trust. The website also states: 'Applications relating to core funding, operating costs, salaries or revenue expenditure will be considered in the same way as requests for general funding and will, therefore, be eligible for small grants only.'

Financial information

In 2016/17 the trust had assets of £362,000 and an income of £159,000. Grants to 143 organisations totalled £131,000 (including £15,000 of support costs) and were broken down as follows:

Community service	54	£50,500
Schools/education	47	£39,500
Youth	28	£22,500
Disability	12	£15,500
Special needs education	2	£3,100

Beneficiaries included: Children Ahead Ltd, Nia Project; Rest Bay Lifeguard Club and Urban Synergy (£3,000 each).

Beneficiaries of grants under £3,000 totalled £131,000.

Exclusions

The trust's website states that applications are not considered in support of the following:

- Core funding; General running costs
- Major building works
- Sponsorship or advertising
- Research
- Overseas projects; Travel
- Religious projects; Political projects
- Purchase of second-hand vehicles
- Third party fundraising initiatives (exceptions may be made for fundraising initiatives by Ford Motor Company Ltd employees and retirees)

Applications

Application forms are available to download from the website, where guidance notes are also available. There are two types of grants that can be applied for: small grants (up to £250) and large grants (over £250 and usually up to £3,000). Small grants are considered four times a year in June, October and February. Large grant applications are considered twice a year in March and September. Deadlines are detailed on the website.

Gatwick Airport Community Trust

Children and young people, art, sports facilities, environment and conservation, community facilities, people with disabilities, older people, development of volunteering

Parts of East and West Sussex, Surrey and Kent but particularly communities directly affected by operations at Gatwick Airport. A map of the area of benefit can be seen on the website

£195,500 (2017)

CC number: 1089683

Trustees: Richard Burrett; Michael Roberts; Brian Quinn; John Kendall; Julie Ayres; Joanna Rettie; Alan Jones; Graham Knight; Christopher Townsend.

Correspondent: The Trustees, c/o Kreston Reeves, Springfield House, Springfield Road, Horsham, West Sussex RH12 2RG (tel: 07444 737518; email: mail@gact.org.uk)

www.gact.org.uk

The trust was launched in January 2002 and the first grants were awarded in May 2002. It is an independent charity set up by legal agreement between West Sussex County Council, Crawley Borough Council and Gatwick Airport Ltd.

The following was taken from the trust's website:

> Grants are currently awarded annually for such charitable purposes as the trustees determine within the area of benefit which covers parts of East and West Sussex, Surrey and Kent. They adopt strict criteria and channel funds for deserving projects, particularly in those areas where people are directly affected by operations at Gatwick Airport.
>
> The normal level of grants is from £1,000 to £5,000. Occasional larger grants may be considered if the impact is targeted to benefit a significant number of people and is considered to make a valuable and noticeable difference longer term.
>
> Priority categories for the Trust when assessing a project are set out below:
>
> - Development of young people
> - Art projects including amateur drama, music, art
> - Sporting facilities
> - Environmental improvement and conservation
> - Improvements to community facilities such as village halls
> - Support for the disabled
> - Support for the elderly
> - Encouragement of additional volunteering or giving in the area

Financial information

In 2017 the trust had assets of £16,400 and an income of £213,500. Grants to 107 organisations totalled £195,500 and were broken down as follows:

Community and community facilities	£64,500
Sports and recreation	£35,000
Young children	£28,500
People with disabilities/who are disadvantaged	£26,500
Arts, theatre and music	£16,000
Older people	£13,500
Young adults	£7,100
Environmental	£4,300

Beneficiaries included: Capel Sports Pavilion; Charlwood Sports Pavilion and Tall Ships Youth Trust (£10,000 each).

Exclusions

According to the trust's website, it will not support the following:

- Projects or beneficiaries that are completely or largely outside the area of benefit
- Recurrent expenditure or running costs
- Ongoing costs, maintenance or deficits
- Repeat annual applications for similar projects
- Costs that should be funded from other sources e.g. public bodies
- Applications from organisations that have statutory responsibilities such as local authorities, hospitals, schools, unless it is a project that is over and above their core activities
- The purchase of land or buildings
- Organisations that are working to make a profit for shareholders, partners or sole owners, nor to individuals
- Individuals
- Grants will not normally be made to organisations with excess 'free' reserves
- Salaries

Applications

Application forms can be downloaded from the trust's website. Applications are invited once a year, usually between January and March. Grants are paid by the end of May. Further information can be found on the trust's website. Telephone enquiries are welcomed.

The Golden Bottle Trust

General charitable purposes including: the environment, health, education, religion, the arts and financially developing countries

Worldwide

£1.62 million (2016/17)

CC number: 327026

Trustee: Hoare Trustees.

Correspondent: Hoare Trustees, C. Hoare & Co., 37 Fleet Street, London EC4P 4DQ (tel: 020 7353 4522)

The trust was established in 1985 for general charitable purposes, by C Hoare and Co. bankers, the oldest remaining private bank in the UK. The trust is managed by the company, Hoare Trustees, and continues to receive most of its income from C. Hoare and Co.

The objective of the trust is the continuation of the philanthropic commitments and ideals of the Hoare family. Traditionally the charity has supported causes including the arts, religion, environment, health, education, the developing world and also many charities with whom the Hoare family is familiar.

Grants range from £250 to £10,000 with larger amounts occasionally being granted, usually to the same charities that the Hoare family has funded regularly.

In addition to grant-making the charity has invested in a number of PRIs (Programme Related Investments) in the UK and the financially developing world. In 2016/17 the trust made one further PRI with a £100,000 commitment to the charity Mustard Seed.

Financial information

In 2016/17 the trust held assets of £18.36 million and had an income of £7.5 million. Grants were made totalling £1.62 million, which does not include £161,500 given by the trust to match staff fundraising.

Beneficiaries, receiving £10,000 or more, included: The Bulldog Trust (£300,000); The Henry C. Hoare Charitable Trust (£60,000); Blueprint Trust (£51,000); The Access Point (£20,000); London Library, Prison Reform Trust and Turn to Starboard (£10,000 each).

Exclusions

No grants are given for individuals or organisations that are not registered charities.

Applications

The trust does not normally respond to unsolicited applications.

The Goldman Sachs Charitable Gift Fund (UK)

General charitable purposes, including, community development, education, health, social welfare, arts and culture, and humanitarian relief

Worldwide

£1.08 million (2016/17)

CC number: 1120148

Trustees: Robert Katz; Mike Housden; Peter Fahey.

Correspondent: Jenny Evans, Executive Director, Goldman Sachs, Peterborough Court, 133 Fleet Street, London EC4A 2BB (tel: 020 7774 1000)

The Goldman Sachs Charitable Gift Fund (UK) was established in 2007 for general charitable purposes. The fund is the UK charity of the multinational investment bank and financial services company The Goldman Sachs Group Inc., and is the wholly owned subsidiary of the Goldman Sachs Charitable Gift Fund, which has been recognised by the United States Internal Revenue Service as a tax-exempt organisation.

Grants are awarded worldwide and are used to support a wide range of charitable activities including, community development, education, health, social welfare, arts and culture, and humanitarian relief.

According to the fund's 2016/17 annual report:

> The ongoing strategy of the Fund is to make grants pursuant to its objects from donated funds solicited from The Goldman Sachs Group, Inc., and its predecessors, subsidiaries, affiliates and successors (Goldman Sachs), and current and former senior employees of Goldman Sachs.

Financial information

In 2016/17 the fund had assets of £11.06 million ($14.3 million) and an income of £1.5 million ($1.9 million). During the year, the fund awarded 80 grants totalling £1.08 million ($1.4 million). Grants were distributed as follows:

Education	£581,000
Arts and culture	£216,500
Other	£124,000
Community	£104,500
Medical	£52,500
Humanitarian	£4,000

GBP figures have been calculated using the exchange rate at the time of writing (August 2018).

Beneficiaries included: Rhino Conservation Botswana (UK) Trust (£60,000); The British Museum (£50,000); The Chatham House Foundation, Inc. (£44,000).

Applications

The 2016/17 annual report explains that the fund 'operates as a donor advised fund whereby the directors establish donor accounts for individual donors to make recommendations, although the ultimate decision for the distribution of funds tests solely with the directors of the Fund'.

Goldman Sachs Gives (UK)

Arts and culture, community, education, humanitarian, medical

Worldwide

£18.5 million (2016/17)

CC number: 1123956

Trustees: Jenny Evans; Robert Katz; Mike Housden; Peter Fahey.

Correspondent: Jenny Evans, Trustee, Peterborough Court, 133 Fleet Street, London EC4A 2BB (tel: 020 7774 1000)

Goldman Sachs Gives (UK) was established and registered with the Charity Commission in 2008. The income of the fund is made up of donations from affiliate and subsidiary companies of Goldman Sachs Group Inc., and also from past and present senior employees of these companies.

The charity's 2016/17 annual accounts state:

> The objects of the Fund are to promote for the public benefit the advancement of education, the relief of poverty, the advancement of religion and any other exclusively charitable purpose. In furtherance of those objects the Fund focuses on supporting charities and charitable activities that build and stabilise communities, increase educational opportunities, advance health, relieve poverty, promote the arts and culture, provide humanitarian relief and further any other charitable purposes.

Financial information

In 2016/17 the charity had assets of £93.4 million and an income of £23.2 million. A total of £18.5 million was awarded in 551 grants to institutions, broken down into the following areas of support:

Education	£7.9 million
Community	£3.1 million
Medical	£2.7 million
Humanitarian	£2.6 million
Arts and culture	£1.9 million
Other	£335,000

Beneficiaries included: Greenhouse Sports Ltd (£2.9 million); British Refugee Council (£1 million) New York University (£906,000); Grenada Schools Ltd (£750,000); Cancer Research UK (£688,500).

Applications

Applications can be made in writing to the correspondent. Be aware however that this is a donor advised fund.

Gowling WLG (UK) Charitable Trust

General charitable purposes

UK, with some preference for West Midlands

£124,500 (2016/17)

CC number: 803009

Trustee: Lee Nuttall, Phillip Clissitt, Andrew Witts.

Correspondent: Lee Nuttall, Trustee, Gowling WLG (UK) LLP, Two Snowhill, Snow Hill Queensway, Birmingham B4 6WR (tel: 0121 233 1000)

Registered in 1990 as the Wragge & Co. Charitable Trust, the trust was renamed in 2016 as Gowling WLG (UK) Charitable Trust, following the merger of Wragge Lawrence Graham & Co. LLP, the UK-based international law firm, and Gowling LLP, an international law firm based in Canada. The trust is the corporate charity of Gowling WLG LLP.

The trust's accounts for 2016/17 state that 'the trustees have no fixed policy on grant making and support a wide range of local and national charities [...] however, they do not usually make grants to individuals or organisations which are not themselves charities.'

The company's website states: 'The firm's Charitable Trust makes small grants throughout the year to charities registered in England and Wales and also provides matched funding for our people's fundraising efforts in aid of a wide variety of UK charities.'

Financial information

In 2016/17 the trust had assets of £24,000 and an income of £110,000 which was almost entirely made up of Gift Aid donations. Grants were made to 161 charitable organisations totalling £124,500.

Beneficiaries included: DEC East Africa Crisis Appeal (£10,000); Teach First (£5,800); Help Harry Help Others (£2,900); University of Warwick (£2,000); Bede House Association (£1,800); Chance to Shine Foundation (£1,000); Dress for Success and Independent Age (£500 each); Sense (£250); Severn Hospice Ltd (£100).

Exclusions

The foundation does not make grants to individuals or to organisations which are not charities.

Applications

Apply in writing to the correspondent. The day-to-day management of the trust is carried out by Gowling WLG, including co-ordinating grant applications, which are presented to the trustees for their consideration at meetings throughout the year.

The Greggs Foundation

General charitable purposes

England, Wales and Scotland, with a preference for the north east of England, (Northumberland, Tyne and Wear, Durham and Teesside) and regional divisions of Greggs plc

£3.15 million (2017)

CC number: 296590

Trustees: Andrew Davison; Fiona Nicholson; Richard Hutton; Lindsay Graham; Jane Hartley; Tony Rowson; Roisin Currie; Karen Wilkinson-Bell; Kate Bradley; Mick Thompson.

Correspondent: Justine Massingham, Grants Manager, Greggs House, Quorum Business Park, Newcastle Upon Tyne, Tyne and Wear NE12 8BU (tel: 0191 212 7626; email: greggsfoundation@greggs.co.uk)

www.greggsfoundation.org.uk

The Greggs Foundation was registered with the Charity Commission in 1987 and is the corporate charity of Greggs plc, the UK's largest bakery chain.

The latest annual report and accounts state that, 'Ian Gregg (former chairman of Greggs plc) set up the foundation as a registered charity in 1987 with the aim of giving something back to the communities where Greggs plc trades, and where customers and employees live.'

The foundation makes grants to organisations throughout England, Scotland and Wales to enhance the quality of life in local communities. Divisional Charity Committees based within the regional divisions of Greggs plc also make grants on behalf of the foundation and are located in Newcastle upon Tyne; Glasgow; Gosforth; Leeds; Manchester; Birmingham; Treforest; and Twickenham. According to its website, the foundation's trustees prioritise organisations that support voluntary carers, people with disabilities, homeless people and older people.

Grant programmes

At the time of writing (August 2018), the foundation administered five grant programmes: North East core funding grant, local community projects fund grant, environmental grant, hardship fund grant and breakfast clubs. The following information is taken from the foundation's website:

North East Core Funding

Financial support is offered to help sustain and increase the capacity of organisations that are based in and support people who live in the north east of England. Grants of up to £45,000 (up to £15,000 per year) are available 'to increase the capacity of the organisation to provide quality services', including support for core running costs. Priority groups are: people with disabilities; homeless people; voluntary carers; older and isolated people. Any not-for-profit organisation can apply.

Local Community Projects Fund

Small grants of up to £2,000 are made to 'enable not for profit organisations to do something they otherwise couldn't afford to'. The programme is administered by seven regional charity committees based throughout England, Wales and Scotland. Any not-for-profit organisation can apply as long as the project supports a community and benefits people who: have disabilities; live in poverty; are voluntary carers; are homeless individuals; are isolated older people; or those who have other demonstrable significant need. The website states:

> We are interested in projects that improve resilience within your community of interest. This can include sessional activities/respite support, equipment for sessional activities, trips and residential breaks. We are also interested in new approaches and innovative ideas as well as sustainable approaches to supporting your community of interest.

Grants are more likely to be made to local organisations based near Greggs shops. Organisations 'with a turnover in excess of £300,000 are unlikely to be successful'.

Environment Grants

Funded by the 5p levy on carrier bag sales, this fund is dedicated to 'projects that improve the physical environment in a way that will improve people's lives'. Small grants of up to £2,000 are available on a one-off basis. The fund is administered in a similar way to the Local Community Projects Fund. Any not-for-profit organisation can apply although preference is given to smaller, locally based, community-led organisations with a turnover of under £300,000. The foundation also encourages schools to also apply.

Hardship Fund

Grants of up to £150 are made to individuals and families (via recognised social organisations) who live in extreme financial hardship. The grants are used to provide household goods, such as cookers, fridge freezers, clothing, beds and bedding, baby equipment and flooring.

Breakfast Clubs

The Breakfast Club programme was established to help primary schoolchildren to get nutritious start of their day. As part of the scheme, schools in England, Wales, Scotland or Belfast are provided with fresh bread from their nearest Greggs shop, and a grant to support start-up and ongoing costs of the initiative. There are currently over 465 breakfast clubs operating.

Financial information

In 2017 the foundation had assets of £20.2 million and an income of £3.46 million, including donations from Greggs plc and dividends from the Foundation's investment fund. Grants totalled £3.15 million and were broken down as follows:

Environmental Grants	£904,500
North East Core Fund	£624,500
Local Community Project Fund	£581,000
Breakfast Clubs	£684,000
Hardship Fund	£308,000
Holiday provision and other	£103,000

Beneficiaries included: Cramlington youth Voluntary Project (£36,000); Kilmarnock Road Children and Young People Family Resource Centre, Opengate, Real Deal Plus (£30,000 each); Newcastle West End Food Bank (£20,000); Durham Christian Partnership (£16,400); Wag and Co. North East Friendship Dogs (£13,500); Sunderland Bangladeshi Centre (£12,000); Jubilee Fields Community Association (£11,500).

Exclusions

Exclusions vary between grant programmes, see the website for full details.

Applications

Each grant programme has its own detailed criteria, guidelines and application process, all of which are available to view on the website.

Applications for **Hardship Fund** grants are only accepted via recognised social organisations, such as charities, housing associations and social services acting on behalf of a family or individual in need. Applications are assessed weekly, but at the time of writing (August 2018) they are currently oversubscribed and can only fund around half the requests. The website indicates that applications will be more successful if they can demonstrate significant impact on the following three groups:

- We prioritise families over individuals
- We prioritise the most financially excluded people
- We prioritise items that will make the most difference

The **North East Core Funding** programme is very competitive with around one in five eligible applications being successful.

Similarly the **Local Community Projects Fund** is 'over-subscribed and there is huge competition for the grants available'. The foundation asks not to be too disappointed if it is unable to support your project. It is unable to give tailored feedback on every application but will let you know whether it has been successful as early as possible. In 2017, 27% of eligible applications were awarded.

The foundation also states that the **Small Environment Grants** is 'likely to receive a very high number of applications and an accordingly low success rate'.

Halifax Foundation for Northern Ireland

Social welfare, education and training

Northern Ireland

£1.1 million (2017)

CC number: NIC101763

Trustees: Hugh Donnelly; Janine Donnelly; James McCooe; Imelda Macmillan; Paula Leathem; Aine McCoy; Nuala Dlacz; Gillian Boyd; Ken Simpson.

Correspondent: Brenda McMullan, 11–15 Donegall Square North, Belfast BT1 5GB (tel: 028 9032 3000; email: info@halifaxfoundationni.org)

 www.halifaxfoundationni.org

Previously known as the Lloyds Bank Foundation for Northern Ireland, the foundation was renamed in 2016, due to the strong presence in Northern Ireland of the Halifax, which is part of Lloyds Banking Group. The foundation is one of four Lloyds Banking Group charities, covering England and Wales, Scotland, Northern Ireland and the Channel Islands. The foundation is an independent grant-maker, receiving its income from shares held in the banking group.

Funding objectives

The overall aim of the foundation, as stated on its website is:

> To support charitable organisations within Northern Ireland to enable people, who are disadvantaged or with special needs, to participate actively in their communities.

The foundation has two main target areas to which it seeks to allocate funds: social and community needs, and education and training.

Social and community needs

The foundation supports a wide range of activities and the following examples are listed on the website as a guide:

- **Community Services:** Family centres, youth clubs, older people's clubs, after schools clubs, self-help groups, childcare provision preschools and playgroups

- **Advice Services:** Homelessness, addictions, bereavement, family guidance, money advice, helplines and suicide awareness
- **People with Special Needs:** Residences, day centres, transport, carers, information, advice, and advocacy
- **Promotion of Health:** Information and advice, mental health, hospices, day care, home nursing, independent living for older people
- **Civic Responsibility:** Young people at risk, crime prevention, promotion of volunteering, victim support, mediation, rehabilitation of offenders
- **Cultural Enrichment:** Improving access and skills development in the arts and national heritage for disadvantaged people and those with special needs

Education and training

The foundation aims to enhance educational opportunities for people who are disadvantaged or have special needs through the following:

- **Employment:** Projects which help disadvantaged people develop their potential and secure employment
- **Life Skills:** Promotion of life skills, independent living skills for people with special needs
- **Training and Education:** Accredited, vocational or personal development training

Grant programmes

The Community Grant Programme is the foundation's main focus through which grants are made within its funding objectives. Grants currently average between £3,000 and £4,000.

In order to be eligible to apply, organisations must have an income of less than £1 million in the previous 12 months. For registered charities which have a headquarters based outside Northern Ireland, the foundation will use the figure of the income of their Northern Ireland operation to determine their eligibility.

Community Grants Programme guidelines state that the following list is a guide to the key areas the foundation supports:

- Core costs
- Materials and equipment
- Salary costs
- Volunteer expenses
- Project costs
- Refurbishment
- Activities
- Training
- Disabled access
- Transport Costs

Full guidelines for the programme are available from the website.

The Matched Giving Programme allows employees of Lloyds Banking Group to claim up to £1,000 per year for a charity they have fundraised or volunteered for, within the scheme's eligibility criteria. The foundation matches every pound raised, or donates £8 per hour of voluntary time given, for a maximum of £500 in fundraising or time given. Full guidelines are provided on the foundation's website. During this financial year, 326 awards were made under the programme totalling £120,500.

Financial information

In 2017 the foundation held £3.35 million in assets and had an income of £3.9 million. A total of almost £1.1 million was awarded in 531 grants broken down as follows:

Social and community welfare	£661,000
Education and training	£317,500
Matched giving	£120,500

Previous beneficiaries have included: Appleby Careers Project Ltd and Gleann Amateur Boxing Club (£5,000 each); Loughside FC (£4,100); Child Brain Injury Trust (£4,000); Citizenship Foundation (£3,600); Cathedral Quarter Trust, St John's Parish Church, Strabane Community Unemployed Group and Youth Hostel Association of Northern Ireland (£3,000 each); Greenpower Education Trust (£1,500); Ballynure and District Friendship Club (£700); Ballymacward Preschool Playgroup (£500).

Exclusions

According to the Community Grants Programme guidelines, the following are not funded:

- Organisations which have an income of more than £1 million in the previous year's accounts
- Organisations which are insolvent
- Organisations who have over 12 months reserves would not be seen as a priority
- Individuals, including students
- Animal welfare
- The environment
- Hospitals and Medical Centres
- Schools, universities and colleges (except for projects specifically to benefit pupils with special needs)
- Sponsorship or fundraising events either for your own organisation or another
- Promotion of religion
- Endowment funds
- Activities that are normally the responsibility of central or local government
- Loans and business finance
- Travel or activities outside of Northern Ireland
- Capital build (except in the case of disabled access)

Applications

All applications must be made online via the foundation's website, where full guidelines, including a list of supporting documentation required, are available. The Community Grants Programme is operated on a rolling basis, meaning organisations can apply at any time. It can take at least four months for a decision to be made, and applying organisations may receive a telephone call or visit as part of the application process.

The Hiscox Foundation

General charitable purposes, particularly: education, medical science, the arts, independent living for older people, disadvantaged or vulnerable people

Worldwide, primarily in the UK

£147,500 (2016/17)

CC number: 327635

Trustees: Alexander Foster; Robert Hiscox; Rory Barker; Andrew Nix; Amanda Brown.

Correspondent: Craig Martindale, Hiscox Underwriting Ltd, 1 Great St Helen's, London EC3A 6HX (tel: 020 7448 6505)

www.hiscoxgroup.com/responsibility/communities.aspx

The Hiscox Foundation is the corporate charity of Hiscox plc, a specialist insurance provider.

According to its website, the foundation 'focuses on supporting charities that aid and improve education, science, advancement of the arts and culture, children's rights and that provide services to disadvantaged and vulnerable members of society'.

Financial information

In 2016/17 the foundation had assets of almost £8.2 million and an income of £746,000, including a £500,000 donation from Hiscox plc. Grants were made to 90 charities totalling £147,500.

Beneficiaries included: HART (£50,000); St Helena's Hospice (£12,000); Martin House Children's Hospice (£6,500); Mind (£5,000); Sane (£1,000); Save the Children (£135).

Applications

Apply in writing to the correspondent. Our research suggests that support is mainly given to causes known by the trustees. According to the annual report for 2015/16, 'priority is given to any charitable endeavour by members of staff of the Hiscox group to encourage such activity'. The trustees meet quarterly to consider applications.

The Hudson Foundation

General charitable purposes, care of older people, care of the sick

UK with a preference for the Wisbech area

£208,000 (2016/17)

CC number: 280332

Trustees: David Ball; Stephen Layton; Edward Newling; Stephen Hutchinson.

Correspondent: David Ball, Trustee, 1–3 York Row, Wisbech, Cambridgeshire PE13 1EA (tel: 01945 461456)

The objective of the Hudson Foundation is to provide funds for general charitable purposes, with a particular focus on the relief of ill and/or older people; and the establishment and maintenance of residential accommodation in the Wisbech area. The 2016/17 accounts state that, 'whilst the trustees do make contributions to revenue expenditure of charitable organisations, they prefer to assist in the funding of capital projects for the advancement of the community of Wisbech and district'.

The foundation's principal source of funding is its trading subsidiary, Alan Hudson Ltd, which rents the charity's investment property and donates its taxable profits by way of Gift Aid to the charity.

Financial information

In 2016/17 the foundation had assets £2.3 million and an income of £1.25 million. During the year, grants were made to 11 organisations totalling £208,000.

Beneficiaries included: Wisbech St Mary Sports Centre (£103,000); Wisbech Angles Theatre Council (£60,000); Methodist Homes for the Aged (£7,900); Wisbech Grammar School (£5,000); Guide Dogs for the Blind (£2,000).

Applications

Apply in writing to the correspondent. The trustees meet quarterly.

IBM United Kingdom Trust

Education and training in ICT (Information and Communication Technology)

UK; Europe; Middle East; Africa

£1.24 million (2017)

CC number: 290462

Trustees: Prof. Derek Bell; Anne Wolfe; Naomi Hill; Andrew Fitzgerald.

Correspondent: Mark Wakefield, Trust Manager, IBM United Kingdom Ltd, 1PG1, 76 Upper Ground, London SE1 9PZ (email: wakefim@uk.ibm.com)

The focus areas for IBM's community investment are the strategic and innovative use of Information and Communication Technology (ICT) in education and training and the promotion of digital inclusion, with the broad objective of raising standards of achievement. Most activity is within the compulsory education phase. The vast majority of IBM's community investment is delivered through specific programmes initiated and developed by IBM in partnership with organisations with appropriate professional expertise. The trust gives preference to organisations concerned with people disadvantaged by poverty and/or at risk of digital exclusion. Preference is given to supporting projects and organisations in areas in which the company is based and/or where there is employee involvement.

The trust's annual report gives the following information on its objects and activities:

- The advancement of education, particularly through the use and understanding of information technology
- The advancement of research, with emphasis (though not exclusively) on information technology
- Improving the condition of life for the disadvantaged or disabled through the use of information technology
- Encouraging the use and understanding of information technology in the charitable sector
- Through the provision of information technology and related services, or otherwise, supporting the relief of poverty, the health of the community and the preservation of the environment

Based on the above objects, and with consideration for public benefit, the Trust has the following aims:

- Increasing the scope, usage and understanding of information technology through education
- Providing information technology and other services to enable not for profit organisations and the disadvantaged to acquire skills
- Promoting volunteering by IBM employees
- Providing aid in the form of technology and technical support for disaster relief
- Providing support for research at universities and other educational institutes

The Trust primarily achieves its aims by supporting the development and delivery of IBM's own community programmes, where these meet the charitable objects of the Trust. The support is delivered through the provision of grants of equipment, technical support and cash. The support is provided for IBM's community involvement programmes in the United Kingdom, and across EMEA.

The Trust's approach to grant making falls into two key areas:

- The provision of grants that advance both the aims of the Trust and support IBM programmes
- The provision of small grants in support of charitable organisations in the communities surrounding IBM sites

In this way the Trust seeks to achieve its aims, not only through key longer term programmes, but also through support for smaller scale initiatives by providing direct contributions, and encouraging ongoing links between charitable and educational organisations and IBM.

Financial information

In 2017 the trust had assets of £4.73 million and an income of £2.14 million which was comprised of donations from IBM International Foundation and IBM subsidiaries. Grants were made totalling £1.24 million, and were distributed as follows:

Provision of IT and other services	£1.05 million
Support for research	£167,000
Increasing the use of technology in education	£20,000
Miscellaneous	£3,000

Beneficiaries included: Foodcloud (£57,000); Business in the Community (£36,000); Royal Society of Wildlife Trust (£35,000); Danish Refugee Council (£32,000); University of Aberdeen (£30,000).

Applications

Very few unsolicited requests are considered. If you decide to submit an appeal then it should be done by email or in writing and include a brief resume of the aims of your organisation and details of what assistance is required. Those considering making an application are advised to telephone first for advice.

The Iliffe Family Charitable Trust

General charitable purposes

UK

£86,500 (2016/17)

CC number: 273437

Trustees: Lord Iliffe; The Hon. Edward Iliffe; Catherine Fleming; Lady Iliffe.

Correspondent: Catherine Fleming, Trustee, Barn Close, Burnt Hill, Yattendon, Berkshire RG18 0UX (email: ifct@yattendon.co.uk)

The trust was set up in 1977 by the Iliffe Family who own Yattendon Group plc which is a private British company with interests in printing, agriculture, marinas and property. The Chair of the group, Lord Iliffe and Group Chief Executive, Edward Iliffe are both trustees of the charity.

Grants are given to support general charitable purposes, including: medical causes; heritage; conservation; education and social welfare. The bulk of the grants made are to UK-registered charities already known to the trustees.

Financial information

In 2016/17 the trust had assets of £1.4 million and an income of £32,500. Grants to 18 organisations totalled £86,500 and were broken down as follows:

Education	8	£45,500
Welfare	4	£30,000
Heritage	2	£4,500
Religious	2	£3,500
Conservation	1	£2,500
Medical	1	£150

Beneficiaries included: Berkshire Community Foundation (£15,000); Jubilee Sailing Trust, RNLI and RYS Foundation (£10,000 each); The Bradfield Foundation and The Watermill Theatre (£2,500 each); Innovation for Agriculture (£2,000); Yattendon Parochial Church Council (£500); NCCC (£150).

Exclusions

Grants are not made to individuals and rarely to non-registered charities.

Applications

Applications can be made in writing to the correspondent. Only successful applications will be acknowledged. Grants are considered at meetings of the trustees, held throughout the year.

The Innocent Foundation

International development, food security, sustainable agriculture, food poverty, emergency relief

Worldwide

£798,500 (2016/17)

CC number: 1104289

Trustees: Adam Balon; Jon Wright; Richard Reed; Christina Archer; Douglas Lamont; Sarah-Jane Norman.

Correspondent: Kate Franks, Manager, The Innocent Foundation, 342 Ladbroke Grove, London W10 5BU (tel: 020 3235 0352; email: hello@innocentfoundation.org)

www.innocentfoundation.org

The Innocent Foundation was established by the founders of Innocent Drinks in 2004. Innocent is now majority-owned by The Coca-Cola Company but continues to give at least 10% of its profits to charity, the majority of which is received by the foundation. Trustees of the Innocent Foundation include the three founders of the company – Adam Balon, Jon Wright and Richard Reed – and its current Chief Executive, Douglas Lamont.

The foundation works with partner charities around the world 'so that they can help the world's hungry'. The foundation's website states the following about its partners:

> Our partners have the same core principles we do and are working to help communities on a sustainable path to a better life, a life where they won't be hungry any more. We work with some partners supporting one-off short-term projects, but with the majority the partnership commitment is for three years.

Grant programmes

The foundation makes grants to support four different types of project, as outlined on the website:

- **Food security** – grants of up to £30,000 per year for three years are given to help get new sustainable agriculture projects off the ground. Funding can only be given to support work in countries categorised as 'serious', 'alarming' or 'extremely alarming' on the Global Hunger Index
- **Local food poverty** – the foundation makes grants to charities working on projects to combat food poverty in the UK. It has already worked with the Trussell Trust, Make Lunch and the Matthew Tree Project
- **Breakthrough development** – funding is given to support innovative, 'untested' ideas to 'find new models that over time will become the gold standard to address hunger issues'
- **Emergency hunger relief** – the foundation helps to get food to people affected by humanitarian crises, working with Oxfam to support its emergency relief work around the world. Since 2014, the foundation has given £400,000 towards 15 emergencies

Full information about funding from the foundation is available from the website.

Financial information

In 2016/17 the foundation had assets of almost £2.9 million and an income of £1 million, including a donation of £950,000 from Innocent Ltd. There were grants made to 17 project totalling £798,500.

Beneficiaries included: Action Against Hunger (£323,000); Oxfam (£100,000); Ace Africa (£50,000); Find your Feet (£37,000); ADD (£32,500); Make Lunch (£25,000); Jeevika Trust (£12,000).

Exclusions

Organisations which are not UK-registered charities or which do not have UK representation (some staff based in the UK) cannot be supported.

Food security – the foundation will not support the following: individuals; religious or political causes; general appeals or circulars; events or conferences; seed funding is not given for core costs alone (but these can be included as overheads pro-rated to the project); major capital costs, such as buildings or machinery.

Applications

At the time of writing (June 2018) the foundation was undergoing a strategic review and so was not accepting applications. Check the foundation's website for updates and the latest information.

The KPMG Foundation

Children and young people, young offenders, education and training, employment

England, Scotland and Wales

£1.23 million (2016/17)

CC number: 1086518

Trustees: Robin Cartwright; Peter Sherratt; Christine Gilbert; David Woodward; Fahad Raja; Rachel Hopcroft; Melanie Richards.

Correspondent: Melanie Richards, Trustee, KPMG LLP, 15 Canada Square, Canary Wharf, London E14 5GL (tel: 020 7311 4733; email: kpmgfoundation@kpmg.co.uk)

https://home.kpmg.com/uk/en/home/about/corporate-responsibility/kpmg-foundation.html

@kpmg_foundation

Established in 2001, the KPMG Foundation is the corporate charity of the Audit, Tax and Advisory services company KPMG LLP. The foundation is funded primarily by donations from KPMG LLP, which also covers half of all administrative costs incurred by the foundation.

The foundation's objective is to unlock the potential of children in the UK who, for primarily social reasons, have not achieved their educational potential.

To date, the foundation has helped over 30,000 children improve their literacy, and has awarded £10.8 million to 68 charitable projects.

On its website, former trustee and KPMG UK Chair Simon Collins states that the foundation has a particular focus, 'on early intervention and education significantly helps to unlock the potential of individuals and communities. As trustees, one of our key objectives is to improve the outcomes of children in care and children in deprived families.'

The trustees are particularly interested in funding projects which:

- Focus primarily on improving access to education, training and employment
- Demonstrate that early intervention can prevent problems further downstream
- Build on a thorough understanding of the core issues facing the most disadvantaged children and how their lives could be transformed
- Utilise the Foundation's convening and collaboration power by bringing others together around an issue (funders, policy makers, academics etc.)
- Demonstrate potential to evidence success over the long-term through rigorous evaluation and quantitative metrics
- Enhance the work of the Foundation through leveraging the power of KPMG and the skills of its staff
- Focus on outcomes as opposed to focusing on what is being done
- Have the potential to be scalable; and
- Will leverage other funds and be sustainable

The foundation's impact report is available on its website and gives an extensive list of projects supported in the past as well as currently assisted initiatives.

Financial information

In 2016/17 the foundation had assets of £6.3 million and an income of £851,500. There were 13 grants made totalling £1.23 million. Grants were distributed as follows:

Children and young people in deprived families	9	£1.1 million
Children and young people on edge of care, in care or leaving care	3	£89,000
Young offenders and those at risk of offending	1	£37,000

Beneficiaries included: Barnardo's (£569,000); Future First (£150,000); Working Chance (£101,000 in two grants); Family Rights Group (£50,000); Enabling Enterprise (£40,000); Education Endowment Foundation (£21,500).

Applications

According to the website, the director and advisers to the foundation 'pro-actively seeks projects to support and does not accept any unsolicited applications'. The trustees can also make referrals to the director of the foundation should they identify a programme or charity that fits with the foundation's objectives.

The Lancashire Foundation

General charitable purposes with a particular focus on young people and people who are severely disadvantaged

UK; worldwide

£1.06 million (2017)

CC number: 1149184

Trustees: Michael Connor; Derek Williams; Louise Wells.

Correspondent: Michael Connor, Trustee, Lancashire Insurance Company (UK), Level 29, 20 Fenchurch Street, London EC3M 3BY (tel: 020 7264 4056)

www.lancashiregroup.com/en/responsibility/lancashire-foundation.html

This foundation is the corporate charity of the Lancashire group of insurance companies which operates in Bermuda and London. It receives its income through an annual donation from the group.

The Lancashire Foundation forms a core part of the group's corporate social responsibility commitments and uses its resources to support local and international communities, with a particular focus on assisting young people and people who are severely disadvantaged.

Areas of support

The Lancashire Holdings Ltd website states:

> The work of the Lancashire Foundation is a crucial component of our corporate social responsibility activity. The Foundation is committed to channelling its resources in an effective way to meet the needs of our local communities and also international communities, and is particularly focused on helping young people and those severely disadvantaged in society. The Foundation recognises the financial pressure that charities face and therefore its donations are generally not tied or restricted to particular programmes or activities. We believe that the benefitting charities themselves are best placed to direct funds in the most efficient and effective way to ensure their sustainability and to meet their beneficiaries' needs. We seek to enter into multi-year arrangements with the charities we support to assist in their sustainability.

The foundation's page on the group's website explains that 'in very exceptional circumstances' additional emergency funding can be provided and that 'in certain circumstances' charities suggested by others in its market place can be supported.

Financial information

In 2017 the foundation had assets of £2.58 million and an income of £604,500. Grants to 47 organisations totalled £1.06 million.

Beneficiaries included: Médecins Sans Frontières (£260,000); St Giles Trust (£104,500); The Family Centre (£87,500); Vauxhall City Farm (£43,000); Impetus Private Equity Foundation (£20,000).

Applications

The foundation principally channels its funding through key partner charities and those nominated by staff of the Lancashire group. Its page on the Lancashire group's website explains that:

> Prospective charitable organisations are asked to provide a grant application form to the staff Donations Committee, which considers their funding proposals and, if agreed, provides a recommendation to the Trustees of the Foundation for their approval to release funds accordingly. Donations Committee members and other members of staff act as advocates for the charitable organisations that the Foundation supports throughout the year.

LCFC Foxes Foundation Ltd

General charitable purposes with a focus on health, young people, and the armed forces

East Midlands

£187,000 (2016/17)

CC number: 1144791

Trustee: Simon Capper, Susan Whelan, Tony Lander, Alan Birchenall.

Correspondent: Simon Capper, Trustee, King Power Stadium, Filbert Way, Leicester LE7 2FL (tel: 0116 229 4737; email: lcfcfoxesfoundation@lcfc.co.uk)

www.lcfc.com/fans-community/foxes-foundation

The LCFC Foxes Foundation raises funds and awards grants to charities in the East Midlands. Over the past few years, there has been a strong focus on providing defibrillators and other life-saving equipment to be placed throughout Leicestershire to maximise accessibility. According to its website, the foundation also has a preference for charities which support children and young people, local hospitals and human services and former members of the British armed forces to name a few. Since its formation, the foundation has raised over £1.5 million for good causes.

Financial information

In 2016/17 the foundation has assets of £111,500 and an income of £171,500. During the year, the foundation awarded grants totalling £187,000 to five organisations.

Beneficiaries included: The Royal Voluntary Service, Once We Were Soldiers, Warning Zone and Leicester Hospitals Charity (£37,500 each).

Applications

Application forms can be downloaded from the website and should be submitted by post.

Leeds Building Society Charitable Foundation

General charitable purposes, community projects focusing on social welfare and relief in need, vulnerable people and disadvantaged individuals

Areas where the society's branches are located

£133,500 (2017)

CC number: 1074429

Trustees: Peter Chadwick; Ann Shelton; Robert Wade; Gary Brook; Martin Richardson; Michael Garnett; Gary Hetherington.

Correspondent: Luke Wellock, CSR Manager, Leeds Building Society, 105 Albion Street, Leeds, West Yorkshire LS1 5AS (tel: 0113 225 7518; email: lwellock@leedsbuildingsociety.co.uk)

www.leedsbuildingsociety.co.uk/your-society/about-us/charitable-foundation

The foundation was established by and is closely associated with Leeds Building Society. It supports the communities around the nationwide branches of the society.

According to the foundation's website:

> Generally, we will consider applications for community based projects which aim to provide relief of suffering, hardship or poverty, or their direct consequences.
>
> Some examples of the areas in which we have made donations include:
>
> - Homeless people
> - Adults and children with physical and mental disabilities
> - Older people
> - Underprivileged families
> - Deaf, blind and partially sighted people
> - Community projects benefiting local residents
> - Victims of natural and civil disasters in the UK
> - Scout, Guide & Play groups

Financial information

In 2017 the foundation had assets of £2,100 and an income of £119,500, £118,500 of which came from Leeds Building Society. During the year, 136 grants were made totalling £133,500.

Beneficiaries included: Barnardo's (£6,000) and Skelton Grange (£3,600).

Exclusions

The foundation is unlikely to make donations for:

- The restoration or upgrading of buildings, including churches;
- Environmental charities (unless there is a benefit to a disadvantaged community); and
- Administration equipment such as IT equipment for a charity's own use

The foundation is unable to support:

- Projects with religious, political or military purposes;
- Overseas charities or projects;
- Individuals, including sponsorship of individuals;
- Animal welfare projects; and
- Medical research

Church projects will be considered only where they involve community outreach and benefit (e.g. supporting the homeless, disadvantaged families).

Applications

Apply online through the foundation's website.

All applications will be acknowledged. The trustees meet quarterly in March, June, September and November. Following the meeting the foundation will write to you and let you know whether or not your application has been successful.

If you need more information or advice contact the secretary of the charitable foundation on 0113 225 7518 or foundation@leedsbuildingsociety.co.uk. The foundation operates independently of the Building Society and, as such, local branch staff are unable to answer questions about the foundation.

LHR Airport Communities Trust

Community development, young people, education, skills and employment, environmental protection

The areas surrounding Heathrow Airport (Ealing, Hillingdon, Hounslow, Richmond, Runnymede, Spelthorne, Slough, South Bucks, Royal Borough of Windsor and Maidenhead)

£792,000 (2017)

CC number: 1058617

Trustees: Alison Moore; Jason Holmes; Ian Nichol; Dr Prabhjot Basra; Michael Murphy; Andrew Kerswill; Richard de Belder; Carol Hui; Chris Johnston; Darius Nasimi; Gennie Dearman; Samina Hussain.

Correspondent: Dr Rebecca Bowden, Trust Director, c/o Groundwork South, Colne Valley Park Centre, Denham Court Drive, Uxbridge, Middlesex UB9 5PG (tel: 01895 839662; email: community_fund@heathrow.com)

www.heathrowcommunityfund.com

facebook.com/heathrowcommunityfund

@heathrowairport

The fund is an independent charity which receives funding from Heathrow Airport Ltd, airline noise fines, other funders and airport staff. Its grant programmes look to improve the quality of life for communities near the airport.

Grants programmes

In support of its objectives, the Heathrow Community Fund (HCF) makes grants through five programmes.

Organisations can apply for grants through three programmes. These are:

- **Communities for Youth**: 'invites grant applications from organisations working on projects linked to education and economic regeneration schemes that give young people new skills and help them into employment'. Young people are generally defined as being those between the ages of 13 and 25. Grants range from £2,500 to £25,000 and are given for projects costing no more than £100,000 in total. Projects under this programme must take place in one of the following boroughs: Ealing, Hillingdon, Hounslow, Spelthorne or Slough
- **Communities for Tomorrow**: 'invites grant applications from organisations working on environmental or sustainability projects and schemes that involve recycling, tackling climate change or improving the local environment'. Grants range from £2,500 to £25,000 and are given for projects costing no more than £100,000 in total. Projects under this programme must take place in one of the following boroughs: Ealing, Hillingdon, Hounslow, Richmond, Runnymede, Slough, South Bucks, Spelthorne or Windsor and Maidenhead
- **Communities Together**: 'invites grant applications from organisations looking for small amounts of funding to support projects that draw communities closer together – funding can support all sorts of community activities from gardening to sports or the arts'. Grants are awarded up to £2,500. Projects under this programme must take place in one of the following boroughs: Ealing, Hillingdon, Hounslow, Richmond, Runnymede, Slough, Spelthorne, South Bucks, or Windsor and Maidenhead

More information on these programmes, including full eligibility criteria and guidelines, is available from the fund's website.

There are also two funds to which employees can apply for support with their own charitable involvement:

- **Heathrow Active People Initiative (HAPI)**: 'Employees of Heathrow Airport Ltd are encouraged to actively volunteer for charities and community groups working in their local communities, the Trust supports this with a grant programme awarding up to £2,500 to charities for projects involving Heathrow staff volunteering'
- **Matched Funding**: 'Employees of Heathrow Airport Ltd are also supported in their fundraising for charity by a Matched Fund scheme in which the Trust will match funds raised'

Financial information

In 2017 the trust had assets of £921,500 and an income of £1.2 million (of which £725,000 was received from Heathrow Airport Holdings Ltd). Grants totalled £792,000 and were distributed as follows:

Communities for Youth	£273,000
Sponsored events	£181,500
Communities for Tomorrow	£86,500
Development fund	£83,000
Heathrow Active People Initiative (HAPi)	£73,000
Communities Together	£71,500
Staff matched funding	£14,000
Business Service Centre Activities	£9,000

Previous beneficiaries have included: Surrey Care Trust (£21,000); Catalyst (£17,700); Spark! (£10,000); Venture Trust (£7,000); Trees for Cities (£2,500); Friends of Inwood Park (£2,000); Growing Better Lives CIC (£1,000); Northfields Guide Centre (£500).

Exclusions

Refer to the fund's website. Each of the grants programmes are subject to their own eligibility criteria and restrictions.

Applications

Application forms and guidance notes for each of the grants programmes are available from the HCF website, where important dates for application submissions and decision-making are also listed. There are two application rounds: Round 1 involves the submission of an expression of interest form and Round 2, a full application.

The fund's grants programmes are managed by the charity Groundwork South – the website explains that: 'Trustees and panel members live and work locally and are supported by the Trust Director and a team at Groundwork, who draw on their local knowledge and experience to help you submit a strong bid showing the full value of your work'. Decisions are made by the trustees and the Review Panel according to the priorities and criteria set for the funding programmes.

Lloyd's Charities Trust

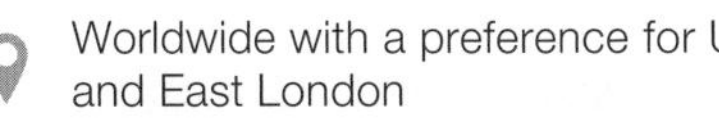

Disasters and emergencies, social welfare

Worldwide with a preference for UK and East London

£687,000 to organisations (2017)

CC number: 207232

Trustees: Graham Clarke; Chris Harman; Neil Smith; Victoria Carter; David Ibeson; Simon Beale; Karen Green; Andrew Brooks.

Correspondent: Michaele Hawkins, Global Corporate Social Responsibility Manager, Lloyd's Building, 1 Lime Street, London EC3M 7HA (email: communityaffairs@lloyds.com)

 www.lloyds.com/lct

The trust was set up in 1953, and is the charitable arm of Lloyd's insurance market in London. The trust makes grants on behalf of the Society of Lloyd's through three main programmes:

General fund

The trust has a policy of working with a small number of selected charities over a three-year period. Current partner charities will be supported until 2019. The following information on the fund's priorities has been taken from its website:

> Insurance plays a valuable role in creating a more confident and secure world and we believe that our charitable funding should extend this role in relevant ways.
>
> Mindful of Lloyd's position as the world's leading specialist insurance market, and given its role in covering global risks including natural disasters, Lloyd's Charities Trust aims to help the global communities most at risk from disasters and emergencies in the following ways:
>
> - We give to charities responding to disasters and emergencies, to help relieve suffering and rebuild lives
> - In areas prone to natural disasters, we fund disaster risk reduction initiatives aiming to build resilience into these communities
>
> Mindful of Lloyd's position as one of the UK's leading financial institutions and a major employer and contributor to the economy, Lloyd's Charities Trust focuses some of its giving:
>
> - To spread the economic and social benefits of the Lloyd's market by supporting projects that tackle disadvantage and foster opportunity
> - To support the individual and collective charitable efforts of those working in the Lloyd's market and the City of London
>
> Around the world our offices also support their local communities through the Lloyd's Together programme.

Smaller donations are available through the **Lloyd's Charity Awards.** The trust's website states:

> Donations of £2,000 are given to charities supported by individuals working in the market in recognition of their fundraising and voluntary work. Awards are also made to charities that have given invaluable support to those in the market whose lives have been affected by difficult circumstances.
>
> Since the initiative was launched in 2007, over £650,000 has been donated to 300 charities.
>
> To apply, you must be a permanent employee working in the Lloyd's market (employed by managing or members' agents, brokers, cover-holders, the Corporation, LMA or LIIBA) on the date the application is made and when the award is announced.

Education fund

The education fund is used to benefit young people in London communities. The fund currently supports students from low-income backgrounds from Cambridge Heath Sixth Form Partnership schools in Tower Hamlets, to study at universities outside London.

Lloyd's Community Programme

Lloyd's Community Programme (LCP) is a sub-fund of the Trust. Lloyd's Community Programme encourages volunteering and acts as a catalyst for the Lloyd's market to empower people in our neighbouring London communities to achieve their potential.

Financial information

In 2017 the trust had assets of £3 million and an income of £647,000, of which £500,000 was a donation by the corporation of Lloyd's. Grants awarded to organisations totalled £687,000 and an additional £65,000 was given in bursaries to individuals. Grants to organisations were broken down in the annual report as follows:

Lloyd's community programmes	£349,500
RedR	£150,000
Build Change	£64,000
Lloyd's Market Charity Awards	£62,000
Whizz-Kidz	£50,000
British Red Cross	£15,000
Other donations	£15,000
LCF Grenfell	£10,000

Applications

Lloyd's Charities Trust makes ad hoc donations and the majority of funds are committed to supporting the partner charities the trust works with. Current partner charities are being supported until October 2019.

Check the trust's website for further information on Lloyd's Charity Awards or contact Sarah Chamberlain at sarah.chamberlain@lloyds.com.

Lloyds Bank Foundation for England and Wales

Dependency, asylum seekers and refugees, care leavers, domestic and sexual abuse, homeless and vulnerably housed, learning disabilities, mental health, offending, prison or community service, sexual abuse and exploitation, trafficking and modern slavery, young parents

England and Wales

£20.1 million (2017)

CC number: 327114

Trustees: Paul Farmer; Dr Neil Wooding; James Garvey; Hilary Armstrong; Prof. Patricia Broadfoot; Helen Edwards; Rennie Fritchie; Catharine Cheetham; Joanna Harris; Lesely King-Lewis; Dame Gillian Morgan; Sara Weller.

Correspondent: Paul Streets, Chief Executive, Pentagon House, 52–54 Southwark Street, London SE1 1UN (tel: 0370 411 1223; email: enquiries@lloydsbankfoundation.org.uk)

 www.lloydsbankfoundation.org.uk

 facebook.com/lloydsbankfoundation

 @LBFEW

The foundation receives the majority of its income from Lloyds Bank plc. There is an agreement with Lloyds Bank that until 2020 the foundation will receive 0.3616% of the group's adjusted pre-tax profits/loss, averaged over three years.

Areas of work

According to its website, the foundation funds charities working on one of the following 11 complex social issues:

- Dependency
- Asylum seekers and refugees
- Care leavers
- Domestic and sexual abuse
- Homeless and vulnerably housed
- Learning disabilities
- Mental health
- Offending, prison or community service
- Sexual abuse and exploitation
- Trafficking and modern slavery
- Young parents

Grant programmes

The grant programmes re-opened in August 2018 with some slight changes to their criteria. A summary of the changes can be found at on the website.

The foundation runs two main funding programmes, 'one for core costs and one for developing your charity'. Details of the programmes have been taken from the foundation's website.

Invest

Our Invest grants provide long-term funding for the day-to-day running of your charity (core costs), and/or the direct delivery of your charity's work.

We can provide a minimum of £30,000 to a maximum of £100,000, delivered across three years. There is also the opportunity for continuation funding, so your charity could be funded by our Invest grant for up to six years in total.

You can apply for either a core costs grant or a project costs grant.

If you are applying for a core costs grant then you will be able to use the funding to cover any of your charity's core or delivery costs. Please be aware that if you are applying for core cost funding, we'll ask you to demonstrate that the majority of your charity's work (more than 50% of your work and expenditure) meets our eligibility criteria.

If you are applying for project costs you will be able to apply for the direct delivery costs of the project. You will only be able to apply for the core costs associated directly with delivering the project.

Enable

Enable grants are awarded to charities which have identified clear development needs, and provide a great opportunity to strengthen charities to deliver more effectively.

Through Enable grants we fund opportunities for your charity to develop, or trial new approaches to service delivery, so you can become more effective in your work. You may want to improve your charity's capability in areas such as business development and planning, monitoring, leadership and governance and communications; an Enable grant could put your charity in a stronger position to deliver services and attract more volunteers, funding and support.

We can provide up to a total of £15,000 across one or two years.

What Enable Grants Fund

- Enable grants fund activities related to the development and improvement of your charity's capability. Examples include:
- Pilot initiatives, to trial new ways of delivering your programmes
- Strengthening your monitoring systems
- Creating stronger business plans and service development plans
- Improving your charity's marketing and communications
- Investigating mergers, partnerships, shared services and contracts
- Developing new streams of income and enterprise for your charity
- Expanding your charity's capacity to reach new audiences and recruit volunteers
- Improving your structures and systems, for example in finance, HR, risk management and volunteer management
- Quality standards (please note that if you already hold a quality mark, you cannot apply for renewal costs under the Enable programme)

Enable grants are awarded to charities that meet our eligibility criteria and have identified clear development areas which will support their growth. The costs covered by Enable grants must be additional to those you would already incur through your charity's regular activities; they are not awarded for core costs or direct delivery costs. If this is what you are looking for, please consider applying to our Invest programme instead.

Basic criteria

The foundation's Funding Application Eligibility Criteria document gives the following three basic application criteria:

- You must be a Charity or Charitable Incorporated Organisation (CIO) registered with the Charity Commission
- Your charity must have an income of between £25,000 and £1 million
- Your charity must work with people aged 17 or over, who are facing one of the complex social issues listed. The only exception is supporting young parents or looked after children and young people with learning disabilities who are moving into independent living

Financial information

In 2017 the foundation held assets of over £50 million and had an income of £52.1 million, of which the Lloyd's Banking Group donated £51.5 million. During the year, the foundation gave around £20.1 million in grants to organisations.

According to the foundation's 2017 accounts, grants were approved in the following categories:

Invest and Enable	£12.95 million
Matched giving	£3 million
National Homeshare programmes	£2.5 million
Enhance	£1.5 million

New Invest and Enable grants in 2017

Invest	184	£12.4 million
Enable	125	£1.75 million

Exclusions

According to the foundation's website, the following cannot be funded:

- Community Interest Companies
- Infrastructure or 'umbrella' organisations. We would consider requests from these organisations only for any direct delivery of support to disadvantaged people
- Organisations whose primary purpose is to give funds to individuals or other organisations. This means organisations using more than 50% or annual expenditure as grants
- Hospitals, health authorities or hospices
- Rescue services
- Nurseries, pre-schools or playgroups
- Schools, colleges or universities
- Animal charities

- Charities working outside England and Wales

Applications

Applications can be made via the foundation's website from where, the following information was taken:

> **Decide which grant to apply for**
> We offer two grant programmes, one for core costs and one for developing your charity. You can apply for either programme, but not both.
>
> Our Invest grants provide long-term funding for the day-to-day running of your charity (core costs), and/or the direct delivery of your charity's work. Invest is open for applications twice a year, please check the funding timetable to find out when we are open for new applications.
>
> Enable grants are awarded to charities which have identified clear development needs, and provide a great opportunity to strengthen charities to deliver more effectively.
>
> Before you apply, take a look at our Funding Timetable to check if the programme is accepting applications.
>
> If you are not sure which programme to apply for, get in touch with us to talk about which one is right for you.
>
> **Check your eligibility**
> Before you apply, please read our detailed eligibility criteria to make sure you are the right fit for our grants programmes. You will also need to ensure you can meet our reporting requirements.
>
> **Prepare your application**
> If you meet all our eligibility criteria, congratulations! You can now apply for a grant.
>
> Check below which programme is right for you and follow the guidelines to create the best possible application.
>
> **Submit your application**
> Once you are familiar with the guidelines and have drafted your application, fill in the Application Form. You will be able to save and return to your saved application if you need to.
>
> **What Happens Next?**
> If you are applying for our Enable grants, you can expect to hear if you are successful within four months of submitting your application.
>
> If you are applying for our Invest grants, you can expect to hear if your Stage One application has been successful within three months. Successful Stage One applicants will then be invited to submit a more detailed Stage Two application. Once your Stage Two application has been received, you can expect to hear back within three months.
>
> We are happy to offer feedback if your application is unsuccessful.

Lloyds Bank Foundation for the Channel Islands

General charitable purposes

Channel Islands

£676,000 (2017)

CC number: 327113

Trustees: Sarah Bamford; Michael Starkey; Timothy Cooke; Katheryn Le Quesne; David Hodgetts; Alison Le Feuvre; John Henwood; Gavin Ferguson; Heather MacCallum.

Correspondent: Johanna Le Poidevin, Executive Director, Sarnia House, Le Truchot, St Peter Port, Guernsey GY1 4EF (tel: 01481 706360; email: jlepoidevin@lloydsbankfoundation.org.uk)

www.lloydsbankfoundationci.org.uk

@lloydsbfci

The foundation was set up by Lloyds Bank in 1986. The foundation derives its income almost entirely from Lloyds Banking Group, but is an independent entity with policies determined by a board of trustees, which meets three times each year, agrees on strategic priorities and distributes funding. According to the foundation's website, grants are made 'to support charitable organisations which help people, especially those who are disadvantaged or disabled, to play a fuller role in communities throughout the Channel Islands'.

The foundation also operates a Matched Giving Scheme – a scheme open to members of staff of Lloyds Banking Group plc based in the Channel Islands, to match fundraising efforts.

Areas of work

According to its grant-giving guidelines, the foundation likes to fund:

> **People with health issues or a disability** – We support charities which create opportunities for people with health issues or a disability to live and work independently.
>
> **People experiencing homelessness –** We help charities which provide accommodation and support for people who are homeless, and support their return into society.
>
> **People with dependency on alcohol or drugs** – We support charities providing education and rehabilitation for people who misuse alcohol and drugs.
>
> **Carers** - We help charities providing support, training, and respite care.
>
> **Challenging disadvantage and discrimination** - We help charities who challenge discrimination and stigma, and promote equality of opportunity for all.
>
> **People with literacy problems** - We support learning programmes for people disadvantaged by poor education and literacy.
>
> **People affected by domestic violence** - We support charities who help prevent and protect people from abusive relationships.
>
> **People leaving institutional care to live independently** - We help charities providing support and accommodation for people who are getting back into society, maybe after leaving care or prison.

Financial information

In 2017 the foundation had assets of £2.3 million and an income of £2.2 million, of which £1.6 million was donated by Lloyds Banking Group. During the year, the foundation awarded £676,000 in grants, supporting 23 organisations. The foundation also paid out £37,000 through their Matched Giving Scheme.

Grants were distributed as follows:

Community support	7	£217,500
Health including mental health	6	£180,500
Support for children and young people	3	£88,500
Relationships including caring	2	£52,000
Victim support	2	£48,500
Support for people with disabilities	1	£48,000
Training, employment and lifelong learning	1	£25,500
Offenders/ex-offenders	1	£15,500

Beneficiaries included: Youth Commission for Guernsey and Alderney (£66,000); Caritas Jersey Ltd (£55,000); Drug Concern (£54,500); The Healing Music Trust (£33,000); Prisoner's Education Trust (£15,500); The Jersey Scout Association (£7,000).

Exclusions

According to the application guidelines, the following fall outside the funding criteria:

- Organisations which are not registered charities
- Individual requests
- Sponsorship request
- International appeals
- Animal welfare
- Environmental charities
- Expeditions or overseas travel
- The promotion of religion
  We might not exclude charities which have a religious element, if their objectives demonstrate a wider benefit to people experiencing disadvantage
- Schools and colleges (except for projects that will benefit disadvantaged students and are clearly additional to statutory responsibilities)
- Activities which are the responsibility of a statutory body or the islands' governments
- Activities which duplicates or overlaps a service already provided
- Applications for salaries which would apply to the applicant

- Charities which have received one of our grants in the previous 12 months, or have received three years continuous funding

Applications

Application forms, along with guidelines, are available to download from the website. Forms should be submitted together with:

- A copy of a recent bank statement
- An income tax letter of exemption
- Your organisation's latest audited accounts
- If you are applying for funding for a post(s), the job description
- If you are applying for funding over multiple years, a business plan

Applications can be returned to the foundation at any time and must be submitted by post. The foundation does not accept forms that have been emailed or faxed.

Applications are assessed on a continual basis. The trustees meet three times a year to approve grants. Deadline dates for these meetings may vary but generally fall in mid-February, mid-June and mid-October. The process of making a decision can, therefore, take up to four months. All applicants are informed of the outcome of their application.

Applicants are encouraged to discuss their project with the Executive Director before completing an application form. This will help to ensure that your project is within the criteria and that you are applying for an appropriate amount.

Man Group plc Charitable Trust

Literacy and numeracy

UK

£412,000 (2017)

CC number: 275386

Trustees: Keith Haydon; Carol Ward; Teun Johnston; Lydia Bosworth; Antoine Forterre; Steven Desmyter.

Correspondent: Bayo Adeyeye, Man Group plc, Riverbank House, 2 Swan Lane, London EC4R 3AD (email: charitable.trust@man.com)

www.man.com/responsibility

This trust, which was registered in 1978, is the corporate charity of the investment management firm Man Group plc. The trust is the vehicle for most of the company's charitable donations and operates as an independent charity.

The trust has two main aims: firstly, it looks to support organisations working to raise literacy and numeracy levels in the UK and, secondly, it looks to facilitate opportunities for Man Group employees to share their time and expertise for charitable causes. It works to achieve these aims by carrying out the following activities, which are outlined on the trust's webpage:

- Providing grants via a two stage application process, or through negotiated partnerships with selected charities
- Tracking success by measuring impact, carefully monitoring all grants to ensure progress against agreed objectives
- Providing volunteering opportunities to Man Group UK employees via the Trust's community volunteering programme, ManKind
- Supporting Man Group UK employees' fundraising activity and charitable donations via the Trust's Sponsorship Matching and Give As You Earn schemes

Funding criteria

The trust supports small to medium-sized charities registered in the UK whose work is focused on the promotion of literacy and/or numeracy. There is a document available to download from the website which sets out full criteria and guidelines for applying for support. It states that, in order to be eligible, a charity must:

- Have an annual income greater than £1 million and less than £10 million
- Raise levels of literacy and/or numeracy with evidence of an increase in attainment in one or both of these areas
- Have a significant impact; changing wider policy and practice or having the potential to be mainstreamed or replicated
- Have clear and measurable outcomes and benefits and use evidence of results to improve performance
- Lead to leverage of additional funding wherever possible

The document further explains that applicants must be able to show that their organisation is 'well run, with good governance and financial management' and that they 'have an ambitious approach to tackling social issues'. The trustees prefer to support activities that provide assistance directly to individuals, families and communities and also those that increase the capacity of organisations and individuals.

Grant-making

The Man Group website explains that the trust is 'currently funding one year grants of up to £50,000, but will consider longer-term support for applications that are deemed by trustees to have particular merit'. Grants are typically given to fund core costs (including salaries and overheads) and project costs.

Financial information

In 2017 the trust had assets of £1.1 million and an income of £81,000, of which £50,000 came from the Man Group plc. Donations were made to organisations totalling £412,000.

Beneficiaries included: Discover Children's Story; Mayor's Fund for London; National Literacy Trust; Vision for Literacy Business Pledge.

Exclusions

The trust's grant guidelines state that the trust does not support:

- Large national charities
- Charities which use external fundraising agencies
- Charities primarily devoted to promoting religious beliefs
- Endowment funds
- Requests to directly replace statutory funding
- Individual beneficiaries
- General media campaigns or campaigning or advocacy work to influence policy debates
- Applicants which have been successful during the last twelve months
- Work which has already been completed
- Capital projects and appeals
- Sponsorship or funding towards marketing appeals or fundraising events
- Organisations or projects whose primary purpose is political

Furthermore, the trust will not consider charities with 'high administration costs relative to the services provided'.

Applications

In the first instance, see the trust's page on the Man Group website, detailing eligibility criteria and guidelines on how to apply.

The trust has a two-stage application process. After reading the trust's eligibility criteria and exclusions, a brief expression of interest (not exceeding one side of A4) should be sent by email, including the following: a brief summary of your organisation's aims and activities and, if relevant, the project for which the funding is intended (including the work you hope to carry out, what the need for this work is, who the beneficiaries are, when the project will be undertaken and where it will be based); details of how your organisation meets the trust's focus; the amount of funding being requested; how funds will be used if the application is successful; and contact details.

If your expression of interest is successful, you will be invited to submit a stage 2 application form for consideration by the trustees, who usually meet twice a year. Successful applicants will be notified by telephone or email. All unsuccessful applicants will be notified and will usually receive an outline explanation for the rejection.

The guidelines also note that 'meeting all of the criteria does not guarantee you will be invited to complete a full application form or that if you are invited to do so, you will receive funding'.

Manchester Airport Community Trust Fund

Environment, social welfare, community development

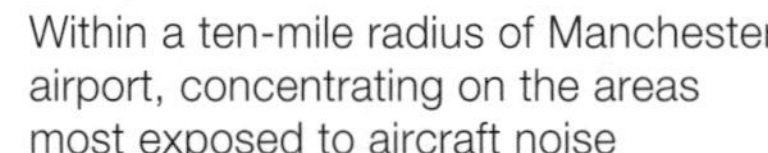
Within a ten-mile radius of Manchester airport, concentrating on the areas most exposed to aircraft noise

£97,000 (2016/17)

CC number: 1071703

Trustees: Cllr Paul Andrews; Cllr Don Stockton; Michael Whetton; Wendy Sinfield; John Twigg; Cllr Bill Fairfoull; Cllr Bob Rudd; Cllr John Taylor.

Correspondent: Diane Stredder, Administrator, Manchester Airport plc, Olympic House, Manchester Airport, Manchester M90 1QX (tel: 0161 489 5281; email: trust.fund@manairport.co.uk)

www.manchesterairport.co.uk/community/working-in-our-community/community-trust-fund

Registered with the Charity Commission in 1998, the Manchester Airport Community Trust Fund is a corporate charity of Manchester Airports Group plc. The trustees are employees of Manchester Airport, as well as trustees appointed by the Manchester Airport Consultative Committee from the council areas of Stockport, Manchester, Trafford, Tameside, Cheshire East and Cheshire West and Chester. The trust receives £100,000 each year from Manchester Airport Group, as well as the proceeds of fines charged for aircraft which exceed noise limits.

According to the accounts for 2016/17, the fund's aims are as follows:

- Promote, enhance, improve, protect and conserve the natural and built environment by projects of tree planting, afforestation and landscaping and other works of environmental improvement and heritage conservation
- Enable within those areas facilities in the interests of social welfare for recreation, sport and leisure time occupation with the object of improving the conditions of life for those living or working in or visitors to those areas
- Promote and provide for the benefit of the public a better appreciation of the natural and urban environment and ways of better serving, protecting and improving the same and education and training in all matters relating to the natural, physical environment and its interaction with the economic wellbeing of the community

Grants

According to the website, grants of up to £3,000 are awarded to charitable organisations based within a ten-mile radius of Manchester Airport (a map is provided on the website) and which are 'community, socially or environmentally focused'.

To be eligible for funding, the website states that projects should:

- Improve, enhance, protect and conserve the natural and built environment; or offer heritage conservation; or promote or advance social welfare; or provide better appreciation of the natural and urban environment; or create a safe habitat for flora and fauna
- Demonstrate lasting benefit to the community
- Benefit all members of the community regardless of race, gender or religion
- Be from an established group or charity able to demonstrate clear banking or financial records, and not an individual or commercial organisation working for profit

Projects must be open to the whole community, or a large section of it, and grants are given only for 'anything which is tangible and long lasting', such as equipment.

Financial information

In 2016/17 the trust held assets of £42,000 and had an income of £129,500, of which £100,000 was a monetary donation and £17,300 an in-kind donation from Manchester Airport Group plc for administration costs. During the year, the trust awarded 61 grants totalling £97,000.

Beneficiaries included: Action for Children and Stockport Wheelchair Racing (£3,000 each); BeeEducated (£2,800); Toft Cricket Club (£2,000); East Manchester Community Boat Club (£1,900); Highway Hope (£1,000); Tameside Armed Services (£600); Platt and Woreley Resident's Group (£300).

Exclusions

Grants are not awarded for:

- Maintenance or running costs (including, for example, repair work, energy costs, salaries, coach fees, uniform or kits)
- Purchase of land or buildings
- Projects which have already taken place
- Individuals

Applications

Application forms can be found on the charity's website, along with guidelines. The trustees meet four times a year, in January, April, July and October and applicants should be informed of a decision within seven to ten days of a meeting.

Successful applicants are encouraged to promote their grant through the local media, and in their own newsletters and publications.

The Mansfield Building Society Charitable Trust

General charitable purposes

Nottinghamshire; Derbyshire; Lincolnshire; South Yorkshire

CC number: 1177151

Trustees: Diana Meale; Irvin Robinson; Gev Lynott; Michael Taylor; Tony Sale.

Correspondent: Gev Lynott, Trustee, Mansfield Building Society, Regent Street, Mansfield NG18 1SS (tel: 01623 676300; email: enquiries@mansfieldbs.co.uk)

www.mansfieldbs.co.uk

The trust is the corporate charity of The Mansfield Building Society and is exclusively for the benefit of registered charities in their core operating territory of Nottinghamshire, Derbyshire, Lincolnshire and South Yorkshire. The trustees consider applications from sustainable charitable causes that benefit the local community.

As well as working in the local area, the trust's objective is to create a legacy of giving to support projects with enduring benefit which:

- Support the disadvantaged (e.g. young, older people, people with disabilities or the homeless)
- Promote and encourage sporting activity
- Support education and/or development
- Benefit the environment (e.g. conservation)

During 2015, the society gifted an initial £50,000 to the trust with the intention that further contributions will be added in future years and in 2016, a further donation of £25,000 was made.

In 2017 the society launched a range of Community Saver Accounts linked to the charitable trust. Every year, the society will contribute to the Charitable Trust based on balances held in the Community Saver account range. So, in addition to the interest paid to savers, a donation equivalent to 0.1% of the average total balances invested in all Community Saver accounts will be donated by the society to the charitable trust each year.

In March 2017, the trust made its first award of £10,000 to the Inspire and

Achieve Foundation to help fund the launch of The Prince's Trust Team Programme for unemployed 16- to 25-year-olds in Nottinghamshire.

According to its Charity Commission record, the trust will make grants to organisations in support of general charitable purposes. As the trust is a newly registered charity, there was no financial information available to view.

Exclusions

The trust will not normally sponsor individuals, party political activities, promotion of religious causes, animal charities or commercial enterprises.

Applications

If you currently work or volunteer for a registered charity in Nottinghamshire, Derbyshire or South Yorkshire, the trust asks you to email (community@mansfieldbs.co.uk) in the first instance with details of your charity and the project you'd like support for, and the trust will let you know how to apply.

Mazars Charitable Trust

General charitable purposes

UK and Ireland

£410,000 (2017/18)

CC number: 1150459

Trustees: Alan Edwards; David Evans; Bob Neate; Philip Verity; Kim Hurst.

Correspondent: Bryan Rogers, Trust Administrator, 1 Cranleigh Gardens, South Croydon, Surrey CR2 9LD (tel: 020 8657 3053)

This trust is the corporate charity of the audit and tax firm Mazars LLP and is largely funded by donations from the company. It makes grants to charities with general charitable purposes that have been nominated by Mazars employees in the UK and Ireland. In 2017/18 grants ranged from £100 to £23,500. Most grants are made towards one-off projects covering a defined period.

Financial information

In 2017/18 the trust held assets of £499,000 and had an income of £463,000, nearly all of which was donated by Mazars LLP. Grants awarded to organisations totalled £410,000 to 208 organisations.

Beneficiaries included: Sense (£23,500); Justice and Care (£22,000); YYY Foundation (£19,000); Malaika Kids UK (£16,000); Woofability Assistance Dogs (£14,400); Bournemouth Hospital Charity (£10,400); St Joseph's Hospice (£10,000); Home-Start Royston and South Cambridgeshire (£7,900); Into the Community – Milton Keynes Food Bank (£6,500); Youth Adventure Trust (£2,300); WellChild (£2,000).

Grants of less than £1,750 were made to 177 other charities and totalled £97,000.

Exclusions

National grants are not generally repeated within three years. The trust does not make grants for core costs.

Applications

The trust does not respond to unsolicited applications. All nominations for grants have to be proposed by staff members of Mazars LLP and no grant applications should be submitted directly to the trust.

Medicash Charitable Trust

Health

North West England

£99,500 (2017)

CC number: 257636

Trustee: Medicash Health Benefits Ltd.

Correspondent: The Trustees, Medicash Ltd, 1 Derby Square, Liverpool L2 1AB (tel: 0151 702 0334; email: ltraynor@medicash.org)

 www.medicash.org/charity

The trust is the corporate charity of Medicash Health Benefits and receives a large proportion of its income from the company.

Grants are made to health-related charities in the North West.

Financial information

In 2017 the trust held assets of £559,000 and had an income of £158,500, of which £128,500 was a donation from Medicash Health Benefits. Grants to 29 organisations totalled £99,500.

Beneficiaries included: Over the Wall (£5,000); Fair for You Ltd (£3,000); The Outward Bound Trust (£2,500); Stick 'n' Step (£1,500); FACT; PSP Association and The Yellow House (£1,000 each).

Applications

Application forms can be downloaded from the trust's website.

The Mersey Docks and Harbour Company Charitable Fund

Seafaring and seafarers, social welfare

Merseyside

£32,000 (2017)

CC number: 206913

Trustees: Mark Whitworth; Ian Charnock.

Correspondent: Caroline Gill, The Mersey Docks and Harbour Company Ltd, Maritime Centre, Port of Liverpool, Liverpool L21 1LA (tel: 0151 949 6349)

Registered with the Charity Commission in 1963, The Mersey Docks and Harbour Company Charitable Fund is the corporate charity of the Mersey Docks and Harbour Company Ltd. The majority of the fund's income comes from the company.

The 2017 accounts state that the charity has the following objectives:

- To reward people that help to save the life of the crew of any ship wrecked in the port of Liverpool, preserve the ship or cargo, or try to save people from drowning
- For the relief of people who are sick, disabled and retired in the dock service or the families of those who were killed in service
- To benefit charities in the town or port of Liverpool

Financial information

In 2017 the trust had assets of £4,900 and an income of £35,500. Grants to six organisations totalled £32,000.

Beneficiaries included: Community Foundation for Merseyside (£12,000); Liverpool Seafarer's Centre (£10,500); RNLI (£5,000); National Museums Liverpool (£2,400); North West Air Ambulance and Radio City Cash for Kids (£1,000 each).

Applications

Apply in writing to the correspondent.

Mills and Reeve Charitable Trust

 General charitable purposes with a preference for medical research and social welfare

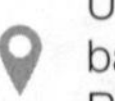 UK, with a preference for charities based near the offices of Mills and Reeve LLP

£96,500 (2016/17)

CC number: 326271

Trustees: Chris Townsend; Greg Gibson; Guy Hinchley; Tom Pickthorn; Dawn Brathwaite; Justin Ripman; Sarah Seed; Alison Bull.

Correspondent: Michelle Wells, Botanic House, 100 Hills Road, Cambridge CB2 1PH (tel: 01223 222273)

 www.mills-reeve.com/charitablegiving

The trust is the corporate charity of Mills and Reeve LLP, which provides a substantial proportion of the charity's income, and each trustee is a member or a former member of the company. The trust's primary objective is to make grants to charitable organisations that support general charitable purposes, but it does express a preference for medical research and charities working with disadvantaged people. The annual report for 2016/17 states that the trust's preference is 'to support good causes which are local to the firm's offices'.

Financial information

In 2016/17 the trust had assets of £229,000 and an income of £89,000, majority of which was donated by Mills and Reeve LLP. During the year, the trust gave almost £96,500 in grants to organisations.

Beneficiaries included: YoungMinds (£13,500); Crisis (£10,000); Dogs for Good (£6,300); IntoUniversity (£5,100); Norfolk Community Foundation (£2,500); St Martin's Housing Trust (£1,500); DEC East Africa Appeal and Shine (£1,000 each).

Exclusions

No grants are given to individuals.

Applications

Apply in writing to the correspondent. According to the annual report for 2015/16, the trust makes smaller grants on an ad hoc basis and favours charities nominated by employees at Mills and Reeve LLP or based near one of their offices.

Morgan Stanley International Foundation

Children's health, education

 Tower Hamlets, Glasgow, and overseas

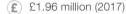

 £1.96 million (2017)

CC number: 1042671

Trustees: Clare Woodman; Hanns Seibold; Maryann McMahon; Stephen Mavin; Fergus O'Sullivan; Sue Watts; Oliver Stuart; Jon Bendall; Simon Evenson; William Chalmers; Mandy DeFilippo.

Correspondent: Anish Shah, Morgan Stanley & Co. International plc, 20 Bank Street, London E14 4AD (tel: 020 7425 1302; email: communityaffairslondon@morganstanley.com)

 www.morganstanley.com/globalcitizen/msif_guidelines.html

 facebook.com/morganstanley

The Morgan Stanley International Foundation (MSIF) was registered with the Charity Commission in 1994 and is the corporate charity of Morgan Stanley and Co. International plc, the financial services corporation. The foundation's trustees are all present employees of the company. The foundation focuses on supporting organisations in the London borough of Tower Hamlets, Glasgow and overseas.

According to the foundation's website, funding is typically given to organisations working in the following areas:

- **Children's Health:** The Foundation looks to invest in innovations and development in children's healthcare. Working with charitable organisations, hospitals and community based initiatives, the MSIF focuses on supporting young people. The MSIF strives to ensure that more children have access to quality healthcare to enable them to have a more meaningful life
- **Education:** The MSIF aims to work with registered charities and state-funded schools which provide benefit to communities across EMEA. The MSIF works with organisations that increase access and opportunity for young people, supporting programmes that address academic achievement and employability skills, by inspiring talented but underserved young people

Funding types

According to its 2017 accounts, the foundation currently gives grants through three different channels: direct charitable grants, employee-nominated charity partnerships and employee matching grants:

- Direct charitable grant applications are invited for the funding of projects in the EMEA region, and are reviewed at the Trustees' meetings against specific grant objectives. Multi-year grants are monitored on an annual basis to ensure the grant criteria continue to be met
- Employee nominated charity partnerships are voted for by Morgan Stanley employees, and the Foundation matches employee fundraising and donations up to a set target
- Employee matching grants focus on creating incentives for Morgan Stanley's employees' fundraising and volunteering efforts in their local communities. The Foundation currently matches fundraising efforts by an employee for a charitable organisation to a maximum of £500 per employee in one given year

Financial information

In 2017 the foundation had assets of almost £2.1 million and an income of almost £1.64 million, of which £1.2 million was a donation from Morgan Stanley and Co. International plc. Grants made during the year totalled nearly £1.96 million, with its employee nominated charity partners, NSPCC and Great Ormond Street Hospital, receiving £901,000 and £52,500. Grants to organisations from the foundation's unrestricted fund totalled £1 million.

Beneficiaries included: The Prince's Trust (£100,000); Marie Curie (£80,000); Bromley by Bow Centre, Glasgow Children's Hospital Charity and London Community Foundation (£25,000 each); Kompania Foundation (£23,500).

Exclusions

According to its website, the foundation does not provide grants for any of the following:

- Organisations which are not registered as a non profit organisation with the appropriate regulatory agencies in their country (unless a state funded school)
- National or International charities which do not operate in the regions we are located
- Grants will not be made to either political or religious organisations, pressure groups or individuals outside the Firm who are seeking sponsorship either for themselves (e.g. to help pay for education) or for onward transmission to a charitable organisation
- Programmes that do not include opportunities for Morgan Stanley employee volunteer engagement

Applications

The foundation's website gives the following details on making an initial approach for funding:

> The Morgan Stanley International Foundation takes a proactive approach to grant making and therefore does not accept unsolicited proposals. If you think your organisation is a match for the criteria set out below, please send an email to communityaffairslondon@morganstanley.com with the following information:
>
> - Program description, including mission, goals and numbers served
> - Measurement strategies
> - Geographic scope
>
> Please note that due to the large number of quality proposals we receive, only applications that have been reviewed and are considered to fit within the MSIF priorities will be contacted directly.

The Morris Charitable Trust

Social welfare, health, education

Islington

£108,500 (2016/17)

CC number: 802290

Trustees: Paul Morris; Jack Morris; Alan Stenning; Dominic Jones; Gerald Morris; Linda Morris.

Correspondent: Jack Morris, Trustee, The Business Design Centre, 52 Upper Street, Islington Green, London N1 0QH (tel: 020 7359 3535; email: info@morrischaritabletrust.com)

www.morrischaritabletrust.com

The Morris Charitable Trust was established in 1989 to provide support for charitable causes. It was founded by the Morris Family, whose principal business – The Business Design Centre Group Ltd – is based in Islington, London. The group contributes a proportion of its annual profits to facilitate the trust's charitable activities.

The following information has been taken from the trust's website:

> The objectives of the Trust are to promote charitable causes, in particular, to relieve the deprived, sick and aged and advance education for the public benefit.
>
> The Trust supports local community projects and other specially selected charities.
>
> Particular emphasis is placed on alleviating social hardship and deprivation and, because of the Morris Family's history and business location, the Trust primarily supports causes within the community of the London Borough of Islington.
>
> The Trust tends to favour capital and 'one-off' projects, although consideration is occasionally given to other innovative charitable projects.

Financial information

In 2016/17 the trust held assets of £200,500 and had an income of £112,500. Grants awarded to organisations totalled £108,500 and were broken down as follows:

£1,001 to £5,000	21	£64,000
£5,001+	1	£35,000
£501 to £1,000	5	£5,000
£0 to £500	11	£4,400

There was no list of beneficiaries included within this year's accounts.

Recent beneficiaries on the trust's website include: Culpeper Community Garden; Drayton Park School; Islington Community Theatre; Islington Outlook; Soul In The City; The Anne Frank Trust; The Parent House.

Exclusions

The following information has been taken from the trust's website:

> We do not generally make donations to applications from individuals. Requests for subsidising the annual, recurring running costs of organisations (e.g. staffing, salaries, or equipment hire) will not be considered either. We do not generally make donations to applicants not registered with The Charity Commission.

Applications

Application forms are available to download from the trust's website. The trustees meet several times a year. Grants are generally not repeated within a 12-month period.

Music Sales Charitable Trust

General charitable purposes, including: health, arts and culture, education and training, religion, overseas and famine relief, disability, children and young people, older people

UK, but mostly Bury St Edmunds and London

£113,000 (2016)

CC number: 1014942

Trustees: Christopher Butler; Ian Morgan; Robert Wise; David Rockberger; Mildred Wise; Mr M. Wise.

Correspondent: Neville Wignall, Clerk to the Trustees, c/o Music Sales Ltd, 14–15 Berners Street, London W1T 3LJ (tel: 020 7612 7400; email: neville.wignall@musicsales.co.uk)

The trust was established in 1992 by the company Music Sales Group Ltd. It supports registered charities benefitting children, older people, people with disabilities and a range of other charitable purposes, particularly organisations benefitting people living in Bury St Edmunds and London.

Grants are given for a variety of general charitable causes, including: medical, health, sickness; arts/culture; education/training; religion; overseas and famine relief; disability.

Financial information

At the time of writing (December 2018) the trust's 2016 accounts were the most recent available. In 2016 the trust held assets of £253,500 and had an income of £115,000, £100,000 of which was donated by Music Sales Ltd. Grants totalled £113,500 and were awarded to 79 organisations in the following areas:

Medical	39	£44,500
Arts/culture	12	£28,000
Overseas and famine relief	6	£17,500
General charitable purposes	9	£8,200
Religion	2	£6,000
Disability	4	£4,900
Education/training	7	£4,100

Beneficiaries included: Bury Bach Society, St Edmundsbury Borough Council, DEC Nepal Earthquake Appeal, East Anglican Children's Hospices, St Nicholas Hospice Care and Westminster Synagogue (£5,000 each).

Exclusions

Grants are not made to individuals.

Applications

Apply in writing to the correspondent. The trustees meet quarterly, usually in March, June, September and December.

The National Express Foundation

General charitable purposes, social welfare, education, sport, children and young people

The former West Midlands county boundary and the Medway, Gravesend and Longfield areas of Kent served by Kings Ferry and Clarke's commuter coach services (postcodes ME1–12, ME14, DA3, DA11 DA12 and DA13)

£95,000 (2017)

CC number: 1148231

Trustees: Anthony Vigor; Ian Fraser; Madi Pilgrim; Ian Austin.

Correspondent: James Donnan, General Manager, National Express Ltd, National Express House, Mill Lane, Digbeth, Birmingham B5 6DD (tel: 0121 460 8423; email: foundation@nationalexpress.com)

www.nationalexpressgroup.com/our-way/national-express-foundation

Established in 2011 following the summer riots in the UK, the charitable foundation is a key part of the National Express Ltd's community support in the UK and is entirely funded by the company. Trustees include directors of the National Express Group. The group's employees play a central role in its community involvement through volunteering, fundraising activities and a payroll giving scheme.

The National Express Foundation's objectives are to promote education, including awarding scholarships, maintenance allowances or grants to those in higher or further education, as well as to provide grants for recreational activities for disaffected and disadvantaged young people, aged 15 to 24, which will in turn develop their skills and harness their potential. Preference is given to areas where the National Express Group operates services – mainly the West Midlands, but also south Essex and East London.

The foundation makes grants to:

- Individual students with challenging personal and financial circumstances to enable them to advance their further and higher education
- Charitable and community groups for projects which support children and young people and promote cross-community cohesion and understanding

The trustees note the following in the application guidance: 'While we do not propose to set restrictions on how the funding would be applied, we will be seeking evidence of innovation in how the projects will be delivered.'

Grants are typically awarded to contribute towards project costs or to help an organisation deliver a particular service. Grants tend to be for £2,500, £5,000, £10,000 or £20,000, although many are for less than £10,000.

Financial information

In 2017 the foundation held assets of £32,500 and had an income of £150,000. During the year the foundation awarded £95,000 to 20 community groups and three educational institutions.

Beneficiaries included: Gospel Oak Community Centre, Let Us Play (£5,000 each); Beacon Evangelical Church, BME United Ltd and Hall Green Youth (£2,500 each).

Applications

Application forms and guidance can be downloaded from the foundation's website, where applicants can find further information on successful projects and deadlines.

The Nationwide Foundation

 Community development, housing, legal assistance, and social welfare

UK

£781,000 (2016/17)

CC number: 1065552

Trustees: Benedict Stimson; Ian Williams; John Taylor; Antonia Bance; Sarah Mitchell; Tony Prestedge; Clara Govier; Sara Bennison.

Correspondent: Jonathan Lewis, Programme Manager, The Nationwide Foundation, Nationwide House, Pipers Way, Swindon SN38 2SN (tel: 01793 655113; email: enquiries@nationwidefoundation.org.uk)

 www.nationwidefoundation.org.uk

Registered with the Charity Commission in 1997, the Nationwide Foundation is principally funded by Nationwide Building Society, which makes annual lump sum donation of 0.25% of its pre-tax profit. Its aims and objectives are to improve the lives of people who are disadvantaged because of housing circumstances by increasing the number of decent affordable homes available to them.

Grants programmes

At the time of writing (July 2018), the foundation operated three separate grant programmes:

Nurturing ideas to Change the Housing System

This programme supports ideas 'for protecting and creating decent, affordable homes and creating changes that lead to an increased number of homes for people in need'.

On its website, the foundation states that it would be willing to fund the researching, testing, developing, or piloting of new ideas as well as the evaluation of existing ideas. They note that ideas should seek to address the root causes of the UK's housing crisis rather than mitigate its effects.

The foundation is willing consider proposals from a wide range of applicants, from academics and think-tanks through to small community groups. Furthermore, projects which are part-funded or delivered in collaboration with other stakeholders in the housing sector, be they other charities, local authorities or funders are strongly encouraged.

The foundation does not set a minimum or maximum grant limit; however, it is unlikely that the foundation would fund a project with less than £5,000.

Backing Community-Led Housing

This programme supports and champions the growth of community-led housing, so that more people who are in need will benefit. At the time of writing (July 2018) the foundation was not accepting applications for this programme but stated on its website that it hoped to reopen the fund in late 2018.

Transforming the Private Rented Sector

This programme helps to 'transform the private rented sector so that it provides homes for people in need that are more affordable, secure, accessible and are better quality'. At the time of writing (July 2018) the foundation was not accepting applications for this programme.

Financial information

In 2016/17 the foundation had assets of £2.77 million and an income of almost £2.64 million of which £2.5 million came from a donation from the Nationwide Building Society. There were nine grants made totalling £781,000 all under the 'Decent Affordable Homes' grant-making strategy.

Beneficiaries included: University of York (£202,000); Wales Cooperative Centre (£130,000); The National Custom and Self Build Association (£110,000); New Economics Foundation and Young Foundation (£83,500 each); DAH Added Value (£4,400).

Exclusions

The foundation will not consider funding for the following:

- Promotion of religion or politics
- Applications which do not comply with the foundation's funding criteria/guidelines

Applications

Proposals should be no more than 500 words and should be sent to applications@nationwidefoundation.org.uk. Your proposal should tell the foundation about the following:

- Your organisation and the work you already do
- The idea you want it to fund and why it will contribute to the foundation's strategy
- The estimated amount of funding you are looking for and proposed timescales

The foundation aims to respond to proposals within ten working days, at which point successful applicants will be invited to submit a full bid for funding.

Nurturing Ideas enquiries should be directed to programme manager, Jonathan Lewis by email: jonathan.lewis@nationwidefoundation.org.uk or phone 01793 652618

There is no deadline for applications.

The NFU Mutual Charitable Trust

Community development, education, social welfare, and research focusing on initiatives that will have a significant impact on rural communities

UK, with a preference for rural areas

£284,500 (2017)

CC number: 1073064

Trustees: Stephen James; Linsday Sinclair; Richard Percy; Meurig Raymond; Stanley Bell; Dr Harriet Kennedy; Andrew McCornick.

Correspondent: James Creechan, Tiddington Road, Stratford-upon-Avon, Warwickshire CV37 7BJ (tel: 01789 204211; email: nfu_mutual_charitable_trust@nfumutual.co.uk)

 www.nfumutual.co.uk/about-us/charitable-trust

The NFU Mutual Charitable Trust is the corporate charity of the National Farmers Union Mutual Insurance Society Ltd (NFU Mutual), one of the UK's leading insurers.

The trust website states:

> The objectives of The NFU Mutual Charitable Trust are to promote, facilitate and support such purposes as are exclusively charitable according to the laws of England and Wales in the areas of agriculture, rural development and insurance in the United Kingdom and in particular:
>
> - Advance the education of the public by means of research and dissemination of information in relation to agriculture
> - Advance the education of young people within rural areas
> - Relieve poverty within rural areas
> - Promote the benefit and social welfare of inhabitants of rural communities by associating together with the inhabitants and local authorities, voluntary and other organisations to advance education and leisure
> - Promote research into agriculture associated activities
> - Advance the education of the public by means of research and dissemination of information in relation to insurance provided that the charity may also promote, facilitate and support any such other purposes as are exclusively charitable according to the laws of England and Wales

Grants range from £1,000 to £50,000. Larger grants are used to support organisations which have a significant impact on rural communities at a national level. The trustees do not normally consider multi-year funding.

Financial information

In 2017 the trust had assets of £305,500 and an income of £323,000. Grants totalled £284,500 were made to 23 charitable organisations.

Beneficiaries included: Farming and Countryside Education (£55,000); The National Federation of Young Farmers Clubs (£30,000); Royal Agricultural Benevolent Institution (£26,000); Rural Support (£20,000); Royal Scottish Agricultural Benevolent Institution (£17,500); The Prince's Countryside Fund and Wales Federation of Young Farmers Clubs (£10,000 each); Open Farm Weekend Northern Islands (£5,000); Farms for City Children (£4,000); Gareth Raw Rees Memorial Scholarship (£1,000).

Applications

Apply in writing to the correspondent either via post or email. The application form is available from the trust's website which states that applications should include the following information:

- The project, initiative or organisation for which funding is sought
- An indication of the amount of the donation requested
- Any business plans
- Details of any other funding sought and or obtained
- Any recognition which would be given to the Trust in recognition of its support
- Confirmation of whether or not the applicant is a registered charity

Following a recent strategic review, the trustees have indicated that in future, the trust will focus on providing funding to larger initiatives, which would have a significant impact on the rural community. The trustees are particularly interested in initiatives in the areas of education of young people in rural areas and relief of poverty within rural areas. The trustees meet twice a year to consider applications received. These meetings are currently held in June and November.

The Nomura Charitable Trust

 Education and training of young people

 London

£280,500 (2016/17)

CC number: 1130592

Trustees: Leila Gomes; Paul Spanswick; Maria Bentley; Charles Pitts-Tucker; Lewis O'Donald.

Correspondent: Naomi Matthams, 1 Angel Lane, London EC4R 3AB (email: communityaffairs@nomura.com)

 www.nomuraholdings.com/csr/society/foundation/nct.html

The trust was established in 2009 and is the corporate charity of Nomura Group headquartered in Asia. The trust is funded by both Nomura and its employees. The trust funds charities provide opportunities for disadvantaged young people.

Areas of work

The trust's website states:

> The Trust's grant giving programme will fund charities which focus on educational achievement, employability potential and aspirations of disadvantaged children and young people – defined as up to 19 year olds living in poverty, deprivation and high risk situations in London.
>
> Our approach is underpinned by three strategic focus areas:
>
> **Educational attainment**
>
> - Raising educational attainment through programmes which address topics such as literacy, numeracy and exclusion/truancy
>
> **Employability potential**
>
> - Enhancing employability potential through programmes which improve hard/soft skills, financial literacy, entrepreneurial thinking and awareness of career opportunities
>
> **Aspirations**
>
> - Raising aspirations through programmes which enhance self-esteem, build social networks and inspire through arts and culture, sports and extra-curricular programmes
>
> **Our Approach**
>
> In considering requests for funding we give preference to projects, programmes and activities that:
>
> - Are located in a community where Nomura has a presence
> - Serve a broad range of community residents and demonstrate impact
> - Provide a significant and measurable impact on quality of life
> - Are managed competently through accountability, cost effectiveness, strong leadership and creativity
> - Work with disadvantaged young people directly and intervene at the individual level
> - Have factored in long-term sustainability; and
> - If appropriate, leverage the talent, skills and action of Nomura employees and resources

Financial information

In 2016/17 the trust held assets of £1.2 million and had an income of £44,000. Grants to seven organisations totalled £280,000 and were distributed as follows:

Raising Aspirations	£192,500
Employability Potential	£54,000
Educational Attainment	£34,000

Beneficiaries included: Into University (£50,000); Greenhouse (£34,000); Chance to Shine (£31,500); Think Forward (£29,000); The Barbican (£25,000); The Brokerage City (£20,000).

Exclusions

The trust's website states that it will not support:

> - Organisations based outside of London and the Middle East region
> - Religious institutions or organisations
> - Organisations that receive donations from, or make payments to, individuals, entities or jurisdictions subject to UK or US sanctions and embargoes. The jurisdictions currently subject to UK and/or US sanctions and embargoes include: Cuba, Belarus, North Korea, Syria, Sudan, Iran, Myanmar and Zimbabwe. The UK sanctions list is administered by HM Treasury (www.hm-treasury.gov.uk) and the US list by the Office of Foreign Assets Control (www.treas.gov/ofac)

- Organisations that discriminate on the basis of race, gender, national origin, sexual orientation or other relevant attributes included in the organisation's non-discrimination policy
- Political parties, campaigns, candidates, or lobbying organisations
- Parent/teacher association fundraisers and alumni associations
- Projects that have not factored in the long term sustainability of the project, including its financing
- Projects that do not have a strong focus on the long-term difference their work will make
- Organisations that have an annual income of less than £50,000 (or equivalent in local currency)
- Organisations that don't have robust accountability, governance and reporting structures/systems

Applications

Applicants are invited to apply by a member of the Nomura Community Affairs team, following a recommendation from an employee. Unsolicited applications are not accepted.

The Norton Rose Fulbright Charitable Foundation

Education, social welfare, medical, disaster relief

Worldwide

£705,000 (2016/17)

CC number: 1102142

Trustees: Simon Cox; Patrick Farrell; Ffion Flockhart.

Correspondent: Patrick Farrell, Trustee, c/o Norton Rose Fullbright, 3 More London Riverside, London SE1 2AQ (tel: 020 7283 6000)

www.nortonrosefulbright.com/corporate-responsibility

The foundation was set up in 2004 and is funded by donations from partners of Norton Rose Fulbright LLP, an international legal practice.

The foundation supports a wide range of general charitable purposes, including education, medical and social welfare. The foundation does this through fundraising, volunteering and grant-making. Many of the charities supported are nominated by the partners and staff of Norton Rose Fullbright. Grants may be made for one-off purchases or for much longer term support.

Financial information

In 2016/17 the foundation held assets of £46,000 and had an income of £502,000, the majority of which was donated by Norton Rose Fulbright. There were 73 grants made totalling £705,000 and distributed for the following purposes:

Social welfare	37	£370,500
Medical	28	£275,500
Educational	8	£59,000

Beneficiaries included: Barretstown (£100,000); London Community Foundation (£62,000); Action for Children (£53,000); MS Society (£39,500); Bhubesi Pride Foundation (£30,000); Project Hope UK (£28,000); Special Olympics (£25,000); Beanstalk (£18,800).

Grants of £15,000 or less totalled £323,500.

Applications

Apply in writing to the correspondent. The 2016/17 annual report states:

> In many cases, the charities we support are those we have supported in the past, but new charities are considered at Trustee meetings. The Trustees also meet on an ad hoc basis to consider specific urgent requests such as the support of major disaster relief appeals.

Oglesby Charitable Trust

General charitable purposes, particularly: arts, education, environment, social welfare, and medical aid and research

North West of England

£3.2 million (2016/17)

CC number: 1026669

Trustees: Jean Oglesby; Michael Oglesby; Katharine Vokes; Jane Oglesby; Chris Oglesby; Kathryn Graham.

Correspondent: Louise Magill, Trust Manager, Lowry House, 17 Marble Street, Manchester M2 3AW (email: welcome@oglesbycharitabletrust.org.uk)

www.oglesbycharitabletrust.co.uk

The Oglesby Charitable Trust was established in 1992 and has been active since the early 2000's. The funding of the trust comes from annual contributions from Bruntwood Ltd, part of a group of North West based property investment companies owned by the founding trustees.

The following information is taken from the trust's website:

> The Trust was set up to support activities in the North West of England to further the well-being of the Region and its people through a very wide range of activities which include the Arts, Education, Environment, Medical Research and tackling Social Inequality. Since its inception the principal activities of the OCT have remained focused in the North of England, although the Trustees have supported a limited number of projects outside both the North West and the UK.
>
> The Trustees take both a grassroots and a strategic approach to their giving, understanding that local approaches tend to reach those most in need, whilst broader initiatives and collaborations are sometimes necessary to drive meaningful change. The Trustees have therefore taken the decision to become focused on root causes, rather than consequences.

Eligibility

According to the website, the trust primarily supports the following

- Registered charities whose activities are based in the north west of England
- Organisations who can demonstrate that the funds are making a real difference, rather than being absorbed into a large anonymous pool, no matter how significant the end result may be
- Organisations that demonstrate both the highest standards of propriety and sound business sense in their activities. This does not mean high overheads but it does mean focused use of funds, directly to where they are needed
- Projects that can be ring-fenced

Areas of work

According to its website, the trust supports the following:

- Artistic development, both on an individual and group level
- Educational – revenue grants, bursaries and building projects
- Environmental projects
- Tackling social inequality, especially projects in which individuals and communities can be enabled to become self-supporting
- Medical aid and research

Financial information

In 2016/17 the trust had assets of £7.9 million and an income of £2.0 million, majority of which was donated by Bruntwood Ltd. Grants were awarded totalling £3.2 million.

Social welfare	£1.1 million
Artistic development	£600,500
Education	£410,500
Medical aid and research	£655,500
Environmental improvement	£451,500

Beneficiaries included: Community Forest Trust (£126,500); Liverpool School of Tropical Medicine (£86,000); Mustard Tree (£50,000); Liverpool Everyman Theatre (£33,000); Oasis centre (£30,000).

Exclusions

The trust does not support:

- Non-registered charities
- Activities which are for the purpose of collecting funds for redistribution to other charities
- Animal charities
- Charities mainly operating outside the UK
- Church and all building fabric materials
- Conferences
- Continuing running costs of an organisation
- Costs of employing fundraisers

- Expeditions
- General sports, unless there is a strong association with a disadvantaged group
- Holidays
- Individuals
- Loans or business finance
- Charities promoting religion
- Routine staff training
- Sponsorship and marketing appeals

Applications

Unsolicited applications are not acknowledged. The trust's website states the following:

> The Trustees are generating, through existing and new relationships, a level of giving that more than matches the Trust's income. This is despite planned growth in the future income over the next few years. The Trustees have taken the decision to develop further this proactive stance to their giving, and only give to charities that they themselves select.
>
> Please do not, therefore, make unsolicited approaches, either by email, letter or in any other form, as they will not be considered or acknowledged.

The Ovo Charitable Foundation

Access to energy, youth poverty, education

Worldwide with a preference for Bristol

£522,500 (2017)

CC number: 1155954

Trustees: Samuel Kasumu; Matthew Owen; Stephen Fitzpatrick.

Correspondent: The Trustees, 1 Rivergate, Bristol BS1 6ED (tel: 0800 599 9440; email: hello@ovofoundation.org.uk)

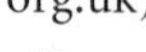

www.ovoenergy.com/foundation

The foundation is the corporate charity of Ovo Energy, an energy supply company based in Bristol. It was established in 2014 and is funded by customer donations which are then matched by the company. Ovo also covers the running costs of the foundation.

The foundation works in partnership with charities on a project-by-project basis. The foundation manager Gaby Sethi explains on the website:

> Our approach to providing grants is different to many other charitable foundations. We're innately curious, so we want to understand the root causes of the problem before we decide what or where we should fund. This approach means that we research important issues so we can work out where the funding gaps are and identify projects where we can have the biggest impact on people's lives.

The foundation has three main areas of work:

- Access to energy
- Youth poverty
- Education

OVO Gives Back

As well as project-by-project partnerships, each year the foundation makes grants of £20,000 to four local charities nominated and voted for by Ovo employees. A further £20,000 is set aside to match any extra money raised by employees. The charities also receive help from employees through volunteering and fundraising.

Financial information

In 2017 the foundation held assets of £1.8 million and had an income of £1 million. Grants awarded to organisations totalled £522,500.

Beneficiaries included: 1625 Independent People (£181,500); Energy 4 Impact (£123,000); Roundabout Ltd (£98,000); Young Bristol (£26,500); Centrepoint Soho (£20,500); Transition Bath Ltd (£5,000).

Applications

The foundation carries out its own research to identify projects to support. The Ovo Gives Back grants are nominated and voted for by Ovo employees.

Parabola Foundation

General charitable purposes, with a particular focus on poverty, arts, culture, and music

England

£770,000 (2016/17)

CC number: 1156008

Trustees: Deborah Jude; Anne Millican; Peter Millican.

Correspondent: Deborah Jude, Trustee, Broadgate Tower, 20 Primrose Street, London EC2A 2EW (tel: 07980 769561)

This foundation is the corporate charity of Parabola Land Ltd, a real estate and property development company. Trustee Peter Millican serves as a director of the company. Peter Millican has had a well-publicised involvement in the arts and was responsible for the development of Kings Place, a London concert venue and office space.

Parabola Foundation operates with general charitable purposes, although there is a particular focus on education; poverty; arts, culture, heritage and science; and environment, conservation and heritage. The annual report 2016/17 states:

> The objects of the charity are to further charitable and cultural projects that will bring benefit to the public. It has been particularly keen to support music and the arts in a way that benefits the community. The charity carefully evaluates all applications for funds based on merit.

Financial information

In 2016/17 the foundation had an income of £11,100 and a total expenditure of £774,500. We estimate that grants totalled around £770,000. Full accounts were not available to view on the Charity Commission website due to the foundation's low expenditure.

Previous beneficiaries have included : Kings Place Music Foundation (£391,000); Aurora Orchestra (£305,000); Poverty Relief Foundation (£56,500); Bowes Museum (£50,000).

Applications

Apply in writing to the correspondent.

Paradigm Foundation

General charitable purposes, community, education, training and employability, financial inclusion

Areas in which Paradigm Housing have homes, mainly South-East and East Midlands. A map of the areas covered is available on the foundation's website

£190,000 to organisations (2016/17)

CC number: 1156204

Trustees: Bob Marshall; Ewan Wallace; Alfred Dench; Jane Harrison; Revd Timothy Yates; Patricia Buckland.

Correspondent: Manjit Nanglu, Paradigm Housing Group, Glory Park Avenue, Wooburn Green, High Wycombe, Buckinghamshire HP10 ODF (tel: 01628 811835; email: enquiries@paradigmfoundation.org.uk)

www.paradigmfoundation.org.uk

This foundation is the corporate charity of the Paradigm Housing Group and was established to help individuals and communities in the area in which the group operates (South East and East Midlands). The foundation is being funded from between 2% and 10% of Paradigm Housing Group's surplus on an annual basis from the group's non-social housing activities.

Projects should benefit Paradigm residents and the local community. According to its 2016/17 accounts, the objects of the charity are:

> To further projects and initiatives within the geographical areas in which Paradigm Homes Charitable Housing Association Ltd or any other entity in the Paradigm Housing Group operates:
>
> - the prevention or relief of financial hardship
> - the relief of unemployment
> - the advancement of education

- the maintenance or improvement of public amenities
- the provision of recreational facilities for the public or those who by reason of their youth, age, infirmity or disablement, financial hardship or social and economic circumstances, have need of such facilities
- the protection or conservation of the environment
- the promotion of public safety and prevention of crime
- and to carry out such other charitable purposes as the Charity may think fit from time to time

The foundation has two grant streams: small-scale community projects up to £3,000 and larger projects over £3,000. For grants of over £5,000 applicants should not submit a form. Instead they may submit an expression of interest to the trustees. Individual grants are also made to Paradigm residents for up to £1,500. The Paradigm Housing website has a map which shows where Paradigm manages housing stock.

Financial information

In 2016/17 the foundation held assets of £260,500 and had an income of £350,500, majority of which was donated by Paradigm Homes Charitable Housing Association. Grants awarded to organisations totalled £190,000 with a further £8,100 given to individuals.

Beneficiaries included: Citizens Advice – Welwyn Hatfield (£61,000); The Oasis Partnership (£25,000); The Chesham and Community Association (£14,500); Chesham Rugby Club (£10,000); Sudbury Neighbourhood Centre (£9,000).

Applications

Applicants to the small and large community project schemes can apply online or download application forms available from the foundation's website. Those applying for £5,000 or more should not complete an application form but send the trustees an expression of interest form. This should outline the purpose of your bid and how you consider it will support one or more of the foundation's priorities. The foundation will let you know if a full application is then required. Applications may be submitted by post or via email, but if applicants are successful a signed version of the application will be required before funds can be released.

All applications will be acknowledged within seven working days of receipt. Decisions on larger grants will normally be made within ten weeks of the application being received. Applications for smaller grants are usually decided within eight weeks. Successful and unsuccessful applicants will be notified of the outcome. The trust conducts monitoring and evaluation of all grants.

The Performing Right Society Foundation

 Music

UK

£2.3 million to organisations (2017)

CC number: 1080837

Trustees: Simon Platz; Ameet Shah; Vanessa Swann; John Reid; Richard King; Julian Nott; Mark Poole; Caroline Norbury; Hannah Kendall; Susannah Simons; Chris Butler.

Correspondent: Fiona Harvey, Secretary, 2 Pancras Square, London N1C 4AG (tel: 020 3741 4233; email: info@prsformusicfoundation.com)

 www.prsfoundation.com

 facebook.com/PRSforMusic

 @PRSFoundation

 @prsfoundation

The PRS Foundation is an independent charitable foundation established in 2000 by the UK's largest collection society PRS for Music Ltd, from which it receives an annual donation of £3 million.

The foundation is currently the UK's largest independent funder of new music of any genre. The principle objectives of the foundation are to support, sustain and further the creation and performance of new music and to educate the public in order to augment its appreciation in the UK. The foundation awards grants and works in strategic partnerships with like-minded organisations.

Grant-making policy

The foundation awards grants under a variety of themes, which are currently listed on its website. Of these, only three are available for charities and not-for-profit organisations:

The Open Fund

The Open Fund provides funding for organisations and music creators and is suitable for a wide range of new music projects across all genre. The fund supports new music projects led by promoters, talent development organisations, venues, curators and large performance groups (which includes orchestras, choirs, jazz bands or folk groups with 12 or more performers). Projects must involve the creation, performance and promotion of new music and enable songwriters, composers, solo artist, bands and performers of all backgrounds to develop creatively and professionally. Grants are available for up to £10,000 and can be provided to support the touring, recording, marketing and commissioning of new music by UK-based creators, community projects, residencies, and live programmes.

Beyond Borders

Grants of up to £15,000 to organisations working with at least two other partners based in the UK or Ireland that want to co-commission or tour new music across the UK. Funding is available for projects that include new commissions, recordings and repeat performances of music written in the past five years.

Full details of the foundation's grant schemes including, grant-making priorities and application forms are available on the website.

Resonate

Grants of up to £10,000 are available to orchestras who commit to exploring contemporary UK repertoire as part of a season/tour and longer term audience development programmes. The programme supports projects that benefit audiences, composers and players in the UK and overseas.

Financial information

In 2017 the foundation held assets of £1.5 million and had an income of £4.5 million. During the year, a total of £3.3 million was awarded including £2.3 million in 315 grants to organisations and £1 million in 236 grants to individuals.

A list of beneficiaries for the year was not available; however, details of previous beneficiaries are available on the foundation's website.

Previous beneficiaries have included: Birmingham Contemporary Music Group; Birmingham Royal Ballet; FACT; Halle; London Sinfonietta; Merseyside Arts Foundation; Parr Street Studios; Small Green Shoots; Unity Theatre Liverpool.

Exclusions

The foundation will not offer funding for:

- Technological development if it does not contain a significant aspect of new music creation
- Projects that contain no element of live performance (unless applying for recording costs only)
- The purchase of vans and cars
- Bursaries, tuition/education costs, or scholarships
- Capital projects (e.g. building work)
- Any project raising funds for another charity
- Buying equipment/building a studio
- Organisations or projects that have been running for less than 18 months and musicians that have not been active for 18 months
- Retrospective activity

- Activity that falls before our decision date
- Organisations based outside the UK
- Artists and music creators based outside the UK
- British artists no longer permanently resident in the UK
- International tours/recording internationally (see the foundation's International Showcase Fund scheme)
- Radio stations/broadcasting costs
- Start-up companies or labels
- A roster of artists on a record label
- Editing, mastering or distribution of work
- Salary and living costs
- Core organisational costs
- Individuals in full-time education or who are under 18 unless represented by an adult with a valid DBS check

Note that companies limited by shares applying for funds will be considered on a case by case basis.

Applications

Apply via the foundation's website. The application forms for each programme also include full guidelines for applicants. Deadlines for applications vary from programme to programme. Contact the foundation or go to the website for further information. Note that the foundation only accepts one application per calendar year to The Open Fund.

The Persimmon Charitable Foundation

General charitable purposes, including: community and economic development, sustainable development, education, youth work, sport, health, social welfare

 England and Wales

£749,000 (2017)

CC number: 1163608

Trustees: Marion Sears; Mike Killoran; Richard Stenhouse; Roger Devlin.

Correspondent: The Trustees, Persimmon plc, Persimmon House, Fulford, York YO19 4FE (tel: 01904 642199; email: contact@persimmonhomes.com)

 corporate.persimmonhomes.com/corporate-responsibility

Established in 2015, this foundation is the corporate charity of Persimmon, a large housebuilding company. The foundation receives its income from independent financial advisers (IFAs) and the Persimmon group. The IFAs who made donations were those companies or firms who gave advice on mortgage products to customers of Persimmon Homes Ltd when they were buying a home.

The foundation makes grants to charities, particularly small local charities, and community groups to promote urban regeneration in areas of economic and social deprivation. The trustees' aim is to improve local communities in the UK by improving health, relieving poverty, advancing amateur sport, improving the local environment and supporting arts and culture.

There are currently two programmes, the Community Champions campaign, which supports small local charities and community groups, and the Healthy Communities campaign, which aims to improve and provide sporting facilities for young people under age 21. The Persimmon Group matches donations made by the foundation under the Community Champions campaign.

Community Champions

Organisations can apply for funding of up to £1,000 to match funding they have raised themselves to support local charitable purposes. Two organisations per operating business (of which there are around 30) are selected each month to receive funding. Information on successfully funded organisations can be found at persimmonhomes.com/community-champions/winners

Healthy Communities

In May 2017 the trustees launched this campaign, which gave 30 donations of £750 per month for sports kits or equipment to various clubs and organisations which provide sporting facilities and to individual amateur sportspeople under the age of 21. Each applicant was then entered into a national competition to receive a prize of £200,000 to create a sporting legacy, with two runner up prizes of £50,000 each and 27 finalist prizes of £5,000. The public then voted for the winning organisations, which in 2018 was the Heart of England Boxing Club.

Financial information

In 2017 the foundation held assets of £971,000 and had an income of £1.4 million. Grants were made to over 900 charities and totalled £749,000.

Recent beneficiaries of the Community Champions campaign include: Action for Children, Blood Bikes Cumbria, Kentish Town City Farm, RNIB, Saltash Community School and Zante Strays (£1,000 each); Brent Carers Centre (£720); Little Rascals Foundation (£750); Dunbar RNLI and Macrobert Arts Centre (£500 each).

Applications

Applicants need to complete the online form. Included in your application the foundation needs to know how much you have already raised and how much money you need. Applications are accepted each month and charities and groups that were previously unsuccessful can apply again.

The trustees prefer to support local charities. Go to www.persimmonhomes.com/contact to find your nearest Persimmon office.

Personal Assurance Charitable Trust

General charitable purposes, social welfare, health

UK

£98,400 (2017)

CC number: 1023274

Trustees: Michael Dugdale; Philip Yates; Sarah Mace.

Correspondent: Sarah Mace, Trustee, Personal Group Holdings plc, John Ormond House, 899 Silbury Boulevard, Milton Keynes MK9 3XL (email: sarah.mace@personal-group.com)

The Personal Assurance Charitable Trust (PACT) was registered with the Charity Commission in 1993. It is the corporate charity of Personal Group Holdings plc, a provider of employee benefits and financial services. The trust's 2017 annual report states that:

> There are no geographical or other restrictions on the type of donations that can be made. However preference will be given to recommendations made by policyholders of Personal Assurance Plc, their employers, and employees of Personal Group Holdings Plc and its subsidiary undertakings. In addition the trustees prefer to make donations that benefit the wider community rather than individual causes [...]

Financial information

In 2017 the trust had assets of £107,500 and an income of £100,000, the majority of which was received as a donation from Personal Assurance Group Holdings plc. Grants were made totalling £98,500.

Beneficiaries included: Memusi Foundation (£68,000); BBC Children in Need (£6,000); TransAid (£5,000); Keech Hospice Care (£3,000); Young's Foundation (£1,000).

Donations under £1,000 totalled £10,000.

Exclusions

Grants are rarely made to individuals.

Applications

The trust makes grants to charities recommended by staff and policyholders. The trust's 2017 accounts state:

> In view of the limited sources of income available the trustees have restricted donations to other charities and charitable organisations recommended by

policyholders of Personal Assurance Plc, their employers and employees of Personal Group Holdings Plc and its subsidiary undertakings.

The Persula Foundation

Homelessness, people with disabilities, human rights, animal welfare

Worldwide

£1.3 million (2016/17)

CC number: 1044174

Trustees: Hanna Oppenheim; Julian Richer; David Robinson; Rosie Richer; Robert Rosenthal; Jonathan Levy.

Correspondent: Teresa Chapman, Secretary, Gallery Court, Hankey Place, London SE1 4BB (tel: 020 7551 5343; email: info@persula.org)

The Persula Foundation was established in 1994 by Richer Sounds plc, the UK home entertainment retailer. Trustees include Julian Richer, founder of the company, and David Robinson, the Managing Director. The trust supports general charitable purposes, but its main aim is the relief and prevention of poverty. At present, the trust is focusing on providing funding for charities that are supporting the following causes:

- Homelessness
- People with disabilities
- Human rights
- Animal welfare

The Persula Foundation also manages three projects: 'Storytelling Tour', which annually provides 100 free sessions of storytelling and music to the visually impaired, older people and children and adults with disabilities; 'ACTS 435', a website that allows people to give money directly to those struggling financially; and 'ASB Help' which provides advice and support to victims of anti-social behaviour.

Financial information

In 2016/17 the foundation held assets of £97,500 and had an income of £1.4 million, mostly from donations from Richer Sounds plc (5% of the yearly profit is donated to the trust). There were grants made to a variety of organisations totalling £1.3 million and were distributed as follows:

Human welfare	166	£573,000
Human rights	37	£339,500
Animal welfare	59	£236,500
People with disabilities	39	£123,000
Homelessness	16	£37,000

Beneficiaries included: Civil Liberties Trust (£60,000); Amnesty International (£50,000); Prison Reform Trust (£34,000); Changing Faces, Crossways Women's Centre and Friends of the Earth (£30,000 each); Hope and Homes for Children and Christians Against Poverty (£25,000 each); Soil Association (£20,000); PETA (£17,500).

Applications

Apply in writing to the correspondent.

Petplan Charitable Trust

The welfare of dogs, cats, horses and rabbits, veterinary research and education

UK

£538,500 (2016/17)

CC number: 1032907

Trustees: John Bower; Clarissa Baldwin; David Simpson; Patsy Bloom; Ted Chandler; Peter Laurie; Kathryn Willis; Jamie Crittall; Gary Davess; Prof. The Lord Trees.

Correspondent: Catherine Bourg, Trust Administrator, Great West House (GW2), Great West Road, Brentford, Middlesex TW8 9EG (tel: 020 8580 8013; email: catherine.bourg@allianz.co.uk)

www.petplantrust.org

The trust was established in 1994 by pet insurance company Petplan Ltd which is a subsidiary company of Allianz Insurance plc. Petplan gives its policy holders the option of making a small annual donation to the trust, which they are able to increase from the suggested £2 per year should they wish to do so. The trust aims to promote the welfare of dogs, cats, horses and rabbits by funding clinical veterinary investigation, education and welfare projects. Since its creation the trust has awarded almost £10 million in grants.

Grant programmes

Scientific grants

The trust awards two types of specific grants:

- Full grants for in-depth research for up to three years
- Pump priming/Pilot grants of up to £10,000 over a period of no more than one year to fund initial research which should ideally lead to further research

Support is given for clinical research that will potentially help vets in practice to treat and care for animals. Only work which involves the study of companion animals will be funded. Applications for these grants are invited from the major veterinary schools.

Welfare grants

According to the trust's terms and conditions document, the following grants are given:

- One major welfare grant of up to £20,000 towards an innovative project which will improve animal care and welfare
- Up to £40,000 to be distributed in general grants of between £5,000 and £7,500
- Up to £40,000 to be distributed for general grants of up to £5,000
- Grants to assist with vehicle purchase

General grants can include items such as neutering, kennelling and veterinary costs but not general overheads. Projects involving pet therapy have previously been supported.

Capital grants

When funds permit, grants for major projects may be awarded to veterinary schools.

Financial information

In 2016 the trust had assets of £714,000 and an income of £790,500, of which £700,000 was donated by Petplan policy holders and £50,000 by Petplan Ltd. Grants were paid totalling £538,500 and were distributed as follows:

Scientific grants	£337,000
Welfare grants	£201,500

Beneficiaries included: Animal Health Trust (£181,000 five grants); Royal Veterinary College (£105,000 three grants); Lincolnshire Trust for Cats (£20,000); Headway Suffolk Brainy Dogs (£12,000); Dogs for Good for Disabled (£9,000); Canine Partners, Carla Lane Animals in Need, Dogs Trust, Yorkshire Cat Rescue (£5,000 each); Blue Cross (£1,500).

Exclusions

Grants are not made for individuals, non-registered charities and studies involving invasive procedures. The trust cannot consider applications for funding for overheads such as rent or general staff costs etc.

Applications

Application forms, eligibility criteria, full terms and conditions, and the dates for application rounds for each grant programme are available via the trust's website.

The PwC Foundation

Employability, healthcare, education

UK

£1.76 million (2016/17)

CC number: 1144124

Trustees: Neil Sherlock; Kevin Ellis; David Adair; Zelf Hussain; Kalee Talvitie-Brown; David Walters; Emma Cox.

Correspondent: Lucy Gresswell, Foundation Manager, PricewaterhouseCoopers, 1 Embankment

Place, London WC2N 6RH (tel: 07718 098321; email: lucy.gresswell@uk.pwc.com)

www.pwc.co.uk/corporate-sustainability/the-pwc-foundation.jhtml

The PwC Foundation was established in 2011 and is the corporate charity of PricewaterhouseCoopers LLP (PwC), which was formed by a merger between Coopers and Lybrand and Price Waterhouse in 1998.

The objectives of the PWC Foundation are to promote sustainable development and social inclusion and environmental awareness for public benefit. The foundation is also the company's vehicle for providing matched funding whereby the foundation matches an individual's fundraising to a maximum of £250 per person, per year.

Financial information

In 2016/17 the foundation held assets of £378,000 and had an income of £1.8 million, of which £1.1 million was donated by PwC. There were 440 grants made totalling £1.56 million. An additional £197,500 was awarded through the PwC matched funding programme. Grants were broken down as follows:

Employability	74	£609,500
Healthcare	199	£488,500
Education	44	£278,500
Other	123	£189,000

Beneficiaries included: Wellbeing of Women (£222,500); School for Social Entrepreneurs (£154,500); Teach First (£112,500); Beyond Food CIC (£109,500); Southbank Centre (£60,000); National Literacy Trust (£59,000); Alzheimer's Scotland (£20,000); Enabling Enterprise (£15,000).

Exclusions

The foundation will not fund political organisations, lobbying groups, animal rights groups or religious bodies.

Applications

The foundation's 2016/17 accounts state: 'Currently there is no formal open grant application process. The Steering Committee and Trustees can independently identify recipients for funding who meet the charitable objectives of the Foundation. Recipients are approved by the trustees.'

The Rathbone Brothers Foundation

General charitable purposes, disadvantage children and young people

Areas where the company has an office

£49,500 (2017)

CC number: 1150432

Trustees: Geoffrey Powell; Paul Stockton; Rathbone Trust Company Ltd; Richard Lanyon.

Correspondent: Bianca Martin, 8 Finsbury Circus, London EC2M 7AZ (tel: 020 7399 0000; email: rathbonefoundation@rathbones.com)

This foundation was established in November 2012 and is the associated charitable foundation of Rathbone Brothers plc, a company which is one of the UK's leading providers of investment management services for private clients, charities and professional advisers.

Grants programme

The main objective of the foundation is to help disadvantaged young people in the areas the company has a presence. The following offices receive money from the foundation to be distributed to local charities:

- Aberdeen
- Birmingham
- Bristol
- Cambridge
- Chichester
- Edinburgh
- Exeter
- Glasgow
- Jersey
- Kendal
- Liverpool
- London
- Lymington
- Newcastle
- Winchester

Financial information

In 2017 the foundation held assets of £779,500 and had an income of £177,000, of which £150,000 was a donation from Rathbone Brothers plc. Grants totalling £49,500 were made to 20 organisations.

Beneficiaries included: Homestart and Shelter from the Storm (£5,000); Sefton Opera (£4,000); Brathay Trust (£3,000); Marrick Priory Trust (£2,500); Andover Child Contact Centre (£1,000).

Applications

Apply in writing to your local Rathbone's office or directly to the trustees.

The Rugby Group Benevolent Fund Ltd

Community projects

Barrington (Cambridgeshire); Chinnor (Oxfordshire); Kensworth (Bedfordshire); Lewes (Sussex); Rochester (Kent); Rugby and Southam (Warwickshire); South Ferriby (North Lincolnshire); and Tilbury (Essex)

£440,000 to organisations (2017)

CC number: 265669

Trustees: Graeme Fuller; Norman Jones; Jim Wootten; Ian Southcott; Geoff Thomas; Nigel Appleyard; John Brooks; David Holton; Kevin Murch.

Correspondent: Isobel Watson, Administrator, CEMEX House, Evreux Way, Rugby, Warwickshire CV21 2DT (tel: 01932 583181; email: info@rugbygroupbenevolentfund.org.uk)

www.rugbygroupbenevolentfund.org.uk

This fund was established in 1955 with the aim of supporting employees and former employees of Rugby Group Ltd, and their dependants. The Rugby Group is now a part of CEMEX UK, a global cement manufacturer but the fund has kept its independence and is managed by a group of employees and former employees. The fund receives its income in dividends from the company.

Today, the fund maintains the same objectives with which it was established but has broadened its scope to include charitable causes in communities where employees, former employees and their dependants live. These are: Barrington (Cambridgeshire); Chinnor (Oxfordshire); Kensworth (Bedfordshire); Lewes (Sussex); Rochester (Kent); Rugby and Southam (Warwickshire); South Ferriby (North Lincolnshire); and Tilbury (Essex).

Grants are made to provide capital for specific projects. The applicant organisation does not have to be a charity but it must have charitable objectives, and the project must be fully costed.

Financial information

In 2017 the fund held assets of almost £2.1 million and had an income of £69,500. Grants were made to 52 organisations during the year and totalled £434,000. A further £28,000 was awarded to former employees and their dependants.

Beneficiaries included: Thomley Activity Centre (£50,000); East Anglia Air Ambulance (£30,000); Hill Street Youth and Community Centre (£15,000); Harston Village Hall (£10,000); War Memorial Long Itchington (£5,000); Barton and District Athletic Club

(£3,000); Rugby Christmas Cracker (£2,000); and Cambridge Cancer Help Centre (£1,000).

Grants of less than £1,000 totalled £6,700.

Exclusions

The fund does not support organisations operating outside the areas of benefit. Support is not normally given for day-to-day revenue costs.

Applications

Potential applicants must first complete an expression of interest form, available to download from the fund's website. The trustees meet several times a year to review and approve applications.

Russell Trust

General charitable purposes

UK, especially Scotland

£151,500 (2016/17)

OSCR number: SC004424

Trustees: Fred Bowden; Cecilia Croal; Graeme Crombie; David Erdal; Iona Russell; Alan Scott; C. A G. Parr.

Correspondent: Iona Russell, Administrator and Trustee, Markinch, Glenrothes, Fife KY7 6PB (tel: 01592 753311; email: Russell.trust@tullisrussell.com)

The trust is a shareholder in Tullis Russell Group Ltd. The Russel Trust supports a broad range of local charities in the area of Fife, Scotland. Every year it donates to hundreds of different charities and educational institutions.

The trust's 2016/17 accounts state that 'the majority of the investments of the Trust are in shares of Tullis Russell Group Ltd and are held as the main part of the endowment'.

Financial information

In 2016/17 the trust had assets of £4.4 million and an income of £256,000, £250,000 of which was donated by Tullis Russell Group Ltd. During the year, the trust awarded £151,500 in grants to organisations.

Beneficiaries included: University of St Andrews (£31,000); The Adam Smith Foundation (£15,000); Stoa School (£5,000); Child Bereavement UK, Home-Start Dundee and Cetacean Research and Rescuer Unit (£2,000 each).

Exclusions

Only registered charities or organisations with charitable status are supported.

Applications

Application forms are available from the correspondent. A statement of accounts must be supplied. The trustees meet quarterly, although decisions on the allocation of grants are made more regularly.

Santander UK Foundation Ltd

General charitable purposes

UK, including Guernsey, Jersey, and the Isle of Man

£5.3 million (2017)

CC number: 803655

Trustees: Jennifer Scardino; Sue Willis; Keith Moor; Christopher Fallis; Rachel MacFarlane.

Correspondent: Amy Slack, Santander UK plc, Santander House, 201 Grafton Gate East, Milton Keynes MK9 1AN (email: grants@santander.co.uk)

www.santanderfoundation.org.uk

The Santander Foundation was established by the banking company Santander UK plc. Through Santander UK's flagship community programme, 'The Discovery Project', the foundation provides grants to support knowledge, skills and innovation in the UK. The foundation's annual report 2016 states, 'the majority of donations into the foundation are from Santander plc, in addition Santander UK plc gift in kind £100,000 each year to the foundation which covers the overhead, administration and running costs of the foundation'.

Grant-making scheme

The foundation's Discovery Grants scheme, provides grants of up to £5,000 to small, locally registered charities, CICs, and credit unions in the UK. Grants are awarded for the following themes:

- **Explorer – improving people's knowledge.** Examples include a series of Money Management workshops to help people understand how to budget
- **Transformer – developing skills and experience.** Examples include work-based training and mentors to help socially isolated people develop skills to get back into work
- **Changemaker – innovative solutions to social challenges.** Examples include a new social networking program that uses a specially developed braille laptops to help visually impaired young people access the internet

Grants are available for one year only. The foundation prefers to fund a complete project or item, which should be local in scale and may include salaries, equipment or materials.

Financial information

In 2017 the foundation had assets of £16.1 million and an income of £5.5 million, of which £5 million was donated by Santander UK plc. The foundation made 3,211 grants to charities amounting to a total of £5.3 million, under the following categories:

Social inclusion	2,119	£4.2 million
Health	990	£985,000
Other	102	£36,500

Beneficiaries of grants of £10,000 or more included: Barnardo's (£210,000); Age UK (£191,000); British Red Cross (£55,000); Marie Curie Cancer Cure (£26,500); Small Charities Coalition and Little Art School (£10,000 each).

Exclusions

Grants are not awarded to:

- Individuals
- Multiyear funding
- Fundraising activities
- Unregistered charities, not-for-profit groups
- Other funders and grant-makers
- Religious, ethnic or political charities
- Events, conferences and sponsorship
- Shortfall funding
- Beneficiaries outside the UK, Channel Islands, or Isle of Man
- Start up organisations

Applications

Application forms can be found in any local Santander branch. Once completed applicants should post their applications in the Discovery Grants post boxes at any branch. Applicants are usually informed of the outcome of their application within six weeks.

ScottishPower Foundation

General charitable purposes including education, the environment, community development, arts, heritage, culture and science, social welfare, community development

UK

£1.14 million to organisations (2017)

OSCR number: SC043862

Trustees: Mike Thornton; Sarah Mistry; Keith Anderson; Ann McKechin; Elaine Bowker.

Correspondent: María Sanz Arcas, 320 St Vincent Street, Glasgow G2 5AD (email: scottishpowerfoundation@scottishpower.com)

www.scottishpower.com/pages/about_the_scottishpower_foundation

The ScottishPower Foundation is the corporate charity of ScottishPower, part of the Iberdrola Group, a global energy company and world leader in wind energy with operations focused in the UK, USA, Brazil, Mexico and Spain. The foundation was set up in 2013 in order to reinforce the company's commitment to supporting charitable work throughout Britain and receives the majority of its income from company donations.

Areas of work

According to the foundation's website, charities and non-profit organisations are funded to support the following purposes:

- The advancement of education
- The advancement of environmental protection
- The advancement of the arts, heritage, culture or science
- The prevention or relief of poverty and the relief of those in need by reason of disability or other disadvantage
- The advancement of citizenship and community development

Financial information

In 2017 the foundation held assets £151,500 and had an income of £1.2 million, which largely came from donations from ScottishPower plc. During the year, the foundation awarded £1.72 million in grants and scholarships.

Beneficiaries included: National Museum of Scotland (£150,000); Erskine, Young Scots Climate (£60,000 each); RSPB Scotland (£47,000); Dumfries House (£30,000); Llangollen International Eisteddfod (£10,000).

Applications

Application forms are available to download from the foundation's website. Check the website for details of application deadlines.

The Severn Trent Water Charitable Trust Fund

Debt advice and financial education

The area covered by Severn Trent Water Ltd, which stretches from Wales to east Leicestershire and from the Humber estuary down to the Bristol Channel. A map is provided on the website

£182,500 to organisations (2016/17)

CC number: 1108278

Trustees: Elizabeth Pusey; David Vaughan; Lowri Williams; Clive Mottram; Andrew Phelps; Paul Stone; Craig Simmons; Jane Bleach.

Correspondent: The Trustees, Severn Trent Trust Fund, FREEPOST RLZE – EABT – SHSA, Sutton Coldfield B72 1TJ (tel: 0121 355 7766; email: office@sttf.org.uk)

 www.sttf.org.uk

The Severn Trent Trust Fund is an independent trust established by Severn Trent Water Ltd in 1997 with a donation of £2 million.

The main objects of the trust are to help people out of poverty and debt by helping needy individuals to pay their water bills, as well as making grants to organisations that provide debt and money advice. The aim of the trust is to help individuals in immediate crisis and financial difficulty while also encouraging future financial stability.

Grants are mainly awarded to individuals or families to clear water debt or assist with water charges.

Grants for organisations

The trust also provides grants to organisations in its area of benefit to support the delivery of debt advice and financial education. According to the trust's website, there are two grant schemes for organisations:

Small grant funding

One-off awards are provided for the purpose of developing or enhancing an organisation's activities around money or debt advice and financial literacy. The trust is flexible about how support is provided, but may include capital expenditure, staff training or promotional work.

Revenue project funding

Grants are also provided over a longer term, up to three years, for projects that meet the trust's criteria. In 2016/17 the trust has a particular preference for organisations delivering services in the rural parts of the trust's area of benefit. The website states that current criteria and funding opportunities can be discussed by contacting the trust (see 'Applications').

Financial information

In 2016/17 the trust had assets of £1.04 million and an income of £3.7 million. Grants totalled £2.6 million with the trust making grants of £2.37 million to individuals and £182,500 to organisations that provide debt advice and other support services.

Previous beneficiaries have included: Birmingham Citizens Advice; Community Advice and Law Service – Leicester; Direct Help and Advice – Derby; Gateway to Birmingham Advice Services; The Haven – Wolverhampton.

Exclusions

Only applications from organisations within the Severn Trent Trust Fund area will be considered. A map of this area can be found on the trust's website.

Applications

Organisations interested in applying for a grant should contact the trust on 0121 321 1324 or email office@sttf.org.uk to discuss current funding criteria and future funding opportunities.

Application forms for individuals are provided on the website.

The Simmons & Simmons Charitable Foundation

Social welfare, education and training, access to justice and legal aid

Worldwide, with a preference for the City of London and Tower Hamlets

£251,000 (2016/17)

CC number: 1129643

Trustees: Richard Dyton; Fiona Loughrey; Colin Passmore; Ina Vom Feld.

Correspondent: The Trustees, c/o Simmons & Simmons LLP, Citypoint, 1 Ropemaker Street, London EC2Y 9SS (tel: 020 7628 2020; email: corporate.responsibility@simmons-simmons.com)

 www.simmons-simmons.com

The foundation was established in 2009 by the law firm Simmons & Simmons LLP. The following information was taken from the foundation's 2016/17 accounts:

> The foundation seeks to support smaller charitable organisations which are local to the offices of Simmons & Simmons and which seek to address social exclusion. The Foundation also seeks to provide access to justice, work and opportunities to those less privileged or fortunate, for example by providing direct grants to talented individuals from low income backgrounds.

Preference is given to charities in which the firm's employees can be involved.

Financial information

In 2016/17 the foundation held assets of £150,000 and had an income of £181,500. Grants totalled £251,000.

Beneficiaries included: Battersea Legal Advice Centre (£36,000); The Big Issue Foundation (£22,000); Bingham Centre for the Rule of Law, The Ethical Property Foundation and Working Families (£10,000 each); Spitalfields Music (£6,000); London's Air Ambulance, Prisoners' Advice Service and School Home Support (£5,000 each).

Grants of less than £5,000 totalled £51,000.

Applications

Application forms are available from the correspondent. Applicants must explain how they meet one of the following objectives:

- Social inclusion (increasing access to education and/or work)
- Governance (supporting the rule of law and access to justice)

They must also explain how they will provide support to communities local to where Simmons & Simmons have offices.

Sirius Minerals Foundation

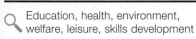

Education, health, environment, welfare, leisure, skills development

North York Moors National Park; Scarborough; Redcar

£300,000 (2017)

CC number: 1163127

Trustees: Neil Irving; David Archer; Gareth Edmunds; Leah Swain; Peter Woods; Richard Hunt; Ian Swales.

Correspondent: The Trustees, Resolution House, Lake View, Scarborough YO11 3ZB (tel: 01723 470108; email: info@siriusmineralsfoundation.co.uk)

www.siriusmineralsfoundation.co.uk

The foundation was established by Sirius Minerals plc to support the communities around its Woodsmith Mine near Whitby. The foundation received an initial £2 million in funding from the company and will receive 0.5% of Woodsmith Mine's revenue once it is operational.

The foundation distributes funds to local community projects such as improving public spaces and facilities, environmental initiatives and community building projects.

The foundation's website states that its objectives are to:

- Advance education, including supporting projects and training that benefit people by enhancing their skills
- Promote the general health of the community
- Advance environmental protection and improvement including the enhancing of the local landscape
- Provide and improve facilities in the interests of social welfare and leisure time with the aim to improve residents' well-being
- Help gain skills to those in need, because of financial hardship by being out-of-work, particularly the long-term unemployed

Financial information

In 2016/17 the foundation had an income of £500 and a total expenditure of £2,600. However the foundation's website states that grants totalling £300,000 were made to 75 organisations in December 2017.

Beneficiaries have included: Castleton Cricket Club; Caedmon College Whitby; Eastside Community Hall; Hawk and Owl Trust; Lingdale Village Hall, The Skill Mill.

Applications

Applications can be made via the foundation's website. Check the website for application deadlines.

Skipton Building Society Charitable Foundation

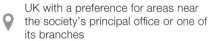

The education and welfare of children, older people

UK with a preference for areas near the society's principal office or one of its branches

£143,500 (2017/18)

CC number: 1079538

Trustees: Rt Revd and Rt Hon. Lord Hope of Thornes; Richard Robinson; Amelia Vyvyan; Alison Davies; Kitty North; John Dawson; Debra Ewing.

Correspondent: Secretary to the Charitable Foundation, The Bailey, Skipton, North Yorkshire BD23 1DN (tel: 01756 705000; email: charitablefoundation@skipton.co.uk)

www.skiptoncharitablefoundation.co.uk

The Skipton Building Society Charitable Foundation was established in February 2000 and is funded by annual payment from the Society.

Areas of support

The foundation's website states:

> We will consider donations:
>
> - To registered charities based in the UK, particularly in areas near the Society's Principal Office or one of its branches
> - Where there is clear and immediate benefit to the recipients in the UK
> - Where charities' objectives are to benefit children, through education and/or welfare, youth schemes and projects, or the elderly and their care
> - Where the charity can provide its last two years' annual accounts
> - Up to £3,000
>
> The Charitable Foundation supports registered charities with donations to enable specific tangible items or activities to be purchased rather than donating to general funds.
>
> The foundation requests that the items are to be used directly by beneficiaries and anticipate that the charity becomes the owner of that equipment, responsible for the on-going upkeep and maintenance.

The foundation considers grants of up to £3,000 but its focus is on smaller grants to ensure as many good causes as possible are supported.

Financial information

In 2017/18 the foundation held assets of £86,500 and had an income of £151,000. Grants awarded to organisations totalled £143,500.

Beneficiaries included: Bridge Care Ltd (£3,000); Blooming Blossoms Trust (£2,900); The Market Place (£2,000); British Disabled Angling Association (£1,900); Blind in Business Trust (£1,700); Follow Your Dreams Ltd (£1,500); Give Youth a Break (£1,000); Deafway (£900); Art Care Education (£600).

Exclusions

The foundation's website states:

> We won't consider donations:
>
> - To non-registered charities or individuals
> - To activities which are primarily the responsibility of central or local government or other responsible bodies
> - Towards running costs including rent or staff wages
> - Towards restoration or upkeep of buildings
> - Holidays, residential trips or overseas travel
> - Towards fundraising events, sponsorship or marketing appeals
> - Towards the cost or maintenance of vehicles
> - To large national charities
> - From charities which have successfully applied to the Foundation within the previous 5 years
> - From charities which have applied to the Foundation within the previous two years

Applications

Application forms can be found on foundation's website. Completed application forms should be returned by post along annual accounts for the last two years.

The Slaughter and May Charitable Trust

Legal advice, education and training, health, social welfare, children and young people and older people

Mainly local to the Slaughter and May offices in Islington and close to Tower Hamlets and Hackney

£385,500 (2016/17)

CC number: 1082765

Trustee: Slaughter and May Trust Ltd.

Correspondent: Kate Hursthouse, Corporate Responsibility Manager, Slaughter and May, 1 Bunhill Row, London EC1Y 8YY (tel: 020 7090 3433;

email: corporateresponsibility@slaughterandmay.com)

 www.slaughterandmay.com

Established in 1991, this trust is the corporate charity of the legal firm Slaughter and May. The trust's annual report for 2016/17 states that it is 'reliant on its key donors, the partners of Slaughter and May with all administrative and other office support being provided by the firm'.

The trust supports a range of legal, educational, health and community projects, with a particular interest in children and young people and older people.

Financial information

In 2016/17 the trust held negative assets of £45,000 and had an income of £405,500. Grants totalled £385,500.

Beneficiaries included: Islington Law Centre (£56,000); National Literacy Trust (£53,500); The Access Project (£40,000); Action for Kids (£30,500); Moreland Primary School (£17,500); Teach First (£11,300); SBA The Solicitor's Charity (£10,000); Bloodwise (£7,000); Shelter (£5,500); The Costa Foundation (£5,000).

Grants for less than £5,000 totalled £38,000.

Applications

The trust's 2016/17 annual report states that it 'makes annual grants at its discretion to a small number of specific charitable causes and does not generally accept unsolicited funding applications'.

Social Tech Trust

Technology projects that transform lives

UK and overseas

£3 million (2016/17)

CC number: 1125735

Trustees: Bill Liao; Sebastien Lahtinen; Elizabeth Murray; Hannah Keartland; Nicolas Temple.

Correspondent: Vicki Hearn, Director, Social Tech Trust, 99 Park Drive, Milton Park OX14 4RY (tel: 01865 334000; email: hello@socialtechtrust.org)

 socialtechtrust.org

 @SocialTechTrust

Established in 2008, this is the charitable foundation of Nominet, the company which runs the registry for all.uk domain names.

Innovate Social Tech

Innovate Social Tech is the trust's new grant programme that supports innovative ventures to transform lives with tech. The fund's initial theme will be Tech to Unite Us:

Tech to Unite Us

Grant of up to £45,000 and technical assistance is available to early stage ventures that use technology to unite people in inspirational and informative ways.

The following criteria have been taken from the trust's website:

> We'll consider your application if your venture has:
>
> - A social mission embedded in your governance
> - Potential to deliver transformative social impact at scale through a deep understanding of the critical social challenge that drives your innovation and an ambition to make a difference through growth
> - An innovative approach to tackling a social challenge; this could be through a creative business model, by harnessing emerging tech, or using existing tech in a new and transformative way
> - A working product or service that you will continue to test and iterate; you are at the demonstration stage of your venture's evolution
> - Evidence of your potential to create user, social and financial value; for example, a theory of change, user co-design and testing, identified social KPIs, or prospective partnerships or routes to market
> - The right team with the critical experience and expertise for success – in-house tech capabilities being an essential
> - Registration as a UK-based organisation and the potential for social impact in the UK

Financial information

In 2016/17 the foundation held assets of £7.8 million and had an income of £5.7 million, £5.4 million of which was donated by Nominet. Grants were awarded totalling £3 million.

Beneficiaries of grants over £50,000 included: Creative England (£250,000); Inspiring Digital Enterprise (£200,000); My Time to Care (£100,000); Run A Club (£81,500); Wavemaker – Stoke (£85,000); Bounce Works (£50,000).

Grants of less than £50,000 totalled £1.45 million.

Applications

Applications can be made through the trust's website. Refer to the website for application deadlines.

Spar Charitable Fund

General, with a preference for children and young people

UK

£92,000 (2016/17)

CC number: 236252

Trustee: The National Guild of Spar Ltd.

Correspondent: Philip Marchant, Administration Committee Member, Spar (UK) Ltd, Hygeia Building, 66 – 68 College Road, Harrow HA1 1BE (tel: 020 8426 3700; email: philip.marchant@spar.co.uk)

Registered with the Charity Commission in 1970, the Spar Charitable Fund is the corporate charity of the retail chain, SPAR (UK) Ltd.

The funds accounts state that:

> The Spar Charitable Fund with the support and assistance of the Spar Benevolent Fund seeks to provide charitable assistance to independent Spar retailers who face adverse problems and difficulties with health, bereavement and social issues. The charitable fund also supports retail industry charitable organisations.
>
> One major objective of the Spar Charitable Fund is to provide a vehicle to enable the Spar organisation through its 2,242 stores across the UK to engage with the public to raise awareness of public charitable needs and raise funding in a wide variety of ways.

Financial information

In 2016/17 it had assets of £929,000 and an income of £59,500. Throughout the year the charity awarded around £92,000 in grants to organisations.

Beneficiaries included: Drink Aware (£24,000); NSPCC (£18,500); Grocery Aid (£14,500); Cancer Fund for Children (£8,000); Retail Trust (£7,100).

Applications

Apply in writing to the correspondent.

St James's Place Charitable Foundation

Disadvantaged children, cancer care, hospices, mental health

UK and overseas

£10.8 million (2017)

CC number: 1144606

Trustees: David Bellamy; Ian Gascoigne; Malcolm Cooper-Smith; Andrew Croft; David Lamb; Michael Wilson.

Correspondent: Mark Longbottom, Foundation Manager, St James's Place plc, St James's Place House, 1 Tetbury Road, Cirencester GL7 1FP (tel: 01285 878562)

 www.sjpfoundation.co.uk

The foundation is the corporate charity of St James's Place Wealth Management, a leading UK wealth management company.

Themes

The foundation's grant-making in the UK is guided by four themes:

Cherishing Children – Cherishing Children is the foundation's largest theme and focuses on supporting children and young people under the age of 25 who are disadvantaged, who are young carers, or who have physical or mental health difficulties or life-threatening degenerative conditions. Grants are made for small capital items, support for staff working directly or hands on with beneficiaries, and support for projects of direct benefit to beneficiaries.

Combating Cancer – Grants are given for capital items of direct benefit to cancer patients, support towards the salary of staff working directly with cancer patients, and grants and support projects aimed at increasing the quality of life for cancer patients.

Supporting Hospices – Grants are given to hospices working with all age ranges. The foundation is currently working with Help the Hospices who will distribute funds to hospices on the foundation's behalf and, therefore, does not invite applications from hospices directly.

Mental Health – The foundation supports mental health charities throughout the UK. Unsolicited applications are not accepted.

Grant programmes

- **Small Grants Programme:** grants of up to £10,000 are available to UK charities with an annual income of up to £1 million
- **Major Grants Programme:** the programme is not currently open to unsolicited applications, instead charities are invited to apply. Grants are usually for more than one year and are awarded to charities with an annual income under £9 million

The foundation's website states: 'Approximately 80% of the money raised goes to supporting UK charities, with the remaining 20% being allocated to charities overseas, particularly those helping children and young people to escape poverty, malnutrition and neglect.'

Financial information

In 2017 the foundation had assets of £8.7 million and an income of £18.2 million. Grants totalled £10.8 million during the year.

Previous beneficiaries have included: Jamie's Farm; Acorns Children's Hospice; Brainwave; Brain Tumour Charity; The Project; Children in Crossfire; Global Child Dental Fund; Hope Support Services.

Exclusions

The foundation does not provide support for:

- Charities with reserves of over 50% of income
- Administrative costs
- Activities primarily the responsibility of statutory agencies
- Replacement of lost statutory funding
- Research
- Events
- Advertising
- Holidays
- Sponsorship
- Contributions to large capital appeals
- Single faith charities
- Charities that are raising funds on behalf of another charity

Applications

Applicants who believe that they fit the criteria are welcome to apply at any time via the foundation's website. The application procedure for all of the programmes can take between four to six months. The following information is given on the foundation's website: 'Applications for a small grant will normally receive a visit from a representative of the foundation, who will subsequently report to the trustees. Following the trustees' decision, successful applicants will be notified.'

Consult the foundation's website for further details.

Standard Life Foundation

Financial resilience and well-being

UK

£24,000 (2017)

OSCR number: SC040877

Trustees: Alistair Darling; James Daunt; Naomi Eisenstadt; David Hall; Lucy Heller; Elaine Kempson; Wendy Loretto; Graeme McEwan; Keith Skeoch; Euan Stirling.

Correspondent: Frances Horsburgh, Secretary, 30 Lothian Road, Edinburgh EH1 2DH (email: enquiries@standardlifefoundation.org.uk)

 www.standardlife.com/sustainability

The foundation was established in 2016 and funded with a donation of assets remaining from Standard Life's demutualisation in 2006.

At the time of writing (May 2018) the foundation was conducting a review of research into financial well-being. Its website states:

> Following a careful process of evaluation, the Foundation will be commissioning a systematic review of research into the topic of financial well-being.
>
> This independent review will form the key focus of the Foundation's activity in 2018. It will provide the building blocks for the Foundation to make a real and lasting impact to improving financial well-being and resilience across the UK.

Financial information

In 2017 the foundation had assets of £85.3 million and an income of £81.3 million, nearly all of which was a donation from the Standard Life Aberdeen plc. During the year, the foundation gave a total of £24,000 grants to one organisation.

Beneficiaries included: Edinburgh University Business School (£24,000).

Applications

The time of writing (May 2018) the foundation was not accepting applications. Its website states:

> At the moment we are not taking unsolicited bids for funding or research projects. However, we do aim to undertake a systematic research review in the future and will be asking for expressions of interests on this project in advance. Please contact the Foundation on enquiries@standardlifefoundation.org.uk if you would like to be informed about this project when it is launched.

The Stewarts Law Foundation

 Alleviating poverty, access to justice, supporting disability, providing educational opportunity

 UK

£573,000 (2016/17)

CC number: 1136714

Trustees: John Cahill; Bennett Townsend; Stuart Dench; Paul Paxton; James Healy-Pratt; Stephen Foster; Julian Chamberlayne; Daniel Herman; Andrew Dinsmore; Kevin Grealis; Keith Thomas; Clive Zietman; Sean Upson; Muiris Lyons; Debbie Chism; Helen Ward; Jonathan Sinclair; Ian Gatt; David Hughes.

Correspondent: John Cahill, Trustee, 5 New Street Square, London EC4A 3BF

 www.stewartslaw.com/about/social-impact/the-stewarts-foundation

Established in June 2010 for general charitable purposes and funded by Stewarts Law LLP, this foundation supports organisations in the UK.

Areas of support

The foundation's website states:

> The Foundation refocused its grant giving principles in 2016 to include four key areas:
>
> - Alleviating poverty
> - Enabling access to justice
> - Supporting disability
> - Providing educational opportunity

Financial information

In 2016/17 the foundation had assets of £89,500 and an income of £658,000. Grants to 12 organisations totalled £573,500.

Beneficiaries included: Access to Justice Foundation (£250,000); Headway (£40,000); Backup Trust, Centrepoint and Coram Children's Legal Centre (£30,000 each); The Children's Trust – Tadworth (£10,000); City Solicitors Horizons (£4,000).

Applications

The foundation does not accept unsolicited applications. The annual report for 2016/17 states: 'It is not the policy of the Trustees to accept direct applications for funds.'

The John Swire (1989) Charitable Trust

 General charitable purposes including: arts, welfare, health, sports, education, medicine and research

 UK and overseas

£1.41 million (2017)

CC number: 802142

Trustees: Barnaby Swire; Jonathan Swire; Michael Craddock Robinson.

Correspondent: Sarah Irving, Swire House, 59 Buckingham Gate, London SW1E 6AJ (tel: 020 7834 7717; email: info@scts.org.uk)

Established in 1989 by Sir John Swire, the trust makes donations at the trustees' discretion to a wide range of organisations, especially in the areas of arts, welfare, health, sports, education, medicine and research. The trust's income is largely derived from investments in John Swire & Sons Ltd, a diversified group of global companies with which it has a strong affiliation.

Financial information

In 2017 the trust held assets of £45.2 million and had an income of £1.49 million. A total of £1.41 million was awarded in donations.

Beneficiaries included: Breast Cancer Haven (£101,000); Mind, Now Teach (Ark UK Programmes) (£25,000 each); Pilgrims Hospices (£5,000); Army Benevolent Fund, British Red Cross; Dover Boat Trust Fund, National Autistic Society and Prostate Research Campaign UK (£1,000 each).

Applications

Although the trustees award some grants without formal applications, they normally require organisations to submit a request explaining how the funds could be used and the outcomes they expect to achieve.

The Adrian Swire Charitable Trust

General charitable purposes

UK and overseas

£1 million (2017)

CC number: 800493

Trustees: Merlin Swire; Sir Martin Dunne; Lady Judith Swire; Martha Allfrey; Richard Leonard; Samuel Swire.

Correspondent: Sarah Irving, Swire House, 59 Buckingham Gate, London SW1E 6AJ (tel: 020 7834 7717; email: info@scts.org.uk)

The trust, formerly known as the Sammermar Trust, was established in 1988 with general charitable purposes. It has a strong affiliation to John Swire & Sons Ltd, a diversified group of global companies. Grants are made to a wide range of causes at the trustees' discretion.

Financial information

In 2017 the trust had assets of £34.3 million and an income of £1.4 million, including that obtained from investments in John Swire & Sons. Grants totalled just over £1 million during the year.

Beneficiaries included: Ashmolean Museum (£125,000); Prior's Court Foundation (£50,000); Wings for Warriors (£30,000); Young Musicians Symphony Orchestra (£20,000); Air Pilots Trust (£10,000); Nilgiris Adivasi Trust (£4,000); Cardinall's Music (£2,500); Shipwrecked Mariners' Society (£500).

Grants of less than £1,000 totalled £2,100.

Applications

Donations are awarded at the discretion of trustees and unsolicited applications are unlikely to meet with success.

The Swire Charitable Trust

General charitable purposes, with a focus on community and social welfare, education and training, and heritage

Predominantly the UK

£2.4 million to organisations (2017)

CC number: 270726

Trustees: Barnaby Swire; John Swire; Sir Adrian Swire; Merlin Swire; James Hughes-Hallett; Samuel Swire; Martha Allfrey.

Correspondent: Sarah Irving, Grants Manager, Swire House, 59 Buckingham Gate, London SW1E 6AJ (tel: 020 7834 7717; email: info@scts.org.uk)

 www.swirecharitabletrust.org.uk

Established in 1975, the trust's core grant-making programme makes grants to UK-registered charities working in the following areas: community and social welfare; education and training; and heritage. This programme is funded by John Swire & Sons Ltd, a diversified group of global companies. As a result of the merger of the Swire Charitable Trust and the Swire Educational Trust on 31 December 2015, the trust also operates a separate graduate and postgraduate scholarship programme for overseas students.

The following information on the trust's grant programmes and funding types is taken from the application guidelines on its website:

Funding programmes

There are three funding programmes available to UK-registered charities working in England, Scotland, Wales and Northern Ireland. The following are currently open and welcoming eligible online funding requests.

- **Welfare** – charities that help to foster long-term positive change in the lives of disadvantaged people and their communities, with a particular focus on those working with young people leaving care, ex-Services, and victims of slavery and human trafficking
- **Opportunity** – charities that help children and adults from all backgrounds to fulfil their potential and make the most of their talents, with a preference for charities that are:
  - Narrow the attainment gap for children from disadvantaged backgrounds
  - Equip young people with the essential skills they need to help them re-engage with education, training, employment or volunteering

- **Heritage** – charities working to restore neglected buildings and monuments which can contribute to community regeneration, particularly in areas of deprivation. The trustees would especially like to hear from smaller heritage charities that focus on providing employment, training or volunteering opportunities for disadvantaged members of their local communities. The trust also funds charities that are focused on keeping traditional and at-risk skills alive

Types of funding

The website notes the following:

> We will fund individual projects that are aligned with our funding priorities but we also recognise that charities themselves are often best placed to allocate resources within their organisations. Therefore our grants can be awarded on a restricted or an unrestricted basis and we are willing to support core costs, capital expenditure and salaries.
>
> There is no maximum or minimum grant size and, although we base our grants on the amount requested and the size of organisation, we may award more or less than you applied for.
>
> Indeed the amount requested will only be used for guidance and the size of the grant will be entirely at the discretion of the trustees.
>
> While most of our grants are for one year only, we appreciate that charities welcome security of funding. So, where a longer-term commitment can be clearly justified, we are willing to consider multi-year grants of up to three years. But these are likely to come with additional conditions, such as reporting requirements.

Financial information

In 2017 the trust had assets of £9.81 million and an income of £2.74 million. Grants to charitable organisations totalled £2.4 million, with an additional £1.45 million awarded through the educational scholarship scheme.

Beneficiaries included: Hope for Tomorrow (£34,000); Historic Royal Palaces (£25,000); Families United Network (£10,000); Deaf World (£6,500); Fife Society for the Blind (£5,000); Children's Hospital at Westmead (£2,500); Crisis UK (£2,000).

Exclusions

According to the trust's application guidelines, it is unable to consider:

- Applications received by post or email, i.e. not via our online funding request form
- Organisations that are not UK registered charities
- Requests from charities that have applied to us in the last 12 months
- Individual applicants or proposals that will benefit only one person
- Activities taking place outside England, Scotland, Wales or Northern Ireland
- Work that has already taken place
- Statutory bodies or work that is primarily the responsibility of statutory authorities *(e.g. residential, respite and day care, housing and the provision of mainstream education in schools, nurseries and colleges)*
- Activities of local organisations which are part of a wider network doing similar work *(e.g. uniformed youth groups, YMCA, MIND, Mencap, Home-start, Wildlife Trusts, RDA, Relate, Citizens Advice Bureau, Age UK etc.)*
- Medical-related activities – such as those offering treatment, care, advice, research or equipment
- Animal welfare charities
- Academic research, scholarships or bursaries

Applications

The trust welcomes funding applications from UK-registered charities which should be made via the online application form on the trust's website. Applications are considered throughout the year.

The Syncona Foundation

Cancer research

UK

£2.4 million to organisations (2016/17)

CC number: 1149202

Trustees: Martin Thomas; Catherine Scivier; Thomas Henderson; Rupert Adams.

Correspondent: Martin Thomas, Trustee, 91 Gower Street, London WC1E 6AB (tel: 020 7968 6460; email: mt@bacit.co.uk)

In 2016 BACIT (Battle Against Cancer Investment Trust) changed its name to Syncona Ltd following the acquisition of Syncona LLP. Syncona is a FTSE 250 company which invests in life sciences. The company makes an donation of 0.3% of its net asset value to charities each year with half going to the Institute of Cancer Research and half going to The Syncona Foundation.

According to its 2016/17 account the objects of the foundation are:

- To support the prevention, treatment, cure and ultimately the eradication of cancer in all of its forms and any allied diseases
- To promote and assist:
  - the study of and research into the nature, causes, diagnosis and pathology of cancer and any allied diseases
  - the development and provision of all forms of preventive, curative, management and palliative treatment of cancer and any allied diseases
  - education and training in subjects relevant to the study of cancer and any allied diseases
- To co-operate with, and promote and assist the work of, the ICR and, or alternatively, such other charitable organisations whose objects include any of those above as The BACIT Foundation may determine in addition to or in substitution for the ICR
- To promote and assist such other charitable objects and charitable organisations as The BACIT Foundation may from time to time consider desirable

Financial information

In 2016/17 the foundation held assets of £2.4 million and had an income of £3.5 million. Grants were made to 22 organisations totalling £2.4 million.

Beneficiaries included: Cancer Research UK (£185,000); The Institute of Cancer Research (£151,500); Maggie's (£110,500); Downside Up (£108,000); Child Women for Women International (£102,000); Beating Bowel Cancer, Scope and The Rwanda Hope Foundation (£99,500 each).

Applications

Unsolicited applications are not accepted. The foundation's Charity Commission record states that: 'The foundation grants those funds to charities selected by its trustees in furtherance of the foundation's objects, in proportions determined each year by shareholders of Bacit Ltd'.

The Thales Charitable Trust

General charitable purposes, education, technology, children and young people, health, people with disabilities

UK

£110,000 (2017)

CC number: 1000162

Trustees: John Howe; Michael Seabrook; Craig Stevenson; Stuart Boulton; Stephen Murray.

Correspondent: Michael Seabrook, Secretary, Thales Corporate Services Ltd, 2 Dashwood Lang Road, Bourne Business Park, Addlestone, Surrey KT15 2NX (tel: 01932 824800; email: mike.seabrook@uk.thalesgroup.com)

Registered in 1990 with the Charity Commission, the Thales Charitable Trust is the corporate charity of Thales Corporate Services Ltd, a major electronic systems company acting in areas such as defence, airlines security and safety, information technology and transportation.

The trust has general charitable purposes but principally supports charitable organisations in the fields of children and youth; technology; education and training; and the care for those with terminal illnesses. The trustees may use their discretion to meet requests from other causes from time to time.

Financial information

In 2017 the trust had an income of £175,000 which was wholly received in donations from the Thales group. Grants were made to 53 organisations totalling £110,000.

Beneficiaries included: Asthma UK; Dream Team; Berkshire Youth; Unique Charity; Victim Support; Able Kidz; Thumbs Up Club.

Applications

Apply in writing to the correspondent. The trust does not generally solicit requests unless for major donations.

the7stars foundation

Children and young people under 16-year-olds – specifically those suffering as a result of homelessness, addiction, abuse and child carers

UK

£13,600 (2016/17)

CC number: 1168240

Trustees: Mark Jarvis; Anuschka Clarke; Liam Mullins; Rhiannon Murphy; Nick Maddison; Jenny Biggam; Helen Rose.

Correspondent: Alexandra Taliadoros, Foundation Director, c/o Mark Jarvis, the7stars, Melbourne House, 46 Aldwych, London WC2B 4LL (tel: 020 3475 3191; email: alexandra@the7starsfoundation.co.uk)

www.the7starsfoundation.co.uk

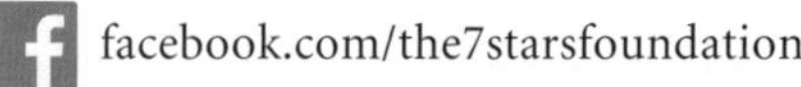

facebook.com/the7starsfoundation

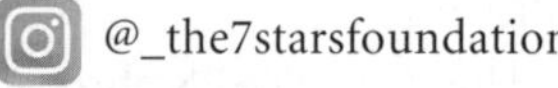

@_the7starsfoundation

Established in 2016, the7stars foundation is the corporate charity of the7stars UK Ltd, the UK's largest independent media agency.

The foundation provided the following information about its objective:

> To be a modern successful business that leads by example by doing the right thing for our clients, staff and the community, the7stars has decided to set up a foundation. the7stars foundation will support the most challenged under 16 year olds in the UK – the forgotten kids who lack the opportunity to achieve their potential. Support will be achieved through grant making to organisations delivery programmes supporting this group. We will donate a minimum of 5% of our profit each year to the Foundation. We collectively feel that as a group we could do more for the community. There is an amplifying effect of pooling together a fund and focusing on causes we all believe in.
>
> **Our goals**
>
> - To donate a minimum of 5% of our profit to good causes each year
> - To support at least one charity in each of the pillars (homelessness, addiction, abuse, child carers) each year
> - To become an active initiative that enables our staff to be involved on a voluntary basis

Grants

The foundation prioritises four areas of work, supporting young people under 16:

- Homelessness
- Addiction
- Abuse
- Child carers

Applications for core costs, including salaries, will be considered as well as project costs and capital funding.

Further information on the foundation's work and causes supported, including its giving policies, is provided on its website. The foundation has also partnered with Coram Chambers LLP to provide grants to individuals. Applications are invited from lawyers involved in children cases, social workers or guardians, in line with the foundation's four funding priorities.

Financial information

As the foundation was established in 2016, the reporting period is 15 July 2016 to 31 March 2017.

In 2016/17 the foundation held assets of £102,000 and had an income of £141,000. Grants were made to five organisations during the period and totalled £13,600.

Beneficiaries listed on the foundation's website included: Create!; Dorset Rape Crisis Centre; Fresh Start; Friends of Chums; Her Centre; National Association for Children of Alcoholics; PACT; Sheffield Young Carers; The Benjamin Foundation; The Jessie May Trust; The Lucy Faithfull Foundation; Wycombe Women's Aid.

Exclusions

The foundation will not support:

- Organisations or individuals residing outside the UK
- Organisations applying on behalf of another organisation – applicants must be legally independent
- Political or religious activities
- Activities or projects already complete at the time of application

Applications

Applicants are directed to the foundation's website, where application forms are available to download. Completed forms can be returned to the Foundation Director by email. The Foundation Director can be contacted with any questions about your application, the application form or the application process. Applications are welcomed at any time, for review at quarterly trustee meetings. They should be submitted via email.

TJX UK Foundation

Children and young people

UK; Republic of Ireland; Germany; Poland

£951,000 (2017/18)

CC number: 1162073

Trustees: Deborah Dolce; Louise Greenlees; Mary Reynolds.

Correspondent: The Trustees, 50 Clarendon Road, Watford WD17 1TX (tel: 01923 47300; email: TJX_Foundation@tjxeurope.com)

This foundation is the corporate charity of TJX, the parent company of TK Maxx and Homesense, and is funded through donations from the company. It makes grants to organisations supporting vulnerable children and young people in the UK and Ireland, Germany and Poland.

Financial information

In 2017/18 the foundation held assets of £4.1 million and had an income of £2.1 million, received from TJX UK. During the year, the foundation awarded 626 grants totalling £951,000 of which £651,000 was awarded to national charities and £300,000 to local charities.

Beneficiaries included: The Prince's Trust (£261,000); British Red Cross (£160,000); Comic Relief (£100,000); Cancer Research UK (£46,000).

Applications

Apply in writing to the correspondent.

Toyota Manufacturing UK Charitable Trust

Children, education, environment, health

Burnastone; Deeside

£259,000 (2017)

CC number: 1124678

Trustees: Sarah Overson; Kevin Reader; Kevin Potter; Gary Newington; Dave Richards; Jim Crosbie.

Correspondent: Jean Sayers, Toyota Motor Manufacturing (UK) Ltd, Derby DE1 9TA (tel: 01332 283609 or 01332 282121; email: charitabletrust@toyotauk.com or external.affairs@toyotauk.com)

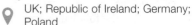

 www.toyotauk.com/the-toyota-charitable-trust/charitable-trust-overview.html

Registered in 2008, this is the charitable trust of Toyota Motor Manufacturing UK Ltd (TMUK). Income is largely derived from company employees through fundraising activities. The trust makes donations to local organisations in the Burnaston (Derbyshire) and Deeside (North Wales) areas with a focus on the environment, children, education and health.

The website notes that the trust has a preference for supporting the following areas:

- **Road Safety**
  - To fund projects which aim to improve the safety of roads in our local community, through either preventative or reactive measures
  - Provide support and resources to reduce road collisions and to reduce recovery time at scene
- **Social inclusion/deprivation**
  - Encourage people to realise their potential by making opportunities possible that are not ordinarily available
  - To support projects providing opportunities to address inequalities in our society and enabling people to improve their social status
- **Health**
  - Supporting projects aiming to promote knowledge of and research into diseases or medical conditions
  - Funding to support those suffering from medical conditions or illness

Member Grants Scheme

The Member Grant Scheme awards grants of up to £5,000 to charities where a TMUK employee holds 'a recognised role' within the charity. Members who undertake a sponsored activity on behalf of a charity are able to request Member Matched funding, where the trust will match up to £1,000 of any sponsorship raised. The website provides a detailed overview of the grants scheme and what the trust is willing to support.

Community Grant Awards

During the year, TMUK employees fundraise to support Toyota's Charity of the Year and other local charities.

Financial information

In 2017 the trust had assets of £351,500 and an income of £336,000. During the year grants were made totalling £259,000.

Previous beneficiaries have included: Welsh Air Ambulance (£8,200); Leonard Cheshire Disability (£5,000); Cruse Bereavement (£4,500); Circus Starr (£3,400); Flintshire Food Bank (£3,000); St John Ambulance – East Midlands (£2,900); Derby Sea Cadets (£2,600); Tiny Tickers (£2,500); Sight Support Derbyshire (£1,500).

Applications

Applications forms can be downloaded from the website. Grants are awarded on a six monthly basis and application periods open in May and October of each year for two months.

The Mike Gooley Trailfinders Charity

Medical research, youth community projects, armed forces

 UK

£7.9 million (2016/17)

CC number: 1048993

Trustees: Tristan Gooley; Michael Gooley; Bernadette Gooley; Fiona Gooley.

Correspondent: The Trustees, 9 Abingdon Road, London W8 6AH (tel: 020 7938 3143)

 www.trailfinders.com

The charity was founded in 1995 by Mike Gooley, the owner of the travel company Trailfinders Ltd. According to the charity's 2016/17 annual report, it supports:

- Medical research
- Community projects which encourage young people in outdoor activities
- Armed forces veteran organisations

Financial information

In 2016/17 the charity held assets of £12.2 million and had an income of £11.2 million, of which £9 million was a donation from Trailfinders Ltd. Grants awarded to organisations totalled £7.9 million.

A list of beneficiaries for the year was not available.

Previous beneficiaries have included: Alzheimer's Society (£400,000); Prostate Cancer Charity (£100,000); and Second World War Experience Centre (£40,000).

Applications

Apply in writing to the correspondent.

UIA Charitable Foundation

Human rights, social welfare, rehabilitation for offenders, people who are homeless, young and older people, victims of domestic abuse

 Worldwide

£20,000 to organisations (2017)

CC number: 1079982

Trustee: UIA Trustees Ltd.

Correspondent: Jackie White, Charity Administrator, UIA Charitable Foundation, Kings Court, London Road, Stevenage, Hertfordshire SG1 2TP (email: charitable.foundation@uia.co.uk)

 www.uia.co.uk/About-Us/Charitable-foundation

The UIA Charitable Foundation is a grant-making body established to provide financial support to formally constituted voluntary organisations and small registered charities that help people in need. It is funded entirely by donations from UIA (Insurance) Ltd, a mutual insurance company, that is provider of insurances to members of UNISON, UNITE and other trade unions.

The objectives to support the relief of poverty, sickness, disability and suffering, the advancement of education and the promotion of other purposes that are beneficial to the community.

The foundation's aim is to support charities that help people in need to improve the quality of their lives. According to the website, the preferred areas for the provision of funding to good causes were those that dealt with:

- Addressing poverty and improving human rights
- Rehabilitation of offenders
- Support for the elderly
- Support for young people
- Tackling homelessness
- Victims of domestic abuse

Financial information

In 2017 the foundation held assets of £43 and had an income of £37,500. Grants totalled £40,000, of which £20,000 was awarded to an individual and the other £20,000 awarded to five organisations.

Beneficiaries were: Banana Link, Ellesmere Port and Romanian Appeal and War on Want (£5,000 each); Stevenage Community Food Bank and Stevenage Haven (£2,500 each).

Exclusions

The foundation's website states that it will not fund the following:

- Work which it believes to be publicly funded
- Retrospective projects
- Organisations that have an annual turnover in excess of £500,000 unless the organisation is acting as a conduit for a partner that fulfils the criteria and may find it difficult to obtain access to funding through independent channels
- Organisations whose combined grant related support costs and governance costs are greater than 10% of their turnover

Applications

The website states that:

> UIA and its key partners, members and staff proactively seek and nominate good

causes all year round for consideration at trustee meetings. At present, trustee meetings are held twice a year in February and September. Receipt of a nomination does not guarantee that it will be considered at the next meeting. You will be informed of the decision in writing as soon as possible after the meeting.

Check the foundation's website for further information.

United Utilities Trust Fund

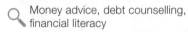

Money advice, debt counselling, financial literacy

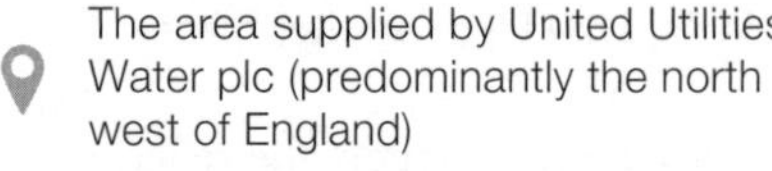

The area supplied by United Utilities Water plc (predominantly the north west of England)

£377,000 to organisations (2016/17)

CC number: 1108296

Trustees: Deborah Moreton; Alastair Richards; Simon Dewsnip; Robert Harrison; Lynne Heath; Sandra McCaughley.

Correspondent: Gay Hammett, c/o Auriga Services, Emmanuel Court, 12–14 Mill Street, Sutton Coldfield B72 1TJ (tel: 0121 362 3625; email: communitygrants@aurigaservices.co.uk)

www.uutf.org.uk

United Utilities Trust Fund is an independent grant-making charity established in early 2005. Its income largely comes from an annual donation from United Utilities Water plc, which has committed to support the trust until March 2020.

Grants are mainly awarded to individuals in financial hardship who have a liability to pay water charges to United Utilities Water (directly or indirectly) and who are unable to pay.

Grants are also given to organisations that can deliver money advice and financial literacy services. The trustees' annual report for 2016/17 provides the following information: 'Trustees recognise the value of offering long-term help and support to individuals experiencing hardship and have adopted a policy of making grants available to organisations that provide free money advice and debt counselling services.'

Financial information

In 2016/17 the charity held assets of £337,000 and had an income of over £5 million. Grants to 4,971 individuals or families totalled £4.4 million and grants to 18 organisations totalled £377,000.

Beneficiaries included: Age UK – South Lakeland (£39,500); Preston and District Citizens Advice (£31,000); Local Solutions (£30,000); Gaddum Centre (£25,500); Centre 63 (£22,000); Involve Northwest (£15,100); Institute of Money Advisors (£8,100); Mind in Salford (£7,800); St Andrews Community Network (£6,300).

Applications

Details of open funding rounds can be found on the fund's website.

UPP Foundation

Higher education

UK

£150,000 (2016/17)

CC number: 1166323

Trustees: Rt Hon David Laws; Dr Paul Marshall; Robin Bailey-Watts; Joanne Midren; Mary Stuart.

Correspondent: Richard Brabner, Head of Foundation, UPP, 40 Gracechurch Street, London EC3V 0BT (tel: 020 7398 7200; email: upp-foundation@upp-ltd.com)

upp-foundation.org

@upp_foundation

This foundation aims to tackle issues facing the UK higher education sector. It was established and is fully funded by University Partnerships Programme (UPP), a UK company which provides student accommodation infrastructure and support services.

According to its website, the foundation:

> Offers grants to universities, charities and other higher education bodies. In recent years, as higher education has expanded, the burden of paying for a degree has shifted towards the individual. This presents difficulties in maintaining the 'University for the Public Good', as well as ensuring there is greater equity in going to, succeeding at and benefiting from the university experience. The UPP Foundation helps universities and the wider higher education sector overcome these challenges.

Grants

The trustees are focusing on four main themes:

- Increasing access and retention to higher education
- Improving employability
- Enhancing civic universities
- Developing global citizens

Further detail on each of these priorities is provided in the eligibility guide on the foundation's website.

Grants can be provided to registered charities and universities, but applications from other organisations with a clear social purpose, such as social enterprises and community groups, will also be considered. Grants are generally between £5,000 and £20,000, although larger grants will occasionally be considered if greater impact and value can be demonstrated.

In particular, the foundation supports applications which can demonstrate:

- A new or innovative approach to tackling relevant issues
- A commitment to collaboration and/or working in partnership
- How the UPP Foundation can measurably add value to the project
- A clear plan for long-term sustainability independent of support from the UPP Foundation

Financial information

In 2016/17 the foundation held assets of £239,000 and had an income of £413,000, all of which was donated by UPP Group Ltd. During the year, the foundation gave a total of £150,000 in grants to organisations.

Beneficiaries included: Universities UK International (£69,000); Reading Real Estate Foundation (£46,000); Queen Mary – University of London (£18,500) and The Bridge Group (£16,000).

Exclusions

According to the website, the foundation will not support:

- Applications from individual students or persons (to clarify we will not accept applications directly from an individual but can accept applications from institutional bodies that meet the 'organisation criteria' wishing to support individuals within the Foundation's themes)
- Organisations directly affiliated to any political party
- Single faith religious organisations – it is understood that many charities have religious affiliations, foundations and history. The restrictions on single faith religious organisations only applies to charities or organisations where the observance to a specific faith is a prerequisite of support from the charity or organisation
- Recipients of funding from The UPP Foundation in the last 6 months, except at the discretion of the trustees

It will not support applications which:

- Risk bringing the name of The UPP Foundation and associated corporate parent UPP Group Ltd into disrepute
- Relate to the purchase of land or existing buildings (including a building's freehold) or the repayment of loans
- Represent a disproportionate percentage of the overall turnover of the organisation
- Relate to non-specific appeals, endowment funds, conduit organisation

Applications

Application forms can be requested by emailing upp-foundation@upp-ltd.com and can be submitted at any time during the year for consideration at quarterly trustee meetings.

Further guidance is provided on the website, refer to the eligibility guidelines.

The Virgin Money Foundation

Community development and regeneration, social enterprise, children and young people

The UK with a preference for the North East, Glasgow, Sheffield and Norfolk

£3 million (2017)

CC number: 1161290

Trustees: Ruth Ibegbuna; Edward Wakefield; Joanne Curry; Timothy Davies-Pugh; Stephen Pearson; Tim Arthur; Emma Morris.

Correspondent: Amy Williams, Programme Support Assistant, Jubilee House, Gosforth, Newcastle upon Tyne NE3 4PL (tel: 0330 123 3624; email: amy.williams@virginmoneyfoundation.org.uk)

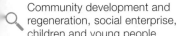

virginmoneyfoundation.org.uk

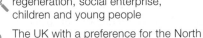

@VMFStartLocally

The foundation established in 2015 following the demise of the Northern Rock Foundation. Its main objective is 'to promote the sustainable regeneration of economically and socially deprived communities in the United Kingdom'.

Grant programmes

At the time of writing (December 2018) the foundation has four funding programmes, details of which have been taken from its website:

The Ripple Fund – The Ripple Fund supports sustainable regeneration in local communities, particularly enabling activity that is likely to have a 'ripple effect', that is activity which will create skills and confidence to tackle other important issues and therefore build stronger communities. Currently applications are by invitation only.

#iwill Take Action Fund – In partnership with the Big Lottery Fund, the #iwill Take Action Fund supports organisations working with disadvantaged young people aged 10 to 20 to encourage them to use their talents and energies to make a difference to their local community. Grants from £10,000 to £60,000 are available under three themes: physical environment, health, and culture. Applicant organisations should be able to provide evidence that young people are involved in the planning and delivery of the project.

Heart of the Community Fund – This fund awards £1,000 every two months to a local charity in Glasgow and Sheffield with two runners-up receiving £500 and £250. Registered charities with annual running costs of less than £500,000 are eligible but must be local to Glasgow or Sheffield and be working to benefit the immediate community. Funds can be used for capital costs, to contribute towards small projects or to pay staff to run an activity.

The foundation's website provides further information on each fund, including application deadlines, examples of successful projects, and detailed eligibility criteria. The foundation supports the charities it works with through its Beyond the Grant programme. The 2017 trustees report notes the following:

> During 2017, 123 volunteers were provided to our funded organisations, including 74 skill-based volunteers offering pro bono support or volunteer placements as trustees or executive coaches for the charities we fund.

Financial information

In 2017 the foundation held assets of £2 million and had an income of £3.3 million, of which £1 million was donated by Virgin Money plc. Grants awarded to organisations totalled £3 million and can be broken down as follows:

Other sustainable regeneration in local communities	£1.4 million
Promoting participation in youth social action	£743,500
Helping disadvantaged young people into employment	£393,000
Helping homeless people find and keep a home	£331,500
Supporting new or existing social enterprises	£109,500

Beneficiaries included: Scotcash CIC (£300,000); Emmaus North East (£250,000); BALTIC Flour Mills Visual Arts Trust (£150,000); YMCA North Tyneside (£58,000 in two grants); Hartlepool Citizens Advice (£49,500); Food Nation (£35,000); Wheels 2 Work Country Durham (£24,500); The Ethical Lettings Agency (£14,200); Barnabas – Safe and Sound (£3,000).

Exclusions

Each fund has specific exclusions, see the website for more details.

Applications

The foundation's website provides further information on each fund, including application deadlines, examples of successful projects, and detailed eligibility criteria.

The Vodafone Foundation

General charitable purposes, with a preference for technology, disadvantaged communities, humanitarian crises and disasters

UK and overseas (where Vodafone operates)

£515,500 (2016/17)

CC number: 1089625

Trustee: N Land, Lord Hastings of Scarisbrick, M. Della Valle, E. Filkin, N. Jeffrey, M. Kirk, H. Lamprell, M. Makamba, R. Martin, F. Roman, R. Schellekens.

Correspondent: Andrew Dunnett, Foundation Director, Vodafone House, The Connection, Newbury, Berkshire RG14 2FN (email: groupfoundation@vodafone.com)

www.vodafonefoundation.org

facebook.com/VodafoneFdn

@vodafonefdn

@vodafonefoundation

The Vodafone Foundation was established in 2001 as the eponymous corporate charity of the mobile telecommunication company.

The 2016/17 trustees' report states that the foundation has a funding partnership with its 28 local foundations to invest in programmes that support communities in which Vodafone has commercial roots. The trustees also allocate funds to global programmes, run in partnership with NGOs.

The 2016/17 trustee's report notes that the foundation funds projects that span the major themes:

> - **Connecting for Good** – connecting our giving to our technology, maximising the impact of our charitable giving by funding projects that can benefit from leveraging Vodafone's technologies and expertise to address some of the world's most pressing humanitarian challenges
> - **Disaster relief** – through our Instant Network programme we aim to deploy Vodafone Volunteers and technology in emergencies to provide free communications and technical support to aid agencies and victims and develop new technologies to support the humanitarian community
> - **In-country Grants** – through the 28 local Vodafone Foundations, we give financial support to projects that benefit local communities in significant and timely ways

UK programme

In the UK the key programmes include:

- **JustTextGiving:** This programme enables charities in the UK to raise money via text donations
- **TecSOS:** This is a specialised handset designed for use by victims of domestic violence by connecting them directly to the police wherever they are
- **Matched Funding:** The Vodafone Foundation gives financial support to UK-based Vodafone employees or teams that fundraise in their own time. This is processed through matched funding of up to £350 per employee, per event, and up to four times per year. In 2016/17 Vodafone employees raised nearly £2.2 million for their chosen causes of which the foundation contributed £661,000

Grant-making

The foundation's grant-making is directed through the 'Connecting for Good' theme and supports charities and not-for-profit organisations working in the areas of health, education and disaster. Projects involving the use of technology are particularly encouraged. Grants are awarded to local Vodafone foundations in the countries where the group has a presence. During 2016/17 around 70% of all giving was allocated to this theme.

Financial information

In 2016/17 the foundation held assets of £4.2 million and had an income of £22 million of which £18 million represents the annual contribution from Vodafone Group plc and Vodafone UK. Grants totalled £20.6 million of which £13.3 million was awarded to local Vodafone foundations. In the UK, grants awarded to organisations totalled £515,500. An additional £84,000 was committed to The Scout Association to deliver the digital skills partnership.

Beneficiaries included: Prince's Trust (£151,500); PK Trust (£120,000); Diana Award (£106,000 in two grants); British Heart Foundation (£1,500).

Applications

Contact the foundation or see the website for further details. A list of local foundations set up in the countries of operation of Vodafone Group subsidiaries and associated companies, with contact details, can be found on the website. The foundation's website states that the foundation:

> Receives an average of 12,000 requests per year for funding and support. While seeking to respond to all requests for information, it normally approaches only those charitable organisations which it believes can help in the delivery of its charitable aims.

The trustees' report states the following:

> All applications are assessed on merit. Proposed projects are then reviewed and, if appropriate, considered and approved by the Trustees of The Vodafone Foundation. For the duration of the grant, The Vodafone Foundation seeks to work with the grantee to build a partnership to achieve the charitable objectives of the programme. Technical advice is provided from resources within the Vodafone Group to advise Trustees on any specific aspects of proposals.

Wates Family Enterprise Trust

Education, employment and training, community projects, social enterprise, sustainability, thought leadership

UK

£791,000 (2017)

CC number: 1126007

Trustees: Andrew Wates; Paul Wates; Tim Wates; James Wates; Andy Wates; Michael Wates; Charles Wates; Jonathan Wates.

Correspondent: Jerry Wright, Director, Wates House, Station Approach, Leatherhead, Surrey KT22 7SW (tel: 01372 861250; email: director@watesfoundation.org.uk)

watesgiving.org

This trust is the vehicle for the philanthropic and charitable activities of the Wates family, owners of the Wates Group.

The trust's charitable grants programme is called Wates Giving. It supports the following causes:

- Education
- Employment and training
- Community building
- Social enterprise
- Sustainability
- Thought leadership

Further information and examples of causes supported in each of these categories are provided on the website.

There are three types of grant which may be made by the trust, according to the 2016 annual report:

- **Major awards** – in support of bids originating from initiatives of the Wates Group and its business units. These fall under the six themes detailed above
- **Family awards** – in support of bids which are the initiative of the Wates family
- **Employee awards** – in support of initiatives of employees of the Wates businesses including staff fundraising efforts, Give As You Earn donations through payroll and volunteering

Financial information

In 2017 the trust held assets of £206,000 and had an income of just over £1.25 million, almost all of which came from the Wates Group. Grants made through the Family Awards programme totalled £264,000. An additional £527,000 was awarded through the Major Projects programme.

Beneficiaries included: Construct a Future (£30,000); Barlow Moor Community Association (£15,000); Joseph Rowntree Foundation, Kensington and Chelsea Foundation (£10,000 each); Beaumont Collegiate Academy and Business in the Community (£5,000 each); St Mungo's (£1,300); Abbey Road Community Centre (£620).

Applications

All proposals come from Wates employees or the Wates family – unsolicited applications are not considered.

Wellington Management UK Foundation

Education and training, young people

United Kingdom, Germany, Luxembourg, Switzerland

£290,000 (2017)

CC number: 1167369

Trustees: Catherine Gunn; Damian Bloom; Devashish Chopra; John Dickson; Nicola Staunton; Joanne Carey; Richard Van Lienden.

Correspondent: John Dickson, Trustee, Cardinal Place, 80 Victoria Street, London SW1E 5JL (tel: 020 7126 6700; email: wmukf@wellington.com)

www.wellington.com/en-gb/community-engagement

The Wellington Management UK Foundation is the UK corporate charity of Wellington Management, one of the world's largest independent investment management firms. Established in 2015, the foundation supports programmes and organisations that improve the education of, and educational opportunities for, economically disadvantaged youth. The foundation prefers to support organisations in London where the company has a presence. It will also support organisations in Germany, Luxembourg and Switzerland.

According to its website, the foundation seeks to achieve this mission by providing grants to organisations of various sizes that work to 'improve academic performance, improve behaviour, reduce absenteeism and develop life skills for economically disadvantaged youth up to 26 years'. Both capital and revenue grants are available. Grants are awarded on an annual basis, although multi-year grants will be considered once a relationship has been established. The foundation will consider applications from newer as well as more established organisations. Furthermore, the foundation notes that it prefers to fund organisations that can demonstrate 'the strength of their management and that have a measurable track record of success'.

Financial information

In 2017 the foundation held assets of £131,500 and had an income of £287,000, the majority of which was a donation from the company. During the year, the foundation awarded grants of £290,000 to 11 organisations.

Beneficiaries included: Action Tutoring; Die Arche (Frankfurt); Doorstep Library; Education and Skills Development Group; Fight For Peace; London Music Masters; MyBnk; Primary Shakespeare Company; Protege DNA; Real Action; Superar Suisse (Zurich).

Exclusions

The foundation does not support scholarship programmes.

Applications

Grant applicants will only be considered for participation in the foundation's grant review process if they have submitted an 'Initial Application Form', which is available to download from the foundation's website. This requirement applies to all new and returning applicants. Applicants who are successful at this initial stage will then be invited to complete a detailed application. Applications are considered on an annual basis.

All applications will be assessed against three essential criteria:

- The programme must support young people
- The programme's focus is educational, this includes the arts
- The programme will have a meaningful impact

The Westminster Foundation

Social welfare

UK with a preference for: Westminster (parts of the Old Metropolitan Borough of Westminster); Cheshire West and Cheshire; north west rural Lancashire (near Forest of Bowland); and north west Sutherland. Overseas grants are awarded in areas where the Grosvenor Organisation operates

£2.52 million (2017)

CC number: 267618

Trustees: Jane Sanders; Mark Preston; The Duke of Westminster.

Correspondent: Jane Sandars, Director, The Grosvenor Office, 70 Grosvenor Street, London W1K 3JP (tel: 020 7408 0988; email: westminster.foundation@grosvenor.com)

 www.westminsterfoundation.org.uk

The foundation was established in 1974 for general charitable purposes by the fifth Duke of Westminster and continues to make grants to a wide range of charitable causes. In 1987 the Grosvenor Foundation, a separately registered charity, transferred all its assets to the Westminster Foundation. The foundation continues to receive regular donations from Grosvenor Group Ltd and supports a wide range of charities through its grant-making, with a focus on the areas in which the group operates.

Grant-making

The foundation's website states that its grant-making is focused on the following two issues:

- **Supporting vulnerable groups:** projects to tackle the challenges faced by people who are isolated or alone whether they are in rural or urban areas. This might include those who are suffering because of the absence of family and social networks to turn to for help and support, such as vulnerable older people. For example, outreach and community groups, befriending schemes, help on the doorstep, nutrition, welfare advice, emergency alarms, learning new skills, access to specialist transport services and communication.
- **Building resilience through strengthening local voluntary organisations:** initiatives such as volunteer training to help organisations develop the skills they need to become better equipped to provide more effective and sustainable support to vulnerable people within our communities.

Types of grants

According to the foundation's 2017 accounts, funding is channelled through two types of grant:

- **Small Grants** – for one-off applications of up to and including £5,000. Applications are via an online application, and reviewed by a Small Grants Panel that meets approximately every ten weeks
- **Discretionary Grants** – Proposals are invited by the Trustees for more substantial grants from a number of other causes of interest to them. Unsolicited applications are unlikely to be successful

Grant-making programmes

According to the foundation's 2017 annual report, there were two themes to the foundation's grant-making in 2017:

- **Supporting Communities** targeted issues of isolation and loneliness, in both rural and urban contexts, and contributes to improved community cohesion within defined geographic focus areas
- **Youth Homelessness** focused on charitable organisations supporting young people who have become homeless or are at risk of doing so, and helping prevent homelessness amongst young adults

Financial information

In 2017 the foundation held assets of £60 million and had an income of almost £56.8 million of which £2.5 million was donated by the Grosvenor Group Ltd. During the year, the foundation awarded 123 grants to organisations totalling £2.52 million.

Beneficiaries of grants over £20,000 included: Black Stork Charity (£107,000); First Light Trust (£40,000); Cardinal Hume Centre (£50,000); Chapter (West Cheshire) (£22,500); Crisis UK (£30,500); LandAid Charitable Trust (£25,500).

Exclusions

The foundation does not consider:

- General appeals or letters requesting non-specific donations
- Organisations that do not have charitable aims (e.g. commercial companies and companies limited by shares)
- Overtly political projects (including party-political and campaigning projects)
- Individuals (or organisations applying on behalf of an individual)
- Student fees/bursaries
- Projects taking place or benefiting people outside the UK
- Projects/work benefiting people outside our specific geographical criteria
- Overseas trips
- Holidays/trips
- Organisations that have applied to us unsuccessfully within the previous 12 months
- Projects where the main focus is website development or maintenance
- Start-up costs, organisations that do not yet have a demonstrable track record

Applications

Applicants should first refer to the website to ascertain whether they are eligible for funding from the foundation.

Applications should be made through the foundation's application form provided on the website, alongside application guidelines. The Grants Review Panel meets around every eight weeks and successful applicants will be notified within two weeks. If you do not hear back in this period, you should assume that you have not been successful.

The WHSmith Group Charitable Trust

General charitable purposes, including medical causes, education and literacy

UK

£228,000 (2017)

CC number: 1013782

Trustees: Faye Sherman; Anthony Lawrence; Natalie Davidson; Sharon Appleton; Clare Skirrow; Nicki Woodhead; Paul Johnson; Clare Skirrow.

Correspondent: The Secretary, WHSmith Ltd, Greenbridge Road, Swindon SN3 3JE (tel: 01793 616161; email: communitygrants@whsmith.co.uk)

www.whsmithplc.co.uk/corporate_responsibility/whsmith_trust

According to its website, the trust aims to support good causes in the local communities where WHSmith operates, and also to promote literacy and a love of reading. Each year the trust supports employees by matching their fundraising and volunteering for charities and schools. The trust also makes donations to hundreds of schools across the UK and funds large scale literacy projects through its long-standing partnership with the National Literacy Trust. The trust benefits from the fundraising efforts of WHSmith employees and also donations.

Community grants

Employees of WHSmith can nominate charities, community organisations or schools to be supported by the trust, through matched funding of up to £1,000 for individual employee fundraising efforts, or £2,000 for team fundraising.

WHSmith also donates some of the funds from the compulsory plastic bag charge to the community grants scheme where voluntary groups, schools, community groups, or any other constituted charitable group of any size can apply for up to £500. Grants can be for capital projects or for revenue and running costs.

The trust's main work is to support the promotion of literacy and reading for pleasure among children. The trust works in partnership with WHSmith plc to support the National Literacy Trust's Young Readers Programme.

Financial information

In 2017 the trust held assets of £136,500 and had an income of £233,000. Grants were made to organisations totalling £228,000.

Beneficiaries included: Cancer Research UK (£5,000); Middlesbrough Football Club Foundation (£2,000); Dartford Grammar School Parents Association, Derwent Valley Cycleway, Miles for Men and National Autistic Society (£1,000 each).

Grants of less than £1,000 totalled £75,000.

Exclusions

According to the trust's website, the following are not eligible for support:

- Party political organisations
- Religious organisations
- Military organisations
- Individuals
- Expeditions or overseas travel

Applications

Applications for a community grant can be made online: blog.whsmith.co.uk/community-grants-application

There are two application rounds each year:

- 1 October to 31 March
- 1 April to 30 September

Grants are reviewed and decided by the trustees at the end of each six-month period.

Any queries should be submitted to: communitygrants@whsmith.co.uk.

The Willmott Dixon Foundation

Young people, people with disabilities

UK

£343,500 (2016/17)

CC number: 326530

Trustees: Richard Willmott; Colin Enticknap; Andrew Telfer.

Correspondent: Wendy McWilliams, Spirella 2, Icknield Way, Letchworth Garden City, Hertfordshire SG6 4GY (tel: 01462 671852; email: company.secretarial@willmottdixon.co.uk)

www.willmottdixon.co.uk/how-we-do-it/the-willmott-dixon-foundation

Willmott Dixon Group is a privately owned construction, housing and property development business. The Willmott Dixon Foundation was set up in 1984 and is chaired by the Group Chief Executive, Rick Willmott.

According to its 2016/17 annual accounts, the object of the foundation is: 'to support projects and causes which promote the training of young people and the welfare of people with special needs'.

Financial information

In 2016/17 the foundation had assets of £26,500 and an income of £350,500. A total of £343,500 was awarded in grants to 41 projects. Donations of less than £2,500 totalled £21,000.

Beneficiaries included: Shelter (£109,500); Chestnut Tree House (£104,000); Action Medical Research (£63,500); Wide Horizons (£9,500); Cancer Research UK (£6,300).

Applications

Applications can be made in writing to the correspondent. Note that the foundation tends to work with a small number of partner charities.

Yorkshire and Clydesdale Bank Foundation

Health, education, social welfare, citizenship and community development, sport, environment, arts, heritage, culture and science, saving of lives, money advice

Areas of England and Scotland where the bank operates

£723,000 (2016/17)

OSCR number: SC039747

Trustees: David Blair; Debbie Crosbie; Sandra Delamere; Lorna Macmillan; Simon Wright.

Correspondent: Graeme Duncan, Secretary, Level 3, 30 St Vincent Place, Glasgow G1 2HL (email: SOTCAwards@cybg.com)

secure.cbonline.co.uk/about-clydesdale-bank/community/charitable-donations-about-us

The Yorkshire and Clydesdale Bank Foundation was established in 2008 and is registered with the Office of the Scottish Charity Regulator. It is the corporate charity of the Clydesdale Bank, a commercial bank formed in Glasgow in 1838.

The foundation's 2016/17 annual report states that it looks to support registered charities, not-for-profit organisations and community and other voluntary organisations under the following categories:

- Prevention and relief of poverty
- Advancement of education
- Advancement of health
- Advancement of citizenship or community development
- Advancement of the arts, heritage, culture or science
- Advancement of public participation in sport
- Promotion of equality and diversity
- Advancement of environmental protection or improvement

- Relief of those in need by reason of age, ill health, disability, financial hardship or disadvantage
- Advancement of animal welfare
- Saving of lives

Activities should take place inside the foundation's beneficial area, primarily areas covered by branches of Clydesdale Bank, its customer banking centres and head office locations.

Spirit of the Community Awards

The foundation also offers grants of up to £5,000 through its Spirit of the Community Awards. In 2018 there were three award categories, details of which have been taken from the award guidelines:

> Awards will be considered for projects in one of the following three categories:
>
> **Help people have a healthy relationship with money** – This category will focus on initiatives that advance financial education including initiatives that promote accessibility to both financial education and financial services.
>
> **Help people into employment** – This category will focus on initiatives that build on and develop skills in individuals to equip them for the workplace and help them become ready for work.
>
> **Help people improve their local environment** – This category will focus on projects seeking to protect or improve the environment.

Financial information

In 2016/17 the foundation had assets of £21,000 and an income of £710,500, largely received in donations from Clydesdale Bank. Grants were made to 322 organisations and totalled £723,000.

Health	£282,500
Education	£158,500
Relief of poverty	£79,000
Sports	£75,500
Citizenship and community development	£61,500
Environmental protection or improvement	£54,500
Arts, heritage, culture or science	£7,600
Saving of lives	£2,000
Animal welfare	£1,000

Beneficiaries of grants over £5,000 included: Hospice UK (£282,500); Money Advice Trust (£50,000); Business in the Community (£39,000); British Red Cross (£20,000); Scottish Waterways Trust and The Tutor Trust (£10,000 each); Charities Aid Foundation (£6,000).

Applications

Application forms and guidelines can be found on the foundation's website.

Yorkshire Building Society Charitable Foundation

General charitable purposes including education and training, health, animal welfare, people with disabilities, children and young people, older people

UK, with a preference for grant-making in the society's branch localities

£229,500 (2017)

CC number: 1069082

Trustees: Christopher Parrish; Richard Brown; Vanessa White; Tanya Jackson; Gordon Rogers.

Correspondent: Fiona May, Yorkshire Building Society, Yorkshire House, Yorkshire Drive, Bradford, West Yorkshire BD5 8LJ (tel: 0345 166 9271; email: corporateresponsibility@ybs.co.uk)

www.ybs.co.uk/your-society/charity/charitable-foundation/apply.html

The Yorkshire Building Society Charitable Foundation is the channel of giving of Yorkshire Building Society (YBS). Its purpose is to support good causes where the society's members and staff live and work, helping to demonstrate the value and support that it provides to local communities throughout the UK.

The foundation's income is acquired from YBS and Small Change Big Difference (SCBD), a scheme promoted by Yorkshire Building Society under which the holders of savings or loan accounts agree to transfer an amount equivalent to the pence of interest received on a savings accounts, or rounding up to the nearest pound, the pence of interest paid on a mortgage account.

Following a full strategic review of the foundation's donations policy in 2016, the foundation redefined the focus of its charitable purposes, as follows:

- The prevention or relief of poverty
- The advancement of health or the saving of lives
- General charitable purposes

According to its website, the foundation considers applications to fund a specific project and/or items that will have a positive impact to the charity's beneficiaries. Examples of these could be: sensory toys for children with special needs, social activities for the vulnerable/isolated older people or training of charity employees to deliver programmes to help their beneficiaries.

Grants generally range in size from £250 up to a maximum of around £2,000.

Financial information

In 2017 the foundation held assets of £220,000 and had an income of £348,500. During the year 325 grants totalling £229,500 were awarded.

Beneficiaries included: Bury Involvement Group in Mental Health, Buttle UK, Caring for Communities and People, Centrepoint, Cheshire Autism Practical Support Ltd, Children's Adventure Farm Trust, Friends of Phoenix, Peterborough and District Samaritans, Sue Ryder (£2,000 each).

Exclusions

The society's website states:

> Applications for general ongoing funding, running costs, contributions towards large funding, research, individual beneficiaries, sponsorship, payment of salaries or expenses are not eligible, nor are the requests for office items/IT equipment for the charity's own use. We are unable to consider requests from charities that only support a specific sector of society based on ethnicity, faith, sexual orientation or political beliefs.

Furthermore, the foundation will only consider donations to UK-registered charities.

Applications

Since the majority of funding available to the foundation is generated by the society's members through the Small Change Big Difference scheme, the foundation has stated that it will only accept recommendations of charities to support from members or employees of the society. Previously applications from charities and good causes with no previous connection to the society were considered.

If you are a Yorkshire Building Society, Chelsea Building Society or Norwich and Peterborough member and would like the foundation to consider supporting a charity, applications can be submitted via the foundation's website.

All applications are reviewed on a quarterly basis by the trustees. Donations are sent directly to successful charities at the end of each quarter (April, July, October, and January).

The Zochonis Charitable Trust

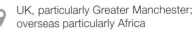

General charitable purposes, particularly youth education and welfare

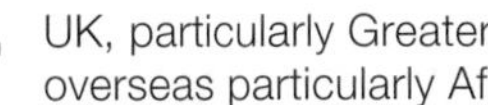

UK, particularly Greater Manchester; overseas particularly Africa

£4.2 million (2016/17)

CC number: 274769

Trustees: Christopher Green; Archibald Calder; Paul Milner.

Correspondent: Marie Gallagher, Manchester Business Park, 3500 Aviator Way, Manchester M22 5TG (tel: 0161 435 1005; email: enquiries@zochonischaritabletrust.com)

This trust was established by the late Sir John Zochonis, former head of P Z Cussons plc, the soap and toiletries manufacturer, with shares in the company. It has general charitable objectives but tends to favour local charities with a particular emphasis on education and the welfare of children.

Financial information

In 2016/17 the trust held assets of £181.7 million and had an income of over £4.9 million. Grants were made to 171 organisations totalling over £4.2 million and were broken down as follows:

Education	£1.36 million
Health	£744,500
Other	£500,000
Overseas	£444,000
Children and youth	£360,500
Social provision	£310,500
Homeless	£135,000
Community	£125,000
Emergency – East Africa famine and Nepal earthquake	£100,000
Armed forces	£46,500
Family	£45,500
Older people	£35,000
Rescue services	£30,000

A list of beneficiaries was not available.

Previous beneficiaries have included: Cancer Research UK, University of Manchester, Manchester High School for Girls, British Red Cross, Breakthrough Breast Cancer, Asthma Relief and National Talking Newspapers and Magazines.

Exclusions

There are no grants awarded to individuals.

Applications

Apply in writing to the correspondent.

Zurich Community Trust (UK) Ltd

Social welfare, community and economic development, people who are disadvantaged.

UK and overseas, with priority given to locations where the company has offices

£1.92 million (2017)

CC number: 266983

Trustees: Ian Lovett; Tim Culling; Vinicio Cellerini; Wayne Myslik; Anne Torry; Andrew Jepp; Conor Brennan; Tulsi Naidu; Richard Peden.

Correspondent: Zurich Community Trust Programme Managers, PO Box 1288, Swindon SN1 1FL (tel: 01793 502450; email: See website for list of contact details for local Zurich Community Trust Programme Managers)

 www.zct.org.uk

The Zurich Community Trust (UK) Ltd is the corporate charity of Zurich Financial Services (UKISA) Ltd, a holding company and part of the Zurich Financial Services Group, which comprises the group's operations in the UK, Ireland and South Africa and provides insurance services.

The trust's main purpose is helping disadvantaged people become more independent by giving time, money and skills donated by Zurich and Openwork and its employees. It focuses on issues that are often overlooked and where the charity can have the biggest impact.

Grant programmes

Social Transformation Programmes

Wholly funded by an annual business donation to the trust, the long-term transformation programmes work in partnership with charities over a minimum five-year period. Grants can be made for core costs and salaries. Applications are by invitation only.

Zurich cares programme

This programme encapsulates the fundraising and volunteering efforts of Zurich employees, with the company matched funding any donations raised by staff.

- **National programme** – The company awards an annual £75,000 grant to its charity partners through this programme – the charities that have been selected by staff to receive this grant for the next three years (2018 to 2020) are Dementia UK and Place2Be
- **Local grant programme** – The programme also funds the Local Grants programme. The application process varies from region to region but generally the trust supports charities situated within 25 miles of its offices. Charities can also apply for volunteers from local offices to tackle practical one-off projects, share their business skills, or take up trustee or school governor positions. Further details about the programme can be found on the trust's website along with a list of local Zurich Community Trust Programme Managers
- **Overseas grant programme** – The programme is open to UK-registered charities operating overseas. Grants of between £2,000 and £10,000 are available for projects where there is a measurable impact and outcome

The Openwork Foundation

Under its theme 'Cares 4 Kids', the foundation supports disadvantaged children and young people up to 18 years of age in the UK and overseas who are disadvantaged either socially, physically or mentally. The current national charity partner is Carers Trust which receives an annual grant of £50,000. Other children's charities are supported through a regional grant programme, but the foundation only considers applications that have been nominated by an Openwork adviser or employee. Grants of between £3,000 and £10,000 are available for capital and revenue funding.

Financial information

In 2017 the trust held assets of £5.25 million and had an income of £3.78 million, of which £2.5 million was a donation from Zurich UK businesses. Grants totalled £1.92 million. The following breakdown is taken from the 2017 accounts:

Zurich Cares – local and overseas	£1.3 million
Transformation programmes	£769,000
Openwork Foundation – local and overseas	£418,000
Openwork Foundation – long-term community partnership	£118,000
Zurich Cares – long-term community partnerships	£11,000

Beneficiaries included: Addaction (£110,000); Saints Foundation (£103,000); Aston Villa Foundation (£102,000); Mental Heath Foundation (£42,000); University of Bath and Volunteering Matters (£30,000 each).

Exclusions

The trust's website states that it will not fund the following:

- Individuals
- Medical research
- Statutory organisations including mainstream schools and hospitals, unless exclusively for a special needs group
- Animal welfare
- Conservation or environmental projects, unless involving disadvantaged people
- Political or military organisations
- Religious organisations
- Sports clubs, village halls, playgroups and mother and toddler groups, unless for a special needs group
- Scouts, girl guides, cadets and other similar organisations, unless specifically supporting disadvantaged children
- Fundraising events including appeals or events for national charities
- Advertising or sponsorship connected with charitable activities

For overseas projects, the trust will not fund:

- Disaster relief or emergency work
- Proposals which show any racial, political or religious bias

- Individuals
- Expeditions or study exchanges
- Medical research
- Fundraising events or appeals

Applications

Applicants must firstly visit the trust's website and follow the links to check eligibility and download the guidelines and application forms. The website provides detailed contact information and deadlines for each of the local communities programme.

If applying for an **overseas grant**, note that the trustees hold a series of meetings from May to September each year. The deadline date for applications is usually in March; check the trust's website for further details.

Glossary

Charity partners and/or Charity of the Year

Charity of the Year programmes support a single organisation typically for a period of a year, however this can be extended. The charity supported is generally chosen by employees. The company will make financial contributions and/or staff members will fundraise or volunteer for the charity. Long-term partnerships are on the rise and we are increasingly seeing more innovative partnerships between companies and charities that are often cause-related.

Community/social investment

These catch-all terms can comprise all types of assistance available: cash; in-kind gifts; employee and customer fundraising; volunteering time; commercially led initiatives; and management costs. Sometimes companies refer to this as 'community contributions'.

Corporate charity

Corporate charities are established by companies as separate legally constituted entities, registered and regulated by the Charity Commission. They may be funded by historic gifts of shares, by direct donations from the profits of the company, or by customer and employee fundraising.

Corporate Social Responsibility (CSR) or charity committee

A CSR or charity committee is a positive indicator of a company's commitment to its role in society beyond the environmental obligations it is required to meet under law. A committee can act as a vehicle for the continuing evolvement of a company's CSR strategy, as well as providing a point of contact for information on a company's CSR practices. Some companies' committees are made up of members of the board of directors, whereas others include employees.

Employee-led support

Employees are often a valuable asset to companies' CSR activities. Staff members lend their fundraising and volunteering efforts to a wide range of local, national and international causes. Fundraising activities can include anything from sponsored runs to employee lotteries, and volunteering can range from individually organised regular commitments to one-off team efforts.

Gifts in kind

Gifts in kind originally referred solely to goods, pieces of furniture or items of equipment (nearly always second-hand). Now, with CSR high on the agenda for many companies, corporates are increasingly offering staff time and skills as gifts in kind, which can be a very valuable asset for a charity and equally provide useful new skills and experience for staff development. The term is often used in relation to physical items alone without reference to professional or support services, and this can cause confusion.

Market-led giving

Market-led approaches to giving include: selling products whereby a percentage of sales is donated to charitable causes; the company sponsors a team, event or organisation; the company funds an initiative that will be of benefit to it in the future, for example an engineering company funding a STEM initiative in a local university.

We include examples of any cause-related marketing initiatives that a company may have undertaken; however, we do not include this in the total community contributions figure for the year because the motivation and priority of such giving is the company's profits and it is not driven by philanthropy.

Notably, many of the companies featured in this edition and specialising in retail, particularly supermarkets, have started to redistribute funds raised from the statutory single-use carrier bag charge to charities. This legislation came in force in England in October 2015 following similar legislation in Wales (2011), Northern Ireland (2013) and Scotland (2014).

Matched funding

Matched funding provides a way for companies to encourage and support their employees' charitable fundraising efforts. Typically, companies will match funding up to a certain amount per employee per year. Some companies match funds on a pound-for-pound basis, whereas others match up to a certain percentage of funds raised.

Payroll giving

Payroll giving allows employees to make donations from their wages in a tax-efficient way. There are a number of schemes on offer, perhaps the best known being the Charities Aid Foundation's Give As You Earn (GAYE) scheme (www.cafonline.org/giving-as-a-company/engaging-employees/caf-give-as-you-earn). The majority of schemes work by taking a monthly donation from the salary of participating employees, although there are some which operate slightly differently. Pennies from Heaven (www.penniesfromheaven.co.uk), for example, works by rounding down to the nearest pound individual employees' monthly salaries.

Pro bono

Pro bono work can provide a way for charities to access invaluable professional skills and knowledge from companies free of charge. Many people think of pro bono work as being the domain of law and accountancy firms; however, companies in this guide from across the corporate sector provide charities with various specialisms, sometimes with remarkably innovative outcomes.

Sponsorship

Sponsorship is vastly different from charitable donations: it is a business arrangement that provides the charity with an opportunity to raise funds and the company with the chance to improve its image and to promote and sell its products or services. Sponsorship is typically given in the form of money, although it can also be in products, services or space.

STEM-focused

Some companies have prioritised the promotion of STEM (science, technology, engineering and maths) subjects as part of their CSR strategy. This could be in the form of special classes or on-site visits for school pupils, or mentoring for university students. A particular focus of companies in this area is the promotion of STEM subjects and careers to young women. This is a direct response to the fact that still only a small proportion of the STEM sector's workforce is made up of women.

Accreditation schemes and membership bodies

Business in the Community

Business in the Community (BITC) is a business-led membership organisation committed to making community involvement a natural part of successful business practice and to increasing the quality and extent of business activity in the community. BITC works with companies in the UK and overseas, who are committed to improving their impact on society. According to its website, BITC offers a combination of expert advice and specialist resources to guides it members on a 'journey of continuous improvement, working across the whole responsible business agenda. From community engagement to employment, diversity and the circular economy'.[1]

Scottish Business in the Community and Business in the Community have merged to form a new network in Scotland called Business in the Community Scotland. Further information on the new network can be found at www.bitc.org.uk/scotland.

CommunityMark

The CommunityMark is the UK's only national standard designed to recognise leadership and excellence in community investment. The standard has been developed by Business in the Community in consultation with the private, public and voluntary sector bodies and is open to UK companies of all sizes and sectors.

According to the BITC website, the CommunityMark 'challenges companies to minimise their negative and maximise their positive impact on society by taking a holistic approach to community investment… The CommunityMark highlights how organisations are transforming their business by integrating responsible business practices and transforming the communities in which they operate, creating positive impacts for society'.[2]

In total, 58 companies have achieved the CommunityMark since its launch. Of these, 34 are currently recognised as upholding this standard of excellence, and are listed in the Accreditation List in the next section.'[3]

Stonewall Workplace Equality Index

The Stonewall Workplace Equality Index is a ranking list of UK companies compiled annually by the lesbian, gay, bisexual and transgender equality charity Stonewall. On its website, Stonewall describes the index as 'the definitive benchmarking tool for employers to measure their progress on lesbian, gay, bi and trans inclusion in the workplace'.[4]

In order to be included in the index, companies must opt in by forwarding detailed documentation to Stonewall. The number of companies that participate each year is estimated to be between 400 and 500. Only those companies which rank in the top 100 are made public. In order to be ranked in the top 100, companies must demonstrate their work in 10 areas of employment policy and practice. Employees from across the organisation must also complete an anonymous survey about their experiences of diversity and inclusion at work. The algorithm used to compile the index is not publicly disclosed, but Stonewall claims to have surveyed over 93,000 employees for the 2018 edition of the index.

In the Accreditation List in the next section, we have highlighted those companies which were ranked in the top 100 of the 2018 edition of the index.

London Benchmark Group

The London Benchmarking Group (LBG) is a group of over 120 companies working together to measure Corporate Community Investment (CCI). There vision is 'a world where every business measures community investment and shares this in an open and transparent way.'[5]

The group's objectives can be broadly said to be to:

- Continue development of a global measurement standard – the LBG model
- Benchmark and share best practice

- Develop and refine measurement tools
- Improve management and implementation of CCI projects
- Better communicate CCI results to stakeholders with LBG centres

The LBG Model, devised by the group, provides a comprehensive and consistent set of measures for CCI professionals to determine their company's contribution to the community, including cash, time and in-kind donations, as well as management costs. The model also captures the outputs and longer-term impacts of CCI projects on society and the business itself. Currently the model is used by hundreds of leading businesses both in the UK and overseas. Companies which are currently members of LBG are listed in the Accreditation List in the next section.

Living Wage Foundation

The Living Wage Foundation is a campaigning organisation which aims to persuade UK employers to pay a Living Wage – an independently-calculated recommended minimum wage to cover workers' basic needs. To achieve this objective the foundation operates an accreditation scheme for UK companies. In order to become accredited as a Living Wage Employer, companies must pay all of their directly employed staff a Living Wage, and have a plan in place to extend that to regular sub-contracted staff as well.

According to the Living Wage Foundation website, the current Living Wage rates are £10.55 per hour in London and £9.00 per hour in the rest of the UK.[6] There are currently over 4,700 Living Wage Employers. In the Accreditation List in the next section we have marked companies which are included in a list of Living Wage Employers on the Living Wage Foundation website.

Armed Forces Covenant

The Armed Forces Covenant is a pledge taken by companies, central and local government authorities, charities and communities to support armed forces personnel, veterans and their families.

The covenant focusses on helping members of the armed forces community have the same access to government and commercial services and products as any other citizen. According to the website, support is provided in a number of areas including: education and family well-being; housing; employment and training; healthcare; financial assistance and discounted services.[7]

To date over 3,000 organisations have signed the covenant. The companies included in this guide which have signed the covenant are listed in the Accreditation List in the next section.

FTSE4Good UK Index

The FTSE4Good UK Index is one of a range of ethical investment indices launched in 2001 by the FTSE Group.[8] The indices are designed to measure the performance of companies demonstrating strong environmental, social and governance (ESG) practices. Inclusion in the indices is based on a range of corporate social responsibility criteria including: environmental sustainability, stakeholder relationships, attitudes to human rights, supply chain labour standards and the countering of bribery. Companies involved in tobacco production, nuclear weapons, conventional weapon systems, or coal power industry are excluded. Research for the indices is supported by the Ethical Investment Research Services (EIRIS – www.vigeo-eiris.com).

In the Accreditation List in the next section, we have marked companies which were included in the FTSE4Good UK 50 index as of November 2018.

Business Disability Forum

Business Disability Forum is a not-for-profit membership organisation that helps to support businesses to employ people with disabilities.[9] It achieves this by providing training, advice and networking opportunities. The organisation also works closely with the government to inform disability policy and runs campaigns to raise awareness around key issues related to disability in the workplace.

References

1 'The Prince's Responsible Business Network – Resources' [web page], Business in the Community, www.bitc.org.uk/resources-training/resources, accessed 26th February 2019.

2 lIntroduction to CommunityMark – Recognising leadership and excellence in community investment' [PDF], Business in the Community, www.bitc.org.uk/resources-training/resources/factsheets/introduction-communitymark-recognising-leadership-and+&cd=1&hl=en&ct=clnk&gl=uk, accessed 22 January 2019.

3 'The Prince's Responsible Business Network – Current holders of the CommunityMark' [web page], Business in the Community, www.bitc.org.uk/resources-training/measurement-reporting/communitymark/current-holders-communitymark, accessed 26th February 2019.

4 'UK Workplace Equality Index' [web page], Stonewall, www.stonewall.org.uk/uk-workplace-equality-index, accessed 26th February 2019.

5 'LBG The Third Generation – Annual Review 2018' [PDF], LBG, www.lbg-online.net/wp-content/uploads/2018/10/LBG-Annual-Review_2018.pdf, p 3, accessed 26 February 2019.

6 'Calculation' [web page], Living Wage Foundation, www.livingwage.org.uk/calculation, accessed 26th February 2019.

7 'About' [web page], Armed Forces Covenant, www.armedforcescovenant.gov.uk/about, accessed 26th February 2019.

8 'FTSE4Good Index Series' [web page], FTSE Russell, www.ftse.com/products/indices/ftse4good, accessed 26th February 2019.

9 https://businessdisabilityforum.org.uk.

Company accreditations

	Business Disability Forum	Living Wage employer	Stonewall employer	Armed Forces Covenant	Community Mark	FTSE4Good	London Benchmarking Group	Business in the Community
3i Group plc		●				●		
Abellio ScotRail Ltd		●						●
Accenture UK Ltd	●	●	●	●			●	●
Admiral Group plc	●							
Adnams plc				●				
Aggregate Industries Ltd				●				
Allen & Overy LLP		●	●					
Allianz Insurance plc	●							
Alun Griffiths (Contractors) Ltd								●
Amey UK plc				●				●
Anglian Water Services Ltd	●	●		●			●	●
Anglo American plc	●	●		●		●		●
Arup Group Ltd		●						●
Asda Stores Ltd	●			●				●
Ashtead Group plc		●				●		
AstraZeneca plc		●				●	●	
Aviva plc		●	●	●		●	●	●
Axis Europe plc								●
BAE Systems plc	●			●			●	
Baillie Gifford & Co Ltd	●							
Balfour Beatty plc	●			●				
Bank of Ireland (UK) plc	●						●	●
Barclays plc	●	●	●	●	●	●	●	●

	Business Disability Forum	Living Wage employer	Stonewall employer	Armed Forces Covenant	Community Mark	FTSE4Good	London Benchmarking Group	Business in the Community
A G Barr plc		●						
Bayer plc								●
Beazley plc		●						
Bettys & Taylors of Harrogate Ltd							●	●
Birketts LLP				●				
Birmingham Airport Ltd	●	●						
A F Blakemore and Son Ltd								●
Boots UK Ltd							●	●
Brewin Dolphin Holdings plc	●							●
British American Tobacco plc				●				
British Land Company plc	●						●	●
Britvic Soft Drinks plc							●	
BT Group plc	●			●		●	●	●
Bunzl plc						●		
BUPA Ltd								●
Burberry Group		●						
Burnley FC Holdings Ltd				●				
Calor Gas Ltd								●
Capgemini UK plc	●	●	●					●
Capita Group plc	●			●				
Capital and Counties Properties plc (Capco)	●			●				
Capital One (Europe) plc					●		●	●
Care UK Health & Social Care Holdings Ltd				●				
Central England Co-operative								●
Centrica plc	●			●		●	●	●
Channel 4 Television Corporation	●	●						
Chelsea FC plc		●						
Clifford Chance LLP		●	●	●				
Cobham plc				●				
Compass Group plc				●		●		
Co-operative Group Ltd	●		●				●	●
Costain Group plc				●				●
Coutts & Co.		●						

	Business Disability Forum	Living Wage employer	Stonewall employer	Armed Forces Covenant	Community Mark	FTSE4Good	London Benchmarking Group	Business in the Community
Coventry Building Society								●
Credit Suisse AG	●	●	●				●	
Cumberland Building Society		●						
Dairy Crest Group plc								●
Deloitte LLP	●	●		●				●
Dentons UK and Middle East LLP		●	●					
Derwent London plc		●		●				
Deutsche Bank AG	●						●	
Direct Line Insurance Group plc								●
Dixons Carphone plc								●
DLA Piper International LLP		●						●
Drax Group plc								●
Dwr Cymru Welsh Water								●
E.ON UK plc				●				
Ecclesiastical Insurance Group plc		●			●			●
EDF Energy plc		●		●				●
Edinburgh Airport Ltd				●				
Esh Group				●				●
Everton Football Club Company Ltd		●		●				
FirstGroup plc							●	
Freshfields Bruckhaus Deringer LLP		●					●	●
Fujitsu Services Holdings plc	●		●	●				●
G4S plc				●				
Galliford Try plc				●				
GKN Ltd				●				
GlaxoSmithKline plc	●	●	●			●	●	●
The Go-Ahead Group plc	●						●	●
Goldman Sachs International	●	●		●				●
Gowling WLG (UK) LLP	●	●						●
Greggs plc				●				●
Hammerson plc							●	
Heathrow Airport Holdings Ltd		●						●
Honda of the UK Manufacturing Ltd								●

	Business Disability Forum	Living Wage employer	Stonewall employer	Armed Forces Covenant	Community Mark	FTSE4Good	London Benchmarking Group	Business in the Community
HSBC Holdings plc	●	●		●		●	●	●
IBM United Kingdom Ltd				●				●
Informa plc		●						
Intercontinental Hotels Group plc						●		●
Interserve plc				●				
intu Properties plc					●		●	●
Investec plc							●	
ITV plc		●						
William Jackson Food Group Ltd				●				●
Jaguar Land Rover Ltd				●			●	●
John Lewis Partnership plc	●						●	●
Johnson Matthey plc								●
Jones Lang LaSalle Ltd	●						●	
Kier Group plc				●				●
Kingfisher plc	●						●	●
KPMG LLP	●	●	●	●	●		●	●
Lancashire Holdings Ltd		●						
Land Securities Group plc				●		●	●	
Leeds Building Society				●				●
Legal & General plc		●				●		●
Eli Lilly and Company Ltd	●							
Lincolnshire Co-operative Ltd								●
The Liverpool Football Club		●		●				
Lloyd's	●	●		●				●
Lloyds Banking Group	●	●	●	●	●	●		●
London Stock Exchange Group plc		●		●		●		
Lush Cosmetics Ltd		●						
Manchester Airport Group plc	●				●		●	●
Marks and Spencer Group plc				●	●		●	
Marston's plc				●				
Mazars LLP		●						●
Sir Robert McAlpine Ltd								●
McDonald's Restaurants Ltd				●				

	Business Disability Forum	Living Wage employer	Stonewall employer	Armed Forces Covenant	Community Mark	FTSE4Good	London Benchmarking Group	Business in the Community
Merlin Entertainments	●			●				●
Michelin Tyre plc							●	●
Microsoft Ltd	●			●				
The Midcounties Co-operative					●			●
Mills & Reeve LLP	●							
Moneysupermarket.com Group plc		●						
Morgan Stanley & Co International plc	●	●						●
Wm Morrison Supermarkets plc				●				●
National Express Group plc		●		●				
National Grid plc	●	●		●		●	●	●
Nationwide Building Society	●	●		●	●		●	●
Newcastle Building Society		●						
Next plc						●		●
Nominet UK								●
Nomura International plc	●	●						
Norse Group				●				
Northern Gas Networks Ltd								●
Northern Powergrid Holdings Company								●
Northumbrian Water Ltd		●						●
Norton Rose Fulbright LLP	●	●	●					
Ovo Energy Ltd		●						
Paddy Power Betfair plc						●		
Paragon Banking Group plc		●						●
Pennon Group plc								●
Pentland Group plc		●						
Persimmon plc				●				
Phoenix Group Holdings plc				●				
Premier Oil plc				●				
PricewaterhouseCoopers LLP	●	●	●	●	●		●	●
Principality Building Society								●
Procter & Gamble UK								●
Provident Financial plc	●						●	●
Prudential plc	●					●	●	

	Business Disability Forum	Living Wage employer	Stonewall employer	Armed Forces Covenant	Community Mark	FTSE4Good	London Benchmarking Group	Business in the Community
Reckitt Benckiser Group plc						●	●	
Redrow Group plc				●				●
RELX plc		●				●	●	
Renishaw plc				●				
Richer Sounds plc	●	●						
RollsRoyce plc	●			●			●	●
Rotork plc				●				
The Royal Bank of Scotland Group plc	●	●	●	●		●	●	●
The Royal London Mutual Insurance Soc. Ltd		●						●
Royal Mail plc	●			●			●	●
RPS Group plc				●				
RSA Insurance Group plc		●						
Saga plc				●				●
The Sage Group plc		●		●				
J Sainsbury plc	●							●
Samworth Brothers (Holdings) Ltd								●
Santander UK plc	●	●		●			●	●
Schroders plc	●	●		●		●	●	●
Scott Bader Company Ltd		●						
ScottishPower UK plc	●						●	●
Severn Trent plc	●			●				
Shaftesbury plc		●					●	
Shawbrook Group plc	●							
Shell (UK Ltd)	●			●				●
Shoosmiths LLP								●
Siemens plc				●			●	●
Simmons & Simmons LLP			●					
Simplyhealth Group Ltd							●	
Skipton Building Society	●			●				
Sky plc	●		●			●	●	●
Slaughter and May (Trust Ltd)	●	●	●					
Smith & Nephew plc		●				●		
Smiths Group plc		●						

	Business Disability Forum	Living Wage employer	Stonewall employer	Armed Forces Covenant	Community Mark	FTSE4Good	London Benchmarking Group	Business in the Community
Sopra Steria Ltd	●							
The Southern Co-operative Ltd							●	●
Southern Water Services Ltd	●						●	●
Spirax-Sarco Engineering plc	●							
SSE plc		●				●		
St James's Place plc							●	●
Stagecoach Group plc				●				
Standard Chartered plc	●	●				●	●	
Standard Life Aberdeen plc		●		●		●	●	●
TalkTalk Group	●			●				
Tesco plc	●			●		●		●
Thales UK Ltd	●			●				●
Thames Water Ltd							●	●
the7stars UK Ltd		●						
Timpson Group plc								●
TLT LLP								●
Toyota Motor Manufacturing (UK) Ltd	●			●			●	●
Travis Perkins plc				●				
Turner and Townsend Ltd				●				●
UBM plc		●						
Unilever plc	●	●				●		●
Unite Group plc	●	●					●	●
United Utilities Group plc				●			●	●
Victrex plc								●
Virgin Money Group	●	●	●	●				●
Viridian International Ltd		●						
Vodafone Group plc			●	●		●		
Warburtons Ltd								●
Wates Group Ltd				●	●			
The Weir Group plc				●				
Wellington Management International Ltd		●						
Wesleyan Assurance Society				●				●
Wessex Water Services Ltd	●							

	Business Disability Forum	Living Wage employer	Stonewall employer	Armed Forces Covenant	Community Mark	FTSE4Good	London Benchmarking Group	Business in the Community
Westmorland Ltd								●
WH Holding Ltd (West Ham United)		●						
Wheatley Housing Group Ltd								●
WHSmith plc	●							
Willmott Dixon Holdings Ltd	●						●	
WPP plc	●	●		●		●		●
Zurich Insurance Group	●		●	●			●	

Useful contacts

Business in the Community

Business in the Community (BITC) is a business-led membership organisation, which offers a combination of expert advice and specialist resources to help businesses increase the quality and scope of their community activities.

137 Shepherdess Walk
London
N1 7RQ

Tel: 020 7566 8650
Email: info@bitc.org.uk
Web: www.bitc.org.uk

Business in the Community Scotland

Previously known as Scottish Business in the Community, the name changed after merging with Business in the Community. Contact details as above.

British Chambers of Commerce

The British Chambers of Commerce (BCC) is the national representative body of the UK's 52 Accredited Chambers of Commerce, which collectively represent over 75,000 businesses. Contact details for local Chambers of Commerce can be found on the website.

65 Petty France
London
SW1H 9EU

Tel: 020 7654 5800
Email: enquiries@britishchambers.org.uk
Web: www.britishchambers.org.uk

Charity Chat

Charity Chat is a podcast that covers various issues affecting the sector and provides commentary on fundraising, learning, and policy.

Email: via the online contact form
Web: www.charitychat.org.uk

Charity Commission

The Charity Commission is the government body responsible for the regulation of registered charities in England and Wales. It also maintains a Central Register of Charities.

London
2nd Floor
One Drummond Gate
Victoria
London
SW1V 2QQ

Liverpool
PO Box 211
Bootle
L20 7YX

Taunton
Woodfield House
Tangier
Taunton
Somerset
TA1 4BL

Newport
Room 1.364
Government Buildings
Cardiff Road
Newport
NP10 8XG

Charity Comms

CharityComms is the membership network for communications professionals working for UK charities.

2–6 Tenter Ground
Spitalfields
London
E1 7NH

Web: www.charitycomms.org.uk

Charity Finance Group (CFG)

CFG champions best practice in finance management in the voluntary sector, providing information and support including education and training for its members and the wider charity sector.

15–18 White Lion Street
London
N1 9PG

Tel: 0845 345 3192
Email: info@cfg.org.uk
Web: www.cfg.org.uk

Charity IT Association

CITA provides free IT services and advice to help charities use technology more effectively.

The Worshipful Company of Information Technologists
39A Bartholomew Close
London
EC1A 7JN

Tel: 020 7600 1992
Email: contact@charityithelp.org.uk
Web: www.charityithelp.org.uk

Charities Tax Group (CTG)

The CTG makes representations to Government on behalf of it members on the issue of charity taxation.

Church House
Great Smith Street
London
SW1P 3AZ

Tel: 020 7222 1265
Email: info@charitytax.info
Web: www.charitytaxgroup.org.uk

Charities Trust

Charities Trust is a donations management organisation. It provides a range of services to help charities raise money for good causes.

Suite 20–22
Century Building
Brunswick Business Park
Tower Street
Liverpool
L3 4BJ

Tel: 01512 865129
Web: www.charitiestrust.org.uk

Chartered Surveyors Voluntary Service

CSVS (Charity Commission no. 1043479) provides professional property advice from a Chartered Surveyor for those who would not otherwise be able to afford it. If you feel that the CSVS could benefit you they can be contacted through your Citizens Advice (www.citizensadvice.org.uk) and other advice agencies.

Tel: 0247 686 8555
Email: csvs@rics.org
Web: www.rics.org/csvs

Common Purpose UK

Common Purpose is a leadership development organization. It runs leadership development programmes that support people to work together across boundaries.

Common Purpose
38 Artillery Lane
London
E1 7LS

Tel: 020 7608 8118
Email: info@commonpurpose.org.uk
Web: www.commonpurpose.org.uk

Companies House

Companies House is the United Kingdom's registrar of companies. It is responsible for incorporating and dissolving limited companies, and maintains a comprehensive record of company information which is made available to the public.

Crown Way
Cardiff
CF14 3UZ

Tel: 0303 1234 500
Email: enquiries@companies-house.gov.uk
Web: www.companieshouse.gov.uk

Confederation of British Industry (CBI)

The CBI works to promote business interests by lobbying, research and networking. It currently has around 190,000 direct and indirect members across the UK.

Cannon Place
78 Cannon Street
London
EC4N 6HN

Tel: 020 7379 7400
Email: enquiries@cbi.org.uk
Web: www.cbi.org.uk

Co-operative and Community Finance

Co-operative and Community Finance provides business loans to co-operatives and social enterprises in the UK.

Brunswick Court
Brunswick Square
Bristol
BS2 8PE

Tel: 01179 166750
Web: www.coopfinance.coop

Corporate Citizenship

Corporate Citizenship is a global consultancy that helps businesses to fulfil their social and environmental responsibilities.

Holborn Gate
26 Southampton Buildings
London
WC2A 1PQ

Tel: 020 7861 1616
Email: mail@corporate-citizenship.com
Web: www.corporate-citizenship.com

Directory of Social Change

London

Resource for London
352 Holloway Road
London
N7 6PA

Tel: 0845 077 7707
Email: cs@dsc.org.uk
Web: www.dsc.org.uk

Liverpool

Suite 103
1 Old Hall Street
Liverpool
L3 9HG

Email: research@dsc.org.uk

The Foundation for Social Improvement (FSI)

The FSI provides training and fundraising opportunities for small charities in order to develop a more sustainable small charity sector in the UK.

The Grayston Centre
28 Charles Square
London
N1 6HT

Tel: 020 7324 4777
Email: admin@thefsi.org
Web: www.thefsi.org

In Kind Direct

In-Kind direct distributes new donated usable consumer goods on behalf of manufacturers and retailers to UK charities working in the UK and overseas.

11–15 St Mary At Hill
London
EC3R 8EE

Tel: 0300 30 20 200
Email: info@inkinddirect.org
Web: www.inkinddirect.org

Institute of Corporate Responsibility and Sustainability

The Institute of Corporate Responsibility and Sustainability is a professional body dedicated to supporting corporate responsibility practitioners.

Durham House
Durham House Street
London
WC2N 6HG

Tel: 020 7839 0199
Email: info@icrs.info
Web: www.icrs.info

Institute of Fundraising (IoF)

The IoF is the professional membership body for UK fundraising and supports fundraisers through training and guidance on best practice.

National Pro Bono Centre
48 Chancery Lane
London
WC2A 1JF

Tel: 0207 092 3942
Email: info@lawworks.org.uk
Web: www.lawworks.org.uk

LawWorks

LawWorks is a charity in England and Wales that works to connect volunteer lawyers with people and not-for-profit organisations in need of legal advice.

National Pro Bono Centre
48 Chancery Lane
London
WC2A 1JF

Tel: 0207 092 3942
Email: info@lawworks.org.uk
Web: www.lawworks.org.uk

London Benchmarking Group (LBG)

LBG is a group of over 120 companies working together to measure Corporate Community Investment.

c/o Corporate Citizenship
5th Floor Holborn Gate
330 High Holborn
London
WC1V 7QG

Tel: 020 7861 1616
Email: lbg@corporate-citizenship.com
Web: www.lbg-online.net

The National Council for Voluntary Organisations (NCVO)

NCVO is the umbrella body for the voluntary and community sector in England. The organisation supports the voluntary and community sector by providing training and networking activities. It also represents voluntary organisations to government and conducts research to inform the development of policy.

Society Building
8 All Saints Street
London
N1 9RL

Tel: 020 7713 6161
Email: ncvo@ncvo.org.uk
Web: www.ncvo.org.uk

National Centre for Universities and Business

The National Centre for Universities and Business supports and promotes collaboration between universities and business in the UK.

Studio 11
Tiger House
Burton Street
London
WC1H 9BY

Tel: 020 7383 7667
Email: ncub@ncub.co.uk
Web: www.ncub.co.uk

National Pro Bono Centre

The National Pro Bono Centre is a "hub" for pro bono charities across the legal sector. It helps to support a wide range of pro bono projects across England and Wales.

48–49 Chancery Lane
London
WC2A 1JF

Tel: 020 7092 3960
Web: www.nationalprobonocentre.org.uk

Reach Volunteering

Reach Volunteering supports charities in the UK to recruit volunteers and trustees.

89 Albert Embankment
London
SE1 7TP

Tel: 020 7582 6543
Web: www.reachskills.org.uk

ShareGift

ShareGift works closely with companies, solicitors, stockbrokers, and financial advisers to create a pool of charitable funds. It does this by accepting donations of small shareholdings from companies, which it then aggregates and sells.

PO Box 72253
London
SW1P 9LQ

Tel: 020 7930 3737
Email: help@sharegift.org
Web: www.sharegift.org

Small Charities Coalition

The Small Charities Coalition provides resources, training, mentoring, support and advocacy for small charities in the UK.

Unit 9/10
83 Crampton Street
London
SE17 3BQ

Email: info@smallcharities.org.uk
Web: www.smallcharities.org.uk

Trades Union Congress (TUC)

The Trades Union Congress is a national trade union centre, a federation of trade unions in England and Wales, representing the majority of trade unions.

Congress House
23–28 Great Russell Street
Fitzrovia
London
WC1B 3LS

Tel: 020 7636 4030
Email: info@tuc.org.uk
Web: www.tuc.org.uk

Volunteering Matters

Volunteering Matters is the UK's leading volunteering charity engaging more than 30,000 volunteers each year through over 180 programmes.

The Levy Centre
18–24 Lower Clapton Road
London
E5 0PD

Tel: 020 3780 5870
Web: www.volunteeringmatters.org.uk

Charitable causes index

Community development

Disability

Disaster relief

Education

Enterprise and training

Environment

Equal opportunities

General charitable purposes